Flash™ MX 2004

Graphics, Animation, and Interactivity

James L. Mohler, M.S.Ed.

THOMSON

DELMAR LEARNING™

Australia   Canada   Mexico   Singapore   Spain   United Kingdom   United States

THOMSON

DELMAR LEARNING

Flash™ MX 2004: Graphics, Animation, and Interactivity
James L. Mohler, M.S.Ed.

Vice President, Technology and Trades, BSU:
Alar Elken

Editorial Director
Sandy Clark

Acquisitions Editor
James Gish

Development Editor:
Jaimie Wetzel

Marketing Director
Cindy Eichelman

Channel Manager:
Fair Huntoon

Marketing Coordinator:
Mark Pierro

Production Director:
Mary Ellen Black

Production Editor:
Thomas Stover

Production Manager:
Larry Main

Technology Project Manager:
Kevin Smith

Editorial Assistant:
Marissa Maiella

Trademarks
Macromedia is a registered trademark of Macromedia, Inc. Flash MX 2004 is a trademark of Macromedia, Inc. Adobe, Adobe Illustrator, Adobe Streamline, and Adobe Photoshop are trademarks or registered trademarks of Adobe Systems, Inc. Swift 3D is a trademark of Electronic Rain, Inc. Microsoft, Windows, Windows 95, Windows 98, and Windows NT are trademarks of Microsoft Corporation. Other brand names may be trademarks or registered trademarks of their respective manufacturer.

For more information contact
Delmar Learning
Executive Woods
5 Maxwell Drive, PO Box 8007,
Clifton Park, NY 12065-8007
Or find us on the World Wide Web at
http://www.delmarlearning.com

NOTICE TO THE READER

Publisher does not warrant or guarantee any of the products described herein or perform any independent analysis in connection with any of the product information contained herein. Publisher does not assume, and expressly disclaims, any obligation to obtain and include information other than that provided to it by the manufacturer.

The reader is expressly warned to consider and adopt all safety precautions that might be indicated by the activities herein and to avoid all potential hazards. By following the instructions contained herein, the reader willingly assumes all risks in connection with such instructions.

The publisher makes no representation or warranties of any kind, including but not limited to, the warranties of fitness for particular purpose or merchantability, nor are any such representations implied with respect to the material set forth herein, and the publisher takes no responsibility with respect to such material. The publisher shall not be liable for any special, consequential, or exemplary damages resulting, in whole or part, from the reader's use of, or reliance upon, this material.

About the Author

James L. Mohler is an Associate Professor in the Department of Computer Graphics Technology at Purdue University. He has authored, coauthored, or contributed to thirteen other texts related to multimedia, hypermedia, and graphics topics. Professor Mohler has presented numerous papers and workshops at local, national, and international conferences, and has published articles in both academic and trade publications.

Mr. Mohler has been awarded several teaching awards and has served as webmaster for the School of Technology at Purdue University, lead developer for the Interactive Multimedia Development specialization within the department, webmaster for the Purdue University Virtual Visit web site, and executive editor for the *Journal of Interactive Instruction Development*.

He also enjoys serving as Praise and Worship Leader at Living Word Ministry Center in Frankfort, Indiana. James and his wonderful wife Lisa have three children, Meisha Danielle, Christian Alexander, and Treyton James. He can be contacted via email at *jlmohler@purdue.edu.*

Acknowledgments

I would like to especially thank the wonderful team at Delmar for all their support on this book. The author is only a part of a much larger team, and thanks go to acquisitions editor Jim Gish (one of the best I have worked with), project manager Carol Leyba, and development editor Daril Bentley (thanks for your patience and help in pulling this out in time), production manager Tom Stover, executive production manager Mary Ellen Black, and editorial assistant Jaimie Wetzel. I would also like to thank the many readers at Amazon and elsewhere who were so supportive of previous editions of this book.

Finally, I would like to thank my wonderful wife Lisa, who has been patient and loving while I have spent endless hours in the office.

*This book is dedicated to my students—past, present, and future.
It is you who keep me "sharpening the saw."*

Contents

Chapter 4: Drawing and Painting Tools   89

Chapter 5: Working with Text   125

Chapter 9: 2D Animation and Effects   223

List of Exercises

Introduction

There are not many technologies I have gotten excited enough about to write a book on. When HTML first came out, I was excited and decided to focus my efforts on learning this "new technology," and writing a book. My coauthor and I had about 30 days to learn, consume, and regurgitate as much as we could about HTML. We were coaxed into riding the wave of technology, and I am grateful I could surf along with an experienced coauthor.

However, this book is different from others I have written. I have spent more time on this book—writing, revising, reviewing, and testing in the classroom. It has been thoroughly updated to Flash MX 2004.

I hope you enjoy using and learning from this book. Flash is a wonderful tool, and I foresee that it will continue to evolve and become more useful as time progresses.

Flash MX 2004 Versus Flash MX Professional 2004

One of the decisions Macromedia made concerning post-MX Flash was that it would be advantageous to split the product into a designer and a developer edition to better meet the needs of these two groups of users. Thus, there are now two different editions of Flash: Flash MX 2004 and Flash MX Professional 2004. Flash MX 2004 is aimed at users who focus on creating visually responsive web content and interactive interfaces, whereas Flash Pro extends Flash MX 2004 by adding a plethora of features aimed at web application development. Note that this book is focused on Flash MX 2004.

Audience

This book is designed for educators, students, and practitioners in the field who really want to get "up close and personal" with Flash. I have designed this book for people who really want to learn how Flash works. The exercises and examples are designed to educate you, not provide you with a quick fix. Within the pages of this book you will find referenced examples from cover to cover. By the time you complete this book, you will know how Flash works and how to go about creating your own Flash movies and Flash-based web sites.

▪ ▪ ▪ Philosophy and Approach

The author's greatest strength is that he is an educator first and a developer second. Most of his time is spent finding ways to help people learn and understand how computer graphics applications work. The philosophy is to go beyond simple button pushing and rote techniques to focus on the larger picture. When someone understands how something works, they can use that knowledge to do much more than reemploy some code or some technique laid out before them. They can apply what they have learned to another problem or another context much broader than the original content presented.

The goal and reason for sometimes-lengthy explanations in this text is to provide you the knowledge derived of many hours of testing, and of many successes and failures. Someone once said that there is no substitute for "drive time" when it comes to learning a new technology or a new piece of software. This is true of any learning situation. Beware of books that suggest that you can learn a software package in hours. You can learn techniques in a matter of hours, but do you really understand what you are doing, and could you replicate it in another context? Probably not. This is the reason for the thorough explanations throughout this book, intended to help you really understand what it is you are doing, and what the software is doing.

Complex examples are often too unwieldy for learners to break down and understand what is actually going on as they are trying to follow them. Thus, many of the examples in this book focus on a single concept, and thus appear simple. The person looking for a quick fix might prefer another approach, but the best way to describe a feature is to separate it and talk about it out of context, so that you understand what the feature does. You can then integrate that learning into a more complex project. That is the philosophy that drives, and the approach taken in, this book.

Finally, the approach taken in this and in the previous editions of this book has been well received. In the words of those who have commented, "It's like having a teacher right there." That is the greatest compliment the previous editions could have received, because it indicates that the goal of the book was achieved. The goal of this book has been to improve on and expand that achievement.

■ ■ ■ Version Specificity and Prerequisites

The files found on the companion CD-ROM are specific to Flash MX 2004 and are not backward compatible. If you have an older version of Flash, you will not be able to open the Flash files.

As to prerequisites, the book really has none. Indeed, prior experience in a vector or raster image editor would be helpful, but it is not imperative. Similarly, prior experience in programming will make writing your own ActionScript and JavaScript easier.

■ ■ ■ Book Features and Conventions

The sections that follow discuss the major features of this book. This edition includes a tear-out quick-reference card of keyboard shortcuts to Flash MX 2004 commands, as well as a companion CD-ROM.

Quick-reference Card

The 2004-updated tear-out quick-reference card at the back of the book contains Flash commands, by category, and their associated "quick keys." This feature is convenient in that you can quickly find that command you do not quite remember. In addition, the use of shortcut keys is an important aspect of becoming more proficient in Flash.

Glossary, Appendices, and Index

You will find at the back of the book and extensive glossary of Flash-specific terms, as well as general terms related to the areas of functionality Flash incorporates. The glossary serves as a study in its own right. The appendices offer information and look-up tables associated with topics covered in chapters (see the table of contents). A thorough index covers all text content, including entries that allow you to locate conceptual material.

Text Conventions

Italic font in regular text is used to distinguish certain command names, code elements, file names, directory and path names, and similar items. Italic is also used to highlight terms and for emphasis.

The following is an example of the monospaced font used for examples of command statements and computer/operating system responses, as well as passages of programming script.

```
var myimage = InternetExplorer ? parent.
cell : parent.document.embeds[0];
```

The following are the design conventions used for various "working parts" of the text. In addition to these, you will find that the text incorporates many exercises, examples, and sidebars. All of these elements are easily distinguishable and accessible. Sidebar material highlights or supplements topics discussed in the text.

 NOTE: *Information on features and tasks that requires emphasis or that is not immediately obvious appears in notes.*

 TIP: *Tips on command usage, shortcuts, and other information aimed at saving you time and work appear like this.*

 WARNING: *The warnings appearing in this book are intended to help you avoid committing yourself to results you may not intend, and to avoid losing data or encountering other unfortunate consequences.*

 CD-ROM NOTE: *These notes point to files and directories on the companion CD-ROM that support exercises or that supplement the text via visual examples and further information on a particular topic.*

■ ■ ■ About the Companion CD-ROM

The companion CD-ROM located at the back of the book is one of the most important things about this book. There are well over 50 example files you will be prompted to use throughout the book. You will find that the CD-ROM is PC and Macintosh compatible, and versions of the example files exist for both platforms.

 NOTE: *See also Appendix D, which provides a complete directory structure of the content of the companion CD-ROM.*

Because some operations in Macromedia Flash MX 2004, particularly the Control | Test Movie command, require Flash to write to the drive of the computer, you may find it more helpful to copy the instructional example files to a local drive.

If you choose not to copy the files to a local drive from the very start, to be able to use Control | Test Movie in Flash, at some point you will have to save the files to a local drive. A Read Me file is located on the CD-ROM that details this information.

Flash™ MX

2004

1

An Overview of Flash

▪ ▪ ▪ ▪ Introduction

The Web is dramatically morphing in appearance every day, and no end is in sight to its evolution. Some people complain of the rate of change. However, many believe the Web is paving the way for faster and better communication, thanks to the wealth of these emerging technologies. Fortunately, we are moving away from pages filled with endless streams of text with limited aesthetic appeal. With the use of tools such as Flash, developers are creating sites with sophisticated animation, effective user interfaces (UIs), and truly web-based applications.

With a wealth of web technologies at your fingertips, you may question where Macromedia Flash fits in and why it is so important. With so many technologies being released and revised, it is difficult to get excited about "yet another technology." However, once you have seen any of the many web sites that contain full-screen animation, sound, or interactive UIs created with Flash, you soon appreciate the implications and excitement that surround this powerful development tool.

The latest release of Flash has some very exciting features to offer, but before you explore them, you need to look at Flash in context. This chapter sets the stage for how you should view Flash in concert with other technologies. It is designed to help you understand why the "Flash phenomenon" has occurred and why so many sites utilize it. Additionally, the chapter concludes with an overview of the new version's features.

Keep in mind as you progress through this book that although this book is about Flash and all the wonderful things it can allow you to create, there is no "wonder application" that is the solution to every problem or that is the "only application you need." When Flash is used alone on a web site, it can allow you to slip into the habit of living with large file sizes and ineffective designs. Flash is often only one part of the design and development equation. The other part of the equation is using Flash in concert with other technologies, based on the solution you are trying to generate.

The integration of Flash with other technologies such as client- or server-side scripting languages or other integrated development environments is key. One should not live by Flash alone; rather, one should view it (along with its strengths and weaknesses) in the context of the range of technologies available and create solutions holistically. Too often those new to Flash see its wonderful potential and ignore all other possibilities. The key is to think, plan, design, and develop with both the micro and macro aspects in mind. A little more on that in a moment!

Objectives

In this chapter you will:

- Discover the realities of delivering web content regardless of media type
- Learn about the nuts and bolts of connection speeds and how to figure out optimum delivery to your audience
- Find out how to develop for the right portion of your audience
- Understand the main features of Flash and why it has taken the Web by storm
- Get a quick overview of the new features of Flash MX 2004

The Realities of Web Delivery

The Web provides several unique advantages over other modes of communication, such as traditional publications and even digital publications such as CD-ROM and DVD. Of all the media that can be used for multimedia content, none is more fluid than the Web. The Web is dynamic in both its editability and in the range of media elements that can be implemented within it. Similarly, web content is accessible almost everywhere and, when a connection can be established, is accessible at all hours of the day and all days of the year.

You probably need no convincing of the advantages the Web offers in delivering a wide variety of information. However, a few cautionary notes (some realism, if you will) are in order as the web design craze and the mad rush of Flash development is occurring.

First, no matter what technology you choose for content delivery, you must always examine how frequently the information changes and how you plan to manage to keep up with it. Which medium is most appropriate for the information depends on how fluid the information is. A key to attracting and keeping users is ensuring that information is fresh.

Concerning the stability of information, too often people believe that one technology or the other (such as print, web, or CD-ROM) is the answer for everything. "Just put it on the Web" is the cry that is heard. But rationally you have to consider whether you are just posting information to be posting information. You must focus your development effort.

Second, when and where information may be needed is also important. There are times when CD-ROM media may be advantageous over web media, or vice versa. There are still computer users out there who are not connected to the Web. The fact is, according to data presented at SIG-GRAPH 2001 in Los Angeles, about 93 percent of the world is not connected to the Web! Given the worldview of technology, there may also be times when traditional print-based publications are best for a particular situation. Always choose the technology based on the audience, the need, and the given resource limitations.

This book is indeed about Macromedia Flash and all of the wonderful things you can do with it. But do not put blinders on when it comes to development. Seldom will you develop web content in a vacuum, and seldom will a single technology meet every project need. As a matter of fact, putting all of your development effort into a single piece of technology, no matter how good that technology is, can be detrimental in the long run.

Definitely Flash is a key technology on the Web today, but it should not be the only tool in your toolbox. To be able to keep up with the rate of change on the Web, you should be versed in many things and, moreover, should understand how to integrate technologies and push them to work together. The most successful web developers are not only masters of specific technologies but gurus of the means by which those technologies are integrated and used jointly.

▪ ▪ ▪ Designing for Your Audience

It would be wonderful if all of our creative endeavors were boundless, but as with every technology, there are limitations. When dealing with multimedia on the computer, half the battle is finding ways to overcome the technical hindrances imposed on our ideas.

With the Web, your primary limitation is bandwidth. Other limitations may include proprietary technologies and plug-ins, browser inconsistencies, display differences, and author and content validity. Nonetheless, your biggest battle in designing for the Web is dealing with the limits imposed on what you can deliver through that narrow pipe leading to your

end users. Indeed, connections are getting better, but there is still a prolif-
eration of users accessing via slow connections if, considering a global
audience, a connection exists at all.

The Nuts and Bolts of Connections and Speeds

High-quality audio, video, animation, and graphics typically require much
bandwidth to download, display, and play back effectively. But in reality,
anything you intend to push over the Web, including Flash content,
requires some knowledge of file sizes, connections, and speeds to design
these assets effectively.

For example, a single high-resolution uncompressed raster graphic at
640 x 480 pixels can require a data rate of up to 900 kilobytes per second
(KBps) to be delivered without any noticeable download time. One minute
of "acceptable-quality," compressed audio (22.05 kHz, 8-bit, monaural)
can require download speeds of up to 1.3 megabytes per second (MBps),
whereas 15 seconds of compressed video (with audio) at 160 x 120 pixels
requires 900 KBps.

The higher the quality of media element, the longer it takes to download or view from the Web. File weight (size) is directly proportional to
user wait. These same considerations are important when dealing with
Flash movies, even though Flash movies are typically quite small. As Flash
developers create more complex creations, file size becomes a bigger issue.

Table 1-1 outlines commonly employed end-user connections, including their associated data rates and bandwidths, as well as how long it
takes to download 100 kilobytes (KB) of data over a particular type of connection. The importance of this table is that devices often claim a high
connection rate or bandwidth when presented in marketing literature. Yet,
actually the data rate is what is important. Similarly, if you are familiar
with CD-ROM development, it is helpful to have a "feel" for the comparison of the speeds of CD-ROMs and network connections.

If you have done multimedia work before, you realize that even mod-
erate multimedia sound and video capability requires speeds of 200 KBps
or greater for adequate playback. Thus, devices appearing further up in
the chart (see table 1-1) will provide unacceptable results, such as video
that plays erratically or audio that inadvertently pauses. As it relates to
Flash development, such connections require that you preload content in
your movies so that those inadvertent pauses are not noticeable.

Given table 1-1, you can calculate the minimum (optimum) time it
will take for a given user to download web content, whether that content
is HTML and graphics, video, or Flash material. For example, imagine you
want to distribute a Flash file that is 300 KB to users on a 14.4 modem.

Table 1-1: Web Connection Types and Rates

Connection	Data Rate	Bandwidth	Time per 100 KB (sec.)
14.4 modem	1.8 KB	14.4 KB	55
28.8 modem	3.6 KB	28.8 KB	27
33.6 modem	4.2 KB	33.6 KB	23
56K modem	7 KB	56 KB	14
ISDN	7–16 KB	56-128 KB	14–6
Frame relay	7–64 KB	56–512 KB	14–1.5
T1	32–193 KB	256–1,544 KB	3.1–.5
1X CD	150 KB	1.2 MB	.66
DSL	188 KB	1.5 MB	.53
Cable modems	188 KB	1.5 MB	.53
2X CD	200 KB	1.6 MB	.5
4X CD	450 KB	3.6 MB	.22
10X CD	1.2 MB	9.6 MB	.08
Fast Ethernet	1.25 MB	10 MB	.08
16X CD	2.4 MB	19.2 MB	.04
24X CD	3.6 MB	28.8 MB	.02
T3	5.5 MB	44 MB	.01
USB	12 MB	96 MB	.0083
Firewire	100-400 MB	800 MB–3.2 GB	.001–.00025

The data rate for a 14.4 modem is 1.8 KBps. Thus, the minimum time it will take those users to download your 300-KB file is 2.7 minutes (300 KB / 1.8 KBps / 60 seconds = 2.78 minutes).

 TIP: *You can easily calculate bandwidth from data rate, or vice versa. Given a bandwidth, divide by 8 to obtain the data rate. Then divide the file size in kilobytes by the data rate. If you are dealing in megabytes, make sure you use equal scales and remember that 1,024 kilobytes is 1 megabyte (not 1,000 kilobytes). You can calculate bandwidth based on data rate by multiplying by 8.*

The key thing to remember is that bandwidth is measured in bits, kilobits, or megabits, whereas data rate is measured in bytes, kilobits, or megabytes. Data rate is what is important because file sizes are provided in byte measurements.

It must be noted that the connection speeds shown in table 1-1 assume optimum conditions; that is, only a single user connected to the data source. As more individuals attempt to access a site, the data rate is split across the total number of connections. This means that even though the user can download data at 188 KBps (assuming a 1.5-MBps DSL or cable modem connection), the server that is supplying the data may be serving 100 other users at the same time.

Speed is also lost in the physical hardware (routers, hubs, and so on) involved in the process. Both decrease the actual amount of data being served to each individual. Nevertheless, the simple download calculation provided can be used as a "rule of thumb" given optimum conditions when planning.

For Whom Are You Developing?

Ultimately, you must design for the end user; that is, according to their limitations and needs. In general, delivery of computer media is always limited by the weakest link, and thus you should always design per the lowest common denominator. There are other approaches, such as specifying a baseline that may or may not be consistent with the lowest common denominator, but more often than not designs are based on some baseline at a predetermined level.

One of the characteristics of good web developers is that they determine (or have in mind) the lowest common technological denominator (through research, knowledge of the audience, usability statistics, or other sources) among the intended audience before they even touch a computer. A good web developer knows a lot more than what looks good and works well. He or she also thinks logically about what can be delivered to that audience in a reasonable fashion.

Statistically, in relation to a normal or bell curve, the people you should design for are the middle 68 percent of your users, as indicated in figure 1-1. They are generally more alike than they are different. You should not design for the upper 16 percent, because they are the advanced users and will more than likely exceed your expectations in hardware, software, and skills. If you design for them, you eliminate 84 percent of your audience from viewing your site.

For example, say you are designing an e-commerce site targeting middle-aged users. This audience probably consists largely of in-home users who are not likely to pay a lot for web connections (thus, modem users) and who probably do not have a lot of computer experience (the 68 percent). A very small minority of them (the upper 16 percent) may be the

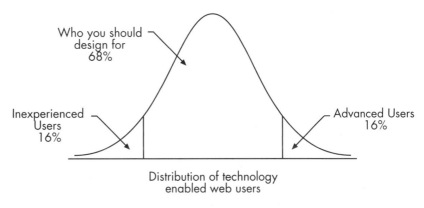

Figure 1-1. For whom should you design?

exact opposite: fast connections and a lot of experience. If you design for the advanced users, you probably will not sell much, because you are ignoring the majority of users. You must design for the middle section of users, who are more alike than they are different. If you design for the middle 68 percent, you can be assured that in reality 84 percent (the middle and upper range) of users will be able to access and use your site.

The lower 16 percent will always be behind the technology curve. They are the ones who may be using an archaic browser, may be afraid of downloading a plug-in due to "viruses," or for whatever reason cannot or will not make use of your site. Often, regardless of the accommodations you make in your web sites, the lowest 16 percent of users will never have the technology, skills, or desire to view and use your site. You cannot socially please or technologically accommodate everyone. The best web sites will be able to satisfy and accommodate the 84 percent. Prior to starting a site design, always try to establish what the majority of your users will have to work with and what they will be able to view.

 NOTE: *Based on research performed by NPD, a division of MediaMetrix, 98.4 percent of web browsers worldwide have the Flash Player installed, which translates to more than 414 million people that can view Flash immediately. Granted this simple statistic does not take into account what version each user has, but it points to the fact that the Flash Player is more widely distributed than most other technologies, including Java. For more information about the particulars of this research, as well as margin of error and other factors, visit: www.macromedia.com/software/flash/survey/.*

Flash: The De Facto Standard

Throughout this book you will discover many of the intricate benefits of using Flash for your creations. However, before you do, it would be beneficial to examine the big picture. For example, what are the most significant advantages of using Flash? Why are so many people choosing it for their web sites? There are seven major attributes of Flash that are the keys to its success and penetration in the web development community. The following sections examine these briefly.

 NOTE: *There are other standards under review for vector-based web graphics. Although space will not permit the discussion of them here, you may wish to research them, as they may have future implications. They include Scalable Vector Graphics (SVG), which you can research at* www.w3.org/Graphics/ SVG/, *and Web Computer Graphics Metafile (WebCGM), which you can research at* www.w3.org/Graphics/WebCGM/. *Of the two, SVG seems to hold the most promise, based on early indications.*

A Vector Environment

The most significant reason people are using Flash so heavily, if we can say there is only one reason, is the fact that Flash files are so small. The predominance of elements created in Flash are vector-based; that is, consisting of points, lines, arcs, and polygons. The alternative, raster or bitmap graphics, consist of individual picture elements, called pixels. Most of the time Flash will yield files that are one-half to one-quarter the size (if not more) of raster-based equivalents when comparing static images. Add to that small animation file sizes, and the file size savings starts to multiply exponentially.

Until the emergence of Flash, almost all content on the Web was raster based and was provided in the GIF or JPG file formats. Although these two file formats use compression to decrease file size, overall they are larger than a vector version of the same file. This is because raster images must define every picture element represented in the image with color, even if that area of the image represents a non-printing color.

Foundationally, it is the difference between vector and raster graphics that makes Flash so progressive in its approach to the content represented within it. That is not to say that Flash cannot include raster elements, but where Flash excels is that much of its content is vector based. As you begin working with Flash and its drawing capabilities in Chapter 4, you will begin to see the power of working with vector imagery and how small the files really are. Exercise 1-1 compares Flash, GIF, and JPG.

Exercise 1-1: Comparing Flash, GIF, and JPG

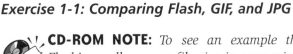

CD-ROM NOTE: *To see an example that highlights Flash's small average file size in comparison to GIF and JPG graphics, open the file* index.html, *located in the* fgai/chapter01/ ch01_01/ *folder on the companion CD-ROM. In the CD-ROM file you will find a web page that shows the file size comparison, as well as the visual comparison of Flash and these two raster image formats. Although this example shows only a static graphic, the file size savings is compounded dramatically when you start creating animation and interactive components.*

Other Benefits of Vector Graphics

Historically, vector graphics emerged as a way of creating graphics for high-resolution printing in the publishing industry without the severe overhead of bulky raster file sizes. Anyone who has tried to print a high-quality raster image from their desktop computer knows how problematic raster images can be when printing, let alone having to be concerned with the other attributes of these images, such as color and resolution. Thus, vector was at first a solution for this.

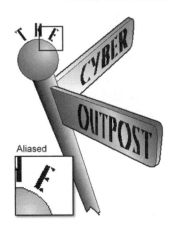

Figure 1-2. Aliased edges typify vector graphics displayed on screen.

However, until Flash, no one really thought about using vector graphics for animated or interactive components on the Web, although Macromedia was well on the way toward that notion with its "Shockwave" branding for FreeHand. The hesitancy to use vector for screen display was primarily due to the aliased edges that typify vector images on screen, as indicated in figure 1-2.

Because vector images presented a deficient, "jaggy" appearance on screen, small file sizes were negated because the visual quality was poor. If a company could create an application that retained the advantage of small file sizes (and the other positive attributes of vector imagery), while finding a way to overcome the "jaggy" nature of vector graphics on screen, they would have the next "hot" application for multimedia development. And that is exactly what Macromedia saw in FutureSplash Animator when the company purchased it and turned it into Macromedia Flash several years ago.

The Birth of Flash

For those interested, the source code for Macromedia Flash was actually created by a small company called FutureWave Software, Inc., in 1996. Based on a vector illustration product called SmartSketch that they had developed, FutureWave demonstrated its new FutureSplash Animator 1.0 product at the January 1997 Macworld Expo.

Soon after, FutureWave, SmartSketch, and FutureSplash Animator all disappeared, or so it seemed. Macromedia purchased FutureSplash and renamed it Flash. SmartSketch was sold to Broderbund Software, who has incorporated its features into some of their PrintShop range of products. Although such buyouts frequently spell doom for small, inventive products, Macromedia's purchase of FutureSplash Animator and the marketing and development that has been devoted to it is one of the main reasons it has had such an impact on the Web.

Antialiasing

The key to transforming vector graphics into an applicable screen delivery mechanism was the inclusion of automatic antialiasing found in the earliest version of Flash. Antialiasing, which (apart from the Web) was not a new concept at the time, is the blurring of the edges of graphic elements so as to create a smoother presentation, in either image or on screen.

When you create raster graphics in packages such as Adobe Photoshop or Corel PhotoPaint, the application will generally antialias elements as you create them. This is particularly important as it relates to text and geometry, such as circles and arcs, as well as angled lines. It is antialiasing that renders a bitmap image having a "smooth" or "photographic" appearance, as shown in figure 1-3. It was exactly this feature, performed automatically and at will, that makes Flash graphics look perfectly smooth, all the time and at any size. (See also exercise 1-2.)

Exercise 1-2: View Antialiasing at Any Size

CD-ROM NOTE: *To see an example that demonstrates Flash antialiasing at any size, open the file* index.html, *located in the* fgai/chapter01/ch01_02/ *folder on the companion CD-ROM. This example shows the same Flash movie displayed at multiple sizes. Note that the antialiasing is perfect at any size, giving it the "bitmap look" automatically.*

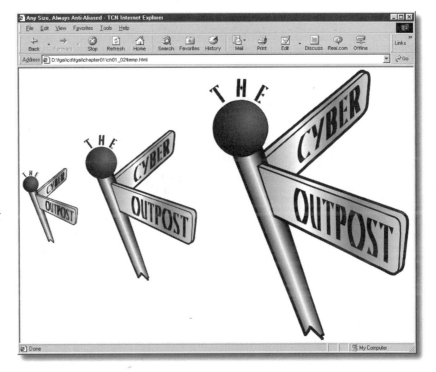

Figure 1-3. Automatically antialiased imagery is what made vector graphics applicable to screen display.

Scalability

Because Flash is vector based, it also has two other interrelated advantages: scalability and resolution independence. Although these two aspects are usually defined as one attribute, here they are defined individually because they mean two different things to the developer.

As to scalability, Flash movies can be placed into a web page at any size without visual degradation and without a change in file size (this can be seen in the example referenced in the previous CD-ROM Note). Additionally, you can permit the end user to dynamically scale, distort, or magnify the Flash asset at runtime if you so desire. These three things cannot be done with web-based raster images.

Let's take scaling (dynamically or otherwise) a raster graphic as an example. Typically, if you had a raster image you wanted to include in a web page, you would need to size it to (or create it at) the exact size it would appear in the web page in pixels prior to integrating it into the page. If the image is created larger than is needed and integrated into the web page, you are just wasting bandwidth, as well as the user's time, in that they have to download more data than is needed to view your image at the size you specified.

If you create the graphic too small and try to scale it up with the HTML < *IMG* > tag width and height attributes (a big no-no in non-Flash web development), the visual clarity of the image will likely fall apart, the result being a poor visual representation of what you have created. In addition, when the end user encounters that in-line graphic, regardless of size, it will only display at the size you have predefined it; there is no dynamic scaling, zooming, or interaction that can occur.

 NOTE: *Newer versions of Internet Explorer will let you "zoom" in and out of raster images in web pages when they are not image maps. But this is generally a woeful approach to what is being discussed here, and it is far from what is possible with Flash.*

Flash movies, on the other hand, are different. First, you need not be concerned with the exact size of a Flash movie when creating it. The key when developing Flash content is to be aware of the need for, and maintain, the appropriate aspect ratio; that is, the width-to-height ratio of the movie or the aspect ratio of the space you intend to place the Flash movie into.

If you are designing a full-screen Flash movie, you do not have to worry about whether the user is viewing at 640 pixels by 480 pixels, 800 pixels by 600 pixels, or whatever. Instead, you simply need ensure that your movie conforms to an aspect ratio of 4:3, because once the Flash movie is created you can define it at any physical size (as long as the aspect ratio remains constant), with no additional file size overhead or visual degradation. You will see examples of how this works as you progress through this book. You will also see that Flash movies are much more powerful, in that the user can interact with your graphical content (see exercise 1-3).

 Exercise 1-3: Interacting with a Flash Movie at Runtime

 CD-ROM NOTE: *To see an example of an interactive Flash movie that permits zooming and panning, open the file* index.html, *located in the* fgai/chapter01/ch01_03/ *folder on the companion CD-ROM. Later in this book you will learn how to create interactive graphics such as this example.*

Resolution Independence

Related to scalability (and in reality the reason Flash movies are scalable) is what is known as resolution independence. Resolution is descriptive of the visual clarity of a graphic, expressed in either dots per inch (dpi) or pixels per inch (ppi). Generally when dealing with screen media, you do not deal with it quite as much, but occasionally resolution becomes an issue.

All vector graphics are resolution independent, meaning that you can quite easily change the resolution to accommodate various output devices with no change in file size. Raster graphics, on the other hand, are called resolution dependent (or device dependent), meaning that the visual clarity (resolution) of the image is fixed the moment the image is created or scanned. Thus, prior to creating or scanning a raster image, you have to know what you want to do with the image so that you know what resolution you need (or do not need, as it relates to the Web). Once a raster image is created, you cannot "add" resolution, as you can with vector graphics. In reality you do not really "add" resolution to a vector image as it is really never "fixed" to begin with.

Where people run into trouble is when they want to reuse a raster image originally designed for the resolution of a particular device. For example, repurposing images designed for print for use on the Web (or vice versa) typically causes the most problems, mainly because the resolution of the images is being "force fit" or reengineered for another purpose.

Generally if you are going from print to the Web all you have to do is scale the image down to some appropriate size and resolution. However, going from the Web to print is much more problematic because in the best-case scenario raster images for the Web have about half as much resolution as images for print. But fortunately with vector-based Flash images you do not have to worry about it, as vector content is relatively portable and does not carry with it these concerns.

 NOTE: *Issues regarding raster resolution are further explored later in the book. As noted earlier, you can use raster images in Flash (preferably sparingly). When you do, you have to deal with raster resolution.*

Like vector imaging packages such as Macromedia FreeHand or Adobe Illustrator, the graphic content you create in Flash will be output at the appropriate resolution for whatever device you are sending the data to. Typically, you will be displaying it on screen, and with Flash's automatic antialiasing everything will look good. But what if the user wants to print your content? Well, that is the point of this discussion: resolution independence allows the printed form to look as good as it does on screen. You do not have to do anything except set your movie up so that the correct material prints, which is examined in Chapter 15.

Bitmap Graphics

As previously mentioned, although the elements you create in Flash are vector based, Flash provides the ability to include bitmap graphics in your movies. You will find that the typical raster formats can be used, including TIF, BMP, PCT (PICT), and many others. Some you will use, and others you probably should not, but it depends on the objective (explored later in the book).

There are some limitations to relying heavily on raster graphics in your Flash movies. Flash treats a raster graphic like any other authoring package; that is, it has no "magic" formula or special feature for overcoming the naturally larger file sizes associated with raster. However, with an intelligent approach to their use, even Flash movies that integrate bitmap graphics will be better than the run-of-the-mill HTML web site. Just keep in mind that the more raster images you add, even in Flash, the greater your file sizes and download times will become. This is discussed in greater detail in Chapter 7. (See also exercise 1-4.)

Exercise 1-4: Dynamically Loading Raster Images at Runtime

 CD-ROM NOTE: *To see an example of a interactive Flash movie that dynamically loads its raster images, open the file* index.html, *located in the* fgai/chapter01/ch01_04/ *folder on the companion CD-ROM. Later you will learn how to create such a movie.*

Animation

Aside from the issues related to the vector nature of Flash, one of its most often highlighted aspects is its animation capability. This is what Flash was originally known for (and still is to a large degree). Before Flash, animation on the Web was either based on GIF files, scripting languages such as JavaScript, or programming languages such as Java. However, Flash provides a completely vector-based environment for creating animations, which allows extremely small, portable files to be created.

Most of these other methods are based on raster images, meaning that they take significantly longer to download because none overcomes the problem of raster image file sizes. From full-screen to icon-sized animations, any dimensional size range can be included with web sites that use Flash. Flash permits the creation of three types of animation: frame-by-frame animation, motion tweening, and shape tweening (explored in Chapter 9). Similarly, you can integrate 3D work (in 2D form) from other programs (discussed in Chapter 10). (See also exercise 1-5.)

Exercise 1-5: Types of Animation in Flash

CD-ROM NOTE: *To see a quick example of the types of animation you can create, open the file* index.html, *located in the* fgai/chapter01/ch01_05/ *folder on the companion CD-ROM. This shows quick demonstrations of frame-by-frame motion tween and shape tween animations that you will learn how to create later in the book.*

Sound

One of the most intriguing things about Flash is its ability to integrate sound. For most sites that use audio, synchronization of the audio with visual data is easier because the audio is contained within the Flash file. It is not perfect, as you will learn, but it permits quite a degree of control over graphic and audio content on the Web. Using the timeline in Flash, which works much like Macromedia Director's timeline, the developer simply associates the sound with a particular frame in the movie. When the frame is encountered, the sound is played. You also have the ability to control sound with scripting, much like you do in Director.

Sound files used within authored Flash movies are stored as SWF files. Inside the Flash file, sounds can be compressed with one of the best sound compression technologies, MP3, as well as standard ADPCM compression. MP3 offers tremendous compressibility, making it possible to create long-playing animations (with voice-overs and/or music) of much smaller file sizes.

Moreover, because the audio is stored within the SWF file, there are no external references or additional HTML code needed. (See exercise 1-6.) Flash can import WAV, AIFF, AU, and MP3 files (as well as a wide range of video files), and can now do so dynamically at runtime, giving developers the choice as to whether to link or embed sound and video files. This and related topics are covered in Chapter 8.

Exercise 1-6: Utilizing Audio in Flash

CD-ROM NOTE: *To see and hear a quick example of audio in Flash, open* index.html, *located in the* fgai/chapter01/ch01_06/ *directory on the companion CD-ROM. You will need to make sure you have headphones or speakers to hear the audio.*

Video Integration

One of the most interesting features in Flash MX was the much improved video support capabilities. Now with Flash MX 2004, Macromedia has added much more to the video arsenal.

This feature, however, does come with one caveat: the overall limitations that exist with the delivery of video over the Web. Although Flash MX 2004 integrates one of the best codes on the market, there are many considerations and much preparation that has to transpire for video to work efficiently and effectively over the Web. Chapter 11 explores issues of video preparation and integration in association with using this new capability wisely. (See also exercise 1-7.)

Exercise 1-7: Utilizing Video in Flash

CD-ROM NOTE: *To see a quick example of a basic integration of video within Flash, open the file* index.html, *located in the* fgai/chapter01/ch01_07/ *directory on the companion CD-ROM.*

Interactivity and UI Componentry

Probably the most exciting long-term effect Flash is having on the Web centers on usability. Flash developers have the ability to create true graphical user interfaces and interactive components well beyond the rudimentary controls available in HTML-based forms or other web technologies. Often information is difficult to navigate due to interface deficiencies and reliance on the Web's "page" metaphor or the browser's UI.

Because every site is different, the user must learn to use and navigate each site, and often the navigation structure is based on the page structure rather than on a custom UI for the site. There is also the additional problem that the browser's functionality is far from a rich and rewarding experience in terms of customization.

Flash excels at being able to deliver rich graphics for exceptional user interfaces, and it provides facilities for more easily creating UI componentry, as shown in figure 1-4. It also now allows developers to build truly web-based applications using Flash as the backbone. From buttons and slider bars to complex original creations, authors can now create a unique experience for the users of their site, without the tremendous file size overhead typically associated with raster graphics or the limitations imposed by other technologies.

Scripting

Finally, Flash MX 2004 provides internal and external scripting capability and is based on a scripting engine that is "rock solid" in comparison with other multimedia authoring applications. The language is maturing rapidly, and is beginning to compete with many integrated development environments (IDEs) and programming languages in terms of functionality. Scripting in Flash is not just for multimedia anymore. Rather, it is nearing the level of a true application programming language (APL).

As you may know, Macromedia introduced significant revisions to its core scripting language in Flash 5, which were dubbed ActionScript. Modeled after the JavaScript Core Language (JCL) specification, Action-Script was well received by the development community and, upon the quick release of Flash 5, was used for everything from simple navigation to programmed animations and pseudo-application development.

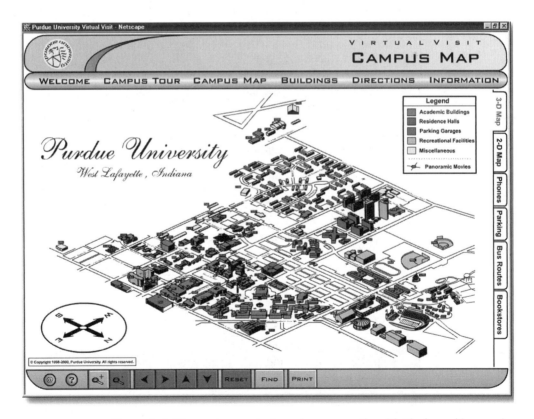

Figure 1-4. UIs can be created much more easily with Flash, making navigation more intuitive and user friendly.

▪▪▪ What's New in Flash?

Notwithstanding its major features—the reasons everyone in the web development community is clamoring for books, classes, and resources about Flash—Flash MX 2004 provides a lengthy list of new and revised features. Although this is not an exhaustive list (the full range and nitty-gritty details of which are explored in subsequent chapters), the following outlines what is new in Flash MX 2004. However, first we must acknowledge the new product split that exists in Flash. Following this discussion, you will read about the specific features of Flash MX 2004.

Flash MX 2004 and Flash MX Pro 2004

One of the decisions Macromedia made concerning post-MX Flash was that it would be advantageous to split the product into a designer and a developer edition to better meet the needs of these two groups of users. Thus, there are now two different editions of Flash: Flash MX 2004 and Flash MX Professional 2004. Flash MX 2004 is aimed at users who focus on creating visually responsive web content and interactive interfaces, whereas Flash Pro extends Flash MX 2004 by adding a plethora of additional features aimed at web application development.

The thing to realize about this dual-focused application is that only one of the two may be installed on a single machine. This is because they are actually the same application; Flash MX 2004 has some disabled features (which are Flash Pro features) and can be upgraded, which allows you to unlock to Flash Pro features in the currently installed Flash MX 2004 software.

Although some may view this as a questionable approach, it is actually quite logical in the evolution of Flash. And indeed, Flash MX 2004 alone has many features that will more than qualify it as a next-generation product. The following section details many of the new features found in Flash MX 2004. As you proceed through subsequent chapters, you will find that these features are elaborated upon further.

Flash MX 2004 Features

Flash MX 2004 includes several new features that can be grouped based on what aspect of the software a particular feature is an improvement upon. The new features can be grouped into productivity features, rich media support features, publishing features, and other new features.

Productivity Features

The following are productivity features new in Flash MX 2004.

- Timeline Effects

  In the past, creating transitions and even creating the most rudimentary animated elements required a lot of work – or at least more work than it should. The new Timeline Effects help you automate the creation of transitions and basic animation.

- Behaviors

  Several of Macromedia's other products integrate something called behaviors. Behaviors are pre-written scripts that simplify the task of assigning rudimentary interactivity to objects and frames. Behaviors provide a straightforward way of adding interactivity with little or no code writing.

- Templates

  With the release of Flash MX, Macromedia included several template files that were designed to help you get started creating content. These templates included pre-built files for various types of movies. Macromedia has extended this, including start-up files for a variety of types of movie files.

- Integrated and Improved Help System

  In times past, Flash included an HTML-based help system that used a Java applet for searching. However, this technique was sometimes difficult to work with in certain scenarios. Flash MX 2004 includes an integrated help system with an expanded ActionScript reference section and integrated lessons.

- Improved Undo and Redo

  Flash MX 2004's Undo and Redo commands can now track up to 1,000 things performed, making it very easy to move backward and forward in a step sequence as you work with a file. When combined with the new History panel, this is definitely a powerful new capability.

- History Panel

  The new History panel tracks all user interactions within the authoring environment. All of these interactions can be converted into reusable commands.

- Spell Checker

  Although spell checkers are certainly not something "new," it is a big improvement in Flash. No more searching through frames to find that misspelled word!

- Document Tabs

  If you are like most designers, when you are working in Flash you may have several Flash files open at a time. When multiple files are open, Flash provides document tabs at the bottom of the screen so that you can easily switch between your open Flash files (and you can instantly see what you currently have open).

- Start Page

  The Start Page features allows you to quickly choose what you want to do when you Start Flash or select New from the File menu. Similar to the dialog box shown in Microsoft Word when you select New from the File menu, this feature is focused in improving productivity.

- Find and Replace

  The Find and Replace command has been improved. Now you can search text strings, as well as font names, defined color, symbol names, sound names, video clip names, or important bitmap names.

Rich Media Support Features

The following are rich media support features new in Flash MX 2004.

- Adobe PDF and Illustrator 10 Support

  Flash can now directly import and export Adobe PDF and Illustrator 10 files. With the feature comes direct support of content contained within these file formats.

- Video Import Wizard

  The Video wizard is designed to help you import and encode video. It also provides presets and limited clip-editing features.

- Small Font Rendering

  The Small Font Rendering capability assists in the appearance of small fonts in your movies.

Publishing Features

The following are publishing features new in Flash MX 2004.

- Detection Kit

  The new Detection Kit makes it easier to distribute your Flash files. No more worrying about if end users have the plug-in or what version they might be running. This will help you deliver the right content without all the guesswork.

- Publishing Settings

  With Flash MX 2004, Publish Settings can now be saved and reapplied to multiple projects.

- Improved Accessibility

  A big addition to Flash MX was the ability to include accessibility information in Flash files. Flash MX 2004 improves on this by allowing greater control over tab order and improved support for screen readers and closed captioning.

- Complete Unicode Support

  This feature provides true multi-language authoring capabilities to Flash. In essence it allows you to author to any character set.

- Strings Panel

  This feature allows you to deploy content into multiple languages by tracking strings for localization.

Other New Features

The following are other features new in Flash MX 2004.

- Improved Performance

  The Flash Player has been greatly improved, with a performance increase of two to five times that of Flash MX. Generally, the performance increase will be seen in video playback, scripting, and general screen refresh rate.

- ActionScript 2.0 Support

  ActionScript has been improved and now adheres to the ECMA-script 3.0 specification. It now supports inheritance and strong typing of variables, and incorporates a revised event model.

▪ ▪ ▪ Summary

This chapter has provided a quick overview of some of the most important peripheral things you must think about when developing with Flash, or for that matter in terms of any type of web development. If you were not aware of the reasons Flash has captured so much attention in the web development community, they should now be apparent.

Flash's advantages range from those of its vector nature (file size, antialiasing, scalability, and resolution independence) to its support of bitmaps, sound, animation, video, and scripting. These are but the most obvious attractions. As is said, "the devil is in the details," and as you begin to look at these details in subsequent chapters you will gain a better understanding of why Flash is such a popular and powerful development tool.

chapter

2

Getting Started

▪▪▪▪ Introduction

Flash continues to be one of the most power web development tools available. In Chapter 1, you read about the new and wonderful things Flash MX 2004 can do and like most people are probably excited about the possibilities. This chapter gets you started by orienting you to the interface and to the environment settings you can establish in the application (settings that are "remembered" each time you open the application), as well as settings specific to an individual movie (settings particular to a specific project).

 NOTE: *As you begin to work, you will see two file types referenced quite often. Files with the .fla extension are native Flash application files; that is, files you create when you author a Flash movie. These can be readily reopened into Flash. Files with the .swf extension are "compiled," web-ready Flash files. Sometimes these can be reopened and sometimes not; it depends on whether they are set to "protected mode" or not.*

▪▪▪▪ Objectives

In this chapter you will:

- Learn about the Flash interface and its primary parts (toolbar, timeline, stage, and panels)
- Discover how you can customize the Flash user interface (UI)
- Find out about the various preference settings you can modify
- Become skilled at customizing document settings that allow you to configure your Flash file's stage size and other characteristics
- Learn how to customize the Flash keyboard shortcuts to your liking

- Understand the font mapping capability
- Find out how to open and play back a movie that contains both scenes and symbols
- Discover the many resources designed to help you get up to speed with Flash

The Flash Interface

If you are familiar with other Macromedia tools (particularly Director and, in some ways, Dreamweaver), you may find Flash's interface somewhat recognizable. If you are familiar with these other Macromedia tools, it has a familiar "feel" to it, as you might expect.

 TIP: *As you read along in this chapter, you might find it helpful to open Flash MX 2004 and interact with it as the text describes the interface and features.*

As a time-based program, Flash's interface is divided into several distinct areas that provide various capabilities. The Flash work area consists primarily of the toolbar, the timeline, the stage, and a variety of panels, as shown in figure 2-1.

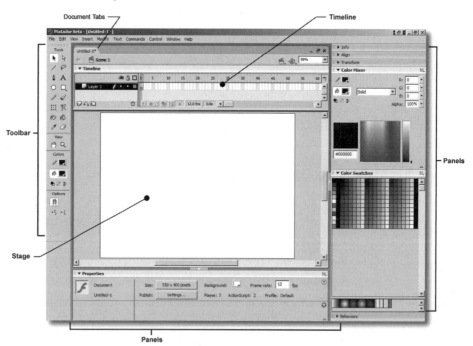

Figure 2-1. The Flash interface includes the toolbar, timeline, stage, and various panels.

One of the most important panels, the Properties panel, functions similarly to the panel of the same name in Dreamweaver. This is a panel you will likely keep open constantly, as it shows you the properties relevant to tools, objects, frames, and even the movie itself. The other panels you will close and open as needed, depending on how you like to work and whether you have multiple monitors.

The Toolbar

The toolbar, shown in figure 2-2, is divided into four sections: Tools, View, Colors, and Options. The Tools section contains the tools used to draw and paint objects on the stage, the tools used to manipulate objects, as well as the tools for selecting objects or portions of objects to be modified. The View section provides access to the Hand (pan) and Zoom tools, and the Colors section provides access to current line and fill colors.

At the bottom of the toolbar is the Options section, which shows the optional settings for the current tool. These options allow you to establish the way a tool behaves. For example, select the Brush tool and settings relevant to it appear in this area, such as Brush Mode, Brush Size, Brush Shape, and Lock Fills, as shown in figure 2-2. Note that as different tools are selected the options change. Only options that apply to the currently selected tool appear in this area.

 NOTE: *When working with tools in the next chapter, keep an eye on the available options. These indicate the current settings for a particular tool, as well as what control you have over the tool.*

The Timeline

Figure 2-2. The toolbar is divided into four sections: Tools, View, Colors, and Options.

The timeline is used to lay out elements in a movie. You define what you want to happen (and when) by defining the "layout over time" in the timeline. If you want something to appear on the stage at frame 5, for example, you do so by going to that time point in the timeline and creating, pasting, or placing that object on the stage. This establishes a keyframe. Depending on the duration you set for that object (how many consecutive frames the object occupies in the timeline), you can vary the length of time the object appears on the stage.

Aside from static objects, the timeline also permits the creation of frame-by-frame animation (similar to traditional cel animation) and something called tween animation. When static objects are added to the stage, keyframes are created that identify a key position, size, orientation, or color. By creating two keyframes with opposing characteristics for a particular object (that is, different sizes, orientations, scales, or colors), you can then tell the computer to automatically generate the in-between frames, called tweens, using a motion tween.

You can also create morph-type animations using a type of tweening called shape tweening. Thus, Flash can be used to create cel animations, motion tween animations, and shape tween animations. Chapters 10 and 11 delve more deeply into the subject of creating both cel and tweened animation in Flash.

The Stage

Most often, Flash files are displayed in the browser. However, Flash also allows you to create "projector files" that can be played totally apart from use of the browser or Web. Regardless of implementation, the stage is the area that will appear to the person looking at your Flash movie. Although it is the timeline that defines sequencing and timing, the stage visually shows the position and orientation of those objects—what the people that look at your movie will see.

For example, when authoring a movie, you choose a particular place you want something to occur in the movie, say frame 5. You set the timeline at that point and then place on the stage the items you want to appear at that point. Thus, while authoring you concurrently use the stage and timeline, placing objects on the stage at various points in the timeline.

Panels

The fourth part of the Flash environment is the various panels used to access and control everything from graphic componentry to coding. When you first start Flash, the panels are logically arranged for you. However, you can also change this arrangement. You can access all of these panels in the Window menu, to turn them on and off. All panels fall into one of three categories: Design Panels, Development Panels, or Other Panels. Also, if you are working at a particular screen resolution, or if you are constantly changing resolution as you work for testing purposes, you can quickly reset all panels to the appropriate size using the Window | Panel Sets submenu.

 TIP: *Some users may find the panel docking feature disconcerting. You can turn this off in the Edit | Preferences | General tab, discussed in material to follow.*

Although you will become familiar with each of the panels in subsequent chapters, the following list quickly describes what each does, as well as in which panel submenu it is located in the Window menu.

Window Menu

- *Properties*: Provides immediate access to all of the characteristics of a selected item, including tools, object properties (such as the characteristics of graphic or text objects), and document properties (the properties of the movie itself).

- *Library:* Used to "hold" and provide access to special Flash objects called symbols (reusable elements).

- *Help:* Provides access to the Flash Help information via a panel.

Design Panels Submenu

- *Align:* Allows you to quickly align or distribute objects on the stage.

- *Color Mixer:* Permits you to create color swatches that can then be used for lines, fills, or the background color of the stage.

- *Color Swatches:* Gives access to all of the defined colors for lines and fills available for objects. Colors are created in the mixer and then saved in the palette for use.

- *Info:* Shows detailed information about an object and the mouse on the stage, such as X and Y coordinate locations and color at the specific location.

- *Scene:* Allows you to organize the "scenes" (specific sections) in your movie.

- *Transform:* Gives you ready access to transforms applied to an object, such as scale, rotation, and skew. Unlike most graphic editors, Flash remembers the transform of an object, which is very handy.

Development Panels Submenu

- *Actions:* Lets you write code for an object to do something. The Actions panel is used to create, modify, and assign actions to objects.

- *Behaviors:* Provides access to predefined code elements called behaviors (similar to those provided in Dreamweaver and Director).

- *Components:* Allows you to more easily create and use complex interactive components such as drop-down menus and radio buttons. Flash comes with many preexisting components, but you can also create and add your own to this panel.

- *Component Inspector:* Provides access to information concerning components. For the panel to contain information, you must select a component on the stage.

- *Debugger:* Provides the capability to analyze what is happening within a movie as it is playing and, as its name implies, helps you debug your movies.

- *Output:* Provides feedback about movies. It can also be used as an aid during scripting.

Other Panels Submenu

- *Accessibility:* Allows you to add accessibility information to the objects in your movie, so as to better support interpretation of your Flash movies via a nonvisual browser.

- *History:* Provides a listing of all of the things you have done in the environment so that you can back up; similar to a selective undo.

- *Movie Explorer:* Allows you to quickly view all elements in the movie, as well as perform a certain amount of editing on those elements.

- *Common Libraries:* This provides access to libraries of Flash symbols. See also Chapter 6.

For now, do not worry about remembering all of the panels and what each one does. All you need to know at this point is where the panels are accessed. Each of these panels is discussed in detail throughout the course of the book.

UI Customization

Flash supports many GUI customization capabilities to help you work more efficiently. One of the first things you will notice is that the area surrounding the stage (including the top, bottom, and left- and right-hand sides) can be used as a "docking area" for panels. By default, the timeline is docked at the top, the toolbar to the left, and panels at the bottom and right. You can reconfigure this, as well as undock items, if you wish.

For example, you can "tear off" the toolbar or any of the panels (see figure 2-1 for default locations) and place these items wherever you want. You do so by click-dragging on the small "textured" area to the left of the item's gray title bar (see figure 2-3a, which shows a panel in default docked location). By detaching the timeline or any one of the panels, you can create more useful configurations within single and dual monitor systems.

Once you have "detached" an item, an additional blue bar is shown (see figure 2-3b), indicating that the item is undocked (floating). When the title bar is blue, grabbing any part of the title bar allows you to move the item. To reattach the item in the docking area, click-drag and release the item near one of the docking areas around the stage. When you release the item (assuming docking is turned on), the item will snap into place in the docking area and the blue bar will be gone, indicating that the item is docked.

 NOTE: *When you want to dock a panel that is currently floating, you must grab the gray textured area to the left of the item's name to get it to dock. If you grab the blue title bar and release it near a docking area, the item will not dock. The blue title is used only for moving. The only exceptions to this are the toolbar, timeline, and stage. When these are detached, there is no gray bar, so you move and redock these by click-dragging the blue bar.*

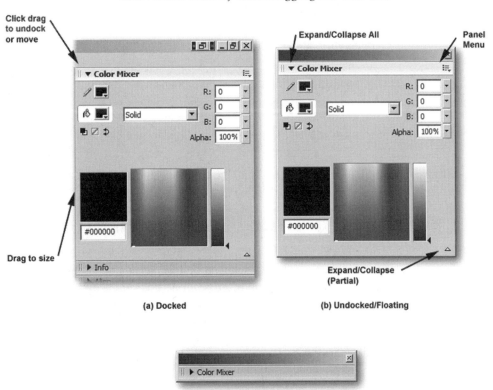

Figure 2-3. Panels can be moved from their default location by clicking to the left of the panel name (a), which makes them float (b). They can also be collapsed in their floating position (c) or in their docked position.

When the timeline or the panels are in their default "docked" locations, note that the separation border between the stage and these items can be sized by click-dragging the area between the item and the stage (see figure 2-3a). Additionally, the small triangle in front of the item name in the title bar can be clicked to compress or expand the item (figure 2-3b). Figure 2-3c shows a compressed, undocked (floating) panel.

Another important thing to take note of is that most panels have a menu of their own, which can be accessed on the right-hand side of the panel's gray title bar (figure 2-3b). Some panels, such as the Color Mixer, have an additional compress/expand feature, as indicated by the small arrow to the lower right of the panel. This allows you to decrease the amount of screen area needed by the panel in that it partially collapses the panel.

 TIP: *If you are a developer and do not currently have a dual-head machine (i.e., a machine that has dual monitors), this could possibly be one of the best investments you could make. Productivity can increase as much as 200 percent by simply having multiple monitors.*

As mentioned, Flash provides predefined panel layouts based on your screen resolution settings. It also allows you to save your panel arrangements and their placement on screen. Notice the Window | Save Panel Arrangement option. By selecting this, you can name and save your panel arrangements however you choose. Once you name and save a panel, it will appear in the Window | Panel Sets submenu. If you wish to delete a panel set, access the Flash MX 2004/Panel Sets folder on your hard drive and delete the name of the panel set you wish to eliminate.

▪ ▪ ▪ Setting Up Your Work Environment

As previously noted, Flash provides many options for customizing the work environment. Some of these options adjust the default settings for the application. Others modify default settings for the file on which you are currently working. The following sections examine ways of customizing the work environment, including settings related to movie files.

Preferences

Several of Flash's operating parameters can be customized. All environment settings are presented in a single tabbed dialog box. You access the settings using Edit | Preferences.

General

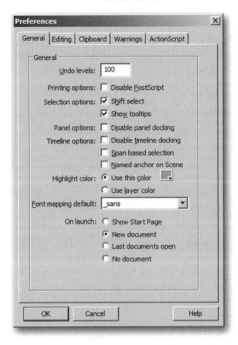

Figure 2-4. The Preferences dialog box allows you to customize many aspects of the Flash environment.

The General tab of the Preferences dialog box, shown in figure 2-4, allows adjustments to be made to general environment variables, including the following.

- *Undo Levels:* Specifies the number of consecutive Edit | Undo commands you can execute. The default is 100, but Flash 2004 can track up to 1000 you do in the environment.

- *Printing Options:* This Windows-only feature disables Postscript output when printing. Select this only when encountering problems printing Flash files.

- *Selection Options:* Defines how multiple objects are selected and whether tool tips are shown. By default, this checkbox is selected, which means that you must press the Shift key to select multiple objects. If you prefer being able to automatically add objects to a selection without holding down the Shift key, deselect this option.

 NOTE: *A tooltip is a descriptor that appears when you hold the cursor over a tool or item in the work area for a couple of seconds.*

- *Panel Options:* Allows you to control whether panels automatically dock when positioned near the Flash application window. Whether this is deselected or not, you can still reconfigure panels by click-dragging them.

- *Timeline Options:* The first checkbox allows you to define whether the timeline can be "docked" above the stage area. Here you can also control how frames and sprites (objects in the timeline consisting of a keyframe and a duration) are selected in the timeline using the second checkbox. If you want Flash to operate like Flash 5, select this checkbox. With the third checkbox, you can force Flash to automatically name the first frame of a scene (a "named anchor"). This is used in conjunction with the Forward and Backward buttons for navigation. All three of these checkboxes are disabled by default.

- *Highlight Color:* This Preference option allows you to determine what color is used for highlighting. You may select a color or allow the layer color to be used.

- *Font Mapping Default:* Sets the default device font used by Flash in the application. Flash includes three generic device fonts: sans, serif, and typewriter. See also Chapter 5.

- *On Launch:* Allows you to determine how the Flash environment starts. When the Flash application starts you can have it automatically start with a new, blank movie, the last movie you were working with, or with no open movie.

Editing

The Editing tab, shown in figure 2-5, allows you to set the default characteristics of the Pen tool, set text defaults (to accommodate non-Roman content creation), and establish general drawing settings. Options on this tab include the following.

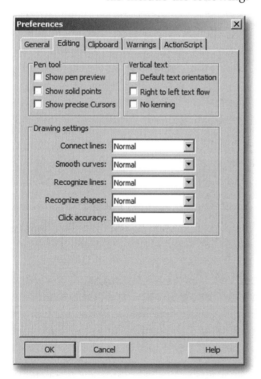

Figure 2-5. The Editing tab allows you to establish defaults for the Pen tool and text, and to establish various drawing settings.

- *Show Pen Preview:* Allows you to preview line segments as you draw them. If you enable this feature, once you select the first point, Flash will display a preview of the line segment as you move the cursor around the screen.

- *Show Solid Points:* In practice, this setting determines whether Flash Bezier points work like Macromedia FreeHand or like Adobe Illustrator. FreeHand displays deselected points as hollow, and selected points as solid. Illustrator is the opposite. If you are familiar with FreeHand, leave this option deselected. If you are familiar with Illustrator, you may want to select this option to make the environment more like what you are used to.

- *Show Precise Cursors:* This setting changes the Pen tool cursor to crosshairs for more precise drawing (as opposed to using a less precise icon).

- *Default Text Orientation:* Sets the default orientation for text in your movies to vertical (rather than horizontal). This option, as well as the two that follow, are for creating movies for Asian and other non-Roman languages.

- *Right to Left Text Flow:* As its name implies, this forces the default alignment of text to be built from the right-hand side of the screen to the left-hand side.

- *No Kerning:* Turns off kerning, which is the special spacing applied to specific Roman letter combinations to achieve more aesthetically pleasing results.

- *Connect Lines:* Controls the distance required before a line or other entity snaps to a point.

- *Smooth Curves:* Determines the smoothing algorithm when using the smooth modifier associated with certain drawing tools.

- *Recognize Lines:* Sets the accuracy of line recognition.

- *Recognize Shapes:* Controls the accuracy of shape recognition.

- Click Accuracy: Defines the accuracy of mouse movements and clicks.

 NOTE: *Flash can automatically recognize certain shapes. In the later chapter on drawing, you will understand how curve, line, and shape recognition works.*

Clipboard

Flash can include bitmaps either through the clipboard or by importing them. In comparison, importing files provides the user with more control. However, by using Preferences, adjustments can be made regarding the input of a pasted bitmap, as well as how vector elements are copied out of Flash. Note that some of these are platform-specific settings.

As shown in figure 2-6, the Bitmaps section allows modifications to be made to the three primary attributes of a raster element from the clipboard. In Chapter 7, you will look at these and other specifics in more detail. For now, just know that the Preferences | Clipboard tab, when on a Windows platform, provides the following control options over content being brought into Flash from the clipboard.

- *Color Depth:* Controls the default bit depth (color fidelity) of images pasted from the clipboard.

- *Resolution:* Controls the default resolution (image clarity) of images pasted from the clipboard.

- *Size Limit:* The file size limit for pasted raster images. When a pasted bitmap is larger than the specification, Flash prompts you.

- *Smoothing:* Establishes whether Flash automatically smoothes pasted bitmaps (more on this in Chapter 7).

- *Gradients:* Controls the quality of vector gradients copied from Flash for pasting into other programs.

On the Macintosh, the Clipboard tab instead provides the following four options for the user to control PICT content pasted from the clipboard.

- *Type:* Lets Flash know what to expect from the clipboard, specifically in regard to vector or raster data.

- *Resolution:* Sets the resolution for imported data (typically only associated with raster data).

- *Include PostScript:* Allows PostScript data to be imported with accompanying raster data.

- *Gradients:* Controls the gradient quality of PICT gradients stored on the clipboard; that is, levels of gradation within fills from other vector programs.

On both platforms, the following option is also available.

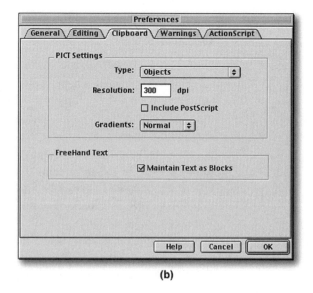

(a)   (b)

Figure 2-6. Adjustments can be made regarding the input of pasted bitmaps, as well as other parameters, but the options you see can vary, depending on if you are (a) a Windows user or a (b) Macintosh user.

- *FreeHand Text:* Controls how text blocks are pasted from FreeHand. If this option is not selected, text is pasted as group vector outlines grouped by character.

Warnings

The Warnings tab, shown in figure 2-7, controls what things will generate user prompts. These settings include the following.

- *Warn on Save for Macromedia MX compatibility:* This warns when you are about to save as an older Flash file, letting you know that Flash MX 2004 features you have used will not work. If the file contains no Flash MX 2004 specific content, you will not be prompted even if this is selected.

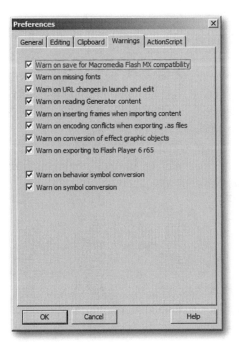

Figure 2-7. The Warnings tab allows you to establish what Flash will alert you about.

- *Warn on missing fonts:* This alerts you if you open a native Flash FLA file that is requesting fonts you do not have on your machine.

- *Warn on URL Changes in Launch and Edit:* Flash content can be launched and edited directly within Dreamweaver (if you have it installed). This setting has a Flash prompt alerting you if you launch and edit the URLs in a Flash movie in Dreamweaver and then return to Flash.

- *Warn on reading Generator content:* Flash MX 2004 does not support Generator content. Thus, this setting makes Flash display a large red X through Generator content contained in a movie.

- *Warn on inserting frames when importing content:* When you import audio or video content, Flash often adds frames to the current timeline. This setting has Flash alert you when frames are added during import of content.

- Warn on encoding conflicts when exporting AS files: This makes Flash warn you when you are attempting to save the external ActionScript file (AS file) as a format other than that specified in Flash's Preferences setting in the ActionScript tab.

- *Warn on conversion of effect graphic objects:* Has Flash warn you when you try to edit a symbol that has a Timeline Effect applied to it (editing the symbol can be detrimental to the applied Timeline Effect).

- *Warn on exporting to Flash Player 6 r60:* This has Flash warn you when you create an SWF file that is for an earlier version of Flash.

ActionScript

One of the nice features of coding in Flash MX 2004 is syntax highlighting. When you start working with ActionScript in Flash, you will find that the color coding used for different parts code you write makes it easier to decipher what you have written. In Flash MX 2004, you can customize the colors used for such highlighting, as well as several other aspects via the Preferences dialog box, as shown in figure 2-8. These preferences include the following.

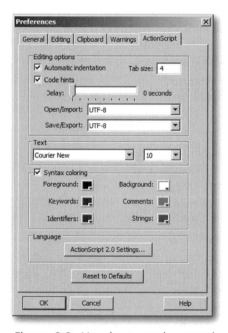

Figure 2-8. You have much control over the formatting of you Action-Script code in Flash MX 2004.

- *Automatic Indentation and Tab Size:* Controls whether or not Flash automatically indents your ActionScript code, as well as the size of the tabs used for indentation.

- *Code Hints and Delay:* Flash MX 2004 incorporates code hints that will help you enter ActionScript code. The Delay option controls how long you must pause your typing for Flash to prompt you with the code hint.

- *Open/Import and Save/Export:* One of the advanced features of Flash is the ability to write your ActionScript code in external text files, named with the *.as* extension. The Open/Import and Save/Export dropdown lists let you define the type of text file that is imported or exported when using external script files.

- *Text:* Allows you to completely control the font style and size used for the ActionScript editor.

- *Language:* This element controls the version of ActionScript you intend on using in your file.

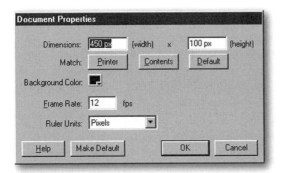

Figure 2-9. The Document Properties dialog box allows modifications to be made to certain parameters of Flash documents (movies).

Document Properties

Just as Preferences allows you to set parameters for the Flash application, the Movie Properties menu option allows modifications to be made to certain parameters of movie files themselves. If the Modify | Document menu option is selected, the Document Properties dialog box is presented (figure 2-9). Here, you can set several of the current file's properties. The Document Properties options include the following.

- *Dimensions:* Defines the size of the stage. You may specify pixel or inch measurements, with sizes ranging from 1 x 1 to 2880 x 2880 pixels. The default is 550 x 400 pixels.

- *Match:* Allows the stage dimensions to be automatically set to match the printer, the content of the stage, or the default.

- *Background Color:* Sets the color of the background of the stage.

 NOTE: *The background color of the stage is one of the most important items in the Movie Properties dialog box. The background color of the stage may be set to any currently defined solid color. To define colors, you must use the Color Mixer panel. Chapter 4 discusses how to define solid colors using this panel, as well as the Swatches panel.*

- *Frame Rate:* Controls the rate at which a movie plays. The frame rate is specified in frames per second (fps), with the default being 12.

- *Ruler Units:* Sets the default units used within your movie. Because Flash movies are typically designed for screen display, Pixels is the default.

Keyboard Shortcuts

Another customization capability Flash MX 2004 provides is the ability to create your own customized set of keyboard shortcuts for commands and features. By default, Flash uses its own built-in shortcuts. Yet, you can modify the existing shortcuts, save sets of shortcuts, rename and delete sets, or select predefined keyboard shortcuts for making Flash work like

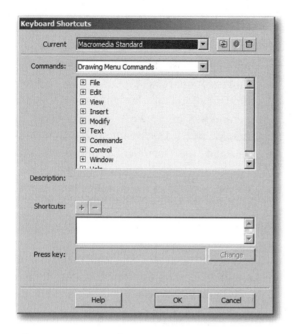

Figure 2-10. Use the Keyboard Shortcuts dialog box to edit the keyboard shortcuts in Flash.

other applications, such as FreeHand, Fireworks, Illustrator, and Photoshop.

To modify shortcuts, use the Edit | Keyboard Shortcuts option to open the Keyboard Shortcuts dialog box, shown in figure 2-10. Note that you cannot change the existing default shortcuts. To create your own set, you must first duplicate one of the existing sets (see the tooltip shown near the cursor in figure 2-10) and then modify the settings within the duplicated set. Once you have duplicated a set, select an item in the Commands section of the dialog, select the Press Key field, and press the keyboard combination you want for the item. The dialog box will indicate whether there are conflicting shortcuts. Use the Rename and Delete buttons to perform those actions on a shortcut set.

Font Mapping

Fonts are one of the most notorious things developers have to work with in regard to multimedia and hypermedia development. Due to differences between platforms, as well as the simple fact that there are so many different fonts that exist, you frequently have to be concerned about fonts when you share FLA files with others.

As it relates to the web-ready files you create from Flash, you do not have to worry, as this is one of the advantages of using Flash for movies intended for the Web. However, when you work in multi-developer environments, fonts in FLA files can be unwieldy. For example, do the other developers you are working with have the fonts you have? Will you have the fonts they have? It is not as simple as "sharing font files with one another," as this is generally illegal.

Flash MX 2004 provides an easy way of reassigning the fonts called for in a movie (for display purposes). When you open a native Flash file (FLA) and you do not have the font faces needed on your computer system, Flash will provide you with the ability to reassign the fonts called for with fonts currently available on your machine. The visual design in your movie may change, but at least you will be able to read the text in the movie. Not uncommonly when font substitutions are made "automatically" by the computer the result is a symbolic font, such as Zapf Chancery, making it impossible to read.

This feature (font mapping) is similar to the feature of the same name in Director. If your machine has all of the necessary fonts, or if the FLA file has the fonts embedded (and you are on the same platform on which the FLA was developed), the font mapping is not needed. If not, you can employ font mapping to at least make "logical" font substitutions, instead of leaving it up to the computer to decide. This issue is discussed in detail in Chapter 5.

▪ ▪ ▪ Working with Flash Movies

As you have read, with the timeline you organize and control when elements are displayed in relation to time in your movies. The visual location and the characteristics of the objects displayed (size, position, orientation, and so on) are set on the stage. Let's examine how to open up basic Flash files and get them to play back.

 NOTE: *One of the new features of Flash MX 2004 is revealed when you open multiple movies at once. When you have more than one movie open at a time, small tabs appear at the bottom of the stage area (between the Properties panel and the stage). The tabs are named according the movie file names. You can easily switch to any file by clicking on its tab.*

Timeline Playback Basics

Frames or cels (in terms of traditional cel animation) are laid out along the timeline, corresponding to the times various objects appear on the stage. In animation, a frame is actually a single instance in time and is the smallest unit of measurement in an animation. The compilation of frames creates the animation during playback. In exercise 2-1, you will work with a Flash file, but first read the following CD-ROM Note.

 CD-ROM NOTE: *You may choose to work from the CD-ROM or from the hard drive. It is recommended, however, that you copy the files to a hard drive or other writable medium. As you get into the later chapters, having the files located on a hard drive will make working with the files easier. One particular function in Flash, the Test Movie command, requires that Flash be able to write to the drive. If you work exclusively from the CD-ROM, the Test Movie option will not be able to function and you will be prompted with an error when you try to use it.*

Exercise 2-1: Working with a Sample Flash File

 CD-ROM NOTE: *To begin working with a sample Flash file, open the file* ch02_01.fla, *located in the* fgai/chapter02/ *folder, installed from the companion CD-ROM.*

As you read the following paragraphs, experiment with the sample file. Figure 2-11 shows an example movie with several frames in the timeline. Note that the movie contains five layers. Each layer contains a different component that appears on the stage over time. Each layer is like an acetate sheet on which you draw. You will learn more about this in Chapter 3.

The small red indicator (shown over frame 15 in figure 2-11) indicates the frame currently being shown on the stage. You can move the playhead to a different frame by click-dragging the playhead or by simply clicking once in any frame in the timeline. As you do so, you see the "state" of the elements on the stage at the chosen instance in time.

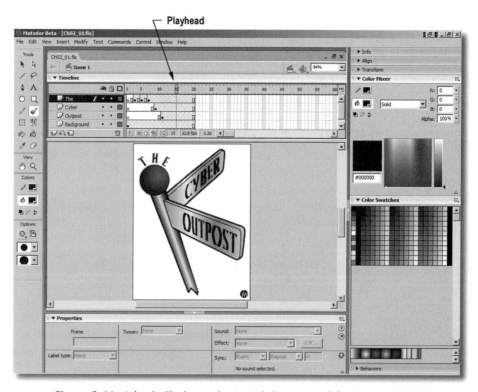

Figure 2-11. A basic Flash movie containing several frames and layers.

One method of playing back an entire movie is to let the Flash application play it for you directly. There are several ways to do this. You can use Control | Play or simply press the Enter key. When you do this, the program will play the movie back once. You can select Control | Loop Playback to get the movie to loop continuously. When a movie is playing in the Flash application, you can use the Escape key (or select Control | Stop) to stop it. Of course, you can simplify all of this by opening the Controller toolbar, by selecting Window | Toolbars | Controller. This opens a small panel that provides "VCR-like" controls, all in one panel.

 NOTE: *Some movies contain special elements called symbols, as well as ActionScript coding, that can only be played back using the Control | Test Movie menu option. This and what the rest of the options in the Control menu are used for are discussed in detail in later chapters. For the exercises in the early chapters of this book, Control | Play and Control | Stop will suffice.*

Movies with Scenes

If frames could only be placed along a single timeline in Flash, it would be quite a limiting tool. Either the timeline would be very long or you would have to jump from one movie to another using coding in order to create lengthy (or "long-playing") movies. Flash allows the developer to work with multiple "main" timelines within a single movie (see exercise 2-2). This provides a means of organizing different parts of a movie within a single, self-contained FLA file. It also helps keep timeline lengths manageable. Appropriately, each timeline in a movie is called a scene. Each scene may contain its own set of objects. Additionally, there may be any number scenes in a single movie.

 NOTE: *In the development community there is much discussion about whether scenes should be used. The reality is that it depends on the situation. There are positives and negatives, as well as alternatives. In Chapter 3 you will read more about this. For now, simply note that some movies may contain more timelines than you can see when you first open the file.*

Exercise 2-2: Working with a Sample Movie with Multiple Scenes

 CD-ROM NOTE: *To see a sample movie that has multiple scenes, open* ch02_02.fla, *located in the* fgai/chapter2 *folder, installed from the companion CD-ROM.*

Figure 2-12 shows an image from the previously cited sample movie. Flash provides quick access to the scenes stored in a movie via the Scene button on the right-hand side of the Edit path, shown in figure 2-12. Clicking on this button reveals the scenes available in the movie. You can easily switch to any scene by clicking on its name in the Scene drop-down list. The name of the scene currently shown on the stage is displayed on the left-hand side of the Edit path.

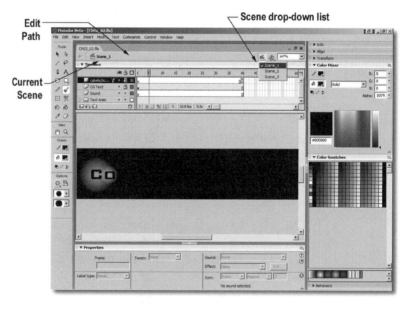

Figure 2-12. Flash movies may contain multiple timelines, called scenes, which are accessible via the Scene drop-down list on the right-hand side of the Edit path. The current scene is displayed on the left-hand side of the Edit path.

When a movie has multiple scenes, you can use the Control menu selection Control | Play to play all scenes in the movie. Typically when scenes are used in a movie there will be ActionScript code that will make Flash jump from scene to scene during playback (and the jumping does not have to be linear). When you use Control | Play All Scenes, Flash plays the scenes in their linear order; that is, as they are arranged in the Scene drop-down list. The movie associated with this exercise also has ActionScript assigned to the last frame of each scene. In this case, you could select Control | Enable Simple Frame Actions to also make the movie play back all of its scenes.

When you want to create a movie with multiple scenes, you add scenes to the movie as you progress through the develop- ment process; that is, you add them as needed. Another way to see the scenes in a movie is to use the Scene panel, shown in figure 2-13. In addition to its use for seeing all scenes in a movie, this panel (as you will learn later) can be used to add, remove, rename, and rearrange scenes.

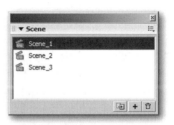

Figure 2-13. The Scene panel can be used to add, delete, rename, duplicate, or rearrange scenes in a movie.

 NOTE: *Most of the files associated with the beginning chapters of this book can be played back using Control | Play. However, not all movie files can be played back this way. Some require the use of Control | Test Movie (specif- ically, movies that contain symbols, and some types of ActionScript code). Remember that to be able to use Test Movie the Flash file must reside on a write-enable drive. You cannot use Test Movie directly on the files contained on the companion CD-ROM.*

Movies with Symbols

Often Flash movies will include particular elements (such as a logo, a graphical button, or an animated segment) that will be needed more than once in a movie. The item may be needed in multiple frames, in multiple scenes, or even across multiple movies. For this purpose, something called symbols can be created and used. Symbols allow you to create reusable components in your movies that can help you keep your file sizes much smaller. They also let you do some pretty powerful things. A symbol is really nothing more than a specialized timeline that is portable (meaning that it can be inserted anywhere in a movie or across multiple movies) and reusable (in that reusing the element does not increase file size).

As you start to dissect the examples in this book, as well as those from other sources, you may not find everything in the movie laid out all nice and neat along the main movie timeline, as you saw in the previous two examples. The early examples in this book are indeed simplified and do not use symbols to make it easier as you start using Flash. However, almost all Flash movies utilize symbols because they are so powerful. Thus, if you start poking around a Flash file from the later chapters or from another source and cannot find the "content" for the file, it is likely the content has been stored as symbols.

Like scenes, one of the quickest ways to get a peek as to whether a file uses symbols is to check the Symbols drop-down list, which is to the left of the Scenes drop-down list on the right-hand side of the Edit path. Later in the book you will learn other (generally more efficient) ways of accessing these items. For the moment, simply note that symbols exist, in case you are tinkering with a file and just cannot figure out what is going on.

■ ■ ■ **The Flash Pipeline**

The "Flash pipeline" refers to a (generally) three-stage process. You begin by authoring your movies in the native Flash MX 2004 format, which on a Windows platform has the *.fla* extension. This is the type of file typically shared among developers, and it can be readily reopened into the application for editing. There are some nifty things in Flash MX 2004 designed to make sharing development files easier, discussed in a later chapter concerning symbols and libraries.

 TIP: *Even if you are using a Macintosh, you should get into the habit of adding file extensions to the end of all files you create, particularly when dealing with graphic or multimedia file formats. If you try to give your files with no extensions to a Windows user, she will not without being told be able to determine what type of file you are providing.*

The second type of file you generate is that created during testing of your movies. While you are working on your Flash movies, you typically test the files frequently, using one of the two techniques described earlier in this chapter. In-process test files (SWF files) are only generated when you use the Control | Test Movie option. When you use Control | Play and Control | Stop to play back a movie in Flash, no web-ready files are created. "Why two methods to do the same thing?" you may ask.

In reality, the Control | Play method of playback is a "quick and dirty" technique for testing the simplest of movies and cannot be used when a movie contains more advanced things such as symbols or more complex

ActionScript. In this regard, the simple Play and Stop commands do not generate an SWF file. You will find that more often than not you will use Test Movie for just about all of your testing.

The last stage of the process is when you are finished with a project and are ready to distribute it. Here, you create a final set of files—sometimes consisting of only a single SWF or EXE (executable) file and at other times consisting of multiple formats from HTML to MOV (QuickTime movie format). The type and number of files created at the end of the process will depend on how you want to distribute your files (discussed in depth in Chapter 12).

As you set out to learn Flash, you should realize the steps in the Flash pipeline and what is typically generated at each stage. More of the details of each of these "phases" are elaborated upon in subsequent chapters.

■ ■ ■ Information/Assistance Resources

Since Flash 4, developers and Macromedia alike have generated a tremendous number of sources of information, several of which you may find helpful in your quest to learn Flash MX 2004. However, before you look at other sources, first become familiar with the materials that come with the Flash software. The software installation CD-ROM is a good place to start, because many times not all of the materials on an installation CD-ROM are automatically installed. Before reading the next section, take a quick look at the materials on your installation CD-ROM. Often there are extra things on it, such as third-party tools and other "goodies."

Sources in Flash

Inside the Flash application you will note several items that will be helpful when working in Flash. These include the following.

- Flash MX 2004 now includes a truly integrated help system that is similar to other non-HTML based help system. There is a wealth of information included in the Help system.

- One of the best developer resources is the Flash Support Center, housed at Macromedia's web site: *www.macromedia.com/support/flash/*. This site contains the latest news about Flash MX 2004, the most important component of which is TechNotes. If you have a problem, this is the first and generally best place to look.

Sources at Macromedia

In addition to the materials that come with the software and that are accessible within Flash, there is a wealth of web sites for developers. Most provide articles, examples, tutorials, and the like. Macromedia maintains a current list of sites designed to help the developer at the following address.

www.macromedia.com/support/flash/ts/documents/flash_websites.htm

In addition to the developer-oriented sites not maintained by Macromedia, there are many newsgroups available for Flash developers. The list is available at the following address, and you are encouraged to take advantage of the mass of information available.

www.macromedia.com/support/flash/ts/documents/tn4149-flashnews.html

 NOTE: *You may also wish to contact the author at* jlmohler @purdue.edu. *Although he may not be able to respond to every question or comment, he will try.*

▪ ▪ ▪ Summary

In this chapter you have been introduced to the main parts of the Flash application and some basics of how Flash movies can be played back. At this point, if the timeline/scenes/symbols discussion is hazy in your mind, do not worry. Subsequent chapters deal with these topics methodically and in depth. For now, simply note the various methods required to play back the example movies.

This chapter also dealt with the preferences and document settings you can manipulate to make Flash MX 2004 and your movie files behave the way you want. In addition, although you likely want to get busy learning more, take some time to examine the wealth of additional resources available in and out of Flash MX 2004. Many of these are invaluable sources of information.

chapter

3

Flash Basics

▪ ▪ ▪ Introduction

In the last chapter, you where introduced to the Flash MX 2004 application interface and its main parts. If you are familiar with other graphics applications, such as Macromedia FreeHand or Adobe Illustrator (or even to some extent features in raster applications such as Photoshop or CorelDraw!) some of this chapter should be review. This applies particularly to the discussion of features such as grouping, locking, and layering, which Flash shares with common graphics applications.

However, there are some particulars specific to Flash that are unlike other applications you have likely used—thus the primary reason for this chapter. In addition, discussion of the methods of selecting and working with graphic objects, as well as transforming graphic objects, are also important aspects of this chapter.

This chapter also examines the Flash drawing hierarchy and how Flash structures its graphical elements in a document. Later in this book, when you will want to create your own graphic elements (as well as use ActionScript coding to communicate or control those items), an understanding of the Flash hierarchy will be quite important.

▪ ▪ ▪ Objectives

In this chapter you will:

- Compare and contrast features in Flash MX 2004 to traditional vector environments
- Learn about the basic tools for viewing, zooming, and panning
- Learn to use the Arrow, Subselection, and Lasso tools for selecting objects on the stage
- Discover features found in Flash MX 2004 that are common to many graphics applications

- Find out about the Flash environment hierarchy and how it affects objects and movies
- Learn how to use scenes, layers, and groups
- Learn how to perform basic object transformations, such as moving, scaling, rotating, and skewing

▪ ▪ ▪ Traditional Vector Versus Flash

Many people involved in web development—many of which are striving to learn Flash—come from other publishing areas, particularly the desktop publishing arena. Therefore, this section notes the major differences between Flash and traditional vector programs. As you progress through the applied exercises later in this book, this is further reinforced by example.

Point Versus Natural Drawing

Flash MX 2004 allows you to work in two different "modes" when creating and editing graphic vector objects on the stage. One functions like typical vector programs; that is, it works with the angular and Bezier points that are the basis of vector lines, arcs, and polygons. In this mode, all vector objects are constructed and edited by modifying the points that define them.

The second is to work in a more free-form way, or what Macromedia terms "natural drawing." This is one of the first major differences you will notice even before you start drawing in Flash. Later, this chapter presents the Arrow tool, which is the natural drawing medium for selecting objects, and the Subselection tool, which functions like traditional vector applications in that it is for object and point selection.

Detached Fills

In most vector environments, only closed polygons can be filled with a color, gradient, or pattern, and the fill is inherently attached to the polygon. In such environments, if the polygon is broken (that is, becomes cut or unclosed in some way), the fill ceases to exist until such time as the polygon becomes closed again.

In Flash, fills are not inherently attached to polygons. Instead, fills are treated as completely unique and separate items that can be disjoined from the original lines that bounded them. Additionally, a polygon or area does not have to be closed to be able to generate a fill. Instead, you can have Flash ignore the gaps between lines and fill the area anyway, even if it is not closed. Although this is not dealt with in depth in this chapter, in Chapter 4 you will see examples of this when you learn about the Paint Bucket tool and the creation of polygons.

Interactions of Base Elements

When working with rudimentary elements such as lines, arcs, and fills in Flash, you will find that they interact in a very special way. To some, this difference from traditional vector applications is quite bothersome, whereas others find it a refreshing approach. This is probably the thing that takes most new Flash users the longest time to get used to. But most find that once they understand how it works they like it better than the traditional vector approach.

In essence, the basic drawing components (lines, arcs, and fills) are not self-contained as in most vector environments. This means that they will automatically react to one another if they overlap. For example, if two lines intersect, they are automatically broken at the point of intersection (eliminating the need for a "knife" tool for trimming lines). Similarly, fills interact with one another in a rather peculiar way. Fills that are the same color, when overlapped, merge, whereas fills of a dissimilar color will subtract (or "knock out") one another.

You will see examples of this in the next chapter as you start to draw elements on the stage using the various tools available. However, before you get there, pay close attention to the discussion at the end of this chapter concerning the drawing hierarchy. It is this explanation that provides insights as to why the environment (and many of these peculiarities) work the way they do.

Shape Recognition

One feature unique to Flash is shape recognition. In Flash, basic elements such as lines or simple geometric primitives (such as circles, rectangles, and triangles) do not have to be drawn perfectly the first time. The application offers Straighten and Smooth tools, allowing you to quickly and easily turn wavy lines into straight lines, or a roughly drawn ellipse or rectangle into a perfect circle or square. As you examine the Arrow tool for selection, you will see this in more detail in an applied exercise.

▪ ▪ ▪ **Basic Tools**

As you read in Chapter 2, the toolbar provides access to the commonly used tools in Flash. The Options section of the toolbar changes when different tools are selected, and indeed some tools have no options at all. Figure 3-1 shows the toolbar with the tools discussed in this chapter identified. In this chapter, you will read about the tools designed for zooming, panning, selecting, and transforming objects. Chapter 4 examines the remaining tools, which are designed for drawing, painting, and editing objects.

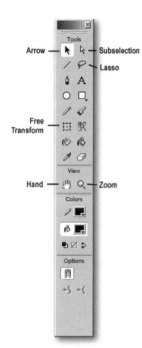

Arrow ——

Subselection

Lasso

Free Transform ——

Hand ——

Zoom

Figure 3-1. Tools discussed in this chapter include those used for selecting, zooming and panning.

If you forget what a tool icon represents, place your cursor over the icon for 1 to 2 seconds, which will reveal a tooltip. You will find that each tool in the toolbar has a keyboard shortcut that is also revealed in the tooltip. Clicking on the letter within the parentheses of the tooltip allows you to select the tool using the keyboard instead of the mouse.

 TIP: *The tear-out card at the back of this book provides a quick reference for all keyboard shortcuts for tools and other commands.*

Exercise 3-1 gives you an opportunity to familiarize yourself with the toolbar.

Exercise 3-1: Orientation to the Toolbar

To orient yourself to the toolbar, perform the following.

- Open Flash MX 2004, which will present the Start page. Select the Flash Document option and then click on OK.

NOTE: *In the Start page, note the different types of new documents you can start. You may want to poke around here and see the start-up files and templates Macromedia provides with the software. As you start different types of projects, these templates can be helpful.*

- Drag the cursor over the tools in the toolbar to view the tooltips that exhibit the name of the tool and its respective keyboard shortcut.

- Try using the shortcut keys to select tools.

... **Controlling the View**

Flash provides multiple ways of changing the view of the stage as you are working. You can use the Zoom and Hand tools located in the toolbar, or you can use the View menu and the Zoom drop-down list on the right-hand side of the Edit path. The sections that follow describe how to control the zoom and pan of the stage using these different methods.

Zoom and Pan Tools

The View section of the toolbar provides the Zoom tool, which can be used to zoom in and out of a drawing, and the Hand tool, which is used for panning the stage. Typically the Hand tool is used when you are zoomed in and cannot see part of the stage you would like. When this is the case, you use the Hand tool to pull or push the stage so that you can see other parts of the stage or work area.

If you click on the Zoom tool, the Options section reveals the "zoom in" (plus sign) and "zoom out" (minus sign) buttons. Depending on which button is selected, clicking in the stage will perform the respective operation.

 TIP: *With the Zoom tool selected, you can quickly toggle between "zoom in" and "zoom out" when the Zoom tool is selected by pressing the Alt key on Windows or the Option key on the Macintosh.*

Even though the Zoom and Hand tools can be selected in the toolbar, it is much faster to use quick keys for zooming and panning. To zoom and pan without the use of the Zoom and Hand tools, use the keyboard commands specified in table 3-1.

Table 3-1: PC and Macintosh Zooming and Panning Keyboard Commands

Function	PC	Mac
Zoom In	Ctrl + spacebar	Command + spacebar
Zoom Out	Ctrl + Alt + spacebar	Command + Option + spacebar
Pan	Spacebar	Spacebar

Other Methods of Stage Control

In addition to the Zoom and Hand tools and their respective shortcuts, two other methods exist. You can use the View menu to access zoom commands and magnification settings or the Zoom Control drop-down menu. For panning, you can use the scrollbars at the right and bottom of the stage.

The Zoom Control drop-down menu is located in the right-hand side of the Edit path, to the right of the Edit Symbols list (the area above the timeline). Here you can select a specific zoom level from the drop-down menu or enter your own numerical value. Numbers greater than 100 (%) zoom in, and numbers less than 100 (%) zoom out.

Magnification level can also be modified in the View menu. Selecting View | Zoom In multiplies the current magnification level by 2; selecting

View | Zoom Out divides the current magnification level by 2. You can also choose a specific Magnification level using one of the options located in the View | Magnification submenu. Note that View | Show All will attempt to zoom to the content on the stage. If the stage is blank, the zoom will be set to the extents of the stage. Selecting View | Show Frame automatically zooms to the extents of the stage.

Like the Zoom and Hand tools, shortcut keys are also associated with the View menu's magnification settings. These keyboard shortcut commands are specified in table 3-2.

Table 3-2: Shortcut Keyboard Commands for View Menu Zoom Settings

Command	PC	Mac
Zoom In	Ctrl + =	Command + =
Zoom Out	Ctrl + –	Command + –
100%	Ctrl + 1	Command + 1
Show Frame	Ctrl + 2	Command + 2
Show All	Ctrl + 3	Command + 3

Exercise 3-2 provides you with an opportunity to practice using keyboard shortcuts for zooming and panning.

Exercise 3-2: Zooming and Panning

CD-ROM NOTE: *To see how zooming and panning works, open ch03_02.fla, located in the fgai/ chapter03/ folder, installed from the companion CD-ROM. For the time being, ignore the content and practice zooming and panning, using the keyboard shortcuts listed in tables 3-1 and 3-2.*

The Work Area

The light gray area surrounding the stage is called the Work Area in Flash. In other vector applications, this is typically called the pasteboard, as it is the area you use during creation to temporarily (or permanently, in some cases) store graphic objects. Pasteboard is basically a carryover term from the days of traditional publishing, in which all print pieces were manually "pasted up" prior to production.

Although there are many uses, the Work Area is often used when you want to animate something on the stage that is at first not visible to the end user. For example, if you wanted to have a car animate across the screen you would start the animation with the car in the Work Area and then have it move on screen at the appropriate time.

The Work Area in Flash is typically viewable when you start a new file, as well as when you open files created by other people. However, it can be turned off. If you open a file and the stage appears locked in the upper left-hand corner and you cannot see or pan to the Work Area, you can easily turn it back on using Ctrl + Shift + W on Windows or Command + Shift + W on Macintosh, or by selecting View | Work Area.

> **NOTE:** *Chapter 12 shows you how to code your HTML such that you ensure that your audience does not accidentally see the Work Area at runtime. Just as you can reveal the Work Area during authoring, you can unintentionally reveal it during playback!*

■ ■ ■ Selecting Objects

As mentioned, Flash provides two primary ways of working with objects: natural drawing and point-based drawing. The next three major sections describe how to select and move objects in these two operational modes. The Arrow tool and Lasso tool are for natural drawing selections, and the Subselection tool is for point-based selection. The Arrow and Subselection tools are examined first. The third section, dealing with object selection, includes discussion of the Lasso tool and its options.

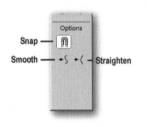

Figure 3-2. When a line, arc, polygon, or fill is selected with the Arrow tool, the Options area of the toolbar reveals the Snap, Smooth, and Straighten options.

Arrow Tool

The Arrow tool provides several important capabilities. Clicking on the Arrow tool reveals the following options, as shown in figure 3-2

- *Snap to Objects (magnet icon):* Controls whether or not objects snap to one another while drawing and editing.

- *Smooth and Straighten:* Control the shape-recognition features of elements.

Moving Endpoints and Shaping Objects

Before examining the Arrow tool options and how they work, a review of how the Arrow tool is used to modify elements in drawings is in order. As mentioned at the beginning of this chapter, Flash does not force you to use the point-based method for editing. It actually allows you to work with either points (using the Subselection tool) or natural drawing capabilities

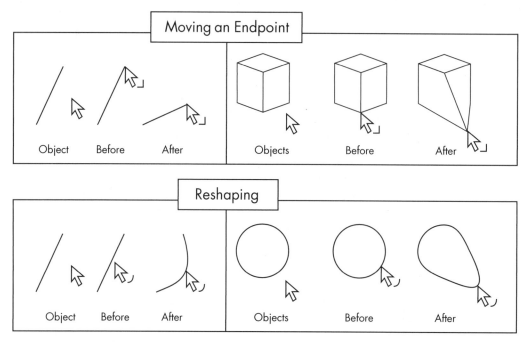

Figure 3-3. Reshaping objects using the Arrow tool makes element modification easier when accuracy is not that important.

(using the Arrow tool). With the Arrow tool, elements are reshaped in a free-form manner and can be moved, selected, and copied.

When the Arrow tool is selected and you move near an object (such as a line), the cursor will change, providing an opportunity to reshape the object. You can move an endpoint or reshape (bend or bow) the middle of the object. Figure 3-3 shows "before and after" views of common transformations.

 NOTE: *An object cannot be reshaped if any portion of it is selected. Instead, click-dragging will move the object rather than reshape it. You can extend an entity by placing the cursor near the endpoint of the entity and click-dragging. (See exercise 3-3.)*

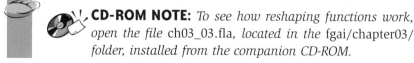 **Exercise 3-3: Modifying Objects with the Arrow Tool**

CD-ROM NOTE: *To see how reshaping functions work, open the file ch03_03.fla, located in the fgai/chapter03/ folder, installed from the companion CD-ROM.*

Perform the following.

- Move the endpoints of the line or curve.

- Bend the center of the line or curve.

- Stretch or modify the box and circle.

Moving Objects

In addition to reshaping objects, you can move all or part of an object to another location on the stage. When selected, objects can be moved, or "nudged," using the arrow keys on the keyboard or click-dragged to a new location. To nudge an object, press an arrow key to move the object a pixel at a time in the direction of the arrow key. If you hold down on an arrow key, the object will scoot across the screen. Holding down the Shift key while pressing an arrow key moves the object 8 pixels per key press.

Figure 3-4. When moving objects using the Arrow tool, first select the object, which displays a pattern over the object signifying that it is selected.

When an object (or part of an object) is selected, a pattern is displayed over it. This signifies that the object is selected. When the cursor is moved near a selected object, the cursor changes to include an arrow, as shown in figure 3-4. This signifies you are about to move the object if you click-drag. Exercise 3-4 provides you with an opportunity to practice moving objects using the Arrow tool.

Exercise 3-4: Moving Objects with the Arrow Tool

CD-ROM NOTE: *To see how moving objects with the Arrow tool works, open the file* ch03_04.fla, *located in the* fgai/chapter03/ *folder, installed from the companion CD-ROM.*

Using the CD-ROM file, select and move the elements from the upper row to the lower row.

By default, to select multiple items on the stage you must hold the Shift key down, as in packages such as FreeHand or Illustrator. Yet, if you prefer the older method, whereby simply clicking on multiple objects selects them, you can use the Preferences option to change this. Remember that this setting can be changed in the Edit | Preferences | General tab using the Selection options. If the Shift Select checkbox is selected, it will make Flash's selection groups work more like FreeHand or Illustrator, in that the Shift key must be held down to add to a selection.

TIP: *If you want to select everything on the current layer, use Select All (Ctrl + A on the PC or Command + A on the Mac). To deselect everything, press the Esc key or click on a blank spot on the stage.*

One of the unusual things about Flash is that when filled objects are created, such as a square with a red fill, the fill is not attached to the bounding lines. Additionally, line segments do not have to be joined to add a fill. To some extent, areas do not even have to be closed to fill them. Flash will automatically ignore all but the most egregious of gaps. This is one of the significant differences between Flash and other illustration programs.

Fills are discrete, editable objects, just like the lines that surround them. Until you get used to this, it may seem odd and cause some frustration. It is important to note this distinction, particularly if you want to move both an object and its fill at the same time. Select the lines that bound the polygon, as well as the fill within the polygon, if you want to move them both. There is a quick way to do this.

To quickly select all line segments that constitute a polygon, instead of having to select each segment individually, double click on any one of the line segments. All of the other line segments will be immediately selected if they intersect and have the same characteristics (line weight, color, and style) as the line on which you originally double clicked. Thus, this double-click selection trick will only work if lines intersect and have similar characteristics.

Like line selection, there is a "double-click" trick for fills and their bounding lines, too. If a fill is bounded by a set of lines, double clicking on the fill selects the fill as well as the line segments that surround it. Exercise 3-5 provides you with an opportunity to practice selecting fills and lines.

Exercise 3-5: Selecting Fills and Lines

 CD-ROM NOTE: *To see how moving lines and fills works, open* ch03_05.fla, *located in the* fgai/ chapter03/ *folder, installed from the companion CD-ROM.*

Using the CD-ROM file, move the objects from the upper row to the lower row. By varying what is selected, you can move just the lines that form the polygon, just the fill, or both at the same time.

While working with selections when using the Arrow tool, be careful when holding down the Ctrl key (Option on the Mac) as you drag a selected object. If you hold down the Ctrl/Option key while dragging with the Arrow tool, a copy of the object will be created and moved, rather than the original object. When Flash is copying, the cursor will show a white plus sign as you drag an element. Those accustomed to using the Ctrl/Option key in FreeHand or Illustrator (to quickly revert to the Arrow tool) may find this feature troublesome. However, it can be resolved by an immediate "undo."

Selecting Parts of Objects

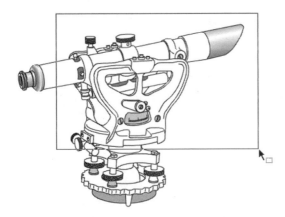

One of the things you may have noticed is that you can use the Arrow tool to not only select an entire object by clicking on it but select a portion of an object. If you click on lines or fills, they are selected in their entirety, as you have seen, but have you noticed what happens if you click-drag across an object with the Arrow tool? Note that when you have the Arrow tool selected and move the mouse off an object the cursor changes to an arrow with a small rectangle next to it.

When you click-drag over a portion of an object—by starting the click-drag off the object and then dragging across an object—only the portion of an object within the drag area is selected, as shown in

Figure 3-5. With the Arrow tool, you can also select portions of an object by click-dragging across objects.

figure 3-5. This is yet another of the flexible things about the Flash environment and how its objects behave. Once you have created a selection consisting of part of an object, it can be modified, just like any other selection.

Snap to Objects

As mentioned, several options appear when the Arrow tool is selected. These include Snap (magnet icon), Smooth, and Straighten. The Snap option forces one object to snap to another. This is helpful when you are trying to get endpoints to line up or objects to snap to specific locations. By default, the Snap option is on. You can toggle it on and off using the button shown in the Options area when the Arrow tool is selected, or by selecting View | Snapping | Snap to Objects (Ctrl + Shift + / or Command + Shift + /).

TIP: *The sensitivity of the snap function can be adjusted in the Edit | Preferences | Editing tab. Connect Lines and Click Accuracy affect the snap function.*

Like other programs, Flash will constrain lines to a horizontal, vertical, or 45-degree increment (independent of the Snap modifier) when the Shift key is pressed as you are modifying an object. If Shift is held down while drawing or moving objects, the objects will automatically constrain as you draw.

 NOTE: *There are several additional snapping options located in the View | Snapping menu. Snap to Pixels is discussed in Chapter 7. The rest are self-explanatory.*

Smooth and Straighten

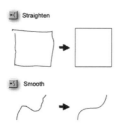

Figure 3-6. The Straighten and Smooth options can be used to quickly adjust objects.

One of Flash's convenient features is its ability to dynamically smooth (simplify curves) or straighten (remove curves) common shapes. For instance, lines that are roughly square (but not perfect) can be corrected using the Straighten modifier to make them into a perfect square, as shown in figure 3-6. Similarly, objects that resemble other standard shapes can be straightened into common shapes or smoothed into more organic forms. For practice using the Smooth and Straighten modifiers, see exercise 3-6.

Exercise 3-6: Using the Smooth and Straighten Options

 CD-ROM NOTE: *To view up close how the Smooth and Straighten options work, open the file ch03_06.fla, located in the fgai/chapter03/ folder, installed from the companion CD-ROM.*

Follow the instructions in the CD-ROM file to smooth and straighten the objects shown. The only thing to remember is that the current zoom level affects Flash's Smooth and Straighten functions. Thus, the extent of adjustments these commands make is dependent on how far you are zoomed in. Also, you can repeatedly use Smooth or Straighten on objects. Thus, if the first time Flash does not recognize the shape or give you what you want, continue to use the Smooth or Straighten option and see if Flash will continue to smooth or straighten the object.

Subselection Tool

Although it is nice to be able to use the Arrow tool for editing in a free-form manner, many people are used to dealing with Bezier curves and the control points that are typical of FreeHand, Illustrator, and other illustration tools. In fact, precise construction of vector drawings is very difficult when you cannot add points to a line and when you cannot modify the points that make up an object. However, the Subselection tool allows you to work at the point level.

When using the Subselection tool, you select an object to reveal the points that define it. Then you select the point or points you want to modify (move or delete). In Chapter 4, you will find you can also add points as well as convert Bezier (curve-based) points to angular. This chapter focuses on selecting, moving, and deleting, which are the operations you can perform with the Subselection tool.

Working with Points

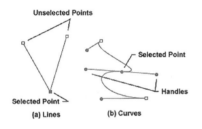

When the Subselection tool is used to select an element on the stage, the control points of the element are revealed. When dealing with lines, control points will appear on the end-points of lines, as shown in figure 3-7a, as well as where the object intersects other objects. Points on a line that are not selected are shown as hollow squares, and points that are selected on a line are shown as filled squares.

Figure 3-7. When you use the Subselection tool, unselected points on a line are shown as hollow squares, and selected points are shown as filled squares (a). When working with curves (b), selecting a point reveals the Bezier handle for controlling the curve.

 NOTE: *If two lines intersect, a point will exist at the intersection. If you delete one of the lines, the point originally created by the intersection will still exist in the remaining line and can be revealed (and subsequently deleted) with the Subselection tool. This behavior is true with all elements (lines, arcs, and polygons).*

When you select a curve, the unselected points appear throughout the curve. The number of points on a curve is based on the complexity of a curve. Figure 3-7b shows a very simple curve. If you click-drag the curve handles, the curve will change. Note that unselected points are displayed as hollow squares, whereas the selected point, to which are attached the Bezier handles, is shown as a black square.

Modifying Points

When the control points of a line, curve, or polygon are revealed with the Subselection tool, you can move a point by click-dragging on it to select and move it. Alternatively, you can select the point and nudge it a pixel at a time using the arrow keys. You can move the entire entity by clicking part of it where there is no point. If you hold down the Shift key, you can select multiple points. Of course, if you click-drag with multiple points selected on an object, all of the selected points will move.

 TIP: *You can quickly select multiple points on an object by selecting the object with the Subselection tool and then click-dragging across the object (start the click-drag off the object). This will select all points on the object that are within the area covered by the click-drag.*

The Subselection tool is also quite handy for cleaning up objects that have unneeded points. As noted, when objects overlap or intersect one another, Flash automatically "breaks" the entity; that is, it automatically adds points to an object when the object intersects something else. Further, if you retain an object that had previously intersected something, the points added to the object due to the intersection are still part of the object. Often this will cause an object to behave strangely when you use the Arrow tool's natural drawing capability. For example, if you try to bow a line, it may not bow like you want due to inadvertent points that were added to the object earlier.

Thus, the Subselection tool can be used to select and delete points on an object. You simply select the point or points you want to delete and then press the Delete or Backspace key. If at some point an object bows or bends in a strange way, there is likely an extra point that was added to the object that is causing the object to behave that way. To get a feel for the Subselection tool and how it works, try exercise 3-7.

Exercise 3-7: Using the Subselection Tool

 CD-ROM NOTE: *Examine the Subselection tool by opening the file ch03_07.fla, located in the* fgai/chapter03/ *folder, installed from the companion CD-ROM.*

Follow the instructions in the CD-ROM file to modify the objects.

The combination of the Arrow tool and Subselection tool in Flash provides complete control of your vector creations. Where accuracy is not a necessity, or where you need to perform general editing such as deleting line segments, use the Arrow tool. When you need complete control over an element, such as accurately controlling a Bezier curve, use the Subselection tool.

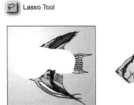

Figure 3-8. The Lasso tool is designed for creating partial selections from a set of objects.

(a) Freeform Mode   (b) Polygon Mode

Figure 3-9. The Lasso tool can be used in (a) free-form mode or (b) polygon mode.

Lasso Tool

In addition to the Arrow tool, you can make natural drawing selections using one more tool: the Lasso tool. Already you saw that with the Arrow tool you could make partial selections of objects by click-dragging across them. The Lasso tool gives you further capabilities in making partial selections.

Figure 3-8 shows an example of how the Lasso tool can be used to make irregularly shaped selections. To make a selection with the Lasso tool, you click-drag around the portion of the objects you want to select. When you drag, you do not have to be concerned with dragging in the shape of a closed polygon. If you stop short of a closed polygon, Flash will automatically close the gap when determining what object portions to select. Like other selections, once you have created a selection, you can move, manipulate, or delete it as you wish.

In addition to free-form mode, the Lasso tool has several specialized options that allow it to function in a manner similar to features found in Adobe Photoshop. You can make the Lasso function in polygon mode, in which only straight lines are defined for the selection. Note the difference between normal Lasso mode, shown in figure 3-9a, and polygon mode, shown in figure 3-9b. When in polygon mode, you single click to define an edge of the bounding polygon. Double clicking finishes the Lasso selection.

 TIP: *When you are working with the Lasso tool, you can add to an existing selection by holding down the Shift key and making a new selection, much like working with masks in Photoshop.*

As you are making selections with the Lasso tool, you can easily switch between Lasso modes (free-form and polygon) using the Alt key. If you begin in free-form mode, pressing the Alt key activates polygon mode. Pressing Alt again reverts back to free-form mode. The functionality of the Lasso tool is comparable to the Lasso tool in Macromedia Fireworks. Try out this feature in exercise 3-8.

NOTE: *The Lasso tool also includes two special options for work-ing with bitmap images, which are discussed in Chapter 7.*

Exercise 3-8: Using the Lasso Tool to Make Selections

 CD-ROM NOTE: *To get a close look at how the Lasso tool works, open the file ch03_08.fla, located in the fgai/chap-ter03/ folder, installed from the companion CD-ROM.*

Follow the instructions in the CD-ROM file to use the Lasso tool to select the fish and copy it to a new location or file.

▪ ▪ ▪ Commonalities with Other Applications

Before examining the Flash hierarchy and graphic object transformation, let's take a look at some features Flash shares with other graphics applications.

Viewing Mode

Flash provides control over the current view of objects on the stage, and incorporates tools designed to help with the creation of graphics. These include drawing quality settings, drawing aids, and other miscellaneous options. Most of these can be found within the View menu.

Quality

The first item for discussion is the quality settings found within the center portion of the View menu, which include Outlines, Fast, Antialias, and Antialias Text. The default setting for quality is Antialias.

Because Flash is a vector-based tool, you can interactively control the display quality of your graphics as you work. How fast the computer redraws the screen depends on the quality setting in the View menu, the speed of the video processor and video RAM of the computer, and the complexity of the graphics on the stage.

The fastest redraw speed is provided via the Outline setting. This shows only the outlines of the vector elements in the movie, without fills or line styles, as shown in figure 3-10. This setting is similar to Keyline viewing mode in FreeHand. The Fast setting shows fills and text, but does not antialias anything. The Antialias and Antialias Text settings show all fills and line styles. The only difference is that Antialias Text also shows text on the stage as antialiased.

You may want to adjust the quality settings as you work. For example, to see if two lines intersect, set the quality to Outlines. Additionally, when drawings become quite complex, you may want to create your graphics in Fast or Antialias mode to speed up redraws. The quality setting chosen will vary, depending on what you are trying to do, the speed of the computer, and the complexity of your drawing.

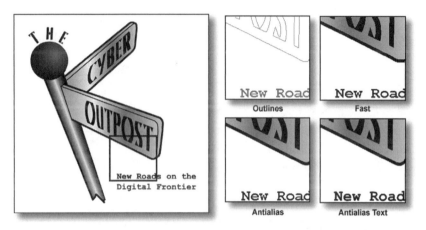

Figure 3-10. The various View | Quality settings can be interactively controlled during authoring.

 NOTE: *You can also adjust display quality at runtime. Chapter 12 takes a closer look at this.*

Other View Menu Options

Aside from the quality settings, the View menu includes the following options worth noting.

- *Goto:* Allows you to quickly jump between scenes.
- *Rulers:* Displays rulers along the edges of the stage in the current units. Remember that the default units are set via the Modify | Document Properties dialog box.
- *Grid:* This submenu provides access to Show Grid, which turns the stage grid on and off; Snap to Grid, which determines whether the selection and drawing tools snap to the grid; and Edit Grids, where you can modify all properties of the grid, including spacing, color, and accuracy.
- *Guides:* The Guides submenu provides access to Show Guides; Lock Guides, which prevents existing guides from being inadver-

tently moved; Snap to Guides; and Edit Guides, where you can modify all properties of the guides, including color and accuracy.

- *Snapping:* Allows you to select from various snap options.
- *Hide Edges:* Allows you to edit objects without viewing their highlighting. This way, as you are editing, you can see how objects will appear in their final state. The closest analogy to this is Photoshop's capability of hiding selection edges.
- *Show Shape Hints:* Shape hints are used for shape tweening and allow you to control how one object morphs to another. Shape tweening is discussed in detail in Chapter 9.

Grouping Objects

Working with groups in Flash is just like working with them in FreeHand, Illustrator, or other vector applications. Groups allow several objects to be temporarily worked on as a single unit or entity. At any point, the collection can be ungrouped such that it returns to separate drawing objects.

To group objects, select several objects and use the Modify | Group menu option (or Ctrl + G on the PC or Command + G on the Mac). To ungroup, use the Modify | Ungroup command (or Ctrl + Shift + G on the PC and Command + Shift + G on the Mac).

 TIP: *To select a group, simply click on it. To delete a group, select it and press the Delete key.*

In Flash, groups may be edited without continually grouping and ungrouping objects. By double clicking on a group with the Arrow tool, all other objects in the drawing will dim slightly, leaving only items for the specified group 100-percent opaque. At this point, anything in the group can be edited. You can delete elements, add elements, or rearrange elements that are part of the group. Once finished, double clicking again restores the stage to its original state, with the elements recomposed as a single, grouped element with the changes made. Exercise 3-9 provides you with practice in modifying elements within a group in this way.

 NOTE: *The double-click trick for groups only works with the Arrow tool. The Subselect tool cannot be used to double click on a group for editing.*

Exercise 3-9: Quickly Editing Groups

 CD-ROM NOTE: *To practice modifying elements within a group, open the file* ch03_09.fla, *located in the* fgai/chapter03/ *folder, installed from the companion CD-ROM.*

Follow the instructions in the CD-ROM file by double clicking on the group, modifying the elements, and double clicking again.

The Flash Environment Hierarchy

Before you begin looking at how to transform objects (scale and rotate), it would be good to take a closer look at how Flash is structured internally. It is important to understand the difference between movies, scenes, and layers, and to be aware of the types of objects that can exist on a layer.

The Flash organizational hierarchy consists of four primary parts: the movie, the scene, the layer, and the objects on the individual layers. The movie is the topmost "object" in this hierarchy, and objects on layers are the bottommost. Movies contain scenes, scenes contain layers, and layers contain objects. When you build your movies, this is how the movie is structured, which affects how you build your movies and how you use ActionScripting to control those elements. Let's take a closer look at each of these.

Movies

Already you have gotten the basics of working with movies under your belt, so elaboration is unnecessary. Chapter 2 focused on how you play back movies and the fundamentals of how you navigate them in the authoring environment. In subsequent chapters you will learn one more very important thing about movies: how to create movies that play back other movies.

Scenes

In Chapter 2, you saw that a movie could be divided into component time-lines, called scenes, all accessible via the Scene drop-down list or the Scene panel. Again, scenes allow you to organize your movie such that you can split the main timeline into parts, to keep the length of the time-lines manageable. Long timelines are not necessarily detrimental—it can just make finding things quickly more difficult, as you have to continual-ly scroll left and right to find what you are looking for.

Generally you add scenes to your movie during the creation process based on some division of the content you are going to present. When you are planning your movie, you should think about ways to divide your content, and scenes are one way to do this. Often where there are breaks in the con-tent logic, flow, hierarchy, chronology, task, or topic, these are places where a new scene may be needed. However, let the situation dictate the solution.

You add scenes to a movie by selecting Insert | Scene. Alternatively, you can use the Scene panel. Later in the book you will learn some simple ActionScript that can be used to "link" the scenes and create navigation structures for them.

 TIP: *If you use scenes, name them something logical. In addition, do not start the name with a number and do not have spaces in the scene name. Instead, replace spaces with an underscore character.*

A final note about scenes is that they are also a nice way to keep all parts of a web site in a single Flash file. Some web sites may use a hundred or more small Flash movies. If each of these Flash movies is stored as a separate source file, managing the total can become unwieldy. Thus, scenes can be used to store many small components (even though they will be used separately in the site) together during authoring. Then you can output individual web-ready versions of each scene to be used as a component somewhere in the web site. There is much debate in the development community whether or not it is a good idea to use scenes. There are positives and negatives to both approaches.

Layers

Just as each movie can contain multiple scenes, each scene can contain multiple layers. Layers in Flash work more or less like layers in any other graphics package. Layers are like transparent sheets on which you draw; that is, unless you draw something on a layer, the layer is blank. The next couple of sections orient you to how layers work in Flash.

Working with Layers

You use the timeline area of the interface to work with layers in Flash. Layers are represented as individual rows (or Director's term, channels) within the timeline. Objects on layers higher in the layer order display in front of objects on layers lower in the layer order. In figure 3-11, for example, objects on layer 1 would be displayed in front of objects on layer 3.

Flash's layer ordering is the same as FreeHand, Illustrator, and Photoshop. Uppermost layers are higher in the stage order. Director, however, is the exact opposite. In Director, uppermost layers (channels) are furthest back in the stage order.

Note the small button at the far right of the timeline bar (labeled in figure 3-10). Clicking on this button (Modify Frame View) reveals a drop-down menu that lets you customize the way the timeline is displayed. If there are many frames in a movie, you can use this drop-down to reduce the width of the frames to allow more of them to be viewed within the

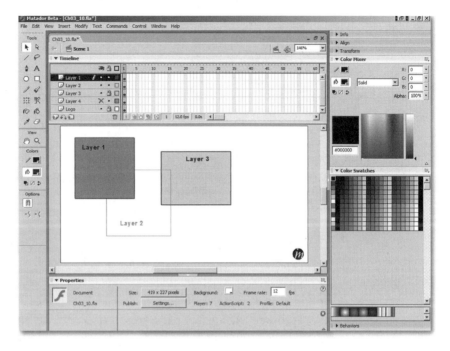

Figure 3-11. Objects on layer 1 are displayed in front of objects in layer 3.

width of the timeline area. To view more layers, you can either drag the bottom of the timeline down the screen or, if you have multiple monitors, detach the timeline altogether and place it in a second monitor.

Layer States

When looking at a layered movie, the first things you will notice are the small icons and dots to the right of the layer names. These icons and dots indicate the current state of the layer. Above layer 1 in figure 3-12, you see three icons. The "eye" indicates whether the layer is hidden. The "padlock" indicates whether the layer is locked. The small rectangle indicates the preview color for the layer when it is in outline mode. An examination of figure 3-12 reveals the following.

- The small pencil icon indicates that layer 1 is the current layer. This means that anything drawn or pasted into the movie will be placed on that layer. Only one layer can be the current layer. When a layer is the current layer, black shading also identifies it.

- The square in layer 2 (which is red) indicates that the layer is currently in outline mode. Outline mode displays only the outlines of the content of the layer. This is like the View | Quality setting of

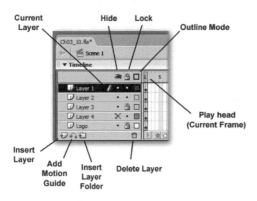

Figure 3-12. The timeline controls allow you to work with the layers in your movie.

the same name, except that it is applied by layer. Here, layer 2 has been set to red outlines. Although the items on layer 2 are simple, understand that by-layer outlining is used when a particular layer contains elements that take a while to redraw. You can speed up authoring performance by setting layers (those with complex elements) to outline mode. Note also that there are a variety of colors you can use for outlining. Double clicking on the icon to the left of the layer name provides a dialog box in which you can set the color.

- The padlock icon in layer 3 means that it is locked. When a layer is locked, the items on the layer are visible, but you cannot select, edit, or move items on that layer. This is helpful when you are creating complex images or animations and want to see a layer's content but not accidentally select it.

- The X icon in layer 4 indicates that the layer is hidden, in which case none of the elements on that layer can be seen or edited.

To change the state of any given layer, you simply click on the dots under the eye, padlock, or rectangle icon for that layer. Note that layers can also have multiple states. For example, a layer could be in outline mode, as well as locked. The current layer can also be locked and/or hidden. However, to be able to paste or draw, the current layer must be unlocked and visible. Otherwise, Flash will tell you it cannot perform the operation.

 TIP: *When you select an object on the stage, Flash will change the current layer to match whatever layer the selected item is on.*

Pay close attention to which layer is current when you start drawing in the next chapter. Invariably, at some point you will start drawing only to find that you are on the wrong layer. Do not worry, however; this happens to everyone. Just keep in mind that anything drawn or pasted is created on the current layer, whatever that is. The sections that follow discuss how to add, delete, and manipulate layers. For practice in working with the Layer modes, see exercise 3-10.

TIP: *You can quickly hide all layers by holding down the Ctrl key (Option on the Mac) and clicking in any layer, under the eye icon. If you hold down the Alt key (Command on the Mac) and click under the eye, all layers except the one you clicked in will be hidden. This same trick works for locking or outlining layers.*

Exercise 3-10: Working with Layer States

 CD-ROM NOTE: *To see how the layer modes work, open the file ch03_10.fla, located in the fgai/chapter03 folder, installed from the companion CD-ROM.*

This file contains five layers currently set to various modes. When opening the file, you may have to adjust the separation line between the timeline and stage to view all of the layers. Perform the following.

- Adjust the various layer states.

- Experiment with elements on specific layers by making a layer current and then drawing on it.

- Turn the layers on and off to see that the elements were placed on the current layer.

Adding, Deleting, and Modifying Layers

Adding, deleting, and modifying layers is a relatively easy task due to the Add Layer and Delete Layer buttons found at the bottom of the timeline. Use them to add and delete layers (see figure 3-12).

To add a layer, click on the Add Layer button. The layer will be inserted above the currently selected layer. You can also use the Insert | Layer menu option, which will instead add a layer at the bottom of the timeline. To remove a layer, select the layer you want to delete and click on the Delete Layer button.

Note that when you add layers they are given a default name. Renaming is accomplished by double clicking on the layer name or by selecting the layer and using Modify | Timeline | Layer Properties, which opens the Layer Properties dialog box, shown in figure 3-13. Here you can adjust any of the layer's properties. As you can see, this is where you determine the color used when the layer is set to outline mode.

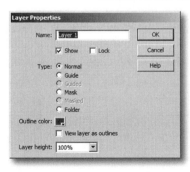

Figure 3-13. The Layer Properties dialog box shows you the attributes of the selected layer.

The Layer Height drop-down list (see figure 3-13) allows you to adjust the display height of the layer in the

Figure 3-14. Use the layer's context menu to access its options.

timeline. As you will see in later chapters, when you add sound, actions, or labels to a layer, they have a visual representation in the timeline. Adjusting the height of the timeline makes reading the timeline easier when a layer or keyframe has such elements associated with it.

 NOTE: *For now, ignore the other options in the Layer Properties dialog box. These are explored in later chapters.*

After some layers have been created in your drawing, you may want to rearrange their order. To move a layer higher in the ordering, click and drag it to where you want it. Use click-drag to move layers up and down in the timeline order.

In addition to the functionality previously described, Flash offers a context menu that can be used to quickly perform many of these operations. Figure 3-14 shows the context menu, accessed by right-clicking on a layer. Exercise 3-11 provides further practice in working with layers.

Exercise 3-11: Adding and Deleting Layers

 CD-ROM NOTE: *To continue examining how layers work, open ch03_11.fla, located in the fgai/chapter03 folder, installed from the companion CD-ROM.*

Using the CD-ROM file, perform the following steps.

1. Click on the Insert Layer button to add a new layer to the drawing. Note that when adding a layer the new layer becomes the current layer and is added above the currently selected layer.

2. Double click on the default name of the layer you just created and enter a new name for it.

3. Draw some elements on the new layer.

4. Delete layer 3 by selecting it and clicking on the Delete Layer button. When deleting, the layers below shift up to fill the space left by the deleted layer.

5. Click-drag on layer 2 in the timeline and move it to the top of the layer order. Note that because layer 2 is now at the top of the layer order its rectangle appears in front of all other items on the stage.

6. Select the rectangle labeled layer 1 on the stage. When you select it, notice that frame 1 turns black. When selecting items

on the stage, the frames associated with those items turn black, indicating in which layer and frames they reside. If multiple items are selected and they reside on multiple layers, frames respective to each item will appear black but the current layer will be the one on which the last selected item resides.

NOTE: *The steps that follow are vitally important because they are where most confusion concerning layers comes into play.*

7. Set the state of all layers to visible and unlocked by right-clicking on any layer and selecting Show All in the context menu. This makes all layers visible and unlocked.

8. Use Edit | Select All (Ctrl + A or Command + A) to select all items. When you do a select all, all items on all layers are selected, in addition to items that may be on the current layer. The only way to keep items in other layers from being selected is to lock their respective layers.

9. Deselect the items by clicking in a blank spot on the stage.

TIP: *Make sure you have the Arrow tool selected when you perform step 9. To select or deselect you must have the Arrow tool selected.*

10. Select the square on layer 1 and use Modify | Ungroup (Ctrl + Shift + G or Command + Shift + G) to ungroup it. Repeat this for the square on layer 2. Hide the remaining layers.

11. Select several items that make up the objects contained on layers 1 and 2. When multiple layers are unlocked and visible, their elements can be selected. Generally, this ability is what causes confusion when making selections. If you do not get in the habit of locking or hiding layers, making specific selections in a multilayer movie may be difficult.

TIP: *The easiest way to keep from selecting objects unintentionally is by locking or hiding the layer.*

12. Examine one more thing concerning layers. Notice that the elements on layers 1 and 2 are ungrouped. Although these elements still reside on their respective layers, they are ungrouped on those layers. Use Modify | Select All (Ctrl + A or Command + A) to pick all of the elements. Frames in layers 1 and 2 will turn black, indicating that the selected elements are contained on those layers.

13. Use Modify | Group to group the elements. After this step, note that two groups are created. Selected elements on layer 1 are grouped and remain on layer 1. Selected elements on layer 2 are grouped and remain on layer 2. When items from multiple layers are grouped, groups are created for each layer. Other programs, such as FreeHand, shift all elements to a single layer. Flash, however, does not.

NOTE: *As you worked through the previous section you may have seen options or items related to guide or mask layers. These are two special types of layers, usually used for animation. These are examined in Chapter 9.*

Grouping Layers with Layer Groups

One of the interesting features in Flash MX 2004 is the ability to group folders using layer folders. Often when you are developing movies, you will use many layers. A single movie or scene may need as many as 50-plus layers for complex creations. When this is the case, the timeline becomes very "deep." If you want to access a particular layer you must either expand the separation border between the timeline and stage (which often results in a miniscule stage that is difficult to work with) or constantly scroll the timeline up and down using the scrollbar on the right side of the timeline.

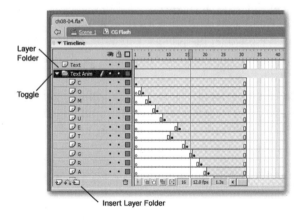

Layer Folder

Toggle

Insert Layer Folder

Figure 3-15. The new Layer Folders feature allows you to group layers together to help minimize the height of the timeline.

Layer folders combat this problem by allowing you to group layers into folders in the timeline, as shown in figure 3-15. You can use the Insert Layer Folder button at the bottom of the timeline (shown in figure 3-15) or the Insert | Timeline | Layer Folder menu option to insert a layer folder. When you do this, the layer folder is inserted above the currently selected layer. You can then put layers in the layer folder by click-dragging them into the folder.

Layer folders can be expanded or contracted by clicking on the small toggle arrow to the left of the folder name and, like normal layers, layer folders can be renamed by double clicking and entering a new name. To delete a layer folder, right-click on the layer folder and select Delete from the context menu.

Objects in Layers

The lowest level of the Flash hierarchy includes the objects you place on layers. There are essentially two classes or types of objects in a layer: overlay objects and stage objects. Overlay objects include symbols, groups, and text, whereas stage objects include lines, arcs, polygons, and fills. Up to this point you have been mainly working with stage objects.

 NOTE: *As this chapter discusses overlay objects, you will be predominantly dealing with groups. Chapter 5 explores text objects, and Chapter 6 deals at length with symbols. All three (symbols, groups, and text) are overlay objects, and discussion of groups in this chapter is applicable to text and symbols, discussed later in the book.*

To better understand this concept, examine figure 3-16a. You see that each layer can include overlay objects and stage objects. Stage objects include ungrouped objects, such as lines and fills, and items that have been

Figure 3-16. The Flash hierarchy provides an explanation of why the environment works the way it does.

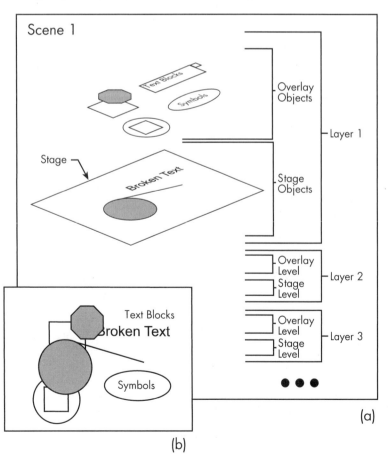

broken apart (to be discussed later in this chapter) or that are ungrouped. The overlay level contains grouped elements, symbols, and text.

Yet, on the screen, as shown in figure 3-16b, it is difficult to visually perceive this hierarchy until you begin working with the object. Also note that scene 1 consists of layers 1, 2, and 3. Thus, each movie can have multiple scenes, each of which has its own set of layers. In addition, each layer can contain both an overlay and stage objects. To better understand these concepts, perform exercise 3-12.

Exercise 3-12: Exploring Overlays and Groups

 CD-ROM NOTE: *To see the distinction between overlays and groups, open the file* ch03_12.fla, *located in the* fgai/chapter03 *folder, installed from the companion CD-ROM.*

Using the CD-ROM file, perform the following steps. As you begin this exercise, note that a filled oval and a filled rectangle currently exist as ungrouped elements on the stage. As such, they are stage objects.

1. Select the oval outline and its fill (double click on the oval fill to quickly select both) and group them (Ctrl + G or Command + G). This makes the oval line and fill a group and thus an overlay object.

2. Move the grouped oval so that it overlaps the rectangle. Note that the oval is visually in front of the square.

3. Try to use the Modify | Arrange | Send to Back menu command with the oval selected. The oval will not move behind the rectangle because the oval is an overlay object, whereas the rectangle and its fill are stage objects.

4. If you try to use the Modify | Arrange command on the rectangle or its lines you will notice that the Arrange menu commands are dimmed and cannot be used.

 NOTE: *The Arrange commands cannot be used on stage objects.*

5. Double click on the rectangle fill (which also selects its lines) and group it. When you group the rectangle, it moves in front of the oval because it is now a group and an overlay object. Anytime you group an element, it will move to the front of the overlay object order.

6. Deselect the rectangle and select the oval.

7. Select Modify | Arrange | Bring to Front. Because the oval and rectangle are now both on the overlay objects, you can rearrange them at will using the Modify | Arrange menu commands.

8. Select both the oval and the rectangle.

9. Select the Modify | Ungroup menu option and click on a blank spot on the canvas to deselect both the rectangle and oval.

10. Try to select the rectangle or oval and move it away from the rest of the objects. Notice that part of one of the objects has been erased. When both entities were ungrouped, they both converted to stage objects. Once on that level, deselecting caused it. Stage objects behave this way, which you will read more about momentarily.

NOTE: *It is vitally important to understand these distinctions between the overlay and the stage levels before moving on to layers.*

Stage Objects: Unioning and Subtracting

As you saw in the last exercise, ungrouped objects in Flash have the peculiar nature of deleting or merging with other objects on the same layer when you overlap them. For new users this is difficult to get used to, particularly in comparison to other vector environments.

Figure 3-17 shows the basics of what happens. When viewing figure 3-17a-1, note the two separate objects in the first cell. If the ungrouped object is moved over the top of the other ungrouped object and deselected, as in figure 3-17a-2, the forward object deletes the object behind it. When you move the object back to its original position, as shown in figure 3-17a-3, notice the "knockout" that is left in the background object.

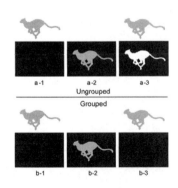

In the example displayed in figure 3-17 (series a), the ungrouped objects are different colors. Thus, the shape of the upper object is knocked out of the lower object. If the objects were the same color, the two objects would meld or merge (a Boolean union) to create a single object. Think of the example shown in the progression of figure 3-17a as a Boolean subtraction caused by the difference in color.

Figure 3-17. The results of (a) ungrouped and (b) grouped objects moved over one another.

The deletion effect shown in figure 3-17 (series a) can be overcome through the use of groups. It could also be overcome by using separate layers for the cheetah and the rectangle. When objects are grouped, as shown in the progression in figure 3-17 (series b), the knockout (or merging) effect does not occur.

 NOTE: *One of the most difficult things to become accustomed to as you learn to draw and paint in Flash is its additive and subtractive property concerning stage objects. However, it will help if you get into the habit of using groups or layers as you acquaint yourself with the drawing editor in the next chapter. (See exercise 3-13.)*

Exercise 3-13: The Additive and Subtractive Property of Stage Objects

 CD-ROM NOTE: *Learn more about the additive and sub-tractive property by opening the file ch03_13.fla, located in the* fgai/chapter03/ *folder, installed from the companion CD-ROM.*

Follow the instructions in the CD-ROM file and move the objects to see the results.

In the previous exercise, you saw how stage-object fills interact with one another; that is, fills of the same color union and fills of different color subtract from one another. Before leaving this issue, we need to address how lines interact with fills. You know that when lines intersect each other, they are automatically broken at the intersection (thus no knife tool is needed in Flash). But what about when a fill is placed over a line or a line over a fill?

When a line is placed over a fill, the effect on the fill depends on the length of the line. If a line does not completely stretch across the fill, the line does not cut the fill. However, if the line stretches across the fill, such that the line intersects two edges of the bounding area for the fill (the fill's outline when in outline mode), the line will cut the fill into two pieces. This is a nice trick to remember if you need to quickly split a fill into two pieces!

In summary, although the following could be said about all three types of overlay objects (symbols, groups, and text), these are the main things you will discover that are a result of the difference between overlay and stage objects.

- Overlay objects do not interact (subtract or union). Thus, grouping, the use of symbols, and the use of levels are all ways to keep stage objects from interacting.
- Stage-level objects interact (subtract or union) with one another when overlapped.

- When you group objects, they suddenly appear in front of other elements. If you have two ungrouped objects, grouping one will bring it in front of the ungrouped object. When you convert objects to symbols, they behave the same way.

- An overlay object cannot be sent behind a stage object. The Arrange commands only apply to overlay objects (symbols, groups, and text). For example, a group cannot be sent behind a fill object. Nor can a fill object be arranged in front of a group.

... Working with Overlay Objects

Before we move on, we need to address a few more issues regarding overlay objects. The following sections discuss subjects relevant to overlay objects and working with them.

Arranging (Z-Order)

Earlier you saw that the Modify | Arrange submenu commands could be used on overlay objects, but not stage objects. Arranging allows you to change the Z-order of symbols, groups, and text objects in the current layer. Within a single layer, multiple items can be overlaid on top of one another, similar to other drawing programs. Although the stage looks like a flat drawing, it is not. Some objects are closer to the screen, and others are farther away, as shown in figure 3-18. Using commands such as Move to Front and Move to Back allows you to selectively arrange your grouped objects so that they appear the way you want.

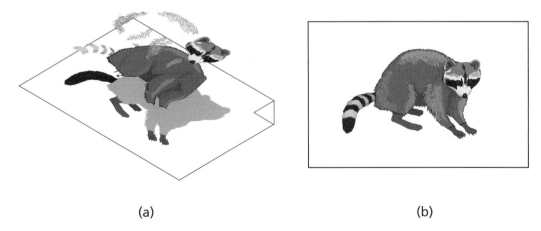

(a)   (b)

Figure 3-18. Arranging objects controls (a) the Z-order within a layer, creating (b) the illusion of a flat drawing.

TIP: *Use combinations of the Ctrl (Command), Shift, and Arrow keys to quickly perform the Arrange submenu commands.*

Locking and Aligning

The Arrange submenu also provides a Lock and Unlock feature, which allows you to lock items at their current size and in their current position on the stage. Recall that you can lock all items on a layer using the Layer mode lock, but you can also lock individual objects. This is typically useful if you are trying to align several objects to the current position of another object using the Align panel. Once an object is locked, it cannot be selected on the stage. In most other programs, although an item is locked you can still select it so that you can unlock it. In Flash you can individually lock overlay objects on the stage, but to unlock items you must use Unlock All; you cannot unlock the items one at a time.

 NOTE: *If you do not have an overlay object selected, the menu options in the Arrange submenu will be dimmed and inactive.*

 TIP: *All of the Align commands can be accessed via the Modify | Align menu. You do not necessarily need to have the Align panel open to align things. Do it directly via the Modify menu.*

Breaking

The Modify | Break Apart command is designed to be used on overlay objects. In essence, the Break Apart command quickly breaks an overlay object (symbol, group, or text) into its stage object components. It can also be used in a special way on bitmaps that are imported into Flash, which you will read about in Chapter 7. In Chapter 5 you see how Break Apart affects text objects, and in Chapter 6 you will see its effect on symbols.

Note that Break Apart, when applied to a group, is not the same as the Ungroup command. Indeed, if you have a set of stage objects and group them, Ungroup and Break Apart will yield the same results, as shown in figure 3-19a. However, what if you have a group that contains subgroups? Note that in figure 3-19b ungrouping leaves the subgroups, whereas Break Apart skips the subgroups and returns everything to its stage object components. This is an important point to remember and is a point often confused by newcomers to Flash.

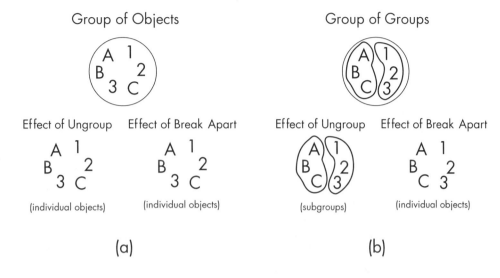

Figure 3-19. Using Break Apart on a group is different from using Ungroup.

Distributing Objects to Layers

The Distribute to Layers command, found in the Modify | Timeline sub-menu (Ctrl + Shift + D or Command + Shift + D), allows you to easily put items in a selection set into their individual layers. This command applies to selection sets containing stage objects as well as overlay objects.

For example, imagine you have three objects on the stage (overlay, stage, or any combination) you want to have placed on separate layers. You could manually create each layer and then copy and paste each item. However, the Distribute to Layers command makes this operation much easier.

To use Distribute to Layers, select the objects on the stage that you want to be placed on individual layers and choose the command from the Modify | Timeline submenu. Flash creates new layers for each object and uses the default layer naming convention for them. It is that easy!

Transforming Objects

Flash provides several methods of transforming stage and overlay objects. Already you have discovered how to move an object directly on the stage with the Arrow tool and the Subselection tool. The following sections detail the other methods of transforming objects; that is, an additional way to move an object, as well as how to scale, rotate, and skew an object. You will also read about some important things you should know regarding object transformations in Flash.

 NOTE: *Although the Transform Fill tool is for transformations, it is related to fill objects and will be discussed in Chapter 4, following discussion of the Paint Bucket tool.*

Moving with the Info Panel

Earlier you saw that you could move objects on the stage using the Arrow and Subselection tools. You can also move an object using the Info panel. When you start doing your own ActionScript coding, often you will want precise control over the coordinate location of objects on the stage. Using the Info panel, shown in figure 3-20, you can enter in an absolute value for the stage position of an object. Thus, you can move an object to any location you like using this panel. Note that the origin (0,0) for the stage is the upper left-hand corner.

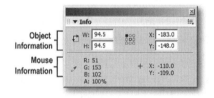

Figure 3-20. The Info panel, shown "undocked," can be used to move an object to a specific stage location. This panel provides information as well.

Figure 3-20 also shows that the Info panel provides more information, including the absolute width and height of the object, the current mouse location (denoted by the + and the X and Y fields in the lower section of the panel), as well as the specific color specification for an exact point on the stage. Note the small array of rectangles near the X and Y fields in the upper part of the panel. This is the registration point of the selected object or objects, discussed in Chapter 6 in regard to symbols.

Free Transform Tool

In the center of the toolbar you will find the Free Transform tool. This tool allows you to move, scale, rotate, and skew objects on the stage. When you select the Free Transform tool and make a selection of objects on the stage (either a single object or multiple), handles or points appear around the selection, as shown in figure 3-21a. Additionally, a small white circle appears in the center of the selection.

 TIP: *You can move a selection while using the Transform tool by moving the cursor toward the center of the object until the arrow cursor is shown instead of a transform cursor. Click-drag and the object will be moved.*

When using the Free Transform tool, as you move near the revealed handles, as well as the boundaries of the object, the cursor changes to reveal the transform that will take place if you click-drag at that location. Figure 3-21b shows the cursor representations and what they mean.

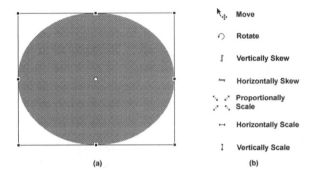

TIP: *With the Free Transform tool selected, note the options in the tool-bar. To limit the functionality of this tool, use the buttons in the Options section to rotate and skew, or scale, only.*

Figure 3-21. When you select the Free Transform tool and make a selection on the stage, handle points are revealed around the object (a). When you movie the cursor near the handles or boundary of the selection, the cursor changes to show what transformation you can do if you click at that point. Different cursors represent difference transformations (b).

If you place the cursor over the corner handles of the selection, you can proportionally scale or rotate. If you place the cursor over a handle at the midpoint of the sides of the object, you can disproportionately scale the selection. If you place the cursor near the selection boundary and not directly on a handle, you can skew the object. Again, as you move the cursor around the selection, the normal arrow cursor will change to a transform cursor, showing the transform about to take place if you click-drag. Exercise 3-14 provides practice in scaling, rotating, and skewing objects with the Free Transform tool.

Exercise 3-14: Transforming an Object with the Free Transform Tool

CD-ROM NOTE: *To take a closer look at the Free Transform tool, open ch03_14.fla, located in the fgai/chapter03/ folder, installed from the companion CD-ROM.*

Follow the instructions in the CD-ROM file to scale, rotate, and skew the object shown.

Note in exercise 3-14 that the origin for the transformation is represented by the white circle, which is typically in the center of the object, as shown in figure 3-21a. You can change the origin for the transform my moving this point. For example, imagine you wanted the object to rotate around or scale from the lower left-hand corner of the selection. Prior to rotating or scaling, you would move the origin of the transform (the white circle) to the lower left and then perform the rotate or scale. You will find that the transformation origin (the fixed point for the origin) will be wherever the white circle is. To practice changing the origin of a transform, try exercise 3-15.

Exercise 3-15: Changing the Origin of a Transform

 CD-ROM NOTE: *To learn about changing a transforms origin, open the file* ch03_15.fla, *located in the* fgai/chapter03/ *folder, installed from the companion CD-ROM.*

Follow the instructions in the CD-ROM file to scale, rotate, and skew the object shown.

Modify | Transform Menu Options

Flash also provides access to transformation commands via menus. The Modify | Transform menu options provide the ability to perform the previously discussed transformations, as well as additional functions. In all cases you must select an object on the stage before these commands, as follows, are active.

- *Free Transform:* Performs the same thing as the Free Transform tool in that you can scale, rotate, or skew an object.

- *Distort:* This feature allows you to freely manipulate and deform an object by moving any of the object's handle points in any direction. This command is only applicable to stage objects (lines, arcs, polygons, and fills).

- *Envelope:* This feature provides Bezier points along the sides and corners of an object, allowing you to deform an object. Like Distort, this command is only applicable to stage objects.

NOTE: *The Distort and Envelope commands are also available as options in the toolbar (Options section) when you select stage objects with the Free Transform tool.*

- *Scale:* Performs the same task as scaling with the Free Transform tool.

- *Rotate and Skew:* Identical to the same tasks that can be accomplished with the Free Transform tool.

- *Scale and Rotate:* Provides a dialog box for entry of numerical values for scaling and rotation.

- *Rotate 90° CW:* Rotates the object 90 degrees clockwise.

- *Rotate 90° CCW:* Automatically rotates the object 90 degrees counterclockwise.

- *Flip Vertical:* Mirrors the object across a horizontal axis.

- *Flip Horizontal:* Mirrors the object across a vertical axis.

- *Remove Transform:* Removes all transforms previously assigned to an overlay object. It has no effect on stage objects.

Exercise 3-16 provides you with practice using the Distort and Envelope commands.

 ### Exercise 3-16: Using the Distort and Envelope Commands

 CD-ROM NOTE: *Open the file* ch03_16.fla, *located in the* fgai/chapter03/ *folder, installed from the companion CD-ROM.*

Try using the Distort and Envelope commands (in the Modify | Transform menu) on the stage objects in the CD-ROM file.

The Transform Panel

In addition to the methods already described, you can access information about the transformations applied to an object using the Transform panel. Select Window | Design Panels | Transform to open this panel.

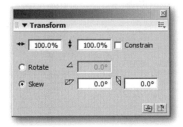

Figure 3-22. The Transform panel, shown "undocked," allows you to apply transforms to object on the stage or copies of them.

Using the Transform Panel

In the Transform panel, shown in figure 3-22, you can numerically transform an object by making a selection on the stage and then entering a scale, rotation, or skew and pressing the Enter key. Pressing the Enter key applies it to the current selection.

 NOTE: *If you want to use the Transform panel to modify an object, you must press the Enter key once you have entered a value. Otherwise, the new transform will not be applied to the object (even though the field will show what you just entered).*

The Transform panel also allows you to apply the transform to a copy of the object that is selected. If you wish to apply the transform to a copy of the object, instead of the original, use the Copy and Apply Transform button, located in the lower-right hand corner of the panel (see figure 3-22).

Remembering Transforms

One of the interesting things about transformations applied to overlay objects in Flash is that Flash remembers the transformation applied to an object. It even remembers compound transformations; that is, for example, when you apply a scale and a skew or a scale and a rotation.

For example, if you apply a scale, skew, or rotation to an object (or any combination of them), you can modify the transformation value using the Transform panel and actually see the prior transformation. In most environments, once a transformation has been applied to an object, you cannot restore the original state of the object in its untransformed state. In Flash, you can. However, note the following special situations.

- Transformations are not remembered for stage objects. Once you apply a transformation to a line, arc, polygon, fill, or combinations of these, the transformation is forgotten.

- Transformations for groups are "temporarily" remembered. Although groups are overlay objects, they are a special case. If you group a set of stage objects and apply a transformation to the group, the transformation will be remembered for the object, as long as you do not ungroup or double click and modify the group. If you ungroup, the objects will remain in their transformed state, and the transformation will be forgotten (will not appear in the Transform panel). Similarly, if you apply a transform to a group and then double click and edit the group, the transformation will no longer show up in the Transform panel.

- Transformations for text and symbol objects are always remembered. Thus, with text or symbols, you can always revert to the untransformed version of the object.

Neat Tricks for Transformations

Transformations of objects are pretty important when you want to develop sophisticated illustrations in Flash. With Flash, you can create very complex technical pictorial representations using transformations as the basis. Most organic (or free-form) drawing is made easier due to the natural drawing tools (as you will see in the next chapter), but for those people who wish to do advanced technical drawing in Flash this brief section is provided to point out some very important information for creating these types of drawings.

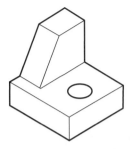

Figure 3-23. Creation of non-organic drawings can be aided by transformations.

Although the limits of this book do not permit a lengthy explanation of axonometric drawing (such as isometric, dimetric, or trimetric drawing; that is, paralline drawing), imagine you wanted to create an object in a particular illustrated pictorial representation, such as the cut block shown in figure 3-23. This is presented as an isometric projection, where all faces are equally exposed to the viewer (the true exposure is approximately 35.2667 degrees). Of course, much more complex illustrations can be created; this example is simple to make it straightforward.

A technical illustrator will typically choose the type of drawing she wants to create based on what she wants to show in the pictorial. The easiest type of pictorial projection is the isometric projection. She may also choose a dimetric projection (in which two object planes are equally exposed to the viewer) or a trimetric projection (in which all planes have a different exposure).

Once the type of projection is chosen, the technique for creating the axonometric pictorial in Flash becomes a four-step process. You begin by creating 2D views (orthographic views) of an object, as shown in figure 3-24a. You then transform those views to orient the planes in their skewed orientation, as shown in figure 3-24b. Using transformations, there are two techniques for doing this in Flash, discussed in material to follow.

As shown in figure 3-24c, you then overlap the planes so that you can project points among the planes, with the exact overlapping depending on the object. Note in figure 3-24c that the top plane is oriented in the middle for easier projection. Finally, you project points from each view of the object, and where they intersect you find a point on the actual 2D pictorial. When you project enough points, you end up with a pictorial representation of the object, as shown in figure 3-24d.

This projection technique is a nifty way to be able to illustrate any object, although organic forms are much more difficult. This technique is very helpful for creating mechanically oriented objects, or objects that have sharp edges and few curvilinear surfaces.

The key to using this technique is knowing the values for skewing the planes for the object orientation you want. There are two ways to arrive at the properly transformed 2D planes. The first method is to use Flash's skewing capability. You simply group the lines that make up the 2D view of the object and then apply a horizontal and vertical skew for the object. Table 3-3 outlines the values required to skew 2D orthographic views into an isometric orientation.

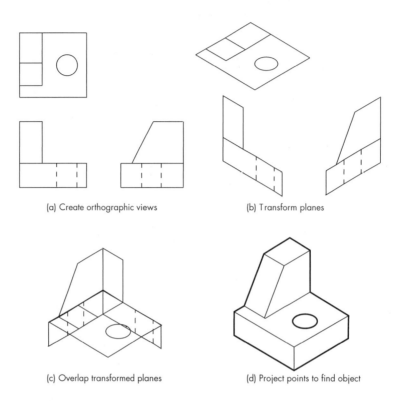

(a) Create orthographic views   (b) Transform planes

(c) Overlap transformed planes   (d) Project points to find object

Figure 3-24. The steps for creating a pictorial representation of an object using projection.

Table 3-3: Horizontal/Vertical Skew Values for Transforming 2D Planes.

Isometric Plane	Horizontal Skew	Vertical Skew
Top plane	60	30
Left plane	0	30
Right plane	0	30

Because isometric projection displays an object rotated 45 degrees and tilted forward 35.2667 degrees in 3D terms, all you need worry about is skewing when creating 2D representations of the projected planes. If you were creating dimetric or trimetric views, you would need to adjust skew and scaling.

NOTE: *Appendix A includes tables that include data for trans-forming any 2D plane into numerous axonometric orientations for projection. Appendix A contains data for the skew method only.*

A second way to transform planes to create projected images is to use a combination of scaling and rotation (which results in an appropriate skew). To create the top isometric plane you would perform the following steps.

1. Group the lines.

2. Rotate the group by 45 degrees using the Transform panel.

3. Group the object again. If you do not group the object a second time, step 4 will not work correctly. This is due to the way Flash applies the second transformation.

4. Apply a vertical scale of 57.73 to the group. Use the Transform panel and enter the value in the Height field. Also, make sure the Constrain checkbox is deselected.

 TIP: *If you apply a rotation and then try to do a non-proportional scale to an object (a group or symbol), the object will scale using the original height of the object (in its original orientation) rather than basing the scale on the rotated height of the object. To see what this means, repeat the previous steps but skip step 3.*

To create the left isometric plane, you would perform the following.

1. Group the lines.

2. Rotate the group by 45 degrees using the Transform panel.

3. Group the object again.

4. Apply a horizontal scale of 57.73 to the group. Enter the value in the Width field and make sure the Constrain checkbox is dese-lected.

5. Rotate the group by –30 degrees.

 NOTE: *Notice here that you do not need to group the object a third time before steps 4 and 5. Scaling is the only operation that seems to revert to the original position of an object when basing the trans-formation.*

To create the right isometric plane, you would perform the following steps.

1. Group the lines.

2. Rotate the group by –45 degrees using the Transform panel.

3. Group the object again.

4. Apply a horizontal scale of 57.73 to the group. Enter the value in the Width field and make sure the Constrain checkbox is deselected.

5. Rotate the group by 30 degrees.

Summary

This chapter has covered a lot of ground, from the basics of making selections to how you perform transformations. You read that the Arrow, Subselection, and Lasso tools can be used to make selections. Likely the Subselection tool was familiar if you have worked with other vector packages, but it is the Arrow and Lasso tools that make working in Flash really interesting.

You also discovered many of the peculiarities of how Flash graphic objects function, as well as the reason they behave they way they do; namely, the Flash environment hierarchy. As you move into later chapters, the hierarchy will become more important as you learn how to write ActionScript code to control various overlay objects.

Finally, you have read about layers, scenes, and transforms. Transforms in Flash are really interesting simply because, unlike other editors, Flash remembers the transforms you apply to overlay objects. Hopefully you found the nuggets about tricks for transforms informative as well.

In the next chapter you will dive into using the drawing and painting tools. You will also learn how to define and work with color in Flash. Let's move on!

4

Drawing and Painting Tools

▪▪▪ Introduction

In the last chapter you looked at the tools in Flash used to select and transform objects. This chapter reviews the drawing and painting tools. Some tools are for the creation of objects, and others are for simply editing objects. The examination here begins with the creation of color. The chapter then takes a look at the tools for creating and editing stage objects. All of these tools are designed to create or edit lines and fills.

This chapter presents a bottom-up approach to using Flash's tools, but if you want to create complex drawings, or if you have extensive experience in FreeHand or Illustrator, you may find it easier to compose vector drawings in those packages and then import them into Flash. The primary difference between Flash (as a drawing environment) and FreeHand or Illustrator is accuracy.

You will find that Flash is not quite as accurate as FreeHand or Illustrator as it relates to positioning and transformations. In addition, one of the biggest things Flash lacks is the ability to perform "power duplication," in which use of the Duplicate command can duplicate a series of operations on an object. Power duplication makes creating linear or circular arrays of graphic objects much easier in packages that support it.

Although Flash has a few limits as a vector drawing tool, it does provide some things that other editors do not. One example presented in the last chapter was shape recognition. In this chapter you will see some unique things as well, such as the ability to optimize (reduce the number of points that define) vector objects, which can be used to reduce file size. The chapter concludes with a look at special menu commands that apply to stage objects. You will also learn some helpful tips on importing vector graphics from other programs.

Objectives

In this chapter you will:

- Revisit the Properties panel and see what type of information it yields
- Learn to define and use colors for tools and objects
- Examine the tools designed for drawing lines, including the Line, Pencil, and Pen tools
- Look at the tools designed for drawing lines and fills, including the Oval, Rectangle, and Brush tools
- Learn about the editing tools, including the Ink Bottle, Paint Bucket, Transform Fill, Dropper, and Eraser tools
- Discover other important editing commands in Flash
- Find out about importing vector graphics files into Flash MX 2004

▪ ▪ ▪ The Properties Panel

Before you jump in and starting using the drawing and painting tools, you first need to know how to control the properties of the stage objects you create and edit. In previous chapters, you read that the Properties panel, which is usually located directly below the stage, provides information about things in Flash.

Let's be more specific. Depending on what you select, it may provide general information about the movie itself, information about stage objects, or characteristics of the object you are about to create with the selected tool. Thus, depending on what you are doing, the content of the Properties panel will change.

In the last chapter (when you were working with the Arrow, Subselection, Lasso, Hand, and Zoom tools), you may have noticed that when these tools are selected the Properties panel simply shows general information about the movie. When these tools are selected (and you have no objects selected on the stage), you can quickly access the movie size, background color, frame rate, and version of the movie via the Properties panel, shown in figure 4-1. (In Chapter 12 you will learn more about versions of a movie.) These are basically some of the same options available via the Document Properties dialog box (Modify | Document).

Did you notice when you selected a group in Chapter 3 that part of the information from the Info panel (W, H, X, and Y) was displayed in the

Figure 4-1. General movie parameters are displayed in the Properties panel when the Arrow, Subselection, Lasso, Hand or Zoom tool is selected.

Properties panel? You will continue to see that the Properties panel changes as you select different things, and often provides quick access to the most commonly used elements from other places. The thing to note is that the Properties panel usually does not show all options. For example, the Document Properties dialog box and the Info panel provide more information than the Properties panel in the two previously cited cases.

Nevertheless, as you start to work with the drawing and painting tools in this chapter, as well as throughout the rest of the book, the Properties panel will become more important. Later in this chapter you will see how the Properties panel can be used to modify the properties of an already-existing stage object, but for now let's see what it does in relation to the drawing and painting tools.

If you select one of the drawing tools (the Line tool, for example), you will see that the Properties panel reveals the characteristics of the line you are about to draw, as shown in figure 4-2. Thus, you can use the Properties panel to set the properties for the object you are about to draw with a tool.

As you move into the discussion of each of the drawing and painting tools, you will read more about the individual options for each of the tools.

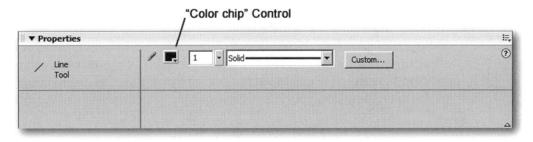

Figure 4-2. When a tool is selected, the Properties panel reveals the characteristics of the object you are about to create.

However, there is one item that is common to most of the tools and is found in many other places besides the Properties panel. This is the "color chip" control. Because this is a common element, and because assigning color is common to both drawing and painting, you need to examine how you define and utilize colors in Flash. To explore the Properties panel, try exercise 4-1.

 NOTE: *Like all applications, one of the things that makes Flash difficult for newcomers is the fact that you can access many of the same things in different locations. This section has tried to simply acknowledge this, and where applicable this book continues to point out where commonalities such as this exist.*

 Exercise 4-1: Exploring the Properties Panel
Open Flash MX 2004 and try clicking on various things to see what is shown in the Properties panel. Note that the items shown change as you select different things.

Color in Flash

With any of the drawing or painting tools selected, you will notice the "color chip" control in the Properties panel (see figure 4-2). You will also find "color chips" in the Properties panel when you select stage objects, in the Colors section of the toolbar, and within the Document Properties dialog box. What a color chip refers to depends on where it is located, but it does the same thing in all cases: it lets you access the currently defined colors in the movie. When you click on any color chip control (again, regardless of where it is located), it will "open up" to show you all of the defined colors in the movie (as well as some other miscellaneous items discussed later).

The important thing to know about color and its use in Flash is that before you can use a color in Flash you must first define (or select) it, much like you do in traditional vector programs such as FreeHand or Illustrator. However, Flash provides two ways to select color. One way allows you to quickly select a color (using a dialog box) and use it immediately, whereas the other requires that you select the color and save it as a swatch (using a panel) before using it.

Note that a swatch is nothing more than a saved color in Flash (for those familiar with Adobe Photoshop, swatches work similarly in Flash). The former method is quicker because you do not "store" the color as a swatch before use. However, this method has a drawback in that you do not have instant access to the color if you want to use it later in the development process. The latter method (pick, save as swatch, and then use) is actually the preferred method, but both methods are described here.

Once you have defined a color using either method, you can then use it to draw with (with a tool), assign it to an already-existing object (using the Properties panel), or assign it to the background color of the stage (using Document Properties or the Properties panel). All of this is covered in material to follow. However, a few more details are in order before that examination. Given this "process" for defining and using color, the following is an overview of "where" you do each.

- To choose a color and save it as a swatch, you use the Mixer panel.

- To simply choose a color without saving a swatch, you use the Color dialog box.

- Once you have saved colors, you view the resulting colors using the Color Swatches panel.

Now that you have a basic understanding of the overall process, let's start looking at some details. The following section explores default colors in a movie and how you get to them.

Default Colors

By default, every Flash movie starts with a predefined set of basic colors saved as swatches. The Color Swatches panel provides access to these colors.

The Color Swatches Panel

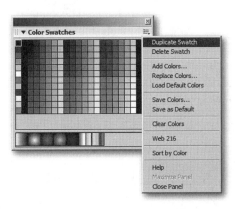

Figure 4-3. The Color Swatches panel and its menu shown undocked.

You can access the Color Swatches panel at any time to see all of the currently defined colors in a movie. By default, the Color Swatches panel should be directly available in the docking area on the right-hand side of the stage. Figure 4-3 shows this panel in its undocked position, as well as its menu.

Ignoring the menu for a moment, note that the Color Swatches panel shows two types of swatches: solid and fill colors. Solid colors are at the top, and fill colors are at the bottom.

Solid colors can be used for lines or fills, whereas fill colors (gradients) can only be used for fills. When you create fill colors they are based on combinations of solid colors, which you will see later.

One of the things you should notice about the default colors shown in the Color Swatches panel is that they are the 216 web-safe (or browser-safe) colors. The browser-safe color palette consists of 216 specific colors, as well as 40 other colors (256 total). The colors selected for the additional 40 colors depend on the browser or the operating system for which the palette is designed. These are the colors used for the interface of the browser or operating system. Note that specific palettes were first used for multimedia development—circa 1990—when computer-based multimedia as we know it today truly started to emerge. Thus, the browser-safe color palette is a continuation of this and serves a similar purpose.

The basic premise of using any 256-color palette is that you are trying to control the way the content will look for the audience members who are viewing in 256 colors. Whenever a computer is set on 256-color display, everything in that environment must be rendered and displayed using the same 256 colors. If you happen to run into an image that uses colors that are not in the current palette being used for the system, the image can range in quality from slightly affected to rainbow soup! The goal of using a specific palette, then—in the case of web development, the goal of using the browser-safe palette—is to try to stay on the "slightly affected" end of the continuum, rather than the "rainbow soup" end.

You will also note that there is a pattern to the colors in the Colors Swatches palette. Notice that there are six groups of 6 x 6 colors. The first chip in each 6 x 6 set is the transformation of black to red, and the last chip is the transformation of cyan to white. These are in essence "slices" through the RGB color cube used to define color on the computer, as shown in figure 4-4. The actual colors selected are based on specific combinations of hexadecimal values, which it is unnecessary to examine in detail. Simply note that there is a pattern to the colors, as this may help you find a color later on.

 NOTE: *In a later section you will see how to select and use the colors in the Color Swatches panel.*

Working with Sets of Colors

In figure 4-3, you saw the embedded menu in the Color Swatches panel. Let's explore this for a moment. In the menu you see that you can duplicate and delete existing swatches in the palette. To do this, you select the color in the palette and then select the appropriate option (Duplicate

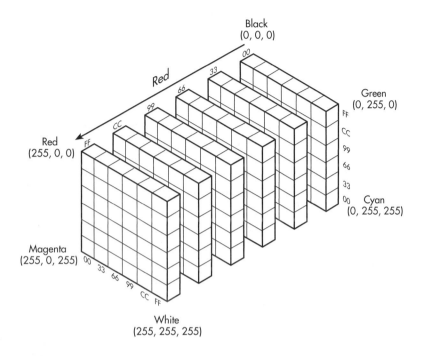

Figure 4-4. The default colors in the Color Swatches panel are slices through the RGB color model.

Swatch or Delete Swatch) from the menu. This will become more relevant a little later.

The important thing to note is that you can add, replace, and save entire palettes of colors, instead of always having to work with the default web-safe set of colors and adding your own. Of course, you can also revert to the default web-safe colors associated with the Load Default Colors option if something goes awry. These features allow you to manage and use sets of colors and give you a lot of flexibility.

"What do I need to know about saving or loading color sets?" you may ask. Flash stores saved sets of swatches in its own proprietary format, denoted with a *.clr* extension (*.fclr* on the Mac). Thus, you can save a palette of custom colors from one movie and import it into another. You can also export your Flash colors to other programs, such as Photoshop. Flash can save in the Photoshop .act format, which can then be imported into Photoshop's Swatches palette. Additionally, you can import color palettes from other sources. In short, Flash allows you to import colors from its own CLR format, Photoshop's ACT format, or from an existing GIF graphic (in that GIF files by nature are 256-color images).

Also in the menu shown in figure 4-3, you see three other options: Clear Colors, Web 216, and Sort by Color. The Clear Colors option lets you delete all colors in the Color Swatches panel color list, leaving only black and white.

If you prefer you can create your own set of colors and have them be the default colors shown every time you start a new movie in Flash (using the Save as Default option). Even if you use this to replace the default colors in Flash, you can always get back to the 216 web-safe colors using the Web 216 option. Thus, the results of the Load Default Colors and Web 216 options are the same unless you have changed the default colors to be used by Flash. The Sort by Color option sorts the colors in the Swatches panel color list by luminosity, as opposed to their default "slice" order described previously. To practice working with the Swatches panel, try exercise 4-2.

 TIP: *There are a few other color sets that are installed with Flash. These include a grayscale, Macintosh system, and Windows system color set. They are located in the* Macromedia/Flash MX 2004/en/First Run/Color Sets/ *folder.*

 Exercise 4-2: Working with the Swatches Panel

Open Flash and examine the default colors defined in Flash. Try loading other color sets (mentioned in the previous Tip) into the Color Swatches palette.

Defining Colors

Now that you have taken a look at the default colors that are automatically available in Flash, as well as how you work with sets of swatches, let's examine the two ways you can define a color. Again, the preferred way is to use the Mixer panel to define and store a color as a swatch. The second is to use the Colors dialog box.

Mixer Panel

To define your own custom color you use the Mixer panel, shown in figure 4-5. Figure 4-5 shows the Mixer panel undocked, and completely expanded. Remember that the small white arrow in the lower right-hand corner of the panel allows you to partially collapse the Mixer panel.

Within the Mixer panel you see several controls. Note first the Stroke color and Fill color "chips." These show you the current colors assigned to lines and fills in the drawing environment. Note that one of them will be highlighted, meaning that as you define a new color in the Mixer panel

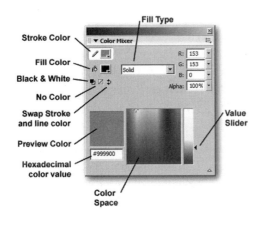

Fill Type

Stroke Color

Fill Color

Black & White

No Color

Swap Stroke
and line color

Preview Color

Hexadecimal
color value

Color
Space

Value
Slider

Figure 4-5. Use the Mixer panel to define and save colors as swatches.

the new color will be assigned to the highlighted item. Stroke color is the current element being modified in figure 4-5.

Also in figure 4-5 you see three small buttons beneath the Fill color chip, as well as a drop-down menu in the center of the panel. The drop-down menu is used to define the Fill type of color you mix. You can define Solid, Linear, or Radial gradients, as well as Bitmap fills.

NOTE: *Bitmap fills are discussed in Chapter 7.*

The three small buttons are designed to perform specific things. The first button sets the current Stroke and Fill colors to Black and White. The second button allows you to define "no color" for either the Stroke or Fill color. You would use this if you wanted to create an oval with no fill, or a rectangular fill with no line. The third button allows you to swap the current Stroke and Fill colors.

Defining a Solid Color in the Mixer

To define a color in the Mixer panel, you begin by selecting Solid from the Fill Type drop-down list. Then you can either interact with the Color Space and Value slider to define the color or you can numerically enter the color using the text fields. When using the Color Space and Value slider, you define the hue and saturation in the Color Space area and the lightness (amount of white or black added to the color) using the Value slider via the mouse. As you modify these two elements, the preview color will change to show you the color selected.

If you choose to numerically enter a color specification, you can do so using the red, green, and blue (RGB) components of the color, or entering the hexadecimal value for the color. When you enter RGB values, they will range from 0 to 255, but the hexadecimal field beneath the preview color swatch will expect the hexadecimal (Base16) representation of the RGB value. If you prefer working with HLS (hue, light, and saturation) values, you can select HLS from the Mixer panel's menu, shown in figure 4-6. When entering color this way, hue is a value from 0 to 360 degrees, whereas light and saturation are values that range from 0 to 100.

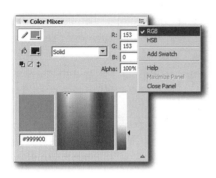

Figure 4-6. The Mixer Panel's menu provides several options.

 NOTE: *When the Mixer panel is partially collapsed, the Preview Color area and the Hexadecimal field are not shown. Also, the Color Space area will be compressed in size.*

Once you have a color defined in the Mixer panel, you can add it to the Color Swatches panel (so you can use it again later without having to remix it) quite easily. You simply select Add Swatch from the Mixer panel menu (see figure 4-6). Once added to the Color Swatches panel, you can easily retrieve the color for use for tools and other things. Exercise 4-3 provides you with practice in defining and saving a solid color.

 Exercise 4-3: Defining and Saving a Solid Color

Try using the Mixer to define a color. Make sure you experiment with both the color controls and entering numerical values for colors. Once you have a color defined, save it as a swatch and view the Swatches panel to see that it was added.

 NOTE: *When you use the Add Swatch option in the Mixer, the swatch is added at the bottom of the swatches in the Swatches panel.*

The Alpha Field

You may be wondering, "What is the purpose of the Alpha field?" The Alpha slider allows you to define the level of transparency (or opaqueness) of a solid color. Flash supports 8 bits of transparency for any defined color. Thus, a color could have 256 levels of transparency. However, the slider is based on percentages, so the actual number of levels is 100. The important point is that a color could be 53 percent transparent, 1 percent transparent, or 93 percent transparent. This provides a tremendous amount of flexibility when creating graphics for the Web.

Transparent GIF files, which only offer 1-bit transparency, pale by comparison. In a transparent GIF, a pixel is either 100 percent transparent or 100 percent opaque. There are no gradations or variations of transparency allowed. Chapter 9 focuses on animation and discusses the use of the Alpha feature for creating objects that have varying levels of transparency.

Defining a Linear or Radial Fill

Solid colors, as you have already seen, are mixed in the Mixer panel, but you can also mix linear and radial gradients to be used for fill objects. If you change the Fill Style drop-down in the Mixer to Linear or Radial, you can create a gradient, as shown in figure 4-7. After a gradient has been defined, you can use it in a tool or apply it to an object.

 NOTE: *The Bitmap option is discussed in Chapter 7.*

When you select the Linear or the Radial option, the panel will look similar to that shown in figure 4-7. The small boxes, called markers, that appear beneath the gradient bar in the center of the panel define the colors that compose the gradient. You can drag the markers to change the sharpness of the transition between the two colors. You can also add more markers to create multicolor gradients, as shown in figure 4-8. If you place your cursor over the top of the gradient bar, the cursor will change to an arrow with a plus sign, indicating that if you click there a new marker will be created. You remove a color marker by click-dragging it away from the color bar, or by pressing the Ctrl (Windows) or Command (Macintosh) key and clicking on a marker.

Note that any of the colors represented by a marker can be changed to another color. The currently selected marker is identified by a black, filled triangle above it. With a marker selected, if you change the color assigned to the color chip (see figure 4-7), the current marker will change to the newly selected gradient.

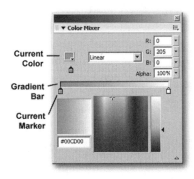

Figure 4-7. Selecting Linear in the Fill Style drop-down list provides controls for creating a gradient.

Figure 4-8. You can add multiple markers to a gradient to create a multicolor fill.

TIP: *Sharp whites and blacks typify shiny objects. To create a gradient that looks like highly reflective metal, you will generally have a lot of markers in the fill. Put a touch of brown on one end and blue at the other to give the perception of a reflected horizon in an object.*

Once you have defined a gradient you wish to save as a swatch (so that you can use it over and over), select Add Swatch from the Mixer's menu. Once you do so, the gradient will be available in the lower portion of the Color Swatches panel. To practice creating multicolor gradients, try exercise 4-4.

 ### Exercise 4-4: Creating Multicolor Gradients

Open Flash and use the Mixer panel to create some gradient colors. Try using both the linear and radial gradients to see the results of each. Add each to the Swatches panel.

Using Transparency in Colors and Gradients

One of the unique things you can do in Flash is define a solid or gradient that utilizes transparency. For example, to create a drop shadow on an object, you define a linear or radial gradient that blends from an opaque color to a transparent color. To utilize transparency within a solid color or gradient, you use the Mixer, set the Alpha value to 0 percent (or other value), and then save the swatch.

When you set the Alpha to 0 percent, the chip and gradient preview will display a grid behind the color, as shown in figure 4-9a. Note that the marker on the left end of the gradient defined in figure 4-9a has been set to 0-percent Alpha. When applied to an object, where there is transparent color, background objects will show through the gradient (see figure 4-9b). Exercise 4-5 provides you with practice in using transparency in gradients.

Figure 4-9. Transparency appears in the Mixer panel as a grid shown behind the color (a). When applied to an object, where there is transparent color, background objects show through (b).

Exercise 4-5: Using Transparency in Gradients

Try creating a linear or radial gradient that uses transparency. Experiment with various combinations to see the results of each.

Color Dialog Box

The key to working with color in Flash is understanding that there are two ways of defining colors: via the Mixer and Color Swatches panels (described in the prior section) and via the Color dialog box. Within the Mixer panel, you define a color and then save it as a swatch so that you can reuse it later. The Color dialog box also allows you to quickly define a color. However, this dialog box does not give you the option of saving the color as a swatch. Thus, these two approaches are somewhat discontinuous and disconnected. Nevertheless, it is important to be aware of both.

Accessing the Color Dialog Box

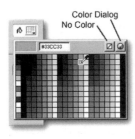

Figure 4-10. Expanding the color controls to view and select swatches or to access the Color dialog button.

You access the Colors dialog box by clicking on any color control chip. The most accessible is within the View section of the toolbar. If you click on a color control chip (either Stroke or Fill color), the currently available colors defined as swatches will appear, as shown in figure 4-10. Note the small button in the upper right of the expanded control that looks like a color wheel. This button provides access to the Color dialog box.

Once the Color dialog box (figure 4-11) is open, it gives you access to a default set of colors. There is not necessarily a correlation between these and the swatches you looked at earlier. In general, the two are not directly related. The colors shown in the Color dialog box are independent of the swatches. Clicking on any of the colors in the Color dialog sets the current color to the one you have selected. Clicking on OK will allow you to start using the color immediately as the stroke or fill, without saving the color as a swatch.

Creating Custom Colors

In the Color dialog box, you can also create your own custom color, which is sort of like creating a swatch (but not really). To do this, adjust the parameters of one of the already-existing basic colors or start from scratch (black) and define your own new color.

Color Space   Value Bar

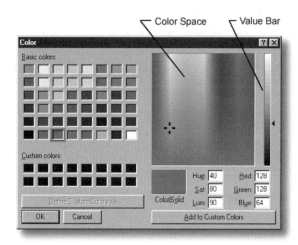

Figure 4-11. The Colors dialog box allows you to quickly select color, but is independent of the Mixer and Color Swatches panels.

To start from scratch, you begin by clicking on one of the boxes under Custom Colors. To modify one of the existing default colors to create a new color, click on a color box under the Basic colors set. In either case, use the Color Space and Value controls to visually adjust the color, or use the HSL or RGB fields to modify the numerical values. Once you get the color you want, click on the Add to Custom Colors button to add the color to the Custom colors section. Then click on OK to set the stroke or fill color to your newly defined color. Keep in mind that the color is not automatically added as a swatch. Colors defined in the Color dialog box are only available in the Color dialog box. To practice using the Color dialog box, try exercise 4-6.

Exercise 4-6: Using the Color Dialog Box

So that you are familiar with the Color dialog box, try accessing it and defining a few custom colors.

Using Colors

Although some may favor using the Color dialog box, the preferred method is to use the Mixer to save a swatch, and then use the swatch for something. The next three sections discuss using colors you have defined as swatches.

Assigning Color to the Background of a Movie

One of the first things people commonly ask is how you change the background color of a movie. Once you have a solid color defined, you can assign it as the background of the stage using either the Properties panel or Modify | Document selection. Note that you cannot set a gradient as the background. If you want a gradient as the background, you must create a rectangle with a gradient fill on a layer in the background and scale it up to the size of the stage.

Similar to this, a frequent second question when discussing background colors is "How do you make the background transparent, such that when the movie is in a web page, the web page background shows through the Flash movie?" Knowing how to create transparent colors, the first thought is to create a transparent color and assign it to the background. But unfortunately this does not work. To make the background of a movie transparent, you must use some special web page coding. Chapter 12 explores this in detail. To see how changing the background color of the stage works, try exercise 4-7.

Exercise 4-7: Changing the Background Color of the Stage

Open Flash and try changing the background color of the stage. Create a few colors of your own and try reestablishing the background color.

Assigning Color to a Tool

You can establish the stroke and fill color with which the tool will draw for all drawing and painting tools. Some tools use both a stroke color and a fill color. Others simply require a stroke color.

There are fundamentally two ways to set the current stroke or fill colors. One way is to use the Colors section of the toolbar itself. The current stroke color and fill color are always shown there. But you can also change the color after a tool is selected using the Properties panel. When you select one of the drawing tools, the Properties panel provides controls for changing current colors as well. Whether or not both Stroke and Fill are accessible depends on the tool. For example, the Line tool only provides Stroke, whereas the Oval and Rectangle tools provide both stroke color and fill color.

Assigning Color to a Stage Object

A last way in which you can use defined swatch colors is when you want to change the stroke or fill color of an already-existing stage object. If you select objects on the stage, the Properties panel provides controls for changing the stroke and fill colors of the selected object. Like assigning color to tools, you can also use the Colors section of the toolbar to do this.

▪ ▪ ▪ Creating Lines and Arcs

Now that you have examined the definition and use of color in Flash, it is time to start looking at the tools for drawing and painting. Let's begin with the simplest of tools—those designed for drawing lines and arcs. The sections that follow explore the Line, Pencil, and Pen tools, and provide applied exercises.

Line Tool

Among the most basic of elements you will want to create are lines. When you select the Line tool, the Properties panel provides access to the characteristics of the line you are about to draw, as shown in figure 4-12. These include stroke color, stroke height, and stroke style. When you want to draw straight-line segments, you select the Line tool, set the characteristics, and then begin drawing.

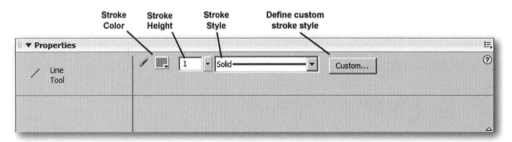

Figure 4-12. When the Line tool is selected, you can control stroke color, stroke height, and line style.

The Properties panel will also allow you to create custom stroke styles, such as your own sizes for dashed lines, and so on. If you click on the Custom button, you access the Stroke Style dialog box, shown in figure 4-13. Use the options to create your own line styles. To practice working with lines, try exercise 4-8.

Figure 4-13. Clicking on the Custom button reveals the Stroke Style dialog box, in which you can define your own stroke styles.

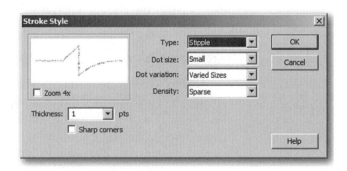

Exercise 4-8: Experimenting with Lines

 CD-ROM NOTE: *Open* ch04_08.fla, *located in the* fgai/ chapter04/ *folder, installed from the companion CD-ROM.*

Use the Properties panel and Line tool to practice creating lines with various stroke styles, widths, and colors.

TIP: *You should minimize the number of custom line styles used, as they can increase file size when used in large quantities.*

Pencil Tool

Pencil Mode Option

The Pencil tool allows you to draw free-form lines. Again, the stroke attributes (Stroke Color, Stroke Height, Stroke Style, and Custom) are set in the Properties panel. However, you should note that an additional option—the Pencil Mode option of the Pencil tool—appears in the toolbar options (not in the Properties panel), as shown in figure 4-14. Use the Pencil Mode options to define the following types of lines.

- *Straighten:* Automatically forces the line you draw to be composed of straight-line segments.
- *Smooth:* Will automatically simplify drawn segments, attempting to make smooth arcs.
- *Ink:* Leaves lines exactly as they are drawn. No smoothing or straightening occurs.

Figure 4-14. When the Pencil tool is selected, an option appears in the Options section of the toolbar.

Keep in mind that in Flash you do not always have to be concerned with drawing exactly what you want the first time. The Smooth and Straighten modifiers associated with the Arrow tool can always be used to smooth or straighten a line, as you saw in Chapter 3. In addition, with the added control it provides, you may find the Pen tool more advantageous when constructing line or arc segments, as described in the next section. To practice using the Pencil tool, try exercise 4-9.

Exercise 4-9: Using the Pencil Tool

Start a blank drawing in Flash and try using the Pencil tool with the various Pencil modes. See how each affects lines you draw.

Pen Tool

Recall from Chapter 3 that Flash allows you to work in two ways: natural drawing and traditional point-based mode. The two previously discussed tools are "natural drawing tools," whereas the Pen tool is akin to traditional vector drawing tools in that it allows you to work directly with the points that define vector objects.

Creation with the Pen Tool

To use the Pen tool to create lines or arcs, you begin by clicking points on the stage. If you use a single click, the Pen tool will add straight-line points, which will result in line segments. If you click-drag as you add a point, handles will appear, creating Bezier curves. By varying single clicks and click-drags, you can create continuous strokes consisting of straight and Bezier segments. Double clicking on a point will end the stroke you are creating.

 TIP: *You can also hold down the Ctrl key (Option key on Mac) and click to end the line.*

By default the Pen tool does not show a preview of the stroke as it is being created. You can use the Edit | Preferences | Editing tab to turn on the Show Pen Preview option. This allows you to see what you are drawing as you draw it. In addition, for greater accuracy, you can turn on Show Precise Cursors in the Editing tab.

In addition to creating strokes, you can use the Pen tool to add, subtract, and modify stroke points on existing line and arc segments. You can use the Pen tool to subtract a point from a straight segment between two points. However, one drawback is that you cannot add a point to a straight segment. To subtract a point, click with the Pen tool on the desired line to make it active. Then move the Pen tool close to an existing point. The cursor will change to reveal a minus sign. Click on the point and it will be removed from the segment. Exercise 4-10 provides you with the opportunity to practice drawing with the Pen tool.

 TIP: *With the Pen tool selected, if you hold down the Ctrl key (Option key on Mac), you can select a Bezier point and then work with its balance handles to modify the curve.*

 Exercise 4-10: Drawing with the Pen Tool

Open Flash and use the Pen tool to draw some elements. Try clicking and click-dragging to get a feel for how the tool works.

Modifying Points with the Pen Tool

The Pen tool also offers two functions in regard to Bezier segments. First, you can add points to a Bezier segment by moving the Pen tool over a selected segment and clicking. Unlike other vector environments, however, you cannot click-drag to instantly move the Bezier handles. Rather, you click to add the point, and then hold down the Ctrl key (PC) or the Option key (Mac) to select the point and change the position of its handles.

The second thing you can do is turn a Bezier point into a straight-segment point (an angle). If you move the Pen tool over an existing Bezier point, the cursor will change to reveal a small angle icon next to the cursor's arrow. If you click on the point, it is turned into a straight-segment point (a sharp angle). The angle created is based on the angle between the two line segments. For practice in working with the Pen tool, try exercise 4-11.

Exercise 4-11: Using the Pen Tool

 CD-ROM NOTE: *To learn more about the Pen tool, open the file* ch04_11.fla, *located in the* fgai/chapter04/ *folder, installed from the companion CD-ROM.*

Use the Pen tool to create and modify the segments shown in the CD-ROM file.

··· Creating Lines with Fills

The last three tools you looked at were for creating lines only. Now turn your attention to tools that create lines and fills simultaneously.

Oval Tool

The Oval tool can be used to create filled or unfilled ellipses and circles. When you select the Oval tool, the Properties panel is used to set the stroke color, stroke height, and stroke style. You will also notice the Fill color chip beneath the Stroke color chip, as shown in figure 4-15. Use this chip to assign a color for the fill inside an ellipse or circle.

TIP: *If you want to draw a perfect circle with the Oval tool, hold down the Shift key as you draw.*

Although most of the attributes for strokes and fills for tools are available in the Properties panel, you can access and set stroke color and fill color in the toolbar as well, using the Colors section, shown in figure 4-16.

Directly beneath the controls for stroke and fill color in the toolbar are three small but important buttons you examined earlier. However, these were in the Mixer panel when you saw them last (figure 4-5). No matter where these buttons are located, they do the same thing. The important one here is the middle button, or the "no color" assignment. The No Color button is also available within the color control selector, as shown in figure 4-17.

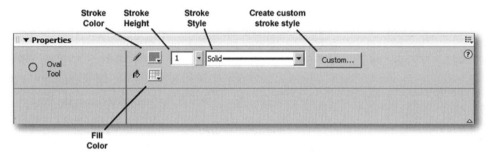

Figure 4-15. The Properties panel shows the options for the Oval tool.

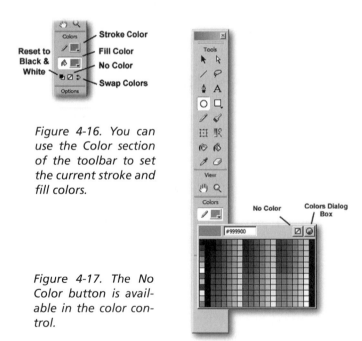

Figure 4-16. You can use the Color section of the toolbar to set the current stroke and fill colors.

Figure 4-17. The No Color button is available in the color control.

When drawing items such as ovals and rectangles, it is important to note how you create an oval (or circle) with no fill and how you create an oval fill (or circle) with no line. The No Color button is important because it is what provides this capability. If you wish to create an oval with no fill, select the Oval tool, and then click on the fill color in the Colors section (or the Properties panel). Click on the No Color button to set the fill to no color. Use a similar process for creating a fill with no line. Exercise 4-12 provides practice in creating different types of ovals.

Exercise 4-12: Experimenting with Ovals

CD-ROM NOTE: *Open the file* ch04_12.fla, *located in the* fgai/ chapter04/ *folder, installed from the companion CD-ROM.*

Use the Oval tool to practice creating ovals with various stroke styles, widths, and colors. Try creating at least one circle or ellipse without a fill and one circular or elliptical fill without a line.

Rectangle and PolyStar Tools

The sections that follow describe the Rectangle and PolyStar tools.

Rectangle Tool

One of the unique things about the Rectangle tool is that it is actually two tools in one. You will note a small black triangle on the Rectangle tool (a carryover from other software tools indicating that there are multiple tools that can be accessed from that button in the toolbar). Let's first deal with the Rectangle tool.

As with the Oval tool, the attributes for the stroke and fill characteristics of the Rectangle tool are set in the Properties panel. However, there is one exception: the Round Rectangle Radius option, which appears in the toolbar options when the Rectangle tool is selected. Figure 4-18a shows the location of this item. Clicking on the Round Rectangle Radius button accesses a dialog box in which you can enter a radius for the rectangle's corners (figure 4-18b). Exercise 4-13 provides practice in working with the Line, Oval, and Rectangle tools.

TIP: *As you are in the process of drawing a rectangle, you can adjust the rectangle's radius by pressing the up arrow or down arrow.*

Figure 4-18. The Rectangle tool provides the Round Rectangle Radius button.

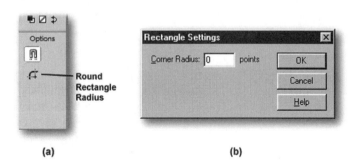

(a)　　　　　　　　　　(b)

Exercise 4-13: Using the Line, Oval, and Rectangle Tools

CD-ROM NOTE: *Get a better idea of how the Line, Oval, and Rectangle tools work. Open* ch04_13.fla, *located in the* fgai/ chapter04/ *folder, installed from the companion CD-ROM.*

Follow the instructions to create the entities suggested in the CD-ROM file.

TIP: *If you want to draw a perfect square with the Rectangle tool, hold down the Shift key as you draw.*

PolyStar Tool

If you click and hold on the Rectangle tool, you will be able to access the PolyStar tool. This tool allows you to create various polygons and stars. When you select this tool, the Properties panel reveals an additional button (labeled Options), use of which allows you to establish the style (polygon or star) as well as the number of sides and star point sides.

▪ ▪ ▪ "Drawing" Fills Using the Brush Tool

Now that you have examined drawing elements, let's look at one more tool that allows you to draw in Flash: the Brush tool. The Brush tool basically lets you draw fills. Aside from drawing individual lines with the Pencil tool, the Brush tool can be used to draw wider strokes, which are actually fill objects. Predominantly, the Brush is used to fill enclosed areas with color by painting in the fill.

Although the visual difference between elements drawn with the Pencil and Brush may seem minute on screen, a more detailed look reveals why you might use one over the other. As shown in figure 4-19, a curve drawn with the Pencil and a curve drawn with the Brush are not alike. The biggest difference between these elements is that objects created with the Pencil are individual strokes with a thickness. Brush objects are really closed polygons (fill objects) that can be seen when the viewing mode is changed to outlines (View | Preview Mode | Outlines). Exercise 4-

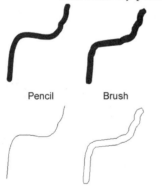

Pencil   Brush

Figure 4-19. The difference between a Pencil and Brush object is revealed when viewed in outline mode.

14 provides practice in working with the Pencil and Brush tools so that you can see the difference.

Exercise 4-14: The Pencil Versus the Brush

CD-ROM NOTE: *To learn more about the differences between the Pencil and Brush tools, open the file ch04_14.fla, located in the fgai/chapter04/ folder, installed from the companion CD-ROM.*

Follow the instructions in the CD-ROM file to manipulate the entities as suggested.

Figure 4-20. The Brush tool reveals four options in the toolbar.

When you select the Brush tool, you will find that four items appear in the toolbar options, as shown in figure 4-20. The fill color for the Brush tool is located in the Properties panel. The options in the toolbar include Brush Mode, Brush Size, Brush Shape, and Lock Fills, which are described in the sections that follow.

Brush Modes

Similar to the Pencil modes, the Brush modes determine how paint is applied with the brush. You can apply paint in a "normal" manner, inside a fill, behind other objects, and so on. The options of Brush Mode are Paint Normal, Paint Fills, Paint Behind, Paint Selection, and Paint Inside. Figure 4-21 shows sample images of the three most commonly used Brush modes. To gain greater familiarity with Brush modes, try exercise 4-15. The various Brush modes perform the following functions.

- *Paint Normal:* Draws on top of any existing lines or fills.
- *Paint Fills:* Affects only fills on the stage, leaving lines unchanged.
- *Paint Behind:* Renders behind any existing lines or fills.
- *Paint Selection:* Makes drawing occur within the selected fill only.
- *Paint Inside:* Paints only the fill area where you began the stroke. Paint Inside will not go over lines. If nothing exists where you start painting, nothing will be applied.

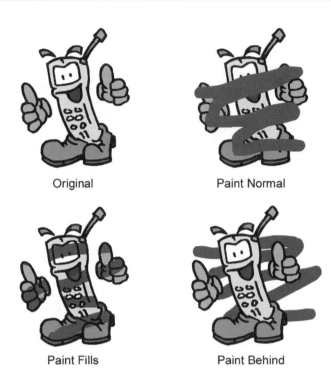

Original   Paint Normal

Paint Fills   Paint Behind

Figure 4-21. The Brush modes allow you to paint in a variety of ways.

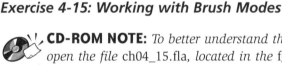

Exercise 4-15: Working with Brush Modes

CD-ROM NOTE: *To better understand the Brush modes, open the file ch04_15.fla, located in the fgai/ chapter04/ folder, installed from the companion CD-ROM.*

Follow the instructions in the CD-ROM file to paint in various modes.

Locking Fills

The Lock Fills button in the toolbar options is a useful feature that locks the angle, size, and origin of the current gradient or fill. This button permits you to easily extend an existing fill into adjacent areas of the drawing. When using the Dropper tool (which allows you to pick up a line, fill, or gradient color), Lock Fills is automatically selected. This is discussed in greater detail later in this chapter.

▪ ▪ ▪ Tools for Editing

Now that you have examined all of the drawing tools, let's begin looking at the tools designed for editing. All of the tools discussed in this section are generally designed to work with already-existing stage objects.

Ink Bottle Tool

The Ink Bottle option is used to change the characteristics of already-existing lines. To change the color of a line or set of lines, click on the Ink Bottle tool and, in the Properties panel, set the characteristics for the style, height, and color to which you would like to change the lines. Click on the line or lines you want to change and they will be changed to match the characteristics you established in the Properties panel.

As you have already learned, when lines intersect, Flash automatically recognizes them as line segments instead of continuous lines. In terms of vector programs such as FreeHand or Illustrator, lines are automatically "broken" (or "cut") when they intersect.

The advantage of this Flash feature is that lines do not have to be trimmed. Just select them to delete them. However, the negative aspect is that when you want to change a line's color or style using the Ink Bottle you have to apply the change across each segment that constitutes the line. To get several segments to fill at once, double click on them and then use the Ink Bottle on the selection. For practice using the Ink Bottle tool, see exercise 4-16.

Exercise 4-16: Using the Ink Bottle Tool

CD-ROM NOTE: *Discover more information about using the Ink Bottle tool. Open the file ch04_16.fla, located in the fgai/chapter04/ folder, installed from the companion CD-ROM.*

Use Ink Bottle and the settings in the Properties panel to adjust the characteristics of the lines in the CD-ROM file drawing.

Paint Bucket Tool

Gap Size

Lock Fills

Figure 4-22. The Paint Bucket tool provides two options: Gap Size and Lock Fills.

You can easily add a solid or gradient fill to an area using the Paint Bucket tool. To create a fill, the set of lines does not necessarily have to be a closed polygon, as you will see in the following section. The Paint Bucket offers two options that control its behavior, as shown in figure 4-22. These are Gap Size and Lock Fills, discussed in the sections that follow.

Gap Size

In Flash, polygons do not have to be closed before they can be filled. Gaps are one of the most difficult things to deal with in most vector drawing programs. Fortunately, Flash can automatically "close gaps" so that fills can be more quickly applied. This does not mean, however, that it adds a line to close the gap, as you will see.

TIP: *Because Flash works so uniquely with fills, it may be more efficient to import line drawings from other packages and then render them in Flash. Complex drawings with many fills are often easier to render in Flash than in traditional vector illustration packages.*

Gap Size determines the size of the gaps you want Flash to ignore. To close gaps manually, select the Do Not Close Gaps option. The Gap Size option is very effective for complex drawings or for line drawings imported from other sources. To experiment with the Gap Size option, see exercise 4-17.

Exercise 4-17: Color and Gap Size Options

CD-ROM NOTE: *To find out more about the Gap Size option, open the file* ch04_17.fla, *located in the* fgai/chapter04/ *folder, installed from the companion CD-ROM.*

Try the various settings on the objects shown in the CD-ROM file.

Lock Fills

The Paint Bucket provides another useful option for working with fills: Lock Fills. Lock Fills works in a manner similar to the Lock Fills option used with the Paint Brush tool. It allows you to select a fill and extend that fill into a new area. When using the Paint Bucket tool, you can always tell if Lock Fills is on by looking closely at the cursor. When this option is on, a small padlock is displayed as part of the Paint Bucket tool's cursor.

Transform Fill Tool

The Transform Fill tool lets you rotate, scale, or move the linear or radial gradation within a fill that has been created on the stage. To transform a fill's gradient, you select the Transform Fill tool and then select a fill object on the stage. When you do so, Flash represents the bounding box of the fill on the stage, as shown in figure 4-23. By grabbing handle points that appear on the side of the bounding box, you can scale or rotate the fill's gradation, very much like grabbing the handles on the sides of an object on which you are using the Free Transform tool (except that the Transform Fill tool does not provide skewing). If you move the center point with the Transform Fill tool, the gradation will change its location within the fill.

As shown in figure 4-23, the corner handle that appears on the gradation's boundary allows it to be rotated. The side handle allows you to scale the gradation within the fill. The center handle allows you to move the fill. As the cursor moves near these handles, it will change to indicate that the transformation is available. Note that if the gradation is linear the bounding shape is rectilinear. If the gradation is radial, the bounding shape is a circle, as shown in figure 4-23.

The one thing to note about the Transform Fill tool is that often when you select an object you may not be able to see the bounding box for the gradation. For example, imagine you selected on a radial fill object with the Transform Fill tool and you cannot see the circular bounds for the gradation. This commonly happens when you are zoomed in on an object. If this happens, just zoom out until you can see the bounds for the fill.

With the Transform Fill tool, the gradation within a fill can be shaped almost infinitely. To practice working with the Transform Fill tool, try exercise 4-18.

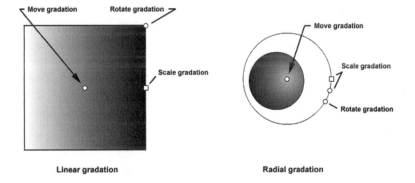

Figure 4-23. The Transform Fill tool reveals the bounding box of the gradation within a fill object. The shape of the bounding area depends on whether the fill's gradation is linear of radial.

Exercise 4-18: Working with the Transform Fill Tool

CD-ROM NOTE: *Learn more about the Transform Fill tool. Open the file* ch04_18.fla, *located in the* fgai/chapter04/ *folder, installed from the companion CD-ROM.*

Use the Transform Fill tool to adjust the fills you apply to the objects of the CD-ROM file.

Dropper Tool

The Dropper tool, much like similar tools found in raster editors, allows you to quickly select the line and fill characteristics of an existing stage object so that they may be applied to another object. Thus, this tool is par-

Line   Fill

Figure 4-24. The Dropper tool's cursor indicates the item being sampled.

ticularly handy for editing tasks. The Dropper tool has no options, and when selected, the Properties panel shows the general movie properties.

After selecting the Dropper, dragging the cursor over an object reveals the characteristics you are about to pick up; that is, line or fill attributes. Figure 2-24 shows the difference between the two cursors. Once you click on a fill or line, the Paint Bucket or Ink Bottle is selected. Using the characteristics (acquired by the Dropper) in the Paint Bucket or Ink Bottle, you can modify other elements in your drawing to match one another. See exercise 4-19 for practice in using the Dropper tool.

 TIP: *When you select the Dropper tool, the Lock Fills button is automatically active in the Fill tool. This allows you to quickly and easily extend or continue a fill into other areas of your drawing.*

Exercise 4-19: Using the Dropper Tool

 CD-ROM NOTE: *To find out more about the Dropper tool, open the file* ch04_19.fla, *located in the* fgai/chapter04/ *folder, installed from the companion CD-ROM.*

In the CD-ROM file, use the Dropper tool to render the object on the right by picking up line and fill characteristics from the rendering on the left. Once you pick up a fill from the object on the left, you must deselect Lock Fills.

Eraser Tool

The Eraser tool in Flash provides a means of deleting portions of objects from a drawing. The Eraser tool provides three options, as shown in figure 4-25. These are Eraser Mode, Eraser Shape, and Faucet.

 TIP: *If you want to start your drawing over, double clicking on the Eraser tool will clear the entire canvas. If you accidentally erase your drawing, you can use Edit | Undo to restore it.*

Eraser Modes and Shape

As with previous tools, the Eraser Mode option provides settings that control what the Eraser will affect. You can perform a "normal" erase, as well as erase only specific elements. Figure 4-26 shows the results of the commonly used Eraser modes on an

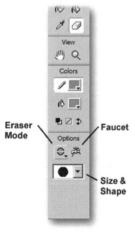

Eraser Mode — Faucet — Size & Shape

Figure 4-25. The Eraser tool has three options in the toolbar.

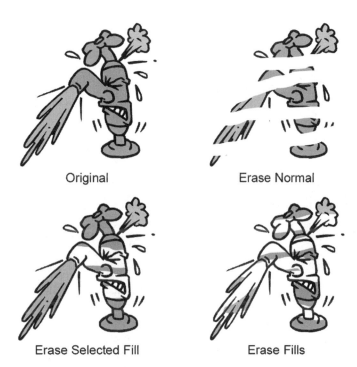

Original   Erase Normal

Erase Selected Fill   Erase Fills

Figure 4-26. The Eraser modes control what is erased.

image. The Eraser Shape option permits the size and shape of the Eraser to be changed.

The Eraser Mode options include the following. To experiment with the Eraser modes, see exercise 4-20.

- *Erase Normal:* Deletes both lines and fills.
- *Erase Fills:* Erases fills only.
- *Erase Lines:* Gets rid of lines only.
- *Erase Selected Fills:* Removes portions of a selected fill.
- *Erase Inside:* Deletes inside an object. The inside is defined as where you start erasing within the bounds of the lines of a closed shape.

The Eraser tool will only work on stage objects. If an object is grouped, you can double click on it with the Arrow tool for editing, instead of using Modify | Ungroup. Once you have double clicked on it, you can then use the Eraser tool. Double clicking again restores the group with the changes. To completely erase a grouped object, select it and press the Delete key.

Exercise 4-20: Working with Eraser Modes

CD-ROM NOTE: *To find out more about the Eraser modes, open the file* ch04_20.fla, *located in the* fgai/chapter04/ *folder, installed from the companion CD-ROM.*

Follow the instructions in the CD-ROM file to erase in various modes and see their effects.

Faucet

The Faucet option allows you to quickly erase large areas of color within your drawings. For example, if you wanted to replace one of the large filled areas shown in figure 4-27, the Faucet option would be most effective. With the Faucet selected, you could click once and the entire filled area would be erased. See exercise 4-21 for practice in using the Faucet option.

Figure 4-27. The Faucet option allows you to erase filled areas in one click.

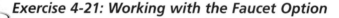

Exercise 4-21: Working with the Faucet Option

CD-ROM NOTE: *Understand how to use the Faucet modifier better by opening the file* ch04_21.fla, *located in the* fgai/ chapter04/ *folder, installed from the companion CD-ROM.*

Follow the instructions in the CD-ROM file to erase the filled areas.

Direct Selection and Editing

In regard to this introduction to the drawing, painting, and editing tools in the toolbar, realize two important things. First, if you have objects selected on the stage, you can immediately change their Stroke or Fill colors by changing the respective colors in the Colors section of the toolbar. In addition, you can use a similar process and instead use the Properties panel to do the same thing. Thus, you do not always need to select the Ink Bottle tool to change line characteristics. Neither do you always need to select the Paint Bucket tool to change fill characteristics. You can do so directly by selecting stage objects and changing the object's attributes in either the Properties panel or the Colors section of the toolbar.

▪ ▪ ▪ Other Editing Features and Notes

To this point, this chapter has covered the various tools used for drawing, painting, and editing. It seems appropriate to acknowledge some of Flash's other editing features used with the painting and drawing tools. The sections that follow briefly cover rulers, grids, and guides; the Align panel; and the Shapes submenu.

Rulers, Grids, and Guides

It goes without saying that any good graphics package includes features that help the user draw and paint accurately. Three options you should be aware of are rulers, grids, and guides. Each of these is accessed via the View menu.

When the rulers are turned on, you can click-drag guides onto the stage, in a manner similar to packages such as FreeHand, Illustrator, and Photoshop. The only thing to note about the grids and guides in Flash is that the Snap to Grids and Snap to Guides options are submenus of the Snapping selection.

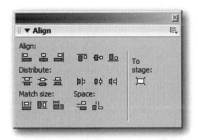

Figure 4-28. The Align panel allows you to align or distribute objects on the stage.

Align Panel

While drawing, it is often helpful to be able to align several objects or to equally space objects across a given area on the screen. Much like other vector editors, Flash provides a utility that will quickly allow you to align or distribute objects consistently, without having to use a grid, snap, or rulers. If you select multiple objects and open the Align panel, shown in figure 4-28, you can quickly align or distribute the selected objects.

 TIP: *Quickly open the Align panel by using Ctrl + K on the PC or Command + K on the Mac.*

In addition to aligning objects (Align) and distributing objects (Space Evenly), Flash can size several objects so that their heights or widths (or both dimensions) match, all in one operation. Additionally, you can align objects to one another and justify them on the page (stage) at the same time. The Match Size feature is particularly useful when creating web interfaces. This causes all selected elements to be aligned and sized to match one another. To explore the Align feature, see exercise 4-22.

 NOTE: *You cannot use Lock in conjunction with Align, as you can in programs such as FreeHand or Illustrator. Once an object is locked, it cannot be selected. You must use Modify | Arrange | Unlock All to select the item that was locked.*

Exercise 4-22: Using Align

CD-ROM NOTE: *To find out more about the Align panel, open the file ch04_22.fla, located in the fgai/chapter04/ folder, installed from the companion CD-ROM.*

Use Align to try various configurations to see what they do. Pay particular attention to Match Size and what it does.

Shapes Submenu

The Modify | Shape submenu contains several useful options. We have already discussed the Straighten and Smooth option. Here we will explore the Optimize Curves, Convert Lines to Fills, Expand Fill, and Soften Fill Edges menu commands.

Optimizing Curves

As mentioned in the first chapter, file size is an important consideration when creating all web content. Even though Flash is a vector drawing tool, complex drawings and movies can push the limits of reasonable delivery. Therefore, even with Flash, file size as regards object creation must be monitored to make sure your files are as small as possible.

Flash offers the Modify | Shape | Optimize menu option, which smoothes curved lines and fill outlines by reducing the number of points used to define them. This can significantly reduce the size of a file in very complex drawings.

Figure 4-29. The Optimize Curves dialog box is a utility that smoothes curved fills and lines.

To use this feature, which is similar to the Smooth modifier, select a stage object or objects and then access the Modify | Shape | Optimize menu option, which accesses the Optimize Curves dialog box, shown in figure 4-29. Using the slider, specify the degree of smoothing desired. This is often a trial-and-error process to get the right balance between object quality and point reduction. The results of curve optimization depend on the curves selected and the current zoom level.

The Optimize Curves dialog box provides two options in addition to the slider that controls the level of smoothing. The Use multiple passes option allows the optimization process to be repeated until the curve can no longer be optimized. This is similar to the process of multiple smoothing operations. The Show totals message option displays an alert box that provides information about the optimization process. Use this data to determine how much smoothing has occurred.

NOTE: *Optimize Curves is just one way of creating small and efficient Flash files. Other means of "working smart" and optimizing your files for distribution are covered in Chapter 12.*

Convert Lines to Fills

The Convert Lines to Fills option takes all selected lines and converts them to fills, making it as if they had been painted with the Paint Brush tool. The width of the fill is determined by the thickness associated with the line before employing the Convert Lines to Fills option.

The Convert Lines to Fills option is useful for special effects, such as filling a line with a gradient. However, converting many of the lines in a drawing to fills will significantly increase the size of your movie files. Therefore, use this feature cautiously.

Expand Fill

The Expand Fill option allows you to quickly expand or inset a fill by a specified distance per the current drawing units. This option does not work on lines, grouped elements, or symbols, but does allow you to quickly expand a fill area. If you select a fill and use Expand Fill, the fill will grow or shrink by the extended value. For example, if you expand a rectangular fill by 10 pixels, the rectangle grows in size and its corners become rounded, as shown in figure 4-30.

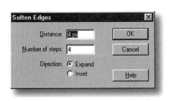

Figure 4-30. The Expand Fill feature allows you to expand or inset singular filled areas.

Soften Fill Edges

The Soften Fill Edges option allows you to create special elements, such as soft-edged drop shadows. With a fill selected, you can use the Soften Fill Edges option to generate a series of repeating elements that expand and become more transparent. Similar to the Expand Fill option, the Soften Fill Edges option works best with a single fill that has no line style.

To use Soften Fill Edges, select a fill and then access Modify | Shape | Soften Edges to open the Soften Edges dialog box, shown in figure 4-31. Use the Distance field to enter the amount of expansion (or inset), and the Number of steps field to define the number of steps in the area. Figure 4-31 shows an example of the effect of the Soften Fill Edges option.

Depending on the number of steps you specify in the dialog box, file size may vary drastically. The Soften Edges option adds several outline elements to your file to create the drop shadow effect.

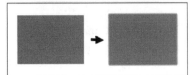

Figure 4-31. Effect of the Soften Fill Edges option.

NOTE: *The Add Shape Hint and Remove All Shape Hints commands are discussed in Chapter 9, as they are related to animation creation.*

▪ ▪ ▪ Importing Vector Graphics into Flash

For importing vector graphics into Flash, you will find that FreeHand is simply the best choice. However, Flash MX 2004 does offer extended import and export support for Adobe PDF and Adobe Illustrator 10 files as well. However, FreeHand remains the best choice because Flash automatically recognizes the layers in a FreeHand file. Additionally, FreeHand offers the particularly useful features Blend (which will create iterative steps between two shapes) and Release to Layers (which will automatically separate a blend to separate layers). These supplementary features in FreeHand make creating Flash animations and movies faster. FreeHand also provides the ability to convert CYM(K) files to RGB with decent color fidelity.

Importing vector graphics into Flash is performed using the File | Import menu option. When you import a vector graphic, the image is brought into Flash as a group in the current layer.

Although vector graphics have many advantages on the Web and for print, file formats related to vector graphics are often tricky. The biggest problem is that vector formats such as Encapsulated PostScript (EPS), Computer Graphics Metafile (CGM), Windows Metafile (WMF), Enhanced WMF (EMF), and Macintosh Picture format (PICT) can contain more than just vector data. This is why many of them are called (and even have in their name) metafile formats.

Metafile formats are special in that they can contain vector, raster, or both. As if this were not enough, there are also different "flavors" of many of these formats; that is, the way in which a format is written. For example, you may have an EPS file that favors Adobe Illustrator and dislikes Macromedia FreeHand, or vice versa. Generally, to find the best path from software A to software B requires some trial and error. In an effort to assist you in this area, reference the following tips and tricks related to file vector file formats.

- *In general, the Adobe Illustrator EPS format and the Macromedia FreeHand EPS format are different "flavors."* If you import an EPS file into FreeHand and it is placed as a box with an X in it, understand that you are dealing with an Adobe Illustrator EPS file.

- *Windows Metafiles (WMF) do not retain arcs and circles.* These elements are broken into individual line segments. It is preferable to avoid this format if possible. Use an Enhanced WMF (EMF) file instead. This format does retain arcs and circles. It also allows you to create images that are completely scalable, with no degradation, in the entire range of Microsoft products.

- *Although the PICT format works very well on the Macintosh, it can be somewhat unpredictable on the PC.* Obviously, you can take a Photoshop PICT on the Mac to Photoshop on the PC with little difficulty. However, in general, PC applications do not care for PICT files because of PICT files' capacity to contain metadata. If you are going cross-platform, stay away from PICT.

- *Computer Graphics Metafiles (CGM) are characteristic formats from high-end workstation programs.* For desktop users, CGM format may present many of the same "flavor" differences as the EPS format. Just because your program will read CGM does not mean it will be able to parse every CGM file. Perhaps the best program for interpreting CGM files (as well as a host of other formats) is CorelDraw!. It is not necessarily the best for drawing and creation, but it supports a wide array of file formats for importing and exporting and is thus a nice "utility" program. It is worth purchasing even if you only use it as a file translator.

- *When taking static vector images from Flash to FreeHand, use the Adobe Illustrator (AI) format or the AutoCAD Data Exchange Format (DXF).* Note that mask layers will not transfer and thus once in FreeHand objects will not retain their "paste inside" effect. But that is true regardless of which vector format is chosen.

- *Frequently, when you export from FreeHand to the SWF format, FreeHand will tell you that you have fills, lines, or strokes that Flash does not support.* This message can appear even though you have not used a paste inside, arrowheads, line styles, or custom fills. Nonetheless, even when you are prompted with this message, the generated SWF file will probably still contain the mainstay of your FreeHand drawing and will likely be an adequate starting place once in Flash.

- *When exporting static images from Flash for use in Microsoft products, use the EMF format.* This format retains arc and circle properties and is scalable.

▪ ▪ ▪ Summary

This chapter has examined defining and selecting colors, the tools for drawing and painting, the tools for editing, and some basic tips on importing vector graphics files. In the next chapter, you will complete your examination of the Flash tool by looking at the Text tool and learning about all the wonderful things you can do with text in your movies. Following that discussion, you will explore symbols, looking at what they are, why you should use them, and how you should use them.

5

Working with Text

▪ ▪ ▪ Introduction

To conclude the discussion of the toolbar tools in Flash, this chapter examines the Text tool and issues related to it. Flash makes working with text easier that many of the concerns you must deal with when designing web pages with raw HTML or even cascading style sheets. However, there are still font issues you must be aware of and that you must work around.

This chapter examines the three types of text objects you can create in Flash. In general you create static text that does not change, and dynamic or input text that can dynamically change during movie playback. Although this chapter does not explore in detail all of the nitty-gritty things you can do with ActionScript and a dynamic or input text field, you will get a feel for how these text types work. The chapter concludes with a discussion of specific font issues you should be aware of, as well as ways of manipulating text in your movies.

▪ ▪ ▪ Objectives

In this chapter you will:

- Examine the types of text objects Flash supports and how they differ from one another
- Learn about the Text tool, its myriad properties, and how you use it to define text objects on the stage
- Discover the difference, albeit small, between text labels and text blocks

- Learn to modify characters and text objects and how to assign hyperlinks to entire text objects
- Examine how to create and use Dynamic Text and Input Text objects in Flash
- Learn to transform and break apart text, as well as what internal HTML support Flash provides
- Find out about fonts and font mapping

Types of Text in Flash

As a quick overview, it would be helpful to understand the three different types of text objects you can create in Flash. All three are created with the Text tool, and you can easily change a text object back and forth between the different types. The three types of text objects are as follows.

- *Static text:* A text object into which you enter content that does not change. There are two types of static text objects: labels and blocks. The primary difference between the two is that labels are single-line elements, whereas blocks are multiline elements.
- *Dynamic text:* Text that changes based on something else in the movie. For example, you could use ActionScripting to change the content of a dynamic text field as something particular happens in a movie.
- *Input text:* Like a dynamic text object, can change based on something else in the movie. However, dynamic text fields cannot be changed by the end user during playback, at least not directly. Input text objects are unique in that the end user can click on and change the text in an input text object during playback. Thus, input text objects function like form fields in HTML, allowing the end user to enter data at runtime.

Each of these text types is generated using the Text tool. Which type of object you create is determined by a single drop-down list in the Properties panel and the selection you make from it. The default is Static text, but as you will see, you can easily change this at will.

 NOTE: *One of the new additions in Flash MX 2004 is the spell checker. Although certainly not a new concept, it is a nice addition to Flash. As well, Flash has an improved Find and Replace feature that not only works on text objects but on all asset names.*

▪▪▪ **Using the Text Tool**

To create text you select the Text tool from the toolbar. All of the options for the Text tool are displayed within the Properties panel. The following sections detail the properties of the text tool, as well as how to enter and edit text objects.

Properties of the Text Tool

Figure 5-1 shows the Properties panel as it relates to the Text tool. Note that by default the Properties panel is partially collapsed. If you click on the small, white arrow in the lower left-hand corner of the Properties panel, it will expand to show all of the options related to the Text tool.

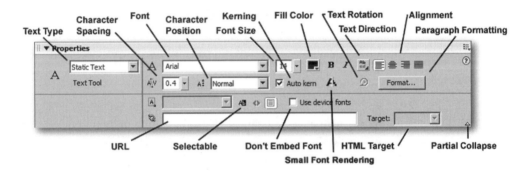

Figure 5-1. The Properties panel, when totally expanded, shows all of the options for the Text tool.

The options shown in the upper portion of figure 5-1 control the general text formatting properties. These are as follows.

- *Text Type drop-down list:* Determines what type of text object you are going to create. Its options include Static Text, Dynamic Text, and Input Text, as previously described.

- *Font drop-down list:* Sets the font face that will be used for the text object. The items shown here are based on the currently installed fonts on your system.

- *Character Spacing field:* Controls the spacing between characters within the created text object.

- *Character Position drop-down list:* Allows you to create subscript and superscript text.

- *Font Size field:* Controls the size of the text within the text object, measured in points.

- *Auto Kern checkbox:* Permits Flash to automatically kern specific pairs of text for increased readability and better aesthetic presentation.

- *Text (fill) Color control:* Defines the color of the text. Fill Color, not Stroke Color, defines the color for text objects.

- *Bold and Italic buttons:* Allow you to style text as bold or italic.

- *Text Direction and Rotation buttons:* These two options work together. They permit you to change the definition of how text "flows" within the field, which is specifically designed for representing Asian text in Flash.

- *Alias Text:* When using small text, you can select this option to improve the visual quality of the text on screen.

- *Justification buttons:* Control the alignment of the entire block of text. The flush left, flush right, and centered options for text produce ragged edges on one or both (in the case of centering) sides of the text block. The Justify button will make the text flush on both sides.

- *Format (paragraph properties) button:* Provides additional paragraph formatting attributes, including indent, line spacing, and left and right margins.

The options in the bottom of figure 5-1 are "special" formatting properties, not necessarily related to "how the text looks." These include the following.

 NOTE: *When the Text Type drop-down list is set to Static text, several of the controls in the lower part of the Properties panel are disabled, as they cannot be applied to static text.*

- *Selectable button:* Makes the text in the object selectable by the end user at runtime. By default, Static Text is not selectable.

- *Use Device Fonts checkbox:* Allows you to tell Flash not to embed the font associated with the text object in the resulting web-ready Flash file. This is discussed in greater detail later in this chapter, as it can significantly affect the visual results of text during playback of your movie.

- *URL Link and Target fields:* Allow you to specify that the entire text object be treated as a hyperlink. When assigning a URL to a text object, you can also specify an HTML target for the link to be loaded into.

Entering Text Labels and Blocks

Once you have the Text tool selected, there are two ways to create the text object, and depending on which method you use there are slight differences in the result. The first way is to single click on the stage, and then enter your text. When you do this, a small circle appears in the upper right-hand corner of the text object-bounding box, as shown in figure 5-2a. This identifies the object as a text label.

The second method of entering text is to click-drag with the Text tool (to create an area for the text entry) and then enter your text. When you do this, you will note that the text object displays a small square in the upper right-hand corner of the object on the stage, as shown in figure 5-2b. This second method creates a text block.

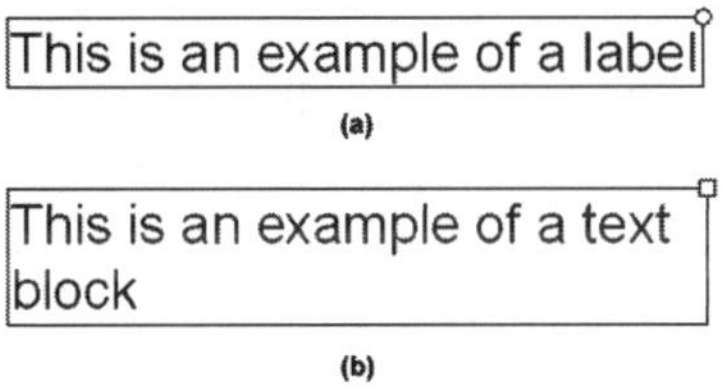

This is an example of a label

(a)

This is an example of a text block

(b)

Figure 5-2. With static text, you can create (a) text labels or (b) text blocks.

"What's the difference between a text label and a text block?" you may ask. As far as manipulating, formatting, and so on, there is little difference. In both cases you can make the object a multiline text object. For text labels you must press the Enter key, whereas text blocks automatically wrap when you read the right bounds of the text object. The real difference relates to accessibility and how the Flash player acknowledges the object.

In the first case, a text label, Flash will assume that something needing a label will follow (or be in close proximity to) the object, such as an input field or other object. Thus, if a nonvisual browser is being used to view the Flash movie, the Flash player will automatically "read" the content of the label for the end user, as it will assume the text label is for another object. Text blocks, on the other hand, function as independent elements and are not tied to anything else in the environment. If you are designing web sites and striving to accommodate web accessibility guidelines, as well as ADA requirements, you should be aware of this difference.

 NOTE: *Chapter 15 deals in depth with accessibility and features specifically designed to accommodate alternative browsers.*

One of the things to note about both types of Static text objects is that you can use the handle on the right-hand side to change the width of the text object. If you click-drag the handle it will size, but when you size a text label in this way it is "converted" to a text block. This is visible in that the handle changes from a circle to a square. If you want to "size" a text label and have it remain as a text label, you must use the Text tool to manually enter carriage returns in the text (using the Enter key). To practice using the Text tool, try exercise 5-1.

Exercise 5-1: Using the Text Tool

CD-ROM NOTE: *To learn more about the Text tool, open the file* ch05_01.fla, *located in the* fgai/chapter05/ *folder, installed from the companion CD-ROM.*

Use the Text tool to add text to the CD-ROM file as instructed.

Modifying Characters

Once you have created a text object, you can easily change the formatting of individual characters. Generally all of the character-level attributes (font face, size, character spacing, color, and so on) can be set per character, per word, or per phrase.

Figure 5-3. You can set character-level formatting in a text object.

To change the formatting at the character, word, or phrase level, select the Text tool and click-drag across the characters you want to change, as shown in figure 5-3. Once selected, changes you make in the Properties panel will be applied to the selected characters. Exercise 5-2 provides practice in modifying characters.

Exercise 5-2: Modifying Characters

CD-ROM NOTE: *Open the file* ch05_02.fla, *located in the* fgai/chapter05/ *folder, installed from the companion CD-ROM.*

Use the Text tool and the Properties panel to change the formatting characteristics of individual words and phrases.

Modifying Labels and Blocks

Items in the lower part of the Properties panel, as well as paragraph formatting, must be applied to the entirety of the object. That is, you select the label or block and then make the assignment. For example, you cannot have a single word or phrase within the text object that is a link. The entire object would have to be a link.

In a similar fashion, paragraph attributes are also assigned at the block level. However, it is possible to have a single text object, which itself contains multiple text blocks (separated by carriage returns) assigned to different paragraph properties, as shown in figure 5-4. The key to Flash letting you do this is to make sure the text within the object is separated by at least one carriage return. To practice modifying blocks, try exercise 5-3.

Exercise 5-3: Modifying Blocks

CD-ROM NOTE: *Open the file* ch05_03.fla, *located in the* fgai/chapter05/ *folder, installed from the companion CD-ROM.*

Use the Text tool and the Properties panel to change the paragraph formatting on the different blocks within the text object.

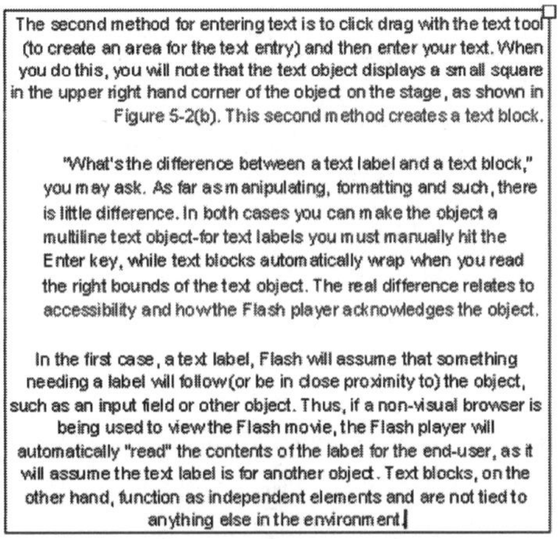

The second method for entering text is to click drag with the text tool (to create an area for the text entry) and then enter your text. When you do this, you will note that the text object displays a small square in the upper right hand corner of the object on the stage, as shown in Figure 5-2(b). This second method creates a text block.

"What's the difference between a text label and a text block," you may ask. As far as manipulating, formatting and such, there is little difference. In both cases you can make the object a multiline text object-for text labels you must manually hit the Enter key, while text blocks automatically wrap when you read the right bounds of the text object. The real difference relates to accessibility and how the Flash player acknowledges the object.

In the first case, a text label, Flash will assume that something needing a label will follow (or be in close proximity to) the object, such as an input field or other object. Thus, if a non-visual browser is being used to view the Flash movie, the Flash player will automatically "read" the contents of the label for the end-user, as it will assume the text label is for another object. Text blocks, on the other hand, function as independent elements and are not tied to anything else in the environment.

Figure 5-4. Blocks of text within a text object may have different paragraph properties assigned to each.

Hyperlinks can be assigned to text.

Figure 5-5. When a text object has a link (URL) assigned to it, it is displayed with a dashed line beneath it in the authoring environment.

Assigning a Hyperlink

As noted, you can assign hyperlinks to text objects in Flash. When you do so, the authoring environment displays a dashed line beneath the text object, as shown in figure 5-5. Although the link is not active in the authoring environment, when you test the movie or place it on the Web the text will be an active web link. Additionally, when the end user rolls over text assigned a hyperlink, the cursor will automatically change, signifying the object is active.

TIP: *When a text object is assigned a URL, Flash does not format the text with typical underlining, nor does it change the color. If you make a text object a link, it is suggested you format it such that the end user will know that it is a hyperlink; that is, with an underline and a color change.*

When you assign a URL to a text object, you will note that the Target drop-down list becomes active. This list includes the four basic HTML targets, the most common being *_blank*, which is used to open a new browser window in front of the existing one. You can also enter your own window name into the Target drop-down list if the page in which the Flash movie you are designing resides in a frame's document or structure. Exercise 5-4 provides practice in creating text object links.

TIP: *When you assign a URL to a text object, you can get away with not entering the protocol information* (http://) *at the beginning of the URL. However, to avoid potential problems, it is recommended you always precede the URL with the protocol.*

 Exercise 5-4: Creating Text Object Links

Open Flash and create a text object on the stage. Then assign a URL to the object using the Properties panel. Use Control | Test Movie to see if the link works.

 NOTE: *You cannot assign a URL to vertically oriented text (that is, text whose Text Direction is set to Vertical).*

▪ ▪ ▪ Dynamic Text

In addition to the ability to create static text objects, you can also create a text object that changes dynamically during movie playback. Dynamic text fields are associated with an ActionScript variable you create. If you change the variable, you change the text displayed in the associated text object. Dynamic text objects can receive content from a variety of places, not least of which is from an external source. However, before examining that, let's look at how you set up a dynamic text field.

Dynamic Text Properties

To set up a dynamic text object, you choose the Text tool and then Dynamic Text from the Text Type drop-down list in the Properties panel. Figure 5-6 shows the options that appear in the Properties panel when you select Dynamic Text.

In addition to the general formatting options you have already examined, several more options are available when Dynamic Text is selected. Descriptions of these options follow.

- *Size and Position fields:* Allow you to view and change the width, height, and stage position of text.

- *Instance Name field:* This is the name of the text object. You use a text object's name to change the object's formatting characteristics using ActionScript. For example, you could change the color (or any other allowable attribute) of a text object using ActionScript.

- *Line Type drop-down list:* Defines how many lines of text can be in the object. Valid options are Single Line, Multiline, and Multiline No Wrap.

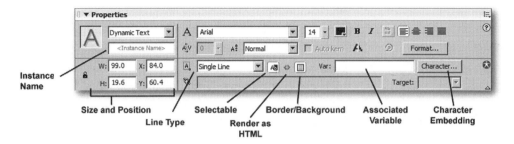

Figure 5-6. The Properties panel reveals several options when
you select Dynamic Text from the Text Type drop-down list.

- *Selectable button:* Determines if the text can be selected by the end user at runtime.

- *Render as HTML button:* Defines whether the content in the text field should be interpreted as HTML code.

- *Show Border button:* Controls the border and background for the field. The default is no border or background.

- *Var field:* Contains the name of the variable or property upon which the text object's content is based. Changing the content in the variable changes the content displayed in the text field.

- *Character button:* Yields a dialog box in which you can specify whether or not font outlines for the field are embedded. By default, font outlines are not embedded for text fields.

Creating Dynamic Text Fields

Follow along with the steps provided in exercise 5-5 to learn how to create dynamic text fields.

Exercise 5-5: Creating Dynamic Text Fields

 CD-ROM NOTE: *Open the file* ch05_05.fla, *located in the* fgai/chapter05/ *folder, installed from the companion CD-ROM.*

Use the following steps to learn about creating dynamic text objects. To see a completed example before following along with the instruction, open the file *ch5_05s.fla*.

The goal of this exercise is to create four dynamic text fields (which track the mouse position) and a draggable object position. The file already has ActionScript code included in it. In the exercise you will simply create fields that "capture" values of the mouse and the object so that you can see the stage coordinates of the objects.

1. Select the Text tool and set the Text type to Static.

2. Begin by creating four text labels with the Text tool; that is, single click on the stage with the Text tool and then enter the text for the specific label. The labels should be named *Mouse X, Mouse Y, Object X, and Object Y*.

3. Visually order the labels on the stage such that you can place another text object to the right of each label. Use the solved example as a guide.

4. Create four text objects, adjacent to the labels that have their Text Type set to Dynamic. You may find it easier to create one and then duplicate and position it.

NOTE: *When you create a dynamic or input text object, the small square that usually appears in the upper right is displayed in the lower right. This identifies it as a dynamic or input field. You do not necessarily have to enter a starting value for a field, either. Unlike normal text elements, if you do not enter text into the entry box the field will remain on the stage.*

5. Set the Var field for each of the dynamic text objects to "receive" the correct value. The *Var* field of the text object next to the *Mouse X* label should be *myX*.

NOTE: *Capitalization is important, as ActionScript is case sensitive. Make sure you enter the values in the Var field exactly as specified.*

6. Set the Var field of the text object next to the *Mouse Y* label to *myY* by typing *MyY* in the field.

7. Set the Var field of the text object next to the *Object X* label to *dragX*.

8. Set the *Var* field of the text object next to the *Object Y* label to *dragY*.

9. Use Control | Test Movie to see the dynamic fields work. Try dragging the green square.

This exercise stepped you through the basics of creating dynamic text fields. There is a little ActionScript going on in the background that makes the entire work. If you check out the ActionScripting in frame 1 you will likely be able to decipher what is happening. If not, do not worry; the

ActionScripting is discussed in detail later in the book. The important thing to understand is that dynamic fields are associated with ActionScript variables: change the value in the variable and the Dynamic Text will also change.

Creating Input Text Objects

Input text objects, like Dynamic text objects, are also associated with variables. In the last example you saw that dynamic text fields are linked to their variables (as the variable changes, so does what is displayed in the dynamic field). However, what makes input text different is that the user can directly change the value in the text object, which in turn changes the variable associated with it. Thus, dynamic fields are "one-way"; that is, they are dependent on the variable. Input fields are "two-way," meaning that changes to the variable change the field, but changes to the field also change the variable.

NOTE: *Another difference between input text and dynamic text is that whereas dynamic text may have a URL assigned to it, input text cannot. Thus, when you select Input Text from the Text Type drop-down list, the URL field is not available in the Properties panel.*

You establish input text fields just as you do for dynamic text. That is, you create a text object, set the Text Type (to *Input text*, instead of *Dynamic text*), and then associate the field with a variable by placing a variable name in the Properties panel Var field. Exercise 5-6 provides further practice with Dynamic and Input text objects.

Exercise 5-6: Using Dynamic and Input Text Objects

CD-ROM NOTE: *Open the file* ch05-06.fla, *located in the* fgai/chapter05/ *folder, installed from the companion CD-ROM.*

Use the CD-ROM file in performing this exercise. To see a completed example before following along with the instructions, open the file *ch5_06s.fla.*

1. Click on the Text tool and create a text element on the stage.

2. In the Properties panel, set the Text Type drop-down to Input Text.

3. Enter myfield in the Var field. If you wish to modify any of the other text options, you may.

4. Create a label to place in front of the Input Text object you just created and enter *Input:* into the text element.

 TIP: *As you create a series of fields, Flash remembers the last text type you set, which can sometimes be frustrating. Make sure you did not inadvertently create the label as an Input text object.*

5. Create an additional text label below the first and enter *Output:* in it.

6. Create another text object to the right of the second label. Set Text Type in the Properties panel to Dynamic Text for this object.

7. Set the new Dynamic Text object's *Var* field to *myfield* also. When you test the movie, data entered into the first field will be posted to the second.

8. Test your movie to see that the value entered into the upper text field is passed to the lower text field.

When working with text objects in Flash, keep in mind that Flash will remember the last setting for the Text Type drop-down, as you saw in the previous exercise. Be careful when creating text objects; make sure they are the type you think they are as you create them.

Manipulating Text Objects

The following sections describe some special things you should know about text objects. The sections are rather brief, but they highlight some important things you should be aware of when working with text in Flash.

Transforming Text Objects

Text objects in Flash are just like any other overlay object. Thus, you can quite easily use the transformations you learned about in the last chapter to create skewed text that appears to be 3D. As it relates to skewed text, you may again find Appendix A helpful when trying to determine skewing values for objects on various planes. The primary thing to keep in mind is that the smaller the exposure of the skew the more difficult the text will be to read. Aside from that, given Appendix A, you should be able to create text on any pseudo-3D plane.

Breaking Text Apart

On occasion, you may want to modify the letters of a string of text in a customized manner. For example, if you have text that says Drip that you want to make look like it is dripping, you are not limited to just the fonts you have. You can convert any text to its base-level fill objects and then edit them using the various painting and drawing tools. Converting text to fills in Flash is akin to the Convert to Paths command in FreeHand, except that the resulting elements are fill objects.

 NOTE: *Break Apart is only active when you select a Static text object. It is disabled when you select Dynamic or Input text objects.*

To convert text to outlines in Flash, select a text block that is set to Static with the Arrow tool and use Modify | Break Apart. The first time you break apart text, it is split into its individual characters, whereby each character is a Static text object. If you use Break Apart again, the individual letters are reduced to their basic fill components. Once you break text apart a second time, it loses its text features, such as the ability to change a word or phrase. Yet, once broken to its basic fills, the fills that make up the text can be modified just like any fill object. You can use the Arrow or Subselection tool to modify the text as you wish.

The only negative thing about breaking text apart is the fact that breaking apart large quantities of text can drastically increase the size of your movie files. In essence, you are converting the letter representations to a multiplied number of fills. Therefore, only break text apart for special effects, and do so sparingly. Exercise 5-7 provides practice in using the Modify | Break Apart functionality.

 Exercise 5-7: Breaking Text Apart for Custom Effects

CD-ROM NOTE: *Learn more about modifying text. Open the file ch05_07.fla, located in the fgai/chapter05/ folder, installed from the companion CD-ROM.*

Use Modify | Break Apart, and then use the drawing or painting tools to modify the look of the text.

HTML Text Support

One of the unique features of text elements in Flash is that they can support a limited number of HTML tags when set to Dynamic Text or Input Text. From the developer's perspective, this means you can create text elements in which specific elements are used as hyperlinks. It also means that you can use the rudimentary HTML formatting capabilities in the text elements in your movie. Flash supports the following basic HTML tags.

- *< A > (anchor):* Used to add hyperlinks to words or phrases in a text object.
- *< B > (bold):* Used to bold the selected text.
- *< FONT COLOR > :* Changes the color of the tagged text.
- *< FONT FACE > :* Changes the typeface used in the tagged text.
- *< FONT SIZE > :* Changes the font size of the tagged text.
- *< I > (italic):* Used to italicize tagged text.
- *< P > (paragraph):* Allows you to define paragraph blocks.

 TIP: *Typically in HTML, adjacent paragraph blocks are separated by a carriage return (line feed), which causes a blank line to be inserted between paragraphs. Flash does not render it this way. It does appear, however, that the < br > tag can be used.*

- *< U > (underline):* Used to underline text.

Note that if you use the anchor tag in a text object you will need to also use the *< FONT COLOR >* and *< U >* tags. When you insert an anchor in a dynamic field, the link does not automatically display as a different color, and is not underlined because it is in a web browser. You must manually set these parameters using all three tags together.

To get the paragraph tag to work, you must close the tag. When people code HTML by hand, they often ignore closing the *< /p >* tag. However, Flash follows the rules of "well-formedness" associated with XML. Thus, you must follow those rules. One of them states that all tags must be closed.

 CD-ROM NOTE: *To see a finished example of a file that utilizes HTML tags in dynamic fields, open the file* ch05-8s.fla, *located in the* fgai/chapter05/ *folder, installed from the companion CD-ROM.*

▪ ▪ ▪ Fonts and Font Mapping

The following sections are designed to provide a little further background on how Flash handles fonts and font mapping. It is important to understand that Flash cannot totally utilize every type of font that exists; some fonts are unusable. The following sections detail what you need to know along these lines so that you do not run into trouble with fonts in your movies.

Embedded and Device Fonts

One of the primary advantages of web-ready Flash files is that they typically include all information necessary to properly render fonts in your movie at runtime. Unlike the HTML < *FONT* > tag or cascading style sheets, you typically do not have to worry about whether the end user has the fonts you used in your FLA movie files. Flash SWF files automatically embed the needed font descriptions when you prepare the movie for the Web (that is, save it as an SWF).

Flash can utilize a wide variety of fonts, including Type 1 PostScript fonts, TrueType fonts, and (on the Macintosh) bitmap fonts. Of these, TrueType fonts are the most common and the easiest to work with. If you are on a PC, you must ensure that you are using Adobe Type Manager (ATM) 4.1 or higher. Otherwise, you might get unexpected results.

Each font embedded in a Flash SWF file increases the file size slightly. This is logical in that each font description includes all of the nitty-gritty descriptions for upper- and lowercase letters of the font, as well as special characters within it. Generally the amount of data added to a Flash file due to font embedding is less than 30 KB, but it depends on the "ornateness" of the font; that is, the complexity of the curves, "feet and tails," kerning, and so on.

 TIP: *One of the best ways to reduce file size as it relates to fonts is to import fonts as symbols and then share the libraries that those fonts reside in across multiple movies. More on that later!*

To Embed or Not to Embed

Flash gives you control over whether or not to embed a font in the resulting SWF file. The default is to include all required fonts, but you can tell Flash not to include a font description if you like. Recall that one of the properties for static text was the Use Device Font checkbox. With dynamic and input text there was a button called Character. These are how you tell Flash not to include a particular font description, or to include only certain aspects of the font description (in the case of the Character button).

When you select Use Device Font, or No Characters (for dynamic or input text), you are in essence assuming that the end user has the particular font on his machine. "What happens if he doesn't?" you ask. When the user does not have a font, Flash will automatically make a choice using font substitution. Sometimes the choice is good, but most of the time the choice is inadequate and your screen designs will look poor as a result.

The immediate thought is likely "Why would I ever choose not to embed a font?" The reality is that there are advantages to not embedding fonts—the primary being smaller file sizes. Another is the fact that at sizes smaller than 10 points, device fonts are displayed more cleanly.

Nevertheless, there are many scenarios in which it might be advantageous to not embed fonts, but the primary question when deciding this is: "Do you absolutely control the playback machine?" If so, do not embed fonts (and you will save some bytes in the size of your file). If not, embed fonts. There is nothing more embarrassing than a font that goes awry in a presentation, making text unreadable or, worse, totally ruining a very aesthetically pleasant design.

Default Device Fonts

Flash provides three default device font options in the Font menu. These are the *_sans, _sans serif,* and *_typewriter* entries at the top of the Font drop-down list. Typically _sans is Arial on Windows, and Helvetica on Macintosh. The *_serif* setting is usually Times New Roman on Windows, and Times on Macintosh. The *_typewriter* setting is typically some derivative of Courier on either platform. Of course, all of this also depends on whether or not the user has made any custom configuration changes to her operating system.

Because so often people are developing for the Web, seldom is there a real need to use the default device fonts. The only exception is when you want the text in your movie to "shift" on one platform or another, or from machine to machine.

There are differences not only among font families, such as Arial versus Helvetica, but even visually significant differences between versions of the same font on different platforms. For example, Helvetica on the Macintosh is about 2 point sizes smaller than Helvetica on the PC. If you have a paragraph that has 10 lines, it may shrink as much as 100 pixels from one platform to another. In short, unless you know for sure that you will absolutely control the end playback machine—and more importantly, the fonts on that machine—device fonts in any scenario cannot be recommended by this author.

Certain Fonts Cannot Be Embedded

A final note in this section regards the fact that not all fonts on a machine are usable by Flash. A quick way to tell if Flash has a problem with a font is to assign it to an object and see if Flash antialiases it (set View | Preview Mode | Antialias Text). If the font appears jaggy on the screen, it means the font is not being properly interpreted by Flash and will not be properly embedded in a resulting SWF file.

Substituting Fonts

One of the nicest things in Flash MX 2004 is its font mapping capability. Chapter 2 referenced this new feature, but let's examine it a little more closely. First, note that font mapping has to do with the sharing of native Flash files, not font issues within web-ready SWF files. It is common for a group of developers or designers to share an FLA file (or set of FLA files) during development. However, often from designer to designer, or from designer to coder, the fonts each has may not be consistent across machines.

In the prior version of Flash, this presented a problem in that you had to either make sure everybody had the same fonts on their machines or embed the font in the native FLA file. The former worked best, as the latter only worked if you stayed on a single platform.

In Flash MX 2004, when you open a file that calls for fonts you do not have on your machine, you have the option of temporarily "reassigning" the font to something you have on your machine. You do this through the Font Mapping utility (Edit | Font Mapping). The nice thing about this feature is that it is "temporary."

For example, let's say a designer has set up all screen designs in a movie and now it is time for the programmer to add code to a file. The programmer, who likely does not have the same fonts as the designer, can open the file, add the coding, and save the file without the original font definitions changing. It is this feature (the fact that font mapping reassignment is temporary, not just the ability to map fonts) that makes Flash powerful. This allows a firm to freely pass files from designer to designer, or to anyone else for that matter, without having to worry about everybody having the same fonts.

Storing Fonts for Authoring

A final feature you should be aware of is the ability to store entire font descriptions and share them across multiple files. As alluded to earlier in this section, on fonts and font mapping, one of the best ways to reduce file size across multiple Flash movies in a site is to store a font in what is know as a shared library. This is examined in detail in the next chapter, which explores symbols and libraries.

▪ ▪ ▪ Summary

This chapter has provided an overview of how you can use text in Flash. You have read about the three primary types of text objects supported in Flash and have observed a few examples that have shown you the basics.

There is much more you can do—the primary thing being controlling not only the content of a text object with ActionScript but the formatting details of the text object itself. This chapter served as a quick overview to getting text into your movie.

In the next chapter you will begin looking at symbols and the library. In the previous section you read how you can create special font symbols so that you can share fonts indirectly with other developers. In the next chapter you will learn about the entire range of symbols and the many things the library can provide during development and at runtime.

6

Symbols and Libraries

▪ ▪ ▪ **Introduction**

Symbols and libraries are quite possibly one of the most powerful concepts and capabilities in Flash. As you read in Chapter 1, the most significant advantage to Flash content is the fact that the files are so small. You have already seen how Flash's vector nature is partially responsible for this. However, as much as the vector nature of Flash contributes to its small file sizes, so does the judicious and proper use of symbols and libraries.

Symbols are reusable graphic objects you store as part of your movie. You create a symbol and then make references to it throughout your movie. Thus, the data for the object is only stored once in your movie.

Up to this point everything you have worked with has either been composed of stage objects or groups, neither of which is a very file-size conscious approach. The text has purposely avoided in-depth discussion of symbols until now. Thus, the files you worked with in the early part of this book were slightly larger than they could have been.

The place where symbols are stored is called the library. In this chapter, you will first examine symbols and how to create them. There are three fundamental types, each of which is designed for a specific type of task. You will also find that when you import certain types of elements, such as bitmaps or sounds, symbols are automatically created to represent them. Following the discussion of symbols you will examine the concept of libraries in Flash and what you can do with them.

▪ ▪ ▪ Objectives

In this chapter you will:

- Discover the importance of using symbols within your movies
- Find out when and where symbols should be used
- Learn how to create graphic, button, and movie clip symbols
- Understand the difference between the standard libraries and the current library
- Figure out how to open other movies as libraries and how to insert symbols from other movies
- Find out about shared libraries and how a single library can share its symbols across multiple files

▪ ▪ ▪ The Power of Symbols and Libraries

When you create elements on the stage, they are written to your native FLA file. Thus, as you add stage objects, as well as text and groups, your file size increases. As you start to define multiple frames to create animation, repetitious definition of these objects in each frame dramatically affects files size because the data of the objects must be written several times within the file; once for each frame.

Symbols combat this problem and make this redundant data unnecessary. When a symbol is used, the data is defined once. All "copies" of the object that appear on the stage are referenced to the symbol, which is where the actual data for the object resides. These "copies" are called symbol instances, or simply, instances.

Converting reoccurring objects to symbols and then referring to them whenever you need them significantly reduces the size of the resulting Flash file, as well as its respective web-ready SWF file. Using symbols can reduce file size by 50 percent or more and is the basis for effective Flash development.

▪ ▪ ▪ Symbol Behaviors (Types)

Flash provides three types of symbols you can use, and all symbols that exist in a movie can be accessed via the file's library. A symbol is defined by a behavior and by a name you assign to it when you create it. The behavior determines the type of symbol, and the name is a unique identifier. A symbol's name can actually be anything, but should be unique, as well as something easily identifiable by you so that you can more easily find it in the file's library.

It is a good idea to develop a standard way of naming your symbols. In the library, the different types of symbols are not only represented by the name you assign but by icons, which you will learn about later. Particularly in complex movies, consistency in symbol naming is very important.

 NOTE: *Try to adopt some personal way of identifying your movie symbols. On the end of your symbol name, add MC for movie clips, _b for buttons, and _g for graphics.*

Figure 6-1. The Library window provides a quick view of the symbols in the current file.

Symbols in the Current File

Once a movie contains some symbols, you can interactively switch between the main movie timeline and the symbol's timeline. At any time, you can edit, delete, and create more symbols. To view all symbols that exist in a file, you use Window | Library to open the Library panel. Figure 6-1 shows the Library panel for a file that contains some symbols. (Libraries are discussed further later in this chapter.) For now, simply note that you can view all symbols in a file, as well as access any symbol's timeline using the Library window. If you double click on a symbol name in the library, you can access its timeline.

Process for Creating Symbols

There are two basic ways in which you can create symbols in your files, regardless of the type of symbol you want to create. You can either convert existing stage objects, groups, or text to a symbol or start a new symbol from scratch.

 NOTE: *Symbols can be created from existing stage objects, groups, or text, and from other symbols. You will learn more about this later in the chapter.*

Convert to Symbol Dialog

When you convert existing objects on the stage to a symbol, you select the objects on the stage and then use Modify | Convert to Symbol (or F8). You are then presented with a dialog box in which you name the symbol and define what type of symbol it will be, as shown in figure 6-2. When you define a symbol, you also select its registration point. The registration point is the origin, inside the symbol.

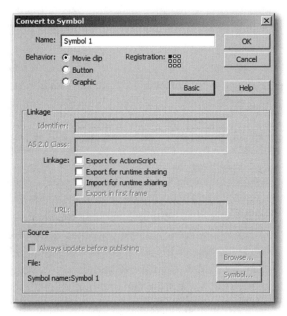

Figure 6-2. The Convert to Symbol dialog box allows you to establish the parameters for the symbol.

In the lower part of the dialog box (shown in figure 6-2) you see some additional parameters for the symbol. If you click on the Basic button, the lower part of the dialog box will not be shown, as the settings in the lower half are for advanced symbol use. In short, the extra information at the bottom relates to whether you want to store the symbol in the current file or whether you want to make the symbol accessible to other SWF files.

After you are ramped up on symbol basics, assume that all symbols will be contained in the current file, and thus that you can ignore the lower part of the dialog box. The discussion on sharing symbols later in this chapter will return to this issue.

Once you have converted objects on the stage to a symbol, the symbol remains on the stage but appears "grouped." If selected, the symbol instance is displayed with a white circle with crosshairs in its center. The crosshairs are the representation of the symbol's registration (origin) point. The white circle is the transformation origin, and by default these two are set equal to each other. You can change the transformation origin using the Free Transform tool. To practice converting objects to symbols, try exercise 6-1.

Exercise 6-1: Converting Objects to Symbols

Open Flash and create a basic filled circle. Select the fill and circle and use Modify | Convert to Symbol to make a symbol. Select any of the behaviors and any registration point. Look in the library to see that the symbol you created is now in the library.

New Symbol

The second method for creating a symbol is to use the Insert | New Symbol command. When you use this command, you begin by defining the attributes of the symbol (behavior, name, registration, and so on) using a dialog box similar to that shown in figure 6-2. Once you accept the attributes for the symbol, the timeline for that symbol is opened (replacing the main movie timeline). You then draw, paint, paste, or import the content you want to be in the symbol directly into the new symbols timeline. Once you have added everything you want in the symbol (which can include static graphics, animation, or even other symbols), you switch back to the main movie timeline by clicking on the Scene 1 link in the Edit path, shown in figure 6-3.

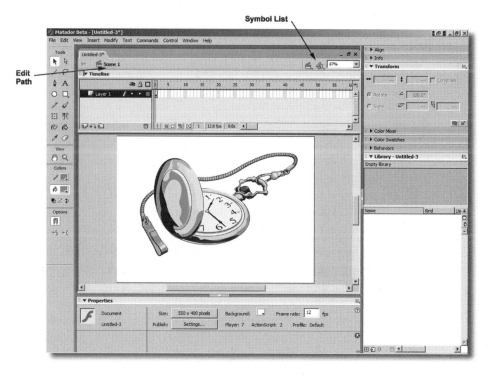

Figure 6-3. The Edit path shows the timeline you are currently editing, as well as a link back to the main timeline.

If you switch back to the main timeline, the first thing you will notice is that the symbol you just created does not appear on the stage. When you use the Convert to Symbol command to create a symbol, an instance of the symbol is automatically on the stage (because the objects from which the symbol was generated originated there). However, the process you just went through—that of creating a new symbol—defined the symbol in the library, but it did not add an instance of the symbol to the stage. You must do that manually. For new users, this is often confusing at first.

Adding Symbol Instances

When you use Convert to Symbol, an instance of the symbol is automatically placed on the stage. When you use New Symbol, you must manually add an instance of the symbol to the stage by opening the library and dragging the symbol to the stage.

To add an instance of a symbol to the stage, open the Library window and find the name of the symbol you want to create an instance of. Click-drag either from the symbol's name or from the Preview window of the library to the stage. An instance of the symbol will be added to the stage. Exercise 6-2 provides practice in creating new symbols.

Exercise 6-2: Creating New Symbols

Open Flash and use the Insert | New Symbol command to create a few different symbols. At this point, do not be concerned with their behaviors (simply select one). Once you have created some symbols, add instances of them to the stage by click-dragging them from the library.

Understanding Instances

It is important to understand the concept of a symbol versus an instance of a symbol. Changes you make to a symbol in the library affect all instances of that symbol that appear on the stage. The symbol is the actual object, and changes to it affect all instances of it.

However, changes you make to an individual instance of a symbol have no effect on other instances of that same symbol, nor on the symbol itself. Thus, you could create a single symbol in the library, create several instances of it on the stage, and then modify each instance by scaling, skewing, and so on—which would have no effect from instance to instance. Each instance of a symbol has its own properties, and is "self-contained" in that regard. As you continue to work through examples in this chapter, you will get a better understanding of how this works. To practice working with symbol instances, try exercise 6-3.

Exercise 6-3: Understanding Symbol Instances

Open Flash and create a basic filled circle and convert it to a symbol. Open the library and create several instances of that symbol on the stage. Apply various transformations to the symbol instances. Note that transformations applied to one symbol do not affect the others, nor do they affect the symbol data in the library.

Editing Symbols

Now that you understand the basic process for creating symbols, let's examine editing symbols. There are a couple of ways to access a symbol's timeline so that you can edit it. If you want to edit a symbol, the quickest way is to double click on an instance of it on the stage. This opens the symbol's timeline, "in place," and allows you to edit the symbol's content. You can also use the Symbol List button at the right in the Edit path to select the symbol on which you want to work, as shown in figure 6-3. The Symbol list provides a quick list of currently available symbols, just like the Scene list provides a quick list of currently available scenes in the movie.

Once you are accessing a symbol, the symbol name appears to the left of the scene name in the Edit path (see figure 6-3). Keep in mind that once you are editing in a symbol's timeline, changes you make will affect all instances of the symbol within the movie. Exercise 6-4 provides you with an opportunity to practice accessing and editing symbols.

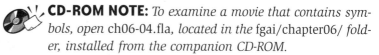

Exercise 6-4: Accessing and Editing Symbols

CD-ROM NOTE: *To examine a movie that contains symbols, open ch06-04.fla, located in the* fgai/chapter06/ *folder, installed from the companion CD-ROM.*

Use the Symbol List button to examine the symbols in the CD-ROM file and try accessing the various symbols in the movie.

As you begin working with symbols, be careful that you know whether you are working in a movie scene or in a symbol. Particularly as you are getting started, it is all too easy to begin and suddenly find yourself working in the wrong place!

Registration of Symbols

Before examining the different types of symbols in more detail, it is important to understand the significance of the registration point of a symbol, particularly when you start using ActionScript to manipulate symbols. The registration point of the main movie timeline is in the upper left-hand corner of the stage, whereas the origin of a symbol is its registration point.

When you define a symbol, one of the attributes you define is its registration. At any point you can change the registration, but you must go inside the symbol and physically move the content in the symbol to do so. In addition, a change such as this (that is, shifting around the content within a symbol) will affect all instances of that symbol on the stage. Exercise 6-5 demonstrates this concept.

Exercise 6-5: The Registration of a Symbol

Open Flash and create a filled rectangle on the stage. Convert the fill and lines to a symbol (either graphic or movie clip). Open the library and create several more instances of the symbol on the stage by click-dragging them to the stage. Double click on any symbol instance to "edit it in place." Select the rectangle and fill inside the symbol and move the items. Note that when you move the items the change to the symbol affects all instances of it on the stage.

Different Symbols, Different Purposes

Flash provides three types of symbols, discussed in the sections that follow. These are graphic, button, and movie clip symbols. Each of these has a timeline that behaves in a certain manner. The main difference between each type of symbol is in the manner in which it behaves in the main movie timeline. Thus, each serves a different purpose and has some special functionality in most cases. You will also see in the sections that follow how each symbol is used within a movie.

Realize that you can easily change a symbol's behavior (type) property in the Library panel. A symbol defined as a graphic can be "redefined" as a button or movie clip, although you usually have to do some editing in the symbol if you make this type of change.

The important thing is that just because the symbol was originally defined one way does not mean its definition cannot be modified. It is not uncommon to change a symbol's behavior during the development of a movie. Later in this chapter you will see how to use the Library panel to perform this function.

Graphic Symbols

A graphic symbol has its own timeline, may have any number of layers, and is often used for static graphics or for static components used in animation. For example, to create an animation of a walking person you might make the legs, arms, and torso of the person each a graphic symbol. You could then animate those static graphic symbols.

Although graphic symbols are normally used for static graphics, they can include animation. Graphic symbols are synchronized to the main movie timeline. Thus, as one frame of the main timeline plays, one frame of a graphic symbol plays. A graphic symbol, because it is coordinated with the main timeline, stops when the main movie it is inserted into stops. This unique feature differentiates the graphic symbol from a movie clip symbol.

 NOTE: *The only limit to graphic symbols is that they cannot include button symbols or sound elements.*

Using Graphic Symbols

Graphic symbols are typically meant for items that will be used in the main movie's timeline for frame-by-frame animation, as previously mentioned. However, they are vital for tween animation work. Additionally, graphic symbols may be integrated into other symbols. You can create compound or nested symbols by embedding one symbol type into another. Subsequent chapters offer a variety of examples of graphic symbols used in other symbols, such as buttons and movie clips.

 TIP: *Most of the time you will use movie clips for symbol-based looping animations. Yet if you use a graphic symbol for animation, sometimes the symbol animation will cut off or stop before it is able to complete a loop, due to the brevity of the main movie. Use Modify | Frames | Synchronize Symbols to automatically adjust the synchronization between a graphic symbol loop and a main movie segment.*

Creating a Graphic Symbol

Already you have discovered the two general ways of creating symbols. The only extension to this is to select Graphic as the behavior. From there, you can begin inserting content into the graphic symbol.

 TIP: *Generally, anytime an object (or set of objects) is to be reused in your movie, you will want to make it into a symbol, rather than creating it in a movie timeline. Indeed, in most of the movies you create almost everything may consist of symbols. In fact, this approach is recommended as the most efficient method of developing movies.*

Button Symbols

Buttons are the second type of symbol. As the name implies, button symbols provide the ability to create a symbol that automatically behaves like a push-button control. Flash makes it very easy to produce these controls in that it provides special frames for the up, over, down, and hit states of the button. By placing objects in these frames, a push button's functionality is automatically created.

In reality there are many things you can do with a button, and you are not limited to using push buttons. Flash MX 2004 provides the capability to create very complex interactive controls much more easily than prior versions. However, you do not create these controls with just a button symbol. Rather, they are an extension of the movie clip symbol, the most advanced of these being components.

To this point, you have been reading about symbols and have learned the basics of creating symbols. In the next three sections you will build a basic button that can be used as a simple interface component. Exercise 6-6 gets you started in creating a basic button.

Exercise 6-6: Creating a Button

CD-ROM NOTE: *A finished version of the button, named* ch06-06s.fla, *is located in the* fgai/chapter06/ *folder, installed from the companion CD-ROM.*

To begin creating a basic button, perform the following steps.

1. Open the file *ch06-06.fla*, located in the *fgai/chapter06/* folder, installed from the companion CD-ROM. Within this file are objects you will make into a button symbol.

2. Select the button and the shadow (currently separate groups) to make these items a symbol (using Modify | Convert to Symbol). Name the newly created symbol Button1 and set its behavior to Button.

3. Switch to the new symbol's timeline using the Symbol List button.

   In the Button symbol's timeline, note that there are four tabs instead of a "numbered" timeline. These frames automatically appear at the top of a button symbol when you edit it. They are synonymous with the four states of the object in relation to the mouse. The Up state is the normal state of the button, when the mouse is not affecting the button. The Over state is what the button looks like when the user rolls the cursor over it. The Down state shows how the button will be when the user clicks on it. The Hit state is the area that will react to the user's mouse. To create a button, you define the stage content for each state of the button.

   In this example, you will leave the Up and Over states as they currently appear. However, you must still build the timeline from left to right. Thus, you need to extend the sprite in the Up frame to the Over frame. Continue with the following steps.

4. Right-click on the Up frame in the timeline and select Insert Frame. This creates a copy of the Up frame in the Over frame.

5. In the Down frame, right-click and use Insert Keyframe.

6. In the Hit frame, right-click and use Insert Keyframe.

7. Click in the Down frame to modify the elements on the stage.

    To make the button look like it presses in when the user clicks on it, you will rotate the button 180 degrees and nudge the shadow up and over, as follows. This simulates the action of the button pressing in by changing the highlights and shadow for the button.

8. Use the Transform panel to rotate the button 180 degrees. You may have to click on the stage (to deselect the button and shadow) and then select the button only.

9. To make the button look more realistic, you need to move the shadow on the down press. Select in the Down frame to select the shadow group.

10. Use the arrow keys to shift the shadow up 5 pixels and to the right 5 pixels.

    Now you need to optimize the Hit frame. All you need in the Hit frame of a button is a basic fill. If you optimize your buttons by removing extraneous objects, your file sizes will be smaller. Continue with the following steps.

11. Select in the Hit frame, and then use Edit | Select All and then Ungroup. Click in a blank area of the canvas to deselect.

12. Again, for the Hit area for the button, the only element you want is the main part of the button. Delete all fills and lines except for the outermost circle that defines the button, by selecting each item and pressing the Backspace or Delete key.

13. Fill the outermost circle with black and then select and delete the line that surrounds it.

14. Switch back to scene 1 of the movie by clicking on the Scene 1 link in the Edit path.

    You will note that because you used Convert to Symbol to create the symbol, the symbol is already on the stage. If you had used Insert | New Symbol, you would have to use Window | Library to drag and drop the newly created symbol onto the stage.

15. Use Control | Enable Simple Buttons and place the cursor over the button. Try clicking on it to see if it works. In Chapter 8, you will learn how to add sounds to this button.

You can perform a wide range of functions with buttons. Buttons do not have to look and behave like a traditional push button. The possibilities are quite endless. Even 3D buttons can be implemented, as can be seen in the Button library found under the Windows | Other Panels | Common Libraries option.

Movie Clip Symbols

The third type of symbol, and quite possibly the most powerful, is the movie clip. A movie clip is a symbol in which the entire timeline independently plays when it is placed inside the main movie. A movie clip can contain almost anything and is different from a graphic symbol in that its animation continues to play even after the main movie into which it is inserted stops. Additionally, movie clip symbols can include all other symbol types within them, including sound.

Movie clips are like having the ability to place a Flash movie inside another movie. The entire timeline of the movie clip can be used to set up animation. The movie clip can then be inserted into the main movie, taking up only one frame in the main movie. Additionally, a movie clip could be inserted into a button's Over state to create a button that animates when the user rolls over a button symbol. With movie clips, the possibilities are almost endless, as you will learn in this and the following chapters.

When to Use Movie Clips

One of the most difficult things for new Flash developers to acquire a sense of is when and where to use the various types of symbols, particularly movie clips. Keep in mind that movie clips are different from a movie scene in that, as a symbol, a movie clip only requires one frame in the main movie, even though a movie clip might consist of several frames itself. Additionally, movie clips differ from graphic symbol animations in that movie clips continue to play even if the main movie's timeline stops. Another difference is that movie clips can include buttons and sounds. Generally, anytime you want a reusable animation to continue playing after the main movie has stopped, a movie clip is your best bet.

Creating and Using a Movie Clip

The simplest example of why you would use a movie clip is in the case of an animated button. In exercise 6-7, you will create a button that has an animated Over state. The animation will be created using a movie clip, which itself is based on a static graphic symbol. It is common to create a series of nested symbols, such as inserting a graphic and movie clip symbol into a button symbol.

Exercise 6-7: Creating an Animated Button

CD-ROM NOTE: *To view the solution before starting, open the file* ch06-07s.fla, *located in the* fgai/chapter06/ folder, *installed from the companion CD-ROM.*

Use Test Movie to preview the finished animation. To create a button with an animated Over state, perform the following steps.

1. Open the file *ch06-06.fla*, located in the *fgai/chapter06/* folder, installed from the companion CD-ROM.

2. Use Insert | New Symbol to create a new symbol named *Spinner Movie*. Set the behavior to Movie Clip.

3. Use Window | Library to open the current movie's library.

   You will create the content for the *Spinner Movie* symbol from the other symbols already in the file. You will notice that there are already a couple other symbols in the file.

4. Click-drag the Spinner graphic symbol to the stage. Position the crosshairs of the *Spinner Movie* symbol on the existing stage crosshairs. The crosshairs in the center of the stage mark the registration point for the *Spinner Movie* symbol. Use the arrow keys to nudge the symbol if needed.

   Although Chapter 9 explores 2D animation at length, in the next couple of steps you will create a quick animation that spins the spinner.

5. Click on frame 1 in the *Spinner Movie* symbol timeline.

6. Press F5 (Insert | Timeline | Frame) to extend the duration of the graphic symbol of the stage. Extend the duration of the sprite to frame 10.

7. Right-click on frame 10 and select Insert Keyframe from the context menu.

8. With the playhead in frame 10, select on the instance of the Spinner graphic symbol on the stage.

9. Select the Modify | Transform | Scale and Rotate (Ctrl + Alt + S or Command + Option + S) menu option.

10. In the dialog box, enter *100* for Scale and *180* for Rotate and then click on OK.

11. Right-click in frame 1 and select Create Motion Tween from the context menu. You have just created a simple tween animation that animates the rotation of the object.

12. To test while in the movie clip, select Control | Play.

 NOTE: *Control | Play works here because you are testing the movie clip's timeline, as opposed to testing the entire movie.*

13. Click on the Scene 1 link in the Edit path to return to the main move timeline.

14. Click-drag the *Button1* symbol from the library to the stage to create an instance of the *Button1* symbol on the stage.

15. Double click on the *Button1* instance on the stage to open its timeline.

16. Right-click on the Over frame in the button's timeline and select Insert Keyframe.

17. Insert the *Spinner Movie* symbol into the Over state of the button. Drag the *Spinner Movie* symbol from the library to the button's timeline. You have just nested a movie clip symbol inside a button symbol.

18. Align the registration point of the *Spinner Movie* clip with the existing button graphic using the arrow keys.

19. Insert a keyframe in the Down and Hit frames of the *Button1* symbol timeline by right-clicking in each frame and selecting Insert Keyframe from the context menu.

20. In the Down frame, delete the instance of the *Spinner Movie* clip.

21. Rotate the button to give the appearance that the button is pressed, as you did in the last exercise.

22. In the Hit frame, remove all elements except a black fill in the largest circle, similar to the previous exercise.

23. Switch back to scene 1 by clicking on the Scene 1 link in the Edit path.

24. Save your FLA file to a local drive.

25. Use Control | Test Movie to see the animated button work.

Note that you must use Test Movie to test a movie that contains movie clips, as noted in Chapter 2. Simply enabling buttons will not work when the button contains a movie clip.

▪▪▪ Special Symbol Issues

As you conclude this section on symbols, a couple of important points should be acknowledged as they relate to working with symbols in movies. Generally, these items seem to cause confusion among people learning how to use symbols. Therefore, they have been reserved for the end of this discussion in the hope that they will make more sense. Typically, if you are having difficulty with a symbol or a specific technique, one of these related issues is likely the root of the problem.

Redefining Symbols

You can easily redefine a symbol's behavior by accessing the symbol's properties in the library and by changing its assigned stage behavior. For it to work properly, you must redefine the symbol in both places.

Redefining a symbol is not an infrequent occurrence. Every symbol has a basic behavior definition in the library. Similarly, when a symbol is placed on the stage from the library, the stage recognizes the symbol's currently defined behavior and sets the symbol instance's behavior to the same. When any symbol is placed on the stage, you can check to see how the stage defines the instance by viewing the left end of the Properties panel, shown in figure 6-4.

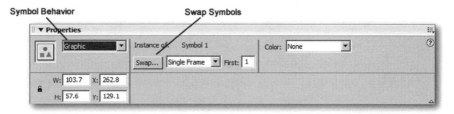

Figure 6-4. The Properties panel reveals the behavior associated with the symbol instance.

The problem with redefining symbols and instances is that the symbol's behavior in the library and the instance's behavior are independent of each other. If you change the behavior of the symbol in the library, you must manually tell the stage, using the Properties panel, that the symbol's definition has changed. If you use Test Movie or Enable Simple Buttons in the Control menu, with no response from the symbols, check their definition on the stage. To practice redefining a symbol, try exercise 6-8.

Exercise 6-8: Redefining a Symbol

Open a new Flash file and create a fill and circle on the stage. Convert these items to a graphic symbol. Then access the library and change the graphic symbol's behavior to Button. Go to the stage and select the item. Note that even though the library behavior changed the stage still thinks it is a graphic symbol.

Swapping Symbols

Another important item in the Properties panel when a symbol is selected is the Swap button (see figure 6-4). Use the Swap button to exchange the symbol associated with a stage instance. This feature is handy if you are trying to get instances of various symbols the same size or transformed in some way. Using Swap, you can create the first symbol instance with some transformation. You can then copy the instance and use Swap to assign a different symbol to the instance. This saves you from having to reassign a transformation. This simple technique can save a lot of time when creating movies.

TIP: *Swap Symbol can also be accessed via menus (Modify | Symbol | Swap Symbol).*

NOTE: *The Swap button has the same effect as Exchange Cast Members in Macromedia Director.*

The "Color" of Symbols

A final item you will note in the Properties panel is the Color drop-down list. This drop-down allows you to assign a color effect to a symbol instance. Color effects are as follows.

- *Brightness:* Adds white or black to the symbol instance.
- *Tint:* Adds a tint of color to the instance.
- *Alpha:* Affects the opaqueness of the instance.
- *Advanced:* Allows you to individually modify all of the previous color effects simultaneously.

In Chapter 9 you will examine the color effects as they relate to symbol instances. By applying color effects, you can create animated transitions and special effects in your movie files.

Compound or Nested Symbols

Symbols are not limited to singular creations. As you have seen, you can insert several symbols into another before inserting them into a scene. As you begin creating, as well as examining, the examples in the latter portion of this book, you will start to see the hierarchy of building effective symbols. For now, the following are some pointers as they relate to compound or nested symbols.

- *Placing a button into a graphic symbol disables the button.* The graphic of the Up state will display, but the button will not function.

- *Placing a movie clip into a graphic symbol will allow the movie clip's animation to play, but any buttons or sounds will not function.* The movie clip will loop as normal, however.

- *A graphic or movie clip may be placed into a button's Up, Over, or Down state.* When the inserted symbol is a movie clip, it creates a button that has an animated state. To preview the animated state, you must use Test Movie. Enable buttons will only show the button states and not play the inserted movie clip.

- *A graphic or button may be placed into a movie clip.* When such a movie clip is inserted into a scene, Test Movie must be run to test the buttons in the movie clip.

Breaking Symbols Apart

If you begin creating symbols and find you need to break apart an instance of a symbol, so as to substantially change the instance's stage objects, you can do so rather easily. Use Modify | Break Apart on a symbol instance to unlink the instance from the symbol into a collection of ungrouped stage objects. When you break apart a symbol instance, the process leaves the original symbol unchanged. Only the instance of the symbol is affected.

This process may be helpful if you have a series of buttons that are fundamentally the same, save one. You could use the button symbol to generate all instances and then simply break apart a single instance to create a new custom version of the button.

▪ ▪ ▪ Understanding Libraries

The term library as it is used within Flash may be, to some extent, a misnomer for those familiar with libraries in other packages. Indeed, Flash symbols that exist in one file may be used in any other file. In this regard, every Flash file can be a library. Yet in most other packages a library is a "special" file that can only be used as a library; it cannot be used for other purposes.

In Flash, however, every file that has symbols can function as a library. By using the File | Import | Open Library for Import menu option, any Flash file that contains symbols can be made to yield its components for reuse in another file. Additionally, symbols you want to share across multiple movies can be defined in a single, shared library, rather than having copies of those symbols in each movie file. You can also use the File | Library | Open Library for Import menu option to work with shared library elements. Setting up a library of shared symbols is relatively easy, as you will discover in this section. First, however, let's begin with the basics of libraries.

Importing Symbols from Other Libraries

You can easily access symbols from any Flash file. Any Flash file that contains symbols can be opened as a library while you work. The symbols can be "imported" into the current file by simply dragging and dropping them into the current file, as you have already seen. In exercise 6-9, you will open one of the startup files and import some symbols from another file to see how this works.

The Library panel allows you to perform myriad maintenance tasks and gives you quite a bit of information, such determining what types of symbols are in the library, how many times a symbol has been used, and when the symbol was last modified. You can also create groups of symbols in folders, for easier management. Exercise 6-9 shows you how to import symbols from another file.

Exercise 6-9: Importing Symbols from Another File

To import symbols from another file, perform the following steps.

1. For this exercise, open the file *ch06-09.fla* from the *fgai/chapter06/* folder, installed from the companion CD-ROM.

2. Use File | Import | Open Library for Import and select the file *library.fla* in the *fgai/chapter06/* folder, installed from the companion CD-ROM. Doing so will open the Library window, as shown in figure 6-5.

 NOTE: *As shown in figure 6-5, the Library panel has been undocked.*

As shown in figure 6-5, three buttons exist above the vertical scroll bar of the Library window: Sort Direction, Wide State, and Narrow State (view). Flash libraries can be sorted by any of the headings listed to the left of the Sort Direction button. Sort Direction determines whether the items are shown as ascending or descending. Note that Sort Direction only applies when you are in Wide State view mode.

The Wide State and Narrow State view mode buttons affect the width and amount of data shown in the library. In Wide State view, the Library window can be sized, and shows more than just the name of the symbol. The Narrow State view restricts the width of the window to the name only, but allows variable height of the window.

3. Once the library is open, note the small icons in the list, which indicate the behavior or type of symbol (see figure 6-5). Begin by inserting a graphic symbol into the current FLA file. Scroll down the list, find the "glass" symbol, and click on it.

4. To place the "glass" symbol into the current movie, click-drag in the Preview window or on the symbol's name and drag the instance of the symbol to the stage so that it is inserted into the current movie.

Once a graphic symbol is placed on the stage, small crosshairs will be present at the center of the symbol. This is the registration point of the graphic symbol. When creating a graphic symbol, you can control where the symbol objects appear in relation to the registration point. Generally, the registration point will be either in the center or aligned to a certain part of the element.

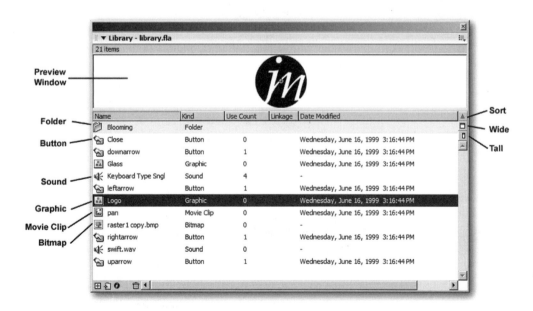

Figure 6-5. When a file is opened as a library, the Library panel opens, revealing the symbols in the file.

5. Symbols placed on the stage can be modified in various ways. You can scale, deform, move, or change color effects without affecting the actual symbol's data. This is because the representation on the stage is an instance or reference to the symbol, as opposed to the data itself. As a demonstration of this, use the Scale modifier of the Arrow tool, or the Transform panel, to disproportionately scale the symbol down on the stage.

6. Use the Window | Library panel to open the current file's library. Note that the symbol in the current file has not changed. It is the instance (or reference) on the stage that has changed.

7. Press Ctrl + L to close the current file's library.

You can group symbols into folders for easier management. To access the symbols within a folder, double click on the folder to expand it. To collapse an expanded folder, double click on it. When you create your own movies, get into the habit of using folders in the library. In large movies with a lot of symbols, organization via folders is key.

8. In the *library.fla* Library window, double click on the Blooming folder to expand its content. Click on the Blooming movie clip. When you do so, the movie clip will appear in the small preview window. You can use the small Play button in the upper right portion of the Preview window to preview the movie clip. Click-drag the movie clip to the stage and scale it down a little.

9. At this point, play the movie to see what happens. Go to the Control menu, where you will see that Play Movie is inactive. When you insert a movie clip symbol on the stage, from that point on you must use Control | Test Movie to see the movie clip play.

10. Insert a simple button from the library. If you closed the *library.fla* panel when you tested the movie, use File | Import | Open Library for Import again to open the *library.fla* file.

11. Scroll down and find the Close button. Click-drag it to the stage.

12. To see the button work, access the Control | Enable Simple Buttons menu option. When authoring movies, you must enable this option to see buttons "work." Once enabled, you can roll the mouse over and click on the button to see it work.

13. You have seen how to import a graphic, button, and movie clip into your movie. Symbols can also be used in other symbols to create compound or nested symbols. With the *library.fla* file open as a library, click-drag the symbol named Pan into the movie. This is a movie clip symbol that has four buttons inserted into it. If Enable Buttons is on, note that the buttons do not work. Because the button symbols are nested within a movie clip symbol, you must use Control | Test Movie to get these buttons to work.

As you have seen, getting symbols from other files is relatively easy. The ability to drag and drop symbols from other files is very powerful indeed. Yet, realize that when you import symbols from other files they become part of the file you drag them into. To see this at work, continue with the following steps.

14. If the *library.fla* Library panel is currently open, close it.

15. In the open file, click on the Symbol List button. Note that all of the symbols you imported from the *library.fla* file are now part of the current file.

16. Save this file to your computer as *mylibrary.fla* and then close.

17. Start a new, blank file.

18. Use Open Library for Import again and select the *mylibrary.fla* file you just saved.

19. At this point, you could start the process of importing symbols into the new, blank canvas again by dragging them from *mylibrary.fla* to this new file.

Symbols are powerful in that they can be reused over and over, just by importing them from existing files. In this way, you can work like the programmer who creates small components that can be reused from application to application. After some time, you can create and collect many reusable components that will reduce your production time.

Using the Library Panel and Menu

When you access the current file's library, there are several control buttons that appear, as shown in figure 6-6. Note the buttons along the lower left of the Library panel, which allow you to quickly add new symbols and folders, find out information about a particular symbol, and delete an existing symbol.

Note the Library panel menu shown in figure 6-6, which provides menu access to several capabilities. The features of the Library panel menu are as follows.

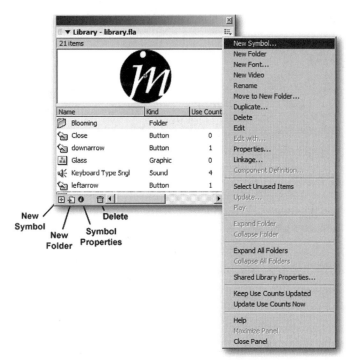

New Symbol

New Folder

Delete

Symbol Properties

Figure 6-6. The Library panel's menu and quick-access buttons

- *New Symbol:* Creates a new symbol by opening the New Symbol dialog box.
- *New Folder:* Creates a folder into which you can place or group symbols.
- *New Font:* Allows you to import a font description into the library.
- *New Video:* Allows you to import a video clip for embedding in the library.
- *Rename:* Allows the developer to rename an existing symbol.
- *Move to New Folder:* Moves a selected symbol into a new folder.

- *Duplicate:* Duplicates the selected symbol and allows you to define a new behavior for the symbol.
- *Delete:* Deletes the symbol from the library.

 NOTE: *A new feature in Flash MX 2004 is the ability to undo a library deletion. That is, if you accidentally delete a symbol from the library, you can undo the deletion.*

Small squares appear on the stage when a symbol that is needed has been deleted. Before deleting a symbol from the library, it is a good idea to check the usage count. The usage count shows how many times a symbol has been used in the movie. Thus, it allows you to quickly figure out which symbols are not used in a movie. See also "Usage Count" in the following list.

 TIP: *If you need to delete multiple symbols or move multiple symbols to a folder, you can select multiple symbols in the Library panel by holding down the Shift key. You can then select Delete or Move to Folder from the Options drop-down menu in the Library panel.*

- *Edit:* Switches the editing environment to the selected symbol.

- *Edit with:* For symbols such as bitmaps or sounds, this option allows you to select the editor (external application) to be used to open a file so that you can edit the symbol within it.

- *Properties:* Brings up the Symbol Properties dialog box, in which you can rename the symbol or change its behavior.

- *Linkage:* Reveals the Symbol Linkage Properties dialog box. This option is used with shared libraries.

- *Component Definition:* Allows you to define the parameters associated with Flash components.

- *Select Unused Items:* Allows you to easily find symbols not used by any of the movie scenes, so that you can delete them.

- *Update:* Allows you to automatically reimport (update) bitmap and sound symbols.

- *Play:* Allows you to play non-nested graphic and movie clip symbols.

- *Expand/Collapse Folder:* Allow you to quickly expand or contract one or all folders.

- *Shared Library Properties:* This dialog is where you enter the URL for the location of a shared library.

- *Usage count options:* Usage counts tell you how many times a symbol is used in a movie. You can set the library to constantly update the counts using the Keep Use Counts Updated option, or you can manually update the counts as needed using the Update Use Counts Now option.

 TIP: *Most of the Library panel menu commands are disabled when you are viewing an external or shared library. To edit those libraries, open them into Flash, rather than opening them as an external or shared library.*

Default Libraries

In the previous sections, you have observed how to import symbols from other files, as well as how to access the current movie's symbols. In addition to this, the Flash software includes several default libraries of symbols. These are accessed using the Window | Other Panels | Common Libraries submenu. You may want to access these to see what is available and to practice importing symbols from them.

You can also customize the content of the default libraries that appear in the Common Libraries submenu. The files used by this menu are found in the *Program Files/Macromedia/Flash MX 2004/en/Configuration/ Libraries* folder on the PC, or in the *Flash MX 2004/en/Configuration/ Libraries* folder on the Macintosh. You can add and delete symbols from the existing libraries, or you can add your own libraries by copying to this folder Flash files that contain symbols.

Shared Libraries

One of the most innovative features in Flash MX 2004 is the ability to share symbols at runtime and during authoring. With this feature, sets of Flash movies that use the same interface components (such as buttons, sliders, and the like) and other symbols that may appear across multiple movies can now be made and used more efficiently. In the following few exercises you will learn how to create a library that has symbols to be shared, as well as how to utilize those symbols in another movie file. To make a shared library work, there are four general things you do, as follows.

- Create a Flash file that contains the symbols you wish to share across movies.

- Define the symbols in that library as items that should be shared, using the Linkage menu option in the Library panel, and save the file.

- Open the file as a shared library and place the items identified as shared elements in the library into the new movie.

- Export both the shared library file and the movie file as a web-ready SWF file.

Let's begin looking at how you can use shared libraries by first opening an existing library and defining components it should share.

Using the Shared Library

For the shared library to work, a web-ready SWF version of the shared library must be created, in addition to the SWF version of the destination movie file or files. By default, the movie file SWF (into which shared components are placed) will look for the shared library SWF in its directory. For example, a file named mymovie.swf will by default look for its shared library in the same directory into which it is placed. However, you can change the directory location for the shared library using the Shared Library Properties option in the menu of the Library panel. This allows you to store a shared library in a single, common location.

Whenever you open an external file as a library or open a shared library (which you will read about in material to follow), you cannot add or delete symbols or folders. You can make these types of modifications only in the current file's library. Thus, if you wish to modify the content of an external library or a shared library, you must open it directly into Flash, make the modifications, and resave it. Also note that when a shared or external library is opened the background color of the panel (behind the symbol names) is grayed, also indicating that you cannot edit the library content.

Defining Components to Be Shared

You can take any flash file and identify the components in that library that should be shared. In exercise 6-10, you will identify the symbols that should be shared and then actually use them in another file. One important note is that if you have symbols that are nested inside one another (such as a movie clip that contains several buttons, or any other nested situation), you must set all of the components to "share," not just the single parent symbol. The exercise highlights this fact.

Exercise 6-10: Identifying Symbols for Sharing

 CD-ROM NOTE: *Open the file* library.fla, *located in the* fgai/chapter06/ *folder, installed from the companion CD-ROM.*

Perform the following steps.

1. With the *library.fla* file open, access the Library panel. You must make sure that you use File | Open (not File | Import | Open Library for Import).

2. Move the Library panel to the center of the screen and drag its borders out so that you can see all of the options (see figure 6-5). Alternatively, you can click on the Wide button (below the Sort Direction button) to quickly maximize the panel.

   In figure 6-5, note the Linkage column. When working with shared libraries, this column is used to indicate the current link status of the symbols to be shared. You will note that nothing is listed there currently, indicating that none of the symbols are currently set up as shared symbols. In this example you will set up the two button components as items to be shared.

3. Begin by clicking on the Close button symbol and selecting Linkage from the Library panel menu (you can also right-click on the symbol's name in the library and select Linkage from the context menu). This will reveal the Symbol Linkage Properties dialog box, shown in figure 6-7.

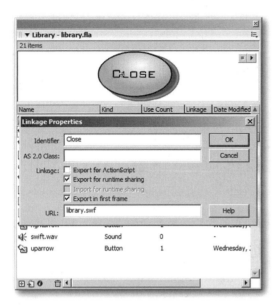

Figure 6-7. The Symbol Linkage Properties dialog box is where you define whether or not a symbol is to be shared.

4. In figure 6-7, note that the default setting is for no sharing, as nothing is selected. Whenever you create symbols, they are not shared by default (unless you set them to be in the Create/Convert Symbol dialog box when you create the symbol, per the advanced settings in the Create/Convert Symbol dialog box). To make an item a shared symbol, select the *Export for runtime sharing* option. Go ahead and click on the *Export for runtime sharing* option for the Close button symbol.

5. Once you have selected the *Export for runtime sharing* option, you are required to enter a name for the symbol in the Identifier field. This name is how the file that uses the shared symbol will refer to it. It is also how you can use ActionScript to manipulate the object. For now, enter Close in the Identifier field.

 NOTE: *The* Import for runtime sharing *option in the Symbol Linkage Properties dialog is for using shared symbols. You will read more about this in the next section.*

6. In addition to entering a name for the symbol, you must also enter the URL where the library will be located. For now, assume that the two files (the shared library and the destination) will be in the same directory. Thus, enter *library.swf* in the URL field and click on OK.

7. Once you click on OK, note the change in the Linkage column that says that the symbol is now set to Export, followed by the item's identifier. You can quickly identify symbols that are set up for sharing by the Export option displayed in the Linkage column.

8. Now let's set up the other "button" element. Select the Pan movie clip, which is actually a movie clip that contains four other button symbols in the file.

9. Use the Linkage option and select the *Export for runtime sharing* option in the Symbol Linkage Properties dialog box. The URL should be automatically entered as *library.swf.* Click on OK.

10. In addition to setting the parent symbol (*Pan* movie clip) for sharing, you must also set its child symbols for sharing. If you do not, the movie clip will be shared, but its child buttons will actually be copied to each file the Pan button is placed into, thus adding extraneous data to all files the Pan button is inserted into. Set the down arrow, left arrow, right arrow, and up arrow symbols for sharing using the Linkage menu option, as you did with the previous two items.

11. Although you would normally set all symbols in a shared library to export, the remaining symbols will use their default non-share setting for purposes of demonstrating something a little later. Save the file as *library_s.fla.* Additionally, select File | Export Movie to save the file as a web-ready SWF file (discussed in detail in Chapter 12).

12. In the Export Movie dialog box, enter *library_s.swf* in the Filename field. Click on OK.

13. In the Export Flash Player dialog box, just click on OK.

Using Shared Symbols

Now that you have set up a shared library, you can use the components from it in another file. Exercise 6-11 takes you through the process of using elements from a shared library.

Exercise 6-11: Importing Elements from a Shared Library

To use the shared library you have set up, perform the following steps.

1. Use File | New to begin a new Flash file.

2. Use File | Import | Open Library for Import to open the file *library_s.fla.*

TIP: *You can quickly tell the difference between a shared or external library and the current movie's library by the color of the background. If it is gray, the library is shared or external. If it is white, it is the current file's library.*

In the shared library window, note the Linkage column of the items you set as shared in the previous file, as shown in figure 6-8. This is a very important thing to pay attention to. Items that say *Import* will be brought in as shared components and will not change the file size of the current movie. Items that say nothing will be brought in and stored in the current movie's file (which adds to the file size).

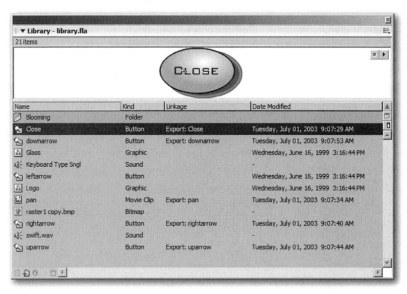

Figure 6-8. When you open a file as a shared library, the Linkage column reveals which items are set up for sharing.

3. Drag the Close, Pan, and "glass" symbols onto the current file's stage.

4. Close the shared library and open the current file's library.

   Note in the library that the items that were set up for sharing are set on Import in the Linkage column. The "glass" symbol, which was not set up for sharing, has nothing in the Linkage column. This means that the current movie will import the shared components from the shared library at runtime. The other item, the magnifying glass, is simply duplicated data in the file and is not a shared component.

5. Before you leave this exercise, right-click on the Close button symbol in the Library panel and select Linkage in the context menu.

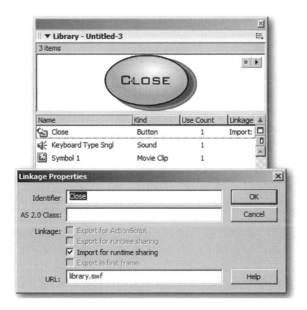

6. As shown in figure 6-9, note that the identifier you set up in the shared library is displayed in the Identifier field. Also note that the selected Linkage radio button is Import for runtime sharing and that the name of the shared library SWF file is named here.

Figure 6-9. The element imported from the shared library is referenced by the identifier entered in the shared library.

▪ ▪ ▪ Other Assets in Libraries

Four special elements are automatically added to the library when they are imported: bitmap graphics, video, fonts, and sounds. The next chapter delves more deeply into issues of bitmaps, including how they are represented in the library. Chapter 8 explores sound symbols, and Chapter 11 deals with video in more detail. However, before leaving this chapter, you need to understand font symbols and why they are useful. You can import fonts into shared libraries to help reduce file sizes across sites that use numerous fonts.

Font Symbols

As mentioned in Chapter 5, some fonts can be imported into an FLA file's library. Font symbols are generated as a result of importing into the library a font available to the system (usually stored in the Fonts folder on the machine). For sites that utilize many fonts in movies and across movies, the ability to include a single font definition in a shared library for use across multiple files is quite advantageous.

However, if you are not using a shared library across your files, this feature will provide little benefit from the standpoint of file size in your web-ready movies. For example, say you have five movies that all use "Doodle" font. With no shared library, when saved as the web-ready SWF format, each of the movies will automatically include the complete description of the font and its characteristics in each of the five files.

If you were to import the font into each file's library, you would gain nothing, because whether or not the font file were stored in the FLA's library the font description data would be automatically included in the SWF anyway. This was one of the original "key features" of Flash web-ready files; that is, you did not have to worry about what fonts the users of your site had on their machines. Fonts used for design purposes would be displayed correctly because the font description was automatically included in the web-ready SWF.

Where importing fonts into a library is advantageous (from a file size perspective) is when there is a shared library. In the previous example, if the five movies use a shared library for common elements, and the "Doodle" font is in that shared library, when the SWF files are generated the font will be written once to the shared library instead of in each of the movie files. Granted, a single font file may only be about 15 K in a single SWF file (not much of a file size savings), but if you had 10 to 12 fonts in 10 to 12 movies the file size savings as a result of using fonts in a shared library becomes more important.

The one caveat to shared font files is that you have to create a font symbol for any font you want to use in your design from the very beginning of your movie creation (or at least at the initial instance you plan to use the font in the movie). In exercise 6-12, you will create a font symbol in a file and use it.

Exercise 6-12: Creating a Font Symbol in a File

To practice creating a font symbol in a file, perform the following steps.

1. Start a new Flash file by selecting File | New.

2. Open the file's library by selecting Window | Library.

3. Select New Font from the Library menu.

4. In the Font Symbol Properties dialog box, shown in figure 6-10, enter a name for the font and select the font (from your system) you want assigned from the Font drop-down. It is recommended you use a name close to the actual font name. If you wish to include bold or italic versions of the font, check the Bold and Italic checkboxes.

5. Close the library.

6. On the stage, create a new text element with the Text tool and enter some text.

7. In the Font drop-down list in the Properties panel, find the name you entered into your font symbol in the library and

select it. Font symbols are identified in the Font drop-down by a small asterisk (*) that appears at the end of the font name.

Figure 6-10. The Font Symbol Properties dialog box allows you to define a font symbol from the available fonts on your system.

 NOTE: *The key to using font symbols is in remembering that you must first define the font as a symbol in the library. Then you are able to select it in the Properties panel.*

Summary of Library Concepts

To summarize this section concerning libraries, keep in mind the following important concepts. Again, be careful that you do not get the Common Libraries submenu and the Window | Library menu options confused as you work. The Common Libraries submenu accesses the default libraries installed with Flash. The Window | Library menu option accesses the current movie's library of symbols.

- Any Flash file that contains symbols can be opened as a library or set up as a shared library.

- Anytime you drag a symbol from another file (using Open Library for Import), the symbol becomes part of the current file's library of symbols. Thus, you do not have to retain the originating file from which the symbols came. They are integrated into the file into which they are placed.

- To use a shared library, you must first, in the Linkage dialog box, identify the symbols in the file you want to share.

- When you drag a symbol that is set up as a shared component, it is linked to the current file. If you open a library as a shared library and drag a symbol that is not set up as a shared component into the current file, the symbol becomes part of the current file's library of symbols and adds data to the file.

- Use Window | Library to insert a symbol that exists in the current file to the current file's stage.

- Use the Window | Other Panels | Common Libraries submenu to open the default libraries installed with Flash.

- Save your own libraries to the *Flash MX 2004/en/Configuration/ Libraries* directory for them to appear in the Common Libraries submenu.

- When you import a bitmap graphic or a sound into a file, the objects are automatically added to the current file's library. If you no longer need the bitmap or sound (i.e., it has been deleted from the stage), make sure you use Window | Library and delete the bitmap or sound symbol from the library. Deleting a bitmap from the stage or a sound from a frame does not delete it from the library. You must manually do this. It is always a good idea to use the Select Unused Items option from the Options menu in the Library panel to clean out unused symbols.

- Insert fonts that are used in a series of movies into a shared library to reduce the file size of your resulting web-ready movies.

▪ ▪ ▪ Summary

This chapter reviewed how symbols and the library are used in Flash. While proceeding through the rest of this book, you will continue to see symbols used over and over. They are one of the most powerful features available in Flash.

7

Bitmap Graphics

▪ ▪ ▪ ▪ Introduction

In previous chapters you dealt with the variety of vector elements that can be used in Flash. It is now time to examine the things you can do with bitmap graphics in Flash, and there are quite a few. From transforming them and tracing them to using them as fills for vector objects (something that works pretty uniquely), you will see that you are not limited to working with vector objects only.

This chapter begins by introducing you to the attributes of raster graphics, much in the way Chapter 3 introduced you to the uniqueness of vector graphics and how Flash works with them. You will also take a look at preparing raster graphics for use in Flash, and then see the variety of things you can do with them in your documents.

▪ ▪ ▪ ▪ Objectives

In this chapter you will:

- Examine the primary attributes of raster graphics
- Learn to prepare bitmaps using a raster editor
- Find out how to set the properties of a raster graphic once you have imported it
- Discover how to transform, trace, break, and use bitmaps in a variety of ways

▪ ▪ ▪ ▪ Attributes of Raster Graphics

Part of successfully integrating raster graphics in Flash is properly preparing them before you import them. To properly prepare them, you must know a thing or two about how they work; that is, about their attributes.

The following sections briefly describe the primary attributes of raster graphics; that is, those things you must tend to prior to importing them into Flash MX 2004. Following this, you will examine how you control these attributes in a raster editor such as Adobe Photoshop, including how to size and change the resolution, modify the color depth, maintain transparency, and choose the applicable file format.

Image Resolution

Resolution in any situation deals with the number of color units per unit of area. When you deal with print, you talk in terms of dots per inch. With screen design (web or multimedia), you deal with pixels per inch (ppi) and with scanners, samples per inch (spi). Regardless of the color unit and the unit of measure, resolution deals with the visual clarity or quality of an image over a given area. In general, the greater number of units over an area, the higher the quality of output.

When you are working with image resolution, you typically talk in terms of ppi. However, when discussing images for screen, you can use dpi and ppi interchangeably. In essence, a bitmap image is nothing more than the compilation of many adjacent color units (pixels) that form a picture. Look very closely at the image and you can see the individual color units, as shown in figure 7-1. Back away from it and look at the entire set of units and your eye blends the color units, allowing you to no longer notice the discrete color units. Instead, you see an image.

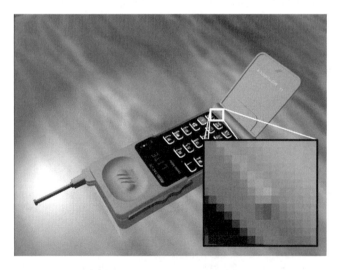

Figure 7-1. Raster images consist of hundreds or even thousands of individual color units called pixels.

Dealing with raster graphics on the Web or for CD-ROM multimedia is much easier than dealing with the myriad issues that arise when you want to print a bitmap. For the Web it is pretty easy: all graphics have a resolution of 72 ppi, because there is a one-to-one ratio between the pixels in the image and the pixels in the monitor on which you display it. Thus, you deal in raw pixel measurements at 72 ppi, as that is the standard resolution for computer monitors.

As you work with programs such as Adobe Photoshop, Corel PhotoPaint, or Macromedia Fireworks, realize that because you are designing primarily for the computer screen, inch measurements (which all of these packages provide simultaneously with pixel measurements) are essentially useless. The only thing that matters is the pixel in screen design.

Where the water gets muddy though is when you want to repurpose images. For example, say you have a raster image that was part of a print publication you now want to use in a web page or Flash movie. Print images require a tremendous amount of data compared to screen images. Thus, it is not as simple as taking the "print image" and plopping it on a web page or in Flash. You must modify the resolution, via sizing, prior to using the image in Flash. You will learn more about how to do this in material to follow.

Bit Depth

The second aspect of bitmap graphics you should be aware of is bit depth. Bit depth is simply the number of bits available in an image for describing each color unit. If the image is a 24-bit image (called RGB color or Truecolor), you have 24 bits that can be used to describe each color unit (in the case of screen images, 24 bits to describe each pixel). This means that each pixel can be one of 16.7 million possible colors. As the number of bits available for describing each pixel in an image decreases (24 is generally considered the maximum), so does the range of possible colors for each pixel and therefore the overall quality of the image.

Thus, bit depth controls the color fidelity in an image; that is, the color quality or "faithfulness" of the color reproduction in regard to an original, if you are scanning an image. When creating an image from scratch, bit depth affects the range of color from which you can select when creating the image. Typically when dealing with color on the Web there are two bit depths you typically deal with: 24-bit (16.7 million colors) and 8-bit (256 colors). Most of the time, however, you will be dealing with 24-bit images.

File Size

The file size of a raster image is a function of resolution, bit depth, and physical size. Ignoring compression, the file size of a raster graphic can be calculated via the following equation.

```
File Size in KB = Resolution² * Width * Height * Bit Depth / 8192
```

Here, width and height are in inches. To determine inch measurements for this equation given pixel measurements for width and height, use the following.

- Width in pixels/resolution = width in inches
- Height in pixels/resolution = height in inches

Knowing these equations is helpful when planning web sites. Being able to determine the size of images you may want to include, particularly in mass, may help you figure out if what you want to do is feasible.

Alpha Data

Another aspect of raster graphics that is important is something called alpha data. In general, alpha data is extraneous data (8 bits, to be exact) added to a file to represent something not typically included in the "normal" color data in the file. Often this is related to transparency data, but alpha data can also be used for a variety of other purposes.

You need only be concerned with alpha data specifically for transparency, typically called an alpha channel or mask in other programs. Flash can utilize the alpha data from other programs that is related to transparency, as you will discover shortly.

Compression

Due to the typically large file sizes of raster graphics, most raster formats can include their data in a compressed format. Many raster graphic file formats support more than one type of compression, and some require that the data within them always be compressed. Most compression schemes in raster graphic files look for redundant colors in the image and then substitute for that redundancy using "tokens." A simple analogy would be the comparison of shorthand used by a secretary to capture notes. Using shorthand reduces the amount of writing and makes what is written shorter.

Although a lengthy discussion is not necessary, the primary thing to know about compression in raster graphics (as it relates to use in Flash) is whether the compression is lossy or lossless. Lossy compression simply means that when the file is com-

Original　　　　　　Quality 50%　　　　　　Quality 10%

Figure 7-2. Lossy compression sacrifices a certain amount of color data to attain smaller file sizes.

pressed a certain amount of color data will be sacrificed to make the file smaller, as shown in figure 7-2. Thus, when you uncompress a lossy file, the resulting file is not exactly the same as the original file prior to compression. You control the amount of data loss in lossy compression when you compress the file. When you use lossy compression, colors can shift slightly in the resulting image.

Lossless compression, on the other hand, does not loose data. When you uncompress a lossless compressed file, the resulting file is exactly the same as the original file prior to compression. Lossy compression typically yields smaller file sizes simply because it not only finds redundancies in color data but deletes some data.

 NOTE: *You should always use lossless compressed formats when importing bitmap data into Flash, discussed further in material to follow.*

File Formats

The final issue of note concerns raster graphic file formats. There are as many bitmap graphic formats as there are graphic applications. You need not be concerned with all of them, as there are only a few you really need to know for Flash. However, for the few that are important, you need to know what is special about each and, by using a particular one, what advantages you have in Flash for using it. Table 7-1 outlines the raster file formats Flash supports, as well as some other details about each. Later in this chapter you will discover some of the special features of certain formats and how Flash handles them.

Table 7-1: Flash-supported Raster File Formats

File	Extension	Compression	PC	Mac	Special Features
Animated GIF	.gif	Lossless	Yes	Yes	Imports as separate images in library
GIF Image	.gif	Lossless	Yes	Yes	1-bit transparency supported
Joint Photographics Experts Group	.jpg	Lossy	Yes	Yes	None
Macintosh Picture*	.pct, .pic	Lossless	Yes**	Yes	Can include vector and raster on Macintosh
MacPaint Image*	.pntg	None	Yes	Yes	None
Photoshop*	.psd	Lossless	Yes	Yes	None
Portable Network Graphics	.png	Lossless	Yes	Yes	256-level transparency supported
Quicktime Image*	.qtif	Lossless	Yes	Yes	None
Silicon Graphics Image*	.sgi	Lossless	Yes	Yes	None
Truevision Targa*	.tga	Lossless	Yes	Yes	None
Tagged Image File Format*	.tif	Lossless	Yes	Yes	None
Windows Bitmap	.bmp, .dib	Optional Lossless	Yes	No	None

▪ ▪ ▪ **Preparing Raster Graphics**

Now that you have examined the attributes of raster graphics, let's examine how you prepare raster images using three of the most common editors: Macromedia Fireworks, Adobe Photoshop, and Corel PhotoPaint.

Sizing Raster Images (Resolution)

The first important thing you must do to a bitmap is to properly size your image before bringing it into Flash. Like most multimedia programs, when you size a bitmap image in Flash (that is, transform it using scale), the amount of data in the image stays the same. That is, it does not extrapolate (reduce) or interpolate (add) data when you scale the image. Thus, scaling a bitmap image in Flash should be avoided unless there is some compelling reason to do so, such as some special animation effect.

 NOTE: *Before sizing an image, make sure the image is in 24-bit color, sometimes called RGB color or Truecolor.*

Why Not Scale in Flash?

Let's examine this more closely. If you import a bitmap and scale it up on the stage, Flash stretches the available data across the stage and "smoothes" it to make it look better (as shown in figure 7-3). If you scale up the image to greater than 130 to 150 percent (give or take), the image may break apart and start to look rather poor (see the area inside the circle in the left-hand image in figure 7-3). Thus, you end up with poorer visual results because you started with too little data.

Alternatively, if you import a bitmap and then scale the image down (see the right-hand image in figure 7-3), you get no negative visual results. However, you actually have more data in your file than you need, partic-

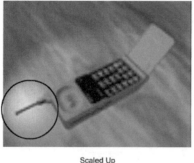

Scaled Up   Original Image   Scaled Down

Figure 7-3. The effect of scaling a bitmap on the stage in Flash.

ularly if the image you are using was originally designed for print! The image on the right (figure 7-3) is scaled down 50 percent; therefore, 50 percent of the data associated with the image serves no purpose.

Given these two examples, you should now realize the importance of sizing your bitmaps prior to importing into Flash. Scaling up can cause visual problems, and scaling down can add wasted data to your file.

Desirable Extra Data

As you have already learned, Flash movies are completely sizeable when you output an SWF file. When you place a raster image in Flash, Flash will attempt to display the image on the stage at true size (pixels by pixels at 72 ppi). However, if the end user scales a Flash movie up (either directly in a web page by changing the browser or frame size, indirectly simply because their resolution is larger, or by sizing the Flash Player or a projector file), you have the potential of running into the "scaling up" problem you saw earlier. Thus, there may be times when you might "have a little more data than you need" to accommodate this potential problem.

Sizing in Fireworks

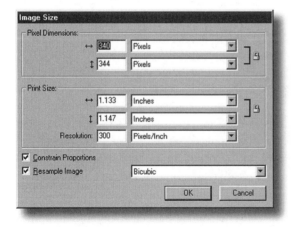

To size an image in Macromedia Fireworks, you use the Modify | Image Size command. This brings up the dialog box shown in figure 7-4. Use the Pixel Dimensions section of the dialog box, and make sure the Constrain Proportions and Resample Image options are selected.

Figure 7-4. To size an image in Fireworks, you use the Image Size dialog box.

Sizing in Photoshop

To size an image in Photoshop, select the Image | Image Size command. This brings up a dialog box very similar to the one shown for Fireworks in figure 7-4. Use the Pixel Dimensions section of the dialog box, and make sure the Constrain Proportions and Resample Image options are selected.

Sizing in PhotoPaint

To size an image in PhotoPaint, select the Image | Resample command. This brings up the dialog box shown in figure 7-5. Use the Image Size section, and make sure the units to the right are set to Pixels, not Inches. Also make sure the Anti-alias and *Maintain aspect ratio* checkboxes are selected, and the *Maintain original size* checkbox deselected.

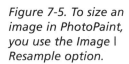

Figure 7-5. To size an image in PhotoPaint, you use the Image | Resample option.

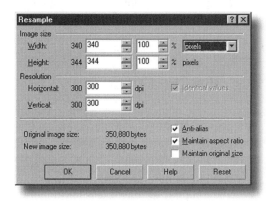

Changing Color Modes (Bit Depth)

When working with bitmaps for Flash, the primary concern is to make sure the image is either RGB (24-bit) or Indexed (8-bit) color, with 24-bit being preferred. Generally 24-bit images can be used for photographic data and 8-bit for non-natural images.

Note that with 24-bit color you should make sure the image is an RGB image, not a CMY image. You generally run into CMY images when you are repurposing images from print publications to the Web. CMY is a special color mode for four-color presswork, whereas RGB is for screen images.

Flash will support the import of CMY PNG files as well as CMY JPG files, but when you import them, the colors in the image may change drastically (much more than they would if you changed color modes in a raster editor). Thus, you should perform all color mode changes in a raster editor before importing the image into Flash.

Changing Bit Depth in Fireworks

Fireworks is a software application designed to specifically work with images for the Web. Thus, when you open an image into it, it automatically converts the image to RGB mode, even if the original image is a CMY PNG or CMY JPG image.

Changing Bit Depth in Photoshop

To change the bit depth in Photoshop, you use the Image | Mode submenu. From that location you can choose the RGB Mode option (24-bit) or the Index Color option (if you are creating a GIF image).

Changing Bit Depth in CorelDraw

To change the bit depth in CorelDraw, you use the Image | Convert To menu option. Select RGB Color (24-bit) or Paletted (8-bit), depending on the file format you intend to use.

▪▪▪ Getting Bitmaps into Flash

Flash can utilize bitmaps by either using the clipboard or via importing. Importing bitmaps is generally a better method. You have more control over the raster data and you can do some special things, such as utilize transparency data. The following sections discuss how to import and use prepared bitmaps in Flash.

 NOTE: *Keep in mind that the Clipboard tab in the Preferences dialog box includes several settings that affect bitmaps you intend on pasting from the clipboard. You may want to return to Chapter 2 to refresh your memory on these settings.*

Importing Images

To import a raster graphic into Flash, use the File Import to Stage menu option and the graphic will be automatically placed on the stage. If you do not want the image to be automatically placed on the stage, use the File | Import to Library command.

 TIP: *If you intend on using a bitmap across several movies, use a shared library. It will significantly improve the speed of download for your end users.*

Choosing a File Format

Although Flash supports a wide array of raster graphic file formats, there are really only two you need for Flash: GIF and PNG. The sections that follow describe these formats and why you should use them. Also addressed is the issue of why you should never use JPG.

PNG

Of all the formats supported by Flash, the most diverse is the Portable Network Graphics (PNG) format. PNG was developed as a patent-free replacement for web graphics, and it provides basically everything that GIF and JPG provide except that (1) PNG compression is lossless (whereas JPG is lossy) and (2) it does not support multiple image storage (which is what makes an animated GIF animated).

PNG was originally designed to be a single format for raster graphics on the Web. The vision was for all web designers to start using PNG in lieu of GIF and JPG. However, it has really not caught on as the full-time replacement for all raster graphics on web pages, mainly because most of the older browsers do not support it. Yet, it has filled a much-needed void in the graphics community: the provision of a single raster image file format that can be used to store high-quality data locally with lossless compression.

The PNG format can be used to store both 24-bit and 8-bit color data and thus matches the capability of both GIF and JPEG in that regard. When compared to JPG, the only difference is that PNGs have larger file sizes. However, PNGs also have better image fidelity than JPG. Thus, PNG files are larger, but higher in quality, than JPG files.

The feature that makes PNG stand out is its support of transparency. PNG provides the ability to include alpha data and, specifically for the Web, transparency. It does so much better than the limited 1-bit transparency of the GIF format. In a PNG file, you can define that a particular pixel color or range of pixel colors should be partially transparent; something you cannot do in GIF.

For transferring bitmaps into Flash, PNG should be the format you use most of the time, whether you need transparency or not. When a PNG has transparency data associated with it, Flash is able to automatically interpret the transparency and transfer it directly to the symbol in Flash such that background objects can show through the transparency assigned to the PNG file. To practice importing a PNG file, see exercise 7-1.

 NOTE: *If you use Fireworks, Flash deals with PNG files from it in a unique way. Flash will recognize most, if not all, of the elements you defined in Fireworks directly, including layers, vector elements, and so on.*

Exercise 7-1: Importing a Portable Network Graphics Image

 CD-ROM NOTE: *Open a new Flash file and try importing the file* circle.png *from the* fgai/chapter07/ *folder, installed from the companion CD-ROM.*

Once you import the graphic, create some Flash elements behind it and move the circle over the top to notice the included transparency in the PNG file.

Animated GIF

Animated GIF files are basically standard Graphic Interchange File Format (GIF) files that contain multiple images. The "animation" capability of animated GIF files are a function of the browser, not the file format itself. The only thing the animated GIF file knows is that there are multiple images defined within it. The interpretation of these individual images as an animation is due to the browser.

When an animated GIF file is imported into Flash, Flash stores each frame of the animated GIF as a separate image in the library. It also takes into account the number of frames assigned with each GIF image and lays out the "animation" appropriately along the timeline. For example, if a frame (image) in the GIF animation is assigned as "three frames long," the duration of the bitmap sprite will be three frames in the Flash timeline.

There may be times when you will want to import an animated GIF to use in your movie directly. If you use this technique, you must be careful because each "frame" in the GIF animation becomes an separate bitmap image in Flash. If you are not careful, you can quickly balloon your file size due to the number of images that may be in an imported GIF animation.

An alternative is to import an animated GIF and then trace the frames of the GIF animation (which converts them to vector) to reduce file size. Either way, realize that when animated GIFs are imported into Flash the file size usually increases. For example, if you compare the file size of an animated GIF to a web-ready SWF file that contains the same animated GIF, you will likely find that the animated GIF file is smaller. Where animated GIFs are most helpful in Flash is in the ability to access each frame of the animated GIF and/or the ability to convert each frame to vector using tracing. To practice importing an animated GIF file, try exercise 7-2.

 NOTE: *Adobe Photoshop does not deal well with animated GIFs. If you need to create or modify an animated GIF, use Macromedia Fireworks.*

Exercise 7-2: Importing an Animated GIF

CD-ROM NOTE: *Open a new Flash file and import the file* mohler.gif, *located in the* fgai/chapter07/ *folder, installed from the companion CD-ROM.*

Note that when you import the animated GIF multiple images are added to the library and the timeline is constructed to represent the timing from the animated GIF.

Standard GIF Files

Standard GIF files do not necessarily provide any major benefits over the use of PNGs, except that it is nice to be able to import GIF files so that you can either do tracing on them or at least use preexisting content. In general, the biggest limitation of GIF (as well as animated GIF) files is the fact that they are limited to 8-bit (256-color) data. Thus, GIF graphics often look "lower quality" because they do not represent gradations or photorealistic data well. However, for abstract or simplified graphics, they are an adequate medium. To practice importing a GIF file, try exercise 7-3.

Exercise 7-3: Importing a GIF File

 CD-ROM NOTE: *Open a new Flash file and import the file* circle.gif, *located in the* fgai/chapter07/ *folder, installed from the companion CD-ROM.*

Note that when you import the GIF the image has an antialias halo due to the fact that transparency in a GIF file is 1-bit.

 NOTE: *Another limit of GIF files is that their transparency is 1-bit, meaning that a transparent color is either 100-percent opaque or 100-percent transparent. There is no "gradation" of transparency in GIF files. Thus, if you need transparency, use PNG.*

Typically all you will use GIF files for is to get already existing data into Flash. If you have a choice for storing your data, you should generally choose PNG when Flash is the authoring tool. In other scenarios, other formats may be most appropriate, but PNG is absolutely the best choice for bitmaps you intend on using in Flash.

JPEG (Not!)

One important thing to realize is that JPG is probably the worst choice you could make for importing data into Flash, or for just about anything else except placing images on an HTML web page. The reason for this is because of the way its compression works; that is, the fact that it is lossy. The color data in a JPG file is always shifted from the original, thus the reason you can never get a JPG image to match the HTML (hex-defined) background color (or any other color, for that matter) of a web page. There is always color degradation in a JPG image.

Beyond that reason, JPGs are also a poor choice for importing data into Flash because Flash can also compress using JPG. Case in point: you create a JPG image. When you do, you degrade the color in the file when you compress it and thus color shifting occurs in the image. You import the file into Flash and choose to compress it again with JPG compression in Flash, which shifts the colors even more and degrades the image even more. Thus, when you recompress JPG data a second time with the JPG compressor, you degrade an image a second time and you decrease the effectiveness of the JPG compressor in Flash.

In short, never use JPG to transfer data into Flash. It is okay to use JPG compression on a bitmap that has never been compressed with JPG. That is, it is fine to import a PNG (which is lossless compressed) and then compress it with JPG. However, when you have a choice, do not choose JPG for anything other than placing a photo or other image into an HTML web page.

Treatment of an Image Series

A final note about Flash and its treatment of imported bitmaps is that it supports the import of a series of images. For example, if you have a series of bitmaps you wish to use as a small, raster-based animation, Flash will automatically recognize them as an animation if they are named sequentially. As long as the files reside in the same folder and have file names that end with a sequence of numbers (such as *myfile001*, *myfile002*, and so on), Flash will import the series automatically and will place them into consecutive frames if you are using the File | Import option.

Setting Default Properties in the Library

Once you imported a bitmap into Flash, you can set the default compression options for the bitmap symbol using the library. Double clicking on the bitmap symbol's icon in the library opens the Bitmap Properties dialog box, shown in figure 7-6. This dialog box allows you to set the compression type, as well as smoothing.

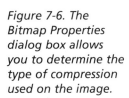

Figure 7-6. The Bitmap Properties dialog box allows you to determine the type of compression used on the image.

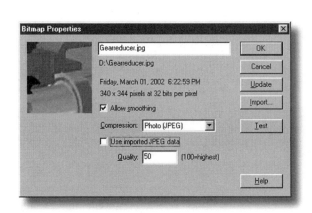

Compression

Flash provides two types compression you can apply to your images: lossy and lossless. The lossy compression used in Flash is based on JPEG, whereas the lossless compression option is based on the Lepel-Ziv (LZ) family of compressors.

Experimenting with Compression

The compressibility of any raster graphic is determined by the amount of repetitive colors within the image. The greater the quantity of repetitive colors, the more the file can be compressed. Often, the best way to determine the appropriate type and, in the case of JPEG, quality for compression is through a little trial and error. Every image varies, and to determine the best method and quality means some experimentation.

 NOTE: *More information concerning bitmap compression settings is found in Chapter 12.*

To determine which type of compression you should use on your imported bitmaps, consider whether you need absolute clarity in an image. If an image is going to be displayed for only a short period of time (at a small size), or if you can sacrifice image quality to a certain degree, select the Lossy option from the Compression drop-down list. Otherwise, select Lossless. Remember that Flash file size, performance, and playback speed may be dramatically impacted by the choice of Lossless or Lossy.

 TIP: *If you need a high-quality image, you may be able to still use lossy (as it will almost always result in better performance). Try selecting the Lossy option and then using a high quality (80 to 100) when you output the file.*

When you select the Lossy option, you can choose to either set the quality (amount of data loss) when you output the web-ready SWF file (when you are done with your movie) or set the quality in the Bitmap Properties dialog box by deselecting the User document default quality. Note that in figure 7-6 the checkbox has been deselected and thus the Quality field appears.

Smoothing

In addition to the Compression drop-down list (shown in figure 7-6), note the Allow Smoothing option. The smoothing option lets Flash attempt to make the image look better by slightly blurring the image. This is most often necessary if you scale a bitmap image in Flash; something the author has not recommended. However, if for some reason you must scale a bitmap image in Flash, or if you know that the movie may be dynamically scaled by the end user at runtime, you may want to select the Allow Smoothing option so that Flash will smooth the scaled image.

 TIP: *When animating a bitmap as part of a movie, such as making a bitmap scoot across the screen, turn off smoothing for better playback.*

▪▪▪ Using Bitmaps in Flash

Once you have imported a bitmap into Flash and have set its properties in the library, you can then utilize it on the stage in a couple of ways. The following sections describe the ways in which you can use a bitmap, once imported.

 NOTE: *Once a bitmap is imported, you can use the Free Transform tool or any of the transformation capabilities on it.*

Tracing Bitmaps

The Trace Bitmap feature allows you to convert bitmaps to a vector representation. As with all raster-to-vector processes, it is not perfect. Most often, the best representation results in an image with a watercolor-type look. However, by tracing a bitmap instead of allowing the bitmap to remain in the file, file size can often be reduced.

To use the Trace Bitmap feature, import a raster image and select it. Use the Modify | Bitmap | Trace Bitmap menu option. You will be presented with the Trace Bitmap dialog box, shown in figure 7-7. The Trace Bitmap dialog box options provide the following controls over tracing.

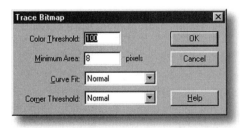

Figure 7-7. The Trace Bitmap dialog box contains features that control how bitmaps are converted to vector images.

- *Color Threshold:* Determines the overall accuracy of the tracing. It does this by comparing two pixels. If the difference between the two RGB values is less than the color threshold, Flash sees the pixels as the same color.

- *Minimum Area:* Controls the number of adjacent pixels compared at one time.

- *Curve Fit:* Specifies how smoothly outlines are drawn.

- *Corner Threshold:* Affects whether sharp edges are retained or smoothed.

TIP 1: *To get the best representation possible from the Trace Bitmap feature, use the following specifications.*

- *Color Threshold = 100*
- *Minimum Area = 1*
- *Curve Fit = Pixels*
- *Corner Threshold = Many Corners*

 TIP 2: *If you just cannot get the trace the way you want, simplify the image in Photoshop or other raster editor. You can often achieve an image that can be more successfully traced by reducing the colors (such as reducing 24-bit to 8-bit) or by simplifying the image using posterization tools.*

Original   Traced Bitmap

Figure 7-8. Example of the best-case representation of a bitmap via the Trace Bitmap command.

Although it may take a couple of iterations to get satisfying results, you may find that the Trace Bitmaps feature is a neat way of creating a custom look, as shown in figure 7-8. However, depending on the complexity of the trace and the number of tracings you do, file size may dramatically increase. File size should always be a consideration. To explore the Trace Bitmap feature, see exercise 7-4.

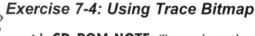
 ### Exercise 7-4: Using Trace Bitmap

CD-ROM NOTE: *To see how the Trace Bitmap feature works, open the file ch07_04.fla, located in the fgai/chapter07/ folder, installed from the companion CD-ROM.*

Use Modify | Trace Bitmap with a variety of settings to see the results.

Breaking Bitmaps Apart

When dealing with bitmaps, you can use the Modify | Break Apart menu option to sample colors from a bitmap and to use a bitmap as a fill. By breaking up an image, certain drawing tools can affect the raster image or can be used in combination with the image.

TIP: *Once a bitmap has been broken apart, you can use the Magic Wand option of the Lasso tool to quickly select adjacent color areas. Use the Magic Wand properties to adjust the sensitivity of the Magic Wand. The Threshold option controls the number of adjacent colors included in the selection, and the Smoothing option controls the roughness of the generated selection.*

When you fill a shape with a bitmap, the shape becomes what is commonly called a "clipping path." This is similar to clipping paths in Photoshop or the Paste Inside feature of FreeHand. Clipping paths show only the part of the inserted element that falls inside the closed path.

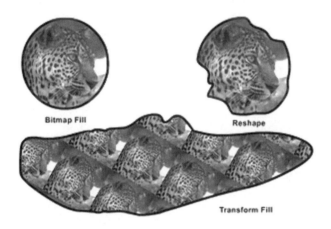

Figure 7-9. Breaking apart a bitmap allows it to be reshaped and to act as a fill.

Figure 7-9 shows an example of a bitmap that has been broken apart. Using the Dropper, the bitmap was sampled (clicked on with the Dropper) to define the bitmap as a fill. A circle was then drawn and bitmap-filled using the Paint Bucket. As the circle is reshaped, the interior image tiles and repeats within the area.

When a bitmap fill is stretched, the image automatically tiles across the fill area. Use the Transform Fill modifier of the Paint Bucket to rotate or scale the image, just as if it were a solid or gradient fill.

 TIP: *One of the noteworthy features of Flash is pixel-level snapping, which allows you to align vector elements more precisely with bitmap elements. Note that a bitmap does not have to be broken before you can use pixel-level snapping. Simply use View | Snapping | Snap to Pixels to turn on pixel-level snapping.*

▪ ▪ ▪ Notes Concerning Bitmaps

In conclusion, keep the following points in mind.

- Once a bitmap has been broken apart, you may use the Dropper to sample the bitmap for use as a fill with the other Flash tools.
- Bitmaps pasted from other applications are generally embedded.

You must break them apart to use them.

- When you import a bitmap, it is defined as a symbol. If you trace and then delete the bitmap, you must make sure you also delete the symbol.

- Ultimately, bitmaps should be used sparingly. If you decide to use a bitmap in Flash, make it as small as possible. On the Web, file size is the biggest limitation to their use.

Summary

In this chapter you have examined the various aspects of preparing and using raster graphics in Flash. Again, the primary format you should use for bitmaps you intend on bringing into Flash is the PNG format. The PNG format provides some special capabilities, which you read about in this chapter. In the next chapter, you will examine sound elements that, like bitmaps, are automatically stored in the library.

8

Sound Elements

▪ ▪ ▪ Introduction

When reviewing various sites, particularly those with dynamic Flash elements, you will find that sound is a vitally important part of the sensory experience. If you strip a site of its audio, something is noticeably missing. Music and other auditory elements added to any visual media engage both sides of the brain and give the audience a true multisensory experience.

Flash provides an advanced way of working with sound. For example, you can effortlessly insert short beeps and whistles associated with buttons in movies. Adding simple sounds to various states of a button is very easy. By using movie clips, you can also create complex music tracks that can be overlaid and controlled from the main movie timeline, just like any other movie clip. You can create sophisticated sound-based movie clips, just as complex hierarchical movie clip structures can be created with graphical data. Although beyond the scope of this book, ActionScript also provides advanced capabilities for working with sound through the Sound object.

This chapter examines the preparatory issues related to the integration of sound on the Web and the specifics of how Flash deals with and uses sound. You will learn to import sound and use the Properties panel to adjust the way the sound is played back.

▪ ▪ ▪ Objectives

In this chapter you will:

- Examine the primary issues related to computer-based audio
- Learn to sample sound from existing analog sources
- Learn to prepare sound for use on the Web
- Find out how to import various sound formats into Flash

- Discover the difference between event and streaming sounds
- Explore the options in the Properties panel that relate to sound
- Find out about compression and how it is used in Flash

▪ ▪ ▪ Understanding Computer Audio

When dealing with digital sound, developers have two options for representing and distributing audio on the Web. Much like the choice for graphics (vector and raster), audio can also be represented in one of two ways: sampled or synthesized. Sampled sound includes WAV and AIFF files and is sometimes called digitized or digital sound, whereas synthesized sound is predominantly delivered via Musical Instrument Device Interface (MIDI) files. The comparative qualities of vector and raster graphics might also be used as an analogy for the similarities and differences between synthesized and digital audio.

Types

The fundamental difference between sampled and synthesized sound is the way in which the audio is defined and played back. Any lengthy discussion of these differences requires an understanding of acoustical physics, but the basics are relatively simple.

When you create a sampled audio clip, you are engaging in the process of sampling, the conversion of analog data into a digital representation. Because audio is a time-based medium, samples (audio states at instances in time) are captured from an analog source and then described digitally. Every pitch and volume characteristic at each instance in time is descriptively written in the file as a specific decibel level. A digital audio file is a description of multiple points over time, which forms a sound curve that is approximated based on certain digital settings at the time of sampling.

Because analog data have an infinite level of descriptiveness, even the best digital recording is still only an approximation, but we can represent the totality of what the human ear can perceive. Even though the computer is limited to discrete, numerical representations, these imperfect representations are still enough for our limited receptors. That is, there is a point at which we usually do not notice missing data. Therefore, the sampled points describe instances in time at regular intervals, as shown in figure 8-1.

Synthesized sound (MIDI files), on the other hand, describes audio much differently. Instead of describing the audio as digitized instances of time, at some base level, MIDI describes the various notes and instruments that should play at any given time. The MIDI description can also contain

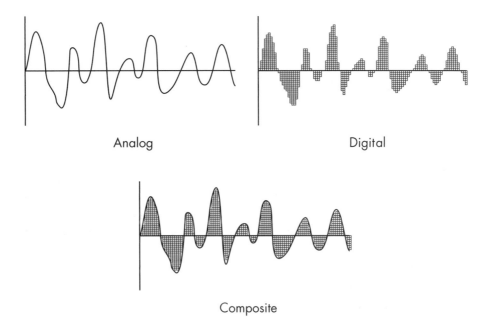

Analog   Digital

Composite

Figure 8-1. The digital representation is only an approximation of the original analog audio clip, yet it is enough to sound perfect to the human ear.

information such as sets of notes that should get louder or softer, as well as special effects such as distortion.

A special chip called a synthesis chip on the computer's sound card then interprets this description. The sound card generates the recreated sound in real time (synthesis). Because MIDI is actually recreating the described audio (rather than playing back a recording), MIDI audio frequently sounds "fake" or "counterfeit" when played back through a "stock" computer sound card.

 NOTE: *Because Flash cannot use MIDI sound, it will not be discussed further. Flash can only use digital audio. However, note that the* < EMBED > *HTML tag can be used to integrate MIDI files directly into a web page.*

Sampling Rate

To create digital audio, an analog source such as a cassette tape or CD-ROM can be used. When the analog audio is sampled, specific, equidistant intervals over time are captured and digitally recorded. The regularity of these capture points is called the sampling rate, measured in hertz (Hz) or kilohertz (kHz). The higher the sampling rate, the denser the number of captured points and thus the more accurate or detailed the description of the audio. In simple terms, sampling rate affects the accuracy or clarity of a sampled sound.

Figure 8-2 shows an example of three captures using three different sampling rates. Note that the highest sampling rate shown, 44 kHz, is extremely detailed (darker/denser) compared to the lowest sample, 11 kHz. As logic dictates, a higher sampling rate results in a larger digital file, but a higher-quality clip.

Sounds that have a sampling rate of 44 kHz are said to be "CD quality." Most audio CDs use 44 kHz because this captures all sounds perceivable to the human ear (22.1 kHz to 20 Hz). When you capture sounds or obtain them from stock galleries or other usable sources, they are often "CD quality."

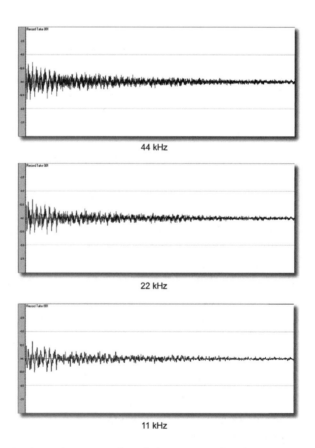

Figure 8-2. These three samples of the same audio clip were captured at different sampling rates.

However, seldom will you use 44-kHz sounds in web-ready Flash files. Due to the amount of detail in these files, you will generally down-sample these files to either 22 kHz or 11 kHz using a sound software program, so that they are adequate in size for web delivery. Down-sampling to 22 kHz reduces data by one-half and provides adequate quality for music. Down-sampling to 11 kHz reduces the file size to one-quarter, but is the lowest resolution for accurate voice transmission. Consequently, 11 kHz does not provide adequate quality for music. Typically music at this resolution has a lot of "metallic" noise within it.

 TIP: *A frequently employed alternative is to import high-quality sound files into your Flash file and then down-sample the sounds when you generate your SWF files using Export Movie or Publish commands.*

As the sampling rate of any digital audio clip decreases, the accuracy of the clip lessens. Because the sampling rate increases the amount of time between captures, certain high and low frequencies are lost in the sample. As the distance between samples becomes greater (a lower sampling rate), more and more frequencies are lost. This is how sampling rate affects the quality of a digital audio clip.

When working with sound on the computer, you must understand how sampling rate affects the clips you play back in Flash. Flash allows you to import and export 44-kHz sound files with movies. However, this is not efficient. Most computer speakers are not able to use or play back all of that data, even though it may exist in the sound clip. Additionally, the size of 44-kHz sound files will drastically increase the size of your files. Generally, use 22-kHz or 11-kHz sound files in Flash. Employ a sound program, such as Sound Forge or Bias Peak (or even a basic sound program such as Sound Recorder in Windows) to down-sample your files.

Export Movie in Flash's File menu allows you to adjust the sampling rate settings when generating web-ready SWF files. However, it may still be preferable to down-sample the files before importing them into Flash so that your native FLA files are smaller. You might import 22-kHz sound files into Flash if that is the highest rate any of your sounds will have on the Web. However, if you are designing Flash files for CD-ROM delivery, 44 kHz may be acceptable. Use your best judgment and plan for the medium you intend to use for delivery.

 NOTE: *Chapter 12 explores varying sound quality while using Export Movie.*

Bit Depth

In addition to sampling rate, digital audio has one other attribute that affects the sampled clip. At each captured instance in a digital audio clip, the computer must represent the captured point's amplitude using bits and bytes. The more bits the computer can use to represent the "snapshot" of amplitude at that point in time the greater the degree of descriptiveness of that point. The number of bits the computer can use to describe any point (instance in time) is called bit depth. As it relates to audio, bit depth controls the fidelity of the sound clip.

If a visual comparison were made between representations of the same audio clip at 16 bits and 8 bits, you would see that the 16-bit file has a greater range of amplitudes, as shown in figure 8-3. Thus, bit depth affects a digital audio clip's dynamic range, which is the range between the loudest and softest audible level. The greater the bit depth, the larger the dynamic range and the more realistic (higher fidelity) the sound.

NOTE: *Sampling rate and bit depth are independent of each other. However, they can affect each other. For example, an audio clip sampled with a high sampling rate and saved at a low bit depth may sound poor, even though it was sampled high.*

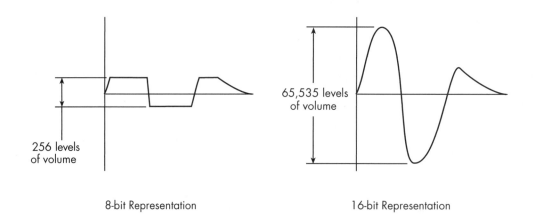

256 levels of volume

8-bit Representation

65,535 levels of volume

16-bit Representation

Figure 8-3. 8-bit and 16-bit sound clips have different levels of descriptiveness.

Sampling for Flash

For the sake of smaller file sizes, always try to use the lowest sampling rate and bit depth required for adequate presentation. Table 8-1 shows file size at various sampling rates and bit depths. As you can see, the higher the quality of sound the greater the file size. Also note the file size commonalities among the various combinations of sampling rate, bit depth, and channels.

Table 8-1: File Sizes per Sampling Rate and Bit Depth

Sampling Rate	Bit Depth	Channels	File Size per 30 Seconds (MB)
44	16	Stereo	5.156
44	16	Mono	2.578
44	8	Stereo	2.578
44	8	Mono	1.289
22	16	Stereo	2.578
22	16	Mono	1.289
22	8	Stereo	1.289
22	8	Mono	.644
11	16	Stereo	1.289
11	16	Mono	.644
11	8	Stereo	.644
11	8	Mono	.322

 TIP: *To calculate the file size of an uncompressed audio clip, use the following equation: File Size in KB = Length of Clip * Number of channels * Sampling rate * bit depth / 8. To determine size in megabytes, divide size in kilobytes by 1,024 (not 1,000).*

When working with files for multimedia, the most common sampling rate is 22 kHz, and the most common bit depth is 16 bits. Variation from these norms depends on the content being recorded or played back, as well as the expectations of the audience. Generally, music with many midtones may be adequately represented with 11 kHz, 8-bit. However, music with many highs or lows may not work well with these settings. Additionally, voice-over usually requires 22 kHz, 16-bit due to its dynamic qualities. Be prepared to do some "trial-and-error" work as you are learning what sampling rate and bit depth work best.

This discussion of audio attributes has purposely ignored multichannel sounds. When you record audio, there are usually two tracks: one for the left speaker and one for the right. You should avoid using multichannel sounds due to their impact on the size of your Flash files. Most sound programs can generate a single channel file from a multichannel file. If you want to incorporate special effects, such as panning from left to right or only playing on one speaker, you should use Flash's "effects" capability to achieve this. The Properties panel offers this capability in the Effects drop-down menu, discussed later in this chapter.

▪ ▪ ▪ Sampling Digital Audio

Sampling audio on your PC or Mac is a relatively easy task, assuming you have a sound card that has an input jack and an appropriate software package. Most PCs and Macs have some type of system software that allows you to sample audio. However, the limits of what you can do are dependent on the utility. Regardless, you should be able to record and manipulate simple clips for use in Flash using what you have.

Tools for Editing and Creation

If you are looking for products to purchase for editing sound, programs such as Sound Forge for the PC or Bias Peak for the Macintosh are efficient for preparing audio for the Web. Although there are myriad packages available, these two products are likely to give you the most for your money. They are excellent for creating special effects. Nevertheless, the following are programs you may want to look into.

- Windows tools:

    — Sonic Foundry Sound Forge (*www.sonicfoundry.com*)

    — Syntrillium Cool Edit (*www.syntrillium.com*)

    — Sonic Foundry Acid (*www.sonicfoundry.com*).

- Macintosh tools:

    — Bias Peak (*www.bias-inc.com*)

    — TCWorks Spark (*www.tcworks.de*)

    — MOTU Digital Performer (*www.motu.com*)

Recording Your Own Clips

The basic scenario for sampling audio is connecting an analog device such as a microphone, tape recorder, or other device to your computer. You will find that a microphone generally gives you the poorest results, particularly if it came with your machine. If you want to do serious microphone sound recordings, invest in a better microphone.

Copyright

If you want to record audio using a tape recording or an audio CD-ROM, do not forget about copyright considerations. Although computers make it easy to use digitized elements, copyright issues are always a concern. Just because the musical score for a particular song may not have a copyright (or has a copyright that has expired) does not mean you can record it and use it for free. More than likely the composer and the group or individual performing the piece have certain rights. Often musical arrangements have multiple copyright considerations, including ownership of the musical score and the rights the individual(s) performing it. Make sure you have the right to use any audio (or other media elements for that matter) you plan to employ.

Sampling Audio

To sample audio from a device such as a tape recorder or stereo, you need to interconnect the two devices so that the device is playing through the sound card of the computer. Find the output jack on the back of the sound card to see what type of jack it is. Most often, it is a patch-type connector. Figure 8-4 shows an example of the three main types of connectors: 1/4-inch patch, 1/8-inch patch, and RCA connector.

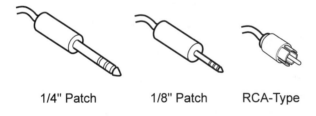

1/4" Patch   1/8" Patch   RCA-Type

Figure 8-4. Various types of audio connections can be found on the back of a sound card or device.

Next, examine the device from which you are recording. Look for a line-out connector. If none exists, you can use a headphone jack. Obtain a patch cable with the proper connectors for your card and device. These can usually be purchased for very little money at a local electronics store. The objective is to have a cable and an established connection between your device and card. The following are guidelines for digitizing audio.

- Begin by checking the settings for the audio levels on the computer. Often, there are separate audio levels for the master volume, line in, CD-ROM, line out, and any other connections for the sound card. Set the volume of these to 50 percent if possible. Then, the volume can be controlled using the device's volume adjuster.

- Before playing any sound from the device, make sure the device volume level is on zero. Insert a tape or other medium. Let it start playing. Then, increase the device volume to 1. This keeps you from overloading, blowing, or getting deafening feedback from the computer's speakers.

- Take a look within your recording software to see if adjustments can be made to the recording level. Both Sound Forge and Bias Peak provide a monitor level indicator, which is similar to a recording level indicator on a home stereo. If your software has monitor level indicators, as the audio plays through the card you will see the LEDs light up. You want the audio volume level to average at the lowest yellow. However, if the audio peaks in the red as it is playing, that is okay. You just do not want it to remain there for lengthy periods.

- When sampling audio, you are usually only able to record as much audio as you have disk space or memory. Some audio packages allow you to record only in RAM memory. Others write the audio directly to the hard disk during recording. Before purchasing any package, make sure it can record audio directly to the hard disk. If it cannot, you will be able to record only a couple of minutes of audio at a time. Both Sound Forge and Bias Peak allow you to record as much as you can store on your hard disk.

- Strive to sample your audio at the highest quality possible, such as 44 kHz, 16-bit, stereo. You can down-sample from this high-quality digital source before importing into Flash. If you have Sound Forge or Bias Peak, having a digital source file at the highest quality allows you to manipulate it by adjusting the lows or highs. You can also do a number of other things, such as adding reverb or tremolo and adjusting EQ-type settings.

- Use the lowest quality sound needed in Flash. More than likely, the highest quality you should use is 22 kHz, 16-bit, mono-aural (single channel) sound clips. Lower-quality settings depend on the content of the clip itself. The only exception is if you plan to deliver your movie files via projector files on a CD-ROM. To reduce file sizes, try to deliver the lowest quality possible without degradation of the sound element.

You do not have to be an audio genius to create "hip" audio clips for your movies. Indeed, sampling clips is quite limited and often you have to be very cautious concerning copyright infringement. There are many programs that can make mixing and creating your own tracks quite effortless.

 TIP: *Programs such as Sonic Foundry's Acid are quite nice for those who know what sounds good, but are not musicians and do*

*not want to have to worry about copyrights. If you need to gener-
ate music loops and effects, this program is definitely worth the
investment.*

Prepping Clips for Use

Before moving on to the actual process of integrating sounds into Flash,
let's examine some things you should do to prepare a sound clip for use.
Some of these things relate only to sounds that have been "recorded" on
your computer, as described in the previous section. Others relate to all
sounds, including those you might generate from programs such as Acid
or that you purchase and use from stock sound CD-ROMs.

 NOTE: *Although there is variation between the capabilities of
sound programs, most include means of performing the basics discussed in the following sections. The following sections use the
Sound Forge software application in referring to components and
processes involved.*

DC Offset

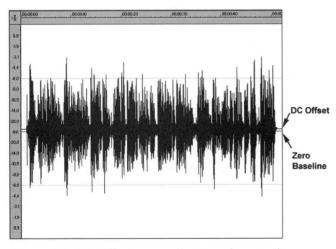

When you record audio on
the computer, either by connecting a microphone or other
device to the input line on
your sound card, the sound in
one channel or the other may
shift due to electrical mis-
matches between the input
device and the sound card.
When a DC offset occurs, the
clip is visually offset from the
zero baseline in the waveform
display on screen, as shown
in figure 8-5. Consequently, if
you try to apply effects (such
as equalization or reverb) or
other manipulations to a clip
that has DC offset, you will
often encounter glitches or
other anomalies in the audio.

*Figure 8-5. DC Offset causes the waveform to be
offset from the zero baseline. Consequently, this
can cause problems for other effects you apply to
the clip.*

When you record audio, the easiest way to visually detect if a DC offset exists is to find a place in the audio where the decibel level is zero. If

the "flat-line" that represents the audio is at the zero point, there is no DC Offset. If there is DC Offset you can select the audio channel and apply a DC Offset filter to shift the waveform into the proper location. You may have to do a little experimentation to get the clip adjusted correctly, but most packages provide "undo" features that permit this. Additionally, some sound packages can automatically detect and correct DC Offset at the click of a button.

 NOTE: *Before doing anything else to a clip, you should correct DC Offset problems first.*

Cropping

An important thing to realize about audio is that silence in an audio clip requires just as much data as the rest of the clip. Thus, once you have adjusted DC Offset, one of the first things you should do is truncate as much of the silence that occurs at the beginning and end of a file as possible. Often when you record you leave plenty of "slop" at the beginning and the end of the file as you start and stop the recording.

Once captured, you should use an audio tool to crop off extraneous silence at the beginning and end of the file. In most packages you can either select the area of the audio you want to keep and "crop" to it, or you can select the beginning silence and delete it, followed by the ending silence. The key is to remember that with audio files, silence is not golden!

Normalizing Audio

Another important modification typically made to recorded audio clips is normalization, usually listed as a Normalize command in the software. Normalization maximizes the volume of a particular clip such that the clip utilizes the entirety of the available dynamic range. In essence, normalization finds the highest volume in the clip and raises all other volumes in the clip so that there is consistency throughout the clip. This is done such that there is no clipping or distortion.

You can also use normalization to make the volume across multiple clips consistent, which is particularly important when you want to mix various clips. Typically, non-normalized clips vary in volume, both compared with one another and even within a single clip. Normalization allows you to correct for the inconsistencies in volume across clips and within clips.

A general approach to normalization (without lengthy investigation into decibel levels and the like) is to attempt to normalize a clip to somewhere between 110 and 120 percent. When you normalize to a value over

100, you are increasing amplitude (volume), as well as any distortion that already exists in the clip. Although you should try to work from a source that is as clean as possible, distortion in a source is always a possibility. If you normalize only to find distortion in the result, try undoing and then normalizing to a value between 90 and 100 percent. If you are trying to match multiple clips, once you have found an appropriate normalization level, apply that level across all clips.

Effects

Most sound packages provide a limited number of effects that can be applied to a clip. The range of effects, usually via filters, is often directly proportional to the cost of the program. Nevertheless, effects such as echo, reverb, flange, delay, and so on can be easily applied to a sound clip. Although you can do a lot of experimentation with these, reverb is specific to clips that are speech based. Often voice-overs can be greatly enhanced by using a slight amount of reverb to the voice. This provides a slightly richer narrative stream than a straight vocal tone.

Resampling

As discussed previously, clips are usually recorded at the highest quality (44 kHz, 16-bit, stereo) and then down-sampled for multimedia. If you are working with Flash movies that will be used to generate CD-ROM content, using 44 kHz, 16-bit, stereo files in Flash may be fine. However, if you are developing for the Web, using files of this quality can make your Flash FLA files quite large. Thus, it may be more effective to down-sample the clips prior to importing into Flash if you know that you will never output at the highest quality.

Most audio editors provide a Resample or Downsample command whereby you can convert a clip from its current sampling rate (resolution) to a lower setting. The best programs include an antialias option where you can have the software more smoothly extrapolate the data reduction (sometimes this happens transparently and automatically). Antialiasing an audio clip has the same effect as antialiasing a graphic. However, one is heard and the other is seen. Antialiasing "smoothes out" the roughness of the data reduction.

Equalization

Equalization is a fairly familiar concept, as most common household stereos include at least a rudimentary equalizer. Equalization allows you to intensify certain frequencies within a sound clip, as well as attenuate others. Figure 8-6 shows the equalization from Sound Forge. The range of fre-

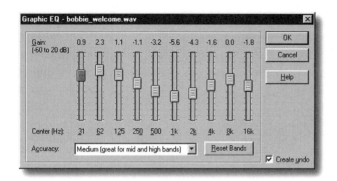

Figure 8-6. Equalization allows you to intensify or attenuate various frequencies in the sound clip.

quency control will depend on the audio program, but most give at least three to seven controls.

The thing to keep in mind about equalization as it relates to web audio is that most computer speakers are quite small and do not have a wide frequency response. Although newer computers are starting to include really nice speaker systems, the quality of the end user's speaker is not something you can assume will be consistent. More often than not end-user speakers will lack much depth of bass (or low frequencies) and will not support a lot of high frequencies either. However, most standard speakers do support the mids to highs better than they support the mids to lows (a lot of this just has to do with physical size and manufacturing quality).

 TIP: *When creating audio for the Web and for your Flash movies, it is best to have a pair of small, inexpensive speakers as well as a pair of nice speakers so that you can truly get a feel for what the range of quality will be on the user's end.*

Where equalization can be pretty effective is after you have down-sampled a clip. When you go from 44 kHz to 22 kHz (or to 11 kHz), you will notice changes in the clip. Some you may want, and others you will not. Many times down-sampling will remove high frequencies and most low frequencies, and may add a noticeable hissing or crackling to the clip. Equalization is a good way to attenuate these undesirable effects as well as add some midtones back to the clip. Poor choice for equalization can also result in "muddy sound" too, so you have to be careful how you use it. The following are some recommendations for using equalization to adjust the frequencies in a clip.

- Most computer speakers lack low-frequency response. To get a richer, deep sound, instead of increasing the low frequencies (on the left end of an EQ), boost the values in the mid-lows, such as the 125- and 250-Hz range.

- If you boost a particular frequency, you may get better results if you simultaneously decrease the adjacent frequencies.

- Increasing the 1-kHz and 2-kHz bands can significantly affect the richness of a clip, particularly if the content is narration or speech.
- If you reduce a clip to 11 kHz, very few high frequencies are left. In this case, try increasing the 4-kHz or 8-kHz bands.

Saving

The final aspect of preparing sound for use in Flash is that of saving the file. In some programs, as in Sound Forge in particular, it is when you save the file that you define the number of channels the sound will include (stereo or mono) as well as its bit depth. When the author is working on sound files for Flash, he typically uses 22 kHz, 16-bit, mono files (where only one channel is needed) or 22 kHz, 8-bit, stereo (where two channels are needed). Again, the need for multichannel files has to be considered very carefully. Out of 100 projects, you may have as few as five that truly need stereo. Of those five, three of them could likely be accomplished using Flash's ability to incorporate speaker panning or other effects.

■ ■ ■ Importing Sound into Flash

Importing and using sound in Flash is a two-step process. You begin by using File | Import to Library to add the sound to the movie's library. You can then assign that sound clip to a frame in some timeline. Sounds are always added to frames, whether in the main timeline or in a symbol.

 NOTE: *Remember that graphic symbols will not play sounds that are assigned in them.*

Concerning clip quality, Flash can import almost any sound quality. When importing sound, you can export an SWF movie for the Web with lower quality (down-sampled sounds). Thus, your native Flash files (FLA) can contain high-quality source sounds, whereas the exported movies (SWF) files can contain lower-quality sounds. If you are trying to create multiple movies appropriate for various connection speeds, the ability to store high and export low can be a useful facility.

In addition to various qualities, Flash can import a variety of file formats, including Windows Waveform (WAV), Audio Interchange File Format (AIFF), Sun audio (AU) and MP3 files. You should find that all of these formats are usable on both the Macintosh and PC versions. On either platform you should also be able to use the QuickTime 4 import option to support additional formats. However, QuickTime 4 must be installed to be able to use these types of files. For practice in importing a sound, see exercise 8-1.

 WARNING: *With all the hype concerning the MP3 audio format on the Web, including discussions of copyrights and the legalities associated with distributing them, always ensure you have the right to use any sound files you decide to integrate into your movies. Although MP3 is the format causing the biggest stir, really with any sound you want to use you need to obtain permission. Even if the source you got it from says it is "royalty-free," do your homework. Avoid litigation by covering your bases!*

Exercise 8-1: Importing Sounds into Flash

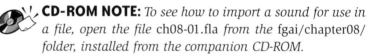

CD-ROM NOTE: *To see how to import a sound for use in a file, open the file ch08-01.fla from the* fgai/chapter08/ *folder, installed from the companion CD-ROM.*

To import a sound into file *ch08-01.fla*, perform the following steps.

1. Select File | Import to Library to reveal the Import dialog box, shown in figure 8-7.

2. Note the types of file you could import (WAV, AIF, AU, MP3, and MOV) from the Files of Type drop-down list, shown in figure 8-7. You could also use the All Sound formats to see all valid sound formats that can be imported. Select WAV, AIF, or AU from the list.

3. Find the file named beep in the *fgai/chapter08/* directory. The file extension will depend on which format you have chosen to use.

4. Double click on the file name in the window or click on the name and then on OK. Either technique adds the audio clip to the current movie's library.

5. Although you do not have to verify that it has been added to the library each time, go ahead and select Window | Library to open the library. Note that the file now exists in the library. However, it has not been assigned for use in the timeline yet.

6. Save your file.

 NOTE: *As with bitmap images, sounds you do not end up using in your movie should be removed from the current movie's library to make the native Flash file smaller.*

Figure 8-7. Select the audio file format in the Files of Type drop-down list.

One of the things you should note about the various sound formats is that there are many types of compression algorithms that can be used in them. Basic WAV and AIFF formats provide several, but the most common algorithm is PCM, which is the compression format Flash works with most easily. Therefore, if you try to import a WAV or AIFF file into Flash and it tells you it cannot read the file, convert the file to a PCM compressed WAV or AIFF file using a sound program such as Sound Forge or Bias Peak. You should then be able to import the file.

■■■ Associating Sounds with Frames

Once a sound clip has been imported into a movie, assigning it to play in a particular frame (or frame in a symbol) is a relatively easy process. In either case, the sound is assigned using the Properties panel. Exercise 8-2 takes you through the process of assigning a sound to a frame.

 TIP: *To import a sound from another library, use either the Library menu or the File | Open External Library command to open a library. With the library open, select a sound symbol from the list and click-drag from the symbol preview to the stage. This adds the sound clip to the current movie's library.*

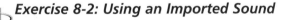

Exercise 8-2: Using an Imported Sound

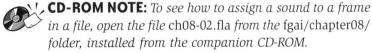 **CD-ROM NOTE:** *To see how to assign a sound to a frame in a file, open the file* ch08-02.fla *from the* fgai/chapter08/ *folder, installed from the companion CD-ROM.*

If you did the previous exercise, you could continue using that file. In this exercise, you will assign the beep sound to a button press. You do this by attaching the sound to a frame in the button symbol. All sounds are assigned to frames. To assign the sound, perform the following steps.

1. Right-click on the button on the stage and select Edit in Place from the context menu, or simply double click on the button to access its timeline.

2. Select the Down frame in the *Button* layer in the timeline.

     NOTE: *Keep in mind that sounds are attached to frames, not to symbol instances. Thus sounds are a frame property.*

3. In the Properties panel, change the Sound drop-down list to the beep sound currently in the library. For now, do not worry about the other options that become available when you select beep from the drop-down list.

4. Click on Scene 1 in the Edit path to return to the main time-line.

5. Save the file.

6. Select Control | Enable Simple Buttons to enable the button.

7. Click on the Play button to verify that the sound does play.

Instead of Enable Simple Buttons, you could have used Test Movie. If you use Test Movie and the sounds are played back poorly, change the audio settings in the File | Publish Settings dialog box. Select the Flash tab and use the Audio Stream | Event Set buttons to set the properties. The Publish Settings dialog box affects all output SWF files, including those from Control | Test Movie as well as from the File | Export Movie menu option. Note that most of the sounds integrated into the sample FLA files on the companion CD-ROM are at 22 kHz, 16-bit, mono.

 NOTE: *The Publish Settings dialog box is discussed in Chapter 12.*

When you assigned the sound in the exercise, you probably noticed the other options that were available in the Properties panel. The following sections describe the various options found there. Often the default values may work, particularly if you are using short sounds associated with user-initiated events. However, more complex creations will require adjustment of the optional settings in the Properties panel.

▪ ▪ ▪ Synchronization of Graphics and Audio

Before looking at the other options in the Properties panel, you need to know about one other important thing: synchronization of graphics and audio. Exact synchronization of specific graphic components on the stage with lengthy sound components is a difficult task. Often it is impossible to get timing exactly right on every machine, given the wide performance differences that can exist on playback machines. The playback speed of Flash movies is highly dependent on the delivery computer, particularly that computer's video card. Let's look at this a little more closely.

Sound is a time-based medium, whereas the graphical components in Flash movies are frame based. This means that a sound must play consistently over time (time being a constant), regardless of machine performance. When you insert a sound in Flash, the sound will play consistently on every machine on which you play it. Unlike some digital video formats, AVI specifically, Flash does not drop portions of the sound if machine performance degrades. Thus, sound will always play back consistently.

However, the playback of graphical components is not based on a constant, per se. The number of frames played back (per second) in a Flash movie varies depending on the performance of the playback machine. Thus, if sound and graphics are in a movie at the same time and the performance of the machine degrades, the sound will remain constant, whereas the graphic playback (number of frames played per second, or fps) will vary. In this scenario, sound clips will be heard before their screen counterparts are visible.

On machines that are faster than the development machine, graphics may occur on time or before they are needed. This is always the most troublesome aspect of creating synchronized graphics and audio in Flash. You will find that the human senses are somewhat forgiving. That is, you may notice a lapse (because you have seen it a hundred or so times on your machine timed just right as you were developing it), but someone else may not notice this. There is a "sweet spot" at which people viewing your work will not notice the lag, but it is generally less than a second.

However, all is not lost. Flash does offer some basic options for keeping synchronization somewhat consistent. It is not 100-percent exact, however. If you are used to the relative preciseness of tools such as Director, you will find that Flash is not quite as accurate. But consistency is a relative term and depends greatly on the performance difference between the development machine and the playback machine. Nonetheless, the Properties panel provides several options, as discussed in the following section.

▪ ▪ ▪ Sound Settings in the Properties Panel

Once you select a sound from the Sound drop-down in the Properties panel, Flash displays the attributes of the sound clip below the Sound drop-down menu. Sampling rate (22 kHz), number of channels (mono), bit depth (16 bit), length (0.3s), and file size (15.2 kB) are all presented, as shown in figure 8-8. You also have several options within the Properties panel. The following sections discuss how each of these settings (Edit, Effect, Sync, and Loops) affects the playback of sound.

Figure 8-8. The Properties panel offers several optional settings that affect the playback of the clip.

Sync: Event Versus Streaming Sounds

The single most important sound setting in the Properties panel is the Sync drop-down. Within Flash, two types of sounds exist: event and streaming. The primary difference between these two types is that event sounds must be entirely downloaded before they can play, whereas streaming sounds can begin playing before they are entirely downloaded.

There is also a significant difference between these options concerning playback. Streaming sounds can be synchronized (at least as closely as possible in Flash) with the timeline. Event sounds, once started, play independently of the timeline. Let's examine these a little further.

Event Sounds

An event sound plays when the keyframe to which it is attached is encountered. Once the keyframe is encountered, the sound plays in its entirety. If a sound is set to repeat or loop, the looped sound continues to play even if the movie is stopped. Additionally, if the frame the event sound is attached to is encountered several times, multiple instances of the sound will play. The Start option in the Sync list is similar to the Event option except that only a single instance of the sound will play, even if the frame is encountered several times. To examine these options, try exercise 8-3.

Exercise 8-3: Event Versus Start Sync Options

 CD-ROM NOTE: *To hear the difference between the Event and Start options, open and play the file ch08-03.fla, located in the* fgai/chapter08/ *folder, installed from the companion CD-ROM.*

Select Test Movie to hear the difference.

The Stop Sync option found in the Sync drop-down allows you to stop individual sounds. For example, if you have several sounds playing, each based on a different sound symbol, you can use Stop Sync to stop an individual sound clip.

 TIP: *Most often, the Event and Start options are best for short sounds, such as a click for a button or other brief segments.*

Streaming Sounds

Streaming sounds, as opposed to event sounds, do not have to be fully downloaded before they start playing. They begin playing almost immediately because the sound is divided into chunks that coincide with frames in the movie, a process called interleaving, which is much like digital video formats such as QuickTime (MOV) or Video for Windows (AVI).

Streaming clips allow you to begin playing a sound clip immediately, and provide the most accurate means of timing graphical components with sound in Flash. One negative aspect to streaming sounds is that if the download stream lags the sound may stop playing until the next portion of sound data reaches the playback computer. However, this type of problem can be overcome through the use of preloading sequences. To practice using streaming sounds, try exercise 8-4.

Exercise 8-4: Using Streaming Sounds

 CD-ROM NOTE: *To see (and hear) an example created using the Stream option, open the file ch08-04.fla, located in the* fgai/chapter08/ *folder, installed from the companion CD-ROM.*

This file is rather large due to the music clip used within it. Thus, it would need quite a bit of optimizing before it would be ready for the Web.

Effect

The Properties panel includes several common special effects that may be quickly assigned to a sound clip. Earlier it was suggested that you do not import multichannel sounds because you can do this within Flash. This is what the Effect drop-down allows. Within Flash, you can quickly create fade-ins and fade-outs at the beginning and ending of your clips, as well as speaker panning. The effects in the drop-down are as follows.

- *Left Channel:* Plays the entire sound in the left speaker channel.
- *Right Channel:* Plays the entire sound in the right speaker channel.
- *Fade Left to Right:* Makes the sound pan from the left speaker to the right speaker.
- *Fade Right to Left:* Makes the sound pan from the right speaker to the left speaker.
- *Fade In:* Sets up the beginning of the sound so that it fades in.
- *Fade Out:* Automatically fades out the end of the sound.
- *Custom:* Allows you to create your own custom effect by click-dragging the volume control using the Edit button.

When you select one of the effects from the Sound panel, the sound-editing controls of the clip are modified. The sound-editing controls are accessible via the Edit button, found in the Properties panel (see figure 8-8).

Edit (Envelope)

If you apply an effect to a clip, or if you want to create your own custom effect, you click on the Edit button in the Properties panel. When you click on the Edit button, you are presented with the Edit Envelope window, in which you can use the sound-editing controls to apply volume changes to the clip, as shown in figure 8-9. These controls allow you to define a volume, per left and right speakers, as well as control how much of the clip is played.

To adjust the volume of either speaker, click-drag the volume controls in the window, shown in figure 8-9. By adding multiple points within the Preview window, fade-in and fade-out effects within the window are created, as shown in figure 8-10. If you were to select Fade In or Fade Out from the Effect drop-down, a similar set of points would be created for you automatically at the beginning or ending of a clip. Fade-ins and fade-outs on a single clip must be manually created.

To control clipping, in other words how long the clip plays, click-drag the In or Out points as needed. This allows you to play only a specified portion of a clip, even though the entire clip exists in memory. Note that even if you use clipping the entire sound clip will be output in the resulting SWF. Thus, it would be more effective to edit the clip in a sound editor and import only the part you need.

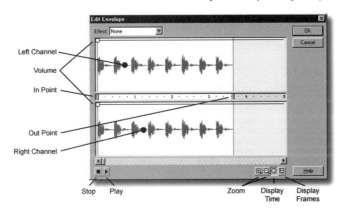

Figure 8-9. The sound-editing controls are accessed via the Edit Envelope window.

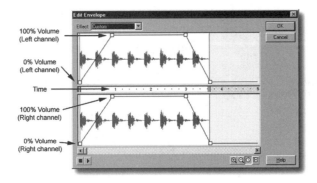

Figure 8-10. By setting the volume in both channels from 0 to full and full to 0 creates a fade-in and fade-out.

Located below the Preview window are controls for playing and stopping the sound, in addition to zoom controls and display options, as shown in figure 8-9. The Display Frames button is helpful when you are trying to synchronize a sound clip with specific graphical components in specific frames. Additionally, you normally use it with streaming sounds only, not event sounds, because only streaming sounds are "timed" or synchronized with the timeline. When you click on this button, the Preview window shows the sound clip in relation to the current frames. The Display Time button, the default, shows the length of the sound clip in relation to time.

When you select the Display Frames button, the playback speed is assumed to be the currently set frame rate (as defined in the Modify | Movie dialog box). Thus, the sound clip is displayed against the current frames, based on the movie frame rate. Yet, remember that sound is time based and will play consistently. The frame rate will vary, depending on the complexity of elements being displayed and the speed of the computer on which it is being played.

Although you can use the Display Frames button to help you synchronize audio and graphics, it is not 100-percent accurate. The best-case scenario when designing movies is to try to shoot for a target machine.

Then, test, test, and test some more on both faster and slower machines. In reality, there is no way of creating an audio and graphics presentation for the Web using Flash that is 100-percent the same on every computer. Machine performance, at least as far as video cards are concerned, varies too greatly. The only thing you can do is shoot for the middle 50 percent of the audience. They are more alike than they are different.

 TIP: *To remove a previously assigned sound from a frame, select the frame and use the Sound panel. Set the Sound drop-down list to None. If the sound is no longer being used, do not forget to delete it from the movie's library as well.*

Looping and Repeating

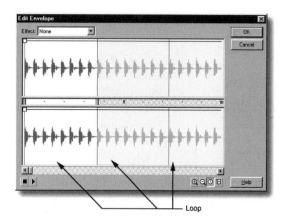

Figure 8-11. Repeats are displayed within the Edit Envelope window as grayed repetitions of the original.

Often you will want a sound to repeat a specific number of times, or at times ad infinitum. Thus, the small drop-down menu to the right of the Sync drop-down allows you to establish the sound as repeating a certain number of times or as looping infinitely. The maximum number of repeats is 999. Greater numbers entered in the repeat field may cause unexpected results.

As you increase the number of repeats, the Edit Envelope window shows the repetitions of the clip. If you switch the Preview window to Display by Frames, you can see an approximation of how long the looping sound will play, as shown in figure 8-11.

∎ ∎ ∎ Flash Sound Settings

When you import a sound clip for placement into a movie, you can control the sound's default sampling rate and compression. Additionally, sound settings exist within the Publish Settings dialog box, in which you can override the default settings that exist in the library.

Both of these options are helpful when creating multiple versions of files for delivery to various connection speeds. In addition, when trying to optimize file size, the ability to control sound quality is important. As it relates to file size, more than any other elements, bitmaps and sound drastically affect file size. Flash provides tremendous flexibility as you prepare movies for the Web or other means by allowing modification of the output quality of sound clips.

 NOTE: *To examine issues surrounding optimization as they relate to sounds, see Chapter 12.*

Library Sound Properties

For each sound imported into your movie, default quality settings can be established, which are very similar to those identified for bitmaps discussed in the last chapter. As with bitmaps, sound clips are automatically added to the movie's library when you import them. The default quality settings take effect when the movie is exported. However, they can also be overridden when you export the SWF. For example, if you have a music clip that needs to have relatively high quality, combined with snippets and effects of lower quality, you can set these defaults in the current movie's library. Exercise 8-5 explores sound properties in the library.

 Exercise 8-5: Sound Settings in the Library

 CD-ROM NOTE: *To learn about the library properties, open the file* ch08-05.fla, *located in the* fgai/chapter08/ *folder, installed from the companion CD-ROM.*

To set the default sampling rate and compression for a sound clip in Flash, perform the following steps.

1. Select Window | Library to access the current movie's library.

2. Find one of the sound clips in the symbol list and double click on its icon to open the Sound Properties dialog box.

3. In the dialog box shown in figure 8-12, set the Compression option as desired. As different options are selected in the

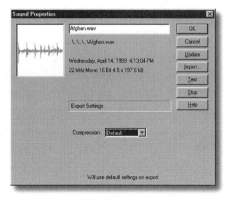

Figure 8-12. The Sound Properties dialog box, accessed via the library, allows you to set the default compression settings for the sounds in your movie.

Compression drop-down, other related options will be shown. The settings established in the dialog box will be used as the default when the movie is exported (assuming you do not override them in the Publish Settings, Publish, or Export Movie operations).

In the dialog box shown in figure 8-12, aside from the OK, Cancel, and Help buttons you see four buttons that can be very helpful when working in the library. The Test and Stop buttons allow you to test the sound clip while in the Sound Properties dialog box with the current settings. This is a nice method of hearing what the clip will sound like without having to jump out and use Test Movie or the other means of generating an SWF file.

The other two buttons are also helpful. The Import button allows you to replace the current sound with another sound, and the Update button allows you to automatically update the sound. The Update button is nice if you are working with a group of developers. Assuming the sound file resides in a shared area and was imported from that storage location, you can make changes to the external sound file and then click on the Update button to update the version in the Flash file. This allows you to work with "in-progress" sound clips.

Compression Options

Flash offers three types of sound compression: linear (RAW), Speech (ADPCM), and MP3. The Default option is equivalent to no compression. If you plan to determine sound output settings when you generate your SWF files, you can leave the Sound Properties option in the library set to Default and then set the properties when you output your SWF files.

The Raw option provides no real compression for your sound clips and is the default. When you select Raw from the Compression drop-down, you have control over the sampling rate and the number of channels in the sound. The Raw option simply inserts the sound into Flash files as raw clips defined in AIFF format.

 NOTE: *One of the things you should notice as you are selecting different compression types is that the Sound Properties dialog box indicates the properties of the clip at the bottom of the dialog box. When selecting compressors, of particular interest is the percentage shown at the end. This shows how much you are reducing the clip by the options you are selecting.*

The Speech compressor is specifically designed for voice-overs and narration. It provides several sampling rates for output, including 5, 11, 22, and 44 kHz. Although you may want to test the various settings with a particular clip, 11 kHz is a good general setting for applications.

When the ADPCM compressor is selected, you can set the sample rate and the bit rate of the clip (see figure 8-13). You have already seen (and heard) in previous examples how sampling rate affects an audio clip. The bit rate option controls the amount of compression applied to the clip. The lowest compression setting is 2 bits, and the highest is 5 bits. The result of the compression applied during export will depend on the similarity of amplitudes within the sound clip, much like the fact that the compression of a bitmap is based on the similarity of pixels in the image. More than likely, testing will be necessary to determine the best bit rate (compression) using ADPCM.

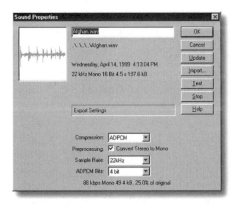

Figure 8-13. The options provided when ADPCM is selected from the compression drop-down list include sampling rate, ADPCM bits, and pre-processing.

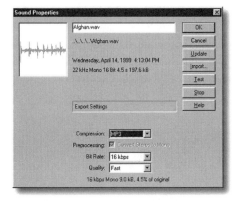

Figure 8-14. Selecting MP3 compression provides control over preprocessing, bit rate and quality.

The last compression option, MP3, was introduced in Flash 4 and has taken the Web by storm. No doubt you have heard of the many copyright concerns regarding the MP3 format expressed by the recording industry, as well as its capabilities for compressing audio for end users. When you select the MP3 option, you can control preprocessing (channel control), bit rate, and quality, as shown in figure 8-14.

As with ADPCM compression, when you select the Convert Stereo to Mono checkbox, the sound clip is converted to a monophonic clip. One thing you should note is that if the bit rate is set too low in an MP3, stereo sound is not possible. Thus, if you select a bit rate of 16 or 8, the Convert Stereo to Mono option is automatically selected.

The Bit Rate option allows you to determine the size of the chunks of data that are compressed. Much like JPEG compression in bitmap images, ADPCM and MP3 are both lossy compression schemes. This means that they sacrifice a certain amount of data to attain higher compressibility. The amount of data loss depends on the size of the chunks of data averaged (called subsampling) and the amount of averaging that occurs (called quantization).

The bit rate option controls the subsampling, and the quality option controls the quantization. It really does not matter whether you are discussing image compression and pixels or sound compression and amplitudes. The compression schemes in both select a block of information and then average the information.

In sound clips, the size of the block selected is chosen by the bit rate option. If you choose a smaller bit rate, the block of data is smaller and the compression will be less effective. If you choose a large bit rate, the data selection is larger and the compression will be more effective, at least from a file size standpoint.

As for the Quality setting, this option controls the amount of averaging that occurs within each selected block of information. The Quality settings range from Fast to Best and also affect the speed of playback on the delivery computer.

All of this regarding subsampling and quantization really says nothing of the aural quality of the clip. Regardless of the compression and options you choose, you will inevitably have to use trial and error to determine the best compressor for the job. The reason is that the compressibility of any digital file depends on the amount of redundant data in the file. Unless you are really into the basics of repetitive amplitudes of a file and have software to do that type of analysis, your best bet is to try the various compression options to get the optimum quality-to-file-size ratio.

Export Movie Options

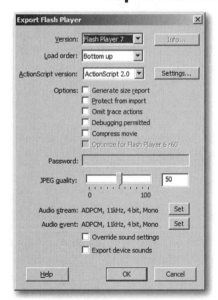

When exporting a movie to prepare it for distribution on the Web, you can assign sound compression options in File | Export Movie, as shown in figure 8-15. By default, the settings applied in this dialog box will only affect sounds that do not have properties assigned to them in the library. Sounds that already have defaults assigned to them in the library will use those settings. You can override the settings applied in the library by clicking on the Override Sound Settings checkbox. If this checkbox is selected, the settings assigned in the library will be ignored.

Flash has two means of creating movies: File | Export Movie and File | Publish. The Publish feature allows you to output the standard SWF files (as well as HTML, GIF, Projector, and QuickTime movie files), whereas Export Movie only outputs the web-ready SWF file.

Both the Export Movie and Publish menu options derive their default settings from those

Figure 8-15. The Export Movie dialog box provides the ability to override the default settings established in the library.

established within the File | Publish Settings dialog box. The Publish Settings dialog box also affects movies that are executed through the Control | Test Movie option.

 NOTE: *For more information concerning Export Movie options, see Chapter 12.*

Summary

This chapter examined the major concerns of using audio within your Flash movies. Obviously, sound is not something to ignore. In many cases, it is audio and small sound bites that complete and add interest to a site. Judiciously decide where, when, and how much sound to include. Too much sound use may make your site a bandwidth hog, whereas too little usage of sound does not satisfy the aural senses and makes the presentation boring. Synchronization is the trickiest part of sound in Flash. Allow enough time for testing when a significant amount of audio is incorporated within a movie, particularly streaming sound.

9

2D Animation and Effects

∎ ∎ ∎ Introduction

To this point we have not delved into the creation of animation, primarily because there was first a lot of ground to cover regarding media support. At this point, having examined vector, raster, and sound objects (as well as symbols and libraries), most of the introductory stuff should now be old hat and you are undoubtedly ready to get started animating.

Thus, this chapter is designed to familiarize you with the three primary types of animation Flash can create: frame-by-frame, motion tweening, and shape tweening. Many of the basic things presented in this chapter are the foundation for more complex creations. As in previous chapters, this chapter presents simpler applied examples that show concepts in the hope that the concepts are easier to grasp. Then the later part of this chapter focuses on more complex examples that show specific techniques and special effects.

∎ ∎ ∎ Objectives

In this chapter you will:

- Learn the basic concepts and principles involved in animation creation in Flash
- Discover the cel animation tools found in Flash and how you can create frame-by-frame animation
- Learn how to create motion tweens and shape tweens
- Use layer guides to create path-based animation and mask layers to create masked content

- Find out about Flash's new timeline effects
- Learn to create a variety of text effects
- Examine how you construct transitions in Flash

▪▪▪ Creating a Basic Animation in Flash

The animation examples that follow are quite simple. While continuing to build on concepts, you will learn how to create more complex animations. The first sample is the Cyber Outpost image, shown in figure 9-1. The goal of this animation is to make the words *The*, *Cyber*, and *Outpost* appear on the screen using frame-by-frame techniques. Exercise 9-1 serves as an introduction to basic animation and frame concepts.

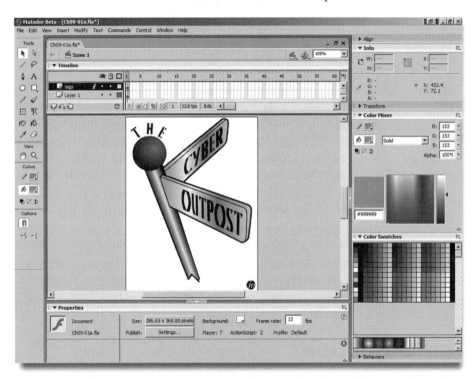

Figure 9-1. A basic example to help you get familiar with frame identifiers and frame-by-frame animation in Flash.

 Exercise 9-1: Creating a Basic Frame-by-Frame Animation

 CD-ROM NOTE: *Open the file* ch09_01a.fla, *located in the* fgai/chapter09/ *folder, installed from the companion CD-ROM.*

The image shown in figure 9-1 has already been created. Your task will be to animate it. To render your own version of the image for practice, the file *ch09_01b.fla* contains only lines. In this file, you can color your own version of the Cyber Outpost image to be animated.

 NOTE: *As you get started with this series of exercises, to simplify the explanations you will be working with grouped objects instead of symbols.*

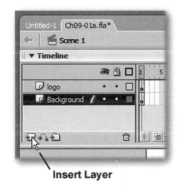

Insert Layer

Figure 9-2. Adding layers to a file is accomplished using the Insert Layer button in the timeline.

Creating Layers

In regard to exercise 9-1, upon starting the movie file, recognize that the file has a single layer and a single frame, as shown in the timeline. The text elements are broken apart and grouped. You can see this if you click on them. You want to first create some layers for each of the elements to help organize the movie. It is easier to make objects appear on the stage if they are distinguished by layer. Use the Insert Layer button to produce three more layers for a total of four, as shown in figure 9-2.

Naming Layers

Once you have some layers, you will need to name them. It is important to name layers because the more layers you get the easier it is to become confused about which object is on what layer. Rename each layer, as follows, by double clicking on the layer's name in the timeline.

- Name one layer *The*.
- Name another layer *Cyber*.
- Name the remaining layer *Outpost*.
- When you have renamed all layers, reorder them in the following order:
  — *Logo*
  — *Outpost*
  — *Cyber*
  — *The*
  — *Background*

"Moving" Objects to a New Layer

You now want to move the elements from the *Background* layer to each of the named layers you created. To do this, use the cut and paste options to move the objects from one layer to another. In exercise 9-2, which follows, you will position each object on the appropriate layer.

Exercise 9-2: Moving Elements to a New Layer

The steps that follow take you through the process of moving elements to a new layer.

1. Click on the Arrow tool. Select the The text on the stage. Frame 1 in the *Background* layer turns black, indicating that the text resides on that layer.

2. Select Edit | Cut (Ctrl + X or Command + X).

3. Click on layer The to make it the current layer. Remember that when you paste or draw, elements are placed on the current layer. Clicking on a layer makes it the current layer, as indicated by the pencil icon next to the layer.

4. Select Edit | Paste In Place (Ctrl + Shift + V or Command + Shift + V) to insert the object in the exact stage position it was cut from. If you were to use the default paste procedure (Ctrl + V or Command + V), the object would be placed in the center of the stage.

5. Repeat this process and place the *Cyber* text on the *Cyber* layer and the *Outpost* text on the *Outpost* layer.

6. After moving the objects to their appropriate layers, if it happens that the background layer is "hiding" the other layers, click-drag the *Background* layer to the bottom of the layer order so that you can see the text components in front of it.

7. Save the file, as you will continue working with it in material to follow.

In exercise 9-2, the Modify | Timeline | Distribute to Layers command was purposely not used so that you could see the effect of using the Paste In Place command. The Distribute to Layers command could have been used to quickly place each of the three objects on a separate layer. You would have selected the three objects and then used Modify | Timeline | Distribute to Layers, which would have immediately distributed the items to three new layers (you would still have had to rename the layers). Either is acceptable, but often Distribute to Layers will be quicker.

Working with Frames

With the objects already separated onto layers, the next step is to start working with frames. Working with the timeline's frames can be a little disconcerting at first. Nevertheless, once you get the hang of it, the process will become second nature. One of the first things you must understand, though, is how Flash represents the different types of frames in the timeline.

Frame Identifiers

There are five basic frame representations that can exist in the Flash timeline, as shown in figure 9-3. These frame representations clue you in to what is defined in the frame. It is important that you remember each so that you can quickly know what is defined in the timeline.

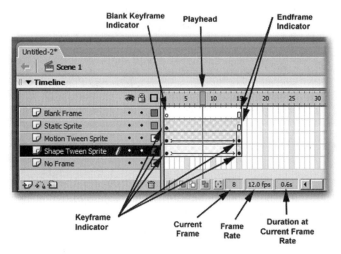

Figure 9-3. The various frame identifiers assist the user in the development and identification of frames.

As shown in figure 9-3, the first layer, named *Blank Frames*, shows the representation for a set of frames that contain no objects. When creating animations in Flash, you build the timeline from the left side using blank frames. For example, if you want an object to appear at frame 10, you insert blank frames up to frame 10 and then place a keyframe in frame 10.

The second layer shown in figure 9-3, named *Static Sprite*, shows a sprite that simply exists on the stage, beginning at frame 1 and ending at frame 15. Note that it begins with a keyframe, which is an initial definition of objects' respective locations, sizes, orientations, and colors as defined on the stage. A black circle identifies a keyframe. The sprite extends to frame 15, in which there is the endframe indicator (a small, hollow rectangle).

Sprites in the timeline are completely adjustable as far as their starting point (keyframe) and duration (endframe) are concerned. You can click-drag a keyframe to move the point at which the objects (represented by the keyframe) appear on the stage. Similarly, if you hold the Ctrl key (Command on the Mac) and click-drag the endframe indicator, it changes the duration of the sprite, which is the amount of time the objects appear on the stage.

If you click-drag the endframe indicator and do not hold Ctrl or Command, the sprite is extended, but a keyframe is placed in the last frame. Clicking on the center of a sprite selects a single frame within a sprite, and double clicking on a frame within a sprite selects the entire sprite. When an entire sprite is selected, you can click-drag it to another location in the timeline.

The third and fourth layers shown in figure 9-3 (layers named *Motion Tween Sprite* and *Shape Tween Sprite*, respectively) are the two types of tweened animation Flash can create. Notice that both types of tween sprites begin and end with a keyframe. As with static sprites, you can click-drag these keyframes to adjust starting time and duration. Because this book is printed in grayscale, you do not see the one significant difference between these two representations, which is that motion tween sprites are displayed as blue in the timeline, whereas shape tweens are displayed as green.

Also note the last layer, *No Frames*. This layer currently has no frames defined within it. Usually when you create a new layer a keyframe is automatically added to frame 1. The important thing to note is that when a layer has no frames at all, if you select it and try to draw, paste, or import, Flash will tell you it cannot perform the operation because no frame exists. Thus, you can do nothing with a layer if it has no frames.

Let's return to the example file you saved from the last exercise. If it is not open, open the working file for the *Cyber Outpost* animation. Notice that four keyframes exist: one for each on each layer you created. Again, keyframes are frames that define primary position, orientation, size, or "color" of objects on the stage. In the timeline, keyframes containing graphical components are displayed as a filled black dot. Again, frames that do not have graphical elements in them ("blank keyframes") are displayed as white areas. By continuing with the exercises, you will see how the frame identifiers change during the creation of the animation.

One final note: if you edit objects on the stage, the editing affects the nearest left keyframe of the current layer. If the playback head is between a keyframe indicator and an endframe indicator, the objects in the keyframe to the left are modified. Thus, when you want to edit a keyframe, such as change the position of an object on the stage for that keyframe, you can select any frame between the keyframe identifier and the endframe indicator to make the change.

NOTE: *Pay close attention to where the playback head is located and what layer you have selected when transforming objects on the stage.*

Adding and Deleting Frames

Continue with the example you were working on to learn more. The *Cyber Outpost* animation will occur over 20 frames. The background of the animation stays the same over those 20 frames, whereas the remaining three layers will change to create the animation. In exercise 9-3, you will practice adding frames.

Exercise 9-3: Adding Frames

To begin, add copied frames to the background so that they exist on the stage for the entire duration of the 20 frames. Frames can be inserted into the timeline using the context menu, the Insert menu, or the mouse and timeline. You will see how to perform all three methods.

1. Add frames to the *Background* layer by selecting the first frame of the *Background* layer and right-clicking the mouse.

2. In the context menu that pops up (see figure 9-4), select Insert Frame. This adds a copied frame to the *Background* layer. Note that many of the commands in the context menu can be executed on the selected frame with function keys (see the Insert menu for the keyboard combinations).

 NOTE: *To bring up the context menu when using a Macintosh and single-button mouse, hold down the Command key and click and hold on a frame.*

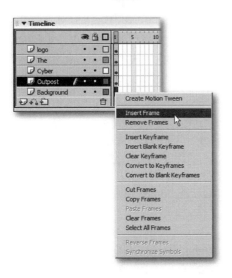

Figure 9-4. Using the context menu is one method of inserting a frame.

3. In addition to using the context menu, frames may also be added using the Insert menu. Click on frame 2 in the *Background* layer. Use the Insert | Timeline | Frame menu option to insert a frame. You can also quickly add frames by selecting a specific frame in the timeline and pressing the F5 function key.

4. Often the quickest method of adding frames to an animation is to drag the endframe indicator to a specific location in the timeline. However, if a keyframe is only one frame long, you must first use the context menu, the Insert menu, or the F5 key to extend the sprite to two frames (so that there is an endframe marker to grab). For example, hold the Ctrl or Command key and click-drag on frame 3 in the *Background* layer and drag the frame out to frame 20, as shown in figure 9-5.

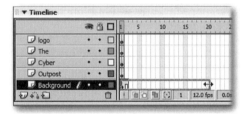

Figure 9-5. When the endframe indicator is shown in a sprite, you can click-drag it to extend the duration of a sprite by holding the Ctrl key on Windows or the Command key on Macintosh.

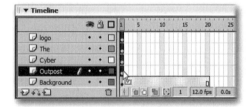

Figure 9-6. You can select a frame across multiple layers by click-dragging across it or by holding Shift and clicking on each frame.

 NOTE: *When there is only a single keyframe in the sprite, click-dragging it will move the keyframe, as opposed to extending its duration.*

5. Once the *Background* layer is extended, you need to extend the other four layers (counting the *Logo* layer), which can be done in one operation. Click in frame 1 of the *Logo* layer, hold down the Shift key, and click on the other three keyframes or click-drag from frame 1 of the *Logo* layer to frame 1 of the *Outpost* layer. This will select the frames across all four layers, as shown in figure 9-6.

6. Press and hold the F5 key to extend the duration of the frames out to frame 20.

7. Save your work.

 NOTE: *You cannot click-drag the endframe indicator of multiple layers to extend them all at once. Click-dragging the endframe indicator only works on single layers.*

Working with Blank Frames and Keyframes

To finish the animation, you will insert some keyframes and delete some elements so that each of the text components appears on the stage at two frame increments. Exercise 9-4, which follows, takes you through this process.

Exercise 9-4: Inserting Keyframes and Deleting Elements

To make each text component appear on the stage at two frame increments, perform the following steps.

1. Begin by clicking on frame 3 of the *The* layer.

2. Right-click and select Insert Keyframe from the context menu.

3. Repeat this process in frames 5 and 7 of the *The* layer, as shown in figure 9-7.

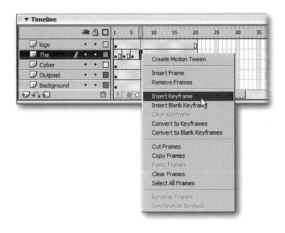

Figure 9-7. Keyframes should be added to the The *layer in frames 3, 5, and 7.*

4. With the keyframes in place, you next need to modify the text contained in each keyframe. You will change the text element so that the first keyframe has no text, the second displays the *T,* the third shows *Th,* and the fourth reveals *The.*

5. Select the first sprite in the *The* layer by clicking on frame 1 or frame 2. You can select either frame 1 or 2 to edit the objects in the keyframe in frame 1, because changes in frame 2 are applied to the left keyframe.

6. Press the Delete key to remove the text from the stage and the definition of it in the timeline. Note that the frame identifier changes to a blank frame representation.

7. Unlike programs such as Director, "blank" spaces (no frames) cannot be placed between sets of frames. To make an element appear or start at a particular time, build blank frames to that point and then enter a keyframe. For example, for entities such as the *T* for the second keyframe to appear on the stage at frame 3, blank frames must be built to that point. You cannot simply insert a keyframe at frame 3 with nothing in front of it.

8. Click on frame 3 in layer *The.*

 TIP: *To help you identify which frame the playhead is in, notice that the timeline displays the current frame in the timeline's status bar (beneath the* Background *layer and approximately vertical with frame 15).*

9. Ungroup the text using Modify | Ungroup (Ctrl + Shift + G or Command + Shift + G).

10. Delete the *h* and *e* on the stage.

11. Repeat this process in frame 5 by ungrouping and deleting the *e* on the stage.

12. Once this is completed, use the Control | Rewind and Control | Play menu options to view the animation.

To finish the animation, you will modify the *Cyber* and *Outpost* layers so that they appear on the stage at the appropriate time.

13. Select frame 9 in the *Cyber* layer and right-click to insert a keyframe.

14. Click between frame 1 and frame 9 (to select the sprite) in the *Cyber* layer and press the Delete key, to delete the *Cyber* text in frames 1 to 9.

15. Repeat this process for the *Outpost* layer by adding a keyframe in frame 11, and removing the *Outpost* text in the first sprite of the *Outpost* layer.

16. Save your file.

17. Use the Rewind and Play options in the Control menu to view the final animation.

Note that you can speed up or slow down an animation such as the one you just created by adjusting the playback speed of the movie or by adding or deleting frames. Adjust the playback rate of an animation through the Modify | Document Properties dialog box to change the overall playback speed. In general, playback rates can be set higher than the default of 12 frames per second. However, the number of elements, the view quality settings, and the playback machine for the animation affect the maximum playback speed.

To change the playback speed of a specific portion of an animation by modifying the number of frames, you add or delete frames as needed. In the example you created, change the timing of any of the elements by clicking the playhead to a specific location (click where the numbers are). Then use Insert | Timeline | Frame or the F5 function key to add frames across all layers, or use Insert | Timeline | Remove Frame or Shift + F5 to delete frames. Adding frames will slow down the animation, and deleting frames will speed it up.

CD-ROM NOTE: *A completed example of the* Cyber Outpost *animation is found in the* fgai/chapter09/ *folder, installed from the companion CD-ROM. The file is named* ch09_01c.fla. *Open this file if you want to compare your results with the example.*

Cel Animation Tools

In the previous exercise, the simple animation displays items on the stage at different times. Using similar techniques combined with Flash's cel animation tools, movement can be created. The instructions in this section will help you create another cel-type animation. However, this time some useful "traditional" tools will be highlighted, as well as interesting frame manipulation techniques. Figure 9-8 shows the image with which you will be working. Exercise 9-5 takes you through the process of creating an animated telephone.

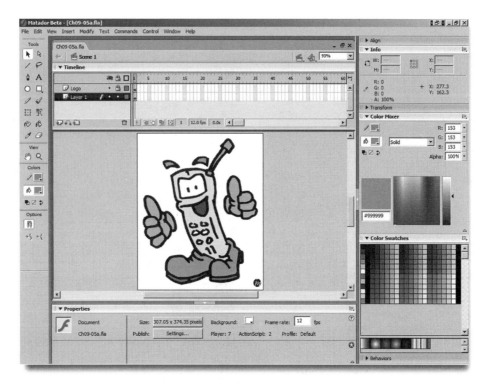

Figure 9-8. Cel animation tools are used to create an animated telephone.

Exercise 9-5: Creating an Animated Telephone

CD-ROM NOTE: *Open the file* ch09_05a.fla, *located in the* fgai/chapter09/ *folder, installed from the companion CD-ROM.*

Follow along and create the example animation described in this section. As with the previous exercise, if you would rather render your own version of the image for practice, the file *ch09_05b.fla* contains only lines. By beginning with this file, you can color your own version of the phone. Similarly, a finished version of the animation is also found on the companion CD-ROM (*ch09_05c.fla*). Look at the finished version to preview what you are about to create.

Structuring the File

To begin this animation, you will first layer the items. In this exercise, you will animate the hands, eyebrows, and eyes of the telephone. The steps that follow take you through the process of creating separate layers for each of these items.

1. Name the existing layer *Background*.

2. Create three new layers and give them each a name: *Hands*, *Eyebrows*, and *Eyes*.

3. Select the objects that constitute the right hand. Group them, cut them, and paste them in place on the *Hands* layer.

4. Repeat this process for the left hand. Place it on the *Hands* layer as well.

5. Select the objects that constitute the right eyebrow and group them. Cut and paste these elements in place on the *Eyebrows* layer. Repeat the process for the left eyebrow and place those elements on the *Eyebrows* layer as well.

6. Select the right eye, group it, and put it on the *Eyes* layer. Repeat with the process for the left eye, placing it on the *Eyes* layer as well.

7. Set the playhead to frame 1 if it is not there already (click on frame 1 where the timeline frame numbers are), and then use the F5 function key to move the duration of all the frames out to frame 15.

8. Save your work.

Animating the Eyes and Eyebrows

With the objects on different layers, start animating by working with the eyes and eyebrows first. In the finished animation, the eyes will move from side to side and the eyebrows up and down. The following steps take you through the process of animating the eyes and eyebrows.

1. Insert a keyframe in frames 2, 3, and 4 in the Eyes and Eyebrows layers.

 TIP: *You can add the keyframe to both layers at the same time by clicking in a frame in one layer, holding down the Shift key, and clicking in the same frame in the second layer. Then use the F6 function key to insert a keyframe.*

2. Move the playhead to frame 2. Using the Arrow tool on the stage, move the eyes on the stage so that they look toward the left.

3. Move the playhead to frame 3 and move the eyes so that they look toward the right, again using the Arrow tool. Leave frame 4 in the original position.

4. Move the playhead to frame 2 and, using the arrow keys, move the left eyebrow down on the stage.

5. In frame 3, move the right eyebrow down. Again, leave frame 4 alone.

6. Using Control | Rewind and then Control | Play, play the animation to see what you have created.

7. While the animation played, you probably noticed that it was so quick that it was difficult to see what was happening. To slow it down a little, add some frames. Move the playhead to frame 1.

8. Use function key F5 to insert one frame.

9. Repeat this process in the other two keyframes in which the eyes and eyebrows move.

10. Play the animation to see what you have created.

11. Adjust the positioning of the elements to get the animated image to look the way you want. To alter an object, pick the respective keyframe and layer corresponding to the object, select the object on the stage, and then move the object. Do not forget that you can use the arrow keys to nudge the objects, instead of click-dragging. If you want to rotate the

eyebrows a little, you can use the Arrow tool modifiers or the Transform panel to help you.

12. Save what you have completed thus far.

Creating the Frame-by-Frame Movement

The previous steps were nothing more than an extension of the steps used in the *Cyber Outpost* animation. The only difference is that you adjusted stage position rather than the time at which the object appeared.

Now you will animate the hands of the phone. This is a little trickier because the motion needs to be smooth across three frames. In exercise 9-6, which follows, you will begin by roughly positioning the hands.

Exercise 9-6: Animating the Hands of the Object

To begin animating the hands of the telephone, perform the following steps.

1. Insert keyframes in frames 10 and 11 of the *Hands* layer.

2. Move the playhead to frame 10.

3. Use the Arrow tool to move and rotate the left hand and right hand, as shown in figure 9-9.

NOTE: *When rotating objects, the default location for the center of rotation is the center of the object. This can be changed using the Free Transform tool. After selecting the object with the Free Transform tool, move the small white circle to change the center point for rotation.*

Figure 9-9. The hands are moved and rotated into position.

Figure 9-10. The hands are moved and rotated a little more.

4. Move the playhead to frame 11.

5. Move and rotate the hands a little more, as shown in figure 9-10.

6. Save your file.

7. Use Control | Play to see what you have thus far.

When you played the animation, the motion of the animation may not be as smooth as you would like. Flash provides a special tool called Onion Skin to help arrange elements so that they animate more smoothly.

Onion Skin and Onion Skin Outlines

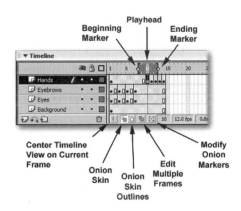

Figure 9-11. Using the Onion Skin feature allows smoother animations to be created in Flash.

The Onion Skin and Onion Skin Outlines buttons, shown in figure 9-11, allow you to create frame-by-frame animations by showing a representation of "before and after" frames beside the current frame. Surrounding frames are shown transparently with the current frame.

When you click on the Onion Skin button, two small markers (called onion markers) appear around the playhead, as shown in figure 9-11. Move the onion markers to reveal more or less frames concurrently on the stage. When building frame-by-frame animations, you can turn Onion Skin on to see the frames around the current frame. However, you can only edit the current frame, which is displayed opaque. Semitransparent objects are not editable. In Onion Skin mode, you can move the playhead to the point (frame) you want to edit while still being able to see the frames immediately adjacent to it.

In exercise 9-7, you will use the Onion Skin feature while continuing to work on the phone animation. The Onion Skin Outlines button is similar to the Onion Skin button except that instead of showing transparent objects for the neighboring frames it shows the surrounding frames as outlines.

Exercise 9-7: Using the Onion Skin Capability

To practice using the Onion Skin feature, perform the following steps.

1. With the playhead in frame 10, click on the Onion Skin button in the timeline.

2. Change the onion markers so that you can see the frames you have been working with.

3. Adjust the positions of the hands so that they appear to move more smoothly. Onion Skin mode becomes more important in regard to the number of frames you have to compare.

4. Once you are finished modifying your animation, turn off the Onion Skin mode by clicking on the Onion Skin button.

5. Save the file.

6. Play your movie to view the changes you made.

Before you begin using the tweening features of Flash, it is important to review a few other concepts, including copying and pasting frames, reversing frames, and editing multiple frames. The sections that follow explore these processes.

Copying, Pasting, and Reversing Frames

In the same manner that items on the stage are copied and pasted, frames can be copied from one position to another in the timeline. When you copy a frame, all objects within that frame are copied. Similarly, when you paste, all items are pasted. However, note that copying and pasting frames is not the same thing as copying and pasting objects on the stage. Understanding this difference is important.

 NOTE: *Pay special attention to whether you have been instructed to copy and paste in the timeline (frames) or on the stage (objects).*

In the telephone animation, you created three hand positions. Using those keyframes you created, in the reverse order, you can make the hands return to their original position. This allows the animation to be looped without having to manually position the hands on the stage. Exercise 9-8 takes you through this process and shows you how to use what you already have to quickly generate the remaining frames.

Exercise 9-8: Using Reverse Frames

If you have been following along to this point, continue to use the file with which you have been working. Otherwise, see the following CD-ROM Note.

 CD-ROM NOTE: *Load the sample file* ch09_08.fla *from the* fgai/chapter09/ *folder, installed from the companion CD-ROM.*

NOTE: *If you were just working with Onion Skin, turn it off by clicking on the button in the timeline.*

1. Right-click on frame 1 in the *Hands* layer.

2. Select Copy Frames from the context menu.

3. Right-click on frame 12 in the *Hands* layer.

4. Select Paste Frames in the context menu. The keyframe copied from frame 1 is now pasted in frame 12.

5. Select frames 10 and 11 in the *Hands* layer by either click-dragging across both or holding the Shift key and clicking on each.

6. Right-click and select Copy Frames from the context menu.

7. Right-click in frame 13 and select Paste Frames from the context menu. The two frames you just copied should now be in frames 13 and 14.

8. Finish the process by click-dragging the endframes of the sprites on the other layers to extend them out to the same duration as the *Hands* layer.

9. Save your file.

10. Play your animation. Notice that the animation is not quite right yet. You need to reverse the order of frames 12, 13, and 14 to make it look right.

11. Click-drag across frames 12, 13, and 14 to select all three frames.

12. Use Modify | Timeline | Reverse Frames to reverse the order of the frames, or right-click on one of the selected frames and select Reverse Frames from the context menu. This reverses the sequence of the frames, such that what was at frame 14 is now at frame 12. However, you will notice that the duration of the sprite in frame 12 is not right.

Note that when you use reverse frames it actually reverses the sprites, not just the individual frames. The sprite in frame 12 was originally at the end and was greater than a single frame. Thus, when you reverse it, the sprite stays the exact same length. There are a number of ways of correcting this. For example, prior to performing the reverse, you could copy the keyframe in frame 1 and paste it in frame 15. Alternatively, you can fix the duration of the sprite after the fact, as you will do in the next few steps.

NOTE: *Be careful of what you select when using Reverse Frames. It is easy to accidentally select the wrong frames (or wrong layers).*

13. Click-drag the endframe in frame 17 back to frame 12.

14. Select frames 18 and 19.

15. Click-drag the selection back to frames 13 and 14.

16. Click on frame 14 and use the F5 function key to move the endframe out. See the following Tip to delete the blank frames at the end of the sprite.

 TIP: *Quickly delete blank frames by selecting them and pressing the Backspace key.*

17. Save your file

18. Play the animation. Notice that the hands move back and forth in a more natural progression.

 NOTE: *To make the animation loop when it reaches the end, use the Control | Loop Playback menu option.*

Edit Multiple Frames: Sizing Entire Animations

A common question people ask is how to scale an entire animation once it has been created. As simple as it may sound, scaling the telephone animation requires you to select all elements on all layers at one time, across multiple frames.

Flash provides a feature similar in function to Onion Skin, called Edit Multiple Frames, which allows you to view the content of a number of frames at the same time. Unlike Onion Skin, in the Edit Multiple Frames mode all objects are shown as opaque and are editable at the same time.

 NOTE: *If Edit Multiple Frames and Onion Skin are enabled, Edit Multiple Frames overrides Onion Skin.*

Because all objects are opaque, it is difficult to tell what is on each layer. In addition, it is easy to mistakenly move the wrong objects, so you do have to be careful when using this feature. However, Edit Multiple Frames is the simplest means of scaling all objects in a movie at the same time. See exercise 9-9 for practice in using the Edit Multiple Frames feature.

TIP: *Keep the Edit Multiple Frames mode from affecting a particular layer by hiding or locking the layer.*

Exercise 9-9: Sizing a Finished Piece with Edit Multiple Frames

For this exercise, use the file you have been working with, or see the following CD-ROM Note.

 CD-ROM NOTE: *Open the file ch09_09.fla, located in the fgai/chapter09/ folder, installed from the companion CD-ROM.*

Begin working with Edit Multiple Frames by performing the following steps.

1. Click on the Edit Multiple Frames button (see figure 9-12).

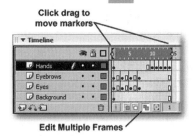

Figure 9-12. The beginning and ending markers can be moved while in Edit Multiple Frames mode.

2. Move the beginning and ending markers in the timeline so that they include the frames that require editing, which in this case is all frames in the animation. Move the pointers so that they are at the beginning and ending frames of the timeline, as shown in figure 9-12.

 NOTE: *If you move the playhead while in Edit Multiple Frames mode, the position of the markers will also change. They are positioned relative to the current location of the playhead.*

3. Click on the stage and use Edit | Select All to select all elements of all frames.

4. Click on the Free Transform tool.

5. Click-drag the scale handles on the outer edge of the selection on the stage to scale the items.

6. If your purpose is to scale all objects in the movie, make sure you get them all. If you scale and notice that you missed something, use Edit | Undo and try performing the Select All again.

7. Deselect the objects by clicking on a blank spot in the canvas.

8. Click on the Edit Multiple Frames button again to turn it off.

9. Play the animation to see the results. The only difference is that the animation is now smaller!

TIP: *You can also use the Transform panel to scale the objects numerically.*

Although the telephone animation is quite simple, it has covered several of the basic concepts you will need to understand before you create more complex animations. Sometimes cel animation techniques are the only way of solving an animation problem or of implementing a certain design. However, Flash would be quite limiting if cel were the only method of creating animations. The next section examines tween animation, which is a very powerful capability. Tweening allows much flexibility and makes creating complex animations easier.

Motion Tweens

As is evident from the last section, creating frame-by-frame animations is quite tedious. Although it is good to know, cel animation requires tremendous amounts of time when creating complex animations. This section examines Flash's tweening ability. With tweens you can create animations that center on movement, rotation, scaling, and color (called a motion tween), or on shape blends (morphs), called a shape tween. You can also use special layers that can be helpful with specific animation tasks. Let's begin with motion tween animations.

Setting Up a Motion Tween

The process for creating a motion tween animation is to begin with an overlay object, preferably a symbol. As you read in Chapter 6, symbols provide many advantages, the primary being file size savings. Due to this, motion tweens you create should use symbols, not groups or text.

 NOTE: *Motion tweening cannot be used on stage objects.*

To show how motion tweens work, exercise 9-10 involves the creation of a simple ball that moves across the screen. It provides a basis for more complex tweened animation examples later.

 Exercise 9-10: Creating a Motion Tween

To begin creating a motion tween, perform the following steps.

1. Start with a new file in Flash. Use the Oval tool to create a circle with a gradient fill. You may want to use the Transform Fill tool to move the center point for the gradient of the circle so that it looks more like a 3D ball.

2. Delete the line around the circle.

3. Make a symbol out of the "ball" by selecting the fill with the Arrow tool and using Modify | Convert to Symbol (or function key F8) to make it a symbol.

4. Set the behavior to graphic and the registration point to the center. Name the symbol *ball* and click on OK.

5. Once the symbol is created, you can work with it on the stage. However, recall that you cannot edit it directly with the painting and drawing tools in the main movie. To edit a symbol, such as changing its color or fill, you access the symbol's timeline. To do this, select the symbol on the stage and use Edit | Edit Symbols or simply double click on the symbol on the stage.

   Now that you have created the symbol, you will establish two key positions of the ball on either side of the stage. Continue with the following steps.

6. In the timeline, click in frame 1 and press F5 to create an endframe indicator on the sprite.

7. Click-drag the endframe indicator out to frame 20. Do not hold the Ctrl or Command key while you extend the duration. If you do not hold Ctrl or Command, a keyframe will be automatically created in the ending frame.

8. Move the playhead to frame 1 and move the ball to the left side of the stage.

9. Move the playhead to frame 20.

10. Define a new position for the ball somewhere on the right side of the stage by dragging it.

11. Save your file.

 TIP: *If you prefer to use numerical values for instance placement on the stage, you can use the Info panel or the Properties panel to define the location of the instance in frame 20. Entering values into the X or Y fields will move the currently selected object.*

Setting Up the Tween in the Frame Panel

In the timeline, tweening automatically creates interpolated frames (in-between frames) between two keyframes. Size, position, orientation, and color of the two surrounding keyframes can be automatically tweened. You have already created two keyframes in your sample file. The difference between the two keyframes is the location of their instances on the stage.

At this point, all you have to do is tell Flash to "tween" these instances to create an animation of the ball moving across the stage. Exercise 9-11 takes you through this process.

Exercise 9-11: Setting Up the Tween

For this exercise, use the file you have been working with, or see the following CD-ROM Note.

CD-ROM NOTE: *Open the file ch09-011a.fla, located in the* fgai/chapter09/ *folder, installed from the companion CD-ROM.*

A finished example of the animation is also available (*ch09-011b.fla*). Set up the tween between two keyframes by performing the following steps.

1. Right-click on any frame between 1 and 19 in the layer that contains the ball symbol. Notice the Create Motion tween shortcut in the menu. You could use this to quickly create the tween. However, you should know where you could manually set it up as well.

2. In the Properties panel, notice in the center section the Tween drop-down list. Set the Tweening drop-down to Motion, as shown in figure 9-13.

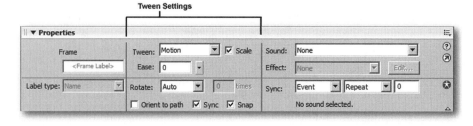

Figure 9-13. When a frame is selected, the center of the Properties panel is where you set up tween animation properties.

TIP: *When setting up tween animations, you can actually right-click on any part of the sprite to set up the tweening. However, when working with multiple layers, make sure you select the correct sprite. Even the best user occasionally selects the wrong layer when dealing with numerous layers.*

Once you have set the Tweening drop-down, note that the area between the two keyframes is represented with a blue background and an arrow. This frame identifier denotes motion tween animation, as shown in figure 9-14a. If the tween is not successful, for whatever reason, the timeline will display the frames as a dashed line, as shown in figure 9-14b.

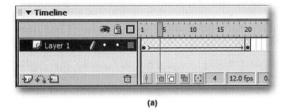

(a)

 NOTE: *When a tween is unsuccessful (see figure 9-14b), the Properties panel will display a small icon (yellow triangle with an exclamation point in it) in addition to the timeline representation.*

3. Save the file.

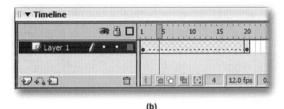

(b)

Figure 9-14. The Tween frame identifier shows that a tween animation was (a) successful or (b) unsuccessful.

4. Play back the movie using Control | Play to see the animation that has been automatically created.

 TIP: *Use the Enter key as a shortcut to start and stop animations, rather than the Control menu.*

When working with basic tween animation, you should keep the following in mind.

- Motion tweening only works on symbols, text, bitmaps, or groups, and you should strive to use symbols as much as possible.

- Tweening has no effect on stage objects. If tweening is applied to objects on the stage level, the timeline will represent the tween as a dashed line with no arrows. Additionally, when the animation is played, nothing will happen.

- Tweening only works on individual symbols, text elements, bitmaps, or groups. To tween several items at once, each must reside on an individual layer.

- Tweening is a frame property. To set up tweening, you must click in a frame and use the Properties panel.

- Tweening is often a quick means of setting up animations. However, once a tween has been created you can define additional keyframes within the tween. This allows you to further modify and tweak a sequence. For example, in the previous exercise you could make the ball "bounce" by selecting frame 10 and pulling the ball down on the stage. The tweening would then be occurring between three keys instead of two.

Other Tween Settings in the Properties Panel

When you assign tweening with the Properties panel, several other options become available, as shown in figure 9-15. These include the items that follow. Exercise 9-12 provides practice in using the Scale, Rotate, and Easing options.

Figure 9-15. The Properties panel provides several optional settings for motion tweens.

- *Scale:* Assuming the size of an instance changes between two keyframes, this setting determines whether the size of the object is tweened.

- *Easing:* Often when creating animation, you may want an animated object to speed up or slow down during its tween. Easing allows you to adjust the speed of the tween. Ease In slows the beginning of the tween, whereas Ease Out slows the end of the tween.

- *Rotate:* This option specifies whether the object rotates during the tween. It also allows you to set the number of times the object rotates during the tween.

 TIP: *You can manually control rotation by transforming the symbols on the stage, as opposed to having to use the Rotate option in the Properties panel.*

- *Orient to Path:* When the instance is asymmetric in shape, the Orient to Path option determines how the object travels along a path. See the section "Understanding Guide Layers" in this chapter for more information regarding the effects of this setting.

- *Synchronize:* If the number of frames in a graphic symbol's animation is not an even multiple of the scene's timeline, the symbol animation may play sporadically. The Synchronize option restarts the graphic symbol when the main timeline loops.

- *Snap:* Forces the motion tween to follow the guide associated with the layer. You will read more about guide layers later in this chapter.

Exercise 9-12: The Scale, Rotate, and Easing Options

CD-ROM NOTE: *View how the Scale, Rotate, and Easing options work. Open the file* ch09-12.fla, *located in the* fgai/chapter09/ *folder, installed from the companion CD-ROM.*

Adjust the tweening options for the ball to see how they affect the animation.

Applying Color Effects

Motion tweens alone are a nifty feature of Flash. As you have seen, you can use a motion tween to animate position, location, and size using the Properties panel. However, you can do one other thing when you are using motion tweening via the Properties panel. The "color" properties of a symbol instance can be adjusted on the stage, thus making it possible to animate the instance as part of a motion tween. This is how you make objects appear and disappear during a movie, as well as create a wide range of other effects.

The term color is used broadly here, covering the ability to adjust brightness (amount of black or white applied to an instance), tint (the pureness of the colors in an instance), and alpha characteristic (opacity). Flash also provides a mechanism for modifying all three of these characteristics simultaneously. In exercise 9-13 you can take a closer look at how this works.

Exercise 9-13: Using Color Effects

CD-ROM NOTE: *See how color effects can be animated using motion tweens. Open the file* ch09-13a.fla, *located in the* fgai/chapter09/ *folder, installed from the companion CD-ROM.*

Follow along with the exercise. The completed file is named *ch09-13b.fla*. Figure 9-16 shows the example with which you will be working in this exercise. You will use the Alpha color option in the Properties panel to make objects disappear by setting the first keyframe to 100-percent alpha (also the default) and the last keyframe to 0 percent. In this example, you will make objects 1 and 3 go from 100-percent opaque in frame 1 to 100-percent transparent in frame 20. Object 2 will go from 100-percent transparent to 100-percent opaque. To create a color-effect animation, perform the following steps.

1. Move the playhead to frame 20 so that you are working in keyframes in frame 20.

2. Click on object 1 on the stage.

3. Locate the Color drop-down list in the Properties panel and select Alpha.

4. At frame 20, object 1 needs to totally disappear; therefore, set the slider next to the Color drop-down menu to 0, as shown in figure 9-17. Object 1 should disappear on the stage.

5. Move the playhead to frame 1 and click on object 2 on the stage.

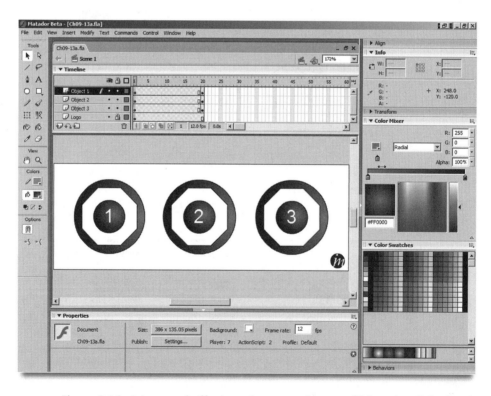

Figure 9-16. A tweened effect can be created by modifying the alpha levels of a symbol instance.

Figure 9-17. When Alpha is chosen from the Color drop-down list, the slider controls the percentage of transparency.

6. Set the instance's Alpha to 0 in the Properties panel.

7. Repeat the process on object 3 and set its Alpha to 0. Make sure to move the playhead to frame 20 before adjusting the Alpha for object 3. Otherwise, the instance in frame 1 will be changed instead of the instance in frame 20.

8. Now that you have applied effects to the symbol instances in various frames, quickly assign the motion tween by right-clicking somewhere between frames 2 and 18 on each of the sprites in each layer. Select Create Motion Tween in the context menu.

9. Save your file.

10. Play the animation to see the effect of the motion tweens on the applied color effects.

You can change the Brightness, Tint, or Alpha setting during any tween. Use varying combinations of the three during any tween animation using the Advanced option. Keep in mind that objects can also change size, location, or orientation at the same time as an effect. Each of these effects means different things in terms of the effect it can create or manipulate, as follows. To explore these other effects, see exercise 9-14.

- *Brightness:* The lightness or darkness of an instance. The instance is lightened by adding white and darkened by adding black.

- *Tint:* Actually the saturation or purity of the instance. Using the Tint option allows you to overlay percentages of other colors over the instance. This changes the purity of the instance, more accurately known as saturation.

- *Alpha:* Describes the level of opaqueness or transparency of the instance. By varying the opacity, such as reducing the Alpha setting to 0, the object disappears.

- *Advanced:* Allows any combination or all of the other three effects to be changed at the same time, so that tint and alpha changes can be made at the same time.

NOTE: *The section of the Properties panel will only work on symbols. It has no effect on groups, text objects, or stage-level objects.*

Exercise 9-14: Applying Brightness and Tint Changes

CD-ROM NOTE: *Open the file* ch09_14.fla *located in the* fgai/ chapter09/ *folder, installed from the companion CD-ROM.*

Try some of the other effects to see how they can be used to create animations.

Understanding Guide Layers

Earlier in this chapter, it was mentioned that you could animate along a path in Flash. This is done by using a special layer called a motion guide. This section examines motion guides and how they can be used to constrain tweened instances to a path. See exercise 9-15 to begin to explore motion guides.

Exercise 9-15: Using Motion Guides

CD-ROM NOTE: *Learn about motion guides. Open the file* ch09-15a.fla, *located in the* fgai/chapter09/ *folder, installed from the companion CD-ROM.*

The completed file is named *ch09-15b.fla*. When creating animations in which you want an object to travel along a specific path, guide layers are very helpful. In this exercise, use a guide layer to define a path for the boat, shown in figure 9-18, to travel along. When creating a guide layer, draw the path you want the object to travel on, just like drawing any other object. To practice using guide layers, perform the following steps.

1. Make the boat a graphic symbol by selecting it and using the F8 function key. Although you could work with it as is (because it is a group), it is best to always work with symbols whenever possible.

2. Extend the duration of the boat and logo symbols out to frame 20.

3. With the *Boat* layer as the current layer, click on the Add Motion Guide button, which is next to the Insert Layer button at the bottom of the Timeline window.

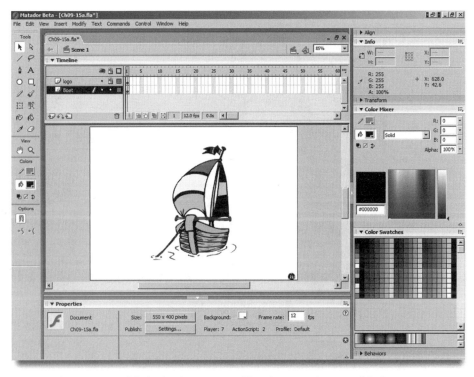

Figure 9-18. This is the boat you will animate using a guide layer.

4. With the *Guide: Boat motion guide* layer as the current layer, draw a line across the screen, as shown in figure 9-19. You will want the line to extend well beyond the stage and thus you may have to zoom out so that you can see more of the work area. In addition, make sure to use the Smooth modifier for smoothing the path of the Pencil, or use the Pen tool.

5. Select the Arrow tool and make sure the Snap (Magnet) option is on.

 NOTE: *When using motion guides, be aware of the state of the Snap option.*

6. Select the boat and click-drag it to the path, as shown in figure 9-20. You may want to click on the symbol's insertion point (small crosshairs) and snap the insertion point to the path.

7. Right-click in frame 20 in the *Boat* layer and select Insert Keyframe.

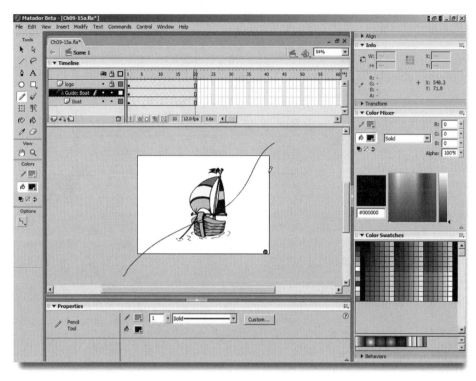

Figure 9-19. A path for the boat needs to be created on the new Guide: Boat
motion guide *layer.*

8. Drag the boat to the lower left of the screen. By click-dragging
    from the insertion point, it will continue to snap to the line.
    You may have to lock the motion guide layer so that you do
    not accidentally grab the endpoint of the line.

9. Set up the tweening. Right-click on a frame between 1 and 18
    in the *Boat* layer.

10. Select the Create Motion Tween option.

11. Save the file.

12. Play the animation to see the results.

13. Modify the boat so that it appears to be coming toward the
    screen. Place the playhead in frame 1.

14. In frame 1, scale the boat instance down using the Free
    Transform tool on the stage, or by using the Transform panel.
    The boat instance should scale around its center point.

15. To make it more realistic, turn off the path by clicking under
    the eye in the guide layer. An X indicates that the layer is hid-
    den.

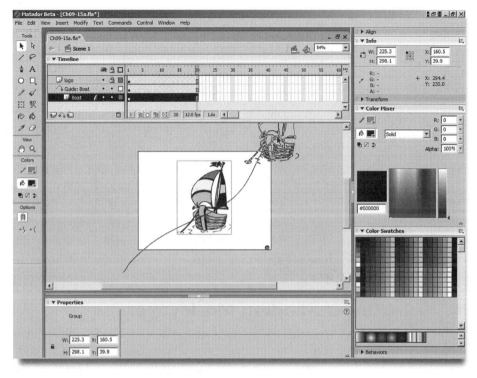

Figure 9-20. With Snap to Objects turned on, drag the boat until it snaps to the motion guide layer.

16. Save the file.

17. Use the Enter key to play the animation.

The Orient to Path option in the Properties panel was mentioned earlier in the chapter. When you use motion guides, Orient to Path becomes important. To see what Orient to Path does, continue with the following steps.

18. Click a frame somewhere within the tween you just created (in the timeline).

19. In the Properties panel, enable the Orient to Path option by clicking on the checkbox.

20. Save the file.

21. Replay the animation to view the results. Notice how the boat now rotates to remain perpendicular to the path.

Motion guide layers give you tremendous freedom when creating animations. The following is a list of things to consider about guide layers.

- Once a tween object has been created, it can always be modified. As long as the tween has the Snap option selected in the Frame panel, the object will travel along the path during the animation.

- Closed polygons, such as ellipses or rectangles, can be used as guide layers also. However, when using closed polygons for guides, you will inevitably have to use more keyframes in the tweened object to ensure it moves in the proper orientation around the path.

- You could adjust any of the other instance properties (including color effect) during the path-based motion tween, just as you set up a scale during the tween animation you just performed. Anything you define in the keys related to position, size, orientation, or color will be tweened.

- A motion guide layer can be applied to multiple layers at the same time.

Understanding Mask Layers

Similar to masks in other packages, mask layers offer the ability to use one layer as a mask for another layer. When combining masks with tweened animation, you can get a variety of special effects. Exercise 9-16 provides practice in working with mask layers.

Exercise 9-16: Using Mask Layers

 CD-ROM NOTE: *Learn about layer masks. Open the file ch09-16a.fla, located in the fgai/chapter09/ folder, installed from the companion CD-ROM.*

The file that you open contains some basic text elements and a red circle, as shown in figure 9-21. If you play the animation, you will see that a tweened animation has been set up in which the circle passes over the text. At this point, if you make the circle a mask for the layer beneath it, the resulting effect is that of a spotlight passing over the text. Set up the layer mask by performing the following steps.

1. Right-click on the *Spotlight* layer (on the layer name, not the sprite in the layer) and select Mask from the context menu. This option defines the layer as a mask, and the layer beneath it as masked.

2. Press the Enter key to play the animation. Notice that the text only appears where the opaque fill passes over it.

Figure 9-21. Two layers are needed for creating a simple spotlight effect.

3. When a layer is going to be used as a mask, it really does not matter what color (hue) the objects on the layer are, nor does it matter what the Alpha (transparency) setting of those objects are. When a layer is a mask, it is 100-percent opaque.

4. To make the animation just a little more interesting, insert a layer beneath the *Text* layer and name it *Background*.

5. As with guides, mask layers can be used to mask multiple layers. Thus, be careful that the new layer is not inserted as a mask. If so, right-click on the layer name and select Properties in the context menu. Change the Type from Masked to Normal. Click on OK.

6. Right-click on frame 1 of the *Text* layer and use Copy Frames in the context menu.

7. Right-click on frame 1 in the *Background* layer and select Paste Frames.

 TIP: *Even though a layer is locked, you can still copy frames from it.*

8. Click on the text on the stage and change its color to about 50 percent gray using the Fill Color option in the Colors section of the toolbar.

9. Save the file.

10. Press the Enter key to play the animation and see the effect.

By combining motion tweening and masks, you can create unique effects. The latter part of this chapter continues to examine a variety of effects that can be created using motion tweening, motion guide layers, effects, and mask layers.

Shape Tweens

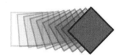

Just as motion tweening can be applied to overlay objects, shape tweening can be used on stage-level objects. Shape tweening allows elements to be created that morph from one object to another, as shown in figure 9-22.

Figure 9-22. Shape tweening allows you to produce elements that morph from one thing to another.

Using Shape Tweening

Shape tweening is created in a manner similar to motion tweening, except that it uses stage-level objects instead of overlay objects. You define keyframes for shape tweening, just as you do for motion tweening. To further explore shape tweening, see exercise 9-17.

Exercise 9-17: Creating Shape Tweens

 **CD-ROM NOTE:** *Learn more about shape tweening by opening the file ch09-17a.fla, located in the* fgai/chapter09/ *folder, installed from the companion CD-ROM. The completed file is named ch09-17b.fla.*

In this exercise, you will create a shape tween using the author's initials. Each letter will morph to the next in a circular manner. This animation could be easily looped on a web page. However, if you want, you can create your own file and use your own initials. When adding your own text, break it apart before trying to perform the shape tween. Shape tweens work only on stage objects. Begin creating a shape tween by performing the following steps.

1. Click on the first keyframe in layer 1.

2. In the Properties panel, select Shape in the Tweening drop-down list. You can accept the default settings for the Shape Tweening options, as shown in figure 9-23.

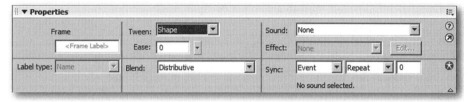

Figure 9-23. Default settings for the shape tween.

3. When Shape Tween is selected, two Blend options are available for your morphing animations: Distributive and Angular. Distributive attempts to create intermediate shapes that are smoother and more irregular. Angular attempts to preserve corners and straight lines. Therefore, use Angular for shapes that have sharp corners and straight lines. You will also notice the Easing option, which works the same for both motion and shape tweens.

4. Repeat this process for the remaining keyframes in layer 1. Consider trying some different settings in the Properties panel to see their effects.

5. Save the file.

6. Press the Enter key to play your animation. To turn on looping, use the Control | Loop Playback option.

7. When you play back the animation, notice that it pauses slightly due to the last keyframe, which is a copy of the first. To fix this, right-click on frame 29 and select Insert Keyframe.

8. Right-click on frame 30 and select Remove Frame.

9. Click-drag the endframe indicator in the *Logo* layer back to frame 29.

10. Replay the animation to see that there is no longer a pause in the looping animation.

Once a shape (or motion) tween has been set up, you can insert and delete keyframes within the tween. However, in the last step of the previous exercise, you first inserted a keyframe next to the existing keyframe before deleting the last keyframe. Had you deleted the last keyframe first, the last tween would not have worked. For tweens to be maintained after creation, they must have a keyframe at the beginning and at the end. If either keyframe is deleted, the tween will not work.

Depending on the letters used in the last exercise, you probably noticed that at least one of the letters did not morph quite right. To control what points in the starting keyframe are morphed to points in the ending keyframe, use Shape Hints.

 TIP: *Blend color in a shape tween, too. Just fill the shapes with different colors, and the color of a fill will "morph" as well.*

Shape Hints

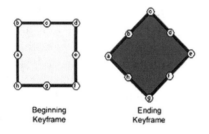

Figure 9-24. Shape hints allow you to control the shape metamorphosis.

Shape hints provide control over complex or awkward morphs by presenting labels (points) used to perform the interpolation of frames. Even simple shape blends can benefit from shape hints, as shown in figure 9-24. By synchronizing the points on the beginning and ending keyframe objects, you control how the object goes through its metamorphosis. Shape hints are useful for basic morphs as well as more complex ones, such as morphing one bitmap to another.

For any shape tween, 26 shape hints (points) can be defined. In the starting keyframe, shape hints are yellow. In the ending keyframe, they are green. Additionally, shape hints are red when they have not been defined. For practice in working with shape hints, see exercise 9-18.

Exercise 9-18: Using Shape Hints

 CD-ROM NOTE: *Learn more about shape hints by opening the* file ch09-18a.fla, *located in the* fgai/chapter09/ *folder, installed from the companion CD-ROM. The completed file is named* ch09-18b.fla.

In this exercise, you will morph some simple objects. Before beginning, play the animation to see how it is currently morphing.

1. Begin by selecting the first keyframe in the shape tween.

2. Use Modify | Shape | Add Shape Hint (Ctrl + Shift + H or

Figure 9-25. Click-drag the shape hint to the left side of the square.

Command + Shift + H). A small, red circle with the letter *a* appears over the top of the object. Red shape hints indicate that they have not yet been defined.

3. Click-drag the shape hint to the first identification point, as shown in figure 9-25.

4. Click on the ending keyframe.

5. Define the location for the shape hint by dragging it on the stage. When you do so, the shape hint will turned green, meaning that it has been identified in the beginning and ending frame. If it remains red, this indicates a problem and you need to go back to the first keyframe and try to reassign the position.

6. Play the animation and see the difference the shape hint has made.

7. Return the playhead to frame 1 and use Modify | Shape | Add Shape Hint to add another point.

8. Define the point in the beginning and ending keyframes.

9. Repeat this process until the morph is the way you want it.

10. Play the animation and see the difference the shape hints have made.

Figure 9-26. Eight shape hints are enough to per-form this example.

In this exercise, eight shape hints should be sufficient to gen-erate the morph shown in figure 9-26. Remember that a maximum of 26 shape hints can be used for each shape tween.

If you define some shape hints and then decide results are not satisfactory, use Modify | Shape | Remove All Hints to delete them. This reverts to the original shape tween. Additionally, you can remove an individual hint by right-clicking on it and selecting Remove Hint from the context menu. You can show and hide the shape hints by deselecting the View | Show Shape Hints menu option.

 NOTE: *If you leave shape hints in a file, they will not be shown when the web-ready file is output.*

If you are a FreeHand user, you can also use FreeHand's blending capability to quickly and easily create frame-by-frame shape morphs. If you use the Blend Xtra in FreeHand, a second Xtra (Release to Layers) can be used to move each blend step to a separate layer. When you export the Flash file from FreeHand, select the Animate Across Layers option to define each layer as a Flash frame. Although you do not have as much control over FreeHand blends as you do with Flash shape hints, this is another way of creating shape blends using Macromedia tools.

▪ ▪ ▪ Timeline Effects

One of the new features of Flash MX 2004 are something called timeline effects. Timeline effects are designed to make creating basic animations easier. As such, they are prebuilt animations that can be applied to text, graphics, bitmaps, and buttons. This section describes the basic timeline effects you will find in Flash MX 2004 and how to use them.

You apply a timeline effect by selecting an element on the stage and then selecting Insert | Timeline Effect. Once you apply a timeline effect, the objects to which the effect is applied are "encased" in a self-contained graphic symbol.

 NOTE: *Currently, Macromedia includes eight effects. There may be more effects available as Flash MX 2004 evolves.*

There are essentially two types of timeline effects. Some actually create animation, whereas others are more along the lines of "utility" items that can used to create visual elements on the screen. The effects currently included in Flash MX 2004 are:

- *Blur:* Animates the edges of the selected objects such that they blur, with an eventual fadeout of the object. You can control the duration, direction, and resolution (visual quality) of the blur.

- *Copy to grid:* Allows you to quickly create a rectangular array of an object. This timeline effect aids visual object creation. In essence, the effect duplicates the selected objects based on your entry of number of columns and rows and the associated spacing between them.

- *Distributed Duplication:* This timeline effect is a great addition to Flash. In other packages, such as FreeHand or Illustrator, this feature would be called "power duplication." It lets you create duplicated items that subsequently vary in spacing, size, and color.

- *Drop shadow:* As another "utility" effect, this allows you to quickly create a drop shadow of selected objects.

- *Expand:* This timeline effect allows you to create an animation of two or more symbols expanding or contracting (as it relates to their position on the stage). You can control starting and stopping positions, scale factors related to height and width, and duration of the animation.

TIP: *The Expand effect is the only one that will not work with stage-level objects. Also, you must select more than one symbol for the Expand effect to work.*

- *Explode:* As its name implies, this effect can be used to make items visually disassociate from one another.

 TIP: *If you use overlay objects with the Explode effect, the objects will visually disassociate and shrink, but the objects will not be broken into subsequent pieces. However, if you stage object, Flash will automatically break the object up into small pieces as a part of the Effect process.*

- *Transform:* The Transform effect allows you to easily create basic transformation animations (that is, a change in position, size, orientation, or color). You can control the animation duration, beginning and ending alpha settings, and easing.

- *Transition:* This effect allows you to create basic fade and wipe transitions automatically. You can control the duration, direction, and easing.

▪ ▪ ▪ Manually Creating Animated Effects

While examining "how-to" examples created in Flash, one of the significant aspects is animated effects. How are transitions and cool text effects created? What about methods for creating background effects and advanced guide layers and masks? Although timeline effects are a neat addition to Flash MX 2004, there is still a need to know how to create animation manually. Indeed, timeline effects will help you perform some rudimentary (but helpful) things, but most animations you will likely want to create will not be as simple as a "single click."

Therefore, after having reviewed some simple examples of how Flash can be used to create basic animations, this section reviews more complex animations. From text effects and manual transitions to advanced guide layers and mask layers, these examples should get your creativity flowing.

 CD-ROM NOTE: *Many samples on the companion CD-ROM are not covered in this chapter; they are provided for further study. Make sure to examine the* fgai/chapter09/ *folder, installed from the companion CD-ROM, for examples that are not specifically discussed in the chapter. These examples include more tips, techniques, and nuggets of how-to information.*

∎∎∎ Animated Text Effects

One of the benefits of working with text objects in Flash is that once a single text effect is constructed it can generally be reused over and over. When the basis of a text effect is a graphic symbol, a series of text blocks can be created that uses the same effect, without having to recreate the effect multiple times.

This section describes three common text effects used on the Web. Granted, not every effect possible can be described in this book. Nevertheless, with the information provided, you should be able to get started.

Hard Blurs

One of the most basic text effects is the hard blur. In the previous section you reviewed the Blur timeline effect, but it is also helpful to know how to create it manually.

Blurs are generally used on a mouse-over or some other menu or button effect. Most of these effects are components that are intermixed with other items, such as buttons. Few of these effects stand alone. These effects are generally part of a larger animation, which is why they are created as symbols. As such, they can be easily inserted into other movies. Exercise 9-19, which follows, takes you through the process of creating a hard blur effect.

 CD-ROM NOTE: *To visually understand what a hard blur looks like when animated, open* hardblur.fla, *located in the* fgai/chapter09/text effects/ *folder, installed from the companion CD-ROM. Consider starting there if you learn better by dissecting movies.*

Exercise 9-19: Creating a Hard Blur Effect

To create a hard blur effect, perform the following steps.

1. Start a new movie in Flash.
2. Select Insert | New Symbol (Ctrl + F8) to create a new symbol. This symbol will be the text on which the movie symbol (which will actually be the effect) will be based. Select Behavior as Graphic and name the symbol *Hard Blur*.
3. Use the Text tool to insert some text into the *Hard Blur* symbol. Center the text on the crosshairs on the stage. You may also want to adjust the size, color, or font of the text element. Then click on the Scene 1 link in the Edit path to switch back to the main movie timeline.

4. Select Insert | New Symbol again, and select Movie Clip as the Behavior. Name the symbol *Hard Blur MC*.

5. Open the library for the current movie by selecting Window | Library.

6. In the library preview window, click-drag the graphic symbol *Hard Blur* to the stage. Line up the instance of the *Hard Blur* symbol with the new movie clip's crosshairs on the stage.

7. Close the Library window.

8. The symbol you just placed is on layer 1. Rename layer 1 *Static*.

9. Click-drag the duration of the sprite, or use the F5 function key to insert frames in the timeline, to extend the sprite to frame 10.

10. Set up the top and bottom blurring tweens. Insert two layers and place one above, and one below, the Static layer in the timeline. Name the upper layer *Top Blur* and the lower layer *Bottom Blur*.

11. Right-click on the sprite in the *Static* layer and select Copy Frames from the context menu.

12. Paste the copied frames in frame 1 of the *Top Blur* layer. You may need to adjust the endframe marker so that the *Top Blur* layer ends at frame 10.

13. Repeat step 12 on the *Bottom Blur* layer.

14. Hide the *Static* layer.

15. Insert a keyframe in frame 10 in the *Top Blur* layer and the *Bottom Blur* layer.

16. Select frame 10 in the *Top Blur* layer and use the arrow keys or the Info panel to move the text on the *Top Blur* layer up 30 pixels and to the right 30 pixels.

17. Select frame 10 in the *Bottom Blur* layer and use the arrow keys or the Info panel to move the text on the *Bottom Blur* layer down 30 pixels and to the left 30 pixels.

    When you turn on the *Static* layer, the stage should look as it does in figure 9-27. Continue with the following steps.

18. If you turned the *Static* layer on, hide it again. Also hide the *Bottom Blur* layer.

19. In frame 10 in the *Top Blur* layer, click on the symbol instance (on the stage) in the *Top Blur* layer.

Figure 9-27. Move the text to create the blur effect.

20. Set the instance's Alpha to 0 in the Properties panel (Color drop-down list). This should make it "disappear" from the stage.

21. Repeat step 19 for the symbol on the *Bottom Blur* layer.

22. Right-click on frame 1 in the *Top Blur* layer and select Create Motion Tween.

23. Repeat step 22 on the *Bottom Blur* layer.

24. Turn the *Static* layer back on.

25. Click on the Scene 1 item in the Edit path to return to the main movie timeline.

26. Insert the movie clip symbol you just created onto the stage.

27. Use Control | Test Movie to play the animation and see the effect.

    Before finishing this example, take a look at one more thing. Note that because you built your movie clip based on a graphic symbol, any changes you make to the graphic symbol will appear in the movie clip. Continue with the following steps.

28. Access the *Hard Blur* graphic symbol using the Symbol list button.

29. Change the color of the text to a 40-percent gray by selecting on it and using the Fill color swatch in the Properties panel.

30. Switch back to scene 1 and then test the movie again. Notice how the modification to the graphic symbol is automatically incorporated into the movie clip symbol. This is one of the powerful things about using symbols for everything!

31. To finish this movie, add some sound effects to add interest. A gong sound was added to enhance the CD-ROM example. Do not forget about the aural element. It adds a new dimension to movies!

 TIP: *If you only want the clip to play once, place a Stop action in the last frame of the movie clip.*

Soft Blurs

Similar to the last example, adding more tween layers to a movie clip can create a soft blur. In exercise 9-20, which follows, you will create a graphic and movie clip symbol, similar to the previous exercise. However, this time the movie clip will have more layers, to create a softer effect.

CD-ROM NOTE: *To see what a soft blur looks like when animated, open the file* softblur.fla, *located in the* fgai/chapter09/texteffects/ *folder, installed from the companion CD-ROM. This file was developed according to the procedure outlined in exercise 9-20.*

Exercise 9-20: Creating a Soft Blur Effect

To create a soft blur, perform the following steps.

1. Start a new Flash file.

2. Make a graphic symbol that contains a string of text, similar to the last exercise.

3. Create a movie clip symbol and insert the graphic symbol on the stage of the movie clip.

4. Name the existing layer in the movie clip *Main*.

5. Build three new layers, named *Fade*, *Medium*, and *Tall*.

6. Copy the *Soft Blur* symbol from the *Main* layer.

7. Use Paste in Place (Ctrl + Shift + V) to paste the symbol to the three new layers.

8. Extend the duration of the four layers to frame 25.

9. Insert keyframes at frames 15 and 25 in the *Medium* and *Tall* layers.

10. Add a keyframe at frame 15 of the *Fade* layer.

11. Turn off all layers except the *Fade* layer. Your environment should look like that shown in figure 9-28.

Figure 9-28. Set up the keyframes and hide the layers.

Figure 9-29. Scale the instance of the text on the Medium *layer.*

12. Prepare the fade-in for the text. Change the Alpha of the symbol instance in frame 1 in the *Fade* layer to 0 using the Properties panel.

13. Right-click on frame 1 and select Create Motion Tween from the context menu.

14. Hide the *Fade* layer.

15. Unhide the *Medium* layer and click on frame 1.

16. Scale the instance of the text, as shown in figure 9-29, using the Free Transform tool. Make sure to grab the handle on the edge, not on the corner.

17. Change the Alpha of the symbol instance in frame 1 in the *Medium* layer to 0. Right-

Figure 9-30. Scale the instance of the text on the Medium *layer, using the corner point.*

Figure 9-31. Scale the instance of the text on the Tall *layer.*

click on frame 1 in the *Medium* layer, copy it, and paste it into frame 25.

19. In frame 25, scale the instance up slightly by using the Free Transform tool and a corner of the instance, as shown in figure 9-30.

20. Right-click on frame 1. Select Create Motion Tween from the context menu.

21. Right-click on frame 15 and select Create Motion Tween from the context menu.

22. Hide the *Medium* layer.

23. Unhide the *Tall* layer and click on frame 1.

24. Scale the instance of the text, as shown in figure 9-31. Note that the symbol is scaled more than that of the *Medium* layer.

25. In frame 1 in the *Tall* layer, change the Alpha of the symbol instance to 0.

26. Right-click on frame 1, copy it, and paste it into frame 25.

27. In frame 25, slightly scale up the instance using the Free Transform tool and a corner of the instance, similar to step 12.

28. Right-click on frame 1 and select Create Motion Tween.

29. Repeat step 24 in frame 15.

30. Hide the *Tall* layer and reveal the *Main* layer.

31. Click on the instance in layer *Main* and set its Alpha to 30 percent in the Properties panel.

32. Reveal all layers.

33. Because the animation is a movie clip, insert it into the main movie timeline and use Control | Test Movie to see the animation.

 TIP: *To stop the clip from looping when it plays, add a stop in frame 25 of the* Tall *or* Medium *layer.*

After completing the soft blur, try to modify the text. Access the graphic symbol the movie clip is based on and change the text. Reinsert the symbol into the main movie and play it again. This is how you can create one effect and reuse it over and over, simply by changing the text!

Rolling Credits

Of all the text effects you will want to create, rolling credits is one of the easiest to do. Many people see this effect and believe it is achieved with a mask layer. However, it is much simpler. Exercise 9-21, which follows, takes you through the process of creating rolling credits.

Exercise 9-21: Creating Rolling Credits

To create rolling credits, perform the following steps.

1. Create a layer named *Background*.

2. Create a solid fill that spreads across the entire stage. Use the Rectangle tool and set its Stroke to No Color. Set its fill color to one of the existing swatches in the Color palette.

3. Draw a rectangle consisting of lines only (no fill) in the area of the screen where you want the rolling credits to appear, as shown in figure 9-32.

4. Because the stroke rectangle and fill rectangle reside on the same layer, the stroke will "cut into" the fill, allowing you to delete the fill area that falls within the stroke. Select the fill area inside the stroke and delete it, as shown in figure 9-33.

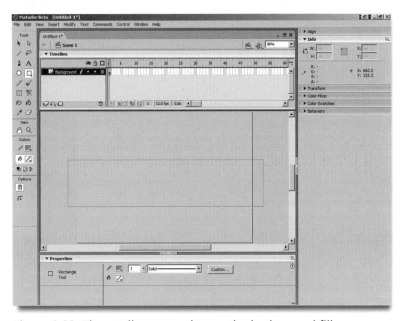

Figure 9-32. The smaller rectangle cuts the background fill.

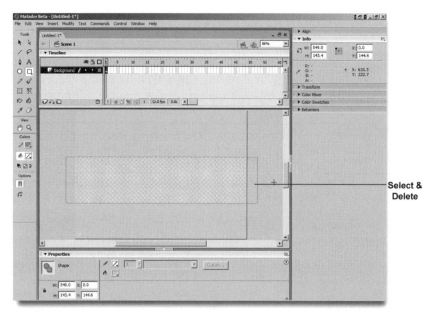

Figure 9-33. Select and delete the portion of the fill inside the stroke.

Now you will fill this area with a linear gradient that fades from the background color to 100-percent transparent and back to the background color. However, first you must create a transparent swatch to be used in the gradient.

5. Open the Mixer panel.

6. Enter *255*, *255*, and *255*, respectively, in the R, G, and B fields.

7. Enter *0* in the Alpha field.

8. Select Add Swatch from the Mixer panel's menu.

9. Open the Fill panel to create a gradient color that fades from the color of the fill (whatever color you chose in step 2) to 100-percent transparent (the "color" you just defined) and back to the fill color. To add color markers to the gradient definition, click along the gradient bar. To change the color of one of markers, use the swatch drop-down list that appears.

10. Fill the rectangle with the new gradient. Use the Transform Fill tool to modify the fill to your liking. You will need to at least rotate the fill so that it goes from top to bottom, as opposed to left to right.

11. Double click the on lines that surround the gradient and delete them so that you see no outline around the gradient area.

12. To simplify things, lock the *Background* layer.

13. Create a new layer for the animated text and create a graphic symbol of the body of text you want to animate.

14. Create a motion tween of the text passing over the gradient area. When setting up the tween, the text should start and end outside the place where the transparency begins.

15. Once the tween is set up, move the text layer behind the *Background* layer and play the animation by pressing Enter.

 CD-ROM NOTE: *Examine the file* rolling.fla, *and several other text effects in files located in the* fgai/chapter09/text effects *folder, installed from the companion CD-ROM. Text effects included are the following animations.*

- *Flipping text*
- *Stretching text*
- *Blooming text*
- *Tumbling text*
- *Exploding text*
- *Rippling text*
- *Shifting text*

▪▪▪ A Mask for Any Occasion: Transitions

Although Flash MX 2004 now includes the Transition timeline effect, there are times you will have to manually create your own transitions. This section outlines the basics of manually creating transitions using masks.

Fading and Dissolving

The first transition to examine is the creation of a fade or a dissolve. Earlier you read about how to adjust the transparency (Alpha) of a symbol on the stage. To create a fade-in or a fade-out, use the transparency settings, directly on the object, combined with a motion tween. Exercise 9-22, which follows, takes you through the process of creating a fade transition.

 Exercise 9-22: Creating a Fade (Dissolve) Transition

To create a fade-in or fade-out, perform the following steps.

1. Start a new Flash file.

2. Begin with some object, such as an imported graphic. Change it into a graphic symbol.

3. Set up a series of frames during which you want the object to fade in or fade out, such as a fade-in over 10 frames. Place a keyframe at the beginning (frame 1) and ending (frame 10) of the frame series.

4. To have the object fade in, set the Alpha at frame 1 to 0 percent. To make the object fade out, set the transparency at frame 10 to 0 percent.

5. Click on an object in the stage and use the Color drop-down in the Properties panel to set the transparency. The Alpha of an object is a property of the instance on the stage.

6. After specifying the transparency of the objects on the stage, right-click in a frame between frames 2 and 9. Select Create Motion Tween from the context menu.

7. Test the transition by pressing the Enter key.

 CD-ROM NOTE: *View an example of a fade (dissolve) transition by referencing the file* fade.fla, *located in the* fgai/chapter09/transitions/ *folder, installed from the companion CD-ROM.*

Wipe or Reveal

Create a wipe, or reveal-type, transition by using an animated mask. All of the transitions that use layer masks require that the mask be a symbol. Keep in mind the rules that govern the use of motion tweens; mainly that symbols are required. Exercise 9-23, which follows, takes you through the process of creating a wipe transition.

 ### *Exercise 9-23: Creating a Wipe (Reveal) Transition*

To create a wipe transition, perform the following steps.

1. After you have created the object you want to transition on the stage, change it to a graphic symbol.

2. On a new layer, draw a rectangular or circular fill. It will be used as the mask. The shape of the mask determines how the final transition will look. Additionally, ensure that the mask is large enough to completely cover the object you want to reveal. Make the fill a symbol in order to animate it.

3. Once the fill is defined as a symbol, animate it using a motion tween. In a reveal transition, the mask moves over the top of the object to reveal it. Thus, to define the animation for the mask, create a motion tween animation in which the mask moves over the top of object, as shown in figure 9-34.

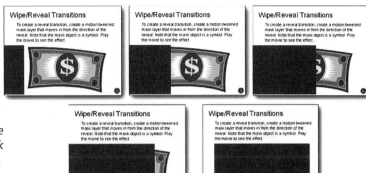

Figure 9-34. Define the movement of the mask for the reveal transition.

NOTE: *Keep in mind that the mask and the object(s) to be masked must reside on different layers.*

4. Once the motion tween for the mask is specified, double click on the layer name to open the Layer Properties dialog box. You can also access this dialog box using the Modify | Layer menu option.

5. In the dialog box, select the Mask radio button, as shown in figure 9-35. Click on OK. When you do this, the layer beneath the layer set to Mask should be set to Masked automatically. This is visually displayed in the timeline by the small arrows that replace the layer icons (see figure 9-36).

6. Play the animation to show the reveal transition.

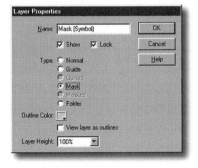

Figure 9-35. Setting the layer to mask using the Layer Properties dialog box.

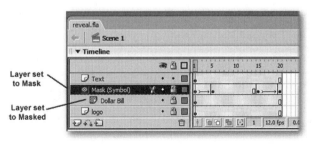

Figure 9-36. The timeline shows which layer is set to Mask and which is set to Masked.

Keep in mind that the mask layer affects the layer directly beneath it. However, a single mask layer may affect multiple layers if you want. Use the Layer Properties dialog box to set the layers that should be masked. Additionally, both the mask and its respective layers become locked when Mask or Masked is chosen in Layer Properties. If either layer is unlocked, the mask will no longer function.

 CD-ROM NOTE: *To see an example of a fade (dissolve) transition, see the* file reveal.fla, *located in the* fgai/chapter09/transitions/ *folder, installed from the companion CD-ROM.*

Push/Cover

Another type of transition worthy of noting is push or cover. In this transition, one object appears to push or cover a background object, as shown in figure 9-37. When creating this transition in Flash, use two masks that simultaneously animate to cover and reveal objects on different layers. Exercise 9-24, which follows, takes you through the process of creating a push transition.

Figure 9-37. The push or cover transition pushes one object over another.

 CD-ROM NOTE: *To view an example of the transition in exercise 9-24, see the file* push.fla, *located in the* fgai/chapter09/transitions/ *folder, installed from the companion CD-ROM.*

 ### Exercise 9-24: Creating a Push (Cover) Transition

In this exercise, you will create an animation in which a faucet image stays on stage for five seconds. Then a cover animation occurs over five frames, revealing the telephone, which remains on-screen for five frames.

1. First, create two objects on two different layers. In this example, the telephone character will push or cover the water faucet character, as shown in figure 9-38. Note that this transition works best if the two objects are close to the same size.

2. Once the two objects are on different layers, turn off one layer, preferably the object that is being covered. In the example, the telephone will cover the faucet; therefore, the faucet layer is turned off.

3. Make a symbol to use as the mask for the animation. Use the same mask for both objects. Make sure the mask is big enough to completely cover both objects.

4. Place the mask symbol over the top of the first object, but on a different layer. This cover will occur over five frames, beginning in frame 5 and ending in frame 10. The mask will be completely over the telephone in frame 10, and in frame 5 the mask will be to the left of the telephone, as shown in figure 9-38.

5. Create a motion tween for the mask to animate it. Right-click in a frame between the keyframes and select Create Motion Tween.

6. To make the mask work, use the Layer Properties dialog box on the layer that contains the animated mask and set it to Mask. Half of this transition is now set up. Press Enter to play the animation to see how it is developing.

7. To finish the second half of this transition, create a mask for the faucet that moves from center to right of the faucet as the mask for the telephone moves from left to center. In the timeline, both masks are tweened at the same time.

8. Make the layer that contains the mask for the telephone the current layer and unlock it. This temporarily turns off its mask characteristics.

Figure 9-38. Placement of the mask for the first object (telephone).

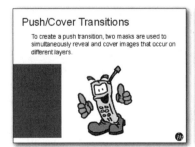

Frame 5   Frame 10

9. Click on frame 10 in the timeline. This should be where the mask is in the center of the screen.

10. Select the mask on the stage and copy it.

11. Hide the telephone layer and lock its mask. This enables you to see the mask but keeps you from inadvertently changing it.

12. Turn on the *Faucet* layer and create a new layer above it. The new layer will be used for the faucet's mask.

13. In the newly created layer, click in frame 5 and create a keyframe. Use the Edit | Paste in Place menu option to paste the copied mask symbol into the center of the screen. The pasted mask and the already existing mask should be next to each other on the stage.

14. Create a keyframe in frame 10 of the faucet's mask layer. Turn off the telephone's mask layer and use the right arrow key to nudge the faucet's mask to the right.

15. Turn on the telephone's mask layer. Click in frame 10 and nudge the faucet's mask to the right so that its left edge is adjacent to the right edge of the telephone's mask.

16. Set the faucet's mask layer to mask mode and lock the telephone and its mask.

17. Press Enter to view the resulting cover transition.

Shape Defines Transition

When it comes to mask transitions, note that the shape of the mask defines the transition. In previous examples, plain rectangular masks were used. Note that you can make the shape of a mask any shape you want, with only a couple of limitations. You cannot use a color blend tween on a mask. If you want an object to fade in or out, make it a symbol and apply the transparency tween to the object. Remember that no matter what the opacity of the object you use as the mask the mask will always be 100-percent opaque. The second limitation: you cannot use a shape tween on a mask.

 CD-ROM NOTE: *To see an example of circular mask transition, see the file* circular.fla, *located in the* fgai/chapter09/transitions/ *folder, installed from the companion CD-ROM.*

▪ ▪ ▪ **More on Masks**

In addition to text effects and transition effects, masks provide three other effects worth noting. These include a more realistic spotlight using partially transparent fills and magnification effects.

NOTE: *The magnification effects described here are a simulated effect as a result of animation and masks. This should not be confused with a movie's ability to zoom via ActionScript or FlashScript Player commands.*

A More Realistic Spotlight

Earlier in this chapter, you saw the basics of how a spotlight effect could be created using a plain circular fill as a mask. The result was not very realistic. Although plain fills can be used as masks, take it one step further by using a mask and another fill object. A second fill object softens the edges of the mask, creating a much more aesthetically pleasing effect. Exercise 9-25, which follows, takes you through the process of creating a push (cover) transition.

 CD-ROM NOTE: *To view an example of spotlight trick described in exercise 9-25, open the file* realspotlight.fla, *located in the* fgai/chapter09/ masks/ *folder, installed from the companion CD-ROM.*

 Exercise 9-25: Creating a Push or Cover Transition

To create a push transition, perform the following steps.

1. Begin by importing or creating an image that you can "reveal" using your spotlight. In this example, the spotlight reveals a cityscape image of Seattle, Washington.

2. Create a new symbol and draw a filled circle with the Oval tool. Make the fill color something other than black.

3. When creating spotlight effects, make sure the spotlight reveals a large enough portion of the background image. If you do not let the audience see enough of the background through the spotlight, they will not able to tell what the image is.

4. Make the second object to create the soft edge around the spotlight. Double click on the line that surrounds the oval and cut it (Ctrl + X or Command + X). This will be used as the basis for the second object.

5. Make a new graphic symbol and paste the copied circle in place so that its position is exactly the same as the previous symbol.

6. Create a new radial gradient that blends from black to transparent. Remember that before you can create a gradient that

uses transparency you must create a transparent color and swatch in the Mixer panel. You can then use the defined swatch to create the gradient.

7. Select the Paint Bucket and fill the circle with the new gradient. Make sure the gradient is perfectly centered within the circle. Then delete the outer line.

8. Switch back to the main movie timeline. Use the mask symbol to create the typical spotlight animation that has sharp edges. Open the Library window and place the mask symbol on the stage.

9. Set the positional keyframes and tween them.

10. Set the layer's mode to Mask. This process is just like the one used to create the spotlight animation earlier in this chapter.

11. To finish the effect, use the soft edge fill you created and place it over the top of the mask, having it move the same way as the mask. Align the key positions of the second symbol exactly over the mask and tween it. You may have to unlock the layer mask so that you can position the upper object.

12 Change the background color of the stage to black to finish the effect.

Magnify

Another effect that is quite easy to create using masks is a magnification effect. By building on the previous example, you can create a movie that has a magnifying glass pass over it. As it does so, the image will appear to magnify right before the viewer's eyes. It is really nothing more than a combination of a mask that reveals a background image and an enlarged image with a more complex symbol for the second object.

 CD-ROM NOTE: *To dissect the magnification example to see how it works, reference the file* magnify.fla, *located in the* fgai/chapter09/masks/ *folder, installed from the companion CD-ROM. Also in this folder is an example of how to use masks for reflections. View the file* reflect.fla *to examine it.*

■ ■ ■ Advanced Motion Guide Layers

Aside from the advanced animations that use masks, guide layers provide the capability for complex creations. In this section, you will read about using closed-path motion guide layers and how to control elements that move along them. Additionally, you will discover ways to simulate 3D objects, shadows, and reflections.

Atom Animation

To demonstrate how to use closed-path motion guide layers, examine a basic animation of a 2D atom, as shown in figure 9-39. In exercise 9-26, which follows, you will animate the looping ball around the layer guide, create one path, and then reuse the path via symbols.

Exercise 9-26: Creating a Closed-guide Animation

To create a closed-guide animation, perform the following steps.

1. Import or draw the basic image, as shown in figure 9-39. All you need is the black fill in the center, one ellipse (in a vertical orientation), and the small ball on the ellipse. These three elements should be graphic symbols so that they can be reused.

2. Begin by placing the center dot in the stage. Then place the ellipse symbol three times, orienting it as shown in figure 9-39. Do not place the "electrons" on the ellipses. You may need to switch to View | Outlines to line up the items. Use the Transform panel to enter numeric information for the rotation of the ellipses.

Figure 9-39. Using motion guide layers to create an animated atom.

3. Create a new movie clip symbol named *Rotating*. This will be the symbol that will be used on the stage for the three rotating electrons. Assign the default layer the name *Electron*.

4. Use Window | Library and place the "electron" on the stage.

5. Using the Add Motion Guide button, create a motion guide layer for the *Electron* layer.

6. Click-drag the ellipse symbol from the Library window to the *Guide* layer.

7. With the ellipse selected on the stage, select Modify | Break Apart. This "detaches" the ellipse from its symbol.

8. Use Modify | Ungroup on the ellipse to make it a stage object.

NOTE: *When using motion guide layers, their content must be stage-level objects to work properly. You cannot use a grouped element or a symbol as a motion guide.*

9. Extend the two existing keyframes out to frame 20. The loop of the electron around the ellipse will occur over 20 frames.

10. With Edit | Snapping | Snap to Objects enabled, drag the electron to the uppermost point on the ellipse, as shown in figure 9-40. When Snap is on, the electron will snap to the ellipse (*Guide* layer).

11. Create a keyframe at frames 5, 10, 15, and 20. In each of these frames, drag the electron to the following locations.
    - Frame 1: 12:00 position
    - Frame 5: 9:00 position
    - Frame 10: 6:00 position
    - Frame 15: 3:00 position
    - Frame 20: 12:00 position

12. After the electrons are in place, set up the tweening between each key position.

13. Press Enter to see the electron pass along the ellipse. If you want to get rid of the pause that occurs between frame 20 and frame 1, insert a keyframe at frame 19 and then delete frame 20.

14. Switch back to Scene 1.

15. Use Window | Library and place the movie clip you just created on the stage. Position it over the top of the existing vertically oriented ellipse.

16. Copy the movie clip and orient it for the other two ellipses. Scale and Rotate can be used to enter numeric information for the rotation.

17. Select Test Movie to view the results.

Snap

Figure 9-40. With Snap to Objects enabled, the object will snap to the motion guide.

 CD-ROM NOTE: *To examine the previous example to see how it works, see the file* atom.fla, *located in the* fgai/chapter09/guides/ *folder, installed from the companion CD-ROM.*

Simulating 3D

The previous exercise demonstrated how you could create a flat representation. When creating 3D effects, the difficulty is dependent on the content to be animated, because these effects are simulated 3D in Flash. For example, figure 9-41a shows an animated object. Figure 9-41b demonstrates how the illusion was created. Because a broken piece of the sphere was placed above the ellipse, the electron appears to pass behind the sphere.

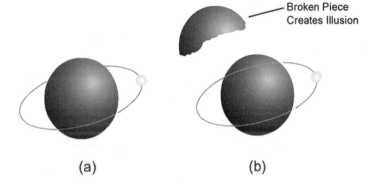

Broken Piece
Creates Illusion

Figure 9-41. To create the 3D effect in Flash requires (a) the creation of an illusion and (b) using a broken piece of the sphere.

(a)   (b)

CD-ROM NOTE: *To see how this illusion works, see the file* sim3D.fla, *located in the* fgai/chapter09/guides/ *folder, installed from the companion CD-ROM.*

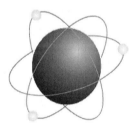

In actuality, this broken technique alone is not enough to do "everything." However, by combining this idea with the ability to create masks, almost anything is possible, as seen in the example in figure 9-42. In each case, masks hide the "behind" area for the elliptical elements.

CD-ROM NOTE: *To see how this illusion works, see the file* sim3D_2.fla, *located in the* fgai/chapter09/guides/ *folder, installed from the companion CD-ROM.*

Figure 9-42. Use masks and guides to create more complex illusions.

Shadows

Using the techniques described earlier in this chapter, you may already understand how to make shadows and reflections. The 3D effect shown in figure 9-42 can be enhanced by the creation of a simple shadow. Using the file *sim3D _2.fla*, quickly create a shadow. First, change the image displayed on the stage to a symbol. Although this is not as easy as pressing the F8 function key or using Modify | Convert to Symbol, it is not a complex process. Once the sphere is created and its rotating electrons are made a symbol, the shadow part is easy! Exercise 9-27 takes you through the process of creating the shadow.

Exercise 9-27: Creating a Shadow

CD-ROM NOTE: *Open the file* sim3D_2.fla, *located in the* fgai/chapter12/guides/ *folder, installed from the companion CD-ROM.*

Perform the following steps.

1. Unlock the layers.

2. Use Edit | Select All (Ctrl + A or Command + A) to select everything.

3. Right-click on one of the frames in the timeline and select Cut Frames.

4. Select Insert | New Symbol and make a movie clip symbol named *Sphere Movie*.

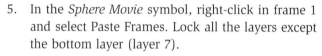

5. In the *Sphere Movie* symbol, right-click in frame 1 and select Paste Frames. Lock all the layers except the bottom layer (layer 7).

6. Switch back to Movie mode and delete everything, layers and all, leaving one layer. Name the remaining layer *Sphere Symbol*.

7. Use the Window | Library menu option and click-drag the *Sphere Movie* symbol onto the stage.

8. Copy the *Sphere Movie* symbol, create a new layer named *Shadow*, and paste the copied symbol instance.

Figure 9-43. Set the Color drop-down to Advanced, with the settings shown.

9. Click on the pasted symbol (the copy).

10. In the Properties panel, access the Advanced option for the Color drop-down and make the settings match those shown in figure 9-43.

11. Arrange the elements on the stage to match figure 9-44.

12. Use Test Movie to view the results.

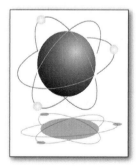

Figure 9-44. Who says Flash cannot create cool 3D tricks?

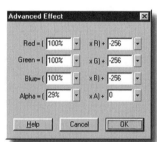

CD-ROM NOTE: *To see a finished example of the 3D shadow, reference the file* sim_shadow.fla, *located in the* fgai/chapter09/ guides/ *folder, installed from the companion CD-ROM.*

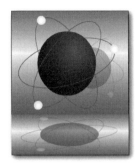

Reflections

Just as you can create interesting shadows, you can create reflections using the technique described for shadow creation, as shown in figure 9-45. By adjusting the Advanced settings or using the Alpha settings, you can also produce reflections. The key is the ability to take items that exist on the stage and convert it all into a symbol.

Figure 9-45. Reflections are as easy as shadows.

 CD-ROM NOTE: *To see a finished example of the 3D reflection, see the file* sim_reflection.fla, *located in the* fgai/chapter09/ guides/ *folder, installed from the companion CD-ROM. In addition, this chapter just touched on some of the effects possible with Flash. Included on the CD-ROM are many more examples of special effects you can examine to learn tips and tricks. The* fgai/chapter09/other/ *folder contains files showing the following effects.*

- Clouds
- Fog
- Smoke/fire
- Rain/snow

In the chapter09 *folder on the companion CD-ROM, you will find a misc folder that contains some miscellaneous effects, such as lens flares.*

▪ ▪ ▪ Summary

This chapter covered many fundamental concepts regarding the creation of animations in Flash. Layers and symbols are two of the most important efficiency features of Flash, no matter what you are creating. Although the animations created were very basic, they demonstrated the functionality of cel animation, motion tweens, color effects, guides, masks, and shape tweening. Building on these fundamentals, you will be able to create almost any type of animation using vector elements.

10

3D Animations and Flash

▪ ▪ ▪ **Introduction**

Many times in this book, you have read about how Flash can do almost anything. However, no software is strong in every area, and the content of this chapter focuses on one of the weaker points of Flash: its inability to efficiently incorporate 3D animation without the aid of other programs. Although it can be manually created in Flash, from scratch, 3D animation can be very time consuming, to the point that it is not worth the means required. When you create a web site that includes 3D animation, the most time-consuming aspect will be the creation of the 3D animation.

Why does it take so long to create 3D animation with Flash? It is because "3D animation" in Flash does not mean rendering out a series of raster images and importing them, as with a package such as 3D Studio Max or form-Z. Although this is one way of getting 3D into Flash, it is not the preferred method, because raster images quickly expand the size of Flash movies. The most effective means of creating 3D in Flash is to use elements that are vector, not raster.

Nevertheless, how do you get the vector representations that appear on the screen in a 3D modeling, animation, or rendering package into Flash in a vector form? Additionally, what about using GIF animations? Which is the most bandwidth savvy, while maintaining maximum visual appeal?

The content of this chapter covers a variety of methods of getting 2D representations of 3D elements into Flash. You will examine which methods of transference are the most effective, as well as which are the most time consuming. You will soon see the correlation between these different priorities. Since the release of Flash 4, two software packages now on the market (Vecta3D and Swift3D) make it easier to get 2D representations from 3D environments into Flash. However, if you are going to use 3D extensively, you need to be sure to include a little extra money in your budget so that you can pick up a copy of one of these software programs.

■ ■ ■ Objectives

In this chapter you will:

- Discover the primary means of incorporating 3D into Flash
- Learn how to use bitmap graphics as a basis for generating vectors
- Find out how to export vector representations from modeling packages such as AutoCAD and Pro/ENGINEER (Pro/E) for use in Flash animations
- Compare three new plug-ins/programs that allow you to use models and animation files from 3D Studio Max
- Take a closer look at how other packages (such as Adobe Streamline, Adobe Dimensions, ITEDO IsoDraw, Microsoft Word, and Viewpoint LiveArt) can assist in the generation of 3D-for-Flash projects
- Explore the advantages, disadvantages, and tips and tricks of using various graphic file formats with Flash

■ ■ ■ Methods of Creating/Simulating 3D

The use of 3D effects and objects in animations is a design trend appearing across the Internet. One of the most frequent questions asked by designers relates to how these effects are generated. It is not as simple as constructing a 3D animation or object in a package such as 3D Studio or form-Z and then rendering out the frames. All rendering packages, including 3D Studio and form-Z, render frames as raster images, not vector. Thus, a method must be established for converting the raster images from these packages to vector. The alternative is to construct 3D animations from scratch in Flash, which is not a simple task.

To create a 3D Flash animation, you will have to construct, photo-trace, or capture the needed vectors in one form or another. Although it is a lot of work, the results of 3D animation in Flash movies have been well received. Hopefully, future versions of Flash will simplify this job. But for now, construction, photo-tracing, and capturing are the means of obtaining 3D vector animations in Flash. Table 10-1 outlines the primary means, as well as the positives and negatives, of each method.

Table 10-1: Methods of Creating Flash 3D Animations

Method	Required Software	Advantages	Disadvantages
Construction	Flash Only	• High visual quality	• Has greatest time input • Complex 3D constructions are difficult • Matching color transformations is difficult
Bitmap: Direct integration	Raster editor, GIF animator, modeling, animation. or rendering package	• Fastest method • Very accurate geometry	• Largest file size (raster) • Images may appear grainy due to compression or color depth
Bitmap: Manual tracing	Modeling, animation, or rendering package	• High visual quality • Small file size	• Large time input • Trace each frame (monotonous) • Matching color transformations is difficult
Bitmap: Automatic tracing	Modeling, animation, or rendering package; Adobe Streamline	• High visual quality • Medium file size • Can generate very stylized images • Can automate rendering	• Time consuming • Files may have many points (larger file size) • Cannot always control rasterization process
3D environment/ static extraction	Modeling package and a converter (depending on file type)	• High visual quality • Small file size • Effects, such as farcles, can be added • Direct generation of vectors • Extremely detailed 3D objects • Easy extraction of animated vectors • Direct to SWF file	• Frames are manually output • Intermediate file formats and conversion software may be needed • Modeling packages are expensive • Modeling packages may be limited to certain platforms
3D environment/ dynamic extraction	3D Studio Max and purchased plug-in (Illustrate! 4.0, Swift3D, or Vecta3D)	• Maintain true arcs and Bezier curves	• Requires knowledge of 3D animation package • Generally spline based, as opposed to polygon based
Other: ViewPoint LiveArt	ViewPoint LiveArt98 (Adobe Streamline also required)	• Very stylized images (preset artistic styles) • "Import" existing models • Full 360-degree rotation of object and lighting	• Only exports raster (tracing required to complete) • Difficult to obtain line-only representations
Other: Adobe Dimensions	Adobe Dimensions, Macromedia FreeHand (optional)	• Extrusions and revolution used to generate 3D • Can determine light source and direction	• Limited to simple geometry • Fills are blended shapes and lines • Causes Flash to generate many symbols
Other: Microsoft Word	Microsoft Word, Macromedia FreeHand (optional)	• Very easy • Readily available package (Microsoft Word)	• Extrusion-only • Limited rotation • Gradients produce large file sizes

In general, all of the methods described in this chapter provide a means of getting the baseline work of an animation into Flash. Aside from directly integrating a series of raster images, in several cases there is no method that will automatically create or transfer an animation into Flash for you. Only two packages currently offer this capability: Swift3D and Vecta3D. When using the other techniques, the best-case scenario is that you will be able to transfer the basic line work of an animation into Flash. From that point, you will then have to render the frames of the animation, or the objects, in Flash.

Construction

3D animations in Flash can be constructed using both traditional cel animation techniques and other facilities, such as motion paths and symbols. In general, this is the most time-consuming method. It can also be tricky to figure out how to implement a specific animation using the capabilities in Flash.

Ultimately, whether or not you can construct an animation in Flash depends on the complexity of the animation. There is no way to work with true 3D elements in Flash. Yet to a certain extent you can simulate 3D in Flash. Due to the amount of time input, this is not a widely used means. In the last chapter you saw a couple of ways to simulate 3D in Flash.

One program of note is ITEDO IsoDraw. This program is well known among technical illustrators in many fields. It is magnificent for constructing vector axonometric and perspective drawings. Although it is expensive, the assistance this specialized package provides for constructing drawings is priceless.

 NOTE: *If you are creating a lot of mechanical, architectural, or other non-organic illustrations, take a look at the ITEDO IsoDraw tool* (www.isodraw.com/).

Raster Images

The first method of creating 3D animations in Flash is through the use of raster images. As highlighted elsewhere in this book, Flash is very capable as it relates to importing raster images, albeit raster images can quickly make file sizes grow. You can quickly and easily import a series of raster images into Flash, or import a GIF animation to get "3D in Flash." If you have a 3D modeling, rendering, or animation package, render out a series of BMP or PCT files to import into Flash. However, if the animation is lengthy, you will find that the movie's file size will grow quickly.

Although you can import GIF animation into Flash, more often than not the subsequent Flash movie will have a larger file size than the GIF animation. The results of a test showed that an SWF file was 10 KB larger than the GIF animation. This is presumably because GIF animations store data at 256 colors, versus Flash, which stores data in near 24-bit quality using the JPEG compressor. The lossless compression fared no better. In addition, GIF images frequently look poor in Flash if JPEG compression is used. This is because the JPEG compressor does not compress 256-color data very well.

Vector via Manual Tracing

Another method of creating animations in Flash is to use bitmap images as a basis for manual tracing, a technique (called photo-tracing) developed by traditional technical illustrators. This method is faster than from-scratch construction and provides better on-screen representation than simply integrating raster images. It also provides smaller file sizes than the integration of raster images. Exercise 10-1 takes you through the process of creating animations using the tracing technique.

Exercise 10-1: Creating Animations with the Tracing Technique

To create an animation in Flash using the tracing technique, perform the following steps.

1. Construct an animation, scene, or object in a 3D package. Render out an animation from the package as a series of images in BMP or Macintosh PCT (PICT) format. In general, you will want to render the images at a pseudo-high resolution, such as 800 x 600. This way, when you trace the vectors, an adequate amount of detail will be retained.

2. In addition to the size of the images, you will also want to make sure you render the images with shadows on and in "Phong" mode. Generally, raytracing and radiosity are not needed, nor are they recommended.

3. Import the raster images into Flash on a single layer and lock it

4. Create a new layer and trace the edges and elements in each frame of the animation. In general, the Pen tool works best for this operation.

5. Using the raster image layer as a reference, render the frames using the painting and drawing tools in Flash. The Dropper and Paint Bucket are the main tools you will use for this operation. Do not forget about the Lock Fills option and Transform Fill tool, because they will be very useful as you render each frame.

6. Once you have finished rendering the frames, open the library for the current file (Window | Library) and delete the raster images.

TIP: *When using the tracing technique, to keep file size down, open the library and delete the raster images when you are done. If you do not delete the raster images, the FLA file will be unnecessarily large.*

Although the tracing method is a valid technique for creating animations, it is by no means the fastest or the most accurate in relation to color transformations across multiple frames. It is very difficult, no matter what technique is used, to get gradients and fills to transform naturally across multiple frames. Using the tracing technique is also laborious because it requires each frame to be traced. Tracing is most effective when the number of frames is low, such as less than 30. As it relates to 3D animations, although the process of tracing is laborious, the typical end results are worth the effort.

Vector Rasterization: Automatic Tracing

Raster-to-vector converters can also be used to generate vector images for 3D animations created in Flash. In general, this technique provides an efficient means of creating vector representations, yet some control over the resulting vector drawing is lost. Raster-to-vector conversion still has a long way to go concerning accuracy. Yet in many cases this process can reduce the time input required for generating source material for 3D animations.

The first place to look for raster-to-vector conversion is in traditional illustration packages. Macromedia FreeHand and Adobe Illustrator both offer autotrace capabilities. In both packages you can import a raster image and then use the autotrace feature to generate a vector representation. Yet, based on testing of these packages, they are only best for very simple line drawings. When raster images contain fills and other complex gradations, the autotrace tools perform poorly at best.

However, Adobe Streamline is a software package specifically designed for changing bitmaps to vector images. The latest version provides the following advanced features.

- Support of major formats such as TIF and BMP
- Multilevel color support, including black-and-white to unlimited colors
- Adequate control over line recognition, accuracy, and path characteristics
- Ability to save both color and conversion settings as a composite setting
- Batch processing capability that can be used to convert multiple images at a time

- Path tools that can be used to edit generated vectors
- Ability to preview and view both raster and vector representations as overlays or individually
- An affordable price for such a powerful tool
- Ability to export in Adobe Illustrator AI format, which can also be successfully imported into Macromedia FreeHand and CorelDraw

As with the manual tracing process, use Adobe Streamline with raster images that are 800 x 600 pixels or larger. If you use an automated raster-to-vector process, do not forget to use the Modify | Optimize command to reduce the point count in your files. If the animation is frame-by-frame animation (likely, it will be), use optimization on each frame to decrease file size. Examination of versions 3.0 and 4.0 of Adobe Dimensions shows that version 4.0 is significantly better in many aspects.

 TIP: *If you are creating 3D Flash animations, Adobe Dimensions may be a smart investment, potentially saving you a tremendous amount of time (and money) in the long run.*

 CD-ROM NOTE: *There are several examples in the* fgai/chapter10/ Streamline Process *folder (installed from the companion CD-ROM) that demonstrate Flash animations that took significantly less time to generate due to Adobe Streamline.*

Vector from 3D Packages

Of all the means for creating 3D animation, probably the most promising as it relates to extremely complex objects is the capture of vector components from a 3D environment. If you have access to packages such as AutoCAD, Pro/E, or another modeling environment, capturing the vectors for use in Flash is much easier.

Additionally, new plug-ins released for 3D Studio Max are advantageous for generating Flash animations. This is not to imply that there are no problems with some of these methods or that it is a one-step process even with the new 3-D Studio Max plug-ins and standalone programs. Nevertheless, these programs do provide the means for using complex images, derived from models or environments, within Flash without having to photo-trace.

Static Extraction

The specifics for capturing the vectors from a 3D environment will vary, depending on the modeling package used. This is predominantly because each CAD-focused modeling package outputs various file formats. The basic procedure is outlined in exercise 10-2.

Exercise 10-2: Capturing Vectors from a 3D Environment

To capture vectors from a 3D environment, perform the following steps.

1. Create a model and orient the viewing angle to a pleasing view.

2. Capture a hidden-line-removed version of the vectors shown on-screen by exporting in a vector format, copying and pasting, or using a plot file.

3. Rotate the object to the next "frame" in the animation and repeat step 2.

4. Continue rotating and capturing until the entire "loop" or animation has been captured.

5. Import the captured files into FreeHand (preferably) or Flash, and then render.

The following sections provide further detail on the process of obtaining vectors from two of the most common modeling packages: AutoCAD and Pro/ENGINEER. Pointers for other modeling packages are included.

Extracting Vector from AutoCAD

In exercise 10-3, you will create an animation using the 3D AutoCAD environment.

Exercise 10-3: Using the AutoCAD Environment to Create an Animation

To use the 3D AutoCAD environment to create an animation, perform the following steps.

1. Create an object you want to animate, as shown in figure 10-1. Using this technique, you can have the object rotate around any of the three primary axes. Additionally, you could have it rotate simultaneously around all three. This example focuses on a simple rotation around one axis.

   The basis for the 3D model shown in figure 10-1 was created in FreeHand. To get vector images into a modeling program such as AutoCAD, the AI (Adobe Illustrator) file format works rather well. Once the line work was in AutoCAD, it was converted to a special line, called a polyline or pline, and extruded.

2. Choose a pleasing view in the modeling environment. Although this example will be a trimetric view, note that most modeling packages (AutoCAD included) can create isometric, dimetric, trimetric, and perspective views.

In this exercise, the logo shown in figure 10-1 will rotate around the Z axis. As with most modeling programs, the location of the object in relation to the origin for rotation is important. In AutoCAD, you can rotate around any point. However, to automate the generation from AutoCAD, the object has been located so that the center of the logo is at the origin (0,0,0). Thus, 0,0 can be entered when a base point for rotation is needed. Keep in mind that in AutoCAD rotation always occurs around the Z axis. If you want to rotate the object in another way (around absolute X or Y), you must reorient the coordinate plane so that the Z axis is aligned parallel to the axis around which you want the object to rotate.

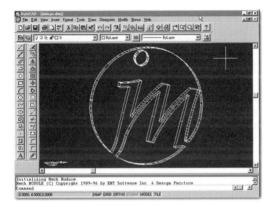

Figure 10-1. Use a program such as AutoCAD to create a 3D object to be transferred to Flash.

3. Before you start extracting and rotating the object, place a locator object in the drawing, such as two intersecting lines.

The locator object will be used as a registration point. As shown in figure 10-1, you will notice a pair of crosshairs in the upper right corner. This is important when you start piecing together the animation in FreeHand.

4. Use the Hide command to generate a hidden-line-removed version of the screen image.

5. Use the File | Export command and select Metafile (*.WMF) from the Save as Type drop-down menu. Name the file and click on OK.

6. You must determine the number of frames desired for the final animation. To determine the rotation of the object in the modeling environment, divide 360 by the number of frames. Keep in mind that more frames yield a smoother animation, but increase file size and the number of frames you must render in Flash.

7. In this exercise, the animation will be 12 frames. Therefore, a WMF file will be saved for every 30 degrees of rotation. Using the Rotate command, rotate the object 30 degrees, and save as a WMF file. Repeat this process for each of the 12 frames.

Because the extracted WMF files from AutoCAD have tessellation lines (lines that define the polygons along the sides of cylinders and other objects), the extracted WMF files will be imported into FreeHand. There they can be aligned, cleaned up, and then exported into Flash for color rendering. If you import the WMF files directly into Flash, many symbols of small line segments will be created automatically. Importing into FreeHand first reduces the number of symbols generated when you get to Flash. Continue with the following steps.

8. Once all of the WMF files have been extracted, import each of the WMF files into FreeHand, and place each one on a separate layer.

9. With all layers turned on, use the Align feature to align the images to the upper right (to the registration point).

10. Turn off all layers and begin working on getting rid of the tessellation lines on each layer, as shown in figure 10-2. Cleaning up the drawings in FreeHand will significantly reduce the file size of the resulting Flash animation.

11. Once all layers are cleaned up, export the file as a Flash Movie, with the Animate Across Layers checkbox selected.

12. In Flash, import the animation file and then use the Paint Bucket to render each frame.

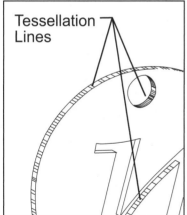

Figure 10-2. Importing the WMF files into FreeHand allows you to remove the tessellation lines and align the images.

If you use WMF or EPS files from AutoCAD (and some other a CAD packages), you will likely find that all arc segments are imported as small line segments. As noted earlier, this significantly increases the resulting Flash file size. In addition, you may find that the drawings exported in these formats provide reduced accuracy. For example, arcs often become "wavy" rather than remaining as smooth Bezier curves.

To provide more accuracy, you may find that using Hewlett-Packard Graphics Language (HPGL) files from AutoCAD yields better end results, although it does take longer because you have to print, rather than export, the files. An HPGL file is the format normally sent to a plotter or printer.

However, by plotting the file to the hard drive, you can actually use it as a method of transferring flat vector drawings out of a CAD package.

In actuality, any CAD package that can print or plot could use this method. However, an added benefit of HPGL files is that FreeHand will attempt to recognize line segments representing arcs and circles, replacing them with true arcs and circles. In this manner, HPGL files may prove to be more effective from AutoCAD, and quite possibly, other modeling programs. Exercise 10-4 takes you through the process of setting up AutoCAD to output appropriate HPGL files for import to FreeHand.

Exercise 10-4: Setting Up AutoCAD HPGL Files for FreeHand Import

To set up AutoCAD HPGL files for import in FreeHand, perform the following steps.

1. Use the File | Printer Setup menu option to open the Preferences dialog box.

2. Use the New button to configure a new printer.

3. In the Add a Printer dialog box, select the Hewlett-Packard (HP-GL) ADI 4.2 driver and click on OK.

4. Select the 7574 model and press Enter. Other printer models may also work.

5. Accept the remaining default options by pressing the Enter key several times.

6. Once you are returned to the Preferences dialog box, you should find the new printer configuration listed in the window. Click on OK to close the dialog box.

Once the printer driver is configured, extracting the HPGL files is a relatively easy process, as outlined in exercise 10-5.

Exercise 10-5: Extracting HPGL Files Imported into FreeHand

To extract HPGL files from FreeHand, perform the following steps.

1. Make sure the entire object is displayed in the current window, and then select File | Print. You can change the zoom level in AutoCAD using the View | Zoom menu options.

2. In the Print dialog box, change the Device and Default Information area to the new printer driver you just configured.

3. In the Additional Parameters area, make sure the Hide Lines and Plot to File checkboxes are selected.

4. Click on the File Name button and assign a path and file name to the HPGL file. Keep in mind that you will be outputting several of these, so choose a name that lends itself to incremental naming.

5. Click on OK. AutoCAD will output a plotter file (HPGL file) to the hard drive.

6. Rotate the object (as before) and use the File | Print menu option to output the remaining "frames" for your animation.

7. To finish the HPGL-to-animation process, import the files in a manner similar to the WMF process. Use the FreeHand Import feature, with the Files of Type drop-down set to HPGL Plot File.

8. Place each HPGL file on a separate layer and then, with all layers visible, align the images using the registration point you created.

9. Clean up each of the layers by removing the tessellation lines, and then export a Flash file from FreeHand.

10. In Flash, use the Paint Bucket to render each of the frames in the animation.

CD-ROM NOTE: *Sample files from the AutoCAD process are located in the* fgai/chapter10/AutoCAD Process *folder, installed from the companion CD-ROM. The original FreeHand, AutoCAD, and Flash files are available. Due to the inaccuracy of the* WMF *file, the* HPGL *file was used instead. This process produced far more accurate arcs and circles in the resulting Flash files.*

Extracting Vector from Pro/ENGINEER

Using Pro/E to extract your animation data is similar to the AutoCAD process, except that a different format for transfer of the data must be used. Pro/E and AutoCAD differ significantly in the way they create models. AutoCAD uses constructive geometry, whereas Pro/E is a parametric-based modeler. Additionally, AutoCAD models are polygonal, and Pro/E models are spline based. Nonetheless, if you have even remote experience in either package, you should at least be able to open a model and extract the basic data needed for a Flash animation. Exercise 10-6 takes you through the process of extracting vector information from Pro/E.

Exercise 10-6: Extracting Vector Information from Pro/ENGINEER

To extract vector information from Pro/E, perform the following steps.

1. Begin by creating or opening your model or scene into Pro/E, such as that shown in figure 10-3.

2. Use Utilities | Environment to turn off labels (such as datum plane notes, axis names, and object names) shown on the screen. If you do not turn them off, they will appear in the files you output (and subsequently increase the file's size tremendously).

3. In the menu bar at the top, set the display mode to Hidden Line Removed.

4. Choose an appropriate view for your animation using View | Spin/Pan/Zoom. This will bring up the dialog box shown in figure 10-4. Set the Type to Dynamic Orient and then use the sliders to get the object into an appropriate view.

   In this animation, a simple "rotate around a single axis" will be performed. As with the AutoCAD process, you can rotate around any axis of the object, or around the origin. In this object, the rotation was set around the center of the object.

5. Once you know what you want to do with the object, decide how many frames you want in the animation. Divide 360 by

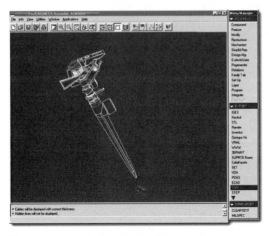

Figure 10-3. Models in Pro/E can also serve as a basis for Flash animations.

Figure 10-4. View | Spin/Pan/Zoom brings up a dialog box in which you can set the starting orientation of the object.

the number of frames to yield the degrees of rotation for each increment.

6. Capture the first frame in the "starting" orientation and save it as a CGM file. In Pro/E, you do this using File | Export | Model. In the Menu Manager, select CGM | Cleartext | Abstract and enter a file name at the bottom of the screen. Keep in mind that you will be exporting multiple images, so your file name should lend itself to incremental naming.

    Pro/E works in a default directory called the working directory. The CGM files you save will be stored there.

 TIP: *If you want your CGM files to be stored in a specific location, use File | Working Directory to set the working directory before you export the CGM files.*

7. Rotate the model to its next orientation (360 divided by number of frames) using View | Spin/Pan/Zoom. For example, if you wanted 12 frames, the rotation would be 30 degrees.

8. Capture another CGM file.

9. Repeat this process until you have all frames for the animation.

In both the AutoCAD and Pro/E processes, if you have multiple objects that need to rotate simultaneously you may find it easier to rotate the view than the objects. Efficiency will depend on how the objects being captured were created.

 CD-ROM NOTE: *Sample files from the Pro/E process are located in the* fgai/chapter10/Pro-E Process *folder, installed from the companion CD-ROM. Two animation files are available. One rotates the object around one axis; the other rotates around all three at one time.*

Other 3D Environments

If you are using a package other than AutoCAD or Pro/E, you will likely find that there is at least one way to capture the vectors. If the package can output to a printer, you can at least use a printer (HPGL) file.

Another package worth noting as it relates to 3D models is a viewing and "rendering" program called LiveArt98 from ViewPoint DataLabs (*www.viewpoint.com*). This relatively inexpensive utility allows 3D models to be viewed in various illustration styles. The most useful feature of the program is that the model can be completely manipulated within the viewer; that is, you can view it from any angle, similar to VRML or VR files.

Originally, the purpose of this program was to provide those who knew nothing about modeling with the ability to use models in the documents they produce on a daily basis. Thus, LiveArt models can be embedded within all sorts of programs, not least of which is Microsoft Word. An added (and undocumented) feature is the ability to drag and drop your own 3DS and DXF files into the viewer, which will render the files using the preset styles.

The one caveat to this program is that there is no way of capturing or outputting the vectors the viewer displays. If there were, all developers using Flash would undoubtedly purchase this program, because it would provide one direct way to go from a 3D model to a 2D vector representation. The only output from the program is the print capability and exporting TIF, GIF, JPG, and PNG files (all raster). Due to this limitation, the program has not yet reached its full potential.

If you do much 3D work in Flash, you need to examine this program, regardless of its limitations. When you combine TIFs from LiveArt with Adobe Streamline's vector conversion capability, you can quickly generate very stylized Flash animations.

Several of the techniques mentioned in this chapter (including the AutoCAD, Pro/E, and Streamline tracing processes) add many symbols to your file when you import the images into Flash. If you use Break Apart to separate the individual frame images from their symbols, you can then delete these extraneous symbols. To delete a large number of symbols without having to right-click on each symbol and delete the symbol in the library, use Window | Library to open the current file's library. Then select multiple symbol names in the window, access the Library menu, and select Delete. This will let you delete multiple symbols easily.

If you have a modeling program other than AutoCAD or Pro/E, there is likely at least one way of obtaining vectors. In general, you should look for the following features.

- *Support for exporting a vector format, such as EPS, CGM, or AI:* These formats are the most widely supported intermediate file formats for 3D-based packages. Generally, these three formats can be imported into FreeHand or Flash. Yet, with the wide variety of graphics file formats available, be prepared to spend a little extra cash for a conversion program such as Hijaak Pro or Debabelizer. Some 3D programs do not support these standard metafile formats.

- *Support of copy-and-paste functionality:* In this scenario, you can select the screen representation of the modeling vectors and copy them to the clipboard. You then paste them into FreeHand or Flash. Some modeling programs do support copy and paste; however, the routine generates bitmaps rather then vector representations. In addition, the complexity of the object(s) being copied and the amount of RAM available may limit the use of this technique.

- *HPGL (printer) output support:* Even though the software can generate hardcopy prints, this is the method that will most likely work for almost any 3D modeling environment. By setting up a printer/plotter driver to write an HPGL file to the hard drive, you can then import the resulting file into FreeHand or Flash for editing to remove any extraneous data. Again, it is preferable to load the file into FreeHand and then export to Flash.

The previous method has one severe caveat: all arcs are plotted as individual line segments. This factor exponentially increases your file size because of the number of points used. When importing an HPGL file into FreeHand, it will attempt to recognize arc components consisting of line segments and replace them with true arcs. However, many arcs will still remain as individual line segments. In this scenario, the best choice is to manually replace arcs in FreeHand.

 TIP: *If you have to use the HPGL process, the latest version of FreeHand has many facilities that can help you. The Cleanup | Simplify filter is invaluable, as is the ability to join and work with layers.*

Dynamic Extraction

3D Flash animations began appearing on the Web not long after the release of Flash 3. Everyone wanted a simple, straightforward method for quickly generating Flash animations from a 3D model. Until lately, all of the other techniques in this book were the only way to generate 3D Flash animations, and they are anything but quick!

Following the release of Flash 4, three supplementary plug-ins/programs that can generate 3D animations in the Flash SWF format were released. They are Illustrate! 5 by Digimation, Inc. (*www.digimation.com*), Vecta 3D by IdeaWorks3D (*www.ideaworks3D.com*), and Swift3D by Electronic Rain (*www.swift3D.com*). All three solutions will generate flat, animated vector files for Flash. As of this writing, Swift3D and Vecta3D are the only solutions that will output gradients. The solution will output flat colors only. Swift3D or Vecta3D might be your best bet.

Vector from Other Packages

As ingenuity is the mother of invention, depending on what software you have available, you could probably discover many ways of creating animations in Flash. Undoubtedly, Swift3D and Vecta 3D should be used if you have many 3D animations to create.

However, for those who are not blessed with finances or software packages and utilities, other programs can also be used to help you more quickly and more easily generate animations. Some packages you may have, and some you may not. Nevertheless, these ingenious methods are worth a brief mention if nothing else.

Microsoft Word

If you are familiar with the data tracked by sites such as MediaMetrix *(www.mediametrix.com)*, you know that Microsoft Office is one package that most people are likely to have. You may not have AutoCAD or Pro/E, but most likely you own or otherwise have access to Word.

With Microsoft Word's 3D tools, you can create, albeit simple, animations. Although it really was not designed for it, you can use Word to generate basic 3D line work from which you can create Flash animations. Exercise 10-7 takes you through the process of using Word to generate 3D images.

NOTE: *Keep in mind that this method has two problems. It works with very simple shapes only, and Word can rotate a shape up to 180 degrees only.*

Exercise 10-7: Using Word to Generate 3D Images

To use Word's 3D tools to generate 3D images, perform the following steps.

1. Open Word's drawing tools by right-clicking on one of the toolbars at the top of the screen. Select the Drawing option in the context menu that appears.

2. Use the Draw menu to create a polygon, or paste a polygon from another package, such as FreeHand or Flash. Figure 10-5 shows a shape that is simple enough for Word to manipulate.

    Word can deal only with very basic, singular polygons. If you have two closed shapes, peculiar overlapping will occur because Word is not really designed for the creation of 3D animation. Keep in mind that Word can handle basic shapes only, such as the shape shown in figure 10-5.

3. In the Drawing toolbar, turn on 3D by clicking on the 3D icon on the far right. Select 3D Settings from the menu that pops up.

4. Use the 3D Settings toolbar to specify the Depth, Direction, Lighting, Surface, and 3D Color settings.

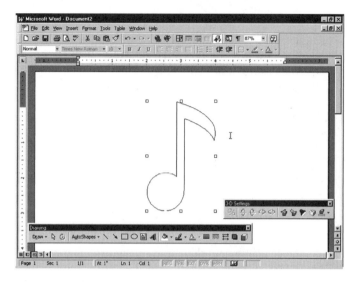

Figure 10-5. A simple shape that can be manipulated in Word.

5. Once you have the first "frame" defined, copy the object to the clipboard and paste it into Flash.

6. Back in Word, use the Tilt options in the 3D Settings toolbar to rotate the simple object.

7. Again, copy and paste the new image to the clipboard. Repeat these steps until all frames are in Flash.

If you decide to use the Word process, it is probably best to use the Wireframe Surface option and then render the object in Flash. The gradients created by Word will generally make files quite large.

Adobe Dimensions

There has been much talk on the Web concerning Adobe Dimensions as a possible tool for outputting material for 3D animations in Flash. No doubt, one of the goals for the program was to easily work in 3D with vector-based, 2D objects. However, Dimensions has several problems. In general, Dimensions works well for simple geometry and basic transformations. It will also handle some animation tasks. Yet, it is a somewhat difficult program to use. Additionally, the files the program outputs require rerendering, because their gradients consist of line and shape blends instead of fills.

Many Flash developers like using Dimensions. However, version 1.0 of the program was better than 3.0 in terms of use with Flash. In addition, as with many of the procedures discussed in this chapter, using many of the automatically generated symbols is a way of reducing file sizes. Unfortunately, Dimensions is notorious for adding hundreds.

Summary

In this chapter, you have examined a wealth of methods for generating 3D Flash animations. Indeed, the best method for creating 3D animations depends on time, task, and the software resources available. Keep in mind that the end results of 3D animations in Flash are usually very impressive, even if the means seem contrived and monotonous. Ultimately, for each project that seems to demand 3D, evaluate that need based on the difficulty of achieving it. Make sure you need 3D before you spend hours generating a Flash representation of it.

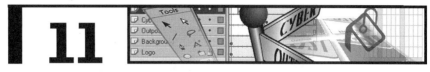

Video and Flash

▪ ▪ ▪ Introduction

Throughout the last couple of chapters you have been examining the wide variety of media elements that can be created in, and imported into, Flash 2004. This chapter concludes with an examination of the video capabilities of Flash 2004.

Flash 2004 offers much improved support for digital video. The new Video Import wizard assists you by providing control over embedding and linking video; editing things such as frame rate, frame size, and so on; as well as the ability to create video profiles. Profiles allow you to establish the settings for a series of clip imports that can be reused.

▪ ▪ ▪ Objectives

In this chapter you will:

- Discover the primary attributes of digital video of which you must be aware
- Learn the primary issues for preparing video for use in Flash
- Find out about the two ways of importing video into Flash

▪ ▪ ▪ Attributes of Digital Video

Over the past couple of years, web-based digital video has been primarily reserved for those who had and could afford high-bandwidth connections. However, today more and more people are able to afford faster connections. Concurrently, compression technologies are getting better and better. Due to these two factors, digital video on the Web, albeit at small frame sizes and with sometimes sporadic playback, is becoming a reality. At the current rate, within the next three years, digital video on the Web will become a reality for the majority home Internet users.

Yet from the creation standpoint, digital video is quite likely one of the trickiest and most time-consuming media elements you will deal with on the computer, regardless of whether you are developing for the Web, CD, DVD, or broadcast. Of these media, the Web has the greatest constraints as it relates to what you create.

Creating digital video content that is technically efficient, effective (as far as what the clip is to show), and pleasing to the audience requires tremendous time input and a lot of know-how. Most people (either developers that have not done video work before or clients who think it is as simple as "point, shoot, and upload") are unaware of the difficulty of "getting that good shot," the technical knowledge needed to get the appropriate balance between quality and file size, and the time required to composite everything in the multiple applications generally necessary to get content from camera to finished media file.

 TIP: *Anytime you are presented with a potential project that uses video, find out as much as you can about how much video will be desired and how much work is involved. Digital video is often the largest consumer of development time in a project.*

Although this single chapter cannot provide all you need to know about video, it will provide a general overview of the things to consider in the process from camera to Web. Given that video consists of bitmap sequences and digital audio, you will find that some of the attributes of those individual elements apply here. But there are other things you must know about that are unique to digital video.

Image Attributes

Because the graphic component of digital video consists of bitmap graphics, the attributes discussed in Chapter 7 apply. If you are simply using raw footage from a camera (discussed further later in the chapter), you do not have to worry significantly about many of the raster image details, such as dpi or color depth. However, seldom is a video clip created from raw footage alone. You usually combine still images with recorded footage to create a finished video clip. In such a case, you do need to be aware of resolution, color depth, and alpha data. Thus, knowledge of basic raster graphic attributes should be well understood before taking on any project that includes video.

File Formats and Compression

As it relates to file formats and compression of the graphic component of video, the primary thing you should keep in mind when compositing a digital video clip for use in any media form is that all of the source material you use should be generated from lossless or uncompressed data. Typically, which of these you choose depends on how much storage space you have.

Nevertheless, the use of lossy compressed data (which, when a digital video clip is generated is lossy compressed again) typically makes video clip file sizes larger and can have any number of effects on the visual quality of the resulting video clip. Thus, you should use lossless compression (or no compression at all) for all aspects of the source media from which you intend to generate a digital video clip.

Additionally, if at all possible, strive to use only digitally recorded footage, as opposed to analog sources. Digital cameras are much cheaper today than even a few years ago, and provide extremely clean video. Analog media always has a certain amount of noise associated with it when you digitize it, not to mention the issue of generation loss that occurs with analog tapes such as VHS and S-VHS. A thousand-dollar digital video camera today can typically provide more than adequate quality, and approaches "prosumer" (in other words, high-end consumer or near low-end professional) quality. Such a camera also provides more than adequate quality for the level of quality necessary on the Web today.

Concerning file formats, aside from the issue of what type of compression is used in the file, you should choose a format supported by whatever video editing software you are using. The most common video editing packages support a variety of formats. What you need to pay attention to is making sure you do not use lossy compressed formats, such as JPG, if at all possible.

Frame Size

One implied attribute that was not discussed at length in Chapter 7 is that of image size or dimension, which in essence controls the video clip frame size. Today, web-based video clips are quite small. Typically for slow connections such as modems, frame sizes are typically 160 pixels by 140 pixels. Anything larger is likely to discourage the end user from spending the time to acquire the clip. If you need larger frame sizes to show something in particular, consider using bitmap images.

Faster connections (such as T1, cable modem, and ADSL or DSL, the latter two of which are becoming more prominent due to decreasing cost) may permit frame sizes up to 320 pixels by 240 pixels. However, using this frame size needs to be carefully weighed against the costs of producing and delivering it to the end user.

In any case, decisions concerning frame size should be made judiciously, with adequate knowledge of your intended user and her connection speed. Regardless of whether you are referring to bitmaps, sound, video, or Flash SWF files in general, everything you do concerning media choices and the quality of those media elements should be based on the available data rate for the end user. Recall from Chapter 1 that it is the middle 68 percent you should shoot for. Too often, the target data rate for media elements is assumed too high because a developer inaccurately projects the technical sophistication or capabilities of his audience. "Know thy audience" is the best advice a developer can heed!

Audio Attributes

Chapter 8 discussed the variety of attributes with which you must be concerned when dealing with digital audio. The primary concern when dealing with web audio is to ensure that the resolution and bit depth are appropriate for delivery over the Web. In most instances the computer speakers of web surfers are not all that good, and therefore anything more than 22-kHz, 16-bit, mono (or 22-kHz, 8-bit, stereo where appropriate) is just wasted. Thus, you can reduce file size significantly by reducing sampling rate, bit depth, and number of channels (reducing each of these by half reduces file size by half).

Chapter 8 also discussed how you can record and manipulate digital audio. An additional note to that discussion is that the file size of a video clip is about half graphics and half video (more or less). You should follow the guidelines provided in Chapter 8 to try to keep the audio in your video clips as small as possible, particularly if you record the sound. In addition, do not forget in regard to all media elements to keep in mind issues concerning copyright.

Video Specifics

In addition to dealing with the basic attributes of graphics and audio, digital video has several attributes unique to it. The sections that follow briefly describe these attributes.

Temporal Components

The temporal attributes of video have to do with time and the playback of the graphic componentry in the clip. The length and frame rate of video clips are considerations when it comes to distributing video over the Web.

Length

Simply put, the length of a video clip ultimately determines overall file size, and affects data rate; that is, the connection speed required for uninterrupted playback. When lengthy clips are put online, even in a streaming capacity many low-bandwidth users are reluctant to utilize the available content. And even when they do, a lagging download stream usually interrupts the playback of the video clip, creating a less than flawless performance.

When choosing to include video in a site, consider the audience and their connection speed. Granted, as higher-speed connections become more prominent within the general consuming public, bandwidth will become less of an issue. But today, you must judiciously choose what to include (and more frequently, what not to include) as it relates to web-based digital video.

If you use video on the Web, make sure there is a reason for doing so; that is, a message that cannot potentially be communicated another way. If you must use video, make clips as short as is possible without affecting the message of the clip. Short, to-the-point clips are much more readily received by the audience. Granted, if the site is focused around entertainment, such as a movie trailer, the user may be more patient about a slow download. But seldom will a user wait for a clip to download unless it is for entertainment value. As it relates to web video: have a point and be to the point.

Frame Rate

Frame rate is essentially the speed at which the frames in the digital clip are played back, which in essence affects the total number of frames in a video clip. The higher the frame rate, the more frames in the movie and consequently the larger the file size.

TV-quality playback is 30 frames per second (fps), which is much more than is needed (or reasonable) for web-based digital video. In most instances, for high-movement web video, 12 to 15 fps is more than adequate. For "talking head" types of clips, you may be able to drop the frame rate of the clip to 10 fps or less, depending on the situation.

Compression

All video formats, for web distribution or not, use some sort of compression. In most cases, digital video formats utilize lossy compression of one form or another. Like the lossy compression used in the JPEG format, data is sacrificed to attain smaller file sizes.

Aside from the "lossy versus lossless" issue, digital video compression formats can be one of two types: spatial (also called *intraframe*) compression or temporal (also called *interframe*) compression. The following sections discuss these briefly.

Spatial

Spatial compression occurs within an individual frame of the clip. Rather than performing comparisons across multiple frames, spatial codecs compress each frame of a video clip as a single unit. In essence, spatial compression operates on each frame of the clip, looking for redundant pixel colors within the frame, as though each were an individual still image.

Typically, spatial compression is best for video clips that have a lot of camera or subject movement; that is, where there are significant changes across multiple frames. In these types of clips, there are many changes from frame to frame, and therefore temporal compression, discussed in the following section, proves ineffective.

Temporal

Unlike spatial compression, temporal compression is based on the unchanging data that occurs between the frames of a video clip. The areas between the frames of a set of adjacent frames that do not change are omitted, thus reducing the size of the file. You could say that temporal compression looks for redundancy across frames (interframe), and spatial compression looks for redundancy within frames (intraframe).

One thing you need to understand about temporal compression (since the standard Sorenson codec in Flash uses temporal compression) is the idea of key frames in a temporally compressed clip. Key frames, as you know them in regard to Flash, are similar, but they are used a little differently in video.

Temporal compression makes note of specific frames in the movie, called key frames, and uses them as a standard for comparing subsequent frames (to find redundancy). When a developer creates a video clip that uses temporal compression, he establishes the number of keyframes. The greater the number of keyframes, the more accurate the visual quality of the clip will be, but the larger the file size. The trick is to find the number of key frames that strikes the best balance between quality and file size. Because the content of a video clip may vary drastically, often trial and error is needed to find the quality/size balance.

 NOTE: *The "trial-and-error" aspect of quality/size balance is one of the things that makes working with video time consuming.*

Frames surrounding a keyframe in a temporally compressed clip, called *delta frames*, are compared to the previous keyframe and are compressed where unchanging pixels are found. Thus, temporal compression is best for video clips in which there is not a lot of camera or subject movement, as is the case with "talking head" types of clips. The more changes from frame to frame in a temporally compressed clip, the less effective the temporal codec is.

Codecs

Many people are familiar with some of the common digital video file formats, such as QuickTime and MPEG, due to the rising number of movie trailers on the Web, as well as the popularity of the MP3 audio format, a near cousin of MPEG video. However, what most people do not realize is that the content of any video compression format, from AVI to QuickTime to MPG (the three most common), can use a variety of different compression algorithms or even no compression.

There are a half dozen or more codecs that can be used in just about any video file format. A few of the most common are Radius Cinepak, Sorenson, and Intel Indeo. At this point, only one needs mentioning (Sorenson), as it is the primary one that is directly supported by Flash 2004. Flash 2004 transparently provides the Sorenson Spark compressor (for encoding video on import) in the Flash 2004 application, and the respective decompressor for playback in the Flash Player. Thus, aside from the Flash Player or the Flash plug-in, nothing else is needed for video playback inside a Flash movie.

The "standard" version of the Sorenson Spark motion video codec provides basic capabilities for including video directly inside a Flash file. The standard version of the code is a temporal compressor, meaning that it excels at video clips that do not have a lot of camera or content movement. In material to follow you will see how to import and use the Sorenson codec to define the compression options, such as number of keyframes and frame size, for an imported video clip.

Sorenson offers a third-party tool to aid in the development and integration of video into Flash. Called Sorenson Squeeze (*www.sorenson.com/*), this small utility and is quite straightforward to use (discussed in material to follow), and is very powerful.

Bit Rate

Of all attributes of video, bit rate is the most important. Bit rate is essentially the download rate required for uninterrupted playback of a media element. Bit rate can be calculated by dividing the file size by the amount of time for playback (in seconds). If the download speed is slower than the required bit rate, the video clip will inadvertently pause during playback, and may do so several times before the clip finishes playing.

Because of the potential for the download stream to overtake the playback rate, you often have to either entirely preload a Flash file that includes video (so that it is totally downloaded before it is needed) or disguise the download stream by using what is known as a preloader with ActionScript.

CD-ROM NOTE: *An example file with a preloader is included in the* fgai/chapter11/preload *directory on the companion CD-ROM. If you open the file into Flash you can view the ActionScript code required to create the preloader. However, if you use Test Movie you will not see the preloader work. Chapter 12 discusses how to use the Bandwidth Profiler, with which you can see the preloader actually work.*

As it relates to video, it is often helpful to have an idea of how much time is needed to preload data. You can use the Bandwidth Profiler and the Generate Size Report tool (discussed in the next chapter) to figure out the appropriate amount of time through testing. You can also calculate the amount of time needed using the following formula.

Preload time = Download time – length (in seconds) + 10% of length

Chapter 1 covered how to establish download time, given a bandwidth. However, to refresh your memory, the calculation is as follows.

Download time = File size in kilobytes / (device bandwidth in kilobits per second / 8)

For example, if you have a clip that is 15 seconds long and you are accessing it that is 100 KB in size on a 14.4 modem, the following calculations can be made.

- Download time: *100 KB / (14.4 kbps / 8) = 55.55 seconds*
- Preload time: *56 seconds – 15 seconds + (15*.1) = 42.5 seconds*

File Formats

Flash supports a variety of file formats, which are outlined in table 11-1. Note that certain formats are supported only via QuickTime 4 (or higher) or DirectX 7 (Windows only).

▪ ▪ ▪ Preparing Video for Use

One of the most time-consuming aspects of working with video is preparing it for use, particularly for use on the Web. The first step in the process is to capture or download the video, depending on the source. There are many ways this can be done, two of which are discussed briefly in the next section: capturing (via a video capture system) and downloading (via a direct connection).

Once you have a digital copy of raw footage, you must then prepare it. Often you want to cut out specific portions, beef up the lightness or contrast, or otherwise prepare the raw footage in any number of ways. Seldom does one use raw footage straight from the camera.

Table 11-1: Flash-supported File Formats Under Macintosh and PC.

File	Extension	Win	Mac	Special Features
Audio Video Interleaved	.avi	Yes	Yes	Most video editing tools support
Digital Video	.dv	Yes	Yes	Standard digital format commonly used in digital video cameras
Motion Picture Experts Group	.mpg, .mpeg	Yes	Yes	Streaming format
QuickTime Movie	.mov	Yes*	Yes	Most video editing tools support
Windows Media File	.wmv, .asf	Yes**	Yes	Long-playing video, live broadcast format, and streaming format

* These formats are supported only via QuickTime 4 or higher.
**These formats are supported only via DirectX 7 or higher.

Once the video is prepared, it is ready for inclusion in Flash directly, or via processing through Sorenson Squeeze. The following sections provide a brief discussion on this process and finish with some tips concerning video content.

Digitizing Video

There are two basic methods of capturing video: using a video capture system, and direct download (sometimes referred to as "direct capture") via a direct digital device connection. The second of these is generally easier. However, it really depends on what medium your source material is on as to which you will want to use. The sections that follow discuss these methods.

Standard Video Editing Equipment

Speaking generally, standard video capture equipment designed for broadcast video work can be used to extract source video for the Web. There are as many types of systems that can be used as there are brands of computers. However, almost all of them are designed for high-quality captures (typically for NTSC 720 x 486 resolution) and are moderately to overtly expensive.

Using these types of systems for capturing web video is like using a dump truck to pull a child's wagon; they represent much more power and functionality than you typically need. However, these systems are often the only way to go if your source material is on analog media (e.g., VHS or S-

VHS) or professional-grade media (e.g., beta or 1/2-inch). In addition, if your company or school has such a system at its disposal, you might be able to put it to work for web video.

Due to the major differences among these systems, it is not possible to delve into the minutiae of "how-to" associated with each, but suffice it to say that most of these types of systems provide hardware for analog and digital video connections for the encoding of video and audio data. With most of these systems you linearly digitize the data, usually storing the file in a local, proprietary digital video format or in a format that stores the file compressed with a proprietary digital video codec. Then, to port to another system you "resave" the file (as well as downsample the video frame size, as applicable) to port it to another machine for integration in multimedia.

The key is: when given the option, use a digital source. Just as compressing a file adds noise to it, there is an inherent amount of noise in most captured material from analog sources, particularly low-quality sources such as VHS or S-VHS. Such noise is always bad when file size is of the utmost importance. Web video files will always be smaller when captured from source material derived from a digital source.

Direct Connection to a Digital Device

One of the more conventional approaches to working with video is to use a digital camera that includes a USB or FireWire connection. If you bought a video camera recently (even if it is for personal home use), more than likely it includes one of these and, if you have not tried it, you should. It is easier than you think to import video using these connections.

Modern digital video devices store video as digital data (usually in a standard format called DV format) and can be directly connected to the computer. Some provide access to the content stored on camera media in the same manner as accessing files on your hard drive, whereas others require you to capture the content using software. Either way, getting content from a digital device to the computer is much easier when USB or FireWire connections are used.

 NOTE: *There are numerous sources on the Web that detail specifics of video capture and video capture equipment. Most are fairly accurate, and are free of charge. The following address is a good place to start a search:* www.google.com.

It All Comes Down to the Source

Ultimately, whichever means you use to get a start on your digital video, how clean that source is will inevitably impact your file size and determine your clip's visual quality. If you sample from a poor analog source or sloppy digital recordings, no matter how good the equipment, you are going to be limited by that source.

The key to successfully utilizing video in Flash is to start with the cleanest possible digital video source when you import into Flash, while also making sure the content you record is worth the effort. This means verifying the quality of the material you retrieve from your source media and avoiding compressing that source before bringing it into Flash. You do not want Flash (or any program, for that matter) to recompress video, as this ultimately results in larger file sizes. Thus, when you digitize, start with a clean, non-lossy compressed source.

Software

There is a wide range of applications that can be used for video editing. Some are designed for working with specific video clips, allowing the developer to cut and manipulate individual clips, whereas others are designed for creating and manipulating special effects. Both generally have a steep learning curve, are often somewhat pricey, and are really focused on broadcast video development. Nevertheless, the following are a few of the most commonly used applications.

- Adobe Premiere (*www.adobe.com*)
- Apple Final Cut Pro (*www.apple.com*)
- Ulead's MediaStudio Pro (*www.ulead.com*)

Sorenson Squeeze

Sorenson Squeeze is designed to provide advanced control over video clips for Flash MX 2004. When video clips are imported into Flash, you have basic control over the video clip's attributes, as you will discover in a later section. However, you do not have control over certain aspects of the compression. In essence, Sorenson Squeeze allows you to produce higher-quality video than the standard compression provided in Flash MX 2004.

In addition, Squeeze provides several other useful features, including capture support (connect a DV camera via FireWire port and you can capture video), video compression for QuickTime MOV file output as well as Flash SWF and FLV, and the ability to prepare clips for use with Sorenson's automated online storage and delivery service, Vcast. Let's look at how Squeeze can be used to create Flash content.

Using Sorenson Squeeze

When you start Sorenson Squeeze, you are presented with the basic interface shown in figure 11-1. The first step is to open a video clip into Squeeze using the File menu. Figure 11-1 shows a clip already loaded, evident in the Preview window. Squeeze will support QuickTime MOV files, standard DV files, and Windows AVI files.

Figure 11-1. The Sorenson Squeeze interface provides simple and straight-forward control over compression and output options.

Once a clip is opened into Squeeze, you can easily select specific presets for the attributes of the file's output. Note the buttons in the interface that allow you to select presets. These presets can be changed via the Compression menu. Once a preset is selected, the files to be output are shown in the Output Files section. The file loaded in figure 11-1 is set to output a QuickTime file, a Flash Video format file (FLV), and an SWF file. Thus, three files and their attributes are shown in the Output window. Once you have the settings you desire, you simply click on the Squeeze It button to generate the files.

One of the biggest advantages to purchasing Squeeze is smaller file sizes. If your site is going to utilize a lot of video, it is probably worth the purchase (current street price is about 300 dollars). The Squeeze application utilizes a two-pass variable bit rate (VBR) compression algorithm, which allows the bit rate to vary, providing better compression.

The program also offers batch processing capability and cropping capability (ability to reduce frame size, which is a must for digital camera uploads). The program also includes filters for functions such as smoothing (similar to smoothing on bitmaps), audio normalization (discussed in Chapter 8), video noise reduction (which reduces outlier pixel colors that can taint visual and compression results), and deinterlacing.

 NOTE: *A trial version of Sorenson Squeeze can be downloaded from Sorenson's web site at* www.sorenson.com.

Tips and Notes About Video

There are several things you should be aware of if you plan on using video in your Flash files. Most, if not all, of these are related to what you do before bringing video into Flash.

- Evaluate the level of detail you need in the video clip.

  Because video clips in Flash are often small in frame size, consider the content you want to show. At a small frame size, will the content be ineffective? Often if you are trying to show details of something in video, the frame size may be so small that it makes the effect of the video negligible. Thus, for details in imagery consider using bitmaps instead.

- Leave out unnecessary content.

  Like white space in bitmap images, unnecessary content in video clips (such as complex fades or transitions, and lengthy periods in which the video has no movement) should be removed. Realize that transitions do not work well with web video due to compression and frame size. Transitions from packages designed for broadcast work are often ineffective at small frame sizes. Consider using straight cuts from video segments to maximize the effectiveness of web video.

- Leave video uncompressed; let Flash do the compression.

  If you are using any package except Sorenson Squeeze (even if you are using another version of a Sorenson compressor in another package), it is suggested that you import only uncompressed video into Flash, if at all possible. Compression in Flash (or any lossy compression, for that matter) will be more effective if Flash works with completely clean source video that has never been lossy compressed.

- Be very familiar with your audience's connection speed.

  Ultimately, everything you do should take the audience into consideration, particularly as it relates to video. Your audience's data rate will dictate frame size, frame rate, movie length, and inevitably the file size you can reasonably deliver to it.

- Break lengthy clips into smaller segments.

   If you have a lengthy or long-playing movie you want to distribute, consider breaking it up into smaller segments.

Importing Video into Flash

Importing video into Flash is a relatively straightforward process. Once you get to the point of importing the clip into Flash, the most difficult and time-consuming part is done already. However, depending on the length of the clip (assuming you are not using Sorenson Squeeze), when the video file is imported into Flash it can take some time for Flash to compress the clip when it is imported.

In general, there are two ways to import and use video in Flash. One is to embed the video directly, in which the video clip is stored inside a Flash file and is compressed with the Sorenson Spark compressor. With this technique, any of the supported digital video file formats mentioned earlier can be embedded within a Flash movie.

The other technique is to link a QuickTime video clip as an external file. The primary limitation to this latter technique is that the Flash file, once it has a linked QuickTime video file, must be published as a QuickTime movie, not a Flash SWF file.

 NOTE: *Chapter 12 discusses how the Publish feature can be used to output QuickTime files directly from Flash.*

Loading to Stage or Library

In addition to the decision of whether to embed or link a clip, you also have the option of loading the clip directly to the stage (as an instance of the video clip) and library simultaneously, or directly to the library only. If you choose to load the clip directly to the stage, it is placed on the stage (again, an instance of it is placed on the stage) and into the library simultaneously. You can use this technique by selecting File | Import | Import.

If you do not want the clip to be automatically placed on the stage when you import, select File | Import | Import to Library. This places the clip into the library, but does not create an instance of it on the stage. For example, if you had a movie with several clips in different locations in the timeline, you might want to load them each to the library (without instances being placed on the stage). You could then go to the different locations in the timeline you desired the video clip instances to be, and manually add them to the timeline by dragging them from the library to the stage.

 NOTE: *These two methods of importing a clip can be used with either linking or embedding of video in Flash.*

Embedding Video

As mentioned earlier, when you embed video into a Flash movie, the video clip becomes an internal element within the Flash SWF file. No other files are needed for playback, and no other plug-ins are necessary. Exercise 11-1 steps you through the process of embedding video in a Flash file.

 NOTE: *To perform exercise 11-1 on a PC or Mac, you will need to make sure that QuickTime 4.0 or higher is installed on your computer. You can get the latest version of QuickTime from www.apple.com.*

 Exercise 11-1: Embedding Video into a Flash Movie

To explore embedding video into a Flash movie, perform the following steps.

1. Open Flash MX 2004 and starting a new movie file.

2. Use File | Import and locate the QuickTime Movie named *atopdh.mov* located in the *fgai/chapter11/* folder, installed from the companion CD-ROM. Select the file in the Import dialog box window and click on the OK button.

3. Once you click on the OK button, you will be presented with the first screen of the Video Import wizard, which asks you whether you want to embed or link the file, as shown in figure 11-2. Select *Embed video in Macromedia Flash document* and click on OK.

   If the video clip has sound that is not supported on your computer (in most cases you will not have the audio codec needed to be able to import the sound), only the video portion will be imported. In such a case, if you need the audio, you will need to open the clip into a video editing package and resave it with a format your computer can read. This will likely be the case only if the file was originally generated on another computer.

4. Once you select embed, you have the option of either embedding the entire clip or embedding only a portion of the clip via the wizard's second screen, shown in figure 11-3. For now,

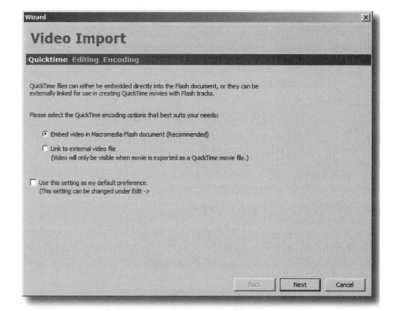

Figure 11-2. The Video Import wizard first asks you whether you want to embed or link the video clip.

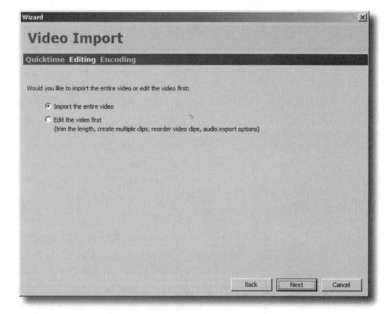

Figure 11-3. The wizard's second screen gives you the option of editing before you import.

select *Import the entire video* (we will discuss the Edit option later). Click on OK.

5. The next wizard screen presented to you asks for you to select a video encoding profile you would like to use, as shown in figure 11-4. In the *Compression profile* drop-down list, select the 56-kbps modem option (like clip editing, we will discuss

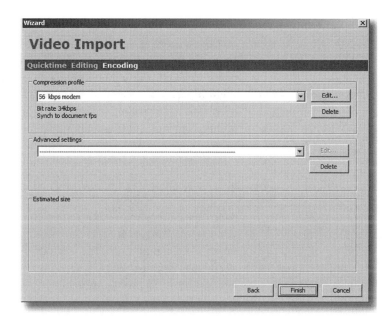

Figure 11-4. The third wizard screen allows you to select a compression profile.

the creation of compression profiles once you are done with this exercise) and click on OK.

6. When you click on the OK button, Flash will begin creating its own internal version of the video clip you entered. The clip you are importing is about 43 seconds long, so it will take a little while to compress (length of time will depend on your computer). If it starts taking too long, you can click on the Cancel button to stop the encoding operation (an already imported version is available on the companion CD-ROM, as described in the next step).

7. Now that you have seen how video is embedded, let's utilize it. If you allowed the video to be imported entirely, you are being prompted with a dialog box stating that Flash needs to extend the frames to frame 513 in the timeline for the video to play in its entirety. Hold that thought. If you did not let the video encode entirely, open the file *ch11_01.fla* from the *fgai/chapter11/* folder, installed from the companion CD-ROM.

8. Once the file is open, open the library, where you will find a video clip symbol named *atopdh.mov*.

9. Click-drag the video clip symbol from the library to the stage. When you do, you will get the same prompt mentioned in step 6.

When you place video clip symbols on the stage, the number of frames needed in the timeline is consistent with the ratio setting you established when the clip was imported. When video plays in Flash, it works like a graphic symbol instance, in that there must be the same number of frames in the instance's representation in the timeline as there are in the video clip symbol itself if you want the clip to play entirely. If there are not enough frames in the timeline, the video clip will be truncated.

To get a video clip to play in its entirety, the sprite in the timeline must be extended such that there is a consistency between the number of frames in the clip and the number of frames in the timeline. The ratio of clip frames to timeline frames depends on what is established in the compression profile you selected (more on that in a moment). For example, the clip you are importing needs 513 frames to play entirely. The clip originally had 513 frames, and the profile you chose used a 1:1 ratio between Flash frames and video clip frames.

Right now, the video clip instance has just one frame in the timeline. If you click on Yes in the dialog box that asks about extending the time, Flash will automatically extend the frames (duration) of the video clip instance's sprite in the timeline so that the entire clip will play. If you click on No, the video clip will be allotted only to the one frame currently in the timeline, and when the movie is tested only the first frame of the video clip will be played.

10. Go ahead and click on Yes. This will place the instance on the stage, but more importantly will extend the instance's sprite in the timeline out such that the entire video clip will play.

11. Use Test Movie to see the video clip play.

 NOTE: *Using Export Movie (see Chapter 12) on files that contain video takes much longer than when used on files that do not contain video.*

In the previous exercise you learned the basics of importing video clips. Now let's turn our attention to two important things: editing clip length when you import (the first item we ignored), and creating and using compression profiles. Creating compression profiles actually includes two things: (1) the settings related to compression and decompression and (2) settings related to clip color, dimension, and tracking. Let's first deal with editing the length of imported video clips.

Editing Clips Upon Import

When you were presented with the wizard screen shown in figure 11-3, we skipped over the edit option. Let's turn our attention to it. If you click on the *Edit video* first button and then on OK, you are presented with the screen shown in figure 11-5.

The wizard screen shown in figure 11-5 allows you to do several things. You can trim the length of the video clip, create multiple clips from the single video source file, and create multiple clips and reorder them back into a single clip.

Figure 11-5. You can edit the clip when you import. This allows you to select a specific section or sections of a clip to import.

Trimming a Single Clip

To trim a clip, you adjust the "in" and "out" points (represented by small right-triangles, shown in figure 11-6). Once you have selected the in and out points, you click on the Create Clip button, which adds the trimmed clip to the list pane on the left. Note that once you have set the in and out points, you can preview the clip using the controls to the left of the *Preview clip* button. Once you have trimmed the original clip to what you want, you click on the Next button to move on to the *Compression profile* section of the wizard. Trimming a clip is that easy in Flash.

Creating Multiple Clips

In addition to trimming a single clip, you can create multiple clips from a single imported source. By setting the in and out points to different sec-

Figure 11-6.
You trim a clip
by adjusting
the in and out
points.

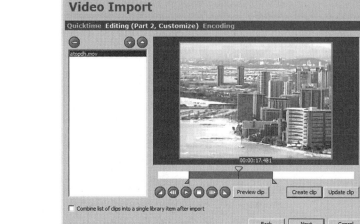

Figure 11-7.
You can edit
the clip when
you import.
This allows you
to select a spe-
cific section or
sections of a
clip to import.

tions and clicking on the *Create clip* button, you can add multiple snippets of the original clip to the list pane on the left (see figure 11-7). Once entries are in the list pane, you can choose to have them embedded as separate items in your library (that is, each is a separate symbol) or you can click on the *Combine list of clips into a single library item after import* checkbox to merge them all back together into a single symbol in the library.

Understanding Compression Profiles

Now that you understand editing clips, let's look at creating compression profiles. In exercise 11-1, you saw how you could use the preexisting profiles on a clip.

When you are presented with the Compression Profile section of the wizard (shown in figure 11-4), there are two parts of a compression profile: the compression settings (accessed via the first drop-down) and Advanced Settings, accessed via the second drop-down (this includes clip "color," clip frame dimensions, and clip tracking).

Compression Settings

In the upper drop-down menu (see figure 11-4), you can edit the existing profiles or create a new one using the *Compression profile* drop-down list. Figure 11-8 shows the settings for the 56-kbps modem setting you chose earlier. This was accessed by choosing the 56-kbps modem setting in the drop-down list and clicking on the associated Edit button.

As shown in figure 11-8, when you are setting up a compression profile you have the option of establishing the profile based on either bandwidth or the desired video quality. As highlighted elsewhere in this book, when you are dealing with compression you are always trying to find the right balance between quality and file size (and file size here is bandwidth). Thus, if you establish the compression profile based on bandwidth you are using a technical approach and Flash lets you see the resulting video quality based on the bandwidth you select in the Clip Preview window.

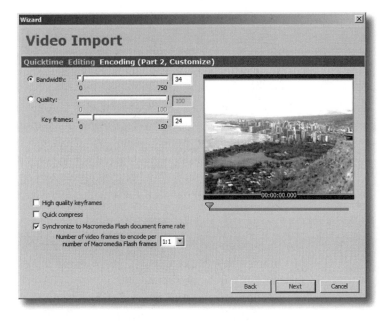

Figure 11-8. Settings for the 56-kbps modem compression profile.

Alternatively, you can choose compression based on quality. Given the large size of video components, it is almost always recommended that you approach video compression from a file size point of view when producing web-based content. If you are developing for CD or other fixed media, you can approach it from a quality standpoint.

The third slider you see in figure 11-8 controls the number of keyframes for the temporal compression. Recall that temporal compression compresses based on the content in keyframes. In essence, a keyframe in a temporally compressed clip is written completely (is a complete description of the frame's image), whereas non-keyframes (delta frames) are "incomplete" descriptions (i.e., only the changing pixels are written).

In general, the greater the number of keyframes the more accurate the representations, but the less effective the compression. If you choose 0 for the number of keyframes, you nullify compression, meaning that a complete description of each frame of the clip will be written in the file. Although this will create a near perfect copy of the digital video clip in Flash, file size will be much larger and playback may be sporadic, depending on the capabilities of the playback machine. Seldom would you set the keyframes to 0, but if you do, make sure the clip is very short.

 NOTE: *The quality-to-file size/compression relationship in an embedded video clip in Flash is the result of a mix of the settings of the first two sliders and the third slider. The first two sliders control the amount of compression in all frames (as in an image), and the other controls the number of frames in each compression set (over time).*

In the bottom part of the *Compression settings* screen (shown in figure 11-8) you see three other items. The *High quality keyframes* checkbox is only applicable if you set compression using the Bandwidth slider. If you set compression using the Quality slider you are already in effect setting the quality for keyframes. When using the Bandwidth method for compression, the *High quality keyframes* checkbox helps ensure consistent image quality across all video keyframes. If you do not select this, quality in click keyframes may vary because amount of compression for any individual frame will depend on the selected bandwidth.

The Quick Compress option is helpful while working on a project, as it speeds compression (and consequently the clip quality may decrease). Use this option as you are working to speed concurrent testing (that is, use of Control | Test Movie). Then, when you are creating your final files for distribution, turn this option off.

The last checkbox in figure 11-8 is very important. This checkbox controls the synchronization between the Flash movie frame rate and the video clip's frame rate. In most instances you will want to sync the video and Flash frame rates. Rare would be the case otherwise.

The *Number of video frames to encode per number of Macromedia Flash frames* drop-down list is pretty important. The file you are importing (see figure 11-8) was prepared using Adobe Premiere and has already had its frame rate reduced to 15 fps. The default setting of 1:1 will further reduce the frame rate so that it matches the current Flash movie setting (12 fps). A change from 15 fps to 12 fps will not be significant in this case, and will not drastically change the playback of the movie.

In our example, however, if you wanted the frame rate of the imported video to remain constant (that is, stay at 15 fps in Flash), you would need to cancel the import, change the Flash movie frame rate to 15 fps, and then import the video.

 TIP: *If you go to the trouble of using an external program such as Premiere (or any of the others listed earlier in this chapter) to prepare your video before importing it into Flash, set the frame rate in that program to the frame rate you will use in Flash. It will save processing time when you import the video into Flash.*

Where the *Number of video frames to encode per number of Macromedia Flash frames* drop-down list is very important is if you bring in raw video (particularly video from a broadcast editing system or a video camera) for which the frame rate of the video clip will likely be higher than 15 (often 30, 29.94, or 24 fps). You can use this drop-down to control the number of frames that actually become part of the Flash movie.

For example, imagine you had a video clip at 30 fps and you import it with the *Number of video frames to encode per number of Macromedia Flash frames* drop-down list set to 1:1. Imagine also that the Flash frame rate is 12 fps.

In this scenario, every twelfth frame will be saved in the Flash movie, and all others will be "dropped" (and in essence not included in the Flash representation of the digital video clip). Visually this will cause the clip to be choppier than the 30-fps version. It will not make the clip play more slowly, which newcomers to digital video often believe.

Continuing with this hypothetical situation, if the *Number of video frames to encode per number of Macromedia Flash frames* drop-down list is set to 1:2, every sixth frame of the clip will be retained and all others will be omitted. The visual result: an even choppier clip!

The number of frames retained in the Flash representation of an embedded video clip will ultimately be limited by the Flash frame rate. The only way to represent all 30 frames of the original clip (not that you would want to do this, but for sake of explanation) would be to set the Flash frame rate to 30 fps, import the clip, and then select 1:1 from the *Number of video frames to encode per number of Macromedia Flash frames* drop-down list.

Advanced Settings

Now that you understand the Compression settings, let's turn our attention to the Advanced Settings (the second drop-down list in figure 11-4). It is through advanced settings that you can adjust the hue, contrast, or gamma of a clip and the dimensions (and frame size cropping), as well as control the tracking options. The wizard screen for Advanced Settings is shown in figure 11-9. This was accessed by selecting Create New Profile from the Advanced Settings section of the wizard shown in figure 11-4.

 NOTE: *As of the beta version of Flash MX 2004, there are no existing Advanced Settings in the second drop-down, shown in figure 11-4. The only option is to create a profile. Presumably there will be some when the software is released.*

 TIP: *One of the advantages of having the Advanced Settings profile is that once established you can apply the settings across an entire series of video clips relatively easily, rather than having to set them up each time for each clip in your project.*

Let's begin by exploring the Color section, shown in figure 11-9. These controls allow you to adjust various attributes of the graphical portion of your clip. Hue allows you to adjust the color balance by specifying a hue shift (the field is based on the 360-degree positions of color around the HSB color model). Zero and 360 are red, 180 degrees is cyan, and the remaining colors are interspersed at 30-degree increments.

Figure 11-9.
Advanced
Settings dialog
box.

Saturation controls the purity of colors. As a color becomes desaturated it moves toward gray and is desaturated by its complement color. The easiest way to describe saturation is that if your colors are too fluorescent you need to desaturate them.

Gamma controls the overall balance of color by allowing you to add neutral gray to a clip. And finally, the brightness and contrast controls allow you to adjust those respective elements in relation to the clip.

 NOTE: *If you use the Advanced Settings when importing a clip, the amount of time it takes to compress and import the clip will take significantly longer, simply because the computer has to work harder—particularly as it relates to hue, contrast, and gamma adjustments.*

The second set of controls in figure 11-9 allow you to control the frame dimensions of the clip. You can scale or crop a clip. A nice feature of the crop capability is that you can perform "offset" cropping; that is, crop on one side only. As shown in figure 11-10, when you set the crop values the clip preview pane shows the crop with crop lines.

Figure 11-10. You can establish offset cropping in the Advanced Settings.

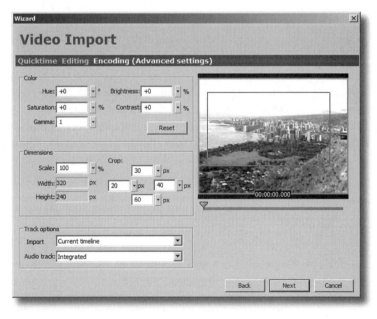

The last section of the Advanced Settings dialog box includes tracking options. The Import drop-down lets you define how the clip will be inserted in the movie. The Current Timeline setting will place it in the current timeline. The other options allow you to insert the clip into a movie clip or a graphic symbol.

NOTE 1: *If you select Graphic Symbol in the Import drop-down, keep in mind that the audio of the video clip will not be supported.*

 NOTE 2: *This chapter assumes you are distributing video in Flash over the Web. If you use Flash for CD-ROM distribution, which is entirely possible, you can go with larger frame sizes and higher numbers of keyframes. However, it is recommended that you still use 15 frames as the maximum frame rate. Even with the tremendous speed available with CD-ROM drives today, frame rates over 15 fps will likely result in sporadic playback.*

The final item in the Advanced Settings dialog box is the Audio Track drop-down which determines whether the audio for the clip will be integrated into the clip, stored separately as a sound symbol, or ignored.

Linking Video

As mentioned earlier, you can also link an external QuickTime video clip to a Flash movie. When you use this technique, there are two significant differences from the process of embedding. The first, and most important, is that when a Flash file contains linked QuickTime video clips, you cannot export and use the SWF version of the file. You must export (or Publish) a QuickTime version of the Flash movie instead. There are some limitations when using QuickTime as the format for distribution. Often ActionScripting and other aspects of Flash do not work when Flash content is output to the QuickTime format.

The second difference concerns the fact that the movie is now dependent on the QuickTime Player for playback, instead of the Flash Player. Thus, if you have a site that uses linked video, you will need to ensure (or notify) the user that she must have the QuickTime Player (or plug-in) to view your site, in addition to the Flash Player.

Even with the limitation associated with linking video, the fact that you can do both linking and embedded of video in Flash makes the application much more extensive for multimedia and web development. Exercise 11-2 walks you through the process of linking a QuickTime video clip to a Flash movie.

 ### Exercise 11-2: Linking a QuickTime Video Clip

To explore linking a QuickTime video clip, perform the following steps.

1. Begin by opening Flash and starting a new document.
2. Select the File | Import | Import to Library command.

3. In the Import dialog box, access the file *atopdh.mov* located in the *fgai/chapter11/* folder, installed from the companion CD-ROM, and then click on OK to import it.

4. When presented with the Import Video dialog box, select the *Link to external video file* radio button and click on Next. When you do this, you will not have to deal with the Editing or Encoding options. The clip is linked in its entirety.

5. Because you used the Import to Library command, the video clip is not automatically placed on the stage. Open the Library window and drag an instance of the video clip to the stage.

   When you do this, note that you are prompted that Flash needs to extend the number of frames for the movie to play in its entirety. Flash consistently handles linked and embedded clips, in that in both cases the number of frames in the timeline must be equal to the number in the clip. Otherwise, the clip will not play in its entirety.

6. When prompted to extend the number of frames in the sprite, select Yes. The sprite will be extended equal to the number of frames in the clip. Note that with linked video there is always exact 1-to-1 synchronization between the video clip frames and the movie frames.

7. Use Test Movie on the clip. When you do, note that the clip is not displayed. When linking video clips, Test Movie does nothing. To see the movie, you must use Control | Play.

Video Clip Instance Properties

Once a video clip is imported into Flash, there are a couple of important things you should know about them. If you select a movie clip instance on the stage, the Properties panel provides sizing information, as well as the ability to swap the symbols associated with clip instances, as shown in figure 11-11. Accessing a video clip symbol in the library provides further capabilities. The following three sections examine these.

Sizing Video Clips

As shown in figure 11-11, as with bitmaps, you have the ability to directly modify the stage location and dimensions of a video clip instance. However, as discussed in Chapter 8, you should not use the W (width) field or the H (height) field to modify the stage dimensions of a video clip. Neither should you use the Free Transform tool on a video clip.

Figure 11-11. The Properties panel provides capabilities related to video clip instances when they are selected on the stage.

Like bitmaps, when you scale a video clip, Flash does not recalculate the data of the media element to accommodate the new size. If you scale a video clip up using the W and H fields, the Free Transform tool, or any of the scale capabilities, the clip will begin to visually break apart (degrade). If you scale a video clip down using any tool, there is more data in the file than is needed (you have wasted data in your file).

For example, the clip you worked with earlier in this chapter, when embedded and output as an SWF file is 2.1 MB in size. The video clip you imported was 320 pixels by 240 pixels in dimension. If you use the W and H fields to scale the video clip down on the stage and output the file as an SWF, you will find that the resulting file size is exactly the same, meaning that concerning the version that was scaled down the file has much wasted data in it.

When you scale a video clip in Flash, Flash does not recalculate the video data based on the new size when it is scaled. In technical terms, it does not interpolate (add data when sizing up), nor does it extrapolate (remove data when scaling down). The most serious case is when you scale down because you have a much larger file size than is needed.

Thus, you should either prepare video clips in a program such as Adobe Premiere or Sorenson Squeeze at the exact dimensions you will need in Flash or use the Advanced Settings in the Video wizard (see figure 11-4) to set the size upon import. You should never scale a video clip (or bitmap) up or down in Flash because in either case there are negative consequences for doing so.

Swapping Video Clips

Chapter 6 discussed how you could use the Properties panel to swap the symbols associated with instances on the stage. This is a handy capability when you want to create a linear array (a row or column of) graphical objects.

As you can see in figure 11-11, you can swap out video clips. This gives you the ability to create a template frame, copy it several times, and then swap out the original video clip so that you can quickly create a set of repeating frames. The only thing to note about swapping video clips is that linked clips can only be swapped with other linked clips in the file. Similarly, embedded clips can only be swapped with other embedded clips.

 NOTE: *If you swap clips, realize that Flash does not update the length of the instances associated with the clip to the length of the new clip. If you swap two clips, you will need to check the length of the instance in the timeline to make sure that it is not too long, or too short, after the swap.*

Updating, Importing, and Exporting Clips

As you have seen in other chapters, the library allows you to access the default settings for symbols that are based on fonts, bitmaps, or sounds. Double clicking on a graphic, movie clip, or button symbol allows you to access its respective timeline.

When you double click on a video clip symbol in the library, you are presented with one of the two dialog boxes, shown in figure 11-12. If you access an embedded clip's properties, you are presented with the dialog box shown in figure 11-12a. Linked video clips produce the dialog box shown in figure 11-12b.

 NOTE: *To open the properties of a symbol in the library, you must double click on the symbol icon. Double clicking on the symbol name lets you rename it.*

Figure 11-12a provides several capabilities you should be aware of. The Update and Import options are pretty straightforward. Update allows you to update the internal version of the clip, which is nice when a group of developers is working on a project and someone other than the Flash

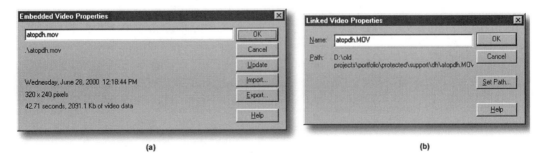

Figure 11-12. The embedded video clip properties dialog box (a) and the linked video clip properties dialog box (b) allow you to access the default properties of the clip.

architect is doing the video. The Import option allows you to replace the library version of the clip with another clip.

Note the Export option in figure 11-12a. Often multimedia authoring tools are "the end of the food chain," meaning that once an asset such as video is in them, getting the media element back out of the file (for use somewhere else) is almost impossible. Flash, however, allows reuse of the video components within it by permitting you to export a video clip symbol back out of a library as a Flash Video format (FLV) file. These files can be reimported and reused in other Flash files, making this feature very handy.

As it relates to linked video, you will find fewer options. In figure 11-12b, note that the only option you have is to establish the path of the video clip. By clicking on the Set Path button, you can reestablish the link to the external file, update the linked file, or link a totally different video clip.

 NOTE: *As when you are swapping clips, if you update a clip (linked or embedded) or if you link or embed a new clip, make sure you check the duration of the timeline instances of the video clips to make sure they are not too long or too short.*

Controlling Video with Actions

Although you have yet to explore ActionScript in this book (see Chapters 13 and 14), once a clip is imported and placed in the timeline, you can use many of the basic actions or behaviors to control it. Actions that can be used with video clips include the following.

- *goto:* Jumps to specific points in a digital video clip by jumping to Flash frames or labels.

- *play() and stop():* Have the video clip play and stop at will by starting and stopping the main movie timeline.

- *_quality:* Affects the visual quality of the clip (if playback wanes) by changing the Flash movie's *_quality* property.

- *stopAllSounds():* stops the sound associated with a video clip.

Each of these actions is discussed at greater length in subsequent chapters. For now, simply keep in mind that once a clip is in Flash you have a lot of control, even with the basics of the ActionScript language. Exercise 11-3 explores the use of ActionScript to control video clips.

Exercise 11-3: Controlling Video Clips with ActionScript

CD-ROM NOTE: *To see an example that uses Action-Script to control video clips, examine the file* ch11_03.fla, *located in the* fgai/chapter11/ch11_03/ *folder, installed from the companion CD-ROM.*

▪ ▪ ▪ **Summary**

In this chapter you have taken a look at the basics of using video in Flash MX 2004. The main thing to keep in mind about video is that it takes a lot longer to produce good video content (including shooting the footage, getting it into the computer, and preparing it technically) than most people think. Allot plenty of time for recording, editing, and preparing video.

This chapter concludes the examination of the various types of media creations you can import and create in Flash. The next chapter explores issues you must deal with when getting your files onto the Web. You will examine testing, integration, and distribution of your movies. Then you will move on to an introduction to basic ActionScripting.

chapter

12

Testing, Integration, and Distribution

▪ ▪ ▪ Introduction

This book has discussed many things concerning the creation of Flash movies, but has not dealt with testing, integration, and distribution issues. Indeed, to be an exceptional Flash developer requires both the ability to aesthetically design and to critically analyze and test. Knowing how to integrate Flash movies and having a sense of when there is "too much stuff in your movies" are also important.

This chapter begins by focusing on how to test movies. Regardless of whether you are developing movies for delivery over the Web or on other media as projector files, testing will be a vital step. Testing is not a "one-shot" occurrence. It occurs over and over, all the time.

Additionally, this chapter will familiarize you with the HTML code for integrating movies into your pages. Flash provides an integrated feature called Publish that can automate much of the process of integration. However, basic HTML tags and attributes that relate to Flash are also covered. Sometimes it may be preferable to code by hand. In fact, you might want to code material using Notepad or SimpleText, two text editors that let you know exactly what is going on in your pages. Nevertheless, knowledge of both methods is necessary.

Flash also provides the ability to critically analyze the way your movies download over the Web. Flash's Size Report feature and

Bandwidth Profiler, combined with several other features, can be used to optimize your movies. This chapter concludes by reviewing the most important things that have to do with optimizing the graphics, bitmaps, and sounds that may find their way into your movies.

▪▪▪ Objectives

In this chapter you will:

- Learn methods for testing your movies in Flash
- Discover the three methods for distributing movies, including how you can specifically develop for each mode of delivery
- Examine the differences between the native FLA file format and the web-ready SWF format
- Use the Export Movie command to create web-ready SWF files
- Learn to convert an SWF file into an executable file called a projector
- Find out about the Publish feature and how it can be used to automate the integration process
- Determine the HTML tags and attributes used to integrate Flash SWF files into web pages
- Use the Size Report and Bandwidth Profiler tools to critically analyze the data within a Flash movie
- Discover optimization techniques that can be used to decrease the size of movies

▪▪▪ Test, Test, and Test Again

Testing is one of the most critical aspects of developing successful Flash movies and sites. Testing is critical because of the range of variables with which you have to deal. The audience's connection, browser, browser version, RAM, video RAM, and processor can all change the way your movies are played back. The main goal in testing is to ensure that a large portion of the potential audience is not eliminated. It is often the end user's hardware, software, or connection that presents limitations. Without keeping these variables in mind, you can quickly develop something that does not run, or runs poorly, for your audience. Without testing, you make assumptions that will most likely be detrimental.

As it relates to web development, two main types of testing occur: concurrent testing and compatibility testing. Concurrent testing takes place the entire time movies are being developed. When completing the exercises throughout this book, you completed this type of testing when you used the Control | Play and Control | Test Movie menu options. Most often developers are the ones who perform concurrent testing. It occurs continually during the entire development process.

On the other hand, compatibility testing is done to determine if the product works under various technical scenarios. Do the page and its movies work in Internet Explorer and Netscape Communicator? Does it work in older versions of these browsers? These are just some of the questions answered through compatibility testing.

You will never be able to accommodate every scenario that exists in the browsing community. There will always be somebody who cannot get that plug-in installed or somebody who is so petrified of computer viruses that downloading anything from the Web is unthinkable. Nevertheless, the goal is to accommodate the middle 68 percent of the distribution. The middle of a normal distribution is more alike than different. This is the audience for whom you should conduct testing.

Testing in Flash

Flash provides two methods for performing concurrent testing, both of which occur within the application environment. The Control | Play or the Control | Test Movie command can be used. You have used these to run the movies included with this book, but all of their settings have yet to be discussed. Nonetheless, as reiterated here, which method you use depends on what your movie contains. Keep in mind that movie clips do not play when you use the Play command. To see and hear movie clips that are inserted into the main timeline, use the Test Movie option instead of the Play option.

Playing in Flash

When a movie does not contain movie clip symbols, use the basic Control | Play command to test the movie. This allows you to see the playhead move across the timeline as elements appear on the stage.

 TIP: *To quickly play and stop a movie that does not contain movie clips, press the Enter key.*

When testing this way, other options found in the Control menu apply, as follow.

- *Rewind, Step Forward, and Step Backward:* Allow you to control the playhead, which changes what is displayed on the stage.

- *Loop Playback:* Forces the movie to loop when it reaches the end of the scene or movie.

- *Play All Scenes:* Forces the movie to play every scene, even if no action is assigned to jump between scenes.

- *Enable Simple Frame Actions:* Implements any actions assigned to frames in the movie. By default, frame actions are not enabled.

- *Enable Simple Buttons:* Allows buttons to function so that you may interact with them. Turn this on to see the states of a button. Turn it off to scale, position, or orient a button on the stage.

- *Mute Sounds:* Disables sounds associated with the main movie timeline when Control | Play is used.

- *Enable Live Preview:* This setting is associated with Flash component objects.

Using Test Movie and Test Scene

The most frequent command used for testing movies is the Control | Test Movie menu option. This command allows you to see all of the movie clips and other symbols within the movie function. The Enable Simple Buttons, Enable Simple Frame Actions, and Mute Sound options have no effect when using Test Movie. Rather, the settings used for Test Movie are established in the Publish Settings menu option found in the File menu.

When the Test Movie menu option is selected, Flash quickly generates a web-ready SWF Flash file. SWF stands for Shockwave Flash. The SWF file is instantly opened into the Flash Player, directly in front of the stage of the currently open movie. The speed of this process depends on the complexity of the movie. The SWF file that is generated is placed in the same directory as the FLA file and has the same name. Each time you use Test Movie, the SWF file is updated and displayed in the player.

If you are developing movies on the Macintosh, be very careful when using the Test Movie option, as well as the Export Movie and Publish options described later in this chapter. Make sure you save your native Flash files with an extension (e.g., *.fla*).

 WARNING: *If you do not save files with an extension, the native FLA file will be overwritten with the SWF file when you use the Test Movie or Export Movie commands. Consequently, if the SWF is protected (via Export Movie), you will render the file useless. The FLA file will be overwritten with a protected SWF file that cannot be reopened into the Flash application. In short, even if you are on a Mac and have no intention of going to PC, use file extensions!*

▪ ▪ ▪ Distributing Your Movies

Macromedia Flash files can be distributed to your audience in one of four ways. The mode chosen is determined by how much content can be realistically included in the intended delivery mechanism. Flash files can be distributed as follows.

- An SWF file to be played back in the standalone Flash player, apart from the Web

- An SWF file to be played back in the browser using a plug-in or ActiveX component

- A projector file that has all code necessary for playback of the Flash movie (does not require the Flash player or the Flash application)

- A QuickTime file

As it relates to multimedia and hypermedia development, your delivery system is only as strong as the weakest link. For your movie files to be perceived as effective, you must design around the limitations that exist for each method of delivery.

When delivering on the Web, the user's connection is usually the weakest link. Lengthy audio segments or many bitmaps will make download times significant. If your audience has a direct network connection, you may be able to get away with larger file sizes. Yet, if your audience has the typical consumer-level modem connection, you must judiciously design movies within the bounds of what is realistically deliverable.

If movies are to be distributed via diskette or CD-ROM, you are less restricted, but still limited in how much audio and graphics can be delivered, even from a CD-ROM or hard drive. Always keep the end user in mind during your decision-making process.

Using the Flash Player

The first method for distributing Flash files is to provide your audience members with web-ready SWF files. These SWF files can be played back on the user's computer either in the standalone player or in the browser's player (as a result of a plug-in ActiveX component). Thus, one of the assumptions you make when providing SWF files is that the audience has the Flash Player in one form or another.

This method of distributing Flash movies is generally used for viewing movies apart from the Web, although the SWF file could very well be integrated into a web page as well. For example, you can show your Flash files to a colleague or friend in the SWF format. As long as the user has the

Flash Player, they do not have to have Flash to view your movies. Conceptually, this is the same idea behind Microsoft's PowerPoint viewer. The viewer allows you to open and play the file, but you cannot edit it.

 NOTE: *The Flash Player for both the PC and Mac platform are located on the software installation CD-ROM. Additionally, you can freely distribute the Flash Player with your movies, much like the PowerPoint presentation player can be freely distributed with your PowerPoint files.*

Creating Projectors

If you are unsure whether or not your audience has the Flash Player (and you do not want to have to worry about it), open a Flash file into the Flash Player and create a projector file. This is probably the best technique if you are going to be distributing your movies via CD-ROM or diskette and are not sure if the person you are giving it to has the player.

Similar to Director's capability of the same name, making an SWF file into a projector converts the file into an executable application that can be run on any computer (of the same platform), regardless of whether the user has the Flash Player. When you convert an SWF file to a projector, the Flash Player adds the appropriate code to the file so that it can "play itself." The file will increase in size slightly when you convert it to a projector. But again, this method is predominantly used to distribute movies apart from the Web, so you have more flexibility in regard to file size. Projectors can be included on most media, such as CD-ROM, DVD, or diskettes.

Projectors created via the player are not cross-platform capable. Thus, a projector created on the PC cannot be run on a Mac, and vice versa. However, Flash's Publish command will allow you to create projectors for both platforms, but you must tell it that you want it to do this.

 NOTE: *For more details concerning cross-platform issues, see the "Cross-platform Issues" section later in this chapter.*

QuickTime

Another means of delivery that can be used on the Web or on CD-ROM media is made possible by QuickTime 4 or 5. If you have Quicktime 4 installed, you can generate Quicktime 4 files from Flash. If you have Quicktime 5 installed, you can generate Quicktime 5 files. QuickTime is one the most far-reaching software technologies that exists. It is installed on millions of computers and helps cross the great divide between Macs and PCs as it relates to the delivery of multimedia assets.

The latest versions of QuickTime (4 and 5) allow for Flash data to be integrated directly within it. Realize that the QuickTime format is much more than a format for digital video. It includes a wide range of data and support for over 30 file formats, not least of which are Flash movies. Think of QuickTime as more of a "container." Flash elements can be intermixed with digital video data, virtual reality components (QTVR), and several other types of assets. For more information concerning the specifics of QuickTime 4 or 5, see Apple's web site.

 NOTE: *For the QuickTime Publish option to work, as well as to be able to import some of the file formats into Flash that are mentioned throughout this book, you must have QuickTime 4 or higher installed. For more information concerning QuickTime or to get the player and required system files, see Apple's site (www. apple.com).*

Within the application, Flash provides the ability to save directly to Apple's QuickTime 4 or 5 formats. The Publish command allows you to generate QT files quickly and easily while you are also generating the other files required for publishing your Flash files. Although this book does not delve into great detail on the use of QuickTime, it is important that you understand the breadth of QuickTime and how it can help you in your development ventures. Just as Flash SWF files are integrated into web pages, so too can QuickTime movies, using the EMBED HTML tag.

As discussed in Macromedia's literature, all of the interactivity of the Flash file should be retained in the resulting QT file. However, if you decide to use the QuickTime distribution option, make sure you test early and often. QT versions of Flash files may work better on the Macintosh than on a PC.

Web Delivery

The final means for distributing your movie, and the most common, is via an HTML page. To do this, generate an SWF file and then include a reference to it using HTML. Although the HTML tags for including Flash files are different and can be more complex, the process is similar to creating references to graphic images within a web page.

To write the required HTML code, you can use the Publish utility that automates the HTML coding process, or you can write the code by hand, using an ASCII-based text editor. Both of these methods are covered later in this chapter.

Once the HTML code has been written, the referenced SWF file will play directly in the browser, assuming the user has the Flash plug-in. When writing the appropriate HTML, you have several options concerning visual placement and formatting of the Flash elements on the web page. The relative HTML attributes and tags are reviewed later in this chapter.

▪ ▪ ▪ SWF Versus FLA

Regardless of which delivery means you use, each begins with exporting the native Flash file (FLA) as a Shockwave Flash (SWF) file. When an FLA file is converted to an SWF file, a couple of things occur. First, Flash removes extra data that may be contained in the FLA file. For example, bitmaps and sounds that are not used within the movie timeline are ignored and are not written in the SWF. Aside from these omissions, the process also applies compression to the sound and bitmap assets within the file, reducing the resulting SWF file size as much as possible.

Shockwave is actually an all-encompassing term used with many Macromedia products. It simply means that the movie file is optimized (as much as possible) for the Web. Flash and Director both provide the ability to generate "Shockwave" (web-ready) files. They are all Shockwave files, even though they are generated from different applications. What you can put in each type of Shockwave file depends on the application used to create it.

The SWF file format has the option of being "protected," so as to restrict others from opening the file back into Flash. SWF files generated from Macromedia FreeHand are not protected. Thus, you can import and use them in Flash. However, when you generate movies for the Web from Flash, make sure you generate protected SWF files. Otherwise, anyone could load and illegally use your Flash elements in their own movies. The Protect Movie option, discussed in the sections that follow, is provided in the Export Movie and Publish dialog boxes.

▪ ▪ ▪ Using Export Movie

Once you have a completed movie and are ready to prepare it for the Web, use the File | Export Movie option. When using this option, you are first required to provide a name for the file. On the PC, the SWF extension is automatically applied to the file. On the Mac, you should get in the habit of adding the *.swf* extension to the end of the file. Once the file is named, the Export Flash Player dialog box is presented, as shown in figure 12-1. The optional settings are described in the sections that follow. Once the desired settings are established, click on OK to generate the SWF file.

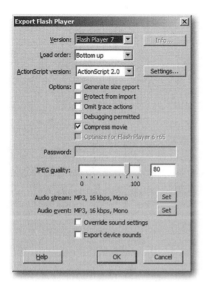

Figure 12-1. The Export Flash Player dialog box presents the optional settings that affect the generated SWF file.

Version

The first option in the Export Flash Player dialog box is the Version drop-down menu. This menu allows you to export movies as older-version Flash files. This feature is particularly useful for exporting Flash movies for use in other programs, such as Director and Authorware. When you select an older version, features supported in newer versions of Flash are disabled.

 TIP: *When you open an older Flash file into Flash MX 2004, you will find that the Export Flash Player dialog box defaults to the older version. It is recommended that anytime you open an older Flash file into 2004 immediately go to the File | Publish Settings | Flash tab and set the Version drop-down list to Flash 7.*

Load Order

The next option presented is the Load Order drop-down. This option affects how each frame is rendered as the file is loaded. This is most evident in the first frame of the movie when the user is connecting via a slower connection such as a modem.

Because Flash files are streaming files, as portions (frames) of the file are downloaded and become available they can be immediately rendered to the screen, even though the rest of the frames from the file have yet to be downloaded. Selecting the Bottom Up option will cause layers further down in the layering order (farthest back in the screen order) to be displayed first. The Top Down option does the opposite. Use the Load Order option to set which layers will be rendered first over slower connections.

ActionScript Version

Similar to the first drop-down, Version, the ActionScript Version drop-down lets you select which version of ActionScript the file will contain. An SWF file from Flash MX 2004, even if it is a version 7 player file, can include Flash MX-style coding; that is, ActionScript version 1.0.

Generate Size Report

Size reports are one of the most impressive parts of Flash. If you select the Generate Size Report option, Flash automatically generates a text file that provides details about the size of each frame and the elements that occur within the movie. See the "Closely Examining the Size Report" section later in the chapter.

Protect from Import

As mentioned earlier, SWF files have the option of being protected. When an SWF is protected, it cannot be loaded back into Flash for editing. If left unchecked, the generated SWF can be imported into Flash and made to yield its graphical and structural components.

 WARNING: *Again, when using a Macintosh, save your files with extensions. Otherwise, an exported SWF may accidentally over- write an FLA file.*

Note that when you select the Protect from Import option the Password field becomes active. This field allows you to create protected SWF files that can be reused, given a proper password. This is a conven- ient safety feature in that if you use the Password field you always have an editable version of your movies, even if the FLA is lost or corrupted.

Omit Trace Actions

The trace action, which you will learn about later, can be used to reveal behind-the-scenes information concerning variables and the state of the application in the Output window. These actions, particularly if there are many of them, can increase the file size of your resulting SWF files. Trace actions do nothing in the resulting SWF file; that is, the information they generate is not shown in the Flash Player or in the browser. However, when you generate your SWF files, you should select the Omit Trace Actions checkbox so that trace actions are not recorded in the resulting SWF file.

Debugging Permitted and Password Field

A new capability in Flash is the ability to debug a movie within the brows- er. If you select the Debugging Permitted checkbox, you can choose to password protect your movie so that you are the only one who can debug the movie remotely.

Compress Movie

Flash MX 2004 gives you a choice of whether you want to compress your SWF file content or not. The compression this option refers to is the compression of the vector elements in the file. Compression of raster and sound components is controlled by the JPEG Quality, Audio Stream, and Audio Event options, discussed later in the chapter.

If you are developing movies for CD or DVD, you may not want to compress vector elements in the movie. Given that file size is not as much a concern on these media, leaving Flash files uncompressed will make them play back more quickly, as the content need not be uncompressed at runtime. However, when developing content for the Web, you do want to make sure you select this option, as you want your files as small as possible for delivery over the Web.

 NOTE: *The Optimize for Flash Player 6 r60 option is available when you are exporting the file as a Flash Player 6 file.*

Image Compression

The JPEG Quality slider and field control the amount of JPEG compression applied to bitmap images. If no images are included in the file, the setting has no effect. Lower settings yield smaller file sizes and poorer visual results concerning the output image. Generally, it is best to experiment with various settings to get the best results, because compressibility and data loss with the JPEG compressor depends on the similarity of colors in the image.

If you change the Compression drop-down list in the Bitmap Properties dialog box (in the library) to Lossless, rather than Default, the JPEG Quality field will have no effect on the exported images in the SWF file. Use the Lossless setting only on bitmap images that must retain complete resolution. Taking advantage of the Lossless setting in the Bitmap Properties dialog box may result in very large file sizes. You may want to revisit Chapter 7 to review the details of setting bitmap properties in the library.

Even if a JPEG setting is established in the library using the Bitmap Properties dialog box, the setting entered into the JPEG Quality field at the time of export will override the Library setting. This allows flexibility by allowing various qualities to be used at the time of export.

See figure 12-2 for an idea of how the JPEG Quality setting affects two images at various qualities. Their associated file sizes also change because of the JPEG Quality setting. Results will vary, depending on the image being compressed.

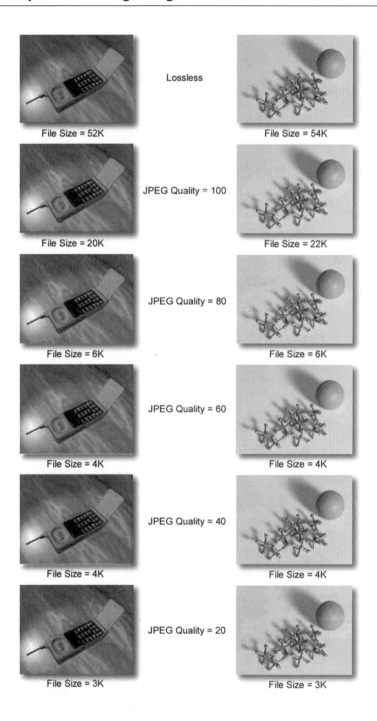

Figure 12-2. These images show the effect of JPEG quality settings on the file size and quality.

CD-ROM NOTE: *As the printing process often masks the true effects of screen data, the versions of the images shown in figure 12-2 are provided in the* ch12_01.fla *file, located in the* fgai/chapter12/jpeg/ *folder, installed from the companion CD-ROM.*

Audio Compression

As you read in Chapter 8, sounds in Flash are either defined as streaming sounds or event sounds. The Audio Stream and Audio Event Set buttons apply to how these two types of sounds are stored in the SWF file. Again, streamed sounds are interleaved with frames as they are saved in the SWF file. This allows the sound to start playing almost instantaneously. Any delay or interruption in streaming of the SWF file will be perceived as a pause in the audio. Event sounds are associated with an event and are downloaded in their entirety before playback. If the stream of data over the Web pauses, event sounds are not affected as far as playback is concerned.

Regardless of the type of sound, the Set buttons can be used to modify the output audio rate, even if the sound is stored in the FLA file at a higher sampling rate. This allows for flexibility as you generate SWF files. You can test various rates to compare file size to audio quality.

You can define the amount of compression used for audio with the Compression drop-down menus associated with the Audio Stream and Event Set buttons. Again, Flash can use either Adaptive Differential Pulse Code Modulation (ADPCM) or Motion Picture Experts Group 3 (MP3), both of which are lossy compression schemes. If the sound clip is speech, use the Speech compression option.

 TIP: *Use the Override Sound Settings checkbox to overrule the audio settings established in the Library Sound Properties dialog box. If this option is selected, the Export Flash Player Audio Stream and Audio Event settings will override the library settings.*

Remember that similar to JPEG compression, ADPCM and MP3 compression loses a certain amount of data to attain higher compression ratios (smaller files). Consequently, the more audio compressed, the less it is like the original file. Experimentation is key to getting the best mix. Just like the JPEG quality setting and colors in an image, audio compressibility is dependent on the range of amplitudes and the number of redundant amplitudes within the sound file.

CD-ROM NOTE: *To hear the effect of various compression rates on audio, examine the file in the* fgai/chapter12/audio/ *folder, installed from the companion CD-ROM. Open the file* ch12_02.fla, *which presents three examples: one voice sample, one music sample, and one sound effect.*

■ ■ ■ SWF to EXE (Projector)

Once you have an SWF file, quickly and easily convert the file to a projector using the Flash Player. Once a file is a projector, the Flash Player is no longer needed to run the file. All of the needed player code is compiled into the projector so that it can be played anywhere. However, note that the generated projector can only be played on the platform on which it was compiled. To generate a projector for multiple platforms, use the File | Publish command. Exercise 12-1 provides practice in generating a projector file.

 Exercise 12-1: Creating a Flash Projector

CD-ROM NOTE: *Open the file* ch12_03.swf, *located in the* fgai/chapter12/ *folder, installed from the companion CD-ROM, into the Flash player.*

To convert the SWF file to a projector, perform the following steps.

1. Open the SWF file into the Flash Player.
2. In the Flash Player, use the File | Create Projector menu option.
3. Name the file and click on OK. The generated projector (executable application) can now be ported to any computer that has the same operating system for playback.

■ ■ ■ Exporting Images

Aside from exporting movies, there may be times when you will want to export a static-image capture of a particular frame. Flash provides the ability to save in many vector and raster formats. Most of the raster formats are pretty straightforward. The formats include Windows Bitmap (PC), PICT (MAC), JPG, GIF, and PNG.

As far as vector export, this can be somewhat tricky. Of the files that exist on the computer, vector files (and even more particularly, metafiles) can be troublesome. Metafiles are those formats that can store raster data, vector data, or both simultaneously. Because metafiles can store data in a variety of ways (depending on the application that is writing the file), getting image A from package B to package C using metafile format D is difficult. Realistically, to find the best path between two packages will require some trial and error with the various vector formats available.

Cross-platform Issues

Aside from the "which browser" question, one of the most important variables you have to deal with is the user's platform. When trying to accommodate users, consider how the operating system will affect your movies. If you want to use or provide SWF or projector files on both Mac and PC, as well as other platforms, how do you do it?

The Web was designed to be platform independent. As wonderful as this sounds, it is not always convenient, especially when you are the developer trying to ensure that movies will work on multiple platforms. Although this section is not intended to be an all-encompassing list of problems you may encounter, it does answer some of the most frequently asked questions, and explores the major hurdles you might encounter.

The SWF file format is intended to be platform independent. For example, you should be able to play SWF files generated on the PC in the Macintosh Flash Player, with few, if any, problems. Keep in mind that font definitions, bitmaps, and sounds should play back and display normally. They are stored within the SWF format. Using "sneakernet" (floppy disks or other media) as well as the Web, you can port an SWF file to any platform and play it back, as long as a player exists on that platform.

Native Flash FLA files are platform independent. However, fonts assigned on the opposing platform can cause problems. Whereas the SWF file retains the font outline for playback, FLA files do not. Thus, the traditional problem of the unavailability of a font on one platform or the other still exists when porting FLA files cross-platform.

For example, if you design an FLA file with a particular font on the PC and save the FLA to the Mac for editing, the specific font must also reside on the Mac. If not, Flash will tell you that the font is not available. Consequently, your text will be substituted with some other font of the system's choosing.

However, even if the font used does reside on the other platform, you will likely have some editing to do. Although the name of a particular Mac and PC font may be the same (even if they visually appear the same), often the size, kerning, letter spacing, and other type attributes will vary. You will almost always have some editing to do when you go cross-platform, so make sure you budget some time for it. In this author's opinion, it is best to do all development on one platform or the other.

NOTE: *Keep in mind tips concerning importing media elements presented in previous chapters. In the PC version of Flash, WAV files are the preferred file format for sound files. In the Macintosh version of Flash, AIF files are the preferred file format for sound files. Remember that the support of some of the file types for importing and exporting is dependent on having QuickTime 4 installed.*

One final note related to cross-platform differences concerns the creation of projectors. When creating a projector file from the Flash player, the SWF file is compiled or prepared for playback on the platform on which it was compiled. Therefore, an SWF compiled on the PC (converted to a projector) can only be played back on the PC. An SWF compiled on the Macintosh can only be played back on the Macintosh. The Publish feature in Flash, however, allows you to create projectors for both platforms.

 TIP: *To create a set of projectors that accommodate both platforms, compile each projector on each platform or use the Publish command. Dual projectors are needed when creating hybrid HFS/ISO9660 CD-ROMs for multimedia distribution.*

▪ ▪ ▪ Web Delivery

Because most work in Flash ends up being delivered over the Web, the rest of this chapter deals with delivery and optimization techniques for Flash files. If the Web is your chosen vehicle, file size is a paramount concern. It does not take a lot of creative thinking to quickly use up bandwidth. What bandwidth you do have can quickly be eaten away by a few sound files, a couple of bitmaps, or a lot of vectors.

Integration Versus Optimization

Before looking at optimization, consider integration. There are two ways of linking your Flash files to an HTML page. Both methods can yield the same results. Nevertheless, which method you choose should depend on your experience with HTML and web-based scripting languages.

If you are new to HTML, consider using the Publish command, Macromedia's automated integration engine. This command makes it easy to embed SWF files. It provides some nice features as well, such as generating projectors, static images, and other files. If you are more of the coding sort, the latter portion of this chapter is for you. However, it is well worth being able to employ both methods.

Publishing with Flash

The Publish feature replaces the software utility called Aftershock, which was distributed with earlier versions of Flash. All of the functionality of Aftershock can now be found within Flash. In fact, the Publish feature is more extensive because it allows the developer to create custom "template" HTML pages that can be used.

However, as its primary function, Publish provides a quick means of getting movies into a web page. With little if any knowledge of HTML code, you can set all of the *EMBED* and *OBJECT* attributes required to get your Flash movies up and running in both browsers. You can also generate a range of other assets that may be needed. The File | Publish menu option provides the following powerful capabilities.

- Add a Flash movie to a new page.

- Provide a Java version of your movie.

- Generate static or animated GIFs, and static JPEG or PNG images of your movies, predominantly for those audience members who happen on your site without the Flash plug-in.

- Quickly generate QuickTime versions of your Flash movies.

- Generate a script that detects the Shockwave plug-in or ActiveX control. If the browser add-on is not found, the user is directed to display a GIF or to get the plug-in.

- Create the code required to give the user a cookie that stores their browsing settings for your site.

- Add code hooks for search engines.

- Create template pages that can be used in the Publish command.

▪ ▪ ▪ Publish Settings

Setting up the parameters for publishing your files is established using the File | Publish Settings command. Much like the tabbed dialog box found in the old Aftershock utility, you determine the media elements you want to generate and the characteristics of those media elements by selecting checkboxes and other controls.

 NOTE: *One of the new features in Flash MX 2004 is the ability to create Publish profiles. In the sections that follow you will learn about the various settings that can be established in Publish Settings. These settings can be saved as reusable profiles that can be applied across many files or projects, and thus you do not have to reset Publish Settings over and over.*

Formats Tab

When you select the Publish Settings menu option, the dialog box in figure 12-3 is shown. In the Formats tab, select the items you want to output. There is a correlation between the tabs shown at the top of the dialog box and the selected checkboxes. For example, if QuickTime (MOV) is not checked in the Formats tab, the QuickTime tab does not appear.

As shown in figure 12-3, note that the names of the media elements shown in the grayed fields to the right of the items are the same as the name of the current FLA file. Additionally, the files are output to the same directory as the FLA file.

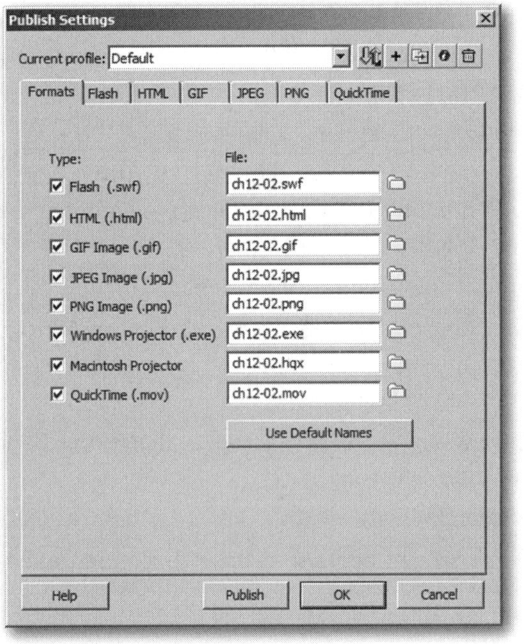

You can change the default names by deselecting the Use default names checkbox. Then, enter a name for the asset being generated. Just be aware of the names you use so that you do not accidentally overwrite existing files. Remember: even on the Macintosh, use file extensions.

Generally, the HTML file created by the Publish command is good for inserting individual Flash movies onto your page. However, if you want to do further editing, such as adding other HTML elements or scripting, you will have to "know the code" or be familiar with a site creation and page-editing tool such as Dreamweaver. Tools such as Netscape Composer, Microsoft FrontPage, and Adobe PageMill can be used, but they may not recognize the code inserted by the Publish command, or even recognize the Flash object itself.

Figure 12-3. The Format tab is used to indicate the elements to be published.

Flash Tab

The content of the Flash tab, shown in figure 12-4, should look familiar, because it is essentially the same as that shown in the Export Movie dialog box. As noted in that discussion, the settings established in the Publish Settings are used as the defaults for the Export Movie, Test Movie, Test Scene, and Publish commands. Use the elements displayed in the Flash tab to set the properties of the generated SWF file. Review the section

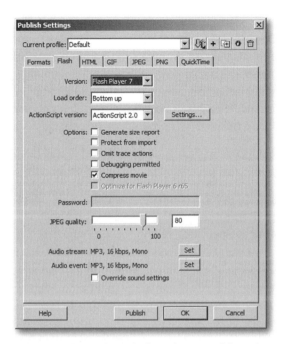

Figure 12-4. The Flash tab resembles the Export Movie dialog box, in which you establish the properties of the exported SWF file.

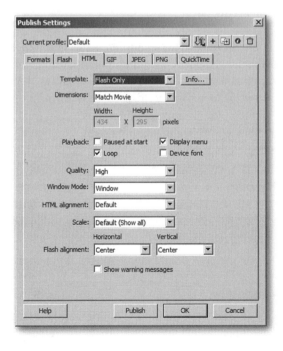

"Using Export Movie" for detailed descriptions of the options found here.

HTML Tab

The HTML tab, shown in figure 12-5, provides the controls necessary to define how the Flash file will be integrated into an HTML page. The Template drop-down provides several default "template" schemes that can be used to quickly assign the most common scripted elements. You can use any of the default templates or create your own. The remaining controls in the dialog box are used to define the HTML attributes used in the < *EMBED* > and < *OBJECT* > tags.

 NOTE: *Because Publishing templates require knowledge of HTML code and some special symbols, discussion of them is reserved for later in this chapter. See the section "Working with Publish Templates" later in this chapter for more details.*

Ignoring the Templates drop-down for now, examine the other controls available in the HTML tab. The first control, Dimensions, is used to define the width and height attributes of your Flash movie. As with other HTML elements, such as raster images, the size can be based on pixels or percentages. When pixels are specified in the

Figure 12-5. The settings in the HTML tab determine the HTML code (and scripting) that will be added to the HTML file that is generated.

Dimensions drop-down, the element is inserted at a fixed size. If the browser display is smaller than the fixed size, scrolling will be necessary.

The Match Movie option is also based on pixel size and is helpful in that you do not have to remember or write down the size of your movie. Selecting Percent (percentages) allows the size of the movie to change as the size of the browser window changes. The object is proportionally scaled to fit into the area of the browser window when percentages are used.

Playback

The Playback checkboxes provide several controls over the movie's playback conditions. Paused At Start and Loop are self-explanatory. The Display Menu checkbox controls the context menu pop-up, which is displayed when you right-click on an embedded movie in the browser. There is no way to totally get rid of the context menu. At a minimum, About Flash Player 6 and the settings options will always be available in the context menu when the user right-clicks on the movie in the web page.

The Device Font option substitutes antialiased system fonts for fonts that are not installed on the user's system. This is not a recommended option because it may negatively affect playback. In addition to the playback parameters, you are provided with six very important drop-down menus (though one applies to Internet Explorer only, as you will see).

Quality

The first drop-down menu is the Quality setting. As mentioned in earlier chapters, you can toggle between various view modes to increase performance within the Flash application. When machine speed slows, you can reduce the view complexity to speed up performance by turning off antialiasing. As your Flash movies play in a page, adjust the visual quality based on machine performance to achieve the same results. The Quality setting provides the following options for visual quality.

- *Auto High:* Tries to balance playback speed and appearance equally. However, if performance decreases, visual quality is sacrificed to increase speed. In general, playback will begin with antialias turned on. Yet, if machine speed degrades, antialiasing is turned off to improve playback speed.

- *Auto Low:* Tries to balance speed and appearance. By default, Auto Low starts with antialiasing off. If performance is favorable, anti-aliasing will be turned on.

- *High:* Favors appearance and continually plays with antialiasing on.

- *Medium:* Tries to favor both appearance and performance by anti-aliasing objects and ignoring text.

- *Low:* Favors performance and continually plays with antialiasing off.

- *Best:* Attempts to choose from among the previous options to display the SWF file based on performance.

Window Mode

The second of these options is Window Mode. This is an exceptional feature; however, currently it only applies to movies played back in Internet Explorer. Nonetheless, it is worth mentioning.

One of the common questions asked is "How do you make the background of a Flash movie transparent so that the background color of the web page shows through it?" This is what the Window Mode feature is all about. Window Mode provides the following three options.

- *Default:* Sets the *WMODE* parameter of the *<OBJECT>* tag to *WINDOW*. This plays the movie "normally" and provides the fastest animation performance.

- *Opaque Windowless:* Sets the *WMODE* parameter to *OPAQUE* and allows you to fluidly move elements behind Shockwave Movies without the moving objects showing. This is typically used in conjunction with Dynamic HTML (DHTML).

- *Transparent Windowless:* Sets the *WMODE* parameter to *TRANS-PARENT* and allows the elements behind the Shockwave movie to show through the blank areas of the movie. Although this is a neat feature, animation performance may decrease when this mode is used.

Currently, if you use the Window Mode setting, *WMODE* will be added to both the *<OBJECT>* and *<EMBED>* tags, as a *PARAM* in *OBJECT*, and as an attribute in *EMBED*. Currently, the *WMODE* attribute is not recognized by Netscape Navigator or Communicator.

HTML Alignment

The Alignment drop-down controls the alignment of other elements on the page in relation to the Shockwave element. Valid options for the Alignment drop-down include LEFT, RIGHT, TOP, and BOTTOM.

Scale

The Scale drop-down menu controls how the Shockwave movie will fit into the area allotted within the Dimensions drop-down. The Default is

Show All. Figure 12-6 shows the results of the various settings on a movie that is wide and a movie that is tall. If the movie is the exact size specified in the *HEIGHT* and *WIDTH* parameters (that is, you are using exact pixel dimensions), a scale will probably not be necessary. Thus, use the default of Show All. However, if you are using screen percentages for your dimensions and your movie has a different aspect ratio than the screen area, a scale setting will probably be required.

Alignment

The final two drop-down menus in the HTML tab allow you to control alignment when the movie does not completely fill the defined area. These two drop-downs are used in conjunction with the Scale drop-down when percentages are used for the dimensions.

Figure 12-7 shows the various results of the Flash Alignment settings. In the HTML code, the single *SALIGN* attribute defines the alignment. Thus, if a movie is aligned left and top, the *SALIGN* attribute is set equal to *LT*. If the movie is aligned right and top, SALIGN is set equal to *RT*. The default when no *SALIGN* attribute is included is center horizontal and center vertical.

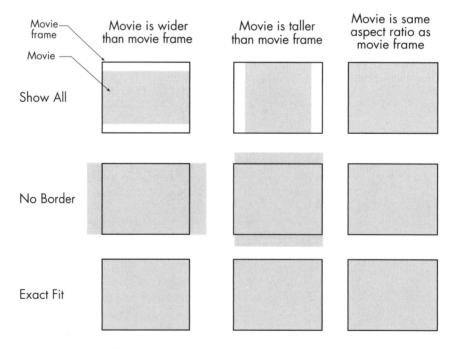

Figure 12-6. If the movie is not the same aspect ratio as the defined HEIGHT *and* WIDTH *parameters (dimensions), a scale setting may be necessary.*

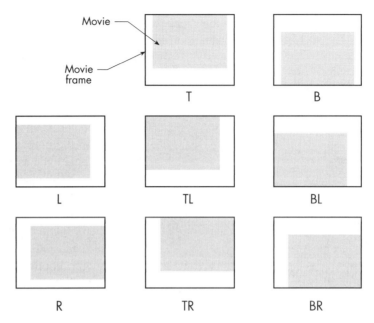

Figure 12-7. If the movie does not completely fill the defined area, the SALIGN *attribute controls the placement of the movie.*

Show Warning Messages

The final checkbox in the HTML tab, Show Warning Messages, is used to indicate any problems that may occur when the Publish command is executed. With so many publishing options, some settings may conflict with one another. If the Show Warning Messages checkbox is selected, Flash will prompt you with errors if they occur. One such message is the QuickTime alert. If you do not have QuickTime 4 installed and you select the QuickTime checkbox in the Formats tab, Flash will prompt you that it cannot create a QuickTime movie.

GIF Tab

As you prepare your movies for web distribution, you always have to consider that there may be users that do not have the Flash plug-in. If so, they will see that ugly broken-link icon in place of your SWF file. For cases when the user cannot view Flash elements, the Publish utility allows you to generate a static GIF, JPEG, or PNG representation of the first frame of your movie, or an animated GIF.

Although the primary use of the GIF, JPEG, and PNG images is for alternative images (when the user does not have the plug-in), you can also use it to create image maps from your Flash movies. The section "Using the Publish Command" discusses this in more detail.

The alternate image generated from Flash is only necessary for Netscape browsers that do not have the plug-in. If Internet Explorer does not have the ActiveX component to interpret the Flash element, it will automatically prompt the user to obtain the plug-in. Consequently, it will automatically show the broken link.

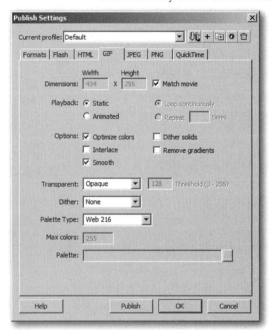

Figure 12-8. The GIF tab is used to define the type of GIF file that will be generated.

If you selected the GIF image option in the Formats tab, the GIF tab is used to define the properties of the file that will be generated, as shown in figure 12-8. As with the size of the embedded SWF file, you begin by defining the dimensions of the image. You then establish whether you want to use a Static or Animated GIF. If you select Animated, you can control the number of loops it plays by either selecting the Loop Continuously option or by entering a number of repetitions.

Other important options shown in figure 12-8 include the following specifications, which affect how the GIF file is generated, as well as how it is saved. Many of these options deal with reducing the colors of the image or animation down to a set of 256 that GIF can define.

The GIF Format and Option

There are three things you should note about using animated GIFs. First, Graphic Interchange Format (GIF) is a graphic file format limited to 256 colors. Thus, you have to define the color characteristics for the file in the lower part of the dialog box. Consequently, the color fidelity of your images will not be as robust as that you see in Flash. Options related to color fidelity are discussed shortly

Second, because animated GIFs consist of raster or bitmap images, the files generated may be quite large, particularly if your Flash movie is very lengthy. Watch your file sizes. It is safe to assume that if a user does not have the Flash plug-in he or she may be a home user and will likely be connecting via a slower modem connection.

Finally, GIF is the only format that provides animation capability. Although free of many of GIF's weaknesses, JPEG and PNG files cannot store multiple images, and cannot be used for animation. If you want an animated image as an alternative to the SWF file, you must deal with the color limitations of the GIF format.

- Optimize Colors attempts to reduce the number of odd colors found in the image.

  By reducing outlier colors via averaging, the colors of the image can be more easily made to fit the 256-color restriction of GIF.

- Dither Solids attempts to reduce colors by replacing solid colors with dithered complements as much as possible.

  This reduces the total number of colors required by the image.

- Interlace allows you to specify that the GIF file is written so that it can be progressively viewed during download.

  Progressive images give the perception that the file downloads from the Web more quickly. Interlacing images neither increases nor decreases file size significantly.

- Much like the Dither Solids checkbox, Remove Gradients attempts to replace gradients with dithered combinations of color to reduce the number of colors required by the image.

- Smooth antialiases vector elements before creating the GIF file.

- Transparent provides the ability to select a color or colors (using Threshold) that will be transparent.

- Keep in mind that GIF transparency is 1-bit, meaning that a pixel can only be 100-percent transparent or 100-percent opaque. The Transparent option sets the background of the image to 100-percent transparent. The Threshold option allows you to choose a number between 0 and 255. Any color in the image with luminosity falling below the number entered will be assigned as transparent.

- Because GIF files can only contain 256 colors, Flash must reduce the colors in the image.

  The Dither option makes the resulting color reduction less noticeable by dithering adjacent pixels. By default, no dithering occurs. The Ordered option presents a patterned replacement, whereas Diffusion presents a fractal or random replacement. Generally, Diffusion will provide the best results.

- When developing images for the Web, remember that some users may be limited to a 256-color display.

  When this is the case, the browser uses a default set of colors, called the Web or browser-safe palette, to display all images. Any color used by an image that is not in the Web palette is interpolated to the closest available color that is in the palette. This means that colors that do not exist in the palette will not display as you designed them. Use the Palette Type option to assign the palette to be used for the 256-color image. The Web 216 option should be used if you are likely to encounter users browsing at 8 bits (256 colors).

The Web 216 option is the palette of browser-safe colors and will force the generated GIF image to use only those colors. If you are not limited by your audience's display, you can use the Adaptive option, which generates a palette of colors from the colors needed in the image. The Web Snap Adaptive option yields colors that are a mix of those generated by Adaptive and those that exist in the browser-safe palette. The Custom option allows you to load Photoshop ACT (Swatch) files for use as the image's palette.

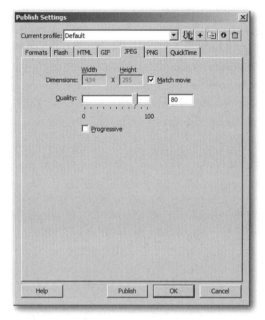

Figure 12-9. The JPEG tab is used to define the parameters for the generated JPEG image.

JPEG Tab

As you have already learned, the Joint Photographic Experts Group (JPEG) format uses a lossy compression scheme. Within the JPEG tab, shown in figure 12-9, you set the dimensions for the image to be generated, as well as the quality of compression. Higher numbers equate to lower compression, larger file sizes, and more visually pleasing images. Lower numbers equate to higher compression, smaller files, and less pleasing images. The Progressive checkbox can be used to create an interlaced JPEG image. Much like the interlaced GIF, progressive JPEG images appear to download more quickly because they can be instantaneously read even though the entire image has not been downloaded.

PNG Tab

The Portable Network Graphics (PNG, pronounced "ping") format is a relatively new format to the Web. Developed as a response to developers wanting a patent-free format, it provides most of the capabilities of GIF and JPEG in one format. Again, it does not support multiple images (animation).

The PNG tab, shown in figure 12-10, contains most of the controls found in the GIF and JPEG tabs. The primary difference between PNG and JPEG images is that PNG's compression is a lossless scheme. This means that PNG's compression does not lose data and creates an exact replica of the original file when uncompressed.

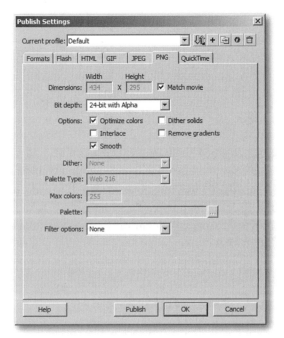

Figure 12-10. PNG provides most of the features of GIG and JPEG, except for GIF's multiple image capability.

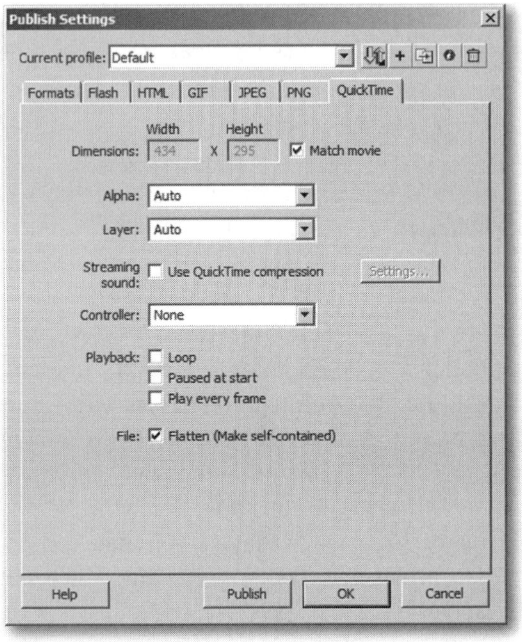

Different, too, are the color capabilities of the PNG format. PNG can contain 24-bit data or 8-bit data. Realistically, GIF is limited to 256, whereas JPEG is usually limited to near 24-bit data. Thus, PNG can do both, and you will find that the Bit Depth drop-down found in the PNG tab allows you to select either. The color options found at the bottom of the dialog box are enabled only when you select the 8-bit option from the Bit Depth drop-down menu.

QuickTime Tab

As shown in figure 12-11, the QuickTime tab provides control over several aspects of the resulting digital video movie. As with other tabs, Dimensions specifies the image size for the video clip. The Alpha drop-down permits you to define portions of the Flash movie as transparent. This is useful if you decide to composite generated QuickTime movies in other packages and technologies. The Layer drop-down lets you set the layer on which the SWF information will reside.

Although Flash uses its own compression techniques for audio, the Use QuickTime compression option allows you to choose from any one of the many QuickTime-accessible compressors that may be on your machine. Codecs (short for compressors/decompressors) such as Sorenson, QDesign, or Qualcomm can be chosen. If you are a digital video developer as well, you will find that the ability to use QuickTime's compressors may provide more flexibility

Figure 12-11. The QuickTime tab is used to define the parameters for the generated MOV file.

and possibly better compression. The remaining checkboxes within the QuickTime tab, as follows, are standard elements you can control.

- Use the Controller drop-down to select the type of control you would like for the movie to display. Options include None (No Controller), Standard, and QTVR.

- Loop and Paused at start are self-explanatory.

- Use *Play every frame* to ensure that graphic components of the QuickTime clip are not dropped to attain synchronization.

- The File option allows you to flatten the generated movie. When working on the Macintosh, QuickTime movies can be made to store data outside the QuickTime movie. This increases playback performance. For movies to be cross-platform, however, make sure you use the Flatten checkbox.

▪▪▪ Using the Publish Command

Once you have established the Publish settings, selecting the File | Publish menu option generates the selected files. The generated files will be created in the same directory as the Flash FLA file, with the names defined in the Formats tab of the Publish Settings dialog box. Again, remember that it is vital that you name your files with extensions.

 WARNING: *As soon as you select the Publish menu option from either the File menu or the Publish Settings dialog box, the respective files are generated. There is no prompt asking if you are sure you want to publish. This is true even if a series of files with the same names already exists in the current directory. Be careful you do not overwrite files you want to keep.*

▪▪▪ Writing HTML

Although this section is not intended to be an extensive HTML indoctrination, knowing enough HTML to be able to integrate a Flash element is pretty straightforward. The two main tags used to integrate Flash movies in HTML are < EMBED > and < OBJECT >. The difference between these two may not be readily apparent. However, it boils down to what is used to support the Flash element in the browser (as far as software components are concerned) and which browser is being used. The difference between the < EMBED > tag and the < OBJECT > tag really centers on implementation. Both tags can also be used for media elements other than Flash.

Embed Versus Object

To successfully integrate a Flash movie into a page so that it will work on both Netscape and Internet Explorer requires the use of both the < EMBED > and the < OBJECT > tags. The < EMBED > tag forces the browser to use a plug-in to support the Flash element, whereas the < OBJECT > tag forces the browser to use an ActiveX control.

Thus, the < EMBED > tag provides the needed information for Netscape, which uses only plug-ins, and the < OBJECT > tag provides the necessary information for Internet Explorer, which uses ActiveX components. Both tags are used simultaneously within one another so that, regardless of browser, only one of the two linked files is displayed in the page.

Plug-ins Versus ActiveX Components

"What is the difference between a plug-in and an ActiveX component?" you may ask. Both plug-ins and ActiveX components are designed to extend the capabilities of HTML because alone the browser supports only JPEG and GIF images. Through add-on software components (plug-ins and ActiveX components), developers can add almost any type of media element, not least of which is Shockwave.

Basically, the difference between plug-ins and ActiveX components relates to scope. Plug-ins are software components that can be used only by the browser. End users download and install a plug-in, which is added to the browser itself. ActiveX components, on the other hand, are much broader in scope. When an ActiveX component is installed to the user's computer, it becomes part of the operating system (Windows). Thus, ActiveX components can be used by (at least theoretically) all applications on the system because they are installed at the system level rather than the application level.

Microsoft's vision was to increase the scope of extensibility by allowing its version of the plug-in (the ActiveX component) to be used in every application, not just the browser. Although the implementation of ActiveX components in applications other than the browser can be tricky, it is an inventive concept nonetheless.

To integrate an SWF file into your web page, use the < OBJECT > and < EMBED > tags within the < BODY > section of the web page. Internet Explorer interprets the < OBJECT > information and ignores the < EMBED > information. Netscape ignores the < OBJECT > information and reads the < EMBED > information. Therefore, it does not matter which browser you are using; only one Flash element will be inserted into the browser. Additionally, depending on what is contained within the Flash file, you may use a variety of attributes within the tags, as discussed further in the next section. Code example 12-1, which follows, provides a basic implementation.

Code Example 12-1: Use of <EMBED> and <OBJECT> Tags to Integrate Flash Files in HTML

```
<HTML>
 <HEAD>
  <TITLE>A Simple Example</TITLE>
 </HEAD>
 <BODY>
  <CENTER>
  <OBJECT classid="clsid:D2/CDB6E-AE6D-11cf-96B8-
444553540000" codebase="http://download.macromedia.com/
pub/shockwave/cabs/flash/swflash.cab#version=7,0,0,0"
WIDTH="250" HEIGHT="300" id="sim_reflection" ALIGN="">
   <PARAM NAME="movie" VALUE="sim_reflection.swf">
   <PARAM NAME="quality" VALUE="high">
   <PARAM NAME="bgcolor" VALUE="#FFFFFF">
<EMBED src="sim_reflection.swf" quality="high"
bgcolor="#FFFFFF" WIDTH="250" HEIGHT="300"
NAME="sim_reflection" ALIGN=""
TYPE="application/x-shockwave-flash"
PLUGINSPAGE="http://www.macromedia.com/go/
getflashplayer"></EMBED>
   </OBJECT>
   <NOEMBED>
    <IMG src="ch9-01.gif" width=250 height=300>
   </NOEMBED>
   </OBJECT>
 </BODY>
</HTML>
```

Exercise 12-2 makes use of the code shown in code example 12-1. In this exercise, you will enter the code into Notepad (or other text editor) and then save the file and open it in a browser. Further notes on the code contained in code example 12-1 follow the exercise.

Exercise 12-2: Creating/Saving Code in a Text Editor and Opening in a Browser

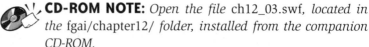

CD-ROM NOTE: *Open the file* ch12_03.swf, *located in the* fgai/chapter12/ *folder, installed from the companion CD-ROM.*

Enter the code shown in code example 12-1 into Notepad or another ASCII text editor. Then save the file with the *.html* extension, place it in the same location as the SWF file, and open it in a browser to see the results. Take a look at the code shown in code example 12-1. Notice how the typical HTML sections are defined, as follows.

- *< HTML >...< /HTML >* defines the document as an HTML document.

- *< HEAD >...< /HEAD >* is known as the header. Miscellaneous document settings are presented here, such as the title that will appear in the browser's title bar.

- *< BODY >...< /BODY >* is the actual content that will be rendered in the browser.

This simple web page contains nothing but the Flash element that is integrated with the *< OBJECT >* and *< EMBED >* tags. The *< OBJECT >* tag contains the relevant information for Internet Explorer. The optional parameters, listed as *< PARAM >* statements, control settings such as the display quality, looping, and autoplay for the Flash file. The *< EMBED >* tag contains the information pertinent to Netscape browsers. There should be congruency between the parameters set for the *< OBJECT >* tag and the attributes within the *< EMBED >* tag. Often a similarity will exist between these two; however, some optional settings may apply to only one browser or the other.

Keep in mind that HTML is not case sensitive. The only exception to this rule is embedded URLs, such as the URL assigned as the *CODEBASE* in the *< OBJECT >* tag and the URL assigned as the *PLUGINSPAGE* in the *< EMBED >* tag. All URLs in HTML are case sensitive.

 TIP: *As far as HTML code is concerned, it is a good idea to adopt some sort of consistent method of capitalization for readability.*

One of the most critical things you should notice in the implementation in code example 12-1 is that the *< EMBED >* tag is nested within the opening and closing *< OBJECT >* tags. This makes the scheme work. It is due to this nesting that Internet Explorer or Netscape Communicator/Navigator ignores the opposing command (*< EMBED >* and *< OBJECT >*, respectively). If the *< EMBED >* is not encased within the *< OBJECT >* tag, errors or two Flash representations may be rendered in the resulting HTML page.

The last thing you should notice is the *<NOEMBED>* tag. This tag provides backward compatibility for older browsers, as well as browsers that do not have the plug-in. If you are manually coding your pages, do not forget this tag. Although you will have to manually create the associated GIF file, the *<NOEMBED>* tag provides a mechanism for supporting rather than eliminating a portion of the web audience.

EMBED Attributes/Object Parameters

The previous section discussed a simple implementation of the *<OBJECT>* and *<EMBED>* tags for Flash elements. Depending on the features your files use, you may need to add more or less optional parameters for your Flash files. Some of the optional settings apply to a particular browser only. Thus, some apply to *<OBJECT>* only or to *<EMBED>* only. Table 12-1 outlines the settings that can be used with both the *<OBJECT>* and *<EMBED>* tags. The various parameters and attributes of the *<OBJECT>* and *<EMBED>* tags are specified in HTML documents. The required parameters in the table are denoted with an asterisk (*). The remaining settings are optional, but they are frequently included.

▪ ▪ ▪ Working with Publish Templates

One of the most interesting features of the Publish command is the ability to use and create templates for integration. Realizing that getting an SWF file into a page is sometimes laborious, Macromedia has attempted to make it easier to get your pages onto the Web.

When you select the HTML tab in the Publish Settings dialog box, you will note that there are several default templates available in the Template drop-down menu. Because coding different functionality requires different tags and scripting, there are several templates. For example, if you use the FS Command action in your movie, special tags are required in the web page. Thus, there is a template for Flash with FS Command. However, if you do not use FS Command, the simple Flash Only template may be all you need.

In addition to the variety of templates provided, you can generate your own templates for use in the Publish Settings dialog box. The files used in the Template drop-down are contained in the *Program Files/Macromedia/ Flash MX 2004/en/First Run/HTML* folder on the PC. The location is similar on the Macintosh within the Flash folder.

Table 12-1: HTML-specified Parameters/Attributes of <OBJECT> and <EMBED> Tags

< OBJECT >	< EMBED >	Function	Description
MOVIE*	SRC*	Provides the URL for the Flash movie that is being included.	Can include both relative and absolute references.
WIDTH*	WIDTH*	Defines the width of the Flash movie window.	Can be specified as a fixed pixel size or a percentage.
HEIGHT*	HEIGHT*	Defines the height of the Flash movie window.	Can be specified as a fixed pixel size or a percentage.
CLASSID*, CODEBASE*	PLUGINSPAGE*	Provides the URL and information for acquiring the ActiveX component or plug-in.	*CLASSID* is specified as a version number; *CODEBASE* and *PLUGINSPAGE* are defined as URLs.
ID	NAME	Specifies a name for the element for scripting.	Permits the object to be controlled via scripting.
N/A	SWLIVECONNECT	Specifies whether Java should be loaded when the Flash Player loads.	A *TRUE* setting forces Java to load. *FALSE* prevents Java from loading. This is required for use of FS commands and JavaScript.
N/A	MAYSCRIPT	Identifies that the object may use scripting.	*MAYSCRIPT="MAYSCRIPT"* is required to use JavaScript and FS Command actions.
PLAY	PLAY	Determines whether the movie plays automatically.	True causes the movie to play after the first frame is loaded. False stops the movie at the first frame.
LOOP	LOOP	Determines whether movie loops when it reaches the last frame.	True causes the movie to loop. False causes the movie to stop on the last frame.
QUALITY	QUALITY	Controls the display quality of the movie during playback.	Options include Autohigh, Autolow, High, and Low (described earlier in this chapter). Best is an undocumented value that allows the Flash Player to choose the quality based on performance at playback.
BGCOLOR	BGCOLOR	Determines the background color of the movie. Note that this attribute will override the background color assigned in the movie.	Six-digit hexadecimal values are entered, two values representing each of the RGB components. See Appendix E for more information.
SCALE	SCALE	Determines how the movie resizes to fit the space allocated by the browser (area defined by *HEIGHT* and *WIDTH*).	Can include *SHOWALL*, *NO BORDER*, and *EXACT FIT*, described earlier in this chapter.
SALIGN	SALIGN	When the movie's aspect ratio does not match the area aspect ratio, this controls the placement of the movie within the area.	Options include *T, B, L, R, TL, TR, BL*, and *BR* described earlier in this chapter.
BASE	BASE	Defines a reference URL/address for relative URLs in a movie (similar to the *BASEREF* HTML attribute).	The value is defined as a URL, on which all other relative URLs are based.
MENU	MENU	Defines what options appear in the context menu when the user right-clicks on a flash movie in a web page.	A value of *TRUE* displays all the menu option and a value of *FALSE* displays the About Flash 5.0 option only.
WMODE	N/A	Provides additional features in Internet Explorer 4.0, including positioning, layering, and transparency.	Options include *WINDOW, OPAQUE*, and *TRANSPARENT*. Window is the default wherein the movie simply plays in its window. *OPAQUE* allows objects to pass behind the opaque Flash movie. *TRANSPARENT* allows objects to pass behind a Flash movie whose background area is transparent.

■ ■ ■ **Examining and Creating Templates**

The HTML files used in the Template capability are special in that they use special characters to represent values substituted during the Publish command. These special characters are a combination of the dollar sign ($) and other alphanumeric characters. Thus, they are "custom" HTML files, but follow the general rules of normal HTML files.

To see what these files look like, open the *Default.html* file located in the *Macromedia/Flash MX 2004/en/First Run/HTML* directory into an ASCII editor. The code for the Default template is shown in code example 12-2. Note the token values represented by the dollar signs ($). These values are replaced when the Publish command is executed.

Code Example 12-2: Default Template File Used in the Publish Settings Dialog Box

```
$TTFlash Only (Default)
$DS
Use an OBJECT and EMBED tag to display Flash.
$DF
<HTML>
<HEAD>
<TITLE>$TI</TITLE>
</HEAD>
<BODY bgcolor="$BG">
<!- URL's used in the movie->
$MU
<!- text used in the movie->
$MT
<OBJECT classid="clsid:D27CDB6E-AE6D-11cf-96B8-444553540000" ¬
codebase="http://active.macromedia.com/flash2/cabs/¬
swflash.cab#version=7,0,0,0" WIDTH=$WI HEIGHT=$HE>
$PO
<EMBED $PE WIDTH=$WI HEIGHT=$HE TYPE="application/x-shockwave-¬
flash" PLUGINSPAGE="http://www.macromedia.com/go/¬
getflashplayer"></EMBED>
</OBJECT>
</BODY>
</HTML>
```

In code example 12-2, note the first two lines. The first line, preceded by *$TT*, is the name of the template as it will be shown in the Publish Settings dialog box. Note the second line, which is preceded by *$DS* and followed by *$DF*. The text between will be shown when the Template Info button is selected in the Publish Settings dialog box.

Using the substitution values, you can create your own templates to be used within the Publish command. You can copy the existing files and use them as a starting place, or write your own from scratch. Table 12-2 outlines the token characters used with the template HTML files and the values they represent. Once you have created a template, all you need do is copy it to the *Macromedia/Flash MX 2004/en/First Run/HTML* directory to begin using it. Its name will appear in the Template drop-down in the Publish Settings dialog box.

▪▪▪ Streaming, Testing, and Playback

As mentioned earlier, Flash SWF files are a streaming file format. This means that the playback of files can begin before the file is completely downloaded. In reality, for the Flash Player to play any frame, all of the elements used in that frame (including vector shapes, bitmaps, and event sounds) must be downloaded.

Although there are many fast connections on the Web, streaming is limited by the slowest connection through which the downloaded frame data must travel. Often, the slowest connection is the user's computer. Network traffic or other variables can also affect this "link." Nevertheless, the speed of the end user's connection often dictates what is reasonably deliverable.

Thus, it is vitally important to closely examine the content of your movies to make sure that the end user perceives what you do. Flash provides a couple of tools that make examining movies much easier, which are described in material to follow.

The perceived effectiveness of Flash's streaming capability during playback depends solely on the amount of data required to render each frame. For smooth playback, the size of the data for each frame should be as small as possible. This is performed through analysis and optimization.

Additionally, the amount of time required to download a series of frames should take no longer than the amount of time required to play those frames. When it takes longer to download a series of frames than to play it back, noticeable pauses or gaps may appear in the presentation, and likely where you do not want them to occur. The goal in analysis and optimization is to reduce any lapses, or at least to control when those lapses occur.

Before you can control or prevent pauses in your presentation, first figure out where they might occur. The next two sections provide a detailed look at the facilities within Flash that allow you to identify potential problems related to downloading and playback.

Table 12-2: Symbol Combinations Used as Placeholders Within HTML Template Files

Name	Symbol	Associated With...
Template Title	$TT	Template Definition
Template Description Start	$DS	Template Definition
Template Description Finish	$DF	Template Definition
Movie Width	$WI	Embed/Object *WIDTH* attribute/parameter
Movie Height	$HE	Embed/Object *HEIGHT* attribute/parameter
Movie Source	$MO	Embed/Object *SRC* attribute/parameter
HTML Alignment	$HA	Embed/Object *ALIGN* attribute/parameter
Looping	$LO	Embed/Object *LOOP* attribute/parameter
Parameters for OBJECT	$PO	Location for the *OBJECT* parameters to be written in the HTML
Attributes for EMBED	$PE	Location for the *EMBED* attributes to be written in the HTML
Play	$PL	Embed/Object *PLAY* attribute/parameter
Movie Quality	$QU	Embed/Object *QUALITY* attribute/parameter
Movie Scale	$SC	Embed/Object *SCALE* attribute/parameter
Movie Alignment	$SA	Embed/Object *SALIGN* attribute/parameter
Movie Mode	$WM	*WMODE* setting (applicable to IE only)
Movie Device Font	$DE	Embed/Object *DEVICEFONT* attribute/ parameter
Movie Background Color	$BG	Embed/Object *BGCOLOR* attribute/ parameter
Image Width	$IW	*<IMG>* tag *WIDTH* attribute
Image Height	$IH	*<IMG>* tag *HEIGHT* attribute
Image Source	$IS	*<IMG>* tag *SRC* attribute
Image Map Name	$IU	*<IMG>* tag *USEMAP* attribute
Image Map Tag Location	$IM	*<MAP>* and *<AREA>* tags (used for client-side image mapping)
Movie Text (location in HTML file to write movie text)	$MT	Flash movie text insertion point; test insert into HTML comment tags <!— —>
Movie URLs (location in HTML file to write movie URLs)	&MU	Flash movie URL list insertion point; text inserted as blank anchor tags
QuickTime Width	$QW	*EMBED WIDTH* of the QuickTime element
QuickTime Height	$QH	*EMBED HEIGHT* of the QuickTime element
QuickTime Filename	$QN	*EMBED SRC* movie file name
GIF Width	$GW	*WIDTH* specified in *<IMG>* tag
GIF Height	$GH	*HEIGHT* specified in *<IMG>* tag
GIF Filename	$GS	*SRC* specified in *<IMG>* tag
JPEG Width	$JW	*WIDTH* specified in *<IMG>* tag
JPEG Height	$JH	*HEIGHT* specified in *<IMG>* tag
JPEG Filename	$JN	*SRC* specified in *<IMG>* tag
PNG Width	$PW	*WIDTH* specified in *<IMG>* tag
PNG Height	$PH	*HEIGHT* specified in *<IMG>* tag
PNG Filename	$PN	*SRC* specified in *<IMG>* tag

Closely Examining the Size Report

One of the two most import features for creating efficient and effective movies is the Size Report option. When you export an SWF file from Flash, you have the option of generating an ASCII text file that provides valuable information about the file. Use Size Report to help you figure out where the bandwidth-intensive portions of your file are, as well as information concerning where some "fat" could be trimmed away. Exercise 12-3 takes you through the process of generating a size report file.

Exercise 12-3: Generating a Size Report File

CD-ROM NOTE: *Open* ch12_04.fla, *located in the* fgai/ chapter12/ *folder, installed from the companion CD-ROM.*

To practice generating a size report, perform the following steps.

1. Select File | Export Movie.

2. Name the SWF file that will be created.

3. In the Export Movie dialog box, make sure the Generate Size Report checkbox is selected.

4. An ASCII text file will reside in the same location as the generated SWF file. Open this into any ASCII text editor, such as NotePad or SimpleText. The generate file should look similar to code example 12-3. The size report for the simulated shadow Flash file (*ch12_04.fla*) allows you to perform extensive frame-by-frame examination of the movie.

The size report generates a frame-by-frame examination of the file, showing entries for Frame Number, Frame Bytes, Total Bytes, and Page (see code example 12-3). The Frame Bytes section reports the number of bytes required for download before the frame can play. Because this sample movie has a movie clip inserted into the main timeline and has only one frame, one frame is reported. This example was used for brevity to show the format of a size report.

In addition to the frame-by-frame information, Flash also reports the total file size of each scene and the file sizes of each symbol. Because this example file is quite brief, there is not much "fat" to trim from the file.

Code Example 12-3: Size Report for the Simulated Shadow Flash File

```
Movie Report
```

Frame #	Frame Bytes	Total Bytes	Page
1	1214	1214	Scene 1
Page		Shape Bytes	Text Bytes

Scene 1	0	0
Symbol	Shape Bytes	Text Bytes

	Shape Bytes	Text Bytes
Broken Piece 1	150	0
Broken Piece 2	168	0
Broken Piece 3	162	0
Dot	75	0
Ellipse	80	0
Rotating	0	
Sphere	114	0
Sphere Movie	0	0

 CD-ROM NOTE: *Look at a more complex example to see how the size report can be used to find out where the most bandwidth will be needed. To do this, generate a size report for the file ch12_05.fla, located in the* fgai/chapter12/ *folder, installed from the companion CD-ROM. Use the sample file to generate your own size report, or follow along with the explanation in the book.*

The following size report has been broken into "chunks," omitting the irrelevant portions. To see the entire report, generate an SWF file using the file *ch12_05.fla* located in the *fgai/chapter12/* folder, installed from the companion CD-ROM. Make sure to select Generate Size Report in the Export Movie dialog box.

Code example 12-4 shows a portion of the frame-by-frame report from a much larger Flash movie. The movie uses a streaming sound, so the Frame Bytes entry associated with each frame is somewhat larger than the previous example. Notice in code example 12-4 that frame 19 has a spike and requires much more data than the previous frames. During testing under target conditions, this spike may indicate a place where there is a lag or problem during playback. If such problems occur during testing, revision of the content of the frame may be necessary, such as optimizing curves (or other techniques).

Code Example 12-4: Partial Report with Spikes in Data

Movie Report

Frame	# Frame Bytes	Total Bytes	Page
1	1190	1190	Scene 1
2	1158	2348	2
3	1158	3506	3
4	1158	4664	4
5	1158	5822	5
6	1158	6980	6
7	1158	8138	7
8	1158	9296	8
9	1158	10454	9
10	1158	11612	10
11	1158	12770	11
12	1158	13928	12
13	1158	15086	13
14	1158	16244	14
15	1158	17402	15
16	1158	18560	16
17	1158	19718	17
18	1158	20876	18
19	3878	24754	19
20	1158	25912	20
21	1158	27070	21

Code example 12-5 shows a more significant spike in the needed data. Take a closer look at frame 126 and notice that it is requiring a tremendous amount of data for playback. This frame may cause problems on slower machines and should be addressed and optimized. Ultimately, some data should be reduced if the file is to be delivered over the Web.

Code Example 12-5: Frame 126 with High Data Requirement for Playback

124	1169	146897	124
125	1169	148066	125
126	192261	340327	126
127	1158	341485	127
128	1158	342643	128

Finally, as shown in code example 12-6, the required bytes for each of the bitmap and sound elements is presented (as is the required byte information for the symbol and font elements). The bitmap elements are the main contributors to the size of the file, because originally they were defined as lossless in the library. Because these graphic elements only appear for a short time on screen, reducing their quality to *JPEG = 50* will more than likely decrease the overall size of the file, as well as the bytes required for frame 126.

Using the Size Report feature, you can easily troubleshoot and optimize your movies. By providing detailed information about your movie's media elements, you can visually determine the trouble spots and attempt to deliver quality appropriate for the given circumstance.

Code Example 12-6: End of the Size Report

```
Bitmap                            Compressed   Original   Compression
--------------                    ----------   --------   -----------
web2 copy.bmp                        30629      120000     Lossless
raster2 copy.bmp                     45124      120000     Lossless
raster3 copy.bmp                     36183      120000     Lossless
web1 copy.bmp                        24371      120000     Lossless
raster1 copy.bmp                     52979      120000     Lossless
Stream sound: 22KHz Mono 5 bit ADPCM
Event sounds: 11KHz Stereo 5 bit ADPCM
Sound Name                          Bytes       Format
--------------------------          -------     --------
sustain.wav                         110505      11KHz Stereo 5 bit ADPCM
```

CD-ROM NOTE: *To see the effect that reducing the bitmap qualities had on the resulting SWF files, open the file ch12_06.fla, located in the fgai/chapter12/ folder, installed from the companion CD-ROM. Generate a report. Compare this report to the report generated from the file ch12_05.fla. Although not all spikes in the data have been addressed, the main problem at frame 126 has been significantly reduced.*

Bandwidth Profiling

The Bandwidth Profiler is the second tool that is quite valuable when you are preparing, testing, and optimizing your movies. A component of the Test Movie command, the Bandwidth Profiler shows a graphic of the amount of data required for the movie over time, as shown in figure 12-12. To turn on the Bandwidth Profiler, select Control | Test Movie to start

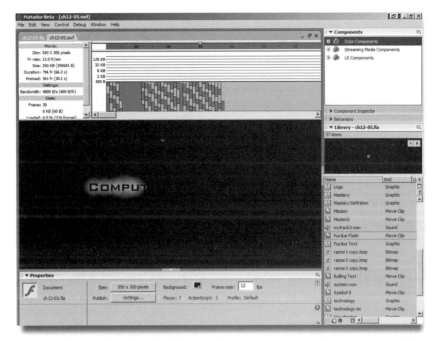

Figure 12-12. The Bandwidth Profiler shows a chart representing the amount of data within each frame.

the movie in test mode. Then select View | Bandwidth Profiler to view the profiler.

The most powerful feature of the Bandwidth Profiler is the View | Simulate Download option. This option provides a means of getting a more accurate simulation of performance over the Web, because it takes into account the downloading of the file.

To use the View | Simulate Download option, select a data rate in the View | Download Settings submenu. Select Control | Rewind and then View | Simulate Download (or Ctrl + Enter) instead of Play. The file will begin to play automatically once enough of the file has been downloaded, which is represented by the green bar.

The Simulate Download option, when selected, reveals a green bar at the top of the timeline in the Bandwidth Profiler. The bar represents how much data has been downloaded over time, using the connection setting in the Download Settings submenu. Once enough of the file has been downloaded to start playback, the playhead begins to play the file while the green bar continues to move. If the playhead reaches the end of the green bar, you know for sure that there will be problems (a pause in the presentation) when the user views it over the Web. This is probably the most effective means of testing, aside from uploading the files to a live server for testing.

Let's examine this a little more closely. With the Bandwidth Profiler open, each bar in the graphic represents the amount of data for that frame, as shown in figure 12-13. The red line through the middle of the graph represents the current target data rate for the end user. Bars that extend above the red median indicate frames that will require greater download times.

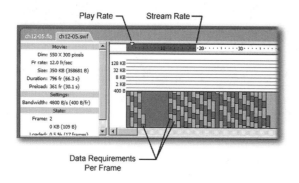

Figure 12-13. Column bars show the amount of data required for the frame; any extending above the target bandwidth may cause delays.

Also shown in figure 12-13 is the comparison of the play rate (represented by the playhead) to the stream rate (represented by a green bar). The stream rate is based on the current connection rate. In general, you do not want the playhead to overtake the stream rate during playback. The number of frames that extend beyond the target bandwidth (the number of frames whose data requirements are greater than the target bandwidth) determines if and when the play rate will overtake the stream rate.

If the playhead "runs into" the stream rate, the movie will pause. This is particularly problematic when streaming sound is involved. In these instances, provide extra time for the data to download by using preloading sequences, called preloaders.

When using the Bandwidth Profiler, you may at any point in the playback of the movie click any bar in the profiler and access the frame. This allows you to determine which sections are the most data intensive. You can then return to the Flash movie and attempt to optimize the frame.

The View menu allows you to view by either a frame-by-frame graph or a streaming graph (the default). The streaming graph shows which frames may cause the movie to pause due to delayed download. The frame-by-frame graph visually illustrates the amount of data in each frame.

The Bandwidth Profiler allows you to specify several data rates, against which you can compare the content of the movie. Use the View | Download Settings submenu to access various default modem settings (data rate settings). Select the View | Download Settings | Customize option to open the Custom Download Settings dialog box, shown in figure 12-14a. Alternatively, you can add your own settings, as shown in figure 12-14b.

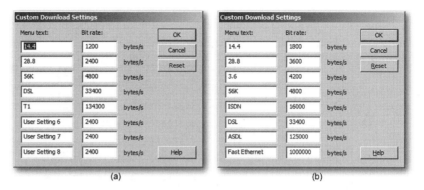

Figure 12-14. Use the Bandwidth Profiler to (a) access the default download settings (data rate settings) or (b) create your own custom settings using the View | Download Settings | Customize menu option.

Again, to create movies that play seamlessly, the primary goal is to make sure the playhead of the movie never intercepts the streaming of data (that is, the normal flow of data from the server over the network connection). If the playhead overtakes the flow of data, the presentation will pause. Because there is no straight pipe from one computer to another on the Net, there will always be the possibility that the presentation may be interrupted. Yet, the Bandwidth Profiler and the streaming options are among the best tools for minimizing the likelihood of this happening.

Optimizing Your Files

A significant portion of this chapter has been devoted to finding problems in your presentation. Features such as the Bandwidth Profiler and Streaming Graph options are used to locate areas where optimization may be necessary. Nevertheless, you can do other things to optimize your files and reduce the data needed to play back your presentation.

In general, the weightiest items in your files will be bitmap images and sound files. Note that as you are constructing the vector elements in your file there are several additional things you can do to help reduce the overall file size. Although optimization of bitmaps and sound files will show the most dramatic effects on file size, optimizing even the vector elements is prudent. When dealing with web delivery, every little "bit" counts.

It is really never too early to start using the Test Movie, Bandwidth Profiler, and Streaming Graph features. Often, most problem areas in a movie can be addressed much easier if they are caught early in the development. It is much more difficult to come back and try to optimize than it is to optimize during the process. Concurrent testing should be an integral part of development.

TIP: *One overriding tip that always applies is to test early and test often.*

The sections that follow provide guidelines for maximizing the outcome of optimization. These sections include general tips and tips for bitmaps, audio snippets, vector elements, and video.

General Tips

The following are tips for maximizing the effect of optimization overall.

- Use shared libraries as much as possible.

- Shared libraries can provide a significant file size savings because they allow you to share symbols across multiple files, including sound, bitmap, and font symbols.

- Do not use or import too many fonts.

  If you add a significant number of fonts to your files, you will find that your files grow quickly.

Tips for Bitmaps

The following are tips for maximizing the effect of optimization regarding bitmaps.

- First and foremost, use bitmap images sparingly.

  The more bitmaps you add to a Flash file, even with JPEG compression, the larger the file size. Use bitmaps only if they are necessary and cannot be easily achieved using vector components.

- Import bitmap images at sizes that are as small as possible.

  Size your bitmaps to the exact size needed before importing them into Flash, just as you would if you were creating bitmaps for the Web. Do not import more data than you need.

- Reduce image quality as much as possible.

  Unless complete resolution needs to be maintained, use JPEG compression in Flash. Because the JPEG compression algorithm discards a certain amount of data to attain smaller file sizes, JPEG compression should be used unless an exact representation of imported bitmap is needed in the presentation. Try various settings for the JPEG Quality to get the optimum size-to-quality ratio. Lossless should be used only if you must retain the exact visual quality and resolution of an image.

- Avoid animating bitmaps at all costs.

  Like most multimedia authoring programs, bitmap images do not scale or rotate very well because of the real-time interpolation and extrapolation that must occur. Additionally, these operations require CPU time to render to the screen. Each time you rotate or scale a bitmap in Flash, you can expect some type of slowing in the playback, because the bitmap must be redrawn through each step.

- Reduce computation (playback) time by turning off the Smoothing option for an image.

  In the Bitmap Properties in the library, you can speed up the rendering of bitmaps to the screen by deselecting the Smoothing checkbox. Although this should not affect file size, it will increase playback speed, depending on the size of the bitmap image.

- Watch the size report for spikes that may be a result of bitmap images.

  As demonstrated with the example earlier in this chapter, one of the spikes in the size report was due to a series of bitmap images that flashed on the screen. After viewing the size report, quality was sacrificed for the sake of delivery. If you have a movie that has bitmaps in it, use the Size Report feature.

Tips for Audio Snippets

The following are tips for maximizing the effect of optimization regarding audio snippets.

- Use the lowest sampling rate and bit depth required.

  As mentioned in Chapter 8, the sampling rate, bit depth, and number of channels (mono versus stereo) can significantly impact the size of an audio clip, which is transferred to the Flash file. As with raster images, test various quality settings to find the optimal ratio of quality to file size.

- Brevity is the key to efficient and effective sounds.

  Even though Flash offers ADPCM and MP3 compression, the longer the clip, the poorer the quality and the larger the compressed file. Try to loop sounds as much as possible. Looping is often a feasible alternative to a large, long-playing sound clip.

- Use the Size Report feature to locate spikes caused by sounds.

  Event sounds do not play until they are loaded in their entirety. Thus, the size report of a movie often shows spikes before the playing of an event sound. Be cautious of bottlenecking caused by several event sounds (look at frame numbers near the location of keyframes that contain event sounds). In some instances, consider using preload techniques, such as those discussed in the next chapter, to ensure that event sounds are loaded well before they are needed.

Tips for Vector Elements

The following are tips for maximizing the effect of optimization regarding vector elements.

- Use symbols exclusively.

  Anytime you have a set of repeating elements, even if they are only repeated once, they should be converted to a symbol. Grouped items, even though they act as a single unit, do not share the symbol's reusable nature. Copied groups add size to a file no matter how simple. Symbols should be used as frequently as possible.

- Use preload techniques to ensure symbol data is present when needed.

  Flash can only render a frame if all of the frame components are downloaded. Similar to problems with bitmaps or audio, even some complex symbols (or having many symbols in a single frame) may cause the movie to pause while the symbol is downloaded.

- Use Flash's Modify | Shape | Optimize command.

  Imported elements from Adobe Illustrator and other packages can often bring with them much extraneous information that is not really needed. This is indicative of many of the processes described in Chapter 10. Make sure to at least attempt to use the Optimize feature of Flash. Additionally, imported images can often be simplified by reducing the number of lines. Fills imported from other programs also frequently cause problems regarding file size. Inspect all of these options as you are working. Again, it is much easier to optimize an image the moment you import it, rather than waiting until it is animated and the movie is half completed.

- Avoid using too many complex tweening operations at a time.

  Although tweening does not necessarily affect file size, it does affect playback. The more complex tweens you have, particularly motion and color effects, the greater chance you will have of significantly slowing playback. Additionally, moving or changing large areas of the screen can also be problematic. Be aware of how many effects you are accruing.

- Avoid breaking apart text or using too many curve modifications.

  Breaking text apart converts outline text into individual line and arc components. The Lines to Fills, Expand Shape, and Soften Edge commands (found in the Modify | Shape submenu) all increase the number of vector elements in your movies. If at all possible, leave text as editable outlines. Be mindful also of the number of curve effects you use. Line and arc components and curve effects can dramatically affect file size.

Tips for Video

The following are tips for working with video.

- Know your audience's bandwidth.

  Video is the largest consumer of bandwidth, much more so than bitmaps and audio. You should pay special attention to the attributes of your video clips and make sure it makes sense to deliver video to your audience. Choose an appropriate frame size and frame rate, based on the bandwidth available to your audience and the content you are trying to deliver. See Chapter 11 for specifics.

- Work with a clean source.

  It is imperative that when working with video (or audio) you start with a clean source that has not already been lossy compressed. If you work with a second-rate capture, or content that has already been lossy compressed, you will end up with less than acceptable video in Flash.

- Keep video clips simple.

  Every frame in a video clip costs you something as far as file size is concerned. Do not waste data on complex transitions or lengthy blank pauses. Also keep in mind that the codec used in Flash is an interframe, meaning that while it will compress high-motion video it excels with clips that do not incorporate a lot of motion.

Summary

This chapter examined the major issues concerning testing, integration, and distribution of your movies. Designing Flash movies is one thing; compiling and preparing them for delivery is another. To be a successful Flash developer you must know how to do both. As you have read, the new Publish utility goes a long way toward getting Flash movies on the Web. Indeed, it is an ingenious tool that can do most of the basic coding. Yet, knowing the code is also vitally important.

13

Introduction to ActionScripting

∎∎∎ Introduction

Flash provides the ability to react to events and create interactivity through its internal scripting language, ActionScript. Already you have seen that the button symbol can be used to generate a functioning button. Yet, thus far all you have read about is making the button work like a button visually. You have yet to connect the scripting necessary to have the button do something constructive.

The most significant thing about Flash MX 2004 is the expansion of its internal scripting capabilities to support the development of not only interactive multimedia content but full-fledged applications. There are two approaches that can be taken when programming in Flash. The way you program ActionScript in Flash depends on whether you are developing basic multimedia content for delivery over the Web (for which you can use the traditional hybrid approach) or Flash-based applications, for which you should use a true object-oriented programming (OOP) approach.

There is no way to present everything about ActionScript in one chapter, let alone in a book designed as an introduction to general Flash development. This chapter provides an introduction to the ActionScript language and constructs, and Chapter 14 provides an overview of actions and putting them to work.

The approach to ActionScript in this book is focused on the development of multimedia content. It is not meant to be an all-inclusive review of ActionScript, nor to focus on the OOP approach to application development in Flash. The intent is to examine how you use basic ActionScript for multimedia development to accomplish those things most people want to develop.

▪ ▪ ▪ Objectives

In this chapter you will:

- Get a holistic view of the ActionScript language and the terminology you need to get up and running

- Learn the generalities of setting up ActionScript code and where you place it in movies

- Find out about the Actions panel and how to use it to add code

- Discover the precedence issues that exist in Flash

- Find out about the basic ActionScript syntax issues, as well as foundational programming constructs such as target structures

- Learn programming fundamentals in ActionScript, including variables, operators, commands, and functions

▪ ▪ ▪ ActionScript: A Holistic View

Much of the scripting in Flash 5 revolved around a hybrid procedural-/event-driven approach, which was appropriate for the development and delivery of multimedia content. However, if you want to create something more than just multimedia content, say a web application in Flash 5, the hybrid approach quickly becomes self-defeating and inefficient.

Flash MX 2004 continues to support the hybrid approach that most developers used in Flash 5, but it also now fully supports class-based, object-oriented programming (OOP) to make the development of Flash applications easier and more efficient. The OOP approach is consequently much more involved and will not be covered in this book. However, to understand the underpinnings of ActionScript functionality (even though this text does not take a true OOP approach to coding Flash movies), it is beneficial to take a holistic look at what OOP is.

Terminology

The following are ActionScript terms, as used in this book, with which you need to be familiar.

- Classes define the methods, properties, and event handlers of the objects that can exist in the environment. They are essentially templates or blueprints for objects. For example, a Vehicle class could contain all code necessary to describe the characteristics (type, color, size, and so on) of a vehicle, as well as how it behaves (moves, starts, stops, and so on).

- Objects are specific instances of a class in the environment. For example, Car, Truck, and Boat are all objects of the type Vehicle.

- Methods are the predefined things an object can do (action verbs for the object). Methods are basically functions specific to a particular object. For example, the method *move()* could be defined for a Car object or for a Boat object. However, individual methods would implement movement in a different way for a particular object. In the case of a Car object, the implementation of the *move()* method would probably turn the wheels of that particular car, whereas in the case of a Boat object it would probably use the propeller and rudder to steer the boat.

- Functions are sets of reusable code that typically receive a value, do something to that value, and either return the result or call another function.

NOTE: *Often the terms method and function are used interchangeably in the Macromedia documentation.*

- Statements are what can be considered "utility" code words that do something in the environment.

- Properties are the characteristics or attributes of an object (adjectives that describe the object). For example, in the case of the Car object color would be a property of the car.

- Event handlers are the events to which an object can respond.

- Arguments are optional bits of information you send to methods and functions. Usually, a method or a function will use the data sent to it in some way, and may return a value.

- A variable is a container for data and is defined by a scope (length of existence) and a data type, such as a string (text) or numeral. Global variables are variables that are active and accessible during the entire movie and are defined using the *_global* keyword. Local variables are temporary variables used within the context of user-defined functions, and they are defined using the *var* keyword. All other variables (any that are defined without the *var* or *_global* keyword) are called timeline variables and exist as long as the timeline they belong to is loaded into the player.

NOTE: *Flash MX 2004 offers the option of strict typing. If you are coming from C, C++, or Java, you know what this means. You can now declare variables to be of a specific data type, much like you can in other strongly-typed/strict-typed language. This forces a variable to store only a particular type of data, in turn preventing compiler errors.*

- Operators are programming elements that perform calculations (operations), comparisons, or assignments.

- An expression is a combination of code statements that may include variables, functions, methods, properties, and operators. Usually, expressions must be evaluated.

- An array is a special type of variable that can store a collection of objects.

What Does Object-oriented Mean?

Object-oriented programming (OOP) environments provide a logical way of creating computer software and developing multimedia materials. OOP languages were designed to more accurately model the real world than prior languages, as well as to allow faster development, greater quality, and enhanced modifiability of computer programs.

As the name implies, OOP provides certain objects that you, the developer, can interact with, control, and manipulate. Additionally, you as programmer can create your own objects and define how they behave, and then create instances of those objects within your environment.

As opposed to other methods of programming, OOP environments offer extensive flexibility. However, the extent to which you can control and manipulate objects is dependent on the characteristics made accessible through the software (by the engineers that actually make the development application). In many instances, there may be objects, but their characteristics may or may not be accessible by developers. In Flash MX 2004, Macromedia has created and exposed many more things than is the case with version MX.

What Defines an Object?

One of the first questions that should come to mind is: What constitutes or defines an object in an OOP environment? What are the "characteristics" you can control, and how do you control them?

Simply put, most objects have three primary things in common: methods (prebuilt functions specific to them), properties, and event handlers, each of which is defined by something called a class. The class is the primary structure that defines everything about an object: the object's methods (things the object can do), the object's properties (the characteristics or attributes of the object), and the object's event handlers (things the object can react to). In reality, event handlers are nothing more than special methods, but in most visual environments such as Flash they are treated as distinct entities separate from methods.

As a basic example, in general terms, you could create a class named dog. Within that class, you could define methods for the dog, such as *bark()*; and *wagtail()*;. You could create characteristics for the dog, such as name, breed, height, and weight (properties). You could also define events to which the dog would respond, such as *on seeCat()*.

Once you define a class for dogs, you could then create an instance of your dog and make it do something by calling one of the methods you set up for the dog (e.g., *bark( )*; or *wagtail( )*;). Additionally, the dog could be made to do something as a response (e.g., *on seeCat()*), and you could have the properties of the dog (e.g., height and weight) change over time.

Although this example may seem rudimentary, it is important to conceptually understand that classes define objects by establishing methods, properties, and event handlers for the object. Various instances of objects, much like instances of symbols, are instantiated during the life of the program and can have various property values. Thus, you could use the dog class to define a multitude of difference instances of the dog, with various names, breeds, and so on. You could tell specific instances of the dog to bark or wag their tails. In addition, each might react at the same time, or individually, if they happened to see a cat!

You will find that understanding the syntax of ActionScript predominantly depends on an understanding of the difference between properties and methods. Generally, methods are distinguishable from properties in code by the parentheses that follow them.

Flash Objects

In Flash, several objects are already defined for you to use, and you have been using them already. Note that you do not necessarily see the classes that define these objects, nor do you have to work with them directly in code. Even though you have been using the GUI tools to draw, paint, and animate, the OOP code objects do exist in the environment and they do affect the way Flash works. These are called environmental, intrinsic, or built-in objects.

For example, the movie is an object. To prove this, what are some of the properties you have modified related to the movie already? Do frame rate, view quality, and background color ring a bell? A frame, a button, and a movie clip are also examples of objects. What are some of the properties of these objects with which you have worked?

Although OOP is not discussed at the beginning of this book, you can see how aspects of earlier chapters and exercises are related to it. Flash also provides special ActionScript programming objects, such as the date, math, and selection objects. They provide special objects for you to work with in ActionScript code. These are called programming or extrinsic objects.

Object Properties

Every object in an OOP environment has properties. Properties are simply characteristics of the object at a given instance in time. You can think of them as adjectives that describe an object. Many of the properties of objects are not absolute. Some properties change over time, as a result of something in the environment or as a result of the programmer forcibly changing it, whereas other properties may be fixed. Fixed properties are often called constants or literals. For now, simply remember that properties are the characteristics (adjectives) that describe or contain information about an object.

Object Methods

If properties are the adjectives that describe an object, methods are the action verbs for the object. As previously stated, methods are the definition of the things an object can do, and are functions (prebuilt code snippets) specific to an object. Generally, by simply calling a method, something happens.

One of the methods you will learn about is the "go to" method. It tells the main movie timeline to go to a specific frame or label in the movie. You call the method by simply writing code in a frame, button, or movie clip using the Actions panel.

When you execute or call a method, it normally requires some additional information. However, whether or not a method needs data obviously depends on what it is supposed to do. If there is needed data, it is called an argument or a parameter. In the "go to" example, when you call the method, it needs to know where you want it to go. That information, the frame or label reference, is known as an argument.

In code, methods are generally called by typing the method name, followed by parentheses. Arguments or parameters are usually passed inside the parentheses. For the "go to" example, the code might look as follows.

```
gotoAndPlay(1); //go to frame 1
    or
gotoAndPlay("mylabel") //go to a frame label
```

 NOTE: *The double slashes in the previous code denote comments. This convention is used throughout this book. Anything following the double slashes (comments) would be ignored by Flash (or by the browser, if you are writing JavaScript).*

Event Handlers

The final OOP construct to be examined is event handlers. They define the events in the environment that an object can respond to. Event handlers contain code segments, added by the developer, that "handle" the events (thus the name). Note that because an object can respond, this does not mean it will respond automatically. You have to add code for it to do so.

In any OOP environment, three things are required to get an object to do something: (1) the object must be able to respond to the event, (2) the object must have code defined for what it should do when the event occurs (handler), and (3) the object must exist in the environment at the point the event occurs. Most coding problems for people new to Flash or Director (as well as other OOP environments) involve not keeping these three "rules" in mind. Let's take a closer look at what happens when an event occurs.

Almost everything in the Flash environment is a result of an event. When the playhead moves from one frame to another, an event occurs. When the user presses a key or clicks the mouse, events occur. When a movie clip is loaded or unloaded, again an event occurs.

Objects know that events occur because notifications are sent out from the environment stating that something has happened. The notification is called an event message (or simply message), which is sent out into the environment and acted upon by an object that can and will handle the event. If an object that can receive the message (can respond to the event) and has code to handle the event (telling it what to do for the event), the object receives the message, does its thing, and terminates the message. If no objects exist (i.e., there is no receiver for the event), the message is terminated and nothing happens.

In most environments, there is a system of precedence for the manner in which messages can be received; that is, a hierarchy of sorts. For example, if two objects exist on the stage and both have programming to handle a particular event, only one can respond. Whichever object has precedence will intercept the message, do its thing, and terminate the message. In Flash, there are events for which precedence is important. We will return to this issue after you have examined a little more introductory information about Flash.

Built-in Objects: Environment Versus Programming

Flash incorporates two generic types of built-in objects. For the sake of a holistic view and understanding of ActionScript, the author identifies these groups as "environment objects" and "programming objects."

The primary environment object in Flash is the movie, but this group also includes movie clips and buttons. Given these objects, you should guess that there are methods and properties associated with them, and indeed there are. Methods such as *gotoAndPlay( );*, *getURL( );*, and

Table 13-1: Core ActionScript Quick Reference

Global Functions

Timeline Control
- gotoAndPlay()
- gotoAndStop()
- nextFrame()
- nextScene()
- play()
- prevFrame()
- prevScene()
- stop()
- stopAllSounds()

Browser/Network
- fscommand()
- getURL()
- loadMovie()
- loadMovieNum()
- loadVariables()
- loadVariablesNum()
- unloadMovie()
- unloadMovieNum()

Movie Clip Control
- duplicateMovieClip()
- getProperty()
- on()
- onClipEvent()
- removeMovieClip()
- setProperty()
- startDrag()
- stopDrag()
- targetPath()
- updateAfterEvent()

Printing
- print()
- printAsBitmap()
- printAsBitmapNum()
- printNum()

Miscellaneous
- clearinterval()
- escape()
- eval()
- getTimer()
- getVersion()
- trace()
- unescape()

Mathematical
- isFinite()
- isNaN()
- parseFloat()

Conversion
- Array()
- Boolean()
- Number()
- Object()
- String()

Properties

Global
- _focusrect
- _quality
- _soundbuftime

Object-Specific
- _alpha
- _currentframe*
- _droptarget*
- _framesloaded*
- _height
- _name
- _rotation
- _target*
- _totalframes*
- _url*
- _visible
- _width
- _x
- _xmouse*
- _xscale
- _y
- _ymouse*
- _yscale

Identifiers
- _global
- _level
- _parent
- _root
- super
- this

*Property cannot be set

Statements

Variables
- delete
- set variable
- var
- with()

Conditions/ Loops
- break
- continue
- do.. while
- if.. else if.... else
- for
- for... in
- switch... case.... default
- while

User Defined Functions
- function
- return

Constants
- -Infinity
- false
- Infinity
- newline
- null
- undefined

Operators

Global

""	String delimiter
()	Parenthesis
.	Dot access
{}	Curly braces
[]	Array access

Arithmetic

+	Addition
*	Multiplication
/	Division
%	Modulo
-	Subtraction

Assignment

-=	Subtraction and assignment
%=	Modulo and assignment
&=	Bitwise And and assignment
*=	Multiplication and assignment
|=	Bitwise Or and assignment
/=	Division and assignment
^=	Bitwise Xor and assignment
+=	Addition and assignment
<<=	Bitwise shift left and assignment
=	Assignment
>>=	Bitwise shift right and assignment
>>>=	Shift right zero fill and assignment

Bitwise

&	Bitwise And
~	Bitwse one's complement
		Bitwise Or
<	Bitwise Xor
<<	Shift left by a number of bits
>>	Shift right by a number of bits
>>>	Shifts right by a number of bits (unsigned)

Comparison

!=	Inequality
!==	Strict inequality
<	Less than
<=	Less than or equal
==	Equality
===	Strict equality
>	Greater than
>=	Greater than or equal

Logical

&&	Logical AND
||	Logical OR
!	NOT

Miscellaneous

--	Decrement
?:	Conditional/Ternary
++	Increment
instanceof	
typeof	
void	

String Escape Characters

\b	Backspace
\f	Form- Feed
\n	Line- Feed
\r	Carriage Return
\t	Tab
\"	Double Quotation
\'	Single Quotation
\\	Backslash
\000-\ 377	An Octal Byte
\x00-\xFF	A Hexadecimal Byte
\u0000- uFFFF	A 160-bit Unicode Char in hexadecimal

loadMovie( ); (to name a few, which Macromedia identifies as Actions in the Actions panel) deal with the main movie timeline, as do properties such as *_currentframe*, *_x*, and *_y*. The first column in table 13-1 lists methods designed to work with movie, movie clip, and button objects. Properties associated with these are listed in the second column.

As shown in table 13-1, ActionScript provides several other conventional core programming items, including functions, constants, command statements, and operators. These are discussed in greater detail later in this chapter.

In addition to the environment objects, Flash provides special "programming" objects that give extended functionality, in one way or another, as you use ActionScript coding. The objects are predominantly designed to facilitate working with data in one form or another (as well as the range of ActionScript functionality) by extending the developer's control within the environment. Unfortunately, the limits of this book do not permit discussion of these objects.

Where Scripts Are Placed

The Flash environment has three objects that can react to events: the frame, the button, and the movie clip. In other words, these are entities to which you can assign ActionScript. These objects can respond to two primary events: events related to the user (mouse or keyboard) and events associated with frames in the timeline.

Frame and Instance Code

ActionScript is assigned within Flash in two ways, depending on whether you want the code to execute when the movie reaches a certain frame (a frame action) or when the user does something to a button (an instance action). Additionally, movie clips, which are also instances, can respond to frame or user events.

You assign ActionScript to a frame by clicking on a frame and then entering code for the frame using the Actions panel. When code is assigned to a frame, it will execute when the frame is encountered by the playhead.

 NOTE: *When you designate code to a frame, a lowercase letter a will appear in the nearest left-hand keyframe. If adjacent frames are to have different code, each frame must be a keyframe.*

Alternatively, to assign code to a button or movie clip symbol, click on the symbol on the stage and enter the code in the Actions panel, shown in figure 13-1. Actions attached to instances of symbols on the stage are a

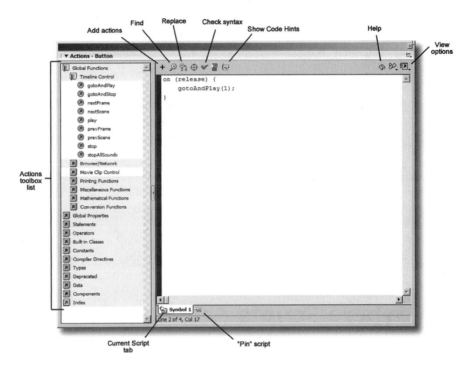

Figure 13-1. The Actions panel is used to assign ActionScript code to frames and instances.

property of the symbol instance, not the symbol itself. Thus, various instances of a symbol throughout a movie may have different actions.

 TIP: *As opposed to the lowercase letter a that appears in a frame when code is assigned to it, there is no visual indicator that tells you that a symbol instance has an action. To find out whether or not an instance has an action, click on it and view the Actions panel.*

Figure 13-1 shows the Actions panel, with code being assigned to a button. The Actions toolbox list on the left provides access to all available Actions in Flash. The actions options are organized according to use, as follows.

- *Global Functions:* Provides access to ActionScript methods that relate to the main movie, movie clips, and buttons. They are arranged in subgroups that include movie control, browser/network, movie clip control, and printing.

- *Global Properties:* Provides access to top-level properties.

- *Statements:* Provides access to command statements such as *if*, *switch*, and *case*.

- *Operators:* Provides access to the global, arithmetic, assignment, bitwise, comparison, and logical operators.

- *Built-in Classes:* Provides access to events, methods, and properties associated with built-in classes (such as array, color, and so on).

- *Constants:* Provides access to commonly used values that do not change.

- *Compiler Directives:* Provides access to special commands within ActionScript.

- *Types:* Provides access to specific data-type keywords.

- *Deprecated:* Provides access to ActionScript items that will likely be unavailable in the next version of Flash.

- *Data:* Provides access to the methods and properties associated with data input/output capabilities.

- *Components:* Provides access to special items related to Flash components.

- *Index:* Provides an alphabetical listing of all available ActionScript elements.

Adding an Action

You add ActionScript by selecting either a frame or a symbol instance and then accessing the Actions panel. In the Actions panel, you either double click on an item in the Actions toolbox list on the left (see figure 13-1) or click on an action in the Actions toolbox list and click on the small plus (Add Action) button. In exercise 13-1 you will attach code to a button instance using this basic technique.

 NOTE: *You will find that certain items in the Actions toolbox list are not applicable to frames or not applicable to objects. Actions that are not applicable to objects are grayed out in the Actions toolbox list.*

Exercise 13-1: Attaching an Action to a Button Instance

To see how a basic action is attached to a button instance, perform the following steps.

1. Open Flash and start a new file.

2. Create a button symbol on the stage.

3. Click on the button and access the Actions panel.

 TIP: *You can also quickly open the Actions panel using function key F9.*

4. In the Actions panel, double click on the Global Functions grouping in the Actions toolbox list.

5. Double click on the Movie Clip Control grouping.

6. Double click on the on item. This adds an *on( )* handler to the code window on the right.

7. Once the on handler is added to the Code window, in the Code window you must specify an event in the Code Hint drop-down list. Select Press from the list.

8. Create a blank line beneath the first line of code (*on (release)* {) in the Code window by the pressing Enter key.

9. In the Actions list, double click on the Timeline Control grouping (inside the Global Functions grouping).

10. Select *gotoAndPlay* from the list. This adds the function to the code listing.

11. You will note that Flash needs you to enter one more piece of data in the code listing: the number or label of the frame you wish to go to. Enter a 1 in the parentheses in the code list.

12. Save this file so that you can return to it later.

As you saw a couple of times in this exercise, once you double click on a code item in the Actions toolbox list, code is automatically added to the Script pane. Let's examine the following code, which you have added to the Script pane.

```
on (release) {
  gotoAndPlay(1);
}
```

As you read earlier, the coding or scripting that responds to an event is called an event handler (or handler, for short) because it has code defined within it that "handles" the event. The handler begins with the event name, such as on (release), as shown in the previous code. The things that are supposed to happen when the event occurs (that is, statements consisting of methods, commands, or expressions) are grouped and appear between the curly brackets. You will also find that the statements between the curly brackets are terminated with semicolons (which are not required unless you have several consecutive statements on a single line).

Using the Actions Panel

When you assign an item to a button (such as Play, Stop, or Go To), it is automatically inserted into the event handler on (*someevent*), where *someevent* is a word such as *release*, *press*, and so on. This is the event that initiates the handler. All actions assigned to a button must be inserted inside an *on ()* handler. Actions assigned to a movie clip must be inserted into an *onClipEvent* (*someevent*) handler, where *someevent* again is some word such as *load, enterFrame*, and so on.

When you insert an action into a frame, you will find that no event handler appears. This is because in a frame there is a single assumed event (the occurrence of the frame); that is, there are not multiple frame events, as in other applications. If you are used to programs such as *Director* (which has *prepareFrame, enterFrame, updateStage, exitFrame*, and other events), note that Flash only has one event as it relates to a frame: the occurrence of the frame. Response to multiple frame events may be something to look for in future versions of Flash.

One thing that may seem confusing at first (particularly for those familiar with Director or other languages that allow event handlers) is the fact that when you use the *on()* handler on a button the Actions panel simply says "*on (someevent)*" not "*on MouseEvent(release)*" (or "*on mouseUp*" or "*on mouseDown*," like Director). The generic title *on()* is a carryover from Flash 3, which could not respond to the keyboard. Just keep in mind that *on()* is for any user-generated event (mouse or keyboard). In exercise 13-2 you will add multiple actions to an instance.

Exercise 13-2: Adding Multiple Actions to an Instance

Once you have added a single action to a button, you can continue adding more code to the current handler. To see how this works, perform the following steps.

1. Open the file you were previously working with.

2. Click on the button you had created and open the Actions panel.

3. Click at the end of the *gotoAndPlay(1)*; code in the Script pane and press the Enter key to add a blank line beneath it.

4. Find the Stop All Sounds action in the Actions grouping in the Actions toolbox list and double click on it. It is located in the Global Functions | Timeline Control grouping.

Note that when you double clicked on the Stop All Sounds action that it was added to the Actions list, as shown in figure 13-2. Once you start adding actions, you can add as many as you want to a single handler.

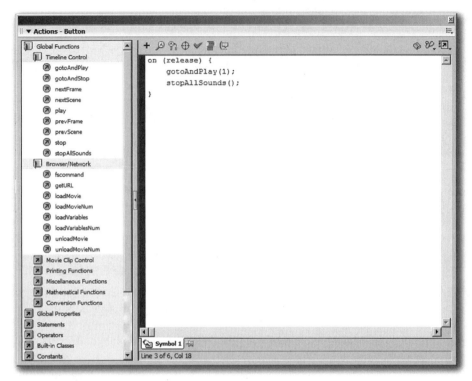

Figure 13-2. Multiple actions can be assigned within a single handler.

The order in which the actions occur is often important. What if you wanted all sounds to stop before going to another frame? You can easily change the order of actions in the list by continuing with the following steps.

5. Click on the *stopAllSounds* action.

6. Using Cut and Paste, cut the *stopAllSOunds()* function and paste it before the *gotoAndPlay()* function.

As you can see, the ordering of actions in the list is fluid and can be changed pretty easily. However, what if you want the button to stop the sounds on the down press and to go to another frame when you release? Currently, both actions are assigned to occur upon release of the button. Let's modify the previous example so that it would do this. Continue with the following steps.

7. By manually entering code into the Script pane of the Actions panel, above the current handler enter a new *on()* handler. Set its event to press.

8. Cut and paste the *stopAllSounds()* function to the new handler, as shown in figure 13-3. Now the Stop All Sounds will occur upon a press of the mouse, and the *gotoAndPlay(1)* upon release of the mouse.

Figure 13-3. Multiple handlers can be assigned to a single object.

Button Events

Before moving on, let's reflect on the button, frame, and movie clip subevents to which you can respond. Just as you can have multiple handlers assigned to an object, a single handler can be set up to handle multiple events. For example, you can specify that certain actions should respond to both a press and a release, as shown in figure 13-4. Thus, the actions contained within the handler will react on both press and release. In other words, the handler will execute twice. For this reason, be careful using compound events in a single handler.

As it relates to mouse events (that is, as it relates to the *on()* handler), actions can be set to take place when any one of the following scenarios occurs.

- *Press:* Causes the actions to execute when the mouse button is pressed down.

- *Release:* Performs the actions when the mouse button is released inside the object.

- *Release Outside:* Implements the actions when the mouse button is released outside the object. However, the user would have had to begin by clicking on the button.

- *Key Press:* Performs the actions when a particular key is pressed. To use the field, click the mouse in the field and press the key to which you want to respond. Note that not all keys or key combinations can be used. This option is generally limited to alphanumeric keys.

- *Roll Over:* Carries out the actions when the user rolls into or within the boundaries of the object.

- *Roll Out:* Executes the actions when the user rolls off the boundary of the object.

- *Drag Over:* Performs the actions only when the user drags across the object. This is generally used for an object such as a slider or scroll bar.

- *Drag Out:* Runs the actions only when the user drags outside the boundaries of the object.

Figure 13-4. Using multiple events in a single handler.

Frame Events

If you decide you want an action to execute based on a specific point in time within a movie, attach actions to frames. As mentioned previously, click in a frame and use the Actions panel to assign actions to frames. The only major difference between assigning actions to frames and objects is that the *on( )* event handler cannot be used in frames. In exercise 13-3 you will practice adding actions to frames.

Exercise 13-3: Adding Actions to Frames

When assigning actions to frames, the only event you can respond to is entry into the frame itself. Thus, the action needs only to be assigned to a keyframe. To have a movie stop at a specific frame, perform the following steps.

1. Click on a frame and access the Actions panel.

2. In the Actions toolbox list, double click on the Global Functions group and then on the Timeline Control group.

3. Double click on the stop action to add it to the Script pane.

   The results of this action cause the movie to stop at the frame in which the action exists. Note in figure 13-5 that the "enterFrame" handler is assumed, but is not shown; no *on( )* handler is present and no curly brackets are used.

Figure 13-5. When actions are assigned to frames, there is no on() *handler, nor are there curly brackets.*

Movie Clip Events

Movie clip events allow you to attach ActionScript code to movie clip instances, practice of which is provided in exercise 13-4.

Exercise 13-4: Attaching Actions to Movie Clip Instances

To attach an action to a movie clip instance, perform the following steps.

1. Start a new Flash movie and create a movie clip symbol.
2. Click on the movie clip instance on the stage and access the Actions panel.
3. In the Actions panel, select Global Functions | Movie Clip Control from the Toolbox list.
4. Insert the *onClipEvent* handler (select the *mouseDown* event in the Code Hint drop-down that appears).
5. Insert a *stopAllSounds* function inside the *onClipEvent* handler.

If you followed along in the previous exercise, the Actions panel should look as it does in figure 13-6. Note that the event handler name for a movie clip is *onClipEvent( )* and that there are several specific events the movie clip can respond to.

When you attach actions to movie clips, you can have the actions respond to the following events.

- *load:* Causes the actions to execute when the movie clip is loaded and appears on the stage.

- *enterFrame:* Causes the actions to execute after the keyframe is played; that is, the keyframe in which the movie clip resides.

- *unload:* Actions associated with this event are initiated in the first keyframe following the frame in which the movie clip was removed from the timeline.

- *mouseDown:* Initiates the actions when the left mouse button is pressed.

- *mouseUp:* Initiates the actions when the left mouse button is released.

- *mouseMove:* Initiates the actions whenever the mouse is moved.

- *keyDown:* Actions in movie clips linked to this event execute when a key is pressed.

- *keyUp:* Actions attached to movie clips linked to this event execute when a key is released.

- *data:* Initiates actions whenever data is received into a movie clip via *loadVariables()* or *loadMovie()*.

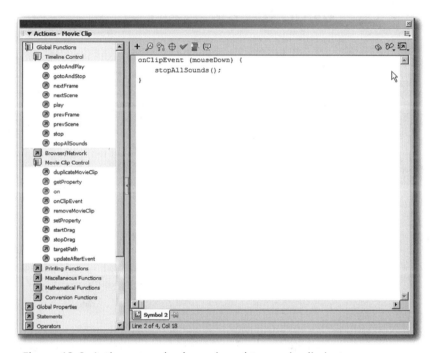

Figure 13-6. Actions can also be assigned to movie clip instances.

▪▪▪ **Behaviors**

In the previous section, you examined the rudiments of adding ActionScripting to your files. However, in Flash MX 2004, Macromedia has added some automation to basic scripting through something called behaviors. This is very similar to behaviors in Dreamweaver and Director. They are designed to make the environment easier to use for those who do not know how to write scripting.

Indeed, the positive thing about behaviors is that they minimize coding. The negative thing about behaviors is that by only learning how to use behaviors you miss out on learning to write your own code. Additionally, when all you know is how to use behaviors you can only "code" the things in Flash for which a behavior exists.

The rest of this book approaches ActionScript coding from the ground up, attempting to get you up and running with writing your own code (rather than depending on behaviors or someone else to write the code for you). However, the author at least wishes to acknowledge this capability so that you know how it works.

Using the Behaviors Panel

In previous exercises you saw how you could add code to buttons, frames, and movie clips. In a similar manner, you can use the Behaviors panel to add code to these entities. If you select a frame and then access the Behaviors panel (shown in figure 13-7), its menu can be used to automatically add the required code to a frame.

Once you select a behavior, you are presented with a dialog box asking you for more information. In the dialog box you define the object you want to apply the code to (by specifying a target, discussed later in the chapter) as well as any other information required by the particular behavior. The behavior added in figure 13-7 was a Go To Frame behavior. Thus, the dialog box in figure 13-8 also asks for a frame label or number. These "extra pieces of information" are actually the arguments for the ActionScript functions that underlie the behavior (behaviors are built upon ActionScript functionality). Recall that when you manually entered the code for a *gotoAndPlay* in an earlier exercise you had to enter the "place to go" (you entered *1*). This is called an argument.

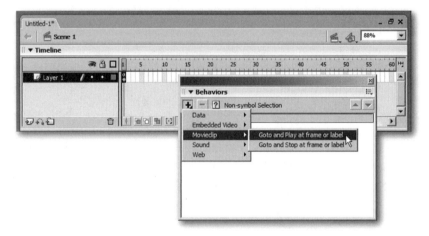

Figure 13-7. The new Behaviors panel allows you to easily add certain code snippets

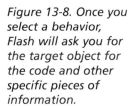

Figure 13-8. Once you select a behavior, Flash will ask you for the target object for the code and other specific pieces of information.

▪ ▪ ▪ **Actions Panel: A Closer Look**

Now that you understand the basics of attaching code to objects and frames, examine the Actions panel a bit more. The Actions panel provides several additional things you can do related to your ActionScript coding.

Code Hints

One of the features of Flash MX 2004 that makes working with ActionScript code easier is code hints. You have seen this feature in previous exercises. As you type code in the Script pane, code hints help you by trying to make suggestions concerning the code you enter. When the small Code Hints drop-down list pops up, all you need do is select from the list rather than type in an entry. This is a good way to make sure you enter the correct capitalization and spelling for ActionScript code words.

Compatibility and Deprecation Highlighting

As you begin working more with the Actions panel, you will note the colorization of certain items in the Actions toolbox list. The Actions panel does two very important things as it relates to this type of colorization. First, the actions shown in the Actions toolbox list may be displayed as green or yellow at different times. Generally, highlighting that occurs in the Actions toolbox list concerns compatibility issues or deprecation. Which color is shown depends on settings in the Version drop-down list in the File | Publish Settings | Flash tab, as follows.

- If you have the Version drop-down list set on Flash 7 (2004), certain actions will be highlighted in green, indicating that the actions are deprecated. Again, deprecated actions will likely be gone in the next version of Flash.

- If you have the Version drop-down list set on Flash 6 (MX) or earlier, certain actions will be highlighted in yellow, indicating that the actions are not able to be used in that version of a Flash file.

Syntax Highlighting

You will also note as you work that the Script pane of the Actions panel shows colorized code to help you identify the various syntactical items you enter. This colorization is also helpful in quickly finding syntax errors. The colors used are as follows.

- *Dark blue:* Commands, keywords, properties, and methods

- *Gray:* Comments

- *Light blue:* Strings denoted by double quotation marks

 TIP: *Although it is not recommended, you can turn off syntax highlighting using the Actions panel's menu.*

Particularly as you begin learning about ActionScripting, as well as programming in general, pay close attention to the colorization. Indeed, half the battle of programming is searching for errors or bugs in your scripts. Syntax highlighting can help in this regard.

 TIP: *Remember that you can set the colors used for coding colorization using Edit | Preferences | ActionScript tab.*

External Authoring of Scripts

A final note concerning working in the Actions panel is that you do not have to use the Actions panel to write your scripts. You can author script files outside Flash and import them using the Import from File option in the Actions panel's menu. Generally, script files are basic text files that follow the normal ActionScript syntax conventions. They are identified with an *.as* extension. This is particularly useful for programmers who are used to a particular editor. The only drawback to this is that you do not see syntax checking. However, for advanced work, this is a convenient feature.

Flash provides an advanced action called *#include* that can be used to include external script files at the time of SWF file generation. If you use the *#include* action, you identify the AS (*.as*) file containing ActionScripting you want compiled with the Flash SWF file. At the time of

SWF file generation (when you use Export Movie or Publish), the AS file specified in the action must be available.

The advantage that such an action would provide is the ability for multiple programmers to work concurrently on complex scripting, or for programmers to set up default script files for specific functionalities. This is much like using *#include* in languages such as C or C + +, as well as the same ability in JavaScript, wherein an externally linked file contains all JavaScript code for a set of pages.

Precedence in the Flash Environment

Earlier in this chapter you read that in most OOP environments messages are terminated once an object intercepts them. Usually if two objects exist in the environment at the same time, and both are able to react to the same event, only one of those objects will be able to react. Which object reacts depends on a hierarchical precedence, or order, of messaging within the environment.

Because many people are familiar with Director, it serves as an example. In Director, there are two types of scripts that can be attached to objects on the stage: cast and sprite. Cast scripts are attached to the objects themselves (in Director's "library," called a cast), whereas sprite scripts are attached to the instances of objects on the stage.

 NOTE: *In Flash there is no equivalent of a cast script. That is, you cannot attach actions directly to symbols in the library. You can, however, place actions inside a symbol, which is very close to this functionality. Sprite scripts in Director are akin to attaching actions to a movie clip or button instance on the stage.*

In Director, both of these scripts can react to mouse events. One such event is *mouseUp*. If both a cast script and sprite script are attached to an object and have a *mouseUp* handler, only one of them will receive the event and do something. The second handler will not execute because the first automatically terminates the event message.

In Director, as it relates to mouse events, the sprite script has precedence and will be the script that executes and terminates the message. Unless you specifically tell the sprite script to pass the event onto the cast script, it will terminate the message and the second script will not execute. In essence, the second handler does not know anything has happened, because the first handler has terminated the message.

Flash, however, is a little bit different. First, event messages are not terminated. If a situation exists in which multiple event handlers can react to an event message, they will both execute, in a defined order. For example, a movie clip's actions react to *enterFrame*, as do actions attached to a frame. Similarly, a movie clip can react to *mouseUp* and *mouseDown*, which coincide with a button symbol's press and release events. In both of these examples, if actions are attached to both items, both sets of actions will execute, with one set occurring before the other.

Thus, when setting up actions, you must keep in mind (1) that event overlap exists, (2) that both sets of actions will execute, and (3) which object's actions will occur first. In the following sections you will read about the cases of overlap that exist between the events handled by the various objects. These sections conclude with a quick summary you can return to later in this book as you are performing more complex exercises.

 TIP: *Anytime you are adding actions and you find something awry when you test the movie, consider the issues presented in the following sections.*

Movie Clip and Button Mouse Clicks

The first overlap exists between the *mouseDown* and *mouseUp* events in a movie clip and the press and release events of a button. Although named differently, in application these events are basically the same thing. Therefore, there is potentially a conflict between the two when you start attaching actions. At the least, you must be conscious of which occurs first when developing your movies.

In the following examples, you will examine some scenarios that display the precedence between a movie clip and button. Note that the examples use the simple *trace()* action to bring up information in the Output window. This window reveals which object is reacting and in what order. Posting information to the Output window with the *trace()* action is a nice way of peering "behind the scenes" of a movie, but it is only effective for simple things. In exercise 13-5 you can practice previewing information in the Output window.

 ### *Exercise 13-5: Precedence Regarding Movie Clips Versus Button Mouse Events*

 CD-ROM NOTE: *Open the file* ch13_05.fla, *located in the* fgai/chapter13/ *folder, installed from the companion CD-ROM.*

Before you start working with the file in the player, let's examine what actions are assigned to the objects.

1. Click on the button and access the Actions panel.

   Note that there are two handlers assigned to the button, one for release and the other for press. Basically, the *trace()* actions in the handlers are set up to provide information to the Output window when you test the movie. The information will be revealed when the button is pressed and released.

2. With the Actions panel still open, click on the movie clip to reveal its actions. Similar to the button, the movie clip has two handlers with *trace()* actions. The handlers are set on *mouseUp* and *mouseDown*.

 NOTE: *The order of the handlers (press and release for the button;* mouseUp *and* mouseDown *for the movie clip) in the Actions panel is not important because each handler is set to a different event.*

3. Select Control | Test Movie to open an SWF file into the player for testing.

4. Begin by clicking down and holding with the mouse on the button. When you do this, the Output window will open, revealing the text from the *trace()* action.

   Note that the movie clip's *mouseDown* was executed before the button's press. Thus, the movie clip has precedence over the button. However, note that they both execute; the event message (*mouseDown*) is not terminated by the movie clip. This is a significant difference from other applications, particularly if you are used to the way Director works.

5. Release the mouse button and note that again the movie clip has precedence over the button, in that the *mouseUp* from the movie clip is acknowledged before the release of the button.

6. With the movie still running, click anywhere in the movie, except on the button.

Note in the previous exercise that the Output window shows that the *mouseDown* and *mouseUp* events attached to the movie clip execute regardless of where you place the mouse. Thus, *mouseDown* and *mouseUp* events attached to movie clips react to any mouse clicks in the environment. The mouse click does not have to be on the movie clip. In regard to buttons, however, for the actions associated with press and release events to execute the mouse does have to be over the button.

 TIP: *You can clear the text in the Output window by selecting Clear from the Output window's Options menu.*

Regarding the precedence of movie clips over buttons, the physical arrangement of the button and movie clip on the stage has no effect over the precedence. You might think that if the button were in front of the movie clip it might affect the precedence, but it does not. For example, if a button overlaps a movie clip on the stage, the movie clip will still have precedence over the button, even if you click directly on the button. Exercise 13-6 provides an example of this precedence.

Exercise 13-6: Precedence Regarding Overlapping Movie Clips and Buttons

 CD-ROM NOTE: *Open the file* ch13_06.fla, *located in the* fgai/chapter13/ *folder, installed from the companion CD-ROM.*

File *ch13_06.fla* demonstrates that even if a button and movie clip overlap on the stage, the movie clip has precedence. Select Control | Test Movie to see the results.

Two additional examples are important to note. First, if a button is nested within a movie clip symbol, the movie clip will have precedence over the button. This is pretty logical, and given the previous examples, you would probably expect this. But what happens when a movie clip is nested within a button? The result may surprise you. If a movie clip is nested within a button, the movie clip will not be able to "hear" the mouse events at all. Placing a movie clip in a button will in essence disable the movie clip's ability to react to the *mouseUp* and *mouseDown* events. Exercise 13-7 demonstrates this principle.

Exercise 13-7: Precedence Regarding Buttons and Movie Clips

 CD-ROM NOTE: *Open the files* ch13_07a.fla *and* ch13_07b.fla, *located in the* fgai/chapter13/ *folder, installed from the companion CD-ROM.*

File *ch13_07a.fla* shows that when a button is in a movie clip the movie clip has precedence. *ch13_07b.fla* shows that when a movie clip is in a button the movie clip cannot respond. Select Control | Test Movie to see the results.

Another aspect of precedence between buttons and movie clips is when you create a drag-and-drop scenario; that is, a situation in which you can drag an element that exists on the stage (usually a movie clip). Movie clips can be set to react anytime the mouse moves, whereas a button can react to a drag off or drag over. As you saw in previous examples, the movie clip has precedence in almost every case.

With issues concerning dragging, you will again find that the movie clip has precedence. Thus, if a button is set to react to a *dragOver* or *dragOut* while a movie clip is set to a *mouseMove*, the movie clip actions will override or take precedence over the button's actions. Both will execute, but the movie clip actions will occur first.

Movie Clip and Button Key Events

Movie clips and buttons can both respond to user interaction with the keyboard. The movie clip can respond to either a *keyDown* or *keyUp* event, whereas the mouse can only respond to a specific *keyPress*. When you start building items that should respond to key presses, the potential exists for uncertainty as to which (movie clip or button) will have precedence. Exercise 13-8 provides practice in determining what has precedence.

Exercise 13-8: Precedence Regarding Movie Clips Versus Button Key Events

 CD-ROM NOTE: *Open the file* ch13_08.fla, *located in the* fgai/chapter13/ *folder, installed from the companion CD-ROM.*

Let's take a look at what takes precedence when a movie clip and button both have key event handlers set up.

1. Once you have opened *ch13_08.fla* into Flash, select the button and view the Actions panel. Note that the button has two handlers, one for a simple press and one for *keyPress*. The *keyPress* event is set up to know when the user presses the P button.

2. Click on the movie clip on the stage. Note the handlers associated with it, which are set up to respond when a key is pressed and released (*keyUp* and *keyDown*).

 NOTE: *The* trace() *action is being used with the Key object to return the key that is pressed (i.e., to return the key's name).*

3. Select Control | Test Movie to open an SWF file into the player.

4. Begin by pressing (once) any key, except P, on the keyboard. Note that the handlers associated with the movie clip return (in the Output window) the key pressed.

5. Press the P key once. Note that the *keyDown* event associated with the movie clip has precedence over the *keyPress* event associated with the button.

6. Press and hold any key, except P. Note in the Output window that the handler associated with the movie clip's *keyDown* event repeats continually while you hold the key.

As you have seen, precedence is important because both buttons and movie clips can respond to the keyboard. Therefore, you would use the movie clip event to intercept or modify the entry of data from the keyboard. For example, when the user entered some data, you could intercept it with the *keyDown* handler attached to a movie clip. You could also globally respond to any key on the keyboard using *keyUp*. With a button's *keyPress* event, however, you would use *keyPress* to set up quick-keys for the buttons in your movie.

Movie Clip and Frame Events

As with other objects that share events, precedence also exists when dealing with the movement of the playhead. Frames in the timeline and movie clips can both be set up to respond to the occurrence of a frame. As previously discussed, when you place actions in a frame you do not see an *enterFrame* event. It is assumed. The movie clip, however, does have an *enterFrame* handler. Exercise 13-9 examines the relationship between frame events and movie clip *enterFrame* events.

Exercise 13-9: Precedence Regarding Movie Clips Versus Frame Events

 CD-ROM NOTE: *Open the file* ch13_09.fla, *located in the* fgai/chapter13/ *folder, installed from the companion CD-ROM.*

Once you have *ch13_09.fla* open, click on the movie clip symbol and use the Actions panel to examine the actions associated with it. Note that the movie clip symbol has a handler set to *enterFrame*.

1. Click on frame 1 of the *Instructions* layer and examine the actions there. Note that the code in this frame is also set up to place information in the Output window on the *enterFrame* (keep in mind that actions in frames are by default set to execute on occurrence of a frame).

2. Select Control | Test Movie to play the movie. Let it play for about a second or two and then press the Escape key to stop it.

3. Examine the data in the Output window using the scroll bars. If you scroll up you will see that the action from the frame occurred before the action from the movie clip. You will also note that the movie clip occurred on every *enterFrame*, whereas the frame action executed only once.

Although it is not common to have a single-frame movie clip (where a movie clip is on screen for only one frame), this and the next step point out something important about the single-frame movie clip.

4. Click in frame 1 of the *Instructions* layer and insert a frame so that it is two frames long.

5. Test the movie. Note that the frame event can be made to continually repeat by looping.

The important thing to note about movie clip *enterFrame* events is that they are global when attached to a movie clip. Anytime a movie clip with this event exists, the actions will execute for every frame the movie clip has on the stage. Frame actions, however, will only execute in the keyframe to which they are assigned. Thus, to repeat them you have to loop, or use the *Go To* action to return to the keyframe that has the action.

Multiple Movie Clips

An interesting case of precedence exists if you have multiple movie clips in a single section of a movie. As you have seen, movie clip events are somewhat global in nature. Movie clips set to mouse events or key events execute their actions on every such event in the environment. The mouse does not necessarily have to be on the movie clip for the clip to respond to all key presses. Similarly, movie clips set to *enterFrame* events execute their actions on the entry of every frame. Therefore, the question arises, what happens when several movie clips are all set to the same event? What determines the precedence? Let's take a look. See exercise 13-10.

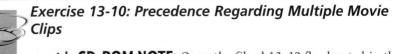

Exercise 13-10: Precedence Regarding Multiple Movie Clips

CD-ROM NOTE: *Open the file* ch13_10.fla, *located in the* fgai/chapter13/ *folder, installed from the companion CD-ROM.*

To see how precedence works in regard to multiple movie clips, perform the following steps.

1. With the CD-ROM file open, begin by examining the actions attached to the three movie clips. Note that each is assigned the *keyDown* event and uses the *trace()* action to indicate which one it is. A with command is used to control the movie clip. It tells the movie clip to go to the next frame (you will learn about this later in this chapter). For now, simply note that each action uses the *keyDown* event.

2. Select Control | Test Movie to start playing the movie. In the Output window, note the order of the objects in regard to their response. MC1 is the upper left, MC2 is the upper right, and MC3 is the lower item. If they are all set to respond to the keyDown event, what controls the order of response?

3. Click on MC2 (upper right).

4. Select Modify | Arrange | Move to Back.

5. Test the movie again.

   Note that the arrangement (in the layer) of multiple movie clips that share the same event determines the order of precedence. If you move an item to the front, it has higher precedence as far as the execution of its actions. An item further back in the arrangement has a lower priority concerning its actions.

A final note concerning arrangement and its effect on script execution is that this also applies across layers. As shown in the previous exercise, within a single layer, precedence is determined by arrangement. Similarly, if objects are spread across multiple layers, precedence is determined by layer order. Thus, the uppermost layer's actions would be executed before layers further back in the order. That is, layers further up in the timeline (layer 1 is in front of all others) have greater precedence.

A Summary of Flash Precedence

In previous sections you explored the issues of precedence that occur among frames, buttons, and movie clips. The following summarize these issues.

- *Mouse clicks:* In general, the *mouseDown* and *mouseUp* events of a movie clip always have precedence over the press and release events of a button. All four will execute on a click, but the movie clip actions will always occur first. The only exception is when the movie clip resides within the button. In this case, the movie clip will not respond to clicks at all. Additionally, buttons only react when clicked on; movie clips react no matter where you click.

- *Button presses:* The *keyDown* and *keyUp* movie clip events are global in nature, meaning that anytime a button is pressed, the actions execute. Button *keyPress* events only occur when a specific button is pressed. When a movie clip has key events and a button has key events, the movie clip's *keyDown* event will supercede the button's *keyPress* event.

- *EnterFrame:* Frame actions take precedence over movie clip actions assigned with the *enterFrame* event. Frame actions only execute when the keyframe to which they are assigned is encountered. Movie clip actions assigned to *enterFrame*, however, will repeatedly execute as long as the movie clip remains on the stage and the playhead is moving.

- *Multiple movie clips:* The arrangement of movie clips in the environment determines the precedence of script execution. If several movie clips share an event, the order of priority is determined by the arrangement. If items are on multiple layers, layer order determines precedence.

ActionScript Syntax Issues

When dealing with any language, whether it is a spoken language or a programming language, there are rules you must follow for communication. There are two types of errors in programming: logical and syntactical. Logical errors are resolved or overcome through knowledge of programming constructs and methodically thinking through a problem. Syntactical errors are overcome by carefully paying attention to the rules regarding the language and vehemently adhering to them. When dealing with Flash, there are four things you need to pay attention to in regard to syntax.

- Structural details such as brackets, semicolons, and parentheses
- Case sensitivity issues
- Comments and what they are for
- Dot syntax

The sections that follow examine each of these points in more detail. In regard to syntax errors, it cannot be stressed enough that failing to follow one of the foregoing items is the most frequent cause of errors in scripts. You cannot depend on Flash to catch all of these problems. The help Flash offers regarding error codes placed in the Output window will often point you in the right direction and tell you the line the error occurs on, but seldom provides the exact solution to the error. This is where knowing the syntax issues and being able to quickly see them in code is important.

Brackets, Semicolons, Parentheses, and Simplification

One of the first things you probably noticed earlier is that curly brackets ({}) are used in ActionScript coding. There is really nothing mysterious about these characters, and indeed JavaScript, Java, and many other languages use them. Much like the logic of HTML angle brackets (< >), which enclose tag keywords, curly brackets are used to denote logical blocks of code that function as a single unit. In this regard, and like the JavaScript standard ActionScript is built upon, curly brackets are always used in matched pairs in coding. Most often, curly brackets are used to define function definitions (i.e., code subroutines and/or handlers you write) and control structures (such as *If* statements).

As you write ActionScript, the location of curly brackets in code is not that important, as long as they enclose (delimit) lines of code that should function together. For example, the three items in code example 13-1 would all be valid and interpreted by Flash the same way. The physical location of curly brackets is not imperative, as long as a pair encloses logical code groupings.

 NOTE: *The two slashes (///) in code example 13-1 are used to denote comments, discussed later in this section.*

Code Example 13-1: Use of Curly Brackets

```
//Item 1
with (_parent.myclip) {
    gotoAndPlay (1);
    stopAllSounds();
}
//Item 2
with (_parent.myclip)
{
    gotoAndPlay (1);
      stopAllSounds();
}
//Item 3
with (_parent.myclip) { gotoAndPlay (1); stopAllSounds();}
```

NOTE: with() *is a command used to direct ActionScript methods to a specific object. The previous code tells a movie clip named myclip to go to frame 1 and play, and then to stop all currently playing sounds.* with() *is discussed later in this chapter.*

The main thing to keep in mind when writing ActionScript is that curly brackets must be in matched pairs. When you are working, it is not uncommon to forget one, particularly when you start interjecting *if, with,* or similar statements. Even though you can write scripts such as any of the three shown in code example 13-1, it is recommended you develop the style represented by item 1, because it is a de facto standard (at least as far as the JavaScript community is concerned).

Another syntax issue you must deal with in Flash is the use of the semicolon (;). Semicolons are not important if you are dealing with the first two methods of writing scripts shown in code example 13-1 (items 1 and 2). Although code example 13-1 shows semicolons following the *gotoAndPlay(1);* functions, you could omit these. However, if you are using the style of notation following item 3 in code example 13-1, semicolons are important because they identify where one method ends and another begins, as shown in the following.

```
with (_parent.myclip) { gotoAndPlay (1); stopAllSounds();}
```

The issue of semicolons and their appearance in Flash and JavaScript is a carryover from Java, in which semicolons are required to separate commands and a variety of other things. The only scenario in Flash or JavaScript for which semicolons are imperative is when you are writing multiple commands in a single line.

A final note concerns simplification of code. Much like working with algebra in mathematics, there are many ways to simplify the code you write. For example, the items listed in the previous examples could be written as follows.

```
_parent.myclip.gotoAndPlay(1);
```

Dot syntax makes it relatively easy to make code shorter through simplification.

Case Sensitivity

A common programming question has to do with case sensitivity. It is always a good idea to be consistent in your capitalization of items, regardless of the rules of a particular language. Most, if not all, ActionScript code words are case sensitive. Properties are the only items that are not case sensitive. Thus, only the items in the Properties column in table 13-1 are not case sensitive. All other code words found in the table are case sensitive.

NOTE: *Macromedia has provided a standard practices document on its web site concerning ActionScript coding for application development. This is accessible at www.macromedia.com/ devnet/. Although much of it is related to advanced coding using the OOP approach, there are some very good recommendations concerning naming conventions and case sensitivity issues.*

Comments

A common practice in programming is to include internal documentation in code. Comments allow you to leave notes for yourself or others in your code so that you can remember what something does, or anything else concerning the code you might later forget. Comments entered into code are ignored by the Flash Player and do not appear when the user views your movie.

In Flash, single-line comments are identified by double slashes that precede them. Code example 13-1 used comments to identify the sections of code that were highlighted. If you need to include multi-line comments, you use a special set of characters. A slash followed by an asterisk (/*) begins the comment, whereas an asterisk followed by a slash (*/) ends the comment. Code example 13-2 shows an example of a multi-line comment format containing these conventions.

Code Example 13-2: Multi-line Comment Format

```
/* This is an example of a multi-line comment.
All of the items written here are ignored by the
player. */
with (_parent.myclip) {
     gotoAndPlay (1);
     stopAllSounds();
}
```

If you are familiar with HTML, multi-line comments are created with the following characters.

```
<!-This is a comment in HTML ->
```

Dealing with Dot Syntax and Targets

One of the most crucial skills related to using Flash is knowing how to specifically target and talk to objects. By targeting objects such as buttons or movie clips, you can control them. For example, you could tell a movie clip to play, stop, or a number of other things. Similarly, by talking to programming objects, you can evoke their methods or access their properties. A target is simply a straightforward way of specifying the location of an object in the movie hierarchy and what you want to do to or with that object. You define a target in dot syntax.

Many of the general actions in Flash do not require the use of targets. For example, the *getURL()*, *play()*, and *loadMovie()* function (as well as others) do not require a target, as they are automatically directed to the main movie timeline (and executed using it as the assumed object). Thus, when you want to execute one of the general functions (see table 13-1), you simply place the action within an event handler, as in the following.

```
on (press) {
      getURL("http://www.purdue.edu/");
}
```

If this code were attached to a button, when the button was clicked a new web page would be loaded into the browser. You could also use the *getURL()* function in a frame.

Accessing Methods and Properties

To access a method property that belongs to a programming object, you use dot syntax to target or call upon the item. For example, one of the programming objects in Flash is the Math object, which allows you to perform a variety of tasks. One such task is the generation of random numbers. For this purpose, the Math object has a method called *random()*.

In dot syntax, to access the *random()* method of the Math object you use *Math.random();*. In general, to access any object method, you use the following form.

```
object.method();
```

Often methods will need to receive some data to be able to execute. The data sent to a method is called a parameter or argument and is typically included within the parentheses of the method. If a method needs more than one argument for execution, each method is separated by a comma. You can create compound statements quite easily. For example, to generate a random number between 1 and 25, you would use the following.

```
Math.Round(Math.random() * 25) + 1;
```

Math.random() generates a random number between 0.0 and 1.0. Thus, to create a whole number you insert the *Math.random()* call inside the *Math.Round()* call.

You use similar syntax to access properties of programming objects. For example, you could retrieve the current width of the stage using

Stage.width;. Thus, for most programming objects, the general form for accessing a property is as follows.

```
object.property();
```

 NOTE: *Some programming objects require instantiation before you can use them. For example, the Color object requires that you use* new Color(); *before you can "talk to" the object. Once the object is instantiated, however, calling a method or property is done as described previously.*

Controlling Movie Clips and Buttons

One of the interesting things about Flash is the level of control you actually have in the environment. In addition to being able to work with programming objects and their methods and properties, you can control movie clips and buttons, as well as other movies (which you will learn about later). Let's deal with the former of these, movie clips and buttons.

When you add instances of movie clips or buttons to the stage, you can easily control them with ActionScript coding. The primary thing you must do to be able to "talk to" a movie clip or button is to name it in the Properties panel. If you select a movie clip or button on the stage, you will find that the Properties panel provides a field called Instance Name. If you enter a name for a movie clip or button, you can direct commands to it.

For example, one of the properties of a movie clip instance is *_alpha*, which is the opaqueness of the instance. If you wanted to change the opaqueness of a movie clip instance using ActionScript coding, you would use a statement such as the following.

```
MC1._alpha=50
```

 NOTE: *Almost all property names are preceded by an underscore.*

This code assumes that the movie clip is named MC1 and would consequently set the opaqueness of the movie clip instance to 50 percent. Thus, the general dot syntax form for accessing the property of an instance is as follows.

```
targetpath.property;
```

Understanding Targets

In most examples to this point you have dealt with the most basic of relationships: single movie clips and buttons within the timeline. However, there are much more complex situations that can exist, particularly when you start thinking about nested movie clips and buttons (that is, symbols inside one another) or layered movies (where movies are loaded into movies using *loadMovie( )*, discussed later in the chapter).

 NOTE: *Targets are required for talking to programming objects (calling their methods or accessing their properties); talking to environment objects such as movies, movie clips, or buttons (directing actions to them or accessing their properties); and creating, accessing, or changing global or timeline variables.*

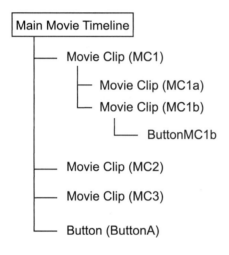

Figure 13-9. Hierarchy of symbols contained within a movie.

Imagine you have a movie with three movie clips and a button loaded into its timeline. The instances of the movie clips are named MC1, MC2, and MC3, and the button is named *ButtonA*. Remember that instance names are assigned to movie clips or buttons using the Properties panel's Instance Name field. To make this example more interesting, nested inside MC1 are two other movie clips, named *MC1a* and *MC1b*. *MC1b* also has a button in it, named *ButtonMC1b*. Figure 13-9 shows a graphical representation of this hierarchy.

Dot syntax makes it possible to communicate from one object to another pretty easily. Later you will also learn about the *with()* command, which also uses targets. The most difficult part of the process is identifying the actual target specification. The next section examines how to talk from one object to another using target specifications, and discusses the issue of absolute and relative targeting.

Absolute Versus Relative Targets

When you want an object to talk to something else in an environment, you have to point the talking object to the receiving object based on (1) the current talking object's location in the hierarchy or (2) a fixed point in the hierarchy. When you specify targets based on the object that is doing the taking, it is called a relative target; that is, where the receiving object is in relation to the talking object. If you specify the location of the receiving object based on a fixed point, it is called an absolute target. When defining absolute targets in Flash, the fixed point is the main movie timeline.

The only time relative versus absolute targeting becomes very important is when you want to create reusable, self-contained movie clips—which is most of the time! For example, let's say you set up a movie clip and you want to be able to drag and drop it into other movies. If you use absolute paths, the clip will likely not work when relocated because its position in the hierarchy has changed. Thus, when absolute targets are used, you have to go back and modify the targets in relation to the object's new location in a movie. If you use relative paths, code can be made so that it is self-contained and not dependent on hierarchical location in a movie. Thus, objects coded with relative paths (and therefore self-contained) are much more portable.

Relative versus absolute targets can be explained another way. An example you may be familiar with (where you deal with absolute versus relative paths) is the *HREF* attribute of the anchor tag in *HTML*. Let's say you have a home page that resides at the root level of your web site. The site URL is *www.somesite.com/*. When you specify URLs (in the < A > tag) off the home page at the URL, you can use either absolute or relative links.

Let's say you have a page (*newpage.html*) that resides in a folder (*myfolder*) at the root level of the server. You can use an absolute HREF based on a fixed point in the web structure. The HREF, then, would look as follows.

```
http://www.somesite.com/myfolder/newpage.html
```

However, you could also use a relative path, from the home page itself, and save a little typing. It would look as follows.

```
myfolder/newpage.html
```

Relative and absolute paths in Flash are basically the same thing and work in much the same way. In the HTML example, the URL (*http://www.somesite.com/*) is the fixed point in the structure. In Flash, you use the keyword *_root* to identify the main timeline in the current movie. Table 13-2 outlines some example targets for talking to the objects in the movie. These absolute paths could be used to have any of the objects shown in figure 13-4 talk to any other object in the movie. (See also exercise 13-11 for examples of absolute targets.)

Table 13-2: Absolute Targets for Accessing Objects

Target	Absolute Target
MC1	_root.MC1
MC1a	_root.MC1.MC1a
MC1b	_root.MC1.MC1b
ButtonMC1b	_root.MC1.MC1b.ButtonMC1b
MC2	_root.MC2
MC3	_root.MC3
MC1a	_root.MC1.MC1a
MC1b	_root.MC1.MC1b
ButtonA	_root.ButtonA

NOTE: *Refer to figure 13-9 when examining table 13-2.*

Exercise 13-11: Examples of Absolute Targets

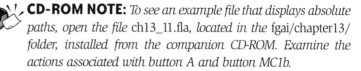

CD-ROM NOTE: *To see an example file that displays absolute paths, open the file* ch13_11.fla, *located in the* fgai/chapter13/ *folder, installed from the companion CD-ROM. Examine the actions associated with button A and button MC1b.*

When working with loaded movies, *_levelX* is used to define a movie level, where *X* is the level of the movie. For example, *_level0* is the main movie, *_level1* is the movie loaded on level 1, and so on. *_levelX* is used in absolute targets for loaded movies, just as *_root* is used for single-level movies.

Now let's examine relative paths. When you use relative paths, you must know the object from which you want to target (the object that is doing the talking), as well as the object you wish to target (or talk to). With absolute targets, you need only know the target object.

Two keywords, *_parent* and this, help you define a relative path. The keyword *_parent* refers to "one step up in the movie hierarchy." The keyword *this* refers to the object the script is attached to.

Let's begin with an example so that you can see how it works. Imagine you wanted *ButtonA* to control movie clip *MC1a* in some way, such as changing its *_alpha* property (see figure 13-9). If you wanted the path to be relative, it would be specified from *ButtonA*'s location in the movie hierarchy to movie clip *MC1a*'s location, as follows.

```
MC1.MC1a._alpha=50;
```

Note that *MC1a* is deeper in the movie hierarchy. To target down to it from *ButtonA* you simply use the name of each movie clip or button down to the object you are targeting. Then you end the statement with the property (as shown previously) you want to manipulate. You could also have a method applied to the object, as follows.

```
MC1.MC1a.stop();
```

You could also access a variable, if it happened to belong to *MC1a*, as follows.

```
MC1.MC1a.myvar="newvalue"
```

As you can see, it is pretty easy to target from an object higher in the movie hierarchy to an object lower in the hierarchy. But what if you wanted to go the other direction? Say you wanted to target movie clip *MC3* from

ButtonMC1b (see figure 13-9), how would you define it? This is where the keyword *_parent* comes in.

To define the location of the movie clip *MC3* in relation to the button *ButtonMC1b*, you have to have a way to "step up" the hierarchy, and *_parent* would be the way to do so. The target would look as follows.

```
_parent._parent.MC3._alpha=50;
```

Note that *_parent* is used twice. The first *_parent* steps up to the timeline contained in *MC1*, and the second steps up to the main movie timeline. To help you better understand this, examine table 13-3, which provides further details on absolute and relative targets in dot syntax.

 NOTE: *Refer to figure 13-9 when examining table 13-3.*

Table 13-3 is quite important, and you must compare it to figure 13-9 to get the gist of what is going on. Again, when specifying absolute paths, everything is referenced from the main movie timeline. Thus, all of the targets in the Absolute Target column begin with *_root*, regardless of which object it is attached to.

You specify relative targets, on the other hand, from a specific object. Note the special term *_parent*, which refers to the parent timeline of the current object (in other words, one step up in the structure). Each time you specify *_parent*, you take one step back (up) in the movie clip (timeline) hierarchy, which can be done multiple times in a single target specification, as shown in the Relative Targets column of table 13-3. Exercise 13-12 provides an example of the use of relative targets.

Table 13-3: Absolute and Relative Targets in Dot Syntax.

Target	From Object	Absolute Target	Relative Target
MC1a	Button A	_root.MC1.MC1a	MC1.MC1a
MC1b	Button A	_root.MC1.MC1b	MC1.MC1b
MC2	Button A	_root.MC2	MC2
MC3	Button A	_root.MC3	MC3
MC1a	Button MC1b	_root.MC1.MC1a	parent.MC1a
MC1b	Button MC1b	_root.MC1.MC1b	parent.MC1b
MC2	Button MC1b	_root.MC2	parent._parent.MC2
MC3	Button MC1b	_root.MC3	parent._parent.MC3

Exercise 13-12: Relative Targets in a Movie

CD-ROM NOTE: *To see an example file that displays relative paths (targets), open the file ch13_12.fla, located in the* fgai/chapter13 *folder, installed from the companion CD-ROM.*

Examine the actions associated with button A and button *MC1b*.

Programming Fundamentals

Although this section is devoted to a discussion of programming fundamentals, you have already had some exposure to the general terminology. The sections that follow deal with a few more conceptual issues, and include simple examples that help with an understanding of these programming concepts.

Variables

One of the fundamental concepts associated with any scripting or programming language is that of variables. Variables are nothing more than containers for data. Throughout the life of a program, variables are used to store information such as a user's name, the date, the time, as well as a wide range of other bits of information that need to be tracked.

Variables are dynamic in that the content they hold can change over time. For example, you could use a variable to keep track of a score in a computer game. As the user kills more beasties or solves more problems, the variable keeps track of such information. At the end of the experience, the score can then be retrieved and presented to the user. You could also dynamically display the score as the user progresses through the game. This would be accomplished by creating a text field that shared the variable's name.

Rules for Variables

In most programming and scripting languages there are many rules associated with the use of variables. The three main concerns in Flash are the variable's name, the scope of the variable, and the type of data contained in the variable. Scope simply signifies how long the variable and its data are active. The data type signifies what type of data is in the variable. Let's begin by examining variable naming.

Variable Names

The way you name your variables is very important. In Flash, variables can generally be anything, but it is recommended you develop a scheme for naming your variables so that you, as well as other readers of your code, can decipher your code more easily. Flash variable names must adhere to the following rules.

- All characters in a variable's name must be a letter, number, underscore (_), or dollar sign ($). Thus, you cannot use other symbol characters, such as an asterisk (*) or a slash (/), in a variable's name.

- Variable names cannot be any of the ActionScript words. (See table 13-1.)

- All variable names must be unique within their scope (see the section "Timeline Variable Scope.")

Data Types

In many programming languages, you must specify the type of data contained in the variable before you can use it. This is not as simple as specifying a variable as a string (text) or a numeral. In most languages, there are several specific data types for string and numeral data. For example, in Java, a variable designed to hold a number can take various forms, such as byte, short, int, or long. You must define the variable as one of these forms before you can use it.

Fortunately in Flash, you do not need to worry about multiple types of strings or numerals, or other data contained in a variable. Flash determines this the moment you assign data to a variable. For example, say you define the following two variables by assigning a variable name to a value.

```
myvar1=10
myvar2="potato"
```

When Flash sees the first assignment, it sees that *myvar1* is assigned to a number, and automatically establishes that the variable *myvar1* should be designed to hold numbers. When Flash sees the second assignment, it sees that *myvar2* is assigned to a string (signified by the set of double quote marks). Thus, the program designs the variable *myvar2* to hold string data. You do not have to worry about telling Flash the general data type, nor any specific data type, for the variable.

There is, however, one exception to the rules governing variables. When a variable or a property has a binary value (on or off), its value can be referenced either as a constant (true or false) or as a numerical value. Thus, if a variable or property is binary (Boolean), you can refer to its value as either true or 1 (on) or false or 0 (off). In this respect, binary variables (and properties) are unique.

One final note in this section is that you must understand the difference between a string and a numeral. In essence, strings are nothing more than basic text elements. With them you can perform special operations, such as searching for specific characters or words in a paragraph, joining two strings (called concatenation), or truncating or extending the characters in a text element. Numbers, on the other hand, can be used to perform mathematical operations and comparisons, as well as a wide variety of other tasks.

Many newcomers think they understand the difference between strings and numerals; that is, until they actually start writing their own code. To get to the fundamental difference, examine the following statements.

```
myvar=1
myvar="1"
```

Although these two statements look similar, they are not the same. The first is a numerical statement, and the second is a string (text statement). The fundamental difference between strings and numerals is evident here: the first line means the numeral 1, whereas the second refers to the 1 as a character.

As previously stated, you do not necessarily have to worry about the intricacies of data types typical of other languages. However, understanding the basic differences among generic data types is important, particularly when you start modifying properties and working with methods.

Methods and properties will expect a certain type of data to be provided to them. For example, if you want to change the _alpha property of a movie clip, Flash will expect you to provide it with a number (numeric value), not a string. This is where it is important to understand the difference between strings and numerals. Later in this chapter you will see how to convert a string to a numeral using the *number();* method, and how to convert a numeral to a string using the *string();* method.

Instantiation and Scope

In most languages, scope refers to the length of time a variable is active or accessible. Local variables are normally active only for a brief period, serving as temporary storage, and are typically used in a function or object script. When the object ceases to exist or the script is finished executing, the variable, too, is removed from memory. Global variables, on the other hand, are usually alive and active during the entire duration of a program, no matter what object initiated them, or when. Flash provides one other type of variable called a timeline variable.

To create a variable, you generally do something called declaring or instantiating the variable. In some languages, you have to declare a variable to reserve space in memory for it, while at the same time specifying its data type. Some programming languages are very stringent in this regard. Flash is not. Although it is good and common practice, you do not have to declare a variable before you use it.

 TIP: *Even though you do not have to, it is recommended that you always use comments to describe the intended use of the variables you create. It is best to do this at the first instance of a variable.*

You can define global, timeline, and local variables in Flash. How and where you write the code determines the type of variable created. Let's first look at global variable declaration in Flash.

Global Variables

When you precede a variable with the *_global* keyword, it is treated in a particular way; that is, it is a true global variable and is not owned by a timeline per se. You do not need to provide a target path to access a global variable's data. Simply precede the variable name with *_global* and you can access it.

In addition, there are two methods of defining a global variable in Flash. The first is to use the *Set Variable* action. The second is to create an expression. Although you cannot define two variables in the same location (scope) with the same name (remember naming rules), for the sake of comparison, the following two lines of code say the same thing, and they both create a global variable called *myvar*.

```
_global.myvar=1;
set (_global.myvar, 1);
```

 TIP: *The* Set Variable *action can be used to define global or timeline variables.*

Similarly, the following two lines of code say the same thing.

```
_global.myvar="Jamie";
set (_global.myvar, "Jamie");
```

In both of the previous two sets of instances, the variable *myvar* is created. The first two lines create a global variable that contains numerical data, and the second set of lines creates a global variable that contains string data. Anytime you use the *Set Variable* action from the Actions toolbox list, or manually use an expression, the variable becomes a global variable, accessible by any other object in the movie. Exercise 13-13 provides practice in working with variables.

TIP: *Once a global variable is created, you can access it from any-where by prefacing the variable name with _global. For example, _global.myvar would provide access to the variables created in the previous code.*

Exercise 13-13: Using Global Variables

 CD-ROM NOTE: *To see an example of how variables are created and incremented, open the file ch13_13.fla, locat-ed in the fgai/chapter13/ folder, installed from the com-panion CD-ROM.*

To practice using variables, perform the following steps.

1. With file *ch13_13.fla* open, note the following. First, the myval variable is initialized in frame 1. Click on frame 1 and view the Actions panel.

2. Note in the Actions panel, shown in figure 13-10a, that the action uses the *_global* prefix to establish the variable.

   Now let's look at the scripting that actually does the variable incrementing. Continue with the following steps.

3. With the Actions panel open, click on the red button on the stage. Note in the Script pane that the variable is incremented (figure 13-10b) by using *_global.myval = _global.myval + 1.*

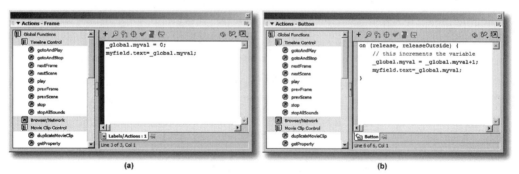

Figure 13-10. A global variable is created (a) and then incremented with script associated with a button (b).

4. Note the second line of code, which transfers the value from the global variable *myval* and inserts it into the text field named *myfield*. If you select the text field on the stage and view the Properties inspector, you will see that the field is named.

Exercise 13-14 provides practice in working with the increment and decrement operators.

Exercise 13-14: Using the Increment and Decrement Operators

CD-ROM NOTE: *An alternative method for incrementing variables (or decrementing variables) is shown in the file ch13_14.fla, located in the fgai/chapter13/ folder, installed from the companion CD-ROM.*

Local Variables

To declare a local variable in Flash you use the *var* keyword. Local variables are usually used for "short-lived" data, such as temporarily storing a value. They are commonly used in for and other types of loops. For example, the following would create a local variable.

```
var mylocal1="blah"
```

The reality is, however, that local variables can only truly be created in user-defined functions you write (not to be confused with the built-in data conversion or evaluation functions listed in table 13-1). Once the user-defined function is done executing its code, the local variable is deleted.

NOTE: *Use of the* var *keyword outside a function container is futile. All variables created outside user-defined functions, whether* var *is used or not, are created as timeline variables.*

Timeline Variable Scope

The last type of variable is the timeline variable. When a variable is created that (a) does not use the *_global* prefix and (b) does not use the *var* keyword inside a function, a timeline variable is created. Global variables exist as long as the Flash player is running. Local variables cease to exist as soon as the user-defined function they are called in ceases. Let's take a closer look at the last of the variable types: timeline variables.

Timeline variables created in Flash are scoped according to timelines. Thus, when a variable is created and it is not a global or local variable, it is "owned" by the timeline that created it. The variable will exist as long as the timeline exists within the player. For example, if a movie clip named *MC1* creates a variable named *gfinal*, accessing the variable's data could be done using an absolute target path, such as the following.

```
_root.MC1.gfinal
```

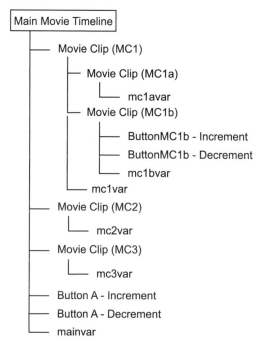

Figure 13-11. A movie structure in which
a variable is defined in each timeline.

If you wanted to use a relative path, the entry would be dependent on the relative position between the object trying to access the variable and *MC1*. Nevertheless, you would undoubtedly use the keyword *_parent*. The next section discusses targets in more detail.

Variables and Target Paths

Let's review one more example. Examine figure 13-11. This example was used earlier in this chapter. However, this time a variable has been added to each of the movie clip timelines, as well as to the main movie timeline. As previously examined, what would the target paths to the variables from the two buttons look like? Table 13-4 reveals the answer.

How do you reference each variable from the two buttons shown in figure 13-11? See table 13-4 for the answer. Exercise 13-15, provides practice in working with target paths.

Table 13-4: Valid Target Paths for Button Variables Using Dot Syntax

From Button A (Increment)				
To	**Relative Path**	**Relative Expression**	**Absolute Path**	**Absolute Expression**
mainvar	*mainvar*	++*mainvar*	*_root.mainvar*	++*_root.mainvar*
mc1avar	*MC1.MC1a.mc1avar*	++*MC1.MC1a. mc1avar*	*_root.MC1.MC1a. mclavar*	++*_root.MC1.MC1a. mclavar*
mc1bvar	*MC1.MC1b.mc1bvar*	++*MC1.MC1b. mc1bvar*	*_root.MC1.MC1b. mclbvar*	++*_root.MC1.MC1b. mclbvar*
mc2var	*MC2.mc2var*	++*MC2.mc2var*	*_root.MC2.mc2var*	++*_root.MC2.mc2var*
mc3var	*MC3.mc3var*	++*MC3.mc3var*	*_root.MC3.mc3var*	++*_root.MC3.mc3var*
From Button MC1b (Increment)				
To	**Relative Path**	**Relative Expression**	**Absolute Path**	**Absolute Expression**
mainvar	*_parent._parent.mainvar*	++*_parent._parent. mainvar*	*_root.mainvar*	++*_root.mainvar*
mc1avar	*_parent.MC1a.mclavar*	++*_parent.MC1a. mclavar*	*_root.MC1.MC1a. mclavar*	++*_root.MC1.MC1a. mclavar*
mc1bvar	*mc1bvar*	++ *mc1bvar*	*_root.MC1.MC1b. mclbvar*	++*_root.MC1.MC1b. mc1bvar*
mc2var	*_parent._parent. MC2.mc2var*	++*_parent._parent. MC2.mc2var*	*_root.MC2.mc2var*	++*_root.MC2.mc2var*
mc3var	*_parent._parent. MC3.mc3var*	++*_parent._parent. MC3.mc3var*	*_root.MC3.mc3var*	++*_root.MC3.mc3var*

Exercise 13-15: Target Paths

CD-ROM NOTE: *To see an applied example of figure 13-11 using absolute targets, open the file* ch13_15a.fla, *located in the* fgai/chapter13/ *folder, installed from the companion CD-ROM. To see an applied example of figure 13-11 using relative targets, open the file* ch13_ 15b.fla, *located in the* fgai/chapter13/ *folder.*

NOTE: *The keywords* _global, _levelX, _parent, _root, *and* this *are called identifiers in table 13-1.*

Expressions

Now that you understand variables, let's examine expressions momentarily. Previously you saw these in a few of the examples. Expressions in Flash are sequences of operators and operands (variable names, functions, properties, and so on) used to compute numerical or string results. Although at this point extensive examples might be more confusing than productive to an understanding of expressions, you should be aware of what is meant by the term expression.

The expressions listed in table 13-5 use the Increment operator to change the value of a variable. When Flash encounters an expression, it evaluates it to a resulting value.

For example, you could create a string expression that concatenates (joins) the user's first and last name, such as "James" + "Mohler". The resultant would be the string result "James Mohler". A numeric expression could be used to add two straightforward numbers, such as 5 + 3, or increase the value in a variable, such as *gscore + 1*. In previous examples, you encountered two "shorthand" operators: increment and decrement. As you can see, operators are vitally important to being able to do anything in ActionScript.

Operators

At the heart of expressions are operators. Depending on the data, and on the results you are trying to obtain, different operators are used. Thus, there are specific operators that apply to numerical expressions only, and specific operators that apply to string expressions only. There are also general, comparison, logical, and bitwise operators. The operators are discussed in the sections that follow.

TIP: *You may find it helpful to reference table 13-1 as you progress through the discussion of specific ActionScript items.*

General Operators

The general operators include several delimiter items, the following of which have been discussed.

- *String delimiters:* Sets of double quote marks (" ") used to signify string data elements
- *Parentheses:* Used to offset arguments that are sent to functions or methods
- *Dot access delimiter (.):* Used to reference hierarchical object order in target paths
- *Curly brackets ({ }):* Used to denote logical code groupings
- *Square brackets ([ ]):* Used to access or assign specific values in an array

General operators not previously discussed include the comma, conditional, and array access operators. The latter two are discussed later in this chapter. The comma delimiter is used when multiple arguments are sent to a method or function. For example, when you use a *getURL()* method, the URL and the target window parameters are sent to the *getURL()* method, as follows.

```
getURL ("http://www.somesite.com", "_blank");
```

Note that a comma is used to separate the values being sent to the method. This works the same way in regard to functions. Imagine you wrote a function to add two numbers and return a result, such as the following.

```
function addme (x, y) {
     x + y = z
     return z;
}
```

Note in this function that the comma is used to separate data being received in the function. To call or utilize this function, you would write the following inside some handler.

```
myvar = addme(1,3);
```

Note again the comma being used to separate the values being sent to the *addme()*; function. In short, this function is written so that it receives values when it is called, which are assigned to two local variables (x and y). The values that will be substituted for x and y are those located within the parentheses when the function is called. Therefore, in essence, the values in the call to the function (1 and 3) are substituted for x and y when the function executes. The function then returns the value z, which is placed within *myvar*. Exercise 13-16 examines commas, functions, and passing values.

Exercise 13-16: Commas, Functions, and Passing Values

CD-ROM NOTE: *To see an example of the use of commas, functions, and the passing of values, open the file* ch13_16.fla, *located in the* fgai/chapter13/ *folder, installed from the companion CD-ROM.*

Equality Versus Assignment Operators

The assignment and equality operators are pretty straightforward. One of the biggest issues concerning the use of operators is the issue of equality versus assignment. ActionScript follows the general rule in which a single equals sign represents "set this equal to this" and a double equals sign means "does this equal that." Thus, the following lines do not mean the same thing.

```
myvar = 1
myvar == 1
```

The first of the previous lines is assigning the value 1 to the variable myvar, whereas the second line is asking, "does *myvar* equal a value of 1?" As you begin writing your code, this is important to remember. Already you have seen examples of assignment (via the variable exercise). Equality (==) operators are examined in greater detail later in this chapter, under a discussion of conditional statements.

Strict Equalities

Flash MX 2004 includes the strict equality operator (===) and strict inequality (!==) operator. Typically when Flash compares two values, if the values are not of the same data type Flash will convert them to the same data type before performing the evaluation of equality. The strict equality operator forces Flash to evaluate the two elements without type conversion. For example, consider the following.

```
1 == "1"
```

This statement says, "Does the numeral 1 equal the string 1?" Typically Flash sees the values on either side of the operator as equal because it converts the latter to a numeral before performing the evaluation. The strict equality or inequality operators allow you to force Flash to evaluate two values without data conversion. Using the strict equality operator on the values in this statement would force Flash to recognize that the two values are not the same.

Operation and Assignment

As you peruse the listing of equality and assignment operators, beyond equality, assignment, and inequality you will find that the remaining operators are shorthand methods for performing certain tasks, called compound operators. They allow you to do two things (usually a mathematical operation and assignment) at the same time.

For example, if you wanted to subtract a known value from a variable, and at the same time assign the new value to the variable, you can write it in a shorthand way. For example, the following pairs of expressions do the same thing.

```
x = x + 7 and x += 7
y = y * 245 and y *= 245
a = a / b and a /= b
```

Numeric and String Operators

Numeric expressions are most often used to perform math operations on numbers. These include addition (+), subtraction (–), multiplication (*), and division (/). Flash also includes Modulo (%), as well as Increment (+ +) and Decrement (– –), which you have already examined. When the function itself returns a numerical value, numeric expressions may also integrate functions. Examples of this include *eval()*, *parseFloat()*, *parseInt()*, and *number()*. Properties may also be used with operators when their values yield numbers.

You have seen some basic numeric expressions in examples and in the text. Generally, numeric expressions follow the standard rules governing mathematics. Thus, multiplication and division occur before addition and subtraction. Parentheses can be used to specify operations that should occur before multiplication and division.

If you use a string in a numeric expression, Flash will attempt to concatenate the string and number before performing the evaluation. For example, adding 6 + "3" ("3" being a string) will result in the number 63. Similarly, "DOG" + 3 results in *dog3*. Similarly, string operations are performed on string values. Any set of characters surrounded by double quote marks (" ") is evaluated as a string. Empty strings are identified by quote marks separated by a space (" "). The only true operational evaluation of a string is concatenation, in which two string portions are added.

Logical

Logical operators differ from other operators in that they are used to concatenate (join) two comparison statements. You should use the double ampersand (&&) for logical and (e.g., if this and that are true), double pipes (| |) for logical or (e.g., if this or that is true), and the exclamation mark (!) for logical not (e.g., if this and that are not true). For example, to see if a variable's value resides between two numbers, you could use the following expression in the condition of an if statement.

```
myscore < 10 && myscore > 100
```

This expression would determine if the variable myscore were between 10 and 100. You could use the or operator to determine if the variable *userpassword* were a certain value, as in the following.

```
userpassword == "dogfight" || userpassword == "chicken"
```

If *userpassword* equaled "dogfight" or "chicken", the appropriate actions could be executed. Finally, you could use the not operator to allow all values except a specific one to respond, by entering the following.

```
myvalue < 100 ! myvalue == 77
```

In this scenario, all values less than 100, except for 77, would evaluate as true. You will see other examples of logical operators later in this chapter.

Comparison

Comparisons (as well as logical operators) are elements used most commonly within if statements and conditional loops. Comparison operators compare two elements, such as those listed in table 13-5. The result of a comparison operation is a binary value of either *TRUE* (1) or *FALSE* (0). When integrated into an if statement or a conditional loop, appropriate actions are either initiated or ignored.

Table 13-5: Comparison of Numerical and String Expression Operators

Comparison	Type	Statement	Result
Two values	Numerical	1 >= 2	*FALSE*
Variable and value	Numerical	*myscore* >= 3	Depends on value in *myscore*
Variable and variable	Numerical	*myscore* > highscore	Depends on values in *myscore* and *highscore*
Property and value	Numerical	_currentframe == 10	Depends on the current frame
Two strings	String	"James" == "Mohler"	*FALSE*
Variable and value	String	firstname != "Mohler"	Depends on value in variable *firstname*
Variable and variable	String	password == userentry	Depends on values in variables
Property and value	String	_droptarget == "/MC1"	Depends on value in *droptarget* property

Bitwise

Bitwise operators are used to internally manipulate floating-point numbers by changing them into 32-bit integers. Bitwise calculations are useful for advanced mathematical operations. They are beyond the scope of this book.

Operators in Summary

As you can see, with operators you can create almost any expression that can be evaluated and reacted to. When you are working with strings or string literals, there may be times when you want to use special characters in your strings. For example, strings are identified by double quote marks. How do you define double quote marks inside a string? To do this requires the use of special sequences of characters, called escape sequences, within the string. Flash supports the following escape sequences.

- \b for backspace
- \f for form feed
- \n for line feed
- \r for carriage return
- \t for tab
- \" for double quote marks
- \' for single quote marks
- \\ for backslash

The following are examples of the use of these characters. *My dog's name is \"Winnie\"* would result in the following string.

```
My dog's name is "Winnie"
```

The code *My name is:\nJames Mohler* would result in the following string.

```
My name is:
James Mohler
```

Although you may never use some of the sequences, \n, \t, \", and \' are very common. The string escape sequences are included in table 13-1 in the lower, right-hand corner.

Statements

Within the main groupings of actions in the Actions toolbox list, the Statements group includes four subgroups examined in the following sections. All of these are command statements. In this book we will examine the Conditions/Loops and Variables sections. Due to the limits of this book, we will not cover Class Constructs or Exceptions.

Conditionals

Being able to respond to certain conditions allows you to control the program flow. There two general types of flow control statements: conditionals and loops. In the Actions panel, these two are grouped under Statements | Conditionals/Loops group.

In Flash, you can use the *if* or *switch* constructs to react to a specific condition in a program. With the *do...while/while* and *for/for...in* constructs you can create repeating segments. Conditional statements allow you to create sets of actions that may or may not execute, depending on the condition. Loops allow you to create sets of actions that repeat themselves with various settings, which in essence is a means of shortening ActionScript code segments.

If...else/else if

The *if* construct provides a tremendous capability within Flash. As a basic programming capability, the *if* statement allows you to write a set of statements that executes if a particular condition is found to be true or false. It also allows you to set up alternatives to the condition. Thus, you can create binary conditions, as well as conditions that respond to a variety of conditions.

For example, if you have a button you want to go to certain URL locations based on the current frame, you could use the *if* statement and a single button. For example, say you want the URL to go to one web site if the playhead is in frame 10. If the current frame is anything else, you want the URL to go to a different web site. The basic *if* structure in simple English would look as follows.

```
If the current frame equals 10 then
     Get this URL
If it does not (Else)
     Get a different URL
End If
```

In Flash, you set up a conditional statement by adding an *if* action to an object. Given the previous English statements, you would convert it to the following ActionScript code:

```
if (_currentframe<10) {
     getURL("http://www.yahoo.com", "_blank");
} else {
```

```
                  getURL("http://www.excite.com", "_blank");
}
```

When you are working with *if* actions, there are four basic scenarios for your statements. They include the scenarios shown in figure 13-12. Because Flash allows both *else* and *else if* clauses to be added to an *if* statement, you can test a condition for any value. When an *else* statement exists, it is a catchall set of statements. If none of the other conditions specified in the *if* or *else if* statements are found to be true, the *else* statements are executed. Exercise 13-17 examines use of the if action based on frames.

(a)	(b)	(c)	(d)

if (condition) {
 	
statement s
 	
}
	if (condition) {
	
	statement s
	
	} else if (
	
	statement s
	
	}
		if (condition) {
		
		statement s
		
		} else if (condition) {
		
		statement s
		
		}
			if (condition) {
			
			statement s
			
			} else if (condition) {
			
			statement s
			
			} else {
			
			statement s
			
			}

Figure 13-12. The scenarios that can be established using the if *statement.*

 NOTE: *If you have a condition for which you want to test many specific cases, you should use the* switch *statement instead (described in the next section), instead of a complex* if *statement. A* switch *statement is more efficient from a processing perspective than complex* if *statements.*

Exercise 13-17: Using the if Action Based on Frames

 CD-ROM NOTE: *To see a simple example of using the* if *action, open the HTML file ch13_17.html, located in the fgai/chapter13/ folder, installed from the companion CD-ROM.*

This CD-ROM file shows how a single button can be used to go to different places using the *if* action. The *getURL()* actions will only work when the HTML file is opened into the browser.

In many programming languages, a second conditional construct is provided. In JavaScript it is called *switch*; in Director, case. In essence, when you use an *if* that has many values you want to test for (let's say greater than 5), you may notice a lag when you run the program. This is because the program must check the condition for each segment of the *if* statement, not to mention that writing lengthy *if* statements can become laborious and confusing (if you have *if* statements nested within *if* statements). Flash MX 2004 provides a *switch* statement, discussed in material to follow. However, before moving on to the next topic, exercise 13-18 explores using the *if* action based on variables.

Exercise 13-18: Using the if *Action Based on Variables*

 CD-ROM NOTE: *To see another example of using the* if *action, open the file* ch13_18.fla *located, in the* fgai/chapter13/ *folder, installed from the companion CD-ROM.*

This CD-ROM file has a button increment, a variable, and an associated field. Using an *if*, when the variable is incremented to a certain number, the main movie timeline reacts.

Ternary Operator

The previous discussion of general operators did not include the conditional operator (often called a ternary operator) consisting of a question mark and a colon (? :) This operator allows you to create conditional statements quickly and easily when there are only two possible values for a condition. In other words, if you have a binary condition, use the conditional operator as a shortcut. The form for the use of the conditional operator is as follows.

```
condition ? do_this_if_true : do_this_if_false
```

Examples of the use of the conditional operator follow.

```
myval == 1 ? gotoAndPlay(1) : gotoAndStop(3);
```

In this example, if *myval* equals 1, the movie will go to and play frame 1. If *myval* does not equal 1, the movie will go to frame 3 and stop.

```
_framesloaded < 100 ? gotoAndPlay("Loop") : gotoAndPlay("Start")
```

In this example, if the *_framesloaded* property (the number of frames loaded) is less than frame 100, the movie returns to a label named *Loop*. If the *_framesloaded* property is greater than frame 100, the movie goes to the frame label *Start*.

```
MC1._x <= 75 ? MC1._x=0 : MC1._x=200
```

In this example, if the *x* location of the movie clip *MC1* is less than or equal to 75, the *x* location of movie clip *MC1* is assigned to 0. If not, the *x* location of movie clip *MC1* is set to 200.

Let's look at the previous examples you have worked with to see the difference. For example, previously the following code was used for a condition.

```
on (release) {
  if (_currentframe < 10) {
   getURL ("http://www.yahoo.com", "_blank");
  } else {
   getURL ("http://www.excite.com", "_blank");
  }
}
```

A shorthand method for writing the same thing using the conditional operator would look as follows.

```
on (release) {
 _currentframe < 10 ? getURL ("http://www.yahoo.com",
"_blank") : getURL ("http://www.excite.com",
"_blank")
}
```

Note the position of the question mark and the colon. As previously mentioned, the use of semicolons is not critical unless you are writing several statements back to back. When you use the conditional operator, it is recommended that you not use semicolons. For example, in the file *ch13-17.fla*, the following code was used for the condition.

```
on (release, releaseOutside) {
  // this increments the variable
  myval = myval+1;
  if (myval>=10) {
   gotoAndPlay ("End");
  }
}
```

A shorthand method for writing the same thing using the conditional operator would look as follows.

```
on (release, releaseOutside) {
 // this increments the variable
 myval = myval+1;
 myval >= 10 ? gotoAndPlay ("End") : gotoAndPlay ("Loop1")
}
```

In this example, note that a second *gotoAndPlay()* had to be added to complete the command. You cannot use a conditional operator unless there are specified resultants for both cases. In this scenario, it causes no ill effects. Exercise 13-19 explores creating a situation in which a movie clip reacts to the timeline.

Exercise 13-19: Having a Movie Clip React to the Timeline

 CD-ROM NOTE: *See an applied example by opening the file* ch13_19.fla, *located in the* fgai/chapter13/ *folder, installed from the companion CD-ROM.*

This CD-ROM file shows an example that displays a movie clip that reacts to the main movie timeline.

Switch...case/default

As previously mentioned, Flash provides a *switch* statement. Like an *if* statement, switch statements allow you to test for any number of conditions and then respond uniquely to each. Where *switch* statements are useful is when you have many conditions for which you would like to perform certain actions. In such cases, *if* statements can become quite lengthy, and at times confusing. The *switch* statement provides a more concise method of creating multi-case conditional statements.

For example, let's use the scenario in which you have a button you want to go to different places at different times. You could create a *switch* statement that detects the current frame and then responds appropriately, as follows.

```
switch (_currentframe) {
  case 10:
      getURL("http://www.google.com/", "_blank");
      break;
  case 20:
      getURL("http://www.yahoo.com", "_blank");
      break;
  case 30:
      getURL("http://www.excite.com", "_blank");
      break;
  default:
      getURL("http://www.lycos.com", "_blank");
}
```

Note here how switch, *case,* and *default* are used. The statement is opened by the *switch* keyword followed by a variable or property. It is the state of the variable or property that is used as the condition. Thus, the first case looks for *_currentframe* to yield 10, the second looks for *_currentframe* to yield 20, and so on. That is, you define the states directly following the case keyword.

In the previous code, note also the *default* keyword. This is like the *else* aspect of the *if* statement. If the *switch* statement checks all cases and finds none that match, it will execute the code in the default section.

A final note about switch statements concerns the use of the *break* command. Note that in each case section *break* is used at the end. *switch* statements are significantly different from *if* statements in that once a matching case is found the code defined in that case will execute.

However, unless a break command is found (which makes the *switch* statement cease operation altogether), the *switch* statement will continue executing the code found in the remaining cases, until it either encounters a *break* or reaches the end of the cases in the *switch*. With *if* statements, once a matching *if* or *else if* section is found, only that section is executed. With *switch* statements, once a matching case is found, all subsequent cases will execute their code unless a *break* is encountered.

 TIP: *When a* default *case is used, it is generally the last item in the* switch *statement. Thus, a* break *is not needed.*

Loops

As you read earlier, in the Actions panel the conditional and loop statements are contained together. In the previous section, you examined the conditional statements. In the following section, you will finish by examining the loop commands that exist in Flash.

for/for...in

As you write ActionScript, you often want to perform an operation on several items at once, or repeat a section of code multiple times. The *for* and *for...in* repeat loops, using a counter, let you repeat something a specific number of times. The form for creating an incrementing or decrementing counter would look as follows.

```
//incrementing counter
for ( var i = minvalue; i <= maxvalue; ++i ) {
   statements you want to repeat with the value of i
}
//decrementing counter
for ( var i = maxvalue; i >= minvalue; --i ) {
   statements you want to repeat with the value of i
}
```

NOTE: *In this code, as well as other places you use* for *loops, keep in mind that the* var *keyword will only work properly if the* for *loop is within a user-defined function. In all other instances, the* var *keyword is ignored and a timeline variable is created.*

Imagine you wanted to repeat something a certain number of times, such as turning a series of movie clip symbols to invisible, or duplicating a certain number of movie clips. As you know, one way to do this is to write multiple lines that manually set each of the items to invisible (*some-clip._visible = 0*). With the for repeat loop, however, you can create a set of looping code that repeats a specific number of times and does the same thing, such as changing the visibility property. Exercise 13-20 examines the use of such a *for* loop.

Exercise 13-20: Using a **for** *Loop*

 CD-ROM NOTE: *To see an applied example of the* for *repeat loop, open the file* ch13_20.fla, *located in the* fgai/chapter13/ *folder, installed from the companion CD-ROM.*

The *for* repeat loop can be used for quite a number of things. You would think the *for* repeat loop could be used to incrementally modify the *_alpha* property to create a transition. However, in Flash the screen is only updated when a frame is encountered and there is no way to use ActionScript to forcibly redraw the screen. Another thing along these lines you should be aware of is that the data output to the Output window is also dependent on the refreshing of the display. Thus, if you place a *trace()* action inside a *for* loop you will not see the *trace()* output in the Output window. Exercise 13-21 examines using a *for* loop for a transition.

Exercise 13-21: Using a **for** *Loop for a Transition*

 CD-ROM NOTE: *To see an example of use of the* for *loop, open the file* ch13_21.fla, *located in the* fgai/chapter13/ *folder, installed from the companion CD-ROM.*

Note in this CD-ROM file that even though the *for* loop is incrementally adjusting the *_alpha* property, because the stage cannot be forcibly redrawn you do not see a smooth transition.

The primary difference between the *for* and *for...in* actions is that *for...in* allows you to find out or modify things relative to a specific object.

When you begin working with programming objects such as the Array object, *for...in* becomes relevant.

while/do...while

The *do...while* and *while* loops repeat a set of actions as long as a particular condition is true. Whereas the *for* and *for...in* loops provide a counter and respond to that internal counter's condition or state, the *do...while* and *while* loops assume a condition is *TRUE* and continually repeat the code statements until the condition is *FALSE*. *while* loops are pretty easy to understand. The following is an example.

```
while ( condition ) {
   statements to perform
}
```

In general, as long as the condition is evaluated as true, the statements will react. The minute the condition no longer exists, the statements cease. The main thing to keep in mind is that the condition must be *TRUE* upon encountering the *while* statement; otherwise, the statements inside will not execute. The *do...while* repeat looks as follows.

```
do {
   statements to perform
} while ( condition )
```

The primary difference between the two types is that *do...while* allows you to execute the statements, once, before the condition is examined. Thus, the condition would not have to be true for the statements to execute once. However, the condition would have to be true for the statements to execute multiple times. When you use the while repeat only, the condition must be true for the statements to ever execute.

Other Conditional/Loop Commands

One of the things you should have noticed when examining the repeat loop commands available is that you must be careful you do not get your users caught in an endless looping scenario. For example, if a user encounters a while loop, you need to make sure there is indeed a way to change the condition causing the loop. In addition to those associated with this issue, several other utility commands are available. These are discussed in the sections that follow.

break and continue

break and *continue* are predominantly used with repeat loops, as well as in *switch* statements. For example, you may find that for a particular value in a *for* loop you want to break out of the loop when the particular case is found. This is very common when using arrays. Arrays are nothing more than variables that can contain multiple values. Most programs call them arrays; however, in Director they are called lists.

Arrays provide a way to see the relevance of the *break* command. Additionally, arrays give you some special capabilities, such as being able to sort values in an array or search for a particular value in the array. When you search for a value in an array, *break* becomes important. For example, imagine you have an array named *grocerylist*, which contains a series of grocery items. Let's say you know that one of the values in the array is *potatoes*. You could create a *for* loop in a function that searches for the value in the array, breaks out of the *for* loop when it finds the value, and returns the index number (position in the list) of the item. The code for creating the array would look as follows.

```
grocerylist = new Array();
grocerylist[0] = "apples"
grocerylist[1] = "oranges"
grocerylist[2] = "potatoes"
The function to find an item would look as follows.
function finditem (myitem) {
        for ( var i = 0; i < grocerylist.length; ++i )
{
                var item = grocerylist[i]
                if ( item == myitem ) {
                        break
                }
        }
        return i
}
```

To call the function and find the index number of *potatoes*, you would enter the following.

```
myindexnum = finditem ("potatoes");
```

When this line calls the *finditem* function, it passes the string value potatoes to the function. When the function *finditem* receives the value, it places it inside the local variable *myitem*. The code inside the function sequentially pulls an item out of the array and compares it to the content of *myitem*. If the item from the list matches *myitem* (that is, the item you were looking for is found), the *break* command is initiated and the loop ceases.

Note the last line, *return i*. This makes the function return the value in *i* to the line that originally called it, *myindexnum = finditem ("potatoes")*;. Thus, the value in *i* is inserted into the variable *myindexnum*. The important thing to remember about *break* is that once you have found the item or value you want, *break* keeps the loop from continuing needlessly, just as earlier you saw it being used to prevent execution of unnecessary case statements in a *switch*. Even though the example array contains just three values, arrays can be extremely long. Using the *break* command saves time funneling through array items unnecessarily. Exercise 13-22 explores using *break* with the Array object.

Exercise 13-22: Using break with the Array Object

CD-ROM NOTE: *To see an applied example of the* break *command, examine the file* ch13_22.fla, *located in the* fgai/chapter13/ *folder, installed from the companion CD-ROM.*

continue, like *break*, serves a special purpose when dealing with looping code segments. *continue* basically tells the repeat to skip the statements contained within it for a particular value. Code that contains a *continue* would look something like the following.

```
for ( var i = 10; i <= 50; ++i ) {
    if ( i == 15 ) | | ( i == 25 ) {
    continue
    }
    // loop statements to be executed with i when i
    // does not equal 15 or 25
}
```

In this code, the variable *i* is incremented from 10 to 50, one value at a time. At each increment, except 15 and 25, the associated statements are executed. When *i* is found to be 15 or 25, the loop is told to continue, meaning "skip the statements and repeat the loop without executing them for the current value of *i* (15 or 25)." *continue* basically means continue the next loop with the next counter value.

Variables

The Statements | Variables group in the Actions toolbox list includes four items, two of which you have already examined (*var* and *set variable*). The following sections discuss the delete and *with()* commands.

delete

As you start working with variables and objects (such as arrays), you have to keep in mind, particularly with large arrays, that they take up memory. It is possible to create so many arrays or variables that you bog down the machine or cause the application to lock up due to using too much RAM.

The delete command, however, allows you to free up memory by deleting a specified variable, array, or other object from memory. It is good and common practice to free up memory by deleting variables or arrays you are no longer using.

Generally when you delete an object, Flash will return a Boolean TRUE if the operation was successful. Therefore, if you wanted to see if an object was successfully deleted from memory, such as the *grocerylist* array used earlier, you could create a temporary variable and check its value to see if it was successfully deleted. The following code does this, using a *trace()* action to print the results of the delete command to the Output window.

```
var tempvar = delete grocerylist;

trace tempvar;
```

If you tell Flash to delete an object and it is unsuccessful, a Boolean *FALSE* will be output. You cannot delete predefined objects, properties, or local variables.

with()

You have seen that you can talk to movie clips, buttons, and movies using dot syntax. However, there may be times when you want to send a series of code statements to an object. The *with()* command gives you a shorthand way of doing so.

For example, imagine you wanted to tell a movie clip named *MC1* to do several things. You could write it out longhand using the following.

```
_root.MC1._alpha=50;
_root.MC1.gotoAndPlay("m1");
_root.MC1.stopAllSounds();
```

Another way to write this is to use the *with()* statement, as follows. Exercise 13-23 explores using the *with()* statement.

```
with(MC1) {

    _alpha=50;
    gotoAndPlay("m1");
    stopAllSounds();

}
```

or more concisely:

```
with(MC1) { _alpha=50; gotoAndPlay("m1"); stopAllSounds(); }
```

Exercise 13-23: Using the with() Statement

CD-ROM NOTE: *To see applied examples of use of the* with() *statement, examine the file* ch13_23.fla, *located in the* fgai/chapter13/ *folder, installed from the companion CD-ROM.*

Functions

The next chapter will get down to business, focusing on global functions, which are the workhorses of ActionScript. However, before we conclude this chapter we should finish with a discussion of Miscellaneous, Mathematical, and Conversion functions (found in the Global Functions section of the Actions panel).

Miscellaneous Functions

The Miscellaneous functions in Flash are, in most cases, designed to perform specialized tasks with data in the environment. The following sections describe these functions.

escape() and unescape()

escape() and *unescape()* are specialized functions for encoding and decoding strings to URL-encoded formats. When this is done, all alphanumeric characters are escaped with various hexadecimal sequences. You would use this function in association with the *loadVariables()* action, or when you use *POST* or *GET* to send data in and out of Flash. Exercise 13-24 points to an example file that is helpful when you want to encode or decode text strings to the URL-encoded format. This exercise also demonstrates what is meant by the term *URL-encoded data*.

Exercise 13-24: Using escape() and unescape()

CD-ROM NOTE: *To see applied examples of the* escape() *and* unescape() *functions, examine the file* ch13_24.fla, *located in the* fgai/chapter13/ *folder, installed from the companion CD-ROM.*

eval()

The *eval()* function can be used to define a variable, property, object, or movie clip in code by entering the respective name as the expression. The *eval()* method provides a means of referring to an object's name in code and is critical for creating generic code. In essence, the *eval()* function forces Flash to evaluate the content of the function before executing the rest of the code in which it is contained. This let's you dynamically generate the names of variables, objects, and arrays on-the-fly in code. Although space does not permit further examination of this method, table 13-6 outlines the ways in which *eval()* can be used to force Flash to evaluate data.

Table 3-6: Examples of Use of the eval() *Method*

To Evaluate as a(n)	Example Code (where *i* is 1)	Hard-wired Equivalent Code if *i* = 1
Variable	*eval("card"+i)=4 or eval("animal"+i)="camel"*	*card1=4 or animal1="camel"*
Object	*eval("ball"+i)._x=25 or eval("plate"+1)._alpha=50 or eval("disk"+1)._visible=false*	*ball1._x=25 or plate1._alpha=50 or disk1._visible=false*
Array	*eval("myarray")[i]="blue" or eval("mylist")[i]=24*	*myarray[1]="blue" or mylist[1]=24*

Exercise 13-25 explores the use of the *eval()* function.

Exercise 13-25: Using the eval() Function

CD-ROM NOTE: *To see applied examples of the* eval() *function, examine the file* ch13_25.fla, *located in the* fgai/chapter13/ *folder, installed from the companion CD-ROM.*

getTimer()

The *getTimer* function provides a facility for measuring time that has elapsed within a movie. It is measured in milliseconds and is based on elapsed time since the movie started playing. The *getTimer()* function returns a numerical value. Exercise 13-26 explores the use of the *getTimer()* function.

Exercise 13-26: Using the getTimer() *Function*

CD-ROM NOTE: *To see applied examples of the* getTimer() *function, examine the file* ch13_26.fla, *located in the* fgai/chapter13/ *folder, installed from the companion CD-ROM.*

getVersion()

The *getVersion()* function is simple. It returns the current version of the Flash Player, as well as the platform the player is running on. Note that it will not work when you use Test Movie. However, you can easily see what the output of *getVersion()* would be by using the Debugger. Use Control | Debugger and click on the Play button once the Debugger starts. Then select the *_level0* object and look at the Variables tab. The value in the *$version* variable is what would be returned from the *getVersion()* function.

targetPath()

The *targetPath()* function provides a means of retrieving the target path to an object specified by the argument. Thus, if you are having difficulty determining the target to an object, this function can be used to determine it. For example, placing the following line of code in an object handler will reveal in the Output window the absolute target to the object.

```
trace(targetpath(this));
```

 NOTE: *Discussion and examples of use of* clearInterval() *and* setInterval() *are beyond the scope of this book. However, in short, they allow you to set a time interval in which a specific set of code executes.*

Conversion Functions

In addition to the global functions, Flash provides two sets of utility functions: conversion functions and mathematical functions. The sections that follow examine these functions.

Boolean()

The Boolean function converts the specified value or expression to a Boolean result. The Boolean values of true or false are returned. For example, if you had a variable you created somewhere in your movie, using the Boolean function, you could "ask Flash" if the value contained in it was a Boolean (true, false, 0 or 1). The function would return a true or false based on the variable's content. The following code demonstrates this.

```
var x=5
var myresult=Boolean(x==10)
trace (myresult)
```

The result of the *trace()* output would be false because the variable *x*, set prior to the variable *myresult*, equals 5, not 10.

Number() and String()

The *Number()* and *String()* functions allow you to convert between strings and numbers. Their forms are as follows.

```
Number(x);
String(x);
```

Here, *x* may be a string, Boolean, or expression. *Number()* and *String()* methods are not the same thing as Number and String programming objects. For example, the following items are not equivalent.

- *new String(); and String (mystring);*
- *new Number(); and Number(myval);*

Exercise 13-27 provides examples that use the *Number()* and *String()* functions.

Exercise 13-27: String() *and* Number() *Functions*

CD-ROM NOTE: *To see applied examples of the* Number() *and* String() *functions, examine the file* ch13_27.fla, *located in the* fgai/chapter13/ *folder, installed from the companion CD-ROM.*

Array() and Object()

The *Array()* and *Object()* functions are for advanced ActionScripting and are designed to convert data to either an array or a custom object. Discussion of them is beyond the scope of this book.

Mathematical Functions

The final type of functions in Flash is mathematical functions, described in more detail in the following sections.

isFinite() and isNaN()

The *isFinite()* and *isNaN()* (not a number) functions are designed to help you evaluate the value of variables, properties, or expressions to determine if they are finite numbers *(isFinite())* or if they are numbers at all *(isNaN())*. The functions return Boolean results acknowledging whether or not the variables contain the type of data being investigated.

parseFloat() and parseInt()

parseFloat() and *parseInt()* are functions designed to be used with numerical entries. They can be used to evaluate strings, numbers, or expressions. *parseFloat()* attempts to convert a string to a floating-point number, whereas *parseInt()* attempts to convert the string to an integer. See exercise 13-28 for examples of these methods.

 TIP: parseInt() *can be used to convert data into specific numbering systems. For example,* parseInt(myvar, 16) *would convert the value in* myvar *to a hexadecimal number. Similarly,* parseInt(myvar, 2) *would convert the value in* myvar *to a binary representation.*

Exercise 13-28: Using parseFloat() *and* parseInt()

 CD-ROM NOTE: *To see applied examples of the* parseFloat() *and* parseInt() *functions, examine the file* ch13_28.fla, *located in the* fgai/chapter13/ *folder, installed from the companion CD-ROM.*

∎∎∎ Summary

In this chapter, you have taken your first step into the world of Flash programming. Granted, some of the nitty-gritty things about programming are not all that exciting. However, knowing about the programming features of ActionScript will become more important as you continue down the path of Flash content creation. Chapter 14 dives into the workhorse actions in Flash that are focused on working with movie, button, and movie clip instances.

14

Working with Actions

▪▪▪ Introduction

The last chapter introduced you to ActionScript and the basics of the language. In it, you reviewed many of the "utility" aspects of it as well as the basic facilities for scripting. In this chapter, you will move on and start doing some functional things using the Global Functions designed to manipulate movies, buttons, and movie clips.

Hopefully you noted the page in the last chapter that contained table 13-1. This is referenced in this chapter occasionally, as it helps one keep a holistic view of what is being discussed. This chapter focuses on the use of what table 13-1 listed as Global Functions. These are the elements that allow you to perform the most common operations needed for multimedia content development.

 NOTE: *The actions grouped under the Actions | Printing group are covered in Chapter 15.*

▪▪▪ Objectives

In this chapter you will:

- Examine some miscellaneous tools for working with ActionScript
- Learn about the movie control actions
- Find out how to utilize the browser and network actions
- Discover the usefulness of the movie clip control actions

▪ ▪ ▪ Additional Tools for Scripting

Before continuing with ActionScripting, there are two tools you need to examine. When you start working with more complex creations, these tools can be helpful in sorting out problems as well as in general construction of movies. They are Movie Explorer and the Debugger, discussed in the sections that follow.

Movie Explorer

One of the items in Flash that will become more important as you start dealing with more complex movies is Movie Explorer. Movie Explorer provides a relatively quick way of getting a holistic view of a movie file. With it you can quickly find scenes, symbols, text, scripts, and media elements such as bitmaps, sounds, and video.

As shown in figure 14-1, Movie Explorer shows two major things about the movie. First, it shows all scenes currently in the movie, and second, it shows all symbols that exist in the movie. Thus, it provides a quick way of examining all elements in a movie and how they are arranged in the movie. You can customize which elements are shown in the panel by using the menu or the buttons displayed across the top part of the panel.

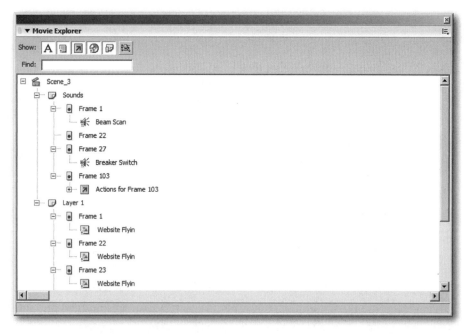

Figure 14-1. Movie Explorer shows the scenes, symbols, text, scripts, and media elements (such as bitmaps, sounds, and video) in a movie file.

In addition to providing an overview, Movie Explorer allows you to quickly perform two very important things. First, you can use Movie Explorer to find, select, and modify almost every aspect of a text element or action. For example, imagine you played back your movie, only to find a typographical error. In the past, you would have had to figure out which frame or symbol the mistake was in, move the playhead to the frame or access the symbol, and then edit the text. With Movie Explorer it is much quicker. Exercise 14-1 shows you how to quickly change text in a movie.

Exercise 14-1: Using Movie Explorer

 CD-ROM NOTE: *To examine how Movie Explorer works, open the file* ch14_01.fla, *located in the* fgai/chapter14/ *folder, installed from the companion CD-ROM.*

To work with Movie Explorer, perform the following steps.

1. Access scene 1 of the movie. Open Movie Explorer by selecting Window | Other Panels | Movie Explorer. Also ensure that all of the optional buttons on the upper part of the panel (Show Text, Show Symbols, and so on) are selected. The Customize button should be the only one that is not pressed in.

2. In Movie Explorer, double click on the Symbol Definition icon to expand it, or single click on the small plus sign to the left of it to expand it.

3. Expand the *CG Text Fly-in* graphic symbol.

4. Expand the *Layer 1* item and then the *frame 1* item.

5. Click on the *Computer Graphics* text item. Use the Text menu to change the font to some other font you have on your machine.

   Note that if you double click on the text in the last step you could also edit the actual text. However, due to the way this movie is set up (small flashes of gold are aligned to each letter in the text), changing the text would require realigning the flasher elements.

   Make sure you pay attention to the status bar of Movie Explorer, as it will provide important information to you, as shown in figure 14-2. For example, when a text element is grouped, you cannot use Movie Explorer to edit it.

6. As an example, try it by accessing the *Purdue Text Fly*-in symbol or the *Website Fly-in* symbol (you will need to switch to scene 2 or 3 in the main timeline). Note that neither of these can be edited because they are in a nested group.

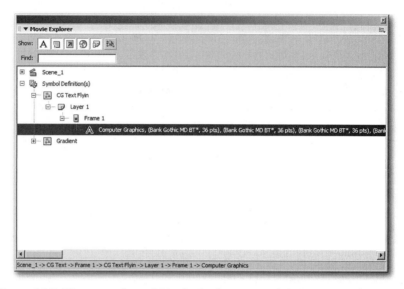

Figure 14-2. The status bar of Movie Explorer reveals important information.

 TIP: *Earlier in the book you read that when actions are attached to buttons, no visual identifier is shown in the time-line or stage. When actions are attached to frames, an a is shown in the frame. You can access text items with Movie Explorer, and you can quickly view and access their actions, finding both their location in the movie structure and the ActionScript associated with them.*

7. Switch back to scene 1 in the main timeline.

8. Expand the *Labels/Actions* item, *frame 40* item, and *actions for frame 40* item, shown in figure 14-3. If you double click on an action in Movie Explorer, the Actions panel will reveal the action so that you can quickly edit it.

The last thing to be done is to use Movie Explorer to find various items. Continue with the following steps.

9. Collapse all expanded items so that all you see are the three scenes and the symbol definitions item.

10. Enter *Purdue University* in the Find field. Note that Movie Explorer automatically reveals the element to you. Thus, you can use the Find field to find almost any item in the movie structure.

In general, there are many things you can do with Movie Explorer. However, most of these things are better understood in the context of particular operations, as explored in the sections that follow.

Figure 14-3. Actions can be revealed and immediately opened into the Actions panel using Movie Explorer.

Debugger

Another tool worth mentioning as you start creating more complex movies is the Debugger window, shown in figure 14-4. With it you can track and watch various aspects of a movie while the movie itself plays in the Flash Player. You can also debug movies while they are playing live from a server.

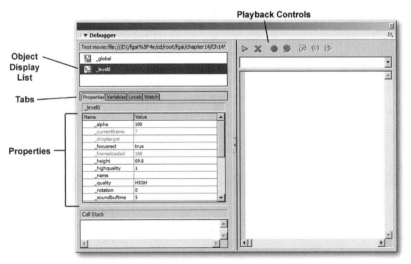

Figure 14-4. The Debugger window can be used to watch all variables or properties in a movie or specific variables or properties.

Debugging in Flash

The Debugger is a highly useful feature of Flash. For those familiar with Director, you will find Flash's Debugger similar. Exercise 14-2 takes you through the basics of using the Debugger in Flash.

Exercise 14-2: Using Flash's Debugger

Flash MX 2004 comes with many samples. Here you will use one of them to explore the basic functionality of the Debugger. The samples are located in the *Flash MX 2004/en/Samples/fla/* folder.

1. Open Flash and access the *paycheck_calculator.fla* file. Once it is open, use Control | Debug movie to start the Flash Player. The Debugger window will be automatically opened.

2. When the Debugger window opens, you must click on the Play button for the movie to begin (see figure 14-4). When debugging, it is helpful to have the movie load but not start playing, so that you can examine the initial state of the file prior to playback.

3. To user the Debugger, select an object in the Display list and then select one of the tabs to find out information. Click on the *_level0* object in the Display list.

4. Click on the Variables tab. It will reveal the variables associated with the object you selected in the Display list, as shown in figure 14-5.

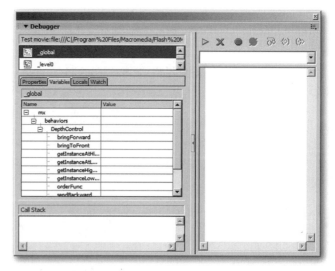

Figure 14-5. The Variables tab shows the variables associated with the object selected in the Display list.

5. Click on some of the buttons in the calculator's interface. Note that the values in the Debugger change as you click on various buttons. This is how you track the state of variables in the movie.

The Debugger is not just for outputting data. You can also modify the value of variables in real time, as the movie plays. Where appropriate you could enter a numerical value in the Value column to see its effect in the movie. Thus, with the Debugger you can view and dynamically change variables.

NOTE: *Just as you can modify variables, you can dynamically enter different values for properties in the Properties tab. Properties that appear grayed out are displayable only. As you will learn a little later, some properties cannot be set; they can only be retrieved.*

One final note about the Debugger is that you can use the Watch tab to specifically view a single variable. It is not uncommon to have many variables in complex movies. Thus, the Variables tab may show more than you want. In the Watch tab, you can enter a specific variable (or property) you want to view.

NOTE: *As you begin learning more about ActionScript, make sure you take the time to look at the other samples in the* Flash MX 2004/en/Samples *folder. There is a lot of good information just waiting to be discovered.*

Using the Debugger in a Web Browser

When you use the Publish or Export Movie commands, a checkbox is provided for you to enable or disable debugging in the browser. If you enable debugging, you can load your Flash movie to a live server and test it directly under the conditions it will be operating. If you perform a "live debug," remember to enable the Debugging Permitted checkbox when you generate the SWF file.

Once you have uploaded your movie to your server for testing, access the page that contains the movie. Once the movie is playing in the web page, right-click on the Flash movie. Select Debugger from the context menu. Because the Debugger option is contained in the Flash context menu in the web page, do not forget to set the *MENU* attribute (for the *< EMBED >* tag) and the *MENU* parameter (for the *< OBJECT >* tag) in your HTML coding. Otherwise, you will not be able to access the *Debugger context* option!

▪ ▪ ▪ Timeline Control Actions

Now that the cursory information is out of the way, let's begin looking at the global functions in Flash. The sections that follow examine each grouping, beginning with the Timeline Control actions (see table 13-1 in Chapter 13). The following sections examine the *gotoAndPlay()*, *gotoAndStop*, *nextFrame()*, *nextScene()*, *play()*, *prevFrame()*, *prevScene()*, *stop()*, and *stopAllSound()* functions.

Most of Flash's basic timeline control actions are relatively straightforward, but some require more discussion than others. The following sections provide an overview of each action, what it does, and the information it needs to work. These sections are followed by some applied examples of the actions.

gotoAndPlay() and gotoAndStop()

The most basic of the actions in Flash is the *goto* action. This action can be used to jump to frames, labels, or named anchors in the current scene or in another scene. An important note is that the *goto* action, when used alone, is limited to jumping to frames and scenes in the current movie.

To set up a *goto* action, select the action from the Actions toolbox list, shown in figure 14-6. The general form for this function is as follows.

```
gotoAndStop(framenumber);
gotoAndStop(frame label);
```

Note that you can also add a second argument, which causes the playhead to jump to a frame number or label in another scene, as follows.

```
gotoAndStop (framenumber, scenename);
gotoAndStop (frame label, scenename);
```

Once you have entered the function name, you must then enter either a number inside the parentheses or a frame label name. Be cautioned about jumping directly to frames in your movies. Instead of jumping to specific frames, it is recommended that you set up your *goto* actions to use labels instead (discussed later). Labels are generally better for setting up looping or "jump-to" locations. If frames are added to a movie, labels shift with the addition of frames. Absolute frame numbers do not. Using absolute frame numbers, such as specifically jumping to frame X, can cause problems if you add frames to the movie late in development. Labels are discussed further in the section "Working with Labels," which highlights this point.

Let's quickly look at some example locations that could be constructed as arguments for the *goto* function. Table 14-1 outlines examples of the

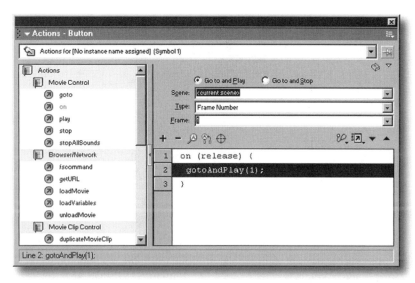

Figure 14-6. When using the goto *action, you have the option to play or stop when the playhead reaches the new frame.*

simple but valid expressions that could be used in the parentheses of the *goto* action.

Table 14-1: Valid Expressions for the goto *Action*

Type	Example	Description
Frame number	24	Jumps to frame 24 in the current movie clip
Frame label	"Start"	Jumps to the frame label *Start* in the current movie clip
Variable	Myvar	Jumps to either frame label or frame, depending on whether the variable contains a string or a number

A final note is in order, regarding the difference between *gotoAndPlay()* and *gotoAndStop()*. The former jumps to the frame defined as an argument continues to play, whereas the latter jumps to the frame (or label) and stops.

play() and stop()

The *play()* and *stop()* actions give you the ability to play or stop the movie at will. There may be times when you want to use these facilities for specific reasons in the main timeline. Additionally, you can direct these actions to specific movie clips within your main movie using the *with()*

command. However, if all you want to do is tell a movie clip to play or stop, you do not really need *tellTarget();* (which is deprecated) or *with();*. Write the ActionScript in the following form.

```
path.instance_name.play();
or
path.instance_name.stop();
```

Always do your best to look for ways to simplify your code. Really the only time you need a *with()* command is when you want to perform multiple actions on an object (instead of having to repetitively write the path and instance every time).

stopAllSounds()

As its name implies, the *stopAllSounds()* action does just that. As with other actions, you can use the *stopAllSounds()* action in combination with a target or the *with()* statement to turn off specific sounds associated with specific objects. The *stopAllSounds()* action is not a permanent setting; that is, it does not permanently turn off the sound in the movie. It stops only the sound or sounds currently playing. Any sounds initiated later in the movie begin playing normally.

∎ ∎ ∎ Applying Movie Control Actions

As discussed in regard to the *goto* action, Flash allows you to create looping segments and jump-to points for navigation using something called labels in the timeline. Rather than jumping to a frame using a *goto* action, you can specifically identify a name for a movie location in the timeline and then jump to it while the movie plays.

 NOTE: *Labels in Flash are akin to markers in Director.*

As previously mentioned, when it comes to jump-to points, labels are better than frames. When frames are deleted from the timeline, the number of frames deleted reduces the frame numbers that follow. Thus, any *goto* actions hard referenced to a frame number get screwed up. This is why labels are preferred. When you use labels, and frames are deleted, the labels shift with the keyframe to which they are attached, meaning that labels are relative points (not absolute points) in the movie.

When using labels and frame actions, it is usually best to create a layer that contains nothing but the labels, actions, and blank keyframes to which they are attached. In this way, you have the choice of deleting frames from other layers without disturbing the defined actions and labels.

Adding Labels to a Movie

In exercise 14-3 you will add a label to a frame in the timeline. When you add a label to a keyframe, a small flag is displayed in the timeline, followed by the label name.

Exercise 14-3: Adding a Label to a Movie

To add a label to a movie, perform the following steps.

1. Start a new Flash file.

2. Create a layer that will contain all of your labels (and frame actions). You might name this layer *Labels/Actions*.

3. Place a keyframe at the location you want to insert a label or comment. Here, you can simply use frame 1 by clicking in it.

4. In the Properties panel, click on the Label field and enter the name for your frame label, as shown in figure 14-7.

5. You could now use the *gotoAndPlay()* or *gotoAndStop()* function to jump to the label you just entered. When you add a label, a small red flag appears in the frame, with the name of the label following. However, if you added the label to frame 1 and it is only one frame long, you will not see the label name. Click in the frame and press the F5 function key to extend the sprite duration. This will reveal the name.

Label Field

Figure 14-7. Frame labels are added by selecting a frame and then using the Properties panel.

Applying play(), stop(), and goto

Creating basic looping segments and establishing navigation are fairly easy. To see how this is done, try exercise 14-4, in which you create a simple movie that has sets of looping frames.

Exercise 14-4: Using Play(), Stop(), and goto

 CD-ROM NOTE: *Begin by opening the file* ch14_04.fla, *located in the* fgai/chapter14/ *folder, installed from the companion CD-ROM.*

Using the CD-ROM file, you will create an underwater scene with sets of fish that swim across the screen. The file already contains several symbols you will use. A completed version of the exercise is also available. Access the file *ch14_04s.fla* in that same folder.

1. Insert a layer above the *Instructions* layer, and name this new layer *Labels/Actions*.

2. Extend all sprites out to frame 20 by moving the playhead to frame 1 and using the F5 function key to extend them. You will create two looping segments: one in frames 1 through 10, and one in frames 11 through 20.

3. Add a keyframe in the *Labels/Actions* layer at frames 10, 11, and 20.

4. Add a label, named *Loop1*, to frame 1 using the Properties panel.

5. In frame 11, add a label named *Loop2*.

 NOTE: *Keep in mind that if you apply an action, label, or other change to the center of a sprite, it is applied to the leftmost keyframe that defines the beginning of that sprite.*

6. Add the following code to frame 10: *gotoAndPlay("loop1");*.

7. Repeat step 6 for frame 20.

8. Save your file.

At this point, if you used Control | Play to play the movie, you would see that the loop is not currently working. You must select Enable Simple Frame Actions from the Control menu. By doing so and using Control | Play, the playhead does loop, even though no animation has been set up yet. Continue with the following steps.

9. To add the items that will loop in these frame segments, create a new layer, named *Fish*, above the *Buttons* layer.

10. Make layer *Fish* the current layer, if it is not already, by clicking in frame 1 on that layer.

11. Use Window | Library to open the current movie's library and drag the symbol named *Fish1* onto the stage.

12. Extend the fish sprite so that its duration extends to frame 10.

13. Insert a keyframe in frame 10 of the *Fish* layer.

14. Set up a motion tween of the fish moving across the stage from right to left. If the animation is too fast, wait until you are done with the exercise to add more frames. If you want, you can play the movie to see the loop.

    Now you will create another fish tween in the second loop area in the timeline, using the *Fish2* symbol. Keep in mind that you cannot drag an item from the library to the stage if there is no keyframe in the frame you are dragging to.

15. Right-click on frame 11 in the *Fish* layer and add a blank keyframe.

 NOTE: *Step 15 is vitally important. If you have no keyframe in frame 11 in the* Fish *layer and you try to drag a symbol from the library, Flash will not let you. The same is true if you try to draw in a frame with no keyframe.*

16. Drag the *Fish2* symbol from the library to frame 11 and create a motion tween similar to the previous one. However, this time make the fish swim from left to right.

17. Save your file.

    With the two sets of looping segments set up, add actions to the buttons so that you can navigate between the looping segments. Instead of *Frame* actions, you will add *Instance* actions to the two buttons that are already created.

18. Begin by adding a keyframe in the *Buttons* layer in frame 11. You do this so that you can add different actions to the button symbol in each set of frames.

19 Move the playhead so that it is located somewhere between frames 1 and 10.

20 Click on the upper red button on the stage and access the Actions panel.

21. In the Actions toolbox list, enter the following code.

```
on (release) {
    gotoAndPlay("Loop2");
}
```

22. Click on the lower red button and add the following code.

```
on (release) {
```

```
        gotoAndStop("Loop2");
    }
```

23. Move the playhead to a location somewhere between frames 11 and 20 so that you can set up the actions in the second section of looping frames.

24. Begin by changing the text for the buttons so that it indicates you will be going to the "1st" loop. To do this, double click on the text and edit it.

25. Assign actions to the buttons. Set the upper button to *gotoAndPlay("Loop1");.* Set the lower button to *gotoAndStop("Loop1");.*

26. Save your file.

Now you will add one more element so that you can highlight a significant thing about movie clips. As mentioned earlier in this book, movie clips are special in that they continue to play even if the main movie timeline stops. Again, this is one way movie clip symbols differ from graphic symbols. Graphic symbols stop when the main movie timeline stops. Movie clips do not. Continue with the following steps to see that movie clips do indeed behave as discussed.

27. Create a new layer, named *Bubbles*, above the *Fish* layer.

28. Use Window | Library to open the current movie's library.

29. Find the movie clip named *Bubbles* and drag it to the *Bubbles* layer. Drag it down and to the left, just off the stage into the work area. You will find that the crosshairs (the registration point for the symbol) are up and to the right of the actual bubble graphics.

30. Place the movie clip's crosshairs in the center of the stage.

31. Save your file.

32. Select Control | Test Movie to view your creation.

 TIP: *If you use Test Movie and the sounds play back poorly, change the audio settings in the File | Publish Settings dialog box. Select the Flash tab and use the Audio Stream | Event Set buttons to set the properties so that the sample rate is higher. The Publish tab affects movies that are tested as well as published. Note that most of the sounds integrated into the sample FLA files of the companion CD-ROM are designed for 22-kHz mono.*

33. As the movie is playing, use the *Go To 2nd Loop (Play)* button and the *Go To 1st Loop (Play)* button to see that the movie

is jumping between the two loop points. In addition, use the *Go To 2nd Loop (Stop)* button and the *Go To 1st Loop (Stop)* button. Do you notice a difference between these two segments and what continues to play?

The *gotoAndStop()* action stops the main timeline of the movie, as it should. However, the *gotoAndStop()* does not stop the *Bubbles* movie clip symbol. Movie clip symbols continue to play even if the main timeline of the movie stops. In essence, movie clip symbols play independently of the timeline. This is why the movie clip continues to play. If the *Bubbles* symbol were a graphic symbol, notwithstanding the fact that the sound would not play, the bubbles would also stop when the main movie timeline stopped.

If you wanted the movie clip to stop when the main timeline stopped, you could add some code to the buttons to tell the *Bubbles* movie clip to stop. You would need to begin this process by giving the *Bubbles* movie clip instance an instance name in the Properties panel (so that you could talk to it). Then you could stop it by using *Bubbles.stop();* or *with(Bubbles) { stop(); }.* These code snippets assume that the instance name of the object is *Bubbles*, but the key is realizing that to talk to the object on the stage (that is, to target it) it must have an instance name.

▪▪▪ Browser/Network Actions

Now that you have examined the basic timeline control actions, let's turn our attention to the browser and network actions. This set of actions is designed to work with external data in the form of URLs, other Flash movies, and data from a variety of sources.

getURL()

The *getURL()* action is probably one of the most frequently used actions. With it, you can load a document specified at a URL into the current browser window that contains the Flash movie. The general form for the *getURL()* function is as follows.

```
getURL(path, target, method);
```

The path argument specified in a *getURL()* can be a relative or absolute URL, as well as a URL in the form of a JavaScript statement or an e-mail statement. An absolute URL is one that contains the entire path and file name of the document to be loaded, such as the following.

```
http://www.tech.purdue.edu/cg/facstaff/jlmohler/
```

Relative URLs, on the other hand, are statements that define a new document based on the placement of the current document on a web server. Most often, specifying relative URLs provides a shorthand method of defining a new document to be loaded. Relative statements entered as the path can include various things, as shown in table 14-2.

Table 14-2: Relative URL Entries for the getURL() *Action*

URL	Meaning
myfile.html	That *myfile.html* resides in the same directory or folder that contains the currently loaded document.
../myfile.html	That *myfile.html* resides in the parent folder of the folder in which the currently loaded document resides. In other words, *myfile.html* is one step backward in the directory structure.
../../myfile.html	That *myfile.html* resides two steps back in the directory structure.
/mystuff/myfile.html	That *myfile.html* resides in a folder named *mystuff,* which is set up as a relative directory on the server.

In addition to using HTTP URLs, you may also specify an e-mail address. This allows the Flash movie to open the user's default mail program with a new message to the location specified. To create a mail link in Flash, assign the path to *mailto:* followed by an e-mail address. For example, if an e-mail to *jlmohler@purdue.edu* is desired, the URL would be *mailto:jlmohler@purdue.edu.*

As mentioned, you can also use the URL field for the insertion of JavaScript commands also. This is really a "back door" technique. Other actions, such as the *fscommand()* action, are more suited to getting Flash to interact with JavaScript. Nonetheless, by entering *javascript:* in the URL field, you can call a JavaScript function using *getURL()*. For example, imagine that the following JavaScript function, which opens a simple dialog box, exists in the HTML page.

```
. . .
<SCRIPT>
<!-
function doalert() {
   window.alert('This is an alert.')
}
//->
</SCRIPT>
. . .
```

This function could be called from the Flash *getURL()* action using the following as the URL.

```
javascript:doalert()
```

As previously mentioned, using a JavaScript command in the *getURL()* action is not a preferred method of calling JavaScript functions, even though many sites use it. An *fscommand()* would be the preferred method. The reason is that the JavaScript command technique (calling a function in a URL) does not work in some older browsers, such as Internet Explorer 3.X. Yet, it does work quite well in most 4.0 versions (or higher) of Netscape and Internet Explorer.

 NOTE: *If you embed JavaScript functions in URLs, make sure you test extensively in multiple browsers and versions.*

The path argument in the *getURL()* function is an example of where you might want to use Flash's expression capabilities. Using it, you could create an expression that constructs the URL to be used from some entered text data and the string value in a variable, such as the following.

```
getURL(http://www.tech.purdue.edu/cg/facstaff/ + facmem + "/");
```

In this manner, you could construct URLs on-the-fly based on the values of variables that exist within a movie. The expression capability adds unique potential to many of the actions, as you will continue to see.

Exercise 14-5: Examples of the getURL() action

 CD-ROM NOTE: *To see an example of these four types of getURL(), open the HTML file ch14_05.html, located in the fgai/chapter14/ folder, installed from the companion CD-ROM.*

You may want to examine the FLA file to see the actions and how they are assigned to the buttons. The *getURL()* actions will only work in the web page, however.

 NOTE: *To be able to test movies that use the getURL() action, you must do so within the browser. The Test Movie facility within Flash will not allow you to see if your links to the Web, mail programs, and JavaScript work. To test relative URLs, the file must also be in the proper folder location to adequately test actions.*

In addition to the path argument, the *getURL()* function allows you to use HTML window naming (the target argument). This argument is used for targeting specific windows, usually when HTML frames are used. For example, if you had a frames page that had a window named Content, you could specifically target the Content window as the window to load the URL into using code such as the following.

```
getURL("http://www.excite.com", "_blank");
```

In addition, Flash provides the following four default HTML target names.

- _self_ opens the URL in the current window or frame.

- _blank_ opens the URL in a new browser window in front of the currently open window.

- _parent_ opens the URL in the parent of the current window. For example, in a frames document that contains two frames, the main document is the parent of both subframes.

- _top_ opens the URL in the topmost document. This is useful in situations in which a frames document has many subframes or has nested frames.

 NOTE: _As with the path argument, expressions could also be used to construct targets based on variables._

 ### _Exercise 14-6: Using the_ getURL() _Target Specifications_

CD-ROM NOTE: _To see a simple example of using the target specification within the_ getURL() _action, open the HTML file_ ch14_06.html, _located in the_ fgai/chapter14/ ch14_06/ _folder, installed from the companion CD-ROM._

The CD-ROM file shows an example of how to target named frame windows, as well as how to use the four default target specifications.

The final portion of the _getURL()_ function is yet another important feature. The method argument provides added flexibility for your movies by allowing you to pass variables from Flash (on the user's end) to the web server delivering the pages. This gives you the capability to very easily create form pages in Flash that pass their values to another technology on the server, such as CGI, ASP, and so forth.

By default, variables that exist in your movie are not passed to the subsequent pages that are loaded. In such cases, the method argument of _getURL_ is omitted. However, when you choose to send the data in variables, you can use standard _POST_ and _GET_ methods to submit data from Flash to a server. When the server receives the information, it could use those values in a CGI script, a Java applet, an Active Server Page, or in myriad other technologies.

For example, imagine you created an editable text field into which the user submitted their name. The user's name could then be placed into a variable within Flash. You could use the _POST_ or _GET_ option for the method argument to submit the user's name and other data to the server.

The server could then use the user's name in the page, such as customizing the address for that particular name.

Fundamentally, the *POST* and *GET* methods are both means of transferring data from a web page (usually from a form) to a web server. Often technologies such as CGI scripts are used to interpret the data being sent from the browser. However, other server-side technologies, such as Microsoft Active Server Pages (ASP), may also intercept data being sent using a *POST* or *GET*, as you will see in material to follow.

The *POST* and *GET* methods encode data as a set of name and value pairs. However, they do it a little bit differently, and the receiving technology normally has to use different techniques to extract the data. The *GET* method encodes the data and appends it to the URL being accessed. A URL that is passing data with the *GET* method looks something like the following.

```
http://www.tech.purdue.edu/index.asp?fname=john&lname=smith
```

Here, the variables *fname* and *lname* are sent to the *index.asp* page residing on the server. The page could use the content of those variables in a variety of ways. The difference between the *GET* and *POST* methods is not the way the data is encoded but how the data is delivered behind the scenes. The *GET* method is sent as a query string (as previously discussed). The *POST* method is sent as part of the HTTP request, as if it were coming from a form. For example, imagine you had a field named *myname* in a Flash movie. If you used the *GET* method to send the data from the form to an ASP, you would use code such as the following.

```
<% Response.Write Request.Query_String("myname") %>
```

This code would write the data from the Flash field to an HTML page. Thus, the *GET* method uses the ASP Request object to retrieve and utilize the data. Note that the *Write()* method of the Response object simply tells ASP to write the data. If you used the *POST* method to send the data, you would use code such as the following to write the data from the field to an HTML page. Exercise 14-7 explores the use of the *GET* and *POST* methods.

```
<% Response.Write Request.Form("myname") %>
```

Exercise 14-7: Using GET and POST

CD-ROM NOTE: *To see examples of use of the* GET *and* POST *methods, open* ch14_07a.html *for an example of the* GET *method and* ch14_07b.html *for an example of the* POST *method. The files are in the* fgai/chapter14/ ch14_07/ *directory, installed from the companion CD-ROM.*

The important thing is to look at the *getURL()* attached to the Send It button. For the examples cited in the previous CD-ROM Note, two ASP pages (copies of them are in the *chapter14 /ch14_07/* directory) have been set up that will receive the data from you and display it in the browser. However, you must be connected to the Internet for this example to work, as ASP is a server-side technology. Thus, the ASP pages must be running on a server that supports ASP for them to work. If you have a server that supports ASP, you could place the ASP files from the CD-ROM on your server and point the *getURL()* actions in the example files to the location on your server.

An important thing to remember concerning the two techniques is that the *GET* method is limited in the characters it can pass. For example, space characters are replaced with plus (+) signs, and other restricted characters are replaced with percentages (%). Thus, to use the passed data, the receiving technology (CGI, ASP, and so on) must interpret the data if spaces or other invalid characters have to be passed. For converting data inside Flash to and from URL encoding, use the *escape()* and *unescape()* functions, discussed in Chapter 13.

If you wish to use CGI or other technologies with Flash, you simply need to make sure which method (*POST* or *GET*) is required. Some technologies can use either and, indeed, *POST* is the most flexible of the two because it does not have character limitations and does not show the data it is passing in the URL, which often looks pretty messy.

loadMovie() and unloadMovie()

The *loadMovie()* function allows you to load one movie into another movie. Similar to the layering capability of Cascading Style Sheets (CSS) and Dynamic HTML (DHTML), as well as the "movie in a window" capability of Director, the *loadMovie()* action can display several movies at once, each of which is layered over another and is identified by a level number.

 NOTE: *The* loadMovie() *and* unloadMovie() *actions work in movies in web pages, as well as in those played within the Flash Player.*

When you use the *loadMovie()* method, the movie doing the loading defines the stage size, background color, and frame rate of all movies. The primary movie is identified as *_level0* in the hierarchy of movies. Subsequent movies loaded by the primary movie using the *loadMovie()* action can be placed on specific layers, such as *_level1*, *_level2*, and so on.

As it relates to layering, _level0 is the background level, with subsequent level numbers proceeding forward.

 NOTE: *If you use the* loadMovie() *and* unloadMovie() *actions, you should design all movies with the same stage size, background color, and frame rate. The primary movie will override settings in movies lower in the hierarchy anyway.*

If you use multilevel movies, the first instance of the *loadMovie()* action will likely exist in a frame action of the primary movie. Subsequent use of the *loadMovie()* action may be used in either object or frame actions. Loading a movie into a level that already has a movie in it replaces the original movie. For example, if _level3 has a movie named *zapper* loaded into it, loading a movie named *zapper2* into _level3 replaces the original movie *zapper*.

After selecting the *loadMovie()* action, you are required to supply a URL argument for the movie, a location for the loaded movie, and parameters for how existing variables are to be passed to the new movie. Thus, *loadMovie()* takes the following general form.

```
loadMovie(url, level, method);
```

Similar to the *getURL()* action, the entered URL may be a relative or absolute. However, the entered URL must be representative of the file structure that exists during authoring and that will exist during playback. You may find it easier to test with all of your movies in the same directory, and then modify the URL entries for placement on a server.

 NOTE: *If you use the* loadMovie() *action, make sure you keep a note of the level on which the movies are loaded. The* unloadMovie() *action allows you to specify only which level to unload, not which movie to unload.*

As with other actions, you can use expressions for the URL and for the level or method arguments. Again, the ability to specify expressions in these allows you to construct their values based on variables and other data that exist at runtime. This allows tremendous flexibility in your movies during playback.

Setting up a basic load and unload scenario in Flash is relatively easy, as long as you know the rules. Two of the first questions that should come to mind are "How are the stages of the two movies aligned?" and "What is, and where is, the registration point?"

Stage Attributes and Frame Rate

In general, the main movie, which loads the other movies, is paramount when it comes to several of the settings at playback. The main movie defines the stage size, background color, and frame rate that will be used for all movies. Therefore, when the movies you load have different stage sizes, background colors, or frame rates, the main movie will override these settings.

Concerning registration, the upper left-hand corner becomes the registration point of all movies, even if they are not all the same size. If a movie with a smaller stage size is loaded into a movie with a larger stage size, the upper left-hand corner point in both movies serves as the registration point, and the smaller movie will fit within the larger. If the reverse is true (that is, a larger movie loaded into a smaller movie), the loaded movie will be cropped to the size of the smaller. Thus, it is easiest to design all movies with the same stage size, to avoid registration problems. To further examine how multilevel movies work, see exercise 14-8.

Exercise 14-8: Using loadmovie() *and* unloadmovie()

CD-ROM NOTE: *To examine how multilevel movies work, open the file* ch14_08.fla *located in the* fgai/chapter14/ch14_8/ *folder, installed from the companion CD-ROM.*

The companion files that will be loaded into *ch14_08.fla* are named *ch14_08_1.fla* and *ch14_08_2.fla*. It is the SWF versions of these files that are loaded. Examine the process of loading and unloading movies a little closer by performing the following steps.

1. Begin by testing the movie to see how it works. Use the Control | Test Movie menu option.

   As with testing movie clips, the *loadMovie()* and *unloadMovie()* actions can only be tested using Control | Test Movie. Additionally, the movies to be loaded must be SWF files created using the Export Movie or Publish menu options. You cannot load an FLA file.

2. Use the Load Movie 1 and Load Movie 2 buttons to load the "child" movies into the current movie.

3. Use the Unload Movie 1 and Unload Movie 2 buttons to unload the movies.

4. Close the Flash Player window to examine other important things you can do with loaded movies.

5. Use Modify | Document to view the main movie's properties. The main movie's frame rate, stage size, and stage background color define the settings that will be used throughout the load and unload process. Mentally note these settings or

write them down. Then, close the Document Properties dialog box.

6. Use File | Open to open the file *ch14_08_1.fla.*

7. Once this file is open, note that the background is black, even though when it was loaded you saw an animation in the main movie. As you read earlier, the background color established in the "child" movie does not apply when the child movie is loaded using the *loadMovie()* action. The main movie's settings override the child movie's setting.

8. Close *ch14_08_1.fla* so that you can examine the *loadMovie()* functions in the main movie.

9. In the file *ch14_08.fla*, click on the button next to the *Load Movie 1* text in the upper part of the small controller and view the Actions panel.

10. In the Actions panel, note how the movie is referenced (see figure 14-11). The *loadMovie()* action works only on SWF files. Thus, when trying to test and "connect" the movies, you must generate SWF files of the movies you want to load. The *loadMovie()* action will have no effect on an FLA (native) Flash file.

When developing and testing a set of movies using the *loadMovie()* and *unloadMovie()* actions, it is best to store all files in a single directory. As long as the parent and child movies reside in the same directory on the web server, you do not have to worry about changing the URL setting to a lengthy absolute HTTP address (such as *www.purdue.edu/cg/facstaff/jlmohler/ch14_08_1. swf*). You can simply leave it as a relative directory.

If the movies will reside in different directories and you want to specify relative directories rather than repetitive HTTP addresses, use ../ to step back a directory and */foldername* to specify a folder deeper in the structure, similar to the techniques used in a DOS or UNIX command line interface.

11. Before leaving the *loadMovie()* action, note the Level field. You can load a movie into any level and you can unload any level. Therefore, movies can be nonlinearly loaded; that is, loaded in any order, using the *loadMovie()* action.

12. Before leaving this example, take a look at the *unloadMovie()* action. With the Actions panel open, click on the button next to the *Unload Movie 1* text. Note that you can only unload movies based on their level number, because in Flash only one movie can be loaded per level.

NOTE: *If you load a movie to a layer that already has a movie on it, the newly loaded movie will replace the previous movie on that layer.*

In both the *loadMovie()* and *unloadMovie()* function you will notice that you can pass variable values from one movie to another if you include a method argument. As discussed earlier with the *getURL()* action, variables and their data can be sent using either *POST* or *GET* methods, with *POST* being the preferred method.

Levels Revisited

Because you cannot load multiple movies on a single layer, you must keep track of which movie is where in the movie hierarchy. Assigning a new movie to a layer that already has something on it may cause you problems (that is, the loaded movie will replace the existing one), particularly where complex structures are concerned. If you are going to use loaded movies in your site, you may want to jot down the hierarchical structure and the level numbers of the movies to help you with designing and testing.

Designing Movies

Due to the dependency of loaded movies on the parent or main movie, designing loaded movie structures will be easier if you begin by designing the main movie. Once the main movie is created, use it as a template for all other movies to be loaded. This will keep you from designing child movies with erroneous stage sizes. It will also enable you to put together the child movies with some knowledge of where the objects in the main movie are located. Use the following suggestions as a guide for creating the parent and child movies.

- Lay out and design the elements that will appear in the main movie.

- Make a copy of the main movie to use as a template for all other movies.

- If you have a complex layout, it may be useful to convert the main movie, in its entirety (as well as subsequent child movies), to a movie clip symbol for insertion as you are working on the design.

If you have a timeline that has many layers and many frames you want to make into a symbol, you cannot simply select everything on the stage and press the F8 function key to convert it to a symbol. Rather, select all frames (in all layers) in the main movie timeline by turning on Edit Multiple Frames. Then, right-click in the frames in the timeline and use Copy Frames from the context menu. Use Insert | New Symbol to create the symbol, and select Movie Clip as the behavior. Right-click in the first keyframe in the newly created symbol and select Paste Frames. All layers and frames will be pasted into the new symbol.

Controlling Loaded Movies

The ability to load and unload child movies into a parent movie is a very useful feature. However, if you use the *with()* command, there is more you can do. For instance, you can control either the main movie timeline or the child movie timeline. This section examines how to use *with()* in several ways. Understanding the hierarchy of elements is paramount to getting *with()* to work.

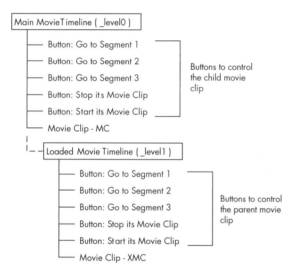

Hierarchy Revisited

The example in exercise 14-9 takes a look at a main movie that loads a child movie. Both the main movie and the child movie have three sets of looping frame segments. Each also has buttons (to control the other), as well as a basic movie clip symbol. The hierarchical structure for the movie scenario is shown in figure 14-8. The visual representation is shown in figure 14-9.

Figure 14-8. Hierarchical structure of the sample movie.

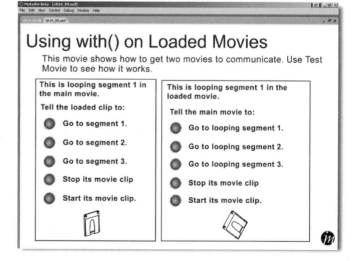

Figure 14-9. Visual representation of the sample movie.

Setting Up Tell Targets

In exercise 14-9, the buttons within the main movie timeline control the child movie, as well as its nested movie clip. The buttons within the child movie will, conversely, control the main movie timeline and its nested movie clip.

Exercise 14-9: Using with() on Loaded Movies

CD-ROM NOTE: *To examine how multilevel movies work, open the file* ch14_09.fla, *located in the* fgai/chapter14/ch14_09/ *folder, installed from the companion CD-ROM. The file loaded into it is named* ch14_09_1.fla.

Examine this example by performing the following steps.

1. Use Test Movie to see how the movies work. Close the Flash Player to return to the Flash application when you are done.

2. One of the first things you should have noticed in the main movie timeline is the action assigned to frame 1. This action loads the child movie into the main movie. If you click on that frame and access the Actions panel, you will see the following code.

   ```
   loadMovieNum("ch14_09_1.swf", 1);
   ```

   Note that the child movie is loaded into *level1*.

   Note in the previous code that the URL in the *loadMovie()* function is assigned to an SWF file. The most frequent error when learning to use the *loadMovie()* action is in trying to load an FLA file. Loaded files must be web-ready SWF files.

3. The main movie timeline is divided into three looping segments, which are set up using labels and *goto* frame actions. In this example, the child movie (*ch14_09_1.fla*) is set up in a similar way. The first three buttons in the main movie and in the child movie control which set of frames is playing in the other movie. Examine the *with()* associated with the Go to Segment 1 button. Click on the buttons and look in the Actions panel to do so.

4. Open the file *ch14_09_1.fla*. In it, access the actions attached to the button next to the *Go to looping segment 1* text. The *goto* action goes to label *Loop1*, which is the label assigned to the first set of looping frames in the main movie.

5. The buttons associated with the Start and Stop buttons control the movie clip in either of the two movies. The child's

buttons control the main movie's clip. The main movie's buttons control the child's movie clip. As you learned in Chapter 13, this process requires that you name the instance of the movie clip. Look at the instance name of the child's movie clip. Minimize the Actions panel if it is open. Click on the movie clip at the bottom (the CD-ROM casing) and view the Properties panel.

6. In the Properties panel, note that the Instance Name field is set to *LoadedMC*. Select the *ch14_09.fla* tab above the timeline to switch back to the main movie (assuming both files are open).

7. In the main movie, click on the button next to the *Stop its movie clip* text and view the Actions panel. Examine the target associated with the *with()* statement, as follows.

```
_level1.LoadedMC
```

To control the movie clip in the child (from the parent), you add the name of the instance to the end of *_level1*, separated by a period for dot syntax. This allows you to send commands from the parent to the child. It also allows you to send commands from the child to the parent.

8. To finish reviewing these movies, examine the instance name of the main movie's clip and compare it to the target used in the child movie.

Loading Movies into Movie Clips

As you have been working with *with()* in this chapter, most of your time has been spent on examining movies loaded into levels. However, within Flash you can also load movies into movie clips, which is particularly useful for printing movies. It is also helpful when you want the entirety of a movie loaded into a specific area of another movie. In this scenario, you are not constrained to having the origin at the upper left-hand corner in all movies.

Thus, the biggest difference between loading a movie into a level, as opposed to a movie clip, concerns registration of the movies. As previously stated, when you load movies into levels, their upper left-hand corner aligns all movies, which is the origin for the environment. Similarly, the primary movie (*_level0*) is the determiner of stage size, stage color, and frame rate.

When you load a movie into a movie clip, the first thing you will note is that the loaded movie will be imported at the size, location, and orientation of the originating movie clip, rather than that of the main movie.

Thus, if a movie clip is small, the loaded movie's stage will be sized to the area already being used for the movie clip and will therefore also be small. The same is true of issues concerning location and orientation.

As you have seen throughout this book, the registration point of a movie clip usually appears in the center of the work area when you begin creating a new movie clip symbol. Similarly, when you convert items on the stage to a movie clip, the registration point defaults to the center of the selected items. Thus, the upper left-hand corner of the loaded movie's stage will be aligned with the movie clip's registration point, wherever it is. Therefore, you may need to design your movie clip so that its content is down and to the right of the registration crosshairs. Exercise 14-10 explores loading a movie into a movie clip.

Exercise 14-10: Loading a Movie into a Movie Clip

CD-ROM NOTE: *To see an example of loading movies into a movie clip, open the file* ch14_10.fla, *located in the* fgai/chapter14/ch14_10/ *folder, installed from the companion CD-ROM. The files* ch14_10_1.fla *and* ch14_10_2.fla *are SWF versions of the movies, loaded into the movie clip.*

loadVariables() and loadVariablesNum()

The *loadVariables()*; method allows you to load data from a text file, or from text generated by a technology such as PHP, ASP, or CGI. The data being imported must be URL encoded. For example, recall the *getURL()* example earlier that used *GET* to pass data to ASP. URL-encoded data looks much like the end of a *GET*, where data is presented in name and value pairs, separated by ampersands (&).

Recall that some characters are replaced by other entities when using *GET*. For example, spaces are replaced with plus signs (+). Because humans do not commonly write text in a "URL-encoded" method, ActionScript provides two actions: one to encode to URL-encoded data (*escape()*), and one to decode URL-encoded data (*unescape()*). These commands were used to write the URL-encoded entries used in exercise 14-11, which explores using the *loadVariables()* method.

Exercise 14-11: Using the loadVariables() Method

CD-ROM NOTE: *To see an applied example of how to load data from an external text file, examine the file* ch14_11.fla, *located in the* fgai/chapter14/ch14_11/ *folder, installed from the companion CD-ROM. The text file* *loaded* (input.txt) *is also included in the* fgai/chapter14/ *folder.*

In exercise 14-11, the file loads a static text file. However that you can send data to a technology (such as ASP or CGI), have it do something to the values, and return the results just by using a single *loadVariables()* action. See exercise 14-12 for an example.

Exercise 14-12: Sending and Receiving Data

CD-ROM NOTE: *To see an applied example of how to send data to an external technology, have it process the data, and send something back, examine the file* ch14_12.fla, *located in the* fgai/chapter14/ch14_12/ *folder, installed from the companion CD-ROM. The ASP files for the exercise are also included in that directory. Note that you have to connect to the Web to make the example work.*

---

fscommand()

As mentioned previously, using the *getURL()* action as a means of calling a JavaScript function (or using any other web technology) is not the preferred method. In general, you can use the *fscommand()* action to send a message to whatever program is hosting or running the Flash Player. Thus, the *fscommand()* action is the action you should use when you want to call a JavaScript or VBScript function from Flash. *fscommand()* is the code equivalent of "FlashScript Command," and it can actually be used to communicate to several things, including the Flash Player.

The fscommand() Method Versus Flash Player Methods

Usually when you start talking about *fscommand()* actions in Flash, many people misunderstand what they are and what they are used for. Before moving into some examples, you need to understand the distinction between the *fscommand()* method (or action) and the Flash Player methods that can be used outside Flash.

The *fscommand()* method in Flash is used to send data out of Flash to JavaScript or other technologies. In essence, the *fscommand()* method causes a single JavaScript function to execute when the *fscommand()* is encountered in the Flash movie. The Flash Player knows that it should respond to an *fscommand()* from a Flash movie because it has an event handler named *fscommand()*. Remember that event handlers are things that happen in an environment that a particular object knows it should respond to.

Flash Player methods, on the other hand, are used in JavaScript to control, as well as send data into, a Flash movie. As you learned previously, a method is a predefined thing an object can do in the environment or to itself. The Flash Player, which in the browser is a plug-in or ActiveX component, is an object and indeed it has many methods you can use to manipulate any Flash movies in the current web page.

Similarly, the Flash Player has events, one of which is the *fscommand()* event, which allows it to respond to the *fscommand()* method called within Flash (as well as other things that may happen in the browser environment). In short, the *fscommand()* method is for communication from Flash to JavaScript. Flash Player methods are for communication from JavaScript to Flash.

The fscommand() Method in Flash

Let's focus on the *fscommand()* method for a moment. When you have a Flash movie embedded in a web page, you can define a JavaScript function in the HTML document that is directly related to the Flash movie. The JavaScript function associated with the Flash movie will be called anytime an *fscommand()* is encountered in the Flash file. Thus, for each Flash movie in a web page, you can have one, and only one, function defined in JavaScript for it. A single Flash movie cannot have two associated JavaScript functions.

"Then how do you set up JavaScript code that will do different things for (or within) the same movie?" you might ask. For example, if a Flash movie has two different buttons and you want each to do something different, how do you write the code, in that you can only have one JavaScript function per embedded Flash movie?

The answer is that the *fscommand()* method has two values that can be sent from Flash to the associated JavaScript function. One value is contained in a variable named *command,* and the other is in a variable named *arguments* (usually abbreviated *args*), as shown in the following code.

```
fscommand(command, args);
```

Whether or not these arguments are defined, when the *fscommand()* method is encountered in the movie, the associated JavaScript function in the web page will execute the scripting contained within it. Keep in mind that it knows to do so because the Flash Player (plug-in or ActiveX component) has an event handler set up to handle the *fscommand()* call from the Flash movie. As long as everything is named correctly, the Flash Player will automatically execute a function associated with a Flash movie. Properly naming the JavaScript function and the Flash movie makes the entire scenario work.

If you want a single function to do different things for different items within the JavaScript function associated with it, you use the *command* and *args* variables to send data out of Flash. Then, in the JavaScript function, you write an *if* statement whose condition is based on either the command or *args* variable (or combinations thereof). Note that the *command* variable is the one normally used, but either variable does the same thing. Let's dissect a quick example to drive this point home.

Working with the fscommand() Method

To better understand the *fscommand()* method, in exercise 14-13 you will examine a button used to open a pop-up window with JavaScript.

Exercise 14-13: Using the fscommand() Method

CD-ROM NOTE: *Open the file* ch14_13.fla, *located in the* fgai/chapter14/ch14_13/ *folder, installed from the companion CD-ROM. To see the button work in the web page, open the file* index.html *(located in the* fgai/chapter14/ ch14_13/ *folder) into a browser.*

To work with the *fscommand()* method, perform the following steps.

1. Click on the button on the stage and view the Actions panel. As you examine the *fscommand()* method, note that the *command* and *args* variables are typically passed to the receiving JavaScript function. In this simple example, these variables are not being passed.

   Generally, the *command* and *args* arguments are used to simply pass name and value pairs to JavaScript. However, if you just want the JavaScript function to execute (as in this example), no values are needed in the *command* and *args* variables. When values are present, JavaScript can do something intelligent with the variables, such as using a conditional statement to interpret the received values and responding accordingly.

   Once an *fscommand()* action is set up in Flash, you are ready to implement it within the web page. When you set up your JavaScript code, you must make sure the *Class ID* and *Embed Name* attributes are similar so that you can write one function for the object.

2. Open the file *index.html,* located in the *fgai/chapter14/ch14-13/* folder. Load this into a text editor such as Notepad or Simpletext.

3. In the HTML file, note that the ID attribute of the *<OBJECT>* tag and the Name attribute of the *<EMBED>* tag match. If they do not match, problems will arise later. Verify that these match.

4. Also note how the object and the embedded name are used in the JavaScript function: *button_DoFSCommand.* Whatever the Flash movie's name is, it needs to precede *_DoFSCommand.* Verify that this is the case.

5. Finally, note in the VBScript code section that the name is used two more times. In all of these instances, the name of the Flash movie, followed by *_FSCommand*, must be written exactly as shown. Verify that this is the case.

6. In the *<EMBED>* tag, note the attributes *LIVECONNECT = "TRUE"* and *MAYSCRIPT = "MAYSCRIPT".* In Netscape, *swLiveConnect* is used to allow the Flash Player plug-in to talk to the Java Interpreter. You must include these two attributes in the *<EMBED>* tag for Netscape to be able to utilize the Flash Player methods and JavaScript. If you forget them, Netscape will just sit there and will not respond to any *fscommand()* methods in the Flash movie. Note that these attributes are not needed in the *<OBJECT>* tag section. Verify that these two attributes are present.

Specific Commands for the Stand-alone Player

Although most of the movies you develop in Flash may be for the Web, you can use the *fscommand()* method to send specific commands to the stand-alone Flash Player. In Chapter 12, you examined how you could play an SWF file in the Player, as well as create a projector file of your movie. These commands are for movies you intend to distribute in either of these two ways. Descriptions of the specific options follow. For example, if you want to set a Flash movie so that it plays full screen in the Flash Player, you add the following frame script.

```
fscommand("fullscreen", true);
```

Thus, the specific *fscommand* options for the Flash Player are as follows.

- *fullscreen:* A binary variable that determines if the movie scales to fit the screen when the user tries to maximize the movie (by double clicking on the title bar or using the window's Maximize button).

- *allowscale:* Determines if the user is permitted to scale the movie during playback (enables or disables the ability to click-drag the borders of the Flash Player window). It is a binary variable.

- *showmenu:* Defines whether or not the Flash Player menu is displayed. It is a binary variable.

- *trapallkeys:* A binary variable that controls whether or not the Flash Player locks all keyboard strokes.

- *exec:* Opens external files and runs external programs. The Args field must contain a path to an application or program file. Blank spaces in the path must be represented with a tab character.

- *quit:* Unloads the movie and causes the Flash Player to close.

In exercise 14-14 you will practice using the stand-alone player.

Exercise 14-14: Using fscommand() *in the Flash Player*

 CD-ROM NOTE: *Open the file* ch14_14.fla, *located in the* fgai/ chapter14/ *folder, installed from the companion CD-ROM.*

Use the file to follow along with the exercise. To see a finished example of the exercise, open the file *ch14_14s.fla.*

1. When you open the file *ch14_14.fla,* you will note that the movie has elements that extend beyond the stage. Use Test Movie to see what the movie does.

    When you test the movie, note that you can see all elements in the movie, even those that extend beyond the stage. The fact that Flash movies can scale is a nice feature; that is, most of the time. When you are trying to render special effects, this aspect can be negative. However, the problem can be easily remedied with an *fscommand()* method.

2. Close the Player, click in frame 1, and access the Actions panel.

3. In the Actions panel, double click on the *fscommand()* method from the Actions group in the Actions toolbox list to add it to the frame.

4. Using the keyboard, modify the function such that it reads as follows.

    ```
    fscommand("allowscale", false);
    ```

5. Use Test Movie to see the results. When you do, you will see little change from the previous test. The special *fscommand()* settings do not work when you use Test Movie in Flash.

6. Close the Player and minimize the Flash application.

7. Locate the SWF file associated with the Flash file you just tested and open it into the Flash Player. You should be able to double click on the SWF file, which should open the external Flash Player.

8. In the Flash Player, the size of the stage area is now constrained and the movie plays without the work area showing. Try to scale it by click-dragging the borders of the Flash Player window.

9. Experiment with the other commands for the Flash Player settings.

Flash Player Methods

The Flash plug-in (or ActiveX component) is an object in the browser environment you can use to talk to Flash movies. Being an object, it has methods, events, and properties available to it. In reality, the Flash Player makes only methods and events accessible to the developer. In the previous sections, the Flash Player was responding to *fscommand()* events sent from the Flash movie.

Let's look at the methods associated with the Flash Player, as well as two other events that exist for the Player. As previously stated, Flash Player methods are used to talk from some technology, usually JavaScript, to a Flash movie. The Flash Player methods include two major groupings: standard methods and *tellTarget* methods.

Standard Methods

The standard methods for the Flash Player are generally associated with the main movie timeline or main movie environment. The following are the standard Flash Player methods.

*   *GetVariable("variablename"):* Retrieves the value in the variable specified by the string *variablename*. For example, *GetVariable("myval")* would return the value in the variable *myval*, which would be owned by the main movie timeline.

*   *GoToFrame(framenumber):* Sends the movie to a specific frame. Note that *framenumber* must be an integer. For example, *GoToFrame(23)* would send the main movie timeline to frame 23.

*   *IsPlaying():* Returns a binary response as to whether the movie is playing (True = playing). This is commonly used in a JavaScript If statement condition.

*   *LoadMovie(level, "URL"):* Allows a movie to be loaded, similar to the *loadMovie* method. The level must be an integer, and URL must be a string. For example, *LoadMovie(1,"mymovie.swf")* would load *mymovie.swf* onto level 1.

- *Pan(X, Y, mode):* Allows the movie to be panned (only when zoomed in). X and Y must be integers. The mode is a binary variable allowing pixels to be entered (0), or percentages to be entered (1). For example, *Pan(25, 25, 0)* would pan the movie 25 pixels down *x* and 25 pixels down *y*.

- *PercentLoaded():* Returns to the browser the amount of the file that has been streamed (ranges from 0 to 100). This, too, is commonly used in a JavaScript conditional statement.

- *Play():* Plays the movie if it is currently stopped.

- *Rewind():* Sends the playhead to the starting frame of the movie.

- *SetVariable("variablename", "value"):* Sets the value of the variable specified by the string *variablename* to the string value specified. For example, *SetVariable("myname", "Jamie")* would set a variable named *myname* (owned by the main movie timeline) to the string *Jamie*.

- *SetZoomRect(left, top, right, bottom):* Permits JavaScript to change the zoom to the specific rectangle. Note that left, top, right, and bottom must be integers, and are specified in twips (1,440 units per inch). To calculate twips, set the units in Flash to Points and then multiply all values by 20 (20 twips = 1 point). For example, *SetZoomRect(0, 0, 400, 400)* would set the zoom rectangle to 0,0 (upper left-hand corner) and 200,200 (lower right-hand corner), in pixels.

- *StopPlay():* Stops the movie.

- *TotalFrames():* Returns the total number of frames in the movie.

- *Zoom(percentage):* Allows the zoom level of a movie to be changed based on a percentage, which must be an integer. Note that the percentage works like the drop-down in most applications, where 50 means 50 percent (stage size doubles/zooms in). A percentage of 200 would zoom out, making the stage area smaller.

The Flash Player methods can use slash syntax (older Flash targeting syntax) or dot syntax. You will recall that in dot syntax, to specify a variable that is owned by a particular timeline you simply include the reference at the end of the dot-separated path. For example, if a movie clip MC1 owns the variable *myname*, to access it you would enter the following path in dot syntax: *_root.MC1.myname*. In slash syntax, to access a variable, the variable is separated from the path by a colon. Thus, to access the *myname* variable, slash syntax would look like *_level0/MC1:myname*.

tellTarget Methods

In addition to controlling the main movie, you can also specifically target individual movie clips and command them. Keep in mind that you can also target the main movie timeline if you specify the target as _level0 or as /. The following are descriptions of the Flash Player methods for controlling movie clips.

- *TCallFrame("target", framenumber):* Executes the actions in frame *framenumber*, located in the target specified by target. The target must be a string, and the frame number must be an integer. For example, *TCallFrame("myMC", 5)* would execute the actions associated with frame 5 of *myMC*, located in the main movie timeline.

- *TCallLabel("target", "label"):* Allows the Call action to be executed by calling a label instead of a frame. Both target and label must be strings. For example, *TCallLabel("myMC", "initvars")* would call the actions associated with the frame label *initvars* in *myMC* (*myMC* would reside in the main movie timeline).

- *TCurrentFrame("target"):* Returns an integer representing the current frame number of the target. The target specification must be a string. For example, *TCurrentFrame("myMC")* would return the current frame number of movie clip *myMC*, located in the main movie timeline.

- *TCurrentLabel("target"):* Returns a string representing the current frame label of the target. The target specification must be a string. For example, *TCurrentLabel("myMC")* would return the current frame label of movie clip *myMC*, located in the main movie timeline. Keep in mind that for a label to be returned the playhead must be in the exact frame in which the label resides.

- *TGetProperty("target", property):* Retrieves a property value from the target. The target is specified as a string, whereas the property is an integer (see table 14-3). For example, *TGetProperty ("myMC", 0)* would retrieve the current *x* position of movie clip *myMC*, located in the main movie timeline.

- *TGetPropertyAsNumber("target", property):* Retrieves a property value as a number from the specified target (see table 14-3). For example, *TGetPropertyAsNumber("myMC", 10)* would return the rotation of movie clip *myMC* as an integer, rather than as a string.

- *TGotoFrame("target", framenumber):* Tells the specified target to go to a specific frame. The target must be a string, and *framenumber* must be an integer. For example, *TGoToFrame ("myMC1/my-MC1a/", 5)* would tell the movie clip *myMC1a* (which is within *myMC1*) to go to frame 5.

- *TGotoLabel("target", "label"):* Tells the specified target to go to a specific label. Both the target and label must be strings. For example, *TGotoLabel("MC1/MC1a", "Print")* would tell movie clip *MC1a*, located within movie clip *MC1*, to go to the frame labeled *Print*.

- *TPlay("target"):* Tells the specified string target to play. For example, *TPlay("MC1")* would tell movie clip *MC1* in the main timeline to play.

- *TSetProperty("target", property, value):* Allows external scripts to set a property in Flash. The target must be a string, whereas the property and value are defined as numbers (see table 14-3). For example, *TSetProperty("bfinder", 0, 200)* would set the *x* location of the movie clip *bfinder* to 200.

- *TStopPlay("target"):* Tells the specified string target to stop. For example, *TStopPlay("MC1")* would tell movie clip *MC1* in the main timeline to stop.

 NOTE: *All of the string targets used by the Flash Player methods follow the standard rules for* tellTarget *paths. These string targets are specified in slash syntax, where the dots of dot syntax are replaced by forward slashes.*

Property Numbers

When setting or retrieving properties, you must use numerical values to represent the various properties available. Table 14-3 outlines the properties and their integer equivalents that can be called using *TGetProperty()* and *TSetProperty()*. Of importance for Flash Player methods are the property numbers on the left. The table also outlines which properties are settable and which are only gettable.

Flash Player Events

The Flash Player provides three standard events to which it can respond. The most widely used is the *fscommand()* event. However, two others exist. For the sake of completeness, they are mentioned here. However, the techniques for using them are undocumented and not widely publicized. The two other Flash Player events are as follows.

- *OnProgress(percent):* Generated as the Flash movie is downloading. The value percentage is provided as an integer.

- *OnReadyStateChange(state):* Generated as the ready state of the movie changes. Values provided via state include 0 = Loading, 1 = Uninitialized, 2 = Loaded, 3 = Interactive, and 4 = Complete.

Table 14-3: Callable Properties/Integer Equivalents Using TGetProperty() *and* TSetProperty().

Nonglobal Properties				
Property Number	*Constant*	*Description*	*Settable*	*Gettable*
0	X_POS	X Position (_x)	Yes	Yes
1	Y_POS	Y Position (_y)	Yes	Yes
2	X_SCALE	X Scale (_xscale)	Yes	Yes
3	Y_SCALE	Y Scale (_yscale)	Yes	Yes
4	CURRENT_FRAME (_currentframe)	Current Frame	No	Yes
5	TOTAL_FRAMES (_totalframes)	Total Frames	No	Yes
6	ALPHA	Alpha (_alpha)	Yes	Yes
7	VISIBLE	Visibility (_visible)	Yes	Yes
8	WIDTH	Width (_width)	No	Yes
9	HEIGHT	Height (_height)	No	Yes
10	ROTATE	Rotation (_rotation)	Yes	Yes
11	TARGET	Target (_target)	No	Yes
12	FRAMES_LOADED (_framesloaded)	Frames Loaded	No	Yes
13	NAME	Instance Name (_name)	Yes	Yes
14	DROP_TARGET (_droptarget)	Drop Target	No	Yes
15	URL	URL (_url)	No	Yes
Global Properties				
Property Number	*Constant*	*Description*	*Settable*	*Gettable*
16	HIGH_QUALITY	High Quality (_highquality)	Yes	Yes
17	FOCUS_RECT	Focus Rectangle (_focusrect)	Yes	Yes
18	SOUND_BUF_TIME	Sound Buffer Time (_soundbuftime)	Yes	No

▪ ▪ ▪ Movie Clip Control

The following sections provide an overview of the movie clip control actions. These include clip duplication, property modification, and drag-gable clips.

duplicateMovieClip() and removeMovieClip()

The *duplicateMovieClip()*; method allows you to make duplicate copies of movie clips on the stage. The *removeMovieClip()*; method allows you to remove copied clips. These methods are particularly useful for, among other uses, drag-and-drop types of games, for which a duplicate copy of an object may be needed. The general form for the *duplicateMovieClip()* function is as follows.

```
duplicateMovieClip(target, name, depth);
```

Within this function, you must define the target movie clip you wish to copy (target), the new name for the copied instance (name), and the depth (level) for the new object.

When a new instance is generated using *duplicateMovieClip()*, the depth of the object becomes important. The simple way of thinking about this is that the copied instance is layered above the original within the parent layer and movie. The instances become part of the parent movie. If the parent movie is unloaded, the instances will also be unloaded.

Specifically, the first generated instance of a movie clip starts at layer offset 16382 (0 x 400 hexadecimal). If the depth is specified as 1, the layer offset of the object is 16382 + 1. A depth of 5 is 16382 + 5. The main thing to keep in mind is that duplicated instances are placed above the original object. Because the *duplicateMovieClip()* and *removeMovieClip()* methods are based on an instance name, only movie clip symbols may be duplicated. Exercise 14-15 explores movie clip duplication.

Exercise 14-15: Movie Clip Duplication

CD-ROM NOTE: *To see an applied example of the* duplicateMovieClip() *and* removeMovieClip() *methods, examine the file* ch14_15.fla, *located in the* fgai/chapter14/ *folder, installed from the companion CD-ROM.*

setProperty()

As you know, properties are the attributes of objects. Objects in your movie, as well as the movie itself, have properties that can be tested and set during playback. The *setProperty()* method expects you to provide the name of the object instance to modify, what property you want to change, and the new value for the property.

Remember that two types of properties exist in Flash: global properties (which apply to the entire movie) and local (or movie clip) properties, which apply to movie clip instances currently on the stage. The following properties are settable.

- *_alpha:* Alpha allows the transparency (opaqueness) of an object to be changed. The value is entered as a percentage, with 0 being fully transparent and 100 being fully opaque.

- *_focusrect:* Show Focus Rectangle is a binary value determining whether the focus rectangle of buttons is displayed.

- *_height:* Height is the height of the referenced object in pixels.
- *_name:* Name is the name of the symbol instance on the stage.
- *_quality:* A string value specifying one of the following concerning display quality: LOW, MEDIUM, HIGH, or BEST.
- *_rotation:* Rotation sets the rotation of a movie clip. The value is entered in degrees.
- *_soundbuftime:* Sound Buffer Time determines the size of the buffer used for sound clips.
- *_visible:* Visibility is a binary value indicating whether the movie clip is visible. A visibility of 0 hides the object, and a visibility of 1 shows the object.
- *_width:* Width is the width of the referenced object in pixels.
- *_x:* X Position changes the X position of a movie clip relative to the parent movie or movie clip.
- *_xscale:* X Scale pertains to the X scaling of a movie clip. A value of 1 indicates no scaling.
- *_y:* Y Position modifies the Y position of a movie clip relative to the parent movie or movie clip.
- *_yscale:* Y Scale relates to the Y scaling of a movie clip. A value of 1 indicates no scaling.

In addition to the settable properties associated with your movies, there are several properties that can be tested but not set. These properties apply only to the *getProperty();* method and conditional statements such as *if*. They include the following.

- *_currentframe:* Indicates the current frame of the movie.
- *_droptarget:* Indicates the target path of an object beneath an object that is being dragged. This permits the developer to determine intersections between two movie clips for such things as drag-and-drop games or exercises.
- *_framesloaded:* Can be used to determine if a frame has been loaded.
- *_target:* The name of a movie clip instance. Note that *_target* provides the reference in slash syntax.
- *_totalframes:* Reveals the total number of frames in the movie.
- *_url:* Contains the URL location from which the movie was loaded.
- *_xmouse:* The *x* location of the cursor.
- *_ymouse:* The *y* location of the cursor.

Exercise 14-16 explores changing properties with ActionScript.

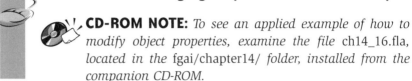

Exercise 14-16: Changing Properties with ActionScript

CD-ROM NOTE: *To see an applied example of how to modify object properties, examine the file* ch14_16.fla, *located in the* fgai/chapter14/ *folder, installed from the companion CD-ROM.*

startDrag(), stopDrag(), and updateAfterEvent()

The *startDrag()* and *stopDrag()* methods allow you to create entities within your movie that can be manipulated with the mouse. The *startDrag()* method is used to start the drag operation, and the *stopDrag()* method is used to cease it. Note that once a drag is initiated it will continue until a *stopDrag()* or another *startdrag()* method is encountered. Note that two dragging operations cannot occur at the same time. If a drag is initiated while one is already underway, the new drag will override the old. The general form for the *startDrag()* function is as follows.

```
startDrag(target, lock, l, t, r, b);
```

The *startDrag()* method requires a target object to drag, defined by the target argument. This can be defined using a standard target path or using an expression. The last four arguments allow you to define a constraining rectangle for the object. The coordinates for the rectangle are based on the parent movie's stage coordinates, and can be absolutely or relatively defined. Thus, *l* stands for left, *t* for top, *r* for right, and *b* for bottom.

The *lock* argument determines where the movie clip appears in relation to the user's mouse. If false is used for the *lock* argument, the point of the movie clip the mouse was over when clicked is the registration point between the mouse and the movie clip. If true is used for the *lock* argument, the center of the movie clip will follow the mouse position.

One of the properties mentioned earlier directly relates to the *startDrag()* and *stopDrag()* methods. The *_droptarget* property is constantly updated while a drag operation is taking place. By checking the *_droptarget* property immediately following a *stopDrag()*, you could determine if the released item intersected another movie clip on the stage. Use the *_droptarget* property to create drag-and-drop games and similar interactive components. Exercise 14-17 explores the use of drag actions.

Exercise 14-17: Using Drag Actions

CD-ROM NOTE: *To see an applied example of how to set up drag-and-drop scenarios, examine the file* ch14_17.fla, *located in the* fgai/chapter14/ *folder, installed from the companion CD-ROM.*

▪ ▪ ▪ Summary

This chapter examined basic actions for movie and movie clip control, as well as access to external browser and network functions. The remaining set of actions (related to printing) are covered in the next chapter, as are Flash's accessibility features.

15

Printing and Accessibility

∎∎∎ Introduction

No introductory book would be complete without coverage of printing issues and the new Flash MX 2004 accessibility features. Thus, this chapter serves to round out and complete this book by introducing you to how you can set up your Flash movies so that they print appropriately for your end users, as well as how to include accessibility information to the users of your site.

∎∎∎ Objectives

In this chapter you will:

- Examine issues surrounding printing screen content
- Discover the basic actions for printing Flash movies at run-time
- Examine the special frame labels for controlling print content
- Learn what accessibility is all about
- Find out more about Flash's new accessibility features and how to use them

∎∎∎ Printing Screen Content

Setting up screen-based content so that it prints properly has plagued multimedia developers for years. Most multimedia authoring tools are not designed to print very well, and often require a lot of work to get effective prints from the content contained within them. Although the web browser can print its content, even the content on most web sites today is not optimized for printing. Frequently you print something out, only to find that the content is truncated on the standard portrait paper orientation. It as only recently that web developers have become "print conscious" as it relates to web development.

The Quandary

Indeed the biggest problem with printing screen content concerns orientation. The first issue you must deal with is ensuring that what you see as a landscape-oriented image on the screen (that is, wider than it is tall) comes out right when printed from a printer oriented in portrait (taller than it is wide). Although the browser can be made to spit information out in a portrait orientation (a quick and dirty solution for making sure you get all the text information in a printer-unfriendly web page), most text-heavy documents are awkward to use in this orientation.

The second issue concerning screen-designed content is that when printed in portrait mode the visual design is often lost. Additionally, the image may be printed smaller or larger than the standard letter-size paper.

Designers often spend countless hours tailoring the text, graphics, and overall look and feel of a site based on the assumption that the landscape screen is all they need worry about. But in reality, much of the web content, whether it is guaranteed that it will be available on the Web tomorrow or not, is printed when people want to retain it. Additionally, much of the content is printed so that it can be used offline and apart from an Internet connection. Albeit indirectly, printing capability should always be an issue to consider in web design.

An Issue of Control

When it comes down to it, printing is an issue of control of information. With your Flash movies and other web content you provide, you can leave the print decision out of the design equation if you like, but there will still be numerous users that will want to print your web content, for any number of reasons. If you leave it to the rudimentary capabilities of the browser, prints of your site will likely leave much to be desired. Thus, the print issue should always be a planned part of your web projects.

Printing in Flash

Setting up your Flash movies so that they have "printing intelligence" provides several advantages over leaving it to the browser to deal with printing (whatever and however it wants). With Flash, you can control exactly what is printed from a movie and how much is printed from a movie. An additional benefit of allowing users to print Flash movies is that the content will inherently have higher quality than that typical of the usual browser prints. Recall from the discussion in Chapter 1 that this is a by-product of Flash's vector nature.

Flash can print any frame that exists in the environment. You can set up a movie so that all frames print (which is unlikely, but can be done), or only specific frames. The frames you print can be in the main movie timeline, a movie clip, or even a loaded movie, if you like. The key with the first two of these is to ensure that the print will be oriented correctly, producing an adequate print.

The latter of these (loading an external movie that is printed) permits you to create customized movies that are loaded and only used for printing. For example, if your Flash movie were a catalog of sorts, you could let the user view products via the web browser. Then, when they wanted to print, you could have Flash print a customized "specification sheet" about the product, totally independent of what the user sees on the screen. Flash specifically permits the following as it relates to printing.

- Define specific frames that are printed from the Flash movie.

  The biggest advantage to this is the ability to disallow printing of specific aspects of the movie. This also lets you create special frames in the movie (that may or may not be viewable) that are tailor made for printing.

- Specify the area of a frame that prints.

  You can set up the frames in the movie to print entirely or partially, by defining the physical area of the frame to be printed.

- Print the content as vector or bitmap content.

  When you print as vector content, you are able to take advantage of the inherent high-quality nature of Flash's vector componentry. Printing as bitmaps lets you retain complex blends and other elements that utilize transparency.

- Print nonvisible content.

  With Flash's printing capability, you can define nonvisible areas for printing. This lets you create custom movies that are specifically for printing, not viewing on screen.

▪ ▪ ▪ **Print-focused Actions**

Setting up a Flash movie so that it is printable requires two things: actions that actually do the printing and frame labels that define what part or parts of the movie print. The following sections deal with the first of these. Flash provides four basic methods for printing.

print() and printAsBitmap()

The *print()* and *printAsBitmap()* methods are designed to print frames that exist in the main timeline, movie clips, or loaded movies. Both methods require an object or level specification, and an optional setting for the bounding box of the print.

The general form for using the *print()* and *printAsBitmap()* methods follows.

```
print(object, boundingbox);
printAsBitmap(object, boundingbox);
```

In both of these methods, the object argument is expected to be a string; that is, the name of the object from which frames are to be printed. As it relates to the *boundingbox* argument, it is expected as a string also. There are three different options for the *boundingbox*, as follows.

- *"bmovie":* Uses a frame in the movie that is specifically designed by the developer to be used as the bounding box for print. Content of this frame does not print. It is only used to define the bounding box (area to be printed). The frame is identified by the special frame label *#b*.

- *"bframe":* Uses the bounding area of each frame's content as the bounding box. In each frame that is printed, Flash finds the maximum rectangle that will fit around all content in that frame and uses it as the bounding box. The bounding box is then scaled to fit the maximum printable area for the printer. You use this setting when the content of frames varies in size and you want them all to be printed so that they fill the page.

- *"bmax":* Uses a composite bounding box determined by comparing all frames in the movie and finding the maximum bounding box from all frames. You use this setting when you want all of the printed frames to be proportionally scaled to one another, as opposed to having them all scale to fit the page when *"bframe"* is used.

As it relates to the difference between *print()* and *printAsBitmap()*, the *print()* method prints the content in the movie as native vector representations. When you use *print()*, the resulting paper copy output by the printer will be higher resolution than that typical of web-based prints. In essence, the resolution of the print will be at whatever quality is currently set for the printer.

The *printAsBitmap()* method allows you to accurately print movie content that has transparency or other color effects applied to items in the movie. Due to the way Flash defines transparency and color effects internally, it must send such content to the printer as a bitmap representation, rather than a vector representation. As logic would dictate, when *printAsBitmap()* is used, it takes longer to print (because it is a pixel-by-pixel definition, rather than a vector one), and the resulting printer file (file sent to the printer queue) is much larger. To better explain these methods, let's examine the following sample code segments and what they mean.

```
print("myclip", "bmovie");
```

This prints the frames in the object *"myclip"* (presumably a movie clip) that are defined as printable. The frame in the movie clip *"myclip"* (labeled *#b*) defines the bounding box (area to be printed), and the content is printed as vector content.

```
printAsBitmap("myclip", "bmax");
```

This prints the content of the object *"myclip"* (presumably a movie clip). It examines all of the frames assigned to print in *"myclip"* and finds the one frame that has the largest bounding box. The frame with the largest bounding box in *"myclip"* is used as the size for all frames to be printed.

printNum() and printAsBitmapNum()

The *printNum()* and *printAsBitmapNum()* methods function similarly to the *print()* and *printAsBitmap()* methods, except that the two methods expect to receive a number for the first argument, instead of a string, as in the following.

```
printNum(number, boundingbox);
printAsBitmapNum(number, boundingbox);
```

The number argument is assumed to be a level number. Recall from Chapter 14 the discussion of loaded movies, where *_level0* is the main movie timeline, *_level1* is the movie loaded on level 1, and so on. The *printNum()* and *printAsBitmapNum()* methods then allow you to print levels of a movie, as opposed to specific objects. The *boundingbox* argument is basically the same, providing the *"bmovie"*, *"bframe"*, and *"bmax"* options. To better explain these methods, let's examine the following sample code segments and what they mean.

```
printNum(0, "bframe");
```

This prints the frames assigned to print in the main movie timeline (the 0 means *_level0*) as vector content. The *"bframe"* bounding box lets each frame define its own bounding box. Each frame is also printed such that it fits to the allowable printable area of the page.

```
printAsBitmapNum(10, "bmax");
```

This prints the content of the movie loaded in level 10. It examines all of the frames set up to print in the movie assigned to the level and finds the one frame that has the largest bounding box. The frame with the largest bounding box in level 10 is used as the size for all frames to be printed.

▪ ▪ ▪ Controlling What Is Printed

The control of what frames are printed, special bounding boxes for printed frames, as well as the ability to disallow printing in a movie is specified by frame labels. Flash reads three special frame labels, described in the following sections.

#p and #b

As described in the previous section, you can define the frames that are printable in the main timeline, a movie clip, or in a loaded movie. You do so by using the special frame label *#p*, which is added in the Properties panel. Any frame in a movie identified as *#p* will print when the print methods are executed. For example, if 10 frames have *#p* in the object being printed, all 10 frames will print when any print method is called.

 TIP: *To print only single elements, the best strategy is to print loaded movies, described later in this chapter.*

The *#b* frame label allows you to define a frame (that may or may not be viewable by the end user) that is used as the bounding frame. Keep in mind that the content of this frame does not print. It is only used to define an area on the stage that will be printed. Then the *"bframe"* argument is used in the print methods to utilize the area defined in the *#b* frame. Exercise 15-1 explores using *#b* to define a bounding box.

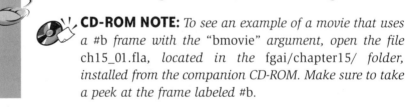

Exercise 15-1: Using #b to Define a Bounding Box

CD-ROM NOTE: *To see an example of a movie that uses a #b frame with the "bmovie" argument, open the file ch15_01.fla, located in the fgai/chapter15/ folder, installed from the companion CD-ROM. Make sure to take a peek at the frame labeled #b.*

You saw earlier that in addition to the *"bmovie"* setting, you also have the *"bmax"* and *"bframe"* settings for the bounding box. Figure 15-1 shows the difference between these two. In one case (*"bframe"*), each frame defines its own bounding box. Thus, the print of the frame scales to fit the avail-

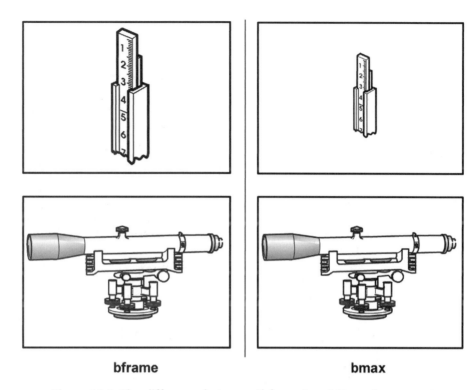

bframe   bmax

Figure 15-1. The difference between "bframe" and "bmax" arguments.

able page area. The *"bmax"* option examines the entire movie to find the frame with the largest content bounding box, and then uses that frame as the definition for the bounding box. An easy way to remember the distinction is that *"bframe"* scales every frame to fit the page, whereas *"bmax"* does not.

!#p

In Flash you also have the ability to disallow all printing. You do so by adding the *!#p* to any frame label in the movie, movie clip, or loaded movie. Note that this only disables printing by the Flash Player. If the movie is contained within the browser, users will still be able to print using the browser's print button.

▪ ▪ ▪ Using Invisible Movies

As you start working with the print capabilities of Flash, you will find that all frames in a movie that have a *#p* will print when a print method is executed on the object. Frequently you may want to have several frames in a movie be printable, but yet you only want the currently viewed frame to be printed each time the user clicks on a print button. Granted, the user can control this in the print dialog box under Print Range, but all too often the end user may not see that he can do this.

Through loading and unloading movies you can set up scenarios in which Flash loads print content in a hidden movie clip. This way you can print individual pages, rather than many frames in a single movie. This also lets you pre-format content specific to the printer, as opposed to using the screen version, which is oriented in landscape mode. Exercise 15-2 demonstrates such a movie.

Exercise 15-2: Using Loaded Movies for Print Content

CD-ROM NOTE: *To see an example of a movie loaded movies for print content, open the file* ch15_02.fla, *located in the* fgai/chapter15/ *folder, installed from the companion CD-ROM. This file makes use of the files* path1.fla, path2.fla, path3.fla, *and* path4.fla.

▪ ▪ ▪ Accessibility

Accessibility is a growing subject as it relates to web-based content, due to legislation concerning web-based information and to basic public awareness of the subject. Accessibility focuses on ensuring that those with disabilities have equal opportunity to access and use information that is commonly available to those who do not have a disability.

In times past, the Web has been a place that the visually impaired may have had little luck in using due to the graphical nature of the media. Similarly, as web audio and video use increases, there is an increasing potential that those with hearing disabilities will also be limited in using web information. Accessibility legislation and guidelines exist to make web information (as well as other media sources) accessible to all people, independent of disabilities.

Limits of this book do not permit a lengthy explanation on the general topic. However, realize that if you are web developer it is an issue on which you should be well informed. The following are some very good web resources with which you should be familiar.

- *www.section508.gov/*

  This web site, maintained by the U.S. government, is the first source you should look to concerning legislation and general information concerning accessibility guidelines. The "About 508" section is particularly useful, as it provides a summary and detail listing of the standards pertaining to usability. Specifications are provided specifically for software applications and operating systems, web-based content, telecommunications products, video and multimedia products, self-contained products, and desktop and portable computers.

- *www.w3.org/WAI/*
  This web site is provided by the World Wide Web Consortium (W3C) and provides further information specific to web technologies.

- *www.macromedia.com/macromedia/accessibility/features/flash/*
  This Macromedia web site details specific information about accessibility and accessibility features inside Flash MX 2004.

- *www.macromedia.com/macromedia/accessibility/*
  This site documents Macromedia's general focus on accessibility throughout their entire software product lines, with information relative to other Macromedia software.

Flash Objects and Accessibility

The two primary means available to those with disabilities for accessing the Web are screen readers and closed captioning devices.

Screen Readers

Screen readers are typically focused at helping the user decipher the navigation capabilities of a site. The text in a web page (that is, text defined by elements such as heading, paragraph, and other block-text tags) is usually directly readable by text readers.

When working with basic text elements, the usual way to make sure navigation elements are "readable" is by either making text-based navigation or by including ALT attributes (for graphical navigation items) that are descriptive of what the graphical item does. However, in the past Flash elements were difficult to describe directly. Flash's new accessibility features take a huge step forward in trying to meet what screen readers need.

Closed Captioning

Closed captioning devices, on the other hand, are focused at translating the audio content of a site into words that are shown on screen. This works in much the same way as closed captioning for television.

Technology

To provide accessibility information, the Flash Player (version 6 and above) uses Microsoft Active Accessibility (MSAA). MSAA is built into all 32-bit platforms (95, 98, ME, NT4, 2000, and XP). Currently, Flash's accessibility information is not available in Netscape on Windows, Windows stand-alone players, or on the Macintosh (Netscape or Internet Explorer). Additionally, MSAA support is not available if WMODE is set to Opaque or Transparent (see Chapter 12 for more about the WMODE parameter of the *<OBJECT>* tag).

 NOTE: *Microsoft provides general accessibility information at* www.microsoft.com/enable/. *For MSAA specifics, see* www.msdn.microsoft.com/library/default.asp?url = /nhp/Default.asp? contentid = 28000544.

Accessible Objects

Flash can expose many of its internal objects to screen readers. Flash can expose the following objects to text readers: the main movie, loaded movies (which are treated as movie clips), movie clip instances, button instances, input text fields, and dynamic text objects. Each of these (as well as child objects contained within a loaded movie, movie clip, or button) is also accessible.

 NOTE: *When auto labeling is used, normal text objects are also readable.*

Setting Accessibility in Flash

The information provided by Flash's accessibility options is typically more than just a terse label. In most cases the information provided about Flash objects can include a name and a paragraph description. With input text fields, dynamic text objects, movie clips, and buttons, you can also choose to expose shortcut keys for the object, if they have been programmed with ActionScript. Let's examine the basic process for setting up appropriate accessibility information.

General Process

As you read, by default Flash is set up so that its objects automatically expose information to text readers. The only thing you must do to make use of Flash's accessibility features is to add extra information about your objects via the Accessibility panel.

NOTE: *You can access the Accessibility panel via the Window menu, or by clicking on the small, blue accessibility icon in the Properties panel.*

Figure 15-2. The accessibility options for the main movie timeline.

Figure 15-2 shows the default accessibility information pertaining to the main movie timeline. If you have no object selected on the stage and access the Accessibility panel, you can set the overall accessibility options for the movie.

As you can see in figure 15-2, you have the ability to control the overall accessibility settings for the movie. The following are the default options presented.

- *Make Movie Accessible:* Exposes the accessibility information related to objects in the movie, as well as the accessibility information about the main movie timeline.

- *Make Child Objects Accessible:* Exposes the child object accessibility information in the movie. In essence, deselecting this option only provides the Name and Description information related to the main movie timeline itself.

- *Auto Label:* Allows the Flash movie to automatically label normal text items (that is, static text) by reading their content. If Auto Label is deselected, Static Text elements will not be read.

- *Name:* Allows you to enter a name for the main movie.

- *Description:* This field allows you to enter a description for the main movie.

Individual Object Information

In addition to setting the accessibility information for the main movie, you can also set it at the object level. As you have seen already, if Auto Label is selected for the main movie, Static Text objects are read automatically. You can also set specific Name and Description information for Input and Dynamic Text fields. If you select on them and access the Accessibility panel, you may establish settings for them.

NOTE: *If you turn off Auto Label in the main timeline, make sure you manually enable large text segments that are content in your movie. To make Static Text objects readable when Auto Label is off, change the text to Dynamic Text.*

Movie clips and loaded movies are treated as special elements regarding accessibility information. First, loaded movies are treated as a movie clip object. To make their content accessible, open the file to be loaded and set the accessibility information as you would in a normal timeline. The content in the loaded movie will then be accessible when loaded.

As it relates to movie clips, selecting a movie clip provides options similar to those found in the accessibility settings for the main movie timeline. You can enable or disable child object accessibility information. If you deselect the Make Child Object Accessible checkbox, only the movie clip's accessibility information will be available. Where you might want to disallow access to a movie clip's content is if it is an animated segment or other dynamic media element. If the movie clip contains buttons, text, or other objects, make sure the accessibility information is available by leaving the Make Child Objects Accessible checkbox selected.

 TIP: *Macromedia provides several tips and suggestions relating to accessible movies on their accessibility web site. See the "Design Tips" section at* www.macromedia.com/macromedia/ accessibility/features/flash/.

▪ ▪ ▪ Summary

This chapter has concluded this book by examining print and accessibility issues in Flash MX 2004. As you look back at all the things you have read about and done in this book, hopefully you have found it rewarding and a good learning experience. This book and the things you have done are just the beginning. There is much, much more to learn. After studying this book, it is suggested you look examine books that include much more on ActionScript, as that is the future of Flash. Do not stop learning! Continue with Flash and web development in general, and make learning a continual process.

glossary

< A > An HTML tag for creating links to other pages or resources; an anchor tag.

< EMBED > An HTML tag for including multimedia elements on web pages; causes the browser to use a plug-in.

< H1 > An HTML tag for creating headings of various sizes; importance of heading is denoted by number. 1 is the most important; 6 is the least important.

< HR > An HTML tag for creating horizontal rules.

< IMG > An HTML tag for including images within a web page.

< OBJECT > An HTML tag for including multimedia elements on web pages; causes the browser to use ActiveX components.

< P > A block-level HTML tag that creates a paragraph of text offset from other elements by a carriage return (line feed).

24-bit color Describes an image that can contain up to 16.7 million colors.

2D animation An animation file created using a package in which every frame's content is defined through either vector or bitmap descriptions.

3D animation An animation file generated from a 3D model or scene.

3-D Studio Max A 3D animation package created by Kinetix (*www.ktx.com*).

8-bit color Describes an image that contains up to 256 colors. All colors are described in a matrix called the Color Look-up Table (CLUT).

acetate Clear plastic film typically used to create traditional cel animation; used as an analogy for how layers work in a graphics program.

achromatic colors Include hues that have no true color, such as black, white, and gray.

ACT The extension assigned to save Photoshop color palettes.

action Feature of Flash that allows you to assign functionality to elements in a movie.

ActionScript Flash's internal scripting language, which is modeled after the ECMAScript technical specification (see *www.ecma.ch*).

Active Server Pages (ASP) A server-side scripting language used in conjunction with Microsoft's HTTP server software, MIIS.

ActiveX Microsoft's approach to plug-ins, in which components are installed at the system level and are accessible by all applications.

adaptive differential pulse code modulation (ADPCM) Compression algorithm commonly used in the WAV file format; a lossy sound compression format.

additive colors Color system used to create projected or displayed images via a cathode ray tube.

additive primaries Red, green, and blue.

address field The portion of a browser into which a universal resource locator (URL) can be typed.

Adobe A company well known for its raster and vector graphics applications (*www.adobe.com*).

affordances The controls in an interface that clue the user in as to functionality.

Afterburner Original name for the filter used to convert image and multimedia files created in Macromedia products to a form that is distributable over the Web. Most newer applications can convert data within the program and do not need the external converter.

AI The extension acronym (*.ai*) for an Adobe Illustrator file.

algorithm A mathematical or logical schemata for solving a problem.

aliasing Characteristic stair-stepped nature of vector lines on a display screen or in an extracted bitmap; caused by the physical limits of the output device as it relates to resolution.

alignment The positioning of text bodies in relationship to other screen elements.

alpha Controls the transparency (opaqueness) of a symbol in Flash.

alpha channels A special part of high-resolution files that can contain masking and gamma information.

alphanumeric character A character (letter or number).

ambient light The amount of light present without any other light sources; representative of sunlight or moonlight; atmospheric light.

analog data Data consisting of a range of frequency variations; what the human senses are able to perceive.

analog degradation The decay of analog information as a result of copying an analog source to another analog device.

analog source A device, such as a VCR or a cassette tape, used to record or play back analog data.

analog to digital conversion (ADC) The process of converting analog data to digital data; often performed by a hardware chip or software.

animation The phenomenon of quickly changing images, which give the perception of movement or change over time.

animator The portion of a 3D animation package that allows the operator to define changes over time.

anti-alias halo Discolored pixels that occur around the edges of an object as a result of previous anti-aliasing.

anti-aliasing The process of blurring the edges of an image or object to make it appear smoother.

Apple Manufacturers of the Macintosh computer (*www.apple.com*).

applet A small, self-contained executable application created in the Java language.

application development The process of creating software designed to perform a task.

array A special type of variable that can contain multiple values.

ASCII text A standard and universal computer text format.

ASP See *Active Server Pages*.

asymmetrical balance Describes a layout in which there is an unequal amount of visual elements on each side of a page.

AU See *Sun Audio*.

Audio Interchange File Format (AIFF) A digital audio file format predominantly used on Macintosh and Silicon Graphics machines.

Authorware An interaction-based authoring program created by Macromedia (*www.macromedia.com*).

Autodesk FLI and FLC A digital animation format that uses frame differencing to write the frames in the animation.

avant garde Generally viewed as a paradigm shift or something that is out of the ordinary.

AVI See *Video for Windows*.

balance The equal or unequal amount of visual elements on a page; described as either symmetrical or asymmetrical.

banding The visual stripes that can appear in 256-color images as a result of interpolation.

bandwidth The amount of data that can be pushed over a network connection; measured in kilobits or megabits per second.

bandwidth profiler Feature available when testing a movie in Flash that allows the developer to simulate performance of a movie by limiting the data delivery rate.

Bezier curves Special spline curves that have control points that can be moved, thus changing the shape of the curve.

binary compression (BIN) A standard Internet external compression scheme.

binary data Data described using series of 0s and 1s; digital data.

binary variable A variable that can contain one only of two values: 0 (False) or 1 (True).

bit depth Determines the number of physical bits that can be used to represent a sample from an analog source.

bit rate The size of the chunks of data that are compressed in an MP3 sound clip.

bitmap A graphic in which the smallest element is the pixel (picture element).

bitmap editor An application designed to edit bitmap images.

bitmap fonts Fonts described using bitmap images.

bitmap graphics See *bitmap*.

blending Merging two or more items to obtain steps between the items.

BMP See *Windows bitmap*.

bookmark A browser convention that allows the user to copy URL locations that can be used at a later time to instantly access a web site.

Boolean operations Logical operations that are used to create unique objects from a set of lower objects. The three primary operations are union, subtraction, and intersection.

browser A special application designed to view HTML pages from the WWW.

bump mapping A special feature of 3D animation programs that allows the user to specify textures through the use of other bitmaps. Depths are generated from grayscale values and applied to an object or surface.

button symbol A symbol that automatically behaves like a push-button control.

byte A series of 8 bits.

cache A special location on the hard drive at which a browser can temporarily store files for future use.

cameras A special view created in 3D animation programs for rendering a 3D scene; a perspective view.

cascading style sheets (CSS) A client-side web technology that provides templates that can be used for a series of web pages; also provides layering and positioning capability.

cathode ray tube A tube that allows images to be projected from special guns to create colored images.

cel A single frame from an animation; derived from celluloid, a substance on which animation frames were first created.

cel animation Traditional method of creating animations in which each frame was hand drawn and painted on a celluloid or acetate substance.

channels Special saved selections (raster editor); a track of music in an audio program (mono versus stereo).

chroma keying A special compositing feature that allows one clip to substitute for a special color in the second clip.

classes Define the methods, preoperties, and event handlers of objects.

clip art Pre-generated and generally public-domain graphics that can be used in derivative works.

clipping paths Objects used to clip or limit the display of other objects; typical in illustration programs.

CLR The extension assigned to saved Flash color palettes saved out of the Colors dialog box.

codec Acronym for "compressor/decompression"; generally used to describe the code that performs compression and decompression.

color The visual phenomenon that occurs as a result of absorption or projection of visible light.

color cycling An animation effect in which colors are substituted in an image, such as cycling from red to blue.

color look-up table (CLUT) The color matrix used in 8-bit images. Each color in the CLUT has a number, and each pixel in the image is associated with one number from the CLUT.

color schemes Sequences of color that look visually pleasing when used together in images.

color shifting An unappealing visual affect in which colors shift from proper to inappropriate colors. Generally occurs when the computer has to interpolate colors.

color space The method of theoretically defining all colors that can be replicated or generated by a specific device.

color wheel A circular arrangement of all colors associated with a particular device.

command line interface An operating environment in which commands are typed in, one line at a time.

comment An action in Flash that permits the developer to add internal documentation to movies; are ignored by the player.

common gateway interface (CGI) A server-side technology that provides a bridge for communication between two dissimilar technologies.

communication The process of sending a message through a communication channel. The message must be received and interpreted correctly for communication to occur.

compact disc read-only memory (CD-ROM) A computer storage medium in which digital data is stored on a plastic-coated silver platter. CD-ROMs can contain from 550 to 650 megabytes.

comparison operators Operators used to compare two values, such as equal, greater than, or less than.

compilation A copyrightable work in which major portions of various works are used together to create a new work, such as combining songs from various artists to create a "Greatest Hits"-type CD-ROM.

complementary Colors that occur across the color wheel from one another such as blue and orange, red and green, and purple and yellow. Most color-blindness problems are the result of the inability to distinguish complementary colors.

compositing The effect of merging media elements into one media element.

compression The process of reducing digital file size by either deleting unneeded data or substituting for redundant data.

compression ratio A description of a codec's effectiveness; obtained by comparing bits before and after compression.

concatenate To join two string elements into a single string element, such as "James" and " Mohler." The resultant would be the string result "James Mohler."

consistency Describes reoccurring elements that appear across multiple pages of a web site.

content The media elements used to convey a message, including text, visuals, and sound.

contrast A description of the value differences between adjacent items or colors.

cool colors Colors that tend to recede in a graphic, such as green, blue, and violet.

copyright The method of protecting creative works in the United States.

CYMK Describes the colors used in four-color process printing.

CYMK color model The conceptual color space used to describe the gamut of colors for printed output.

data rate The speed of the delivery of data, usually inside the computer; measured in kilobytes or megabytes per second.

data type The nature of data contained within a variable; types include string and numerical.

daughter card An add-on computer interface card that connects to an existing card within the computer, rather than to the computer's main system board.

Debabelizer A program used to convert graphic, sound, and digital video files (*www.debabelizer.com/*).

decibels A measure of frequency variations that are not necessarily associated with loudness.

deformation The act of deforming; something that is malformed.

device dependent Descriptive of a media element that has a fixed resolution; designed for output on a specific device.

device independent Descriptive of a media element that does not have a fixed resolution; can be adjusted for output on any device.

device resolution The number of dots per inch for a specific device.

digital audio An audio file that describes a waveform bit by bit as it occurs over time.

digital audio tape (DAT) A digital recording and playback device used in the music industry.

digital data See *binary data*.

digital signal processor (DSP) A special processor found on most sound cards that allows the sound card to process audio functions and commands.

digital-to-analog conversion (DAC) The process of converting digital data to analog data so that it can be interpreted by humans.

Director A time-based authoring program created by Macromedia (*www.macromedia.com/*).

dithering The process of scattering pixels during interpolation to overcome banding.

dots per inch (dpi) A measurement of the number of displayable or printable dots per square inch.

dub A slang term for copying a medium, or the product thereof.

dynamic Describes animated graphics, as opposed to static or unmoving graphics.

dynamic HTML A client-side web technology that provides the ability to include dynamic text and graphics, as well as interactive components.

easing Speeding up or slowing down the beginning or ending of an animation.

edutainment Software with an educational purpose that is entertaining as well.

electromagnetic spectrum The range of waveforms that occur in the environment.

e-mail Electronic mail; the capability to send text messages and other digital files across the Internet.

embedded programs Self-contained applications that can be included in a web page.

Enhanced Metafile Format (EMF) A metafile format developed by Microsoft; predominantly used in Microsoft products.

event Something that occurs during the playback of a movie that can be responded to, such as the click of a button.

executable application A stand-alone program most often designed to perform a specific task. Requires no other programs for execution.

Explorer A web browser created by Microsoft.

expression Sequences of operators and operands (variable names, functions, properties, and so on) used to compute numerical or string results.

Extensible Markup Language (XML) A web technology that permits the data within a web page to be described to enable better search capabilities; does not refer to formatting.

external file compression Compression that occurs independently of any particular type of digital data.

external link A link in a web page that leads outside the current site.

eyeflow The direction in which a user's eyes are drawn or directed across a page.

farcle A sharp and intense flash of refracted light, similar to a starburst.

field A text element that is editable during playback.

field of vision The range or cone of vision.

file size The size of a digital file, usually in kilobytes or megabytes.

File Transfer Protocol (FTP) An Internet service designed to distribute and retrieve files across the Internet.

filter A special add-on program that allows the user to create a special effect or perform some special function.

FLA The acronym for an extension (.*fla*) for a native Flash file that can be opened into Flash.

Flash Player The stand-alone program that can be used to play back Flash SWF files.

FlashScript command (FS command) A specific action in Flash that allows two values to be passed to external web technologies such as JavaScript.

flat shading Rendering in which the scene or model is represented by wires and flat polygonal colors.

FLI See *Autodesk FLI and FLC.*

FLV   Flash Video format; can be exported from a Flash library that contains an embedded video clip.

font See *typefont.*

four-color process Color printing technology that uses cyan, yellow, magenta, and black inks to create full-color reproductions.

fps Frames per second.

frame A single instance in time in an animation; one cel.

frame number The total number of frames in a digital animation or video.

frame rate See *fps.*

FreeHand A vector-illustration program created by Macromedia (*www.macromedia.com/*).

frequency A method of describing a particular sound; measured in hertz.

frequency variations The fundamental basis for analog data; consist of waves.

FrontPage An HTML generator and site management tool created by Microsoft (*www.microsoft.com/*).

functions Special code words that receive a value, do something to that value, and then return the result.

FutureSplash The original name of Flash when owned by FutureWave.

FutureWave The original company that initiated the development of Futuresplash, Flash's predecessor.

general MIDI mode The specification that states the standard MIDI channel and instrument numbers.

generation Used to describe a hierarchy of copies in analog dubbing.

GET A method of sending data from one web technology to another. When defined as a *GET* action, data is sent in the form *Query_String.*

GIF 89a A special GIF file that can contain transparency data.

global variable A variable that exists during the entire life of a program or web page.

Gopher A text- and menu-based Internet search program.

Gouroud A rendering technique in which polygonal faces are rendered using surface normals; no shades and shadows.

graphic (symbol) Symbols that cannot include button symbols, interactivity, or sound. Graphic symbol instances stop playing when the main timeline stops.

Graphic Interchange Format (GIF) A special file format developed by CompuServe that can contain 256-color data as well as transparency information.

grayscale The scale of values from black to white.

group The ability to temporarily cluster elements so that they may be edited as a single object.

guide layers Special layers used as motion paths for symbols in motion tweening.

handles Small, square boxes used in vector illustration programs to represent points.

helper application An external application used to aid the browser in viewing certain types of files.

hertz A measure of waveform cycles per second.

hexadecimal color A base 16 mathematical scheme used to define colors for a web browser.

hierarchical linking The ability to link one object to another so that changes to one object also affect the linked object.

HLS An acronym for hue, light, and saturation.

HLS color model A color model used to describe a gamut of colors by hue, light, and saturation.

horizontal space The width of the capital letter M in a font.

hue A characteristic of color that distinguishes it from other colors; the name of a color such as red, blue, and green.

human-computer interface An area of study that focuses on the development of effective interface design.

hypermedia Media that includes text, graphics, sound, animation, and video and is not confined to a single source medium.

hypertext Text that is nonlinear and nonsequential.

Hypertext Markup Language (HTML) The tag language used to describe the content of web pages; a derivative of the SGML language.

icons Graphic representations or abstractions.

Illustrator A vector illustration program created by Adobe (*www.adobe.com/*).

image bit depth   See *bit depth*.

image maps   Special graphics that can be used in web pages that are divided into regions; each region may be hotlinked to a different site or page.

image resolution   A description of the number of pixels per inch in an image.

image size   A description of an image's physical size in pixels.

in-betweens   Automatically generated frames that occur between the key frames in an animation. Key frames define the positions, sizes, orientations, or color effects of the objects.

indexed   See *8-bit color*.

inline image   An image inserted into a web page using the < A > tag.

instance   The occurrence of a symbol on the stage.

interactive multimedia   Any combination of text, graphics, sound, animation, and video that is controlled by the user and displayed by a computer.

interface   The point of interaction between a user and a computer.

interlaced   A file stored so that it may be downloaded and displayed a chunk at a time.

internal file compression   File compression that occurs as a result of the data in a particular file format.

interpolate   To derive values based on other values.

interpreter   A program that executes lines of code a line at a time.

intersection   A basic Boolean operation in which the overlapping area or volume of two objects becomes residual, with all the remaining area (non-shared) deleted.

intrasite link   A link that jumps you to another page in the current site.

inverse kinematics   The study of interrelationships among mechanical objects and their movements over time.

Java   A universal, platform-independent, object-oriented programming language.

JavaScript   A scripting language that is a simplified derivative of the Java programming language.

Joint Photographic Experts Group (JPEG)   A graphic image file format that uses lossy compression and can contain image data up to 24-bit.

kerning   The amount of space between letters or between words.

keyframe   A frame in an animation in which a key action or change is taking place; primary positions, colors, sizes, or orientations of objects defined within the timeline.

kilohertz (kHz)   1,000 hertz.

kinematics   The study of the relationship of movement as it relates to mechanical objects.

kinesiology   The study of the relationship of movement as it relates to the human body.

labels Special markers associated with timeline keyframes that can be jumped to.

layering The capability of a graphics application to store objects distinctly and separately.

leading The spacing between lines of text.

length String function that determines the number of characters in a string.

Lepel ZivWelch compression (LZW) Lossless compression scheme most often used in the TIFF file format.

letter spacing The spacing between letters of a font.

library Collection of symbols; facility through which the symbols of any file may be accessed and imported into another file.

license A permission to use a copyrighted item, typically based on various parameters of use and for which a fee is paid.

linear Pertaining to progression or straight movement.

linear array An array in which each additional value is indexed by a number.

local variable A variable that exists only as long as the function that called it is executing.

logical operators Operators used to combine conditions within *If* and *Loop* actions.

lossless Compression programs in which no data is lost; the uncompressed file creates an exact replica of the original.

lossy compression Scheme in which certain amounts of data are sacrificed for higher compression ratios.

Macintosh PICT Native Macintosh metafile format that can house both vector and raster information.

mapped Pertaining to 8-bit color mapping.

mask layers Special layers used to mask out portions of other layers.

metafile A file format that can contain multiple types of data.

modifiers Optional settings for the tools in Flash.

metaphor A likeness, construct, or similarity to some other device that is used in an effort to more quickly familiarize the audience with an information device.

methods The things an object can do (action verbs for the object).

modeler The portion of a 3D animation package that is used to create or import modeling data.

mono-aural Describes a single-channel digital audio file.

monochromatic An image using only tints and shades of a single hue.

monospaced fonts Fonts in which there is no letter spacing variations from character to character.

morph The ability to smoothly interpolate between two or more images.

motion guide See *guide layers*.

Motion Picture Experts Group (MPG) A digital video format commonly found on the Web.

motion tween A tween animation based on position, orientation, size, or color changes. Only one object can be tweened per layer and the object being tweened must be a symbol, group, or unbroken text (an overlay object).

mouse event See *event.*

MOV See *QuickTime.*

movie clip (symbol) A special timeline in a movie that permits any object to be inserted within it. Movie clip symbols continue to play even if the main movie stops.

MPEG See *Motion Picture Experts Group.*

MP3 A compressed audio format for the Web; see also *Motion Picture Experts Group.*

multimedia Any combination of text, graphics, sound, animation, and video displayed and controlled by the computer.

Multiple Master A special type of vector font.

multiprotocol Descriptive of the capacity to communicate using various network protocols.

Multipurpose Internet Mail Extension (MIME) The method of associating Internet file types with specific extensions with applications that can open them.

Musical Instrument Device Interface (MIDI) A method of digitally describing audio using instrument and note descriptions.

negative space Describes white space, or areas without visual elements, on a web page.

nested symbols Symbols that contain other symbols.

nonlinear Nonsequential.

nontransient information Information that remains stable or accurate over a period of nine months to a year.

Non-Uniform Rational B-Splines (NURBS) A parametric modeling environment in which surface points may be easily edited; allows for very complex organic surfaces and objects.

numerical operators Operators that perform mathematical calculations.

numerical value A number.

objects Specific instances of a class in the environment.

onion-skinning A carryover technique from traditional cel animation in which the content of adjacent frames are composited (in older technology from sheets of "onion-skin" paper) to enable comparisons of motion.

opacity Describes the visual solidity of surfaces; transparent is the opposite of opaque.

operators Programming elements that perform calculations (operations) or comparisons on two values to reach a third resultant value.

origin In relation to the 3D coordinate system, the origin is the location 0,0,0.

overlay object An object on an organizational level in Flash that contains groups, symbols, and unbroken text elements.

palette See *color look-up table (CLUT)*.

palletized See *8-bit color*.

particle systems A special function within a 3D animation program that allows the animator to create effects such as rain, snow, and tornadoes.

path of motion The path on which animated objects travel; defined by keyframe positioning and orientation.

persistence of vision The visual phenomenon of the eyes and brain perceiving an image after it has been removed from sight.

perspective A pictorial drawing in which the lines in the scene tend to converge to the horizon.

phong A rendering engine capable of generating smooth surfaces and calculate highlights and shadows based on lights positioned in the environment.

Photoshop A raster editing application created by Adobe (*www.adobe.com/*).

PICT See *Macintosh PICT*.

pitch The relative position of a tone in a scale, as determined by its soundwave frequency.

pixel (picture element) The smallest element of a bitmap image, computer monitor, or television display.

pixels per inch (ppi) The number of pixels per square inch.

plug-ins Add-on programs that extend the capability of a web browser by allowing it to view a wide range of files, such as animations, digital videos, or multimedia elements.

point size Describes the size of a font in points.

point A unit of measurement for lines and text; 72 points equals 1 inch.

polygonal mesh A surface model that uses polygons, most often triangles, to define the surface of a model.

Portable Network Graphics (PNG) A nonproprietary graphics format designed to unify the formats used on the Web. Boasts all of the features of both JPEG and GIF in a single format.

positive space The areas of a web page that contain visual elements such as text or graphics.

POST A method of sending data from one web technology to another. A *POST* method is sent as a standard input stream.

Postscript A page description language developed by Adobe that is used by most vector drawing programs.

preloader An introductory portion of a movie that plays while the remainder of a movie is streamed to the end user.

Premiere   A digital video editing program created by Adobe (*www.adobe.com*).

primary color   The main colors of any given color system; all other colors in the system are derived from the primary colors.

procedural mapping   A method of adding surface textures to 3D objects through the use of algorithms.

progressive JPEG   A special type of JPEG image that allows the browser to begin viewing the image before it is fully downloaded.

projector   A stand-alone Flash movie that is executable and does not require the Flash Player.

properties   Attributes of some object.

property array   An array in which each name and value pair can be uniquely identified.

public domain   Media elements or works that can be used freely, without a license or release.

quantization   The process of averaging color based on subsampled blocks.

QuickTime (MOV)   A digital video format, created by Apple, originally designed for use on the Macintosh (*www.apple.com/*).

radiant light   A light source in which light is projected in all directions with no decrease in intensity.

radiosity   The most photorealistic type of 3D rendering; takes into consideration all light within a scene.

random   Numeric function that generates a random number.

random access memory (RAM)   The main memory of the computer that is used to temporarily store data.

raster-based graphics   See *bitmap*.

raytracing   A rendering technique that traces light rays within a scene; does not calculate scattered light rays.

RCA-type   A typical cable connector used with digital video and digital audio.

reflected light   See *additive colors*.

reflectivity   An object property that describes its shininess and how much of the scene is reflected in the surface.

release   A permission to use a copyrighted item; often usage has certain limitations.

remapping   Pertains to changing the color palette of an image.

renderer   The part of the 3D animation program that generates a raster image or animation.

rendering engine   Special code that uses the 3D scene to create a flat raster image; includes wireframe, flat, Gouroud, phong, raytracing, and radiosity.

resolution   The photorealism of an image; describes the ratio of image resolution to image size.

RGB Acronym for red, green, blue.

RGB color See *24-bit*.

RGB color model Theoretical color space used to describe the range of colors available on a computer monitor.

roll Relates to rotation about the Z axis.

run length encoding See *Windows bitmap*.

S-Video A video cable connector commonly found on U.S. devices.

sampling The process of converting analog data to digital data.

sampling rate Measure of how frequently samples in a sound clip or image occur.

sans serif Typefaces (fonts) without serifs. See also *serif*.

saturation Describes the purity of a color, or how much of a color is in a hue.

Scalable Vector Graphics (SVG) A web specification being developed by a W3C working group composed of a variety of leading companies, including Microsoft, Adobe, and Macromedia (*www.w3.org/TR/WD-SVG*).

scan lines The horizontal lines of pixels in a computer monitor.

scenes The main timelines within a movie.

scope The life span of a variable.

serif The stroke projecting from and finishing off the top and/or bottom of a character in some typefaces.

serif fonts Fonts displaying the serif characteristic.

shade Area of a surface opposite the light source.

shadows Areas of a surface blocked from a light source by another feature or object.

shape hints Reference points used within shape tweening to control the way one object morphs to another. See also *in-betweens* and *shape tweens*.

shape tweens Animations consisting of objects that morph.

Shockwave A plug-in created by Macromedia for viewing multimedia and vector elements on the Web. Shockwave components may be generated from Director, Authorware, or Flash.

Shockwave Flash (SWF) The generic movie format used to distribute movies on the Web; requires the Flash Player for playback; can be protected or unprotected.

simple text The standard Macintosh ASCII text editor.

SIT A compressed file create by Aladdin's Stuffit Deluxe.

site map A planning tool for charting the content of a web site.

size report An ASCII text file that details the file size requirements of the objects in a movie.

SND See *System 7 sound files (SND)*.

solid model A model that has theoretical volume and engineering properties.

Sound Blaster Vocal Files (VOC) A digital audio format designed by Creative Labs.

spatial Relating to 3D coordinate space or spacial relationships.

spline A curve with weighted control points.

spot light A directed light source.

sprite An element or object in a 2D animation program.

stage The area of the Flash application that will be viewed by the audience during run-time.

stage-level object An object on an organizational level in Flash that contains ungrouped elements, basic objects (such as lines and fills), and broken elements (such as broken text).

Standard Generalized Markup Language (SGML) An advanced markup language commonly used to produce electronic versions of large texts such as encyclopedias and dictionaries.

static Pertaining to images that do not change or are not animated.

stereo A multiple-channel digital audio file.

stereoscopic field of vision The area created by the overlapping cone of vision from each eye; field in which depth is perceived.

stereoscopic vision The ability to perceive depth.

storyboard A thumbnail representation often used for planning an animation, multimedia, or hypermedia product.

streaming The process of delivering small chunks of a digital file over the Internet for instant execution.

string literal A value entered into an Action field; a variable that is text.

string operators Operators used to manipulate text. Flash has only one concatenate.

string value See *string literal.*

Stuffit Expander A compression program used on the Macintosh platform.

subsampling The process of breaking an image into component blocks that are then color averaged.

substring String function that extracts a portion of a string variable by defining a string, an index (starting position for extraction), and a count (ending position for extraction).

subtraction One of the basic Boolean operations; the volume or area of one object is subtracted from the volume or area of another.

subtractive colors Colors produced on a white page by applying hues.

subtractive primaries Cyan, yellow, magenta, and black.

Sun Audio (AU) Audio format predominantly used on the UNIX operating system.

surface mapping The process of applying qualities to 3D objects so that they look realistic.

surface model A model consisting of surfaces with no volume characteristics.

symbol A special reusable component in Flash that has its own timeline.

symmetrical balance Descriptive of a layout in which there is a relative balance of visual elements in the area of a page and/or between facing pages.

synthesis The ability to create a waveform (analog data).

System 7 sound files (SND) Standard Macintosh system sound format.

system palette The color palette or color look-up table associated with a 256-color environment.

Tagged Image File Format (TIFF) A raster graphic file format designed to contain high-resolution image data for print purposes.

target path The method for identifying objects in Flash; used within the Tell Target action.

text editor A program designed to edit plain ASCII text files.

TIFF See *Tagged Image File Format*.

tiles Bitmaps used as repeating segments over the background of a browser; a tiled background.

timeline The interface component of the Flash application where you define the timing and duration of the elements that appear and disappear during movie playback.

tint Adding white to any hue.

transient information Information that is rapidly changing; generally changes within nine months.

translation A basic manipulation of an object; includes move, rotate, and scale.

translucent The ability of light to pass through a surface.

transparency The ability to see through an object.

triad A color scheme using three colors that are equally spaced from one another on the color wheel.

trigger Slang for a button that has only a hit state.

True color See *24-bit color*.

TrueType A typical type of vector font.

tweens See *in-betweens*.

typeface (font) A unique set of characters that have similar characteristics; examples are Helvetica, Geneva, and Times New Roman.

typography The study of type and its various characteristics.

union A basic Boolean operation in which overlapping volume or area between two objects is joined, or "welded," to create a single object.

Universal Resource Locator (URL) The unique naming address scheme used on the Web.

value Pertaining to the lightness or darkness of a color. Adding black to a hue creates a shade; adding white to a hue creates a tint.

variable A container for data.

VBScript A web-based scripting language.

vector fonts Fonts described using vector descriptions.

vector-based graphics Graphics in which the smaller drawing elements are points, lines, and arcs.

Vector Markup Language (VML) An XML-based format for vector graphics, developed by Microsoft (*msdn. microsoft.com/standards/vml/*).

Video for Windows (AVI) A common digital video format created for use on the Windows platform.

Virtual Reality Modeling Language (VRML) A markup language designed to deliver 3D environment descriptions for viewing on the Web.

visible light The small portion of the electromagnetic spectrum that humans can perceive.

VOC See *Sound Blaster Vocal Files*.

warm colors Colors that tend to come toward the viewer; includes colors such as red, yellow, and orange.

WAV See *Windows Waveform Files (WAV)*.

WebCGM An ISO standard metafile format for the Web that can store raster data, vector data, or both. Currently, no browsers or authoring environments support it (*www.w3.org/TR/REC-WebCGM*).

weight (of a font) The thickness of the lines that constitute the characters of a font.

white space See *negative space*.

Windows Bitmap (BMP) Raster format created by Microsoft for bitmap images.

Windows Waveform (WAV) The standard Windows digital audio format.

wireframe model A model consisting of connecting lines and points but with no surfaces between these elements.

wireframe rendering A rendering in which the lines of the object are rendered but no surfaces are rendered.

WordPad The Windows 95 and Windows NT ASCII text editor.

work area The gray pasteboard area that surrounds the stage in the Flash application.

XML See *Extensible Markup Language*.

yaw Rotation about the Y axis.

ZIP A compressed file created by PKWARE's PKZIP program.

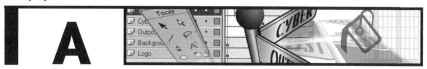

A

Skewing Angles for Elements

The end of Chapter 3 discussed the importance of transformations for the construction of paralline drawings. Table A-1 of this appendix outlines the required skew angles for transforming orthographic views into the proper orientation to the construction of a pictorial using projection. To set up a projection, perform the following steps.

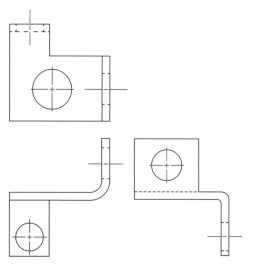

Figure A-1. Begin with orthographic views of an object.

1. Import two or three orthographic (2D) views of an object into Flash, such as those shown in figure A-1. The number of views you will need depends on the object. Sometimes you can get away with only two views. It depends on the object you are trying to construct. Once the views are imported, group the lines that constitute each view.

2. Examine figure A-2 to determine the type of pictorial you want to create. You usually choose the view based on the feature or face of the object you are trying to represent. The numbers at the top are the rotation of the object around the Z axis (in 3D), and the numbers on the left are the tilt toward the view. Once you decide on a view, note the rotation and tilt of the object (this is the data you use to look up skew angles in table A-1).

Rotation of Object Around Z Axis

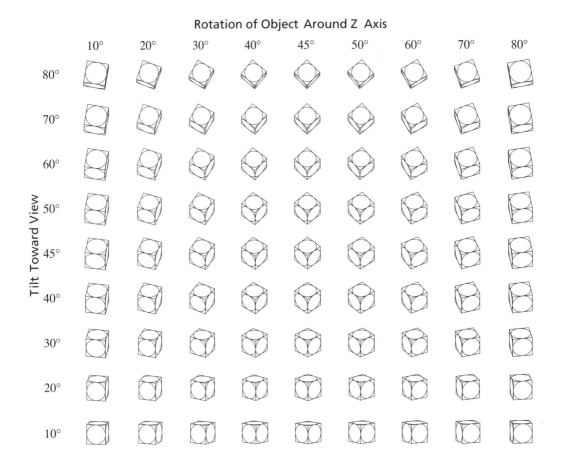

Figure A-2. Manipulation of an object in 3D and the resulting object pictorials.

3. Once you know the rotation and tilt of the object, look it up in table A-1 to find the resulting skew and scale data for each plane of the object.

4. Apply the skew angle data to the orthographic planes. For example, imagine you wanted to construct a pictorial view of the object shown in figure A-1 rotated 40 degrees and tilted 60 degrees. If you look up the rotation and tilt values in table A-1, you find the following.

- For the top plane:

  — Horizontal skew: 44

  — Vertical skew: 36

— Horizontal scale: 101%

— Vertical scale: 98.5%

- For the left plane:

  — Horizontal skew: 0

  — Vertical skew: 36

  — Horizontal scale: 101%

  — Vertical scale: 53.5%

- For the right plane:

  — Horizontal skew: 0

  — Vertical skew: -46

  — Horizontal scale: 98.5%

  — Vertical scale: 53.5%

5. Apply the values provided in the table to each of the planes. Based on figure A-1, the skewed planes are shown in figure A-3.

6. Once you have applied the transformation values, move the planes to that they overlap and share a common side, as shown in figure A-4.

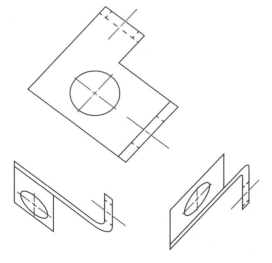

Figure A-3. The result of applying the skew values to the planes.

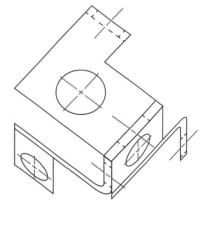

Figure A-4. Overlap the transformed planes.

7. Project lines from the planes to find intersections on the object, as shown in figure A-5.

8. Once the lines are projected and the original planes removed, you are left with a pictorial representation of the object. In this case, the pictorial shows the object rotated 40 degrees and tilted 60 degrees.

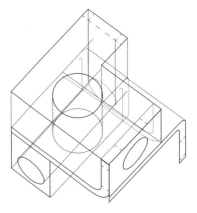

Figure A-5. Projecting points to find the object.

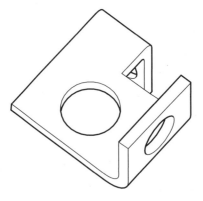

Figure A-6. The completed pictorial.

Table A-1: Transformation Data Given Object Rotation and Tilt, Part 1

Object Rotation and Illustration Data

View Type	Image	3D View		Approximate Exposure			For 10 degree Object Rotation — Top Plane				Skew Method Transformation Data — Left Plane L				Right Plane			
		Rotation	Tilt	T	L	R	H Skew	V Skew	H Scale	V Scale	H Skew	V Skew	H Scale	V Scale	H Skew	V Skew	H Scale	V Scale
Trimetric		10	80	80	10	—	10	10	139.50%	137.00%	0	10	139.50%	24.50%	0	−80	137.00%	24.50%
Trimetric		10	70	70	20	—	11	9	128.00%	120.50%	0	9	128.00%	44.00%	0	−79	120.50%	44.00%
Trimetric		10	60	60	30	—	11.5	8.5	122.00%	106.50%	0	8.5	122.00%	61.50%	0	−78.5	106.50%	61.50%
Trimetric		10	50	50	40	—	13	7.5	119.00%	93.00%	0	7.5	119.00%	77.00%	0	−77	93.00%	77.00%
Dimetric		10	45	45	45	—	14	7	119.50%	86.50%	0	7	119.50%	85.00%	0	−76	86.50%	85.00%
Trimetric		10	40	40	50	—	15.5	6.5	120.50%	79.50%	0	6.5	120.50%	93.00%	0	−74.5	79.50%	93.00%
Trimetric		10	30	30	60	—	19	5	125.50%	66.50%	0	5	125.50%	110.00%	0	−71	66.50%	110.00%
Trimetric		10	20	20	75	—	27.5	3.5	135.50%	52.00%	0	3.5	135.50%	129.00%	0	−62.5	52.00%	129.00%
Dimetric		10	10	10	80	10	45	1.5	152.50%	37.50%	0	1.5	152.50%	152.50%	0	−45	37.50%	152.50%

Table A-1: Transformation Data Given Object Rotation and Tilt, Part 2

Object Rotation and Illustration Data

View Type	Image	3D View		Approximate Exposure			For 20-degree Object Rotation Top Plane				Skew Method Transformation Data Left Plane L				Right Plane			
		Rotation	Tilt	T	L	R	H Skew	V Skew	H Scale	V Scale	H Skew	V Skew	H Scale	V Scale	H Skew	V Skew	H Scale	V Scale
Trimetric		20	80	80	—	—	20.5	19.5	127.50%	125.50%	0	19.5	127.50%	22.00%	0	-69.5	125.50%	22.00%
Trimetric		20	70	70	20	—	21	19	118.00%	112.50%	0	19	118.00%	40.50%	0	-69	112.50%	40.50%
Trimetric		20	60	60	30	—	22.5	17.5	112.00%	100.50%	0	17.5	112.00%	56.50%	0	-67.5	100.50%	56.50%
Trimetric		20	50	50	40	10	25.5	15.5	110.50%	90.00%	0	15.5	110.50%	72.50%	0	-64.5	90.00%	72.50%
Dimetric		20	45	45	45	—	27	14.5	110.50%	85.00%	0	14.5	110.50%	80.50%	0	-63	85.00%	80.50%
Trimetric		20	40	40	50	15	29.5	13	111.50%	80.00%	0	13	111.50%	88.50%	0	-60.5	80.00%	88.50%
Trimetric		20	30	30	55	—	36	10.5	116.50%	70.00%	0	10.5	116.50%	105.50%	0	-54	77.00%	105.50%
Trimetric		20	20	20	65	—	46.5	7	126.50%	62.50%	0	7	126.50%	125.00%	0	-43.5	62.50%	125.00%
Trimetric		20	10	10	70	20	64.5	3.5	144.00%	57.50%	0	3.5	144.00%	149.50%	0	-25.5	57.50%	149.50%

Table A-1: Transformation Data Given Object Rotation and Tilt, Part 3

Object Rotation and Illustration Data

View Type	Image	3D View		Approximate Exposure			Top Plane				Left Plane L				Right Plane			
		Rotation	Tilt	T	L	R	H Skew	V Skew	H Scale	V Scale	H Skew	V Skew	H Scale	V Scale	H Skew	V Skew	H Scale	V Scale
Trimetric		30	80	80	—	—	30	29.5	120.50%	119.50%	0	29.5	120.50%	20.50%	0	-60	120.50%	20.50%
Trimetric		30	70	70	20	10	31.5	28.5	111.50%	108.00%	0	28.5	111.50%	38.00%	0	-58.5	108.00%	38.00%
Trimetric		30	60	60	30	15	33.5	26.5	105.50%	98.00%	0	26.5	105.50%	54.50%	0	-56.5	98.00%	54.50%
Trimetric		30	50	50	35	—	37	24	102.50%	90.50%	0	24	102.50%	70.00%	0	-53	90.50%	70.00%
Dimetric		30	45	45	40	20	39.5	22	103.00%	86.50%	0	22	103.00%	77.50%	0	-50.5	86.50%	77.50%
Trimetric		30	40	40	45	—	42	20.5	103.00%	83.50%	0	20.5	103.00%	85.00%	0	-48	83.50%	85.00%
Trimetric		30	30	30	50	25	49	16	106.50%	78.00%	0	16	106.50%	102.50%	0	-41	78.00%	102.50%
Trimetric		30	20	20	55	—	59	11	115.50%	76.00%	0	11	115.50%	122.50%	0	-31	76.00%	122.50%
Trimetric		30	10	10	60	30	73	5.5	131.00%	78.50%	0	5.5	131.00%	148.00%	0	-17	78.50%	148.00%

For 30-degree Object Rotation — Skew Method Transformation Data

Table A-1: Transformation Data Given Object Rotation and Tilt, Part 4

Object Rotation and Illustration Data

View Type	Image	3D View		Approximate Exposure			For 40-degree Object Rotation — Top Plane				Skew Method Transformation Data — Left Plane L				Right Plane			
		Rotation	Tilt	T	L	R	H Skew	V Skew	H Scale	V Scale	H Skew	V Skew	H Scale	V Scale	H Skew	V Skew	H Scale	V Scale
Dimetric		40	80	80	—	—	40.5	39.5	117.00%	117.00%	0	39.5	117.00%	20.50%	0	−49.5	117.00%	20.50%
Dimetric		40	70	70	10	10	42	38.5	107.00%	106.00%	0	38.5	107.00%	38.00%	0	−48	106.00%	38.00%
Dimetric		40	60	60	20	20	44	36	101.00%	98.50%	0	36	101.50%	53.50%	0	−46	98.50%	53.50%
Dimetric		40	50	50	25	25	47.5	33	97.00%	93.00%	0	33	97.00%	68.50%	0	−42.5	93.00%	68.50%
Trimetric		40	45	45	30	—	50	30.5	96.00%	90.00%	0	30.5	96.00%	76.00%	0	−40	90.00%	76.00%
Trimetric		40	40	40	35	—	52.5	28.5	95.00%	88.50%	0	28.5	95.00%	84.50%	0	−37.5	88.50%	84.50%
Dimetric		40	30	30	40	30	59	22.5	97.50%	86.50%	0	22.5	97.50%	101.00%	0	−31	86.50%	101.00%
Trimetric		40	20	20	45	35	68.5	16	103.00%	90.50%	0	16	103.00%	121.50%	0	−21.5	90.50%	121.50%
Trimetric		40	10	10	50	40	78.5	8.5	115.00%	97.50%	0	8.5	115.00%	146.50%	0	−11.5	97.50%	146.50%

Table A-1: Transformation Data Given Object Rotation and Tilt, Part 5

Object Rotation and Illustration Data

		3D View		Approximate Exposure			For 45-degree Object Rotation — Top Plane				Skew Method Transformation Data — Left Plane L				Right Plane			
View Type	Image	Rotation	Tilt	T	L	R	H Skew	V Skew	H Scale	V Scale	H Skew	V Skew	H Scale	V Scale	H Skew	V Skew	H Scale	V Scale
Dimetric		45	80	80	—	—	45.5	44.5	100.00%	100.00%	0	-45.5	17.00%	100.00%	0	-45.5	17.00%	100.00%
Dimetric		45	70	70	10	10	47	43	100.00%	100.00%	0	43	35.00%	100.00%	0	-43	35.00%	100.00%
Dimetric		45	60	60	15	15	49	41	100.00%	100.00%	0	41	54.00%	100.00%	0	-41	54.00%	100.00%
Dimetric		45	50	50	20	20	52.5	37.5	100.00%	100.00%	0	37.5	72.00%	100.00%	0	-37.5	72.00%	100.00%
Dimetric		45	45	45	25	25	54.5	35	93.00%	93.00%	0	35	93.00%	76.00%	0	-35.5	93.00%	76.00%
Dimetric		45	40	40	30	30	57.5	32.5	100.00%	100.00%	0	32.5	92.00%	100.00%	0	-32.5	92.00%	92.00%
Trimetric		45	35.2667	35.2667	35.2667	35.2667	60	30	92.00%	92.00%	0	30	92.00%	92.00%	0	-30	92.00%	92.00%
Dimetric		45	30	30	35.2667	35.2667	63.5	26.5	100.00%	100.00%	0	26.5	109.00%	100.00%	0	-26.5	109.00%	100.00%
Dimetric		45	20	20	40	40	71	19	100.00%	100.00%	0	19	125.00%	100.00%	0	-19	125.00%	100.00%
Dimetric		45	10	10	50	40	80	10	100.00%	100.00%	0	10	135.00%	100.00%	0	-10	135.00%	100.00%

Table A-1: Transformation Data Given Object Rotation and Tilt, Part 6

Object Rotation and Illustration Data

View Type	Image	3D View		Approximate Exposure			Top Plane				Left Plane L				Right Plane			
		Rotation	Tilt	T	L	R	H Skew	V Skew	H Scale	V Scale	H Skew	V Skew	H Scale	V Scale	H Skew	V Skew	H Scale	V Scale
Dimetric		50	80	80	10	10	50.5	49.5	116.00%	116.00%	0	49.5	116.00%	21.00%	0	−39.5	116.00%	21.00%
Dimetric		50	70	70	15	15	51.5	48	106.00%	107.50%	0	48	106.00%	37.50%	0	−38.5	107.50%	37.50%
Dimetric		50	60	60	20	20	54	46	98.50%	100.50%	0	46	98.50%	53.00%	0	−36	100.50%	53.00%
Trimetric		50	50	50	—	25	57.5	42.5	93.00%	96.50%	0	42.5	93.00%	68.50%	0	−32.5	96.05%	68.50%
Trimetric		50	45	45	25	30	59.5	40	90.50%	90.50%	0	40	90.50%	76.50%	0	−30.5	95.50%	76.50%
Trimetric		50	40	40	30	35	62	37.5	89.50%	95.50%	0	37.5	89.50%	84.00%	0	−28	95.50%	84.00%
Trimetric		50	30	30	—	40	67.5	31	87.50%	97.00%	0	31	87.50%	101.50%	0	−22.5	97.00%	101.50%
Trimetric		50	20	20	35	45	74	22	89.50%	103.00%	0	22	89.50%	122.00%	0	−16	103.00%	122.00%
Trimetric		50	10	10	40	50	81.5	11.5	98.00%	116.00%	0	11.5	98.00%	147.00%	0	−8.5	116.00%	147.00%

Column group headers: *For 50-degree Object Rotation* spans 3D View, Approximate Exposure, and Top Plane. *Skew Method Transformation Data* spans Left Plane L and Right Plane.

Table A-1: Transformation Data Given Object Rotation and Tilt, Part 7

Object Rotation and Illustration Data

View Type	Image	3D View		Approximate Exposure			For 60-degree Object Rotation — Top Plane				Skew Method Transformation Data — Left Plane L				Right Plane			
		Rotation	Tilt	T	L	R	H Skew	V Skew	H Scale	V Scale	H Skew	V Skew	H Scale	V Scale	H Skew	V Skew	H Scale	V Scale
Trimetric		60	80	80	—	10	60.5	59.5	119.50%	120.50%	0	59.5	119.50%	21.00%	0	-29.5	119.50%	21.00%
Trimetric		60	70	70	—	15	61.5	58.5	108.00%	111.50%	0	58.5	108.00%	38.00%	0	-28.5	111.50%	38.00%
Trimetric		60	60	60	10	25	63.5	56	98.00%	105.50%	0	56	98.00%	54.50%	0	-26.5	105.50%	54.50%
Trimetric		60	50	50	20	30	66	53	90.00%	103.00%	0	53	90.00%	69.50%	0	-24	103.00%	69.50%
Trimetric		60	45	45	—	35	67.5	50.5	86.50%	102.50%	0	50.5	86.50%	77.50%	0	-22.5	102.50%	77.50%
Dimetric		60	40	40	—	40	69.5	48	83.50%	103.00%	0	48	83.50%	85.50%	0	-20.5	103.00%	85.50%
Trimetric		60	30	30	25	45	73.5	40.5	78.50%	106.50%	0	40.5	78.50%	102.50%	0	-16.5	106.50%	102.50%
Trimetric		60	20	20	—	50	78.5	30.5	75.50%	114.50%	0	30.5	75.50%	122.50%	0	-11.5	114.50%	122.50%
Trimetric		60	10	10	30	65	84	17	78.00%	130.00%	0	17	78.00%	147.50%	0	-6	130.00%	147.50%

Table A-1: Transformation Data Given Object Rotation and Tilt, Part 8

Object Rotation and Illustration Data

View Type	Image	3D View		Approximate Exposure			For 70-degree Object Rotation — Top Plane				Skew Method Transformation Data — Left Plane L				Right Plane			
		Rotation	Tilt	T	L	R	H Skew	V Skew	H Scale	V Scale	H Skew	V Skew	H Scale	V Scale	H Skew	V Skew	H Scale	V Scale
Trimetric		70	80	80	—	10	70	70	126.50%	128.00%	0	70	126.50%	22.50%	0	−20	128.00%	22.50%
Trimetric		70	70	70	—	15	71	69	112.50%	118.00%	0	69	112.50%	40.50%	0	−19	118.00%	40.50%
Trimetric		70	60	60	—	20	72.5	67	100.50%	112.50%	0	67	100.50%	56.50%	0	−17.5	112.50%	56.50%
Trimetric		70	50	50	10	35	74.5	64.5	90.00%	110.00%	0	64.5	90.00%	73.00%	0	−15.5	110.00%	73.00%
Trimetric		70	45	45	15	40	85.5	62.5	86.00%	110.00%	0	62.5	86.00%	80.00%	0	−14.5	110.00%	80.00%
Trimetric		70	40	40	—	45	77	60.5	80.00%	111.50%	0	60.5	80.00%	88.50%	0	−13	111.50%	88.50%
Trimetric		70	30	30	—	50	79.5	53.5	71.00%	116.00%	0	53.5	71.00%	105.50%	0	−10.5	116.00%	105.50%
Trimetric		70	20	20	—	65	83	43.5	62.00%	126.50%	0	43.5	62.00%	125.00%	0	−7	126.50%	125.00%
Trimetric		70	10	10	20	70	86.5	25.5	57.50%	143.00%	0	25.5	57.50%	149.50%	0	−3.5	143.00%	149.50%

Table A-1: Transformation Data Given Object Rotation and Tilt, Part 9

Object Rotation and Illustration Data

View Type	Image	3D View		Approximate Exposure			For 80-degree Object Rotation — Top Plane				Skew Method Transformation Data — Left Plane L				Right Plane			
		Rotation	Tilt	T	L	R	H Skew	V Skew	H Scale	V Scale	H Skew	V Skew	H Scale	V Scale	H Skew	V Skew	H Scale	V Scale
Trimetric		80	80	80	—	10	80	80	138.00%	139.50%	0	80	138.00%	24.00%	0	−10	139.50%	24.00%
Trimetric		80	70	70	—	20	80.5	79	121.50%	128.00%	0	79	121.50%	44.00%	0	−9.5	128.00%	44.00%
Trimetric		80	60	60	—	30	81.5	78.5	106.50%	121.50%	0	78.5	106.50%	61.00%	0	−8.5	121.50%	61.00%
Trimetric		80	50	50	—	40	82	77	93.00%	119.00%	0	77	93.00%	77.00%	0	−8	119.00%	77.00%
Trimetric		80	45	45	—	45	83	76	86.50%	119.50%	0	76	86.50%	85.00%	0	−7	119.50%	85.00%
Trimetric		80	40	40	—	50	84	75	80.00%	120.00%	0	75	80.00%	93.00%	0	−6	120.00%	93.00%
Trimetric		80	30	30	—	65	84.5	70.5	66.50%	125.50%	0	70.5	66.50%	110.00%	0	−5.5	125.50%	110.00%
Trimetric		80	20	20	—	70	86.5	63	52.00%	136.00%	0	63	52.00%	129.50%	0	−3.5	136.00%	129.50%
Dimetric		80	10	10	10	80	88	45	37.50%	152.00%	0	45	37.50%	152.00%	0	−2	152.00%	152.00%

appendix

B

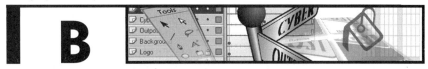

Deprecated Actions

Table B-1 outlines deprecated ActionScript items in Flash MX 2004 and their alternatives. Deprecated simply means that continued support in the next version of Flash cannot be guaranteed and thus you should use other coding methods.

Table B-1: Flash MX 2004 Deprecated ActionScript Items and Their Alternatives

Operators	
Deprecated	**Alternative**
<>	(not equal) !=
add	+
and	&&
eq	=
ge	>=
gt	>
le	<=
lt	<
ne	!=
not	!
or	||

Properties	
Deprecated	**Alternative**
_highquality	_quality
maxscroll	TextField.maxscroll
scroll	TextField.scroll

Table B-1: Flash MX 2004 Deprecated ActionScript Items and Their Alternatives (continued)

Operators	
Deprecated	**Alternative**
<>	(not equal) *!=*
add	+
and	&&
eq	=
ge	>=
gt	>
le	<=
lt	<
ne	!=
not	!
or	||

Properties	
Deprecated	**Alternative**
_highquality	*_quality*
maxscroll	*TextField.maxscroll*
scroll	*TextField.scroll*

appendix

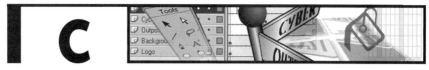

C

Key Code Values

Tables C-1 through C-4 present key code values for alphanumeric, numeric keypad, function, and other keys associated with Flash.

Alphanumeric Keys

Table C-1 presents alphanumeric key code values for Flash.

Table C-1: Alphanumeric Key Code Values

Letter/ Number	Key Code	Letter/ Number	Key Code	Letter/ Number	Key Code
A	65	M	77	Y	89
B	66	N	78	Z	90
C	67	O	79	0	48
D	68	P	80	1	49
E	69	Q	81	2	50
F	70	R	82	3	51
G	71	S	83	4	52
H	72	T	84	5	53
I	73	U	85	6	54
J	74	V	86	7	55
K	75	W	87	8	56
L	76	X	88	9	57

Other Keyboard Keys

Table C-2 presents other keyboard key code values for Flash.

Table C-2: Numeric Keypad Key Code Values

Numeric Keypad Key	Key Code	Numeric Keypad Key	Key Code
0	96	8	104
1	97	9	105
2	98	Multiply	106
3	99	Add	107
4	100	Enter	108
5	101	Subtract	109
6	102	Decimal	110
7	103	Divide	111

Function Keys

Table C-3, which follows, presents function key code values for Flash.

Other Keyboard Keys

Table C-4 presents other keyboard key code values for Flash.

Table C-3: Function Key Code Values

Function Key	Key Code
F1	112
F2	113
F3	114
F4	115
F5	116
F6	117
F7	118
F8	119
F9	120
F10	121
F11	122
F12	123

Table C-4: Other Keyboard Key Code Values

Key	Key Code	Key	Key Code
Backspace	8	Right Arrow	39
Tab	9	Down Arrow	40
Clear	12	Insert	45
Enter	13	Delete	46
Shift	16	Help	47
Control	17	Num Lock	144
Alt	18	; or :	186
Caps Lock	20	= or +	187
Esc	27	- or _	189
Spacebar	32	/ or ?	191
Page Up	33	` or ~	192
Page Down	34	[or {	219
End	35	\ or |	220
Home	36	] or }	221
Left Arrow	37	" or '	222
Up Arrow	38		

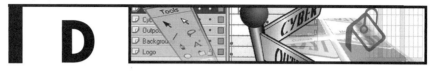

About the Companion CD-ROM

The following is an outline of the example files contained on the companion CD-ROM.

chapter01/

- *ch01_01/*   Example concerning small file sizes
- *ch01_02/*   Example demonstrating antialiasing
- *ch01_03/*   Example that shows scaling
- *ch01_04/*   Demonstrates dynamic image loading
- *ch01_05/*   Overview of animation in Flash
- *ch01_06/*   Use of sound in Flash
- *ch01_07/*   Use of interactivity in Flash

chapter02/

- *ch02_01.fla*   Orientation to the Flash interface
- *ch02_02.fla*   Playing a movie with scenes

chapter03/

- *ch03_02.fla*   Practice zooming and panning
- *ch03_03.fla*   Modifying objects with the Arrow tool
- *ch03_04.fla*   Moving objects with the Arrow tool
- *ch03_05.fla*   Selecting fills and lines

- *ch03_06.fla*   Using the Smooth and Straighten options
- *ch03_07.fla*   Using the Subselection tool
- *ch03_08.fla*   Using the Lasso tool to make selections
- *ch03_09.fla*   Quickly editing groups
- *ch03_10.fla*   Working with layer states
- *ch03_11.fla*   Adding and deleting layers
- *ch03_12.fla*   Exploring overlays and groups
- *ch03_13.flu*   The additive and subtractive properties of stage objects
- *ch03_14.fla*   Transforming an object with the Free Transform tool
- *ch03_15.fla*   Changing the origin of the transform
- *ch03_16.fla*   Using the Distort and Envelope commands

chapter04/
- *ch04_08.fla*   Experimenting with lines
- *ch04_11.fla*   Using the Pen tool
- *ch04_12.fla*   Experimenting with Ovals
- *ch04_13.fla*   Using the Line, Rectangle, and Oval tools
- *ch04_14.fla*   The Pencil versus the Brush
- *ch04_15.fla*   Working with Brush modes
- *ch04_16.fla*   Using the Ink Bottle tool
- *ch04_17.fla*   Color and Gap Size options
- *ch04_18.fla*   Paint Bucket and Transform Fill tools
- *ch04_19.fla*   Using the Dropper tool
- *ch04_20.fla*   Working with Eraser modes
- *ch04_21.fla*   Working with the Faucet option
- *ch04_22.fla*   Using Align

chapter05/
- *ch05_01.fla*   Using the Text tool
- *ch05_02.fla*   Modifying characters
- *ch05_03.fla*   Modifying blocks
- *ch05_05.fla*   Creating dynamic text fields
- *ch05_06.fla*   Using Dynamic and Input text objects
- *ch05_07.fla*   Breaking text apart for custom effects
- *ch05_08s.fla*   Using HTML tags in fields

chapter06/

- *ch06_04.fla*   Accessing and editing symbols
- *ch06_06.fla*   Creating a button
- *ch06_07.fla*   Creating an animated button
- *ch06_09.fla*   Importing symbols from another file

chapter07/

- *ch07_04.fla*   Using the Trace Bitmap function

chapter08/

- *ch08_01.fla*   Importing sounds into Flash
- *ch08_02.fla*   Using an imported sound
- *ch08_03.fla*   Event option versus Start Sync option
- *ch08_04.fla*   Using streaming sounds
- *ch08_05.fla*   Sound settings in the library

chapter09/

- *ch09_01a.fla*   Creating a basic frame-by-frame animation
- *ch09_05a.fla*   Creating an animated telephone
- *ch09_08.fla*   Using reverse frames
- *ch09_09.fla*   Sizing a finished piece with Edit Multiple Frames
- *ch09_11a.fla*   Setting up a tween
- *ch09_12.fla*   The Scale, Rotate, and Easing options
- *ch09_13a.fla*   Using color effects
- *ch09_14.fla*   Applying brightness and tint changes
- *ch09_15a.fla*   Using motion guides
- *ch09_16a.fla*   Using mask layers
- *ch09_17a.fla*   Practice creating shape tweens
- *ch09_18a.fla*   Using shape hints
- *guides/*   Extended guide examples
- *masks/*   Extended mask examples
- *misc/*   Various animated elements
- *other/*   Various animated elements
- *text effects/*   Extended text effect examples
- *transitions/*   Extended transition examples

chapter10/

- *AutoCAD Process/*   Example files extracted from AutoCAD
- *Illustrate sample/*   Sample 3D animation using Illustrate
- *Pro-E Process/*   Files extracted from Pro/ENGINEER
- *Streamline Process/* Examples from Adobe Streamline

chapter11/

- *preload/*   Example showing concept of preloading
- *ch11_01.fla*   Embedding video into a Flash movie

chapter12/

- *audio/*   Examples demonstrating audio differences
- *jpeg/*   Examples showing bitmap compression
- *ch12_03.swf*   Used for various exercises
- *ch12_04.fla*   Generating a size report
- *ch12_05.fla*   Using the Bandwidth profiler
- *ch12_06.fla*   Testing bitmap qualities

chapter13/

- *ch13_05.fla*   Precedence: MC versus button mouse events
- *ch13_06.fla*   Precedence: Overlapping MC and buttons
- *ch13_07a.fla*   Precedence: Buttons and movie clips
- *ch13_08.fla*   Precedence: MC versus button key events
- *ch13_09.fla*   Precedence: MC versus frame events
- *ch13_10.fla*   Precedence: Multiple movie clips
- *ch13_11.fla*   Examples of absolute targets
- *ch13_12.fla*   Relative targets in a movie
- *ch13_13.fla*   Using global variables
- *ch13_14.fla*   Using the Increment and Decrement operators
- *ch13_15a.fla*   Target paths
- *ch13_16.fla*   Commas, functions, and passing values
- *ch13_17.fla*   Using the *with()* statement
- *ch13_18.fla*   Using the If action based on frames
- *ch13_19.fla*   Using the If action based on variables
- *ch13_20.fla*   Having a movie clip react to the timeline
- *ch13_21.fla*   Using a *for* loop
- *ch13_22.fla*   Using a *for* loop for a transition

- *ch13_23.fla*   Using *break* with the Array object
- *ch13_24.fla*   Using *escape()* and *unescape()*
- *ch13_25.fla*   Using the *Eval()* function
- *ch13_26.fla*   Using the *GetTimer()* function
- *ch13_27.fla*   *String()* and *Number()* functions
- *ch13_28.fla*   *ParseFloat()* and *ParseInt()*

chapter14/

- *ch14_01.fla*   Using Movie Explorer
- *ch14_04.fla*   Using *play()*, *stop()*, and goto
- *ch14_05.fla*   Examples of the *getURL()* action
- *ch14_06/*   Using the *getURL()* target specifications
- *ch14_07/*   Using *POST* and *GET*
- *ch14_08/*   Using *loadMovie()* and *unLoadMovie()*
- *ch14_09/*   Using *with()* on loaded movies
- *ch14_10/*   Loading a movie into an MC
- *ch14_11/*   Using the *loadVariables()* method
- *ch14_12/*   Sending and receiving data
- *ch14_13/*   Using the *fscommand()* method
- *ch14_14.fla*   Using *fscommands* in the Flash Player
- *ch14_15.fla*   Movie clip duplication
- *ch14_16.fla*   Changing properties with ActionScript
- *ch14_17.fla*   Using the Drag actions

chapter15/

- *ch15_01.fla*   Using *#b* to define a bounding box
- *ch15_02.fla*   Using loaded movies for print content

macromedia/

swish/

swift/

vecta3D/

sorenson/

Index

License Agreement for Delmar Learning

Educational Software/Data

You the customer, and Delmar Learning incur certain benefits, rights, and obligations to each other when you open this package and use the software/data it contains. BE SURE YOU READ THE LICENSE AGREEMENT CAREFULLY, SINCE BY USING THE SOFTWARE/DATA YOU INDICATE YOU HAVE READ, UNDERSTOOD, AND ACCEPTED THE TERMS OF THIS AGREEMENT.

Your rights:

1. You enjoy a non-exclusive license to use the software/data on a single microcomputer in consideration for payment of the required license fee, (which may be included in the purchase price of an accompanying print component), or receipt of this software/data, and your acceptance of the terms and conditions of this agreement.

2. You acknowledge that you do not own the aforesaid software/data. You also acknowledge that the software/data is furnished "as is," and contains copyrighted and/or proprietary and confidential information of Delmar Learning or its licensors.

There are limitations on your rights:

1. You may not copy or print the software/data for any reason whatsoever, except to install it on a hard drive on a single microcomputer and to make one archival copy, unless copying or printing is expressly permitted in writing or statements recorded on the diskette(s).

2. You may not revise, translate, convert, disassemble or otherwise reverse engineer the software/data except that you may add to or rearrange any data recorded on the media as part of the normal use of the software/data.

3. You may not sell, license, lease, rent, loan, or otherwise distribute or network the software/data except that you may give the software/data to a student or and instructor for use at school or, temporarily at home.

Should you fail to abide by the Copyright Law of the United States as it applies to this software/data your license to use it will become invalid. You agree to erase or otherwise destroy the software/data immediately after receiving note of Delmar Learning termination of this agreement for violation of its provisions.

Delmar Learning gives you a LIMITED WARRANTY covering the enclosed software/data. The LIMITED WARRANTY follows this License.

This license is the entire agreement between you and Delmar Learning interpreted and enforced under New York State law.

This warranty does not extend to the software or information recorded on the media. The software and information are provided "AS IS." Any statements made about the utility of the software or information are not to be considered as express or implied warranties. Delmar Learning will not be liable for incidental or consequential damages of any kind incurred by you, the consumer, or any other user.

Some states do not allow the exclusion or limitation of incidental or consequential damages, or limitations on the duration of implied warranties, so the above limitation or exclusion may not apply to you. This warranty gives you specific legal rights, and you may also have other rights which vary from state to state. Address all correspondence to: Delmar Learning, Box 15015, Albany, NY 12212 Attention: Technology Department

LIMITED WARRANTY

Delmar Learning warrants to the original licensee/purchaser of this copy of microcomputer software/data and the media on which it is recorded that the media will be free from defects in material and workmanship for ninety (90) days from the date of original purchase. All implied warranties are limited in duration to this ninety (90) day period. THEREAFTER, ANY IMPLIED WARRANTIES, INCLUDING IMPLIED WARRANTIES OF MERCHANTABILITY AND FITNESS FOR A PARTICULAR PURPOSE, ARE EXCLUDED. THIS WARRANTY IS IN LIEU OF ALL OTHER WARRANTIES, WHETHER ORAL OR WRITTEN, EXPRESS OR IMPLIED.

If you believe the media is defective please return it during the ninety day period to the address shown below. Defective media will be replaced without charge provided that it has not been subjected to misuse or damage.

This warranty does not extend to the software or information recorded on the media. The software and information are provided "AS IS." Any statements made about the utility of the software or information are not to be considered as express or implied warranties.

Limitation of liability: Our liability to you for any losses shall be limited to direct damages, and shall not exceed the amount you paid for the software. In no event will we be liable to you for any indirect, special, incidental, or consequential damages (including loss of profits) even if we have been advised of the possibility of such damages.

Some states do not allow the exclusion or limitation of incidental or consequential damages, or limitations on the duration of implied warranties, so the above limitation or exclusion may not apply to you. This warranty gives you specific legal rights, and you may also have other rights which vary from state to state. Address all correspondence to: Delmar Learning, Executive Woods, 5 Maxwell Drive, Clifton Park, NY 12065, Attention: Technology Department